Guide to Art Reference Books

Guide to
Art Reference Books

Mary W. Chamberlin

Librarian
Fine Arts Library
Columbia University

American Library Association • Chicago • 1959

Preface

Purpose

This Guide has grown out of the author's experience in art reference work, and her realization of the need for an over-all study of the material potentially available to students of art, professional art historians, and the librarians who aid them in their work.

It is the intention of this book to do what has not yet been done in the English-speaking world: to organize systematically and to evaluate the vast and ever growing literature of art history—the basic reference tools as well as the resources for the most advanced research.

The 2500 entries included range from the earliest books on art printed to the most recent publications. These titles comprise not only the small handbooks and ready-reference works which are found in almost every library and are available to individuals, but also the great encyclopedias, corpus works, and the more rarely encountered sources of highly specialized information. Full bibliographical data are given for each title; contents notes, bibliographies, and various editions have been pointed out; and the annotations describe in detail and explain the scope and limitations of each work listed.

Thus, the requirements of the specialized art librarian as well as the general reference librarian, and even the librarian in the smaller library who must lead readers from the general to the more specific and scholarly texts, have all been kept in mind. Not only will the Guide answer the simplest questions of the college student or the general reader, but at the same time it should facilitate progress in the early phases of advanced research, assist the library school student in the mastery of the bibliography of art, and finally, it is to be hoped, find its place on the scholar's desk.

Scope

In a work of such an ambitious nature, certain criteria for inclusion of titles had to be established. Thus, the Guide covers the literature of architecture, painting, sculpture, prints and engravings, drawings, and the applied arts—roughly, that which is included in the Fine Arts (N) section of the Library of Congress Classification Scheme. The peripheral fields omitted were: advertising art, arms and armor, book arts, calligraphy, caricature, city planning, the dance, heraldry, "how to do it" books, interior decoration (except for furniture and textiles, which are included), landscape gardening, numismatics, photography, postage stamps, posters, and theater arts.

The greater part of the Guide is devoted to reference works, as that term is usually defined. Monographs on individual artists, sites, and specialized subjects have been omitted because they can be found through the use of the bibliographies, handbooks, histories, and other works herein included, or through the catalogs of good libraries. Museum catalogs and catalogs of exhibitions and private collections have also not been listed, in order to keep the volume to manageable proportions. Guidebooks dating from various periods, which can be extremely useful for reference work, have had to be excluded as well. In general, picture books, especially prevalent today, have been omitted, except where they provide the best material on a subject; a few others have been treated in the chapter on "Series," in order to give some indication of the more useful titles.

In the chapter on "Series," as well as in those devoted to "Documents and Sources" and to "Periodicals," materials are treated that are not generally recognized as "reference books"; nevertheless, they are works upon which many reference volumes are based and which provide for scholars and more advanced students essential information usually not to be found elsewhere.

The Guide is concluded by an Appendix devoted to Special Collections and Resources, which lists the main art libraries in the United States and Western Europe. Enough information is given about the purpose and collections of each of these centers of research so that the user of the Guide, in addition to finding out what are the sources for his studies, will be provided with an answer as to where his research—basic or special—may best be carried out.

Throughout the Guide books in the languages of the Western world only have been treated, and those Greek and Russian titles included have been transliterated throughout.

Relation to other fields

Art history is not an isolated field but is closely related to other fields such as general history and literature. For an indication of the reference tools in these overlapping areas the reader is referred to that invaluable work, *Guide to Reference Books* (7th ed.) by Constance M. Winchell (Chicago: American Library Association, 1951) and its supplements.

Selection of titles

Within the established scope of the GUIDE TO ART REFERENCE BOOKS the listing has been a selective one of those titles deemed most important by the compiler in consultation with specialists in the various subjects or periods to which these titles pertain. Further criteria for selection were the amount of use by scholars, as reflected in their bibliographies; actual library demand, as witnessed by the compiler; and the recommendations of the librarians of the great libraries which the author visited in the course of her work on this book.

The Guide, however, has not been compiled with reference to the collection possessed by any one library, or with the needs of any one type of library in mind. Indeed, no single library will possess all the titles listed. The aim has been to survey the whole field of art literature, and importance to research rather than availability has been the main consideration.

Arrangement

The arrangement of entries in the Guide is, basically, by subject. Thus, the first chapters cover general works, grouped by form: e.g., bibliographies, histories and handbooks, indexes, directories, encyclopedias, and iconography. These are followed by chapters devoted to specific subjects, such as architecture, sculpture, or painting. And, finally, there are the chapters on "Documents and Sources," "Periodicals," and "Series," which have been treated separately because they cross all subject fields, yielding specific information on a wide range of topics.

It should further be noted that bibliographies, histories and handbooks, indexes, biographies, and dictionaries and encyclopedias which deal with a particular subject, such as painting, have been treated with the other works on that subject, and come first in the arrangement of materials under the subject. This form division is followed by a division according to chronological periods, for example, Early Christian—Gothic, encompassing, roughly, Early Christian, Byzantine, and Medieval material, and Renaissance—Modern, covering all periods between the Renaissance and the present day. Finally, under each subject, there is a geographical breakdown, alphabetical by country. For convenience, some countries have been grouped together: e.g., Spain and Portugal, the Low Countries, Germany and Austria; and material on England, Scotland, Ireland, and Wales will be found under the heading, "Great Britain."

Code numbers

A code number has been assigned to each entry in the Guide. The numbers run consecutively from the first to the last entry and are intended only as a finding device with no other significance. Certain irregularities of sequence, or letters added after the code number, are merely the result of prepublication revision or inclusion of recent material. Since it was practical to enter any one work only once—for example, a work on both painting and sculpture would be entered in the chapter devoted to painting, with a cross reference to it in the chapter on sculpture—the cross reference by code numbers serves to tie related works together throughout the Guide. And the Index—a detailed author, subject, and title listing, which makes use of these code numbers instead of page numbers—will serve to bring together the various aspects of a subject, so that the reader, in addition to being led to individual works, can be guided also from the general to the more specific.

Current publications

In the case of publications which are still appearing at intervals, the last volume which has appeared is indicated in parentheses, and its date also has been indicated in this manner. Thus, a final entry in parentheses shows that publication is not complete but still in progress.

Closing date

The terminal date for inclusion of new titles was January 1, 1958, at which time the manuscript was completed. A few important items which have appeared since then, or are definitely scheduled for future publication, were added, however, while the Guide was in production.

Acknowledgments

A book of this scope can be successfully accomplished only with the assistance and encouragement of a great many people connected with the various subject areas covered, and I feel that I have been most fortunate in the number of eminent scholars who have been interested in the book's purpose and who have assisted me by offering suggestions and stimulation during its preparation.

The compilation of the book was made possible through a grant by the Eda K. Loeb Foundation to Columbia University for this purpose, and I wish to express my thanks to the Foundation for its great generosity and to Columbia University for its ever thoughtful co-operation. I owe a particular debt of gratitude to two people. One is Dr. Richard H. Logsdon, Director of the Columbia University Libraries, who endorsed my original application and subsequently granted me a leave of absence to accomplish the work. The other is my immediate supervisor, Professor James Grote Van Derpool, Librarian of the Avery Library, who has been untiring in his help and encouragement from the very beginning. Without his support the work could never have been realized. For the administration of the fund Mr. Charles W. Mixer, Assistant Director of Libraries, was responsible, and I am grateful to him for the way in which he handled it, as I am to Miss Nancy Cedrone who assisted him in this task.

Miss Constance M. Winchell, Reference Librarian of the Columbia University Libraries, has given needed encouragement from the start, as well as valuable and detailed advice as the work progressed. Among other people who have encouraged me actively to undertake this work I should like to mention the late Professor Talbot Hamlin of Columbia University; Professor Rensselaer W. Lee of Princeton University; Miss E. Louise Lucas, Librarian of the Fogg Art Museum; Professor Millard Meiss, then of Harvard University; Mrs. Alice S. Plaut, Librarian of Arts and Music of the Public Library of Cincinnati; Professors Meyer Schapiro, Emerson H. Swift, and Everard M. Upjohn of Columbia University; Mr. Bernard Karpel, Librarian of the Museum of Modern Art; and Mr. George Wittenborn, art publisher and book dealer.

I have been most fortunate in having a number of scholars and colleagues who offered valuable suggestions and assistance by checking various sections of the manuscript in the fields in which they specialize. To all of them I wish to express my thanks. Professor Rudolf Wittkower generously checked through the chapter on "Documents and Sources" and made many valuable suggestions in addition to lending his support to the whole enterprise. Dr. Margarete Bieber and Professor Evelyn B. Harrison have gone over the sections dealing with ancient art. Professor Marianna Byram gave advice on the sections dealing with drawings and prints.

Professor George R. Collins has given considerable aid in the Spanish section. Professor Julius S. Held has kindly verified sections dealing with German, Dutch, Flemish, and Scandinavian art. Professor Marion Lawrence checked through the sections of Early Christian, Byzantine, and Medieval art, while Professor Bertha M. Frick of the School of Library Service has read over my listings of medieval manuscript material. Miss Elizabeth McCausland made helpful suggestions regarding the literature in the American field. Professor Jane Gaston Mahler checked through the section on Oriental art and offered many valuable comments. Professor Meiss has lent his knowledge to the Italian section. Professor Paul S. Wingert has given me useful aid in compiling the section on primitive art.

My colleague Adolf K. Placzek, Assistant Librarian of the Avery Library, has been of invaluable help to me in many respects. Not only has he given me numerous suggestions and guidance in covering the field of architecture, but he has continued to offer assistance and encouragement throughout my work, to the point of actual collaboration in some areas.

In the field of the Applied Arts I am indebted to Dr. Gerd Muehsam, Art Librarian of Cooper Union, and Mr. Carl Dauterman of the curatorial staff of the Metropolitan Museum, who both gave invaluable assistance in a field in which I am not as much at home as in others.

Mrs. Olga Masley of the Columbia Libraries staff is responsible for the Russian language entries, while Mrs. Beatrix Van Tijn checked the Dutch and many German citations. Mr. John N. Waddell, Assistant Reference

Librarian of Columbia University, was untiring in calling to my attention new material which did not fall directly in my field and might otherwise have been overlooked.

Miss Eleanor F. Wedge, Reference Assistant in the Fine Arts Library of Columbia, has been most generous in her assistance, and I wish to express my thanks to her for checking and annotating the chapter on "Periodicals" in addition to other time-consuming services too numerous to mention. Not the least of these was her admirable handling of many problems in the library during my leave of absence, thus taking a heavy load off my shoulders.

I have likewise been most fortunate in having two very able assistants on the project. Miss Etta Arntzen, Librarian, Architecture Library of Cornell University, has checked through the major part of the work during her year's leave of absence for graduate work at Columbia. Mrs. Mary Hunt, who substituted admirably for me in the library during my leave of absence, since July, 1957, has undertaken with unerring accuracy the complicated typing of the entire manuscript and many checking and editorial services. The compilation of the Index is also her work. To these two I owe a special word of thanks for their painstaking work and excellent co-operation.

In addition to the persons already mentioned, among my colleagues in this country I want to single out for thanks Mrs. Elizabeth Usher, at that time Acting Librarian of the Metropolitan Museum of Art Library, and Mrs. Lucile Haseman of the General Reference and Bibliography Division of the Library of Congress, who gave untiring help in a place and at a time where it was needed.

During my European trip, when I visited thirty-five art libraries, I was extended warm hospitality by many librarians, which I deeply appreciate and wish to acknowledge. I should like especially to mention Dr. Otto Kurz of the Warburg Institute Library, who gave me very helpful information on several libraries in Europe and their resources. Professor Dr. Ulrich Middeldorf of the Kunsthistorisches Institut in Florence made many useful suggestions regarding the organization of the work. His assistance was especially valuable since he has compiled an exhaustive unpublished bibliography of art reference books which is at present housed at the University of Chicago but which is to be moved to the Institut in Florence. Professor William S. Heckscher, Director of the Ikonologisch Instituut der Rijksuniversiteit in Utrecht, made many advantageous suggestions and introduced me to numerous works in his field with which I was not already familiar. Mr. Robert L. Collison of the Westminster Reference Library in London was extremely helpful.

Research for this book was undertaken in many libraries, and I should like to express my appreciation for all the hospitality and services received in them. The greater part of the work was accomplished in the Avery Library, the Fine Arts Library, and the General Library of Columbia University; the Metropolitan Museum Library; and the Art Division of the New York Public

Library. To the staffs of these libraries and especially to Mr. Rolland Mills, then of the Avery Library, and Messrs. Kelley, Caffrey, Coman, and Sinek of the Metropolitan Museum I owe a very real debt of gratitude for the hundreds of volumes they cheerfully carried to me.

I should like to specify a number of other libraries in which I also worked, namely the Frick Art Reference Library, the Cooper Union Museum Library, the Pierpont Morgan Library, and the Hispanic Society Library, all in New York City. Much time was spent at the Harvard Libraries investigating their wonderful resources, and in Washington, D.C., at the Library of Congress and the Freer Gallery of Art Library. In London I worked in the Victoria and Albert, the Courtauld Institute Library, the British Museum, and the Westminster Reference Library; in Paris at the Bibliothèque Nationale and the Institut d'Art et d'Archéologie de l'Université de Paris; in Rome at the Vatican, the Bibliotheca Hertziana, and the Biblioteca dell'Istituto Nazionale di'Archeologia e Storia dell'Arte. The Zentralinstitut für Kunstgeschichte in Munich and the Kunstgeschichtliche Seminar of the University at Marburg were the German libraries I worked in; the Rijksbureau voor Kunsthistorische Documentatie in the Hague and the Ikonologisch Instituut der Rijksuniversiteit in Utrecht, those in the Netherlands.

Finally, I should like to express my gratitude and appreciation to Mrs. Pauline J. Love, Director of the Publishing Department of the American Library Association, for her co-operation and patience in this difficult undertaking. It has been a real pleasure to work with her.

There would be many others to mention—personal friends who have borne with me, and my mother, who had to give up so many vacations which we might otherwise have spent together. If I have forgotten anyone, I trust I may be forgiven. I can only plead the excuse occasioned by the length of this project and its unceasing demands and contacts.

New York City
July, 1958

Contents

Contents

CHAPTER 1

Bibliography

THE BIBLIOGRAPHIES LISTED IN THIS chapter are the important separate, printed bibliographies covering art history in general. Bibliographies of specific subjects, e.g., Architecture, Sculpture, Painting, the Applied Arts, are listed in those chapters. National bibliographies are, of course, of great importance for art research but they transcend it and are not included in this volume. For them the reader is referred to Constance M. Winchell's *Guide to Reference Books* (7th ed.; Chicago: American Library Association, 1951) and to its supplements.

Historical

1

Cicognara, Leopoldo, *Conte*. Catalogo ragionato dei libri d'arte e d'antichità posseduti dal conte Cicognara. Pisa, Capurro, 1821. 2 v. 20 cm.

A facsimile was published in Leipzig, 1931. A classed bibliography with annotations. Author index at end of v. 2. One of the earliest important bibliographies in the field of art.

2

Comolli, Angelo. Bibliografia storico-critica dell'architettura civile ed arti subalterne.... Rome, Stamperia Vaticana, 1788–92. 4 v. 29 cm.

A classed bibliography with long annotations, covering early historical and theoretical works on art. Classification scheme given at beginning of v. 1; author and title indexes at the ends of v. 2, 3, and 4. Index of v. 2 covers the first two volumes.

3

Duplessis, Georges. Essai d'une bibliographie générale des beaux-arts; biographies indi-viduelles, monographies, biographies générales. Paris, Rapilly, 1866. 144 p. 22 cm.

Useful for listing of editions of early sources.

Contents: Section I, Biographies individuelles, Monographies (nos. 1–2901 listed alphabetically by name of artist); Section II, Biographies générales (nos. 2902–3299 listed chronologically by date of publication): pt. 1, Biographies des artistes (subdivided by schools), pt. 2, Biographies des peintres (subdivided by schools), pt. 3, Biographies des sculpteurs, pt. 4, Biographies des architectes, pt. 5, Biographies des graveurs.

No indexes.

4

Murr, Christophe Gottlieb von. Bibliothèque de peinture, de sculpture, et de gravure. Francfort et Leipzig, Krauss, 1770. 2 v. 18 cm.

An early classified bibliography of the fine arts. Author index p. 779–[806].

5

Vinet, Ernest. Bibliographie méthodique et raisonnée des beaux-arts. . . . Paris, Firmin-Didot, 1874–77. 2 pts. [1.–2. livr.] 25 cm.

A classed bibliography of books published before 1870, with annotations, covering the history of art, archaeology, architecture, sculpture, painting, engraving, and the industrial arts.

Intended as a complement to Brunet's *Manuel du libraire et de l'amateur de livres* and based on the same plan, but never completed.

Divided into "Études générales" and "Études spéciales."

Catalogs of Libraries

6

Amsterdam. Rijksmuseum. Kunsthistorische Bibliotheek. Catalogus der Kunsthistorische

Bibliotheek in het Rijksmuseum te Amsterdam. . . . Amsterdam, Dept. van Onderwijs, Kunsten en Wetenschappen, 1934–36. 4 v. 23 cm.

A classed bibliography, with an outline of the subject classification at the beginning of each volume.

Volume 4 is a "register" containing indexes of authors, artists, illustrators, subjects, places, collectors and dealers, and anonymous works.

7

Amsterdam. Stedelijk Museum. Bibliotheek. Catalogus. [Amsterdam, 1957?] 179 p. 26 cm.

A classified catalog of the Library of Modern Art in the Municipal Museum, compiled by L. Kloet, which contains 5500 entries representing their holdings as of April 1, 1956. Text in Dutch, English, French, German, and Spanish. Indexes: of series p. 147–58; of periodicals p. 159–63; of authors p. 165–79.

8

Annuario bibliografico di archeologia 1952–(54), anno 1–(3). [Modena] Soc. Tip. Modenese, 1954–(56). 25 cm.

Pubblicazioni della Biblioteca dell'Istituto Nazionale d'Archeologia e Storia dell'Arte. Direttore: Guido Stendardo. Subtitle: Opere e periodice entrate in Biblioteca con la data di pubblicazione del 1952. A cura di C. D. Onofrio.

Volume 1 is an annotated, classed bibliography of books and periodical articles bearing the imprint date of 1952 which have been acquired by this library. Generally an abstract of the article or books is given. Indexes of abbreviations, of authors, of proper names, and plan of the classification.

9

Annuario bibliografico di storia dell'arte, anno 1–(4), 1952–(56). Modena, Soc. Tip. Modenese, 1954–(58). 24 cm.

Pubblicazioni della Biblioteca dell'Istituto Nazionale d'Archeologia e Storia dell'Arte.

Volume 1 compiled by Maria Luisa Garroni.

A classified bibliography, with abstracts, of books and periodicals acquired by this library with the imprint date of 1952 (for v. 1). Index of abbreviations also lists periodicals included. There is an index of names.

10

Berlin. Staatliche Kunstbibliothek. . . . Katalog der Ornamentstichsammlung der Staat-lichen Kunstbibliothek, Berlin. Berlin, Verlag für Kunstwissenschaft, 1936–39. 782 p. illus. 31 cm.

At head of title: Staatliche Museen zu Berlin.

Published in 12 parts 1936–39. Introduction by Hermann Schmitz. First issued in 1894. This is a 2d rev. ed., which was reprinted in New York in 1958 by Burt Franklin. 1894 ed. by Peter Jessen contained 2638 entries, while 2d ed. contains 5435 entries.

A classified bibliography of ornamental prints, primarily in book form, comprising the decorative arts collection of the Berlin State Library and its predecessors. The media are specified and items are divided into nine general categories: (1) General collections; (2) Handicrafts; (3) Architecture; (4) Interior decoration; (5) Plastic arts; (6) Nature; (7) Symbolical works; (8) Painting; (9) Calligraphy and printing arts.

"Nachtrag" p. 648–56. "Namenverzeichnis" p. 657–777. "Sachverzeichnis" p. 779.

11

Brussels. Académie Royale des Beaux-Arts et École des Arts Décoratifs. . . . Catalogue annoté de la Bibliothèque artistique et littéraire. Bruxelles, Guyot, 1903. 1170 p. 28 cm.

Gustave François Lagye, editor. At head of title: Ville de Bruxelles. Académie Royale des Beaux-Arts et École des Arts Décoratifs.

First catalog of this library published in 1889. A classed, annotated catalog divided into 39 sections. "Répertoire alphabétique par noms d'auteurs," p. 1071–1168, lists authors and titles.

12

Columbia University. Libraries. Avery Architectural Library. Catalog of the Avery Memorial Architectural Library of Columbia University. Boston, Microphotography Co., 1958. 6 v. 37 cm.

A complete reproduction of every entry prior to May 1958 in the Avery Library catalog, which includes all architectural and art books on the Columbia University campus.

A first catalog of this renowned architectural library was published in 1895, in an edition of 1000 copies. This was an author and title listing only, alphabetically arranged, representing about 13,000 books which were then in the collection.

13

Copenhagen. Kommunebibliotekerne. Litteratur om kunst; kunsthistorie, bygningskunst, billedhuggerkunst, maler -og tegnerkunst, grafisk kunst, fotografi, teater, film. København, Kommunebiblioteker, 1948. 184 p. 23 cm.

A classed bibliography of art books in this library. Includes books in foreign languages as well as Danish. Author index p. 171–184.

14

Deutsches Archäologisches Institut. Römische Abteilung. Bibliothek. Katalog der Bibliothek des Deutschen archäologischen Instituts in Rom, von August Mau; neue Bearbeitung von Eugen von Mercklin und Friedrich Matz. . . . Rom, Löscher, 1913–14; Berlin, de Gruyter, 1932. 2 v. in 4. 26 cm.

_____. Ergänzungen zu Band 1 für die Jahre 1911–1925, bearb. von Friedrich Matz. Berlin, de Gruyter, 1930. 516 p. 26 cm.

Volume 1 issued in two parts, 1913–14, each with a special title page; includes works published before 1911. Volume 2, in two parts, 1932, includes works published before 1925. A classed catalog.

Contents: Bd. 1 (1914), I, Allgemeines und vermischtes. II, Die Altertümer nach ihrem Ort: A. Länder und Städte; B. Museen und Sammlungen, von Hans Nachod. Bd. 2 (1932), III, Die Altertümer nach Klassen (Vasenmalerei, von Elisabeth Jastrow p. 560–732). IV, Die Altertümer nach ihren Inhalt. V, Epigraphik, von Lothar Wickert. VI, Öffentliches und privates Leben. VII, Christliche Altertümer; Berichtigungen und Nachträge; Schlagwortregister, von Gerhard Reincke.

Supplement von Friedrich Matz; Museen und Sammlungen, von Reinhard Herbig p. 415–70; Topographisches Register, von Anton Moortgat p. [475]–516.

List of abbreviations of periodicals cited is given at beginning of v. 1, 2, and supplement.

15

Hague. Koninklijke Bibliotheek. Aanwinsten op het gebied van de beeldende kunsten gedurende het tijdvak 1940–1948. 's Gravenhage, Staatsdrukkerij, 1949. 348 p. 20 cm.

Compiled by Eleonore de la Fontaine Verwey. Introduction by L. Brummel. A classed bibliography of books acquired by this library; contains about 3000 items, covering all languages and countries. Author index p. 319–48.

16

Hague. Koninklijke Bibliotheek. Catalogus van schoone kunsten en kunstnijverheid. 's Gravenhage, Belinfante, 1905. 986 p. 24 cm.

A classed bibliography, with a table at front giving the scheme of classification. Indexes of authors p. 868–919, artists p. 920–53, subjects p. 954–62, countries and places p. 963–73.

17

Istituto Nazionale di Archeologia e Storia dell'Arte, Rome. Bollettino bibliografico [pubblicazioni entrate in Biblioteca, 1935–(39)]. Roma, Arte grafichi, 1938–(43).

Forms pt. 2 of Bollettino del R. Istituto d'Archeologia e Storia dell'Arte, v. 8–(10).

Volume for 1935 (anno VIII) covers books published in 1935 and 1936 which entered the library from Jan. 1 to Dec. 1936. Anno IX covers 1937, and anno X covers Jan. 1 to Dec. 1939.

Each volume contains an alphabetical listing of books received, an alphabetical listing of periodical articles, and a detailed subject index; also a list of periodicals culled.

18

Istituto Nazionale di Archeologia e Storia dell'Arte, Rome. Biblioteca. Catalogo dei periodici della biblioteca dell'Istituto nazionale di archeologia e storia dell'arte, a cura di C. Tanfani e F. Roselli. Roma, Palombi, 1947. 70 p. 26 cm.

A bibliography of 1250 titles of periodicals belonging to this library, arranged alphabetically and indicating the library's holdings of each title. This work is brought up to date by an *Indice dei periodici attivi* (Modena, Soc. Tip. Editrice Modenese, 1956. 24 p. 24 cm.), which is just an alphabetical listing of the titles currently received.

19

London. University. Library. Catalogue of books on archaeology and art and cognate works belonging to the Preedy Memorial Library and other collections in the University Library. . . . London, Univ. of London, 1935–37. 2 v. 34 cm.

_____. Supplement 1937. London, Univ. of London, 1937. 25 p. 34 cm.

A classed bibliography with classification scheme given at beginning of each volume.

Contents: v. 1, Archaeology and ancient art; v. 2, Art. Index. The supplement covers both archaeology and art.

Indexes of "Schedule Headings" and of authors and artists.

20

Paris. Université. Bibliothèque d'Art et d'Archéologie (Fondation Jacques Doucet).

Catalogue général publié sous la direction de Georges Wildenstein. XIV. Périodiques. Paris, Les Beaux-Arts [1937]. 125 p. 32 cm.

A list of periodicals in the library of the Institut d'Art et d'Archéologie, arranged by large groups, i.e., bulletins, annuaires, atti, cahiers, etc.

21

Preussische Akademie der Künste, Berlin. Bibliothek. Katalog der Bibliothek der Königlichen Akademie der Künste zu Berlin. Bearb. vom E. Dobbert und W. Grohmann . . . . Berlin, Asher, 1893. 576 p. 25 cm.

A classed bibliography. "Inhalts-Verzeichnis" (p. xvii–xxxi) gives scheme of classification. Index arranged alphabetically by author p. 562–69. Index of artists p. 562–69; of places p. 570–72.

22

Royal Institute of British Architects, London. Library. Catalogue of the . . . Library . . . . London, The Institute, 1937–38. 2 v. 29 cm.

Original catalog of this library was published in 1889–99; since then the collection has trebled in size.

"The most complete architectural bibliography that has yet been published."—*Pref.*

Contents: v. 1, Author entries for books and manuscripts; v. 2, Classified index and alphabetical subject index of books and manuscripts.

23

Vienna. Österreichisches Museum für Kunst und Industrie. Bibliothek. Katalog. . . . Wien, 1902–1904. 5 v. 20 cm.

A catalog of this important Viennese library.

Contents: v. 1, Gruppe I. C. Zeitschriften, 50 p.; v. 2, Gruppe XII Glasfabrikation und Glasmalerei, 29 p.; v. 3, Gruppe XIII Tonwarenfabrikation (Keramik), 75 p.; v. 4, Gruppe XIV Arbeiten aus Holz, XV Drechslerei, 62 p.; v. 5, Gruppe XVII A. Schmied- und Schosserarbeiten, 18 p.

24

Vinet, Ernest. Catalogue méthodique de la Bibliothèque de l'École Nationale des Beaux-Arts. Paris, École des beaux-arts, 1873. 256 p. 26 cm.

A classed catalog of the books in this library, with entries listed by title rather than by author. Index of authors and of anonymous works p. 233–50. Classification scheme given p. 251–56.

25

Weigel, Rudolf. . . . Kunstcatalog . . . Leipzig, Weigel, 1837–1866. 35 pts. in 5 v. 22 cm.

First seven parts have title "Catalog von Kunstsachen und Büchern, welche in der Anstalt für Kunst und Literatur in Leipzig vorräthig oder durch dieselbe besorgt werden." Beginning with pt. 8, title is "Rudolf Weigel's Kunstcatalog," each part having two title pages.

Includes both books and prints; a total of 25,374 titles of books, drawings, etc., and 3832 portraits of artists.

Index at the end of each volume, and a general index (318 p.) to the five volumes bound at the end of v. 5.

SEE ALSO: Copenhagen. Danske Kunstindustrimuseum. Bibliotek. Møbler (1684) and Tekstil (1937); Lipperheide. Katalog der . . . Kostümbibliothek (1651).

General

26

Bonser, Wilfrid. An Anglo-Saxon and Celtic bibliography (450–1087). Berkeley and Los Angeles, Univ. of California Press, 1957. 2 v. 26 cm.

While this bibliography covers various phases of history, religion, geography, general culture, numismatics and seals, and epigraphy, it also includes archaeology and a sizable section (p. 480–574) on art. It lists both books and periodical articles published up to the end of 1953. "Periodicals and collective works abstracted" v. 1, p. xxiv–xxxvii. Volume 2 consists of author and subject indexes.

27

Borroni, Fabia. "Il Cicognara"; bibliografia dell'archeologia classica e dell'arte italiana. Firenze, Sansoni, 1954–(57). v. 1–(2³) in (4). (Biblioteca bibliografica italiana, v. 6–7, 10–11)

An ambitious attempt at an annotated bibliography, which is expected to run as high as 20 volumes. Complete listings of editions and variants are intended, but not always attained; thorough bibliographical descriptions and—for annotations—quotations from important sources. Books listed chronologically in each section. Illustrated by facsimiles of title pages.

Contents: v. 1 [I]: Opere bibliografiche citate; pt. 1, Bibliografia; pt. 2, Cataloghi di biblioteche d'arte e di libri d'arte; pt. 3, Enciclopedie, lessici e dizionari; pt. 4, Estetica;

[II]: pt. 5, Orazioni, accademiche, dissertazioni, conferenze; pt. 6, Poemetti didascalici e sulle arti; pt. 7, Tecnica; pt. 8, Conservazione e restauro (a) opere generali, (b) applicazioni in ordine topografico, (c) mostre, (d) varie; v. 2 [I]: Archeologia classica; pt. 1, Trattati e letteratura periegetica; pt. 2, Metodologia, manuali, opere generali; pt. 3, Congressi e convegni; pt. 4, Cataloghi; [II]: pt. 5, Musei.

Indexes v. 1, p. 331–443.

28
Essai d'une bibliographie internationale d'histoire de l'art, 1934/35– . Publié sous les auspices de Comité international d'histoire de l'art. Bergamo, Ist. Ital. d'Arti Grafiche, 1936– . v. I. 176 p. 23 cm.

Compiled by Giuseppe Delogu.

Classed bibliography of books in German, French, English, Spanish, Italian, Polish, Czech, Rumanian, Swedish, and Hungarian; with author index. Includes music, exposition catalogs, and sales catalogs. Usually gives prices.

29
Gayley, Charles Mills, and Scott, Fred Newton. A guide to the literature of aesthetics. Berkeley, Calif., 1890. 116 p. 24 cm.

Published as supplement to the Report of the Secretary of the Board of Regents, University of California; also issued as University of California, *Library bulletin,* no. 11.

A classed bibliography making no claim to exhaustiveness or completeness of classification.

30
Gettens, Rutherford J., and Usilton, Bertha M. Abstracts of technical studies in art and archaeology 1943–1952. Washington, D.C., 1955. 408 p. 24 cm. (Freer Gallery of Art. Occasional papers, v. 2, no. 2)

Smithsonian Institution Publication 4176.

"Popular articles are covered as well as highly technical ones."—*Foreword.*

Contents: General literature, Museology, Materials, Construction and conservation of objects, and Technological examination of objects and analysis of materials. Periodical abbreviations p. 4–32; list of contributors p. 1–3.

After Jan. 1, 1953 this material appears in *Studies in conservation* (32), published under the sponsorship of the International Institute for the Conservation of Museum Objects, London.

31
Hammond, William Alexander. A bibliography of aesthetics and of the philosophy of the fine arts from 1900 to 1932. Rev. and enl. ed. N.Y., Longmans Green, 1934. 205 p. 25 cm.

Rev. and enl. by 188 titles from 1933 ed. First published as supplement to the May, 1933 issue of the *Philosophical review.*

"Not confined exclusively to books written since 1900 but includes some old and valuable books republished since then."

A classed bibliography containing books and periodical articles, selective rather than comprehensive. Some annotations are given, and bibliographies indicated. Abbreviations of periodicals p. ix–x.

32
International Institute for the Conservation of Museum Objects. Studies in (études de) conservation. Abstracts. Abstracts of the technical literature on archaeology and the fine arts. v. 1, no. 1–(3), 1955–(56). London, 1955–(56). 21 cm.

A classed bibliography with annotations including books and periodical articles. In most cases the entries are signed with initials. Each number divided into: (1) Museology; (2) Materials and techniques; (3) Conservation and restoration; (4) Analysis and materials and technical examination; (5) Authentication and forgery. At the end of each number is a section on "Books noted."

The intention is to issue two volumes a year and eventually to publish a subject and author index.

Forms a supplement to Gettens and Usilton (30).

33
Internationale Bibliographie der Kunstwissenschaft. 1–15 Bd., Apr. 1902–1917/18. Berlin, Behr, 1903–20. 15 v. in 14. 23 cm.

Covers literature from 1902–18, although the first volume has some items published in 1901.

Includes books, periodical articles, and book reviews, listed under the name of the book. A classified list with author and subject indexes. Outline of classification given at the beginning. Includes prices of books.

34
Istituto Nazionale per le Relazioni Culturali con l'Estero. Archeologia, arti figurative, musica. Roma [I.R.C.E.] 1941. 498 p. 17 cm. (Bibliografie del ventennio)

Lists works published in Italy 1922–41,

covering archaeology, art history, theatre, cinema, and music.

A classed list with author index at back. Section on periodicals p. 353–67; and one dealing with catalogs of the principal exhibitions of Italian art p. 341–52.

35

Karpel, Bernard. Arts of the 20th century; a bibliography. N.Y., Wittenborn, 1959(?). 1000 p. (In preparation)

Subtitle: *A selective guide to the literature of the modern arts, 1900–1950.* A classified bibliography covering painting, sculpture, architecture, design, graphics, photography, the film, theater arts, the dance, and general works. This work will contain 2000 references, 200 pages of illustrations and documents, and have an introduction and captions in English, French, and German.

36

Krienke, Gisela. Bibliographie zu Kunst und Kunstgeschichte; Veröffentlichungen im Gebiet der Deutschen Demokratischen Republik, 1945–1953. Leipzig, VEB Verl. für Buch- und Bibliothekswesen [1956]. 283 p. 25 cm.

A classed bibliography of books and periodical articles published in East Germany 1945–1953. Also includes unpublished university papers. To be published triennially.

Register: (1) Zeitschriften und periodische Veröffentlichungen p. 250–54; (2) Künstler p. 255–59; (3) Orte p. 259–63; (4) Schlagworte p. 263–67; (5) Namen p. 267–69; (6) Verfasser p. 269–83.

37

Lucas, Edna Louise. Books on art; a foundation list. 2d ed. Cambridge, Mass., Fogg Museum of Art, Harvard Univ., 1938. 84 p. 29 cm. (Harvard-Radcliffe fine arts series)

1st ed. published in the *Art bulletin,* v. 11, no. 3, Sept. 1929.

An extremely useful classed list of books in English and foreign languages suitable for a college art library. Most of the material was published before 1936 but a few later titles are included. List of periodicals p. 73–74. Author index.

38

Lucas, Edna Louise. Guides to the Harvard libraries, no. 2: Fine Arts. Cambridge, Mass., Harvard Univ. Lib., 1949. 54 p. 20 cm.

Although intended primarily as a guide to the Harvard libraries, this book contains a useful bibliographical appendix (p. 40–54)

which lists the outstanding reference tools and also refers the student of fine arts to basic reference books outside his specialized field.

39

Lucas, Edna Louise. The Harvard list of books on art. Cambridge, Mass., Harvard Univ. Press, 1952. 163 p. 21 cm.

A revision of the author's *Books on art* (37), but since the emphasis is on "books that a library may acquire without undue difficulty," many important older titles (and much background material) have been omitted. Thus the earlier edition is not entirely superseded.

Covers chiefly architecture, sculpture, painting, and drawing. Periodicals are omitted. Author index.

40

Moon, Brenda E. Mycenaean civilization publications since 1955; a bibliography. [London] Univ. of London Institute of Classical Studies, 1957. 77 p. 28 cm. (*Its* Bulletin supplement, no. 3)

A bibliography of books and periodical articles published between Jan. 1936 and June 1956, dealing with Mycenaean civilization from about 1600 to 1100 b.c. The listings are limited to Minoan Crete and arranged alphabetically with a subject list p. 68–77.

41

Porter, Bertha, and Moss, Rosalind L. B. Topographical bibliography of ancient Egyptian hieroglyphic texts, reliefs, and paintings. Oxford, Clarendon Press, 1927– (51). 7 v. diagrs. 29 cm.

An exhaustive compilation of the literature on the subject, arranged by monuments and their respective details. Contents: v. 1, The Theban necropolis; v. 2, The Theban temples; v. 3, Memphis; v. 4, Lower and Middle Egypt; v. 5, Upper Egypt: sites; v. 6, Upper Egypt: chief temples (excluding Thebes); v. 7, Nubia, the deserts, and outside Egypt. Each volume has its own indexes, list of abbreviations, and list of collections of manuscripts.

42

Reisner, Robert George. Fakes and forgeries in the fine arts; a bibliography. N.Y., Special Libraries Assoc., 1950. 58 p. 28 cm.

Covers books and periodical literature published from 1848 through 1948.

General section includes works which discuss two or more art forms or which deal with the moral, ethical, philosophical, and psychological aspects of forgery. Succeeding sections are devoted to paintings, prints, drawings, miniatures, sculpture, antiques and antiquities, ceramics, and miscellaneous art forms. Within each section the bibliography is subdivided into the following: (1) Books devoted entirely to the subject; (2) Books which contain a section devoted to the subject; (3) Periodical articles.

Author index p. 55–58. Bibliography of articles from the *N.Y. Times*, 1897 to the present, p. 37–54, arranged chronologically with slight annotations.

43

Répertoire d'art et d'archéologie; dépouillement des périodiques et des catalogues de ventes, bibliographie des ouvrages d'art français et étrangers, fasc. 1–(59), 1910–(55). Paris, Morancé, 1910–(58). 27 cm.

A list of articles in periodicals of art and archaeology edited in France and other countries, with a short abstract of each article.

For 1910–14, three fascicles issued each year; 1914–19 issued in three fascicles. Each fascicle arranged under country, by periodical, and at end of year an alphabetical index by author and subject. For 1920–25 each fascicle covers one year, with fascicle 29 an alphabetic index for 1920–24. 1925 has its own index at end. Bibliographies of books arranged by subject; separate section for sales catalogs, arranged by place and date of sale from 1911–31.

From 1926 on, arrangement is by subject classification (outlined at beginning of each volume). Author index at end of volume.

44

Schlosser, Julius, *Ritter* von. La letteratura artistica; manuale delle fonti della storia dell'arte moderna. Trad. di Filippo Rossi. 2. ed. italiana aggiornata da Otto Kurz. Firenze, "La Nuova Italia" [1956]. 766 p. 26 cm. (Il pensiero storico, 12)

At head of title: Julius Schlosser-Magnino. Originally published in German as *Die Kunstliteratur* . . . (Wien, Schroll, 1924); then in Italian in 1935 with an appendix by Otto Kurz (1937).

An extremely valuable manual for the history of art literature up to the early 19th century; especially useful for various editions of early sources. The additions by Kurz have been added to the bibliographies in brackets, bringing the material up to date.

Index of artists p. 711–17 and a general bibliographical index p. 719–57.

45

[South Kensington Museum, London. National Art Library] . . . First proofs of the Universal catalogue of books on art. . . . London, Chapman & Hall, 1870. 2 v. 22 cm.

———. Supplement to the Universal catalogue of books on art. London. Printed for H. M. Stat. Off. by Eyre & Spottiswoode, 1877. 654 p. 22 cm.

Includes "not only the books in the library, but all books printed and published at the date of the issue of the Catalogue, that could be required to make the library perfect."—*p. iv.*

Covers painting, sculpture, architecture, mosaics, enamels, archaeology, coins, anatomy, and photography; also includes books on history, criticism, and instruction in the practice of art.

Listed alphabetically by author or main entry, with location of books (i.e., South Kensington or British Museum, etc.). List of correspondents and contributors to this catalog p. vi–viii.

46

Sturgis, Russell. . . . Annotated bibliography of fine art; painting, sculpture, architecture, arts of decoration and illustration; music, by Henry E. Krehbiel. Ed. by George Iles. Boston, pub. for the American Library Assoc. by the Library Bureau, 1897. 89 p. 26 cm.

A bibliography classed in broad categories, with long critical annotations. Index p. 75–89.

47

Warburg Institute. A bibliography of the survival of the classics. v. 1–2, 1931–1932/33. London, Cassell (v. 1), 1934–38. 2 v. 25 cm.

A descriptive bibliography (with text in German and introduction in English) arranged by subject. It is not confined to art but covers all cultural endeavors.

Author index and index of persons and subjects at end of each volume.

The period 1920–30 is covered by a similar bibliography by Richard Newald entitled *Nachleben der Antike,* published in the *Jahresbericht über die Forschritte der klassischen Altertumswissenschaft,* v. 232, 1931, and v. 250, 1935.

48

Young, Arthur Raymond, ed. Art bibliography, prepared by members of the art staff, Teachers College, Columbia University; comp. and ed. by Professor A. R. Young. [N.Y., Columbia Univ., Teachers College] 1941. 78 p. 28 cm.

Reproduced from typewritten copy.

Considers art in the broadest sense, rather than fine arts. Covers architecture, art appreciation, art education, art books for children, art history, biography, color, commercial art, costume, design, dramatic arts, drawing, esthetics, graphic arts, handcrafts, machine arts, painting, sculpture, magazines.

Tendency toward popular rather than scholarly material. A classed bibliography with an outline at the beginning. "Directory of publishers" with their addresses.

49

Zentralblatt für kunstwissenschaftliche Literatur und Bibliographie. 1. Jahrg. (heft 1–10). Leipzig, Klinkhardt & Biermann, 1909. 347 p. 24 cm.

Subtitle: Begründet als Monatshefte der kunstwissenschaftl. Literatur von Dr. Ernst Jaffe und Dr. Curt Sachs.

Each number contains signed reviews and a classed bibliography of periodical articles and books. At beginning of the volume is an alphabetical list of books reviewed, with names of reviewers and page numbers.

SEE ALSO: Art index (83); Lavedan. Histoire de l'art (449); Praz. Studies in seventeenth-century imagery (328); Tietze. Die Methode der Kunstgeschichte (430); Timmling. Kunstgeschichte und Kunstwissenschaft (431).

National

France

50

Mustoxidi, Théodore Mavroïdi. Histoire de l'esthétique française, 1700–1900, suivie d'une bibliographie générale de l'esthétique française des origines à 1914. Paris, Champion, 1920. 240 p. 25 cm.

A bibliography which includes periodical articles as well as books, arranged chronologically, indicating only the first edition of each work. Alphabetical index at end.

Germany

51

Schrifttum zur deutschen Kunst: hrsg. vom Deutschen Verein für Kunstwissenschaft . . . Jahrg. 1–(17) [okt. 1933]–(1958). Berlin, Deutscher Verein für Kunstwissenschaft, 1934–(58). 31 cm. Annual.

Editors: Hans Kauffmann, Heinrich Appel, Wolf Maurenbrecher, Ewald Behrens, and Angelo Wirtz-Pudelko.

A classified, annotated bibliography of German art in all its ramifications, issued annually to replace bibliographies in the *Repertorium für Kunstwissenschaft* (2323) and the *Internationale Bibliographie* (33). Covers periodical literature, as well as books, and lists reviews.

Volume 1 covers Okt. 1933–Sept. 1934. Author index at end of each volume.

52

Schrifttum zur deutsch-baltischen Kunst, zusammengestellt von Hans Peter Kügler. Beiheft zum Schrifttum der deutschen Kunst hrsg. vom Deutschen Verein für Kunstwissenschaft. Berlin, Deutscher Verein für Kunstwissenschaft, 1939. 42 p. 30 cm.

A supplement to the *Schrifttum zur deutschen Kunst* (51), covering the German Baltic area.

53

Sepp, Hermann. . . . Bibliographie der bayerischen Kunstgeschichte bis ende 1905. Strassburg, Heitz, 1906. 345 p. 25 cm.

———. Nachtrag für 1906–1910. Strassburg, Heitz, 1912. 208 p. 25 cm. (Studien zur deutschen Kunstgeschichte, Bd. 67–155)

A classified bibliography covering Bavarian art history and including periodicals as well as books.

Index of persons and subjects p. 327–29; author index p. 330–45. *Nachtrag* follows same format.

Great Britain

54

London. University. Courtauld Institute of Art. . . . Annual bibliography of the history of British art. v. 1–(6). 1934–(1946/48). Cambridge, Cambridge Univ. Press, 1936–(56). 22 cm.

A classed bibliography with index at end of each volume.

"Includes both books and articles on the history of British art excluding Roman but including Celtic and Viking art, and covering architecture, painting, sculpture, the graphic arts and the applied arts. Writings on British private collections and museums have been noted though the arts discussed may not be British; also writings on foreign artists working in Great Britain. Although the bibliography is primarily concerned with the history of art, writings on modern art and on living artists are included, also contemporary criticism."—*Pref.* The 161 periodicals indexed are principally in English but include some 25 foreign journals.

Beginning with v. 4 certain sections have been omitted or curtailed when they are covered by other bibliographical publications, e.g., heraldry, costume, etc., which are included in Royal Historical Society, London, *Writings on British history, 1934*—(London, J. Cape, 1937—).

Hungary

55

Biró, Béla. A Magyar müvészettörténeti irodalom bibliográfiája; Bibliographie der ungarischen kunstgeschichtlichen Literatur. [Budapest] Képzömüvészeti alap Kiadóvállata, 1955. 611 p. 24 cm.

A classified bibliography listing books and periodical articles dealing with Hungarian art and Hungarian writings on art history. Covers literature from the 18th century to 1954. Table of contents and Foreword in both Hungarian and German.

Contents: (1–3) Art in general as treated in Hungarian literature; (4) Hungarian art to the end of the 18th century; (5) Hungarian art of the 19th and 20th centuries; (6) Exhibitions 1830–1954; (7) Foreign art references; (8) Local history; (9) Applied art.

"Namenregister der Verfasser" (author index) p. 551–88. "Namenregister der Künstler" (artist index) p. 589–612.

Italy

56

Aeschlimann, Erardo. Bibliografia del libro d'arte italiano 1940–1952. Roma, Bestetti [1952]. 380 p. illus., 32 plates. 20 cm.

Gives prices for books and indicates some periodicals which have already died.

Contents: Edizioni di pregio illustrate da artisti contemporanei. Edizioni di pregio tipografico. Edizioni d'interesse bibliografico. Pittura. Bianco & nero. Scultura. Architettura. Archeologia. Arti minori. Pubblicazioni sull'Arte in genere. Cataloghi di mostre d'arte ufficiali (listed by year of exhibition). Itinerari e guide artistiche (arranged by provinces). Scuole d'arte (alphabetically by author). Periodici d'arte. Indice degli autori e degli argomenti (p. 333–80).

57

Annuario bibliografico di archeologia e di storia dell'arte per l'Italia . . . anno 1–2, 1911–1912. Roma, Loescher (W. Regenberg), 1913–14. 2 v. 25 cm.

Compiled by F. Gatti and F. Pellati.

Covers books and periodical articles for the years 1911–12 and some few items which appeared earlier, arranged alphabetically by author, with an "anonimo" section at the beginning. Index of periodicals and of material at end of each volume. No more published.

58

Ceci, Giuseppe. Bibliografia per la storia delle arti figurative nell'Italia meridionale . . . . Napoli, Presso la R. Deputazione, 1937. 2 v. 25 cm.

A detailed, classed bibliography on the art and artists of southern Italy, with emphasis on Naples. References to guides, documents, and literary sources as well as to books or periodicals on art.

Contents: v. 1, L'arte nell'Italia meridionale dal medioevo alla prima metà del secolo XVIII; v. 2, Dalla metà del secolo XVIII ai nostri giorni.

Volume 1 divided into works before 1742 and those beginning with De Dominici. Volume 2 contains a plan of the work (Indice generale), author index, index of artists, index of places, and list of periodical sources including newspapers.

59

Geck, Francis Joseph. Bibliography of Italian art . . . . v. 5–10. Boulder, Univ. of Colorado Book Store [c1932–41].

Volumes 1–4 not yet published.

Covers history, politics, customs and literary achievements as well as the fine arts. Gives lists of principal architects, painters, and sculptors, with dates; charts of historical events and celebrated personages, and lists of important monuments. Popular rather than scholarly. Emphasis on material in English.

Contents: v. 5, Italian Gothic art 1200–1420; v. 6, Italian early Renaissance art—Quattrocento; v. 7, Italian high Renaissance art—Cinquecento, 1 pt.; v. 8, Italian late Renaissance art—Cinquecento, 2 pt.; v. 9, Italian baroque art—Il Seicento; v. 10, Italian rococo art.

SEE ALSO: Borroni. "Il Cicognara" (27); Modigliani. Mentore (426).

Latin America

60

Buschiazzo, Mario José. Bibliografia de arte colonial argentino. Buenos Aires, 1947. 150 p. 25 cm.

9

On cover: Universidad de Buenos Aires, Instituto de Arte Americano, Investigaciones Estéticas. A classified bibliography with short annotations, covering colonial art in Argentina. Contents: Obras de historia del arte argentino p. 1–73; Materiales documentales para la historia del arte argentino p. 74–132; Miscelanea p. 133–34; Indice analitico p. 135–50.

61

Florén Lozano, Luis. Bibliografía de las bellas artes en Santo Domingo. Bogotá, Antares, 1956. 53 p. 24 cm. (Materiales para el estudio de la cultura dominicana, 8)

A classed bibliography with occasional short annotations, including both books and periodical articles. Author index p. 51–53.

62

Giraldo Jaramillo, Gabriel. Bibliografía selecta del arte en Colombia. Bogotá, Editorial A B C, 1956. 147 p. 20 cm. (Biblioteca de bibliografía colombiana)

An annotated, classified bibliography of Colombian art. Author index p. 135–42.

63

Handbook of Latin American studies. Cambridge, Mass., Harvard Univ. Press, 1936–(1951). v. 1–(19). 24 cm. Annual.

Each volume (except v. 1) contains a section of annotated bibliography on art by a specialist in the field.

Volume 2 (1948) covers material published in 1945, and contains an article by Elizabeth Wilder on the general status of Latin-American bibliography and comments on 181 titles.

64

New York. Metropolitan Museum of Art. Books on Latin America and its art in the Metropolitan Museum of Art library, comp. by John B. Montignani . . . . [N.Y.] Metropolitan Museum of Art, 1943. 63 numb. l. 28 cm.

Reproduced from typewritten copy. A classed arrangement with some short annotations, but not for all items. The outline of classification serves as a table of contents.

65

Smith, Robert Chester, and Wilder, Elizabeth. A guide to the art of Latin America . . . . Washington, D.C., U.S. [Govt. Print. Off.] 1948. 480 p. 23 cm. ([U.S.] Library of Congress. Latin American series, no. 21)

A selective, annotated, classified bibliography of books and periodical articles published before 1943, containing about 5000 entries.

Covers museums, art education, and other art activities, as well as architecture, painting, sculpture, graphic arts, minor arts, and photography.

Arranged by periods: (1) Colonial, (2) 19th century, (3) Modern; then subdivided by countries, and under countries by techniques.

If book is in the Library of Congress, its call number is given; if not, its location in some other library if possible. General index at end of volume.

66

Valladares, José. Arte brasileira; publicações de 1943–1953, bibliografía comentada com índice remissivo. Salvador, Bahia, Livraria Progresso Editora, 1955. 78 p. 24 cm.

A classed bibliography with short annotations. "Indice remissivo" p. 71–78, of authors, artists, museums, galleries, and collectors.

SEE ALSO: López Serrano. Bibliografía de arte español y americano (79).

Low Countries

67

Hall, H. van. Repertorium voor de geschiedenis der Nederlandsche schilder- en graveerkunst sedert het begin der 12de eeuw. . . . 's Gravenhage, Nijhoff, 1936–1949. 2 v. 25 cm.

Covers literature in books and periodicals on Dutch art from 12th century to 1946; also painters and engravers of Belgium until 1500.

Deel I covers 12th century to 1932; Deel II, 1933–46.

Subject arrangement with author index. List of works treated (including about 450 periodicals) given at beginning of each volume.

"Lijst van afkortingen der geraadpleegde tijdschriften en verzamelwerken": v. 1, p. [xiii]–xxviii; v. 2, p. [xi]–xxii.

68

Netherlands. Rijksbureau voor Kunsthistorische Documentatie. Bibliography of the Netherlands Institute for Art History. v. 1–(7), 1943–(54). Hague, 1943–[54]. 23 cm. Quarterly.

Published as a supplement to the *Mededeelingen* of the Rijksbureau voor Kunsthistorische Documentatie.

"It is a continuation in another form of van Hall (67)."

"Keeps readers informed of all publications on Dutch and Flemish art of every period, with the exception of sculpture, architecture, and the arts and crafts." However, v. 2 includes sculpture and arts and crafts.

A classed bibliography, issued irregularly, printed on one side of the paper, for clipping. Brief indications of the subjects treated are given, usually in English, and reviews of books or exhibitions are also cited.

Oriental Countries

69
Annual bibliography of Islamic art and archaeology, India excepted . . . v. 1–3, 1935–37. Jerusalem, Divan Pub. House, 1935–37. 24 cm.
Edited by L. A. Mayer.
A classed bibliography with index. Covers books and (predominantly) periodical articles.
"No reviews are noted which, although they appeared in 1935, deal with books or articles published in previous years. Pre-Islamic material is excluded by definition."—*Pref.*

70
Borton, Hugh, comp. A selected list of books and articles on Japan in English, French, and German, comp. by Hugh Borton [and others]. Rev. and enl. Cambridge, Mass., Harvard-Yenching Inst., 1954. 272 p. 24 cm.
Art p. 195–222. A classified list with author, title, and subject index.

71
Boston. Museum of Fine Arts. Bibliographies of Indian art, by Ananda K. Coomaraswamy . . . . Boston, 1925. 54 p. 30 cm.
"Partly reprinted with additions from parts 1, 2, and 4 of the Catalogue of the Indian collections in the Museum of Fine Arts."—*Pref.*
Contents: General; Sculpture; Painting; Textiles; Other minor arts.
Index of places, technical terms, and Indian texts named in book titles.

72
Ettinghausen, Richard, ed. A selected and annotated bibliography of books and periodicals in Western languages dealing with the Near and Middle East with special emphasis on medieval and modern times. Washington, D.C., Middle East Inst., 1952. 111 p. 28 cm. (American Council of Learned Societies Devoted to Humanistic Studies. Committee on Near Eastern Studies)
Includes some art and archaeology. Author index p. 99–111.

73
Instituut Kern, Leyden. Annual bibliography of Indian archaeology . . . 1926–(1940/47). Leyden, Brill, 1928–(50). years 1–(15) in (5) v. plates. 32 cm.
An annotated, classed bibliography of all books and articles dealing with Indian archaeology in its widest sense.
Each volume contains an introduction which describes excavations and recent developments in scholarship. Illustrated with plates and line drawings. List of abbreviations of periodicals and index at end of each volume.

74
Mitra, Haridas. Contribution to a bibliography of Indian art and aesthetics. Santiniketan, Visva-Bharati, 1951. 240 p. 25 cm.
"In the bibliography mainly the source books . . . are included."
Contents: Introduction p. 8–76; Classified list of texts p. 77–237; Additions and corrections p. 238–40.
Introduction contains chapters on Iconography, Table of Linear Measurements, Architecture, Painting, History of Chronology of Masters. List of abbreviations p. 77–82; of annals, journals and quarterlies p. 81; series p. 82.

75
Pearson, James Douglas, and Rice, D. S. Islamic art and archaeology, a register of work published in the year 1954. Cambridge, Heffer, 1956. 38 p. 22 cm.
Processed. Intended to reduce gap caused by the loss of *Annual bibliography of Islamic art and archæology* (69).

76
Rowland, Benjamin, Jr. The Harvard outline and reading lists for Oriental art. Cambridge, Mass., Harvard Univ. Press, 1952. 64 p. 22 cm.
"A complete revision of the same title [i.e., *Outline and bibliographies of Oriental art*] published in 1938, 1940 and 1945. This new edition includes a clarified rearrangement of the periods of Indian art and the introduction of sections on the later periods of Chinese art. Arranged by countries and periods and within these categories under headings of architecture, sculpture and painting."—*Pref.*

11

"Bibliographies intended both for the beginner and as reference lists for the advanced student. Periodical articles are cited only when no books are available on the subject."—*Pref.*

Contents: (1) Outline p. 1–27; (2) Reading lists p. 30–64. List of periodicals and serials in the field p. 28–29.

Scandinavia

77

Bodelsen, Merete (Christensen), and Marcus, Aage. Dansk kunsthistorisk Bibliografi. København, Reitzel, 1935. 503 p. 22 cm.

A classed bibliography, including both books and periodical articles, on Danish art history. Covers architecture, sculpture, painting, graphic arts, museums and collections, art academies, and art historians. Includes material in foreign languages as well as Danish.

No index. List of Danish art periodicals, arranged chronologically by date of first number, p. 14–15.

78

Marcus, Aage. Bibliographie des oeuvres principales de la littérature danoise concernant les beaux arts depuis l'époque romane. (*In* Artes v. I, 1932, p. 17–52)

A classed bibliography with a few annotations, covering Danish literature on the fine arts since the Romanesque period.

Spain and Portugal

79

López Serrano, Mathilde. Bibliografía de arte español y americano 1936–40 . . . Madrid [Gráficas Uguina] 1942. 243 p. 28 cm.

At head of title: Consejo superior de investigaciones científicas, Istituto Diego Velázquez.

A classed bibliography covering books and periodical articles on art and archaeology of Spain, Hispanic America, and the Philip-

pines. Intended to become an annual publication; Portuguese art to be included in future volumes.

Index of persons and places p. 199–240. Outline of classification p. 241–43.

Switzerland

80

Haendcke, Berthold. Architecture, sculpture et peinture. Réd. par le Dr. Berthold Haendcke. . . . Berne, Wyss, 1892. 100 p. 22 cm. (Bibliographie nationale suisse. Répertoire méthodique de ce que a été publié par la Suisse et ses habitants. Pub. avec le concours des autorités fédérales et d'administrations fédérales et cantonales et en collaboration avec de nombreux savants par la Commission centrale pour la bibliographie suisse [fasc. 6^{a-c}])

On p. 4 of cover: Bibliographie der schweizerischen Landeskunde. Architektur, Plastik, Malerei. . . .

A classed bibliography of material on Swiss art with prefatory notes in French and German. Alphabetical index of artists p. 89–100.

United States

81

Dickson, Harold Edward. A working bibliography of art in Pennsylvania. Harrisburg, Pa., Historical and Museum Commission, 1948. 148 p. 28 cm.

Processed.

"Its purpose is to provide a useful bibliography for the study of any or all of the arts as they have developed in the Pennsylvania region."—*Pref.*

Part 1 contains bibliographies and reference material; pt. 2, a selection of writings on American art which deal directly with Pennsylvania subjects; pt. 3, a comprehensive listing of published (and some unpublished) literature on the arts in the Keystone State.

CHAPTER 2

Indexes

LISTED HERE ARE INDEXES OF VARIOUS types useful in answering specific questions of identification and factual information. They include bibliographical and general indexes as well as indexes of artists and of portraits. Indexes to paintings are listed in the chapter on "Painting."

General

82
American Library Association. Art Reference Round Table. A union list of holdings of foreign art periodicals published 1939–46. Chicago, 1950. [22] l. 29 cm.

Typewritten. A useful compilation which lists according to title the holdings of 34 American libraries in the field of foreign art periodicals published during the war years.

83
Art index, Jan. 1929– ; a cumulative author and subject index to a selected list of fine arts periodicals and museum bulletins. N.Y., Wilson, 1930– . 29 cm.

Issued quarterly in Dec., March, and June with an annual cumulation in Sept. and three-year cumulations in 1932, 1935, 1939, etc. One of the basic tools of art research.

Indexes American and foreign periodicals, museum bulletins, annuals, etc., covering the fields of art, archaeology, architecture, arts and crafts, ceramics, decoration and ornament, graphic arts, industrial design, interior decoration, landscape architecture, painting, and sculpture. List of periodicals indexed is given at beginning of each volume. Articles are indexed under author and subject; book reviews are indexed under the author reviewed; exhibitions are entered under the artist exhibiting. Illustrations without text are indexed under the artist's name; and illustrations accompanying an article are listed under the article. Colored illustrations are noted.

84
Deville, Étienne. Index du Mercure de France, 1672–1832, donnant l'indication . . . de toutes les notices, mentions, annonces, planches & c. concernant les beaux-arts et l'archéologie. Publication pour faciliter les études d'art en France. Paris, Jean Schemit, 1910. 269 p. 27 cm.

350 copies printed. Comprises 12,500 entries arranged alphabetically by subject, covering: art in general, monumental archaeology, antiquity, academies, artists, collections and collectors, religious and profane iconography, fêtes and funerals, and minor arts.

85
Ellis, Jessie (Croft). Nature and its applications; over 200,000 selected references to nature forms and illustrations of nature as used in every way. Boston, Faxon, 1949. 861 p. 27 cm. (Useful reference series, no. 74)

A rev. and greatly enl. ed. of her *Nature index* (1930) with a much broader scope and coverage. An index of some 180 books and periodicals, which is useful for finding representations of various forms of nature in art. The greater part of the volumes indexed are in English but some foreign titles are included. Contents: (1) Books and periodicals used in the index p. xi–xii; (2) Nature and its application p. 1–854; (3) Landscapes p. 854–61; (4) Terms used in decorative design p. 861.

86
Ellis, Jessie (Croft). Travel through pictures; references to pictures, in books and periodicals, of interesting sites all over the world. Boston, Faxon, 1935. 699 p. 22 cm. (Useful reference series, no. 53)

"Companion volume to [the author's] *Nature index* (85) and *General index to illustrations.*"—*Pref.* While not primarily an art reference book it is useful for finding views of cities, etc., and many art and architecture books are included among those indexed. Arranged alphabetically by country represented and then by place. Contents: Books and periodicals used in the index p. 1–6; Index p. 7–548; Cross references p. 549–699.

87

Graves, Algernon. A century of loan exhibitions 1813–1912 . . . . London, A. Graves, 1913–14. 5 v. 29 cm.

Edition of 250 copies printed. Includes the most important public exhibitions of the hundred-year period in London and the provinces. For each painting gives gallery where exhibited, year, number and title, size, and name of owner. Arranged alphabetically by artist, then by gallery or museum.

Contents: v. 1, A–G; v. 2, H–Q; v. 3, R–U; v. 4, V–Z and Addenda; v. 5, 2d Addenda and Indexes: Index of portraits p. 2309–440; Index of owners p. 2443–608; List of exhibitions analyzed in the century of loan exhibitions with the different years p. 2609–10.

88

New York. National Academy of Design. National Academy of Design exhibition record, 1826–1860. . . . N.Y., Printed for the New-York Historical Society, 1943. 2 v. 24 cm.

Half-title: Collections of the New-York historical society for the year 1941–1942. The John Watts DePeyster publication fund series, LXXIV–LXXV. Prepared by Miss Bartlett Cowdrey. A complete record of the first 35 annual exhibitions, arranged alphabetically by name of artist exhibiting. Under each artist his exhibited works are arranged chronologically. Index (v. 2, p. 235–365) is a guide to subjects and owners of the works shown.

89

Rutledge, Anna Wells, ed. Cumulative record of exhibition catalogues: The Pennsylvania Academy of the Fine Arts, 1807–1870; the Society of Artists, 1800–1814; the Artists' Fund Society, 1835–1845. Philadelphia, American Philosophical Society, 1955. 450 p. 31 cm. (Memoirs of the American Philosophical Society, v. 38)

Includes painting and sculpture, but not medals or engravings or casts of classical sculpture. Contents: List of catalogs; Index by artist p. 13–291; Index by owner p. 292–371; Index by subject p. 372–450.

90

South Kensington Museum, London. . . . A list of buildings in Great Britain and Ireland having mural and other painted decorations, of dates prior to the latter part of the sixteenth century, with historical introduction and alphabetical index of subjects, by C[harles] E[dward] Keyser . . . [Compiled for the use of schools of art in the United Kingdom] 3d ed., enl. London, Eyre, 1883. 402 p. 22 cm.

1st ed. 1871; 2d ed. 1872. At head of title: Science and art department of the Committee of council on education, South Kensington Museum. Contents: Topographical classification p. vii–xxxii; Historical introduction p. xxxiii–xcii; List (alphabetical) of mural paintings p. 1–296; List of later examples p. 297–99; List of additional examples p. 300–32; Index of objects, subjects, saints, etc., named in the lists p. 333–402.

91

Vatican. Biblioteca Vaticana. Centro Bibliografico della Copia Vaticana del "Princeton art index." Catalogo delle pubblicazioni periodiche esistenti in varie biblioteche di Roma e Firenze; pubblicato con la collaborazione dell' Unione Internazionale degli Istituti di Archeologia Storia, e Storia dell'Arte in Roma. Città del Vaticano, 1955. 495 p. 25 cm.

Compiled by Guy Ferrari O.S.B. At head of title: Biblioteca Apostolica Vaticana, copia Vaticana dell'indice di arte cristiana. A union list of all periodicals in the libraries of Rome and Florence, with indications of the hours of opening, addresses, and telephone numbers of the various libraries included.

"Lista delle biblioteche" p. x–xiii. "Elenco topografico delle accademie, società ecc. e delle pubblicazione da esse edite compreso nel catalogo" p. 437–95.

SEE ALSO: Internationale Bibliographie der Kunstwissenschaft (33); Monro. Index to reproductions of American paintings, and Index to reproductions of European paintings (161 and 162); Répertoire d'art et d'archéologie (43).

Artists

92

British Museum. Department of Prints and Drawings. Index of artists represented in the Department of Prints and Drawings in the

British Museum. . . . London, Longmans, 1893–96. 2 v. 26 cm.

Under each school or country the names of all artists belonging to it are arranged in alphabetical order. Under each artist are specified several classes of work by which he is represented, original works first, and then those executed by other hands after his designs. Includes many names not found in other biographical dictionaries. Contents: v. 1, Dutch and Flemish schools; German schools, by Lionel Cust; v. 2, French schools.

93

British Museum. Department of Prints and Drawings. An index of Chinese artists represented in the Sub-department of Oriental Prints and Drawings in the British Museum, by Arthur Waley. . . . [London] Printed by order of the Trustees, 1922. 112 p. 22 cm.

Contains mostly artists whose work is represented in the British Museum, but a few others are included. Each artist is entered under his family name (in romanized, followed by Chinese, characters), followed by his personal name, style, and *nom de plume*. Dates for each artist are given and, when ascertainable, an indication of the type of work he did and a list of his works in the British Museum, with original works superseding reproductions. Bibliography p. [vii]–xii. A supplement was published by W. Speiser in *Ostasiatische Zeitschrift* (2304), Mai/Aug. 1931, p. 124–39, and Okt. 1938, p. 230–39.

94

Graves, Algernon. A dictionary of artists who have exhibited works in the principal London exhibitions from 1760 to 1893. . . . 3d ed. London, Graves, 1901. 314 p. 32 cm.

1st ed. 1884; 2d ed. 1895. Arranged in tabular form, with one line for each artist. In columns gives town from which artist came, dates of first and last exhibitions, his speciality and exhibitions of ten societies in which he may have exhibited, and symbols indicating to which societies he belonged. Number of works exhibited at each gallery is given, and total number recorded in last column. Contains over 16,000 names and covers painters in oil, water color, architects, engravers, medalists, sculptors, etc. List of abbreviations p. ix. List of exhibitions included in this dictionary p. x. Additions and corrections p. xi–xiv.

95

Graves, Algernon. The Royal Academy of Arts; a complete dictionary of contributors

and their work from its foundation in 1769 to 1904. . . . London, Graves, 1905–06. 8 v. ports. 28 cm.

Artists listed alphabetically. Under each artist gives medium in which he worked, his address, and list of works exhibited, in chronological order of the exhibitions. Each picture is given the number it bore in that exhibition.

96

Index of 20th century artists. v. 1–4, no. 7, Oct. 1933–Apr. 1937. N.Y., College Art Assoc., 1933–37. 31 cm.

Issued monthly. Covers only American artists. Each year a supplement was issued to bring the work up to date. For each artist a short biography, list of awards and honors, affiliations, where represented (excluding private collections), list of exhibitions (arranged chronologically), bibliography, and reproductions (where published). Also includes some earlier artists, i.e., Whistler, Eakins, Ryder, Homer, Chase, St. Gaudens, and Sargent. A cumulative index to v. 1–3 is included in v. 3. A typewritten index to the four-volume set has been issued.

97

Mallet, Daniel Trowbridge. Mallet's Index of artists; international–biographical; including painters, sculptors, illustrators, engravers and etchers of the past and the present. N.Y., Bowker, 1935. 493 p. 26 cm.
———. Supplement. 1940. 319 p. 26 cm.

Both volumes reprinted: N.Y., Peter Smith, 1948. An index to biographical material found in general reference books and other more specialized books. A list of sources of this information is given at the beginning of each volume, as well as an author index to these sources.

Information given includes name, nationality, dates of birth and death, medium (if other than painting), residence if artist is living, and sources in which the biographical information can be found. The supplement contains artists omitted from the original volume, with emphasis on contemporary artists. If no information is available in sources used, a reference is made to an art gallery, museum, or society from which data may be obtained.

Some caution should be exercised in consulting this useful tool, as some inaccuracies occur in names and dates.

98

Witt, *Sir* Robert Clermont. Catalogue of painters and draughtsmen represented in the library of reproductions of pictures and drawings formed by Robert and Mary Witt. London, Privately printed, 1920. 238 p. 25 cm.

―――. Supplement. 1925. 25 cm. 266 p.

An alphabetical list of some 8000 painters and draughtsmen represented in this library, now in the possession of the Courtauld Institute of Art. Gives for each artist his dates and school to which he belongs. Very few cross references. The supplement contains an additional 5000 names. Introduction (called Note) gives description of the library and its scope, which includes reproductions of European pictures and drawings of all schools and periods from the 12th century on.

SEE ALSO: Royal Institute of British Architects. Library. Index of architects . . . (786); Tokyo. Institute of Art Research. Index of Japanese painters (1171).

Portraits

99

A. L. A. portrait index; index to portraits contained in printed books and periodicals . . . ed. by W. C. Lane and N. E. Browne . . . Washington, D.C., Library of Congress, 1906. 1600 p. 25 cm.

An index to portraits contained in 6216 volumes (1181 sets of works) of books and periodicals published before 1905. Gives birth and death dates, artist, engraver, and brief characterization of the subject for 120,-000 portraits of 35,000 to 45,000 persons; and indication of where the portrait may be found in books, excluding local histories, genealogical works, collections of engravings, or portraits of writers in sets of their collected works. List of books indexed at beginning of the volume.

100

Diepenbroick-Grüter, Hans Dietrich von, *firm*, Hamburg. Allgemeiner Porträt-Katalog; Verzeichnis einer Sammlung von 3000 Porträts des sechzehnten bis neunzehnten Jahrhunderts in Holzschnitt, Kupferstich, Schabkunst und Lithographie, mit biographischen Notizen. Hamburg, v. Diepenbroick-Grüter, 1931. xxxiii, xxxii, xxxii, xxxii, xxviii, 902, xvii p. 23 cm.

An index to a collection of 3000 portraits of the 16th to 19th centuries in woodcut, copperplate, mezzotint, and lithograph, with

biographies. Issued in five parts. Each part (representing a section of the alphabet) has its own "Berufs- und Schlagwort-Register; Orts- und Landes-Register." At end of the work an index of hidden names.

101

Drugulin, Wilhelm Eduard. Allgemeiner Portrait-Katalog . . . Verzeichniss einer gewählten Sammlung von 24,000 Portraits berühmter Personen aller Länder und Zeiten (mit biographischen und chälkographischen Notizen), welche zu den beigesetzten billigen Preisen von dem Leipziger Kunst-Comptoir zu beziehen sind. Leipzig, Kunst-Comptoir, 1859–60. 2 v. in 1. 22 cm.

Contains 23,821 entries listed alphabetically under subjects of the paintings. A 52-page index divided into 12 price categories and arranged alphabetically under each price range.

―――. Supplement zu Drugulin's Allgemeinem Portrait-Katalog. Verzeichniss von Portraits welche zu den beigesetzten Preisen durch alle Buch- und Kunsthandlungen von dem Leipziger Kunst-Comptoir (W. Drugulin) zu beziehen sind. Juni 1881. Leipzig, Nies'sche Buchdruckerei (C. B. Lorck), 1861. 52 p. 22 cm.

102

Heinzel, Erwin. Lexikon historischer Ereignisse und Personen in Kunst, Literatur und Musik. Mit 17 Bildtafeln. Wien, Hollinek [c1956]. 782 p. illus. 21 cm.

An index to representations of famous personages as depicted in literature, the arts, and music. Personalities arranged alphabetically, and for each a biographical paragraph or two, followed by the listing of representations.

103

Singer, Hans Wolfgang. Allgemeiner Bildniskatalog. . . . Leipzig, Hiersemann, 1930–36. 14 v. 28 cm.

Continued by his *Neuer Bildniskatalog* (104). An index to engraved portraits of all times and countries up to 1929, from 17 German public collections, which includes roughly 25,000 persons and 180,000 portraits. Arranged alphabetically by subject. Information includes name of artist, medium, and location. At end of each volume is an index of artists and an index of calling or profession of the subjects portrayed, for that volume only. Volume 14 is a complete index to the set, arranged like the indexes in the separate volumes.

104

Singer, Hans Wolfgang. Neuer Bildniskatalog. . . . Leipzig, Hiersemann, 1937–38. 5 v. 28 cm.

A continuation and augmentation of his *Allgemeiner Bildniskatalog* (103). An index to painted and sculptured portraits, also some early photographic and illustrative newspaper material. Same information and format as in the previous work. Volume 1 contains a list of sources from which this catalog was compiled. Volume 5 contains an index of artists and an index of calling or profession of the subjects portrayed.

105

Someren, Jan Frederik van. Beschrijvende catalogus van gegraveerde portretten van Nederlanders, vervolg op Frederik Mullers Catalogus van 7000 portretten van Nederlanders. Amsterdam, Muller, 1888–91. 3 v. 25 cm.

A continuation of an earlier edition of 1853. Volumes 2 and 3 are paged continuously. An index of engraved portraits of Dutch people compiled from sales records, the print rooms of Leyden and Amsterdam, public libraries of the Netherlands, and various private collections.

Volume 1 is a systematic listing of collections of portraits and series of portraits in books, arranged by the profession of the sitter, with an alphabetical index. Volumes 2 and 3 cover separate portraits and are divided into three categories: rulers, nobility who are not ruling, and individual people, arranged alphabetically under each category. Indexes of sitters and of artists at end of v. 3. Under the name of each sitter is given a chronological listing of portraits, bibliographical information regarding the portraits, and information on the states of the prints.

| # Directories

INCLUDED IN THIS CHAPTER ARE GENERAL directories of the art world, and directories of museums and libraries in various countries. The latter will enable the reader to locate individual works of art and to survey the holdings of the more important art collections and institutions. (See also the Appendix on Special Collections and Resources [2490–2565].)

General

106
American art directory, v. 1–(40), 1898–(1957). N.Y., Bowker [etc., 1898–(1958)]. illus., plates, ports. 24–26 cm.

At head of title 1952–55: American Federation of Art. Frequency varies: 1898–1900, 1911–49 irregular; 1904–10 biennial; 1952–triennial. None published 1901–03. Volume 35, 1941–42 covers art activities for 1938–41; v. 36, for July 1941–June 1945; v. 37, for July 1945–June 1948. Volumes 33–37, 1936–1945/48 issued in two parts: (1) Organizations; (2) *Who's who in American art* (305). The latter published as a separate volume after 1952.

Title varies: 1898–1945/48, *American art annual*. Editors: 1899–1948, Florence N. Levy; 1952–55, Dorothy B. Gilbert. Since 1913 published by the American Federation of Arts.

Lists art organizations, national and regional organizations, museums, art schools, universities, and colleges with art departments, in the United States, Central and South America, and Canada. Also includes museum publications, art magazines, newspapers containing art notes, sources for various types of exhibitions, and some information on auctions. General index.

Volume 40 adds a comprehensive list of the leading foreign art museums and art schools in Europe, South America, Great Britain, the Far East, etc.

107
Appleton, Marion Brymmer, ed. Who's who in Northwest art; a biographical directory of persons in the Pacific Northwest working in the media of painting, sculpture, graphic arts, illustration, design, and the handicrafts. . . . Seattle, McCaffrey, 1941. 87 p. 23 cm.

"A directory of professional and amateur artists and craftsmen . . . . Names of many deceased artists and of artists who are no longer living in the Northwest are included. The type of work engaged in by the artist is given at the beginning of the entry. Mediums he uses follow in parentheses and are listed in the order of their relative importance in the artist's work. Information supplied by the artist himself."—*Pref.*

"Art organizations of the Northwest" p. 78–80. "Classified geographical list" p. 80–86. "Artists no longer living in the Northwest" p. 86–87.

108
The British antique trades and collectors' directory. Ed. and comp. by Charles Platten Woodhouse. [1st ed.] London, Woodhouse [1949]. 108 p. illus. 26 cm.

Lists English antique dealers, restorers, art and antique auctioneers, packers and shippers, fine arts and collecting publications, and British collectors. Also includes short essays on the National Trust, art galleries and museums, and other topics of interest to collectors, and reproductions of English antiques.

109
Connoisseurs of the world; being an international biographical dictionary of connois-

seurs, collectors, and patrons of art. London, Mitre Press [1943?]. 96 p. 22 cm.

Compilation was begun in 1939 and interrupted by wartime difficulties, which precludes any claim to completeness. Coverage is extremely uneven. Volume 2 to be issued at a later date. For each entry gives office and home address, position, interests, bibliography of writings if an author, and club affiliation. Entries seem to be mostly British and American and a very few Belgian.

110

Handbuch des Kunstmarktes, Kunstadressbuch für das deutsche Reich, Danzig und Deutsch-Österreich, mit sachlicher Unterstützung reichsbehördlicher, staatlicher und städtischer Institutionen sowie von Vereinen und Fachverbänden. Geleitwort von Dr. Max Osborn. Berlin, Antigua Verlagsgesellschaft, 1926. 792 p. 23 cm.

An art directory covering Germany, Danzig, and German Austria. Now out of date. Geographically arranged with place index p. xvii–xxii.

111

Index generalis; general yearbook of universities and of higher educational institutions—academies, archives, libraries, scientific institutes, botanical and zoological gardens, museums, observatories, learned societies. 21st year, 1954–55. Paris, Dunod, 1955. 1953 p. 23 cm.

Published annually since 1919 except during the war years 1940–51. A useful directory which contains information on libraries, higher educational institutions, and learned societies useful for art research. Under these headings entries are by country and then by city. Under the United States, institutions are arranged alphabetically by name. Academies and learned societies are listed according to subject of research and then by city. Index of personal names p. [1559]–1918 and a geographical index p. [1919]–53 listing all institutions in each town are at end of volume. Supplement, [63] pages of information received too late to be included in the text, also at end of volume.

112

Institute of International Education. Directory of international scholarships in the arts. N.Y., Institute of International Education, 1958. 120 p. 14 x 22 cm.

Foreword by Kenneth Holland. Covers awards in the fields of architecture, creative writing, dance, design, music, painting and sculpture, and theater arts. "Committees on study and training in the U.S." p. 107–14.

113

Internationales Kunst-Adressbuch . . . International directory of arts. Annuaire international des beaux-arts, 1952/53–(1956/57). Berlin, Deutsche Zentraldruckerei [1952–(56)]. 4 v. 25 cm.

Editor, 1952– , Walter Kaupert. "Vereinigt mit Deutsches Kunstadressbuch." Lists associations and societies, museums and galleries, libraries and archives, universities, academies, colleges, art and antique dealers, auctioneers, art publishers, art periodicals, antiquarians and art booksellers, artists (painters, sculptors, and engravers), handicrafts, restorers, art collectors, and a list of names. These categories are usually arranged by country and then by city. For each entry gives the address. Includes advertising matter.

114

The Libraries, museums and art galleries year book, including the Librarians' guide. Advisory editor Lionel R. McColvin. 1954–55. London, Clarke; N.Y., Bowker, 1955. 648 p. illus., fold. plates, tables, etc. 22 cm.

1st ed. 1897; 2d ed. 1900–01; 3d ed. 1910; 4th ed. 1914; 5th ed. 1923–24; 6th ed. 1928–29; 7th ed. 1932; 8th ed. 1933; 9th ed. 1935; 10th ed. 1937; 1948 and 1954–55 not numbered. This last edition, with an introduction by Lionel R. McColvin, lists about 3000 British and 3000 selected world libraries and museums. Contents: (1) Professional organizations and associations; (2) British Isles; (3) Overseas.

115

Maecenas, hrsg. von dr. Joachim Stern. . . . 2d ed. Berlin, Stern [1930]. v. 1. 25 cm.

1st ed. 1927, 594 p., 24 cm. An international directory of public collections, collectors, and dealers in objects of art and antiquity. Arranged geographically. Under each city lists official collections, collectors, and then dealers. Covers Germany, Spain, France, England, and Italy. First edition includes private as well as public collections. Contents: v. 1, Mittel; Nord; Osteuropa. No index but a listing of countries p. 2.

116

Mastai's Classified directory of American art & antique dealers, 1957, 6th ed. Art museums: the U.S., Canada, Mexico, Belgium, the British Isles, France, Italy, the Netherlands, and Switzerland. N.Y., Mastai [1957]. 468 p. 24 cm.

1st ed. 1942; 2d ed. 1944–45; 3d ed. 1947; 4th ed. 1950; 5th ed. 1953. Contains art museums listed by place, and classified lists of antique dealers, art galleries, and interior decorators. Appendix lists paintings sold at auction for over $500.

117

Minerva: Jahrbuch der gelehrten Welt, 1.– (34). Jahrg., 1891/92–(1956). Strassburg, Trübner, 1891–1914; Berlin und Leipzig, de Gruyter, 1920–(56). 21 cm. Annual.

Suspended 1914–19, 1931–32, 1934–35, 1938–55. Lists by names of cities the museums, libraries, universities, colleges, learned societies, and technical schools located there. Included are names of the principal officers of each institution, its size, and publications. An index of personal names is very useful. Published 1927–30 in three volumes; v. 1–2 are main part and v. 3 is the personal index. Volumes 32–34, 1936–56, appear in two sections: 1. Abt., Forschungsinstitut, Observatorien, Bibliotheken, Archive, Museen, Kommissionen, Gesellschaften; 2. Abt., Universitäten und Fachhochschulen.

118

Pantheon, internationales Adressbuch der Kunst- und Antiquitäten-Sammler, und -Händler, Bibliotheken, Archive, Museen, Kunst-, Altertums- und Geschichtsvereine, Bucherliebhaber, Numismatiker. . . . 2. Aufl. bearb. von Dr. Albert Schramm. . . . Esslingen a.N., Neff, 1926. 472 p. 21 cm.

1st ed. 1914. Attempts to cover collections in the entire world. The main body of the work is a directory of collections arranged alphabetically by city. A very useful publication but now out of date. Contents: Adressen p. 1–371; Nachtrag p. 373–84; Sammler nach Schlagworten geordnet p. 385–470; Zusammenstellung fremdsprachlicher Ausdrücke mit deutscher Übersetzung p. 471–72.

119

Philip, Alexander John. An index to the special collections in libraries, museums and art galleries (public, private and official) in Great Britain and Ireland. London, Pub. for the author by F. G. Brown [1949]. 190 p. 19 cm.

A handy subject index to libraries in Great Britain. By no means complete in its coverage.

120

The World of learning, 1947– (1957). London, Europa Publications, 1947– (57). Annual [1]– (8). 25 cm.

A directory of learned societies, research institutions, libraries, museums, and universities. Arranged by country and then by city. The amount of information included varies but usually the date of founding, officers in charge, and faculties of the universities are given. There is an index of the names of the institutions, etc., but no personal index.

SEE ALSO: American architects directory (782); Who's who in American art (305).

Museums

121

American Association of Museums. Handbook of American museums; with an appended list of museums in Canada and Newfoundland. Washington, D.C., The American Assoc. of Museums, 1932. 779 p. 24 cm.

"Compiled by Lewis Barrington and special aides, and edited by L. C. Everard."

A directory of museums, arranged alphabetically by state and then city and museum. For each museum gives address, date of founding, person in charge, description of quarters and collections. Now unfortunately out of date.

122

Arts, musées et curiosité en France. Paris [Éditions Ardo] 1946. 579 p. illus., plates, ports. 25 cm.

A very useful index of French museums, art societies, art libraries, schools, national and regional arts organizations, artist's supply houses, galleries, publishers of art books, awards, etc., including names and addresses. For museums and libraries gives history, name of director, and hours of opening. For artists gives addresses and where they exhibit. Lists of "les artistes disparus depuis 1939" with portraits. Well illustrated.

123

Blair, Dorothy. Preliminary survey of East Asiatic art in the museums of Europe. . . . Ann Arbor, Mich., Edwards, 1937. 200 p. 21 cm.

Processed—lithoprint. An outline, arranged by countries, listing collections of importance to the study of Oriental art. Short descriptions of each collection and its strength.

Names of museums and places given both in English and in the vernacular. Good index at back with many cross references.

124

Blunt, Anthony, and Whinney, Margaret. The nation's pictures; a guide to the chief national and municipal picture galleries of England, Scotland and Wales. London, Chatto & Windus, 1950. 292 p. 64 plates. 22 cm.

A compilation of descriptions of the various picture galleries of the United Kingdom, written by the gallery directors. It is intended as a guide to indicate the special interest to tourists of each collection.

125

Gaya Nuño, Juan Antonio. Historia y guía de los museos de España. Madrid, Espasa-Calpe, 1955. 916 p. illus., 9 col. plates. 22 cm.

A directory of museums arranged alphabetically by geographical location. For each museum gives description of its holdings, historical survey, and bibliography. Well illustrated with many views, both exterior and interior, of various museums as well as of important objects contained in them. Geographical index p. 807–38. Artist index p. 839–61. Index of various names p. 862–98. Index of principal subjects p. 899–901. List of illustrations and color plates p. 902–17.

126

International Museum Office. Répertoire international des musées. Paris, Société des Nations, Institut de Coopération Intellectuelle [1933–35]. v. 1–3. plates. 18 cm.

No more published. Lists collections of art, archaeology, ethnology, folk art, and history. For each museum gives name in the vernacular and in French, hours of opening, and in the case of larger museums, a list of departments and curators. Contents: v. 1, Pays-Bas et Indes néerlandaises, 1933, 64 p.; v. 2, Pologne, 1935, 48 p.; v. 3, France, 1933, 169 p.

127

Netherlands (Kingdom, 1815–). Departement van Onderwijs, Kunsten en Wetenschappen. De Nederlandse musea. . . . 3. druk. 's Gravenhage, Staatsdrukkerij- en Uitgeverij-bedrijf, 1956. 440 p. map. 17 cm.

A directory of Dutch museums, arranged alphabetically by city. For each museum gives the names of director and curators, a short history, bibliography, and list of its publications, as well as indicating whether the museum has a library, and if so its size. Subject index p. 412–17, index of directors and curators p. 418–36. At beginning of volume an alphabetical list of museums and private collections included in the work.

Libraries

128

Adressenverzeichnis deutscher Bibliotheken. Hrsg. von der Auskunftsabteilung der Öffentlichen Wissenschaftlichen Bibliothek, Berlin. 1950. Leipzig, Börsenverein der Deutschen Buchhändler, 1950. v. 1, 248 p. 18 cm.

An address book for German libraries, arranged alphabetically by city. For each library gives the address, telephone number, name of the director, number of books in the collection, and indicates whether the library is open to the public. Supplement p. 224–34. Subject index p. 235–48.

129

Italy. Direzione Generale delle Accademie e Biblioteche. Annuario delle biblioteche italiane, 1949/51–1956. [Roma] 1949–56. 3 v. illus. 25 cm.

At head of title: Ministero della pubblica istruzione. A second edition, begun in 1956, is now up to M, and will be nearly twice as large.

A directory of libraries in Italy, arranged alphabetically by city. Gives for each library name, address, hours, directors, and a description of the collections and holdings, with a bibliography of works about the libraries. Index by subject and collections, of librarians and of addresses. Volume 3 is index volume.

130

Jahrbuch der deutschen Bibliotheken. Hrsg. vom Verein deutscher Bibliothekare. Jahrg. 36, 1955. Wiesbaden, Harrassowitz, 1955. illus. 19 cm.

Jahrg. 1–32 published in Leipzig. A directory of German libraries, arranged by cities and under each listing the libraries and giving the size and a description of each collection, citing specialties and listing publications. "Personalverzeichnis" p. 186–310 lists librarians with a biographical paragraph for each.

131

Nederlandse bibliotheekgids, adresboek van bibliotheken in Nederland. 4. druk bewerkt door Chr. J. Nissink. Amsterdam, Swets & Zeitlinger, 1949. 335 columns. 23 cm.

A directory of libraries in the Netherlands, arranged alphabetically by city. For each library gives date of founding, address, hours of opening, subjects covered, and name of librarian. Subject index p. 263–314 and index of persons p. 315–35.

132

Special Libraries Association. Directory of special libraries, comp. by Isabel L. Towner. N.Y., 1953. 297 p. 25 cm.

An alphabetical listing of special libraries in the United States and Canada, giving for each: (1) a brief description of the library; (2) a detailed subject index; and (3) the conditions under which the resources of the library are available for outside use. Subject index p. 269–97 makes it possible to locate art libraries and special resources in art fields.

133

United Nations Educational, Scientific and Cultural Organization. Répertoire des bibliothèques de France, edité par l'Organisation des Nations Unies pour l'Éducation, la Science et la Culture et la Direction des Services des Bibliothèques de France. Paris [Bibliothèque Nationale] 1950–51. 3 v. 24 cm.

For each library gives address, telephone, hours and conditions of opening, a description of the collections, catalogs, date of founding, and other information. Contents: v. 1, Bibliothèques de Paris; v. 2, Bibliothèques des départements; v. 3, Centres et services de documentation. Each volume has its own indexes.

CHAPTER 4

Sales Records

THIS CHAPTER COVERS THE VARIOUS TOOLS which record the available information on art sales, prices at auctions, collectors' marks, etc., often important for tracing specific works of art.

134

American print prices paid; consolidating the records of America's important print sales. v. 1, 1947. Boston, Holman's Print Shop. 28 cm.

Does not include Japanese prints or prints selling for less than $5. Information on prices supplied by the auction firms. Arranged alphabetically by name of artist. Under each gives title of the print, number of sale and lot, and price brought.

135

. . . Annuaire du collectionneur; répertoire des prix des tableaux . . . estampes, sculpture vendus à Paris et en province . . . Année [1]– (3). Paris, Diffusion Artistique et Documentaire [1949]– (51). v. 1– (3). illus. 25 cm.

Année 2– includes Les grandes ventes de l'étranger. Subtitle varies. Arranged by medium; first part is devoted to painting and second part covers specialties, i.e., sculpture, jewelry, ceramics, rugs, etc. "Répertoire des prix" is arranged alphabetically by artist, with a number referring to the sale and the price realized.

136

Annuaire général des ventes publiques en France. Année 1–2, 1941/42–1942/43. Paris, Art et Technique, 1942–43. 2 v. plates. 27 cm.

Commentaires d'André Fage. Superseded by Les ventes publiques en France (153). At the beginning of each volume a chronological list of sales held in France, then arranged by artist. Année 2 issued in two parts: (1)

Tableaux; (2) Livres, autographes, graveurs, monnaies, sculptures, etc.; also has supplement, "Les ventes en Belgique."

137

Annual price list of the graphic arts. v. 1, 1952. Amsterdam, Minerva Uitg. Mij. 1 v. 27 cm.

Compiled by F. A. van Braam. Only volume published to date. Arranged alphabetically by name of artist. For each item gives description, name of auction house, date of sale, and price realized. List of recorded auction galleries p. vi, and a list of rate of exchange of different currencies.

138

Art price annual. n.s. 4–(12). London, Art and Technology Press, 1948/49–(56/57). 9 v. illus., plates. 22 cm.

Title varies: *European art prices annuary* (or *annual*), v. 4–7, 1948/49–1951/52. German ed. called *Kunstpreiz-Verzeichnis*, Bd. 1– (11), 1941– (56). French ed. called *Annuaire des ventes d'objets d'art.*

Current volume contains the results of important public sales in Europe, the United States, and other countries during the period of July 1, 1956 to June 1957. Contains sections on antiques, pictures, engravings, autographs, and art books. For each item gives prices, description, size, and place and date of sale. Also includes "Bibliography" and "Currency table."

139

Art prices current . . . A record of sale prices at the principal London, Continental and American auction rooms . . . With indexes to the artists, engravers and collectors. v. [1]–9, 1907/08–1915/16; n.s. v. 1–(29), 1921/22–(52). London, The Art Trade Press, 1908–(54). 22 cm.

Subtitle varies. Publication suspended

1917–20. Arranged chronologically by sales. For each object gives the catalog number, price, and name of purchaser. Indexes of pictures, drawings and engravings (the latter by artist and engraver), miniatures and enamel portraits, and collections.

140

Cote des tableaux, ou Annuaire des ventes de tableaux, dessins, aquarelles, pastels, gouaches, miniatures, guide du marchand, de l'amateur, publié par L. Maurice Lang. t. 1–11. Tous les prix des ventes de l'année oct. 1918–fin juillet 1929. Paris, L. Maurice Lang [1919–31]. v. 1–11. 25 cm.

Title varies: 1918–22, *Annuaire des ventes de tableaux;* 1923–29, *Cote des tableaux.* Arranged alphabetically by name of artist. Lists of important sales at beginning of each volume. For each item gives size, sale, and price.

141

Duplessis, Georges. Les ventes de tableaux, dessins, estampes et objets d'art aux XVIIe et XVIIIe siècles (1611–1800); essai de bibliographie. Paris, Rapilly, 1874. 122 p. 23 cm.

A bibliography of sales catalogs of the 17th and 18th centuries arranged chronologically. Index p. [113]–22.

142

Fagan, Louis Alexander. Collectors' marks, arr. and ed. by Milton I. D. Einstein . . . and Max A. Goldstein. . . . St. Louis, The Laryngoscope Press, 1918. 128 p. 50 plates. 25 cm.

300 copies printed. This is a reprint of the 1883 ed. of 688 marks, with 203 supplementary marks added. For each mark it attempts to give collector's name, dates of birth and death, and place of residence, in addition to the date of sale and auctioneer's name. For foreign sales the auctioneer's name is not given. "In most instances the sum total of the amount of sale is given."

Collectors' marks are all reproduced in the plates. An index (8 p.) to the original work and a three-page supplement.

143

Graves, Algernon. Art sales from early in the eighteenth century to early in the twentieth century. (Mostly old master and early English pictures). . . . London, Graves, 1918–21. 3 v. 30 cm.

300 copies printed. A 1137-page repertory of old master paintings, etc., sold at auction. Arranged alphabetically by name of artist

and under each in columnar form: date, auctioneer, owner, lot number and title of picture, purchaser, and sale date. Paintings are arranged chronologically by date of sale.

144

Lancour, Adlore Harold. American art auction catalogues, 1785–1942; a union list. . . . N.Y., The New York Public Library, 1944. 377 p. 23 cm.

"A union check list of over 7000 catalogues of auction sales of art objects held in the U.S. during the period from 1785 to the end of 1943. Books, maps, bookplates, stamps and coins have been omitted."—*Pref.* For each sale gives: (1) date of first day of sale; (2) owner's name; (3) short descriptive title; (4) auction firms; (5) simple collation; (6) number of lot; (7) location of copies. Contains list of American auction houses p. 11–28 and list of catalogs p. 29–319 (listed chronologically). Index of owners p. 321–77.

145

Lugt, Frits. Les marques de collections de dessins et d'estampes; marques estampillées et écrits de collections particulières et publiques. Marques de marchands, de monteurs et d'imprimeurs. Cachets de vente d'artistes décédés. Marques de graveurs apposées après le tirage des planches. Timbres d'édition. Etc. Avec des notices historiques sur les collectionneurs, les collections, les ventes, les marchands et éditeurs, etc. . . . Amsterdam, Vereenigde Drukkerijen, 1921. 598 p. illus. (facsims.) 30 cm.

Arranged alphabetically. Identifies the marks and gives facts concerning, or description of, the collections. Contents: Noms et inscriptions en toutes lettres, et initiales separées ou monogrammées p. 1–505; Figures: armoiries, corps humain, animaux, plantes et fleurs, objets, soleils et étoiles, croix, figures géométriques p. 506–41; Marques difficiles à déchiffrer, et marques japonaises p. 542–55; Numéros p. 556–61; Spécimens d'écritures p. 562–70; Index p. 577–94.

———. Supplément. 1956. 464 p.

About 2350 new marks with historical notes and 810 additions to the articles of the principal volume, and a general index.

146

Lugt, Frits. Répertoire des catalogues de ventes publiques, intéressant d'art ou la curiosité: tableaux, dessins, estampes, miniatures, sculptures, bronzes, émaux, vitraux, tapisseries, céramiques, objets d'art, meubles, antiquités, monnaies, médailles, camées, intailles, armes, instruments, curiosités naturelles etc. . . . La Haye, Nijhoff, 1938–(53). v. 1–(2). 33 cm. (Publications du Rijksbureau voor Kunsthistorische en Ikonografische Documentatie)

Volume 1 covers 1600–1825; v. 2, 1826–60. A chronological list of catalogs of art sales held throughout Europe from 1600. For each entry gives: (1) number given in this catalog; (2) date; (3) place where sale took place; (4) name of the collector, artist, merchant, or proprietor; (5) contents; (6) number of lots; (7) auctioneers; (8) number of pages in catalog; (9) libraries in which the catalog may be found and whether it is priced or not.

Index of names of collectors, v. 1, p. 477–96. List of libraries, v. 2, p. xiv–xvi. Index of names of collections, v. 2, p. 697–726.

147

Mireur, Hippolyte. Dictionnaire des ventes d'art faites en France et à l'étranger pendant les XVIIIme et XIXme siècles. Paris, Soullié, 1901–12. 7 v. 29 cm.

A dictionary of works of art covering "tableaux, dessins, estampes, aquarelles, miniatures, pastels, gouaches, sépias, fusains, émaux, éventails peints et vitraux" arranged alphabetically by artist. Contains about 3000 public sales, names of 30,000 artists, and the prices of about 50,000 pieces.

For each artist it gives dates, country, and type of work, and lists chronologically the public sales in which his works have been sold. For each object it gives dimensions, state of preservation, and description of the subject represented. All prices quoted have been translated into French currency.

148

Monod, Lucien. Aide-mémoire de l'amateur et du professionel; le prix des estampes, anciennes et modernes, prix atteints dans les ventes—suites et états, biographies et bibliographies. . . . Paris, Morancé [1920–31]. 9 v. 26 cm.

Arranged alphabetically by name of artist, giving brief biographical information and record of print prices reached at various sales.

"Graveurs identifiés par leurs monogrammes ou par des designations particulières (XVe et XVIe siècles)" v. 9, p. 61–73. "Bibliographie générale" v. 9, p. 77–109. "Nomenclature des estampes par catégories et par sujets (indication des planches typiques, bibliographies, planches anonymes)" v. 9, p. 113–281.

149

Mühsam, Kurt. Internationales Lexikon der Preise von Gemälden und Handzeichnungen aller Schulen und Länder, nach den Auktions-Resultaten der letzten Jahrzehnte. Berlin, Reiss, 1925. 233 p. 24 cm.

Title page and foreword in French, German, and English. A dictionary of prices of paintings and drawings of all schools and countries realized at auctions in the decade before 1925. Covers the art market in Germany, Great Britain, America, France, Belgium, the Netherlands, Denmark, and Austria. Prices are primarily those of the last decades but a few are earlier.

Arranged alphabetically by name of artist, listing works sold, selling gallery, and price. "Vokabularium" gives in three columns the French, German, and English equivalents of various words used in titles. A list of auction houses mentioned and a list of cities where public sales were held are given in three languages.

150

Print prices current; being a complete alphabetical record of all engravings and etchings sold by auction in London, each item annotated with the date of sale and price realised. . . . v. 1–21, Oct. 1918–Aug. 1939. London, Courville, 1919–40. 21 v. 24 cm. Annual.

Compiled by F. L. and E. L. Wilder. Subtitle varies. Ceased publication. Beginning with v. 13, 1930/31, American prices are included.

151

Redford, George. Art sales; a history of sales of pictures and other works of art, with notices of the collections sold, names of owners, titles of pictures, prices and purchasers, arranged under the artists of the different schools in order of date, including the purchasers and prices of pictures for the National Gallery. Illustrated with autotypes from small sketches of great pictures and water-colour drawings sold, portraits of eminent collectors and views of their residences, objects of ornamental art etc. London, pub. by the Author, 1888. 2 v. illus. 33 cm.

Volume 1 contains an historical account of sales and items relating to specific sales. Volume 2 contains lists of sales of pictures with prices and purchasers. Does not include every picture sold by auction but is a selection from sales catalogs in the British Museum Library, Christie's records, and other sources. Usually lists only pictures valued at more than £100.

152

[Redford, George] Continuation of Redford's Art sales commencing from 1887. . . . All sales are held at Christie's, except when another auctioneer is mentioned. Manuscript record from 1887–1918. Bound in 2 v. 33 cm.

An unpublished manuscript in the possession of the Metropolitan Museum of Art Library, N.Y. Approximately 50,000 handwritten entries on 1500 pages recording sales held in England from 1887 to Dec. 18, 1918. Volume 1 is British schools and v. 2, Foreign schools. Arranged alphabetically according to name of artist, giving a list of his works sold, date of sale, name of picture, size, price realized, and name of purchaser.

153

Les ventes publiques en France; répertoire générale des prix, 1941/42–1946/47. Paris, Bureau International d'Édition et de Publicité [1943–47]. illus. 21 cm.

Supersedes *Annuaire général des ventes publiques en France.* "Sous la direction et avec commentaires d'André Fage." For 1943/ 44 and 1944/45 it is issued in three volumes: (1) Tableaux; (2) Livres et autographes; (3) Meubles, gravures, sculptures, monnaies, céramiques, objets d'art et d'Extrême Orient.

154

World collectors annuary. v. 1–(5/8), 1946/49–(53/56). Amsterdam, Minerva Pub. Co., 1950–[58]. (5) v. illus. 27 cm.

Edited by F. A. van Braam. Arranged alphabetically by name of artist. Under each artist lists paintings, water colors, and drawings sold by auction and gives a description, size, gallery where sold, and the price paid. Beginning with 1952 volume the graphic arts are not included. Contains list of recorded auction houses, rates of exchange, and sometimes articles written by experts on the market. Index of paintings reproduced.

SEE ALSO: Foster. A dictionary of painters of miniatures (1148); Seguier. A critical and commercial dictionary of the works of painters (1152); Slater. Engravings and their value (1554).

| # Reproductions

THIS CHAPTER LISTS THE AVAILABLE sources for locating reproductions of works of art. Included in it are various catalogs and indexes to specific reproductions.

155
Alinari, fratelli, *publishers*, Florence. Catalogo delle fotografie di opere d'arte e vedute. Firenze [1920–40]. 30 v. 24 cm.

A catalog to the collection of 70,000 photographs (size 8″ x 10″) made by this firm, which are available for purchase. The collection contains photographs of architecture, sculpture, painting, and the minor arts. Each volume is arranged by place and includes alphabetical indexes of artists and subjects. Contents: Piemonte, Liguria, Lombardia, Veneto, Venezia, Emilia, Bologna, Marche, Toscana, Siena, Firenze (4 v.), Roma (4 v.), Lazio, Campania, Napoli, Abruzzi, Puglie, Sicilia, Sardegna, Rodi, Paris, Dresden, Greece, Arte moderna.

156
Alinari, fratelli, *publishers*, Florence. Mille pitture di venti secoli. Paintings of twenty centuries. Firenze, Fratelli Alinari [1949]. 186 p. (chiefly illus.) 28 cm.

Text in English, Italian, and French. Cover bears title: A thousand paintings of twenty centuries. A later edition has been issued (n.d., 215 p.). A catalog of color prints made by Alinari, arranged first chronologically and then by countries. Under each section, artists are arranged alphabetically. For each print gives size of the original and of the reproduction, name of artist, title of picture, and location, as well as a small black and white reproduction.

Appendix contains sculpture, architectural views, textiles and tapestries, and flowers from nature. Indexes: "Of greater size" p.

162; "Of artists" p. 163–65; "Of persons represented in paintings" p. 166–67; "Of scenes from the gospel" p. 167; "Index of numbers" p. 168–70; "Topographical index" p. 171–80; "Chronological table of the masters" p. 181–86.

157
Brooke, Milton, and Dubester, Henry J. Guide to color prints. Washington, D.C., Scarecrow Press, 1953. 257 p. 22 cm.

"This guide provides a comprehensive and current compilation of color reproductions available for purchase in the U.S. It lists basic information for more than 5000 color reproductions of over 4000 paintings by more than 1000 artists. Over 150 portfolios are also included."—*Pref.*

Arranged alphabetically by name of artist and then by title. When more than one reproduction of the same picture is available they are listed in order of descending price. For each print gives size of print area to the nearest inch, a symbol for the publisher, and the price.

Contents: Abbreviations and publishers' symbols; List of color prints p. 1–183; Portfolios and sets of color prints p. 184–88; Title index p. 189–243; Artist index p. 244–55; Sources of foreign color prints p. 256–67.

158
Catalogue of selected color reproductions, prepared for the Carnegie corporation of New York. . . . N.Y., Raymond and Raymond, 1936. 2 v. plates. 24 cm.

Choice of prints included is selective and based on quality. Arranged alphabetically by name of artist. For each picture gives, in addition to the reproduction, the date of the original, medium, size, location, publisher, process, size of reproduction, and American distributor. Introduction gives a good short description of various processes of color printing. List of publishers with addresses and distributors. Unfortunately the work is now out of date.

159

France. Direction de la Documentation. Répertoire des collections françaises de documents photographiques. 2. éd. Paris, La Documentation Française, 1955. 142, 46 p. 21 cm.

1st ed. 1949.

A directory of French photographic resources arranged by name of the collection. For each entry it gives the address, description of size and contents, and in the case of museums, the person in charge of the collection.

———. Index analytique—octobre 1955. 46 p.

Gives additions and corrections p. 5–9 and a subject index p. 11–46.

160

Leipzig. Deutsche Bücherei. Fünfjahrsverzeichnis der Kunstblätter 1945–50. Bearb. und hrsg. von der Deutschen Bücherei. Leipzig, Verlag des Börsenvereins, 1952. 171 p. 21 cm.

Contains entries for 2898 reproductions including single prints, folios, and books. Arranged by name of artist. Indexes of artists, subjects and catchwords, and publishers with their addresses.

Since 1847 reproductions of works of art produced in Germany have been listed in the *Börsenblatt für den deutschen Buchhandel*. From 1902 to 1918 they were listed in a supplement, with a hiatus between 1919 and 1943. From July 1944 until mid-January 1945 the *Bibliographie der deutschen Kunstblätter* was issued again as a supplement to the *Börsenblatt*. It was resumed again Dec. 6, 1948, at which time a compilation was issued for all works received by the Deutsche Bücherei between May 8, 1945, and Dec. 31, 1947. Subsequently the bibliography has been issued quarterly and this volume is a quinquennial cumulation from these sources.

161

Monro, Isabel Stevenson, and Monro, Kate M. Index to reproductions of American paintings; a guide to pictures occurring in more than 800 books. . . . N.Y., Wilson, 1948. 731 p. 26 cm.

"Lists the work of artists of the U.S. occurring in 520 books and in more than 300 catalogs of annual exhibitions held by art museums. The paintings are entered (1) un-

der name of artist, followed by his dates when obtainable, by title of the picture, and by an abbreviated entry for the book in which the reproduction may be found; (2) under titles; and (3) in some cases under subject. Locations of pictures in permanent collections have also been included whenever this information was available."—*Pref.*

In the case of a variation of title, the alternate titles are given. Portraits are entered under the name of the sitter as well as the artist. Color plates are indicated. List of books indexed p. 11–26.

162

Monro, Isabel Stevenson, and Monro, Kate M. Index to reproductions of European paintings; a guide to pictures in more than 300 books. . . . N.Y., Wilson, 1956. 668 p. 27 cm.

"A guide to pictures by European artists that are reproduced in 328 books. The paintings are entered (1) under name of artist, followed by his dates when obtainable, by title of picture, and by an abbreviated entry of the book in which the reproduction may be found; (2) under titles; and (3) in some cases under subjects. Whenever permanent locations could be determined, this information has been recorded by symbols . . . Books indexed are general books available in most art libraries (list given p. 11–18). No books on individual painters, few catalogs of exhibitions and few books in foreign libraries were considered."—*Pref.* List of symbols and institutions for which they stand p. 19–22.

163

New York Graphic Society, inc. Fine art reproductions, old and modern masters. N.Y., New York Graphic Society [c1951–54]. 548 p. illus. (part col.) 29 cm.

A catalog of color prints published by this company. Arranged by broad groups, i.e., portraits, marines, modern painting, etc., with an artist index p. 521–31. For each picture gives a small illustration, artist, catalog number, process, size of reproduction, and price. Introduction gives a short nontechnical description of various processes.

164

Nunn, George Walter Arthur, ed. British sources of photographs and pictures. London, Cassell [1952]. 220 p. 21 cm.

Contents: Photographers and photographic agencies; Libraries, museums and art galleries; Special sources; The Royal collection of paintings; National Trust properties containing pictures and other collections; Art institutions; Private galleries and fine art dealers; Publishers of fine art prints; Artists; Commercial photographers; Art journals, magazines and yearbooks; Select list of foreign publishers of fine arts prints; Institute of British photographers; Society of industrial artists; Stock sizes of photographic materials; Copyright of photographs and pictures; Abbreviations of artists' titles; Glossary of printing and process terms. Subject index p. 193–220.

165

Roussel, Jules. Catalogue des clichés des archives de la Commission des Monuments Historiques, avec table analytique . . . Paris, Neurdein, n.d. 624 p. plates. 22 cm.

2d ed. 1st ed. appeared 1916–18. Introduction by C. Enlart. Arranged alphabetically by departments of France and then by city. For each print gives its order number and size.

166

United Nations Educational, Scientific and Cultural Organization. Catalogue de reproductions en couleurs de peintures antérieures à 1860; catalogue of colour reproductions of paintings prior to 1860. . . . [3. ed.] Paris, UNESCO [1955]. 254 p. illus. 23 cm.

Text in French, English, and Spanish. 1st ed. 1950, 180 p.; 2d ed. 1953, 219 p. Preface by Charles Sterling. It is selective on a qualitative basis and contains 641 entries which include Russian and Far Eastern art.

Information given for each entry: name of painter, places and dates of birth and death, medium, size, and collection from which the original comes. For the reproduction it gives: process used in printing, size, UNESCO archives number, printer, publisher, price, and a small illustration. List of printers with addresses p. 243–44. List of publishers p. 247. Index of artists p. 251–54. List of distributors of UNESCO publications p. [258–59].

167

United Nations Educational, Scientific and Cultural Organization. Catalogue de reproductions en couleurs de peintures—1860 à 1957. Catalogue of colour reproductions of paintings—1860 to 1957. Paris [1957]. 365 p. illus. 22 cm.

Rev. and enl. ed. of this catalog first issued in 1949, 1952, and 1955. Text in French, English, and Spanish.

This edition contains 992 entries while the 1955 ed. had 754. "Since its publication 569 new plates have been submitted to us, of which 297 have been rejected, our criteria being the fidelity of the reproduction, the importance of the artist and the significance of the original work."—*Pref.*

This list of reproductions of important paintings is arranged alphabetically by artist and gives: title of the work, medium, dimensions, present location, mode of reproduction and size, UNESCO archives number, printer and publisher, and price (in currency of country where published). Small black and white reference illustrations of each painting are included.

Index of artists p. [359]–60; of publishers p. [361]–62; of printers p. [363]–65.

168

United Nations Educational, Scientific and Cultural Organization. Répertoire international des archives photographiques d'oeuvres d'art. International directory of photographic archives of works of art. Paris, Dunod, 1950–54. 2 v. 24 cm.

"An attempt at as complete a list as possible of the photographic works of art at present existing in various countries." Volume 1 has entries for 1195 collections from 87 countries and v. 2 adds 100 more in 24 countries. Arranged alphabetically by place. For each collection gives subjects included, size, purpose, and sometimes hours of opening and price. Also notes whether publicly or privately owned. Title of the collection is given in the original language as well as in French and English.

169

U.S. Copyright Office. Catalog of copyright entries. Works of art, reproductions of works of art, scientific and technical drawings, photographic works, prints and pictorial illustrations, third series, v. 1–(11), 1947–(57). Washington, D.C., Govt. Printing Office [1948–(57)]. 29 cm. Semiannual.

This is Part 7/11A of the whole *Catalog of copyright entries.* Preceded by U.S. Copyright Office. *Catalogue of copyright entries . . . Part 4 [Works of art, etc.]* (n.s., v. 1–41, 1906–46. Washington, D.C., Govt Printing Office, 1906–[47]. 24 cm.)

Lists together, alphabetically by author and/or copyright proprietor, with registration number and date, title, and often a brief physical description of the material: published and unpublished works of art and designs for works of art; reproductions of works of art published in the United States and abroad; published and unpublished drawings or plastic works of a scientific or technical character; published and unpublished photographs; prints and pictorial illustrations (United States and abroad).

Current registrations and renewal registrations are in separate lists. There are cross references from distinctive titles, subjects of portraits, claimants, joint authors, geographical areas, and scenes.

Currently includes a section "Selected books in art and photography": books of reproductions chiefly, or lists, or catalogs of exhibitions.

170

U.S. Library of Congress. Reference Department. Guide to the special collections of prints and photographs in the Library of Congress, comp. by Paul Vanderbilt. Washington, D.C., 1955. 200 p. 26 cm.

"Compiled to bring together in published form the readily available information on special collections of pictures in the Library, with sufficient annotation to make clear each collection's origin, nature, and scope and thus indicate its usefulness for special reference purposes. The arrangement of the guide is a single alphabet of identifying designations, generally by the name of the originator, or, in the absence of better information, by a concise subject designation."—*Pref.* Lists 802 collections, which include 2,827,398 items. Index to proper names and broad subjects p. 171–200.

171

University prints, Boston: fine art reproductions for students. Newton, Mass., The University Prints, 1907–44 [v. 1, 1931]. 26 v. plates (part fold.), plans. 21 cm.

5500 different fine arts subjects with 108 in color. Small half-tone reproductions (5½" x 8") which are issued in series or bound volumes as an aid to students. The complete series of prints:

Series		Prints
A	Greek and Roman sculpture	539
B	Early Italian art	568
C	Later Italian art	550
D	Flemish, Dutch and German art	584
E	French, Spanish and Modern art	485
F	British art	207
G	European architecture	648
GM	Modern architecture	272
H	American art	434
K	Medieval art	190
L	Graphic arts	120
M	Pre-Greek art	157
O	Oriental art:	
	Early Indian and Indonesian art	85
	Early Chinese art	164
	Japanese art	149
	Iranian and Islamic art	199
	History of painting in colour	108
	20th century painting	100

Basic series A, B, C, G, GM are also available in bound form with prints on both sides of the page; also special art study sets which comprise selections from the above series.

CHAPTER 6

Dictionaries
and Encyclopedias

THE MOST IMPORTANT AND WIDELY USED encyclopedias and dictionaries in the art field in general, and a few general works which are extremely important for art reference work, are listed in this chapter. Dictionaries and encyclopedias covering only one subject (e.g., painting, architecture, etc.) are listed with the other works on that subject. Encyclopedias which are primarily biographical in character, e.g., Thieme-Becker, are included in the chapter on "Biography."

172

Adeline, Jules. Adeline's Art dictionary, containing a complete index of all terms used in art, architecture, heraldry and archaeology; trans. from the French and enl. with nearly 2000 illustrations. N.Y. and London, Appleton, 1927. 422 p. illus. 22 cm.

Reprinted Ann Arbor, Mich., Edwards, 1953.

Many editions of this standard work since it first appeared in 1891. The aim is to give a concise definition of all the terms used in painting, sculpture, architecture, etching, engraving, and heraldry. Material included which is not in the original French work is based on Fairholt (182).

173

Das Atlantisbuch der Kunst; eine Enzyklopädie der Bildenden Künste. Zürich, Atlantis-Verlag [1952]. 897 p. illus. (part col.) 23 cm.

Chapters written by specialists with bibliographies at end of each. Index of artists and people mentioned p. 795–870, with dates and identification. Subject index p. 871–98 with definitions.

Contents: (1) Vom Wesen der Kunst; (2) Die künstlerischen Techniken und ihre An-

wendung; (3) Epochen der Kunst in Europa; (4) Die Kunst der aussereuropäischen Völker; (5) Kunstpflege; (6) Lexicographischer Anhang.

174

Brulliot, Franz. Dictionnaire des monogrammes, marques figurées, lettres initiales, noms abrégés etc. avec lesquels les peintres, dessinateurs, graveurs et sculpteurs ont designé leurs noms. . . . Nouv. éd. rev. et augm. d'un grand nombre d'articles. . . . Munich, Cotta, 1832–34. 3 v. 30 cm.

1st ed. published in 1817.

Monograms arranged alphabetically without regard to size of letter or order in which they appear.

Contents: v. 1, Monogrammes; v. 2, Les lettres initiales; v. 3, Les noms abrégés et estropiés, ainsi que les appendices.

First two volumes have appendix of "Marques figurées," with or without initial letters. Each volume has a separate index of names of the artists cited; at end of v. 3 there is an index of artists covering the three volumes.

175

Daremberg, Charles Victor, and Saglio, Edmond. Dictionnaire des antiquités grecques et romaines d'après les textes et les monuments. Paris, Hachette, 1873–1919. 5 v. and index. illus. (incl. maps, plans, facsims.) 32 cm.

A scholarly work which contains long signed articles written by specialists. Subjects included: arts, costume, furniture, institutions, public and private life, manners and customs, religion, sciences, etc. Biography and literature are excluded. Bibliographical references.

176

Demmin, Auguste Frédéric. Encyclopédie historique, archéologique, biographique, chronologique et monogrammatique des beaux-arts plastiques, architecture et mosaïque, céramique, sculpture, peinture et gravure. . . . Paris, Furne, Jouvet [1873–74]. 3 v. in 5. illus. 26 cm.

Contents: v. 1, General introduction, epigraphy, paleography, coats of arms, letters and marks, church ornaments, art and architecture in general, military and naval architecture, general architecture, mosaics, enamels, mirrors, (pt. 3) sculpture; v. 2, painting; v. 3, engraving.

Gives lists of artists under different categories. General index at end of v. 3. Well illustrated for its period.

177
Dizionario letterario Bompiani delle opere e dei personaggi di tutti i tempi e di tutte le letterature. . . . [Milano] Bompiani, 1947–50. 9 v. illus. (part col.), ports. (part col.), facsims. 22 cm.

A dictionary listing and describing works of art, literature, and music of all times and in all countries, well illustrated with reproductions of works of art and many colored plates. The main body of the work consists of signed articles arranged by the Italian form of the title of the work.

Contents: v. 1, Movimenti spirituali, Opere A-B; v. 2–7, Opere C-Z; v. 8, Personaggi A-Z; v. 9, Indici.

Index volume includes list of titles in the original language with their Italian equivalents, but there are no cross references in the main body of the work. Also an index of illustrations arranged by artist.

178
Ebert, Max, ed. Reallexikon der Vorgeschichte, unter Mitwirkung zahlreicher Fachgelehrter. . . . Berlin, de Gruyter, 1924–32. 15 v. in 16. illus., plates (part col.), maps, facsims. 25 cm.

Scholarly signed articles on archaeology with bibliographies and numerous illustrations.

Contents: v. 1–14, A-Z; v. 15, Register. List of authors, v. 1, p. vi–vii; abbreviations p. viii–xviii; transliteration of foreign alphabets p. xix–xx.

179
Elmes, James. A general and bibliographical dictionary of the fine arts. Containing explanations of the principal terms used in the arts of painting, sculpture, architecture, and engraving, in all their various branches; historical sketches of the rise and progress of their different schools; descriptive accounts of the best books and treatises on the fine arts; and every useful topic connected therewith. . . . London, Tegg, 1826. 760 p. 23 cm.

"A dictionary exclusively devoted to the literature of the fine arts has never before appeared in the English language."—*Pref.*

The longer articles give bibliographical references. Does not include names of artists. Chief sources used are mentioned in the Preface p. viii.

180
Enciclopedia italiana di scienze, lettere ed arti. [Roma] Istituto Giovanni Treccani, 1929–39. 36 v. illus., plates (part col.), maps, plans, facsims. (part col.), geneal. tables, diagrs. 32 x 25 cm.

———. Appendice I. Roma, Istituto della Enciclopedia italiana, 1938. 1147 p.

———. Appendice II, 1938–48. Roma, Istituto della Enciclopedia italiana, 1948–49. 2 v.

While this is a general encyclopedia it is particularly valuable for art reference work because of the wealth of very good illustrations and plates. It is especially strong on Italian art. All articles are signed and many bibliographies are included. Volume 36 is index volume. For a more detailed treatment of the encyclopedia see item D46 in Winchell's *Guide to Reference Books* 7th ed. (American Library Association).

181
Encyclopedia of world art. N.Y., McGraw-Hill, (1959–62). 15 v. illus., plates (part col.) 30 cm. (In preparation)

To be issued in Italian by Sansoni, 1958–61, under title: *Enciclopedia universale dell'arte.*

Volumes are to be issued at three-month intervals until the set is complete; each volume will contain 400 pages of text, 96 color plates, and 400 plates of black and white halftones. Volume 15 will be an index to the whole work.

An alphabetical organization comprising over 1000 items written by internationally known art historians, critics, etc., covering architecture, painting, sculpture, and the decorative arts from their early beginnings to the present time. Factual, biographical, and bibliographical data are to be included.

182
Fairholt, Frederick William. A dictionary of terms in art. . . . with 500 engravings on wood. [London] Virtue, Hall & Virtue [1854]. 474 p. illus. 19 cm.

Includes terms generally used in painting, sculpture, engraving, aesthetics, and also vases, pottery, costume, arms, analysis of color, and artistic implements; descriptions of ornamental woods or precious stones; brief notice of the saints and their symbols.

183

Gay, Victor, and Stein, Henri. Glossaire archéologique du moyen-âge et de la renaissance. Paris. Société Bibliographique, 1887–1928. 2 v. illus. 31 cm.

Each term is defined and accompanied by quotations from documentary or literary sources. Illustrated by line drawings.

Volume 1 originally issued in five fascicles, 1882–87. Volume 2: "texte revu et complété par Henri Stein, illustration dirigée par Marcel Aubert . . . Paris, Picard, 1928."

184

Hansford, S. Howard. A glossary of Chinese art and archaeology. London, China Society, 1954. 104 p. illus. 22 cm. (China Society, Sinological series, no. 4)

Covers metals, gems and stones, sculpture, painting, ceramics, and miscellaneous; under each of which are listed terms in Chinese characters followed by transliteration and English equivalent.

Index p. 97–104 lists transliterations of the words given in alphabetical order, with cross references for related terms.

Pages 89–96 are line drawings of shapes of bronzes, ceramics, and decorative ornament.

185

Harper's Encyclopedia of art; architecture, sculpture, painting, decorative arts, based on the work of Louis Hourticq . . . and trans. under the supervision of Tancred Borenius . . . fully rev. under the supervision of J. Leroy Davidson and Philippa Gerry, with the assistance of the staff of the Index of Twentieth-Century Artists, College Art Association, New York City. . . . N.Y. and London, Harper, 1937. 2 v. illus., plates. 32 cm.

Based on the following work by Louis Hourticq (186).

Contains short articles, biographies, and brief bibliographies. Many small illustrations within the text and on plates. Reprinted as *New standard encyclopedia of art* (N.Y., Garden City Pub. Co., 1937. 2 v. in 1).

186

Hourticq, Louis. Encyclopédie des beaux-arts; architecture, sculpture, peinture, arts decoratifs . . . [Paris] Hachette [c1925]. 2 v. illus., plates. 33 cm.

The work of 12 collaborators.

Aims to be a dictionary, a history, and an album. The dictionary section includes definitions of terms and biography. A section of each page is devoted to history, and attempts are made to trace movements in art, which are illustrated with plates.

There is a list of plates in color and black and white; also a table of contents for the history section. Includes bibliographies. At end of v. 2 there is an addendum on the Louvre, giving its history and its floor plan.

187

Jahn, Johannes. Wörterbuch der Kunst; in Verbindung mit Robert Heidenreich und Wilhelm von Jenny verfasst von Johannes Jahn. 2. durchgesehene und erweiterte Aufl. mit 212 Abbildungen. Stuttgart, Kröner [1943]. 740 p. illus. (incl. plans) 18 cm. (Kröners Taschenausgabe, Bd. 165)

A 4th ed. of 712 pages appeared in 1953.

In one alphabet covers artists, places, terms, works of art, and art movements. Frequently gives bibliographical references at end of entries. Very few illustrations but numerous cross references.

188

Kaltenbach, Gustave Émile. Dictionary of pronunciation of artists' names, with their schools and dates, for American readers and students. . . . 2d ed. [Chicago] The Art Institute [1938]. 74 p. 19 cm.

1st ed. [c1934].

Includes over 1500 names. "Explanations" gives symbols used to denote the pronunciations and a few general rules about stress in various languages.

189

Lacombe, Jacques. Dictionnaire portatif des beaux-arts, ou, Abrégé de ce qui concerne l'architecture, la sculpture, la peinture, la gravure, la poésie et la musique; avec la définition de ces arts, l'explication des termes et des choses qui leur appartiennent; ensemble les noms, la date de la naissance et de la mort, les circonstances les plus remarquables de la vie, et le genre particulier de talent des personnes qui se sont distinguées dans ces différens arts parmi les anciens et les modernes, en France et dans les pays étrangers. Paris, Estienne, 1752. 707 p. 17 cm.

Entries for artists, terms, etc., in one alphabet.

190

Lampe, Louis. Signatures et monogrammes des peintres de toutes les écoles; guide monogrammiste indispensable aux amateurs de peintures anciennes. Bruxelles, Castaigne, 1895–98. 3 v. 26 cm.

Originally issued in 14 parts. Divided according to subjects painted: portraits, history, genre, pastoral scenes, horses and battles, animals, landscape, marine scenes, views of cities and architecture, interiors of churches, bas reliefs, lighting effects, fires, moonlight, still life, musical instruments, plants and insects, fruits and flowers. Under these categories the artists are listed alphabetically. If an artist worked in more than one category he is listed under each. For each artist gives full name, soubriquets, place and date of birth and death, masters under whom he studied, and signatures and marks which he used.

Contents: v. 1, Portraits; v. 2, Histoire; v. 3, Genres divers.

191

Lodovici, Sergio. Storici, teorici e critici delle arti figurative (1800–1940). Roma, E.B.B.I., Istituto editoriale italiano B.C. Tosi, s.a. [1942]. [13]–412 p. illus. (ports., facsims.) 28 cm. (Enciclopedia biografica e bibliografica "Italiana," ser. IV)

Arranged in dictionary form, alphabetically by author. Under each author is given a short biography, a bibliography of his writings, and a discussion of his theories. In many cases there are photographs of the authors.

Alphabetical list of periodicals published in Italy in this period, giving title, place, and dates of publication p. 389–402.

On p. 403 a list of periodicals arranged chronologically, ending with 1930.

192

Lützler, Heinrich. Bildwörterbuch der Kunst, mit 853 Zeichnungen von Theo Siering. Bonn, Dummer [c1950]. 626 p. illus. 19 cm.

A useful small German encyclopedia of art, which gives concise definitions of terms and some proper names associated with the art field. Well illustrated with line drawings. "Wichtige Nachschlagewerke" p. xiii–ix.

193

Meusel, Johann Georg. Teutsches Künstlerlexikon; oder, Verzeichniss der jetztlebenden teutschen Künstler. Nebst einem Verzeichniss sehenswürdiger Bibliotheken, Kunst-Münz- und Naturalienkabinete in Teutschland und in der Schweiz. Verfertig von Johann Georg Meusel . . . 2. umbearb. Ausg. Lemgo, Meyersche Buchhandlung, 1808–14. 3 v. 20 cm.

1st ed., Lemgo, 1778. Covers German artists, musicians, and art galleries, as well as museums and libraries in Germany and Switzerland.

194

Mollet, John William. An illustrated dictionary of words used in art and archaeology; explaining terms frequently used in works on architecture, arms, bronzes, Christian art, colour, costume, decoration, devices, emblems, heraldry, lace, personal ornaments, pottery, painting, sculpture etc., with their derivations. . . . Boston, Houghton Mifflin, 1883. 350 p. illus. 22 cm.

Based on an amended edition of a dictionary by Ernest Bosc of Paris, but completely revised, rewritten, and checked against Fairholt (182). Contains 450 engravings from Bosc and 250 additional ones. A few Indian, Chinese, and Japanese terms in ordinary use in art are included.

195

Müller, Hermann Alexander, and Mothes, Oskar. Illustriertes archäologisches Wörterbuch der Kunst des germanischen Altertums, des Mittelalters und der Renaissance, sowie der mit den bildenden Künsten in Verbindung stehenden Ikonographie, Kostümkunde, Waffenkunde, Baukunde, Geräthkunde, Heraldik und Epigraphik (deutsch, französisch, englisch und lateinisch) für Archäologen, Sammler, Kunsthistoriker, Freunde des Altertums und der Geschichte. Leipzig & Berlin, Spamer, 1877. 2 v. illus. 26 cm.

Contains terms in English, French, German, and Latin with definitions in Latin. Illustrated by line drawings in the text. Contents: v. 1, A-H; v. 2, I-Z. Bibliography on one page before the colored frontispiece.

196

Müller, Iwan Philipp Eduard von. Handbuch der klassischen Altertums-Wissenschaft in systematischer Darstellung. . . . Nördlingen, Beck, 1885–1911. 9 v. 25 cm.

A series of scholarly treatises on subjects in classical literature, antiquities, etc.

Volume vi, Archäologie der Kunst, nebst einem Anhang über die antike Numismatik.

Reprinted in two volumes (Munich, Beck, 1939): I, Text; II, Tafeln.

197

Nagler, Georg Kaspar. Die Monogrammisten und diejenigen bekannten und unbekannten Künstler aller Schulen. . . . München, Franz, 1858–79. 5 v. illus., facsims. 24 cm.

The standard work on monogrammists. Arranged alphabetically by name of artist. Volume 6, Index. "Einleitung" gives bibliography.

———. General-Index zu G.K. Nagler Die Monogrammisten. . . . München, Hirth, 1920. 109 p. 25 cm.

198

O'Dwyer, John, and Le Mage, Raymond. A glossary of art terms, with a foreword by Ruskin Spear. London, N.Y., Nevill [1950]. 148 p. 19 cm.

A popular sort of book with no sources given. Some foreign terms included with translation given in parentheses. Gives names of many movements in history of art. Lists the Bridge Group under *Die Brücke* with no cross reference from *Brücke* or *Bridge*.

✓ **199**

Pauly, August Friedrich von. Pauly's Real-Encyclopädie der classischen Altertumswissenschaft; neue Bearb. begonnen von Georg Wissowa, unter Mitwirkung zahlreicher Fachgenossen hrsg. von Wilhelm Kroll und Karl Mittelhaus. Stuttgart, Metzler, 1894–(1957). v. 1–(23 ¹). 2. Reihe v. 1–(8A ¹) and Suppl. 1–(8). maps. 25 cm.

The standard German classical encyclopedia covering antiquities, biography (including artists), classical literature, and history. Contains long signed articles by specialists, and bibliographies. In English usually referred to as "Pauly-Wissowa" and sometimes cited in German as "R. E." Appears in two series rather than in strict alphabetical sequence.

Contents: Bd. 1–23 ¹, A–Psalychiadai; 2. Reihe (R–Z), Bd. 1–8A¹, R–Vergilius; Supp. 1–8, 1903–56.

200

Pei, Mario A., and Gaynor, Frank, eds. Liberal arts dictionary in English, French, German, Spanish. . . . N.Y., Philosophical Library [1952]. 307 p. 24 cm.

Covers the fields of art, literature, and philosophy.

Basic definitions are given in English followed by the equivalent terms. There is an index of the French, German, and Spanish words.

201

Réau, Louis. Dictionnaire illustrée d'art et d'archéologie. . . . Paris, Larousse [c1930]. 488 p. illus., 16 plates. 22 cm.

Short concise definitions sometimes accompanied by technical and historical explanations. Attempts to cover all periods and includes decorative arts, costume, arms, music, choreography, and theater. For each term equivalents are given in Italian, Spanish, English, and German. Many illustrations.

Short bibliography at end of volume.

202

Réau, Louis. Dictionnaire polyglotte des termes d'art et d'archéologie. [1. ed.] Paris, Presses Universitaires de France, 1953. 247, [5] p. 25 cm.

Organized on a different plan from 1928 ed. All entries are included in one alphabet according to the French terms, thus making a French dictionary of foreign terms. Definitions are not given. Languages included are: Greek, Latin, Italian, Spanish, Portuguese, and some Rumanian, English, German, Dutch, Danish, Swedish, Czech, Polish, and Russian (Greek and Russian in transliteration); but equivalents are not given in all these languages for any one word. Some emphasis on iconographic terms and titles of well-known works of art.

Bibliography p. 251.

203

Réau, Louis. . . . Lexique polyglotte des termes d'art et d'archéologie. . . . Paris, Laurens, 1928. 175 p. 19 cm.

Includes Latin, Italian, Spanish, Portuguese, English, German, Dutch, Danish-Norwegian, Swedish, Czech, Polish, and Russian sections. Under each language the most important terms are listed (according to the French alphabet) and the French equivalent is given. Not intended to be exhaustive but to give the most common terms in these languages.

204

Ris-Paquot, Oscar E. Dictionnaire encyclopédique des marques et monogrammes, chiffres, lettres initiales, signes figuratifs . . . contenant 12,156 marques. . . . Paris, Laurens, 1893. 2 v. illus., 3 plates. 29 cm.

"Concernant les aquafortistes, architectes, armuriers, bibliophiles, célébrités littéraires, céramistes, cisleurs, damasquineurs, dessinateurs, dinandiers, ébénistes, émailleurs, fabricants de papier, fondeurs, graveurs sur bois, cuivre, pierres fines, métaux, horlogers, huchiers, imprimeurs, librairies, maîtres de monnaies, miniaturistes, modeleurs, nielleurs, numismatique, ordres de chevaleries, orfèvres, peintres, potiers d'étain, relieurs, sculpteurs sur bois, pierre, ivoire, albâtre, nacre etc., tapissiers, tisserands, tourneurs etc."

Contents: pt. 1, Ordinary marks and monograms, arranged alphabetically; pt. 2, Figurative or symbolic marks, arranged by a classification; pt. 3, Alphabetical listing of all names cited in the dictionary (p. 579–609 of v. 2); pt. 4, Geographical table listing alphabetically the names of the great industrial cities.

205

Schmitt, Otto. Reallexikon zur deutschen Kunstgeschichte. . . . Stuttgart, Metzler [1937–(58)]. Bd. 1–(4). (In progress) illus. (incl. ports., plans), diagr. 29 cm.

Lfg. 27– hrsg. von Ernst Gall and L. H. Heydenreich.

Long, signed articles with illustrations and bibliographies on subjects in art history, on works of art, and on mythological subjects. Biographical material on artists not included. Covers countries where German is spoken, i.e., Austria, Switzerland, Alsace, Poland, etc., from early middle ages to mid-19th century. Especially good for iconography.

Contents: Bd. 1, Lfg. 1–12, A–Baubetried; Bd. 2, Lfg. 13–24, Bauer–Buchmalerei; Bd. 3, Lfg. 25–36, Buchpult–Dill; Bd. 4, Lfg. 37–(48), Dinanderie–Elle.

206

Sormani, Giuseppe. Dizionario delle arti; compilato da Giuseppe Sormani, con la collaborazione di Vicenzo Ceppellini [et al.] 2. ed. riv. ed ampl. [Milano] Sormani [c1953]. 974p. illus., plates (part col.) 25 cm.

Dictionary arrangement covering all arts of all times and places. Entries are under subjects and movements rather than names of individual artists. Material on artists is found through the index of names.

Contents: Indice alfabetico per materia: Arte, Movimenti e tendenze dell'arte e della cultura, Architettura, Pittura e scultura, Letteratura, Musica, Danza, Teatro, Cinema, Varie (Arte minori, Mitologia, ecc.), Le arti nella storia.

Index of names p. 885–967; of color plates p. 969; of black and white plates p. 971–74.

207

Swanenburg, B. D., ed. Algemeene kunst encyclopaedie; beknopte Samenvatting der beeldende kunsten. Met medewerking van: R. F. P. de Beaufort [et al.] Utrecht, de Haan, 1950. 453 p. illus., col. plates. 24 cm.

A one-volume Dutch encyclopedia of fine arts including names of artists as well as terms. Title page lists the contributors.

208

Trzaski, Everta i Michalskiego. Trzaska, Evert i Michalski s. a. Encyklopedia staropolska Opracował Aleksander Brückner, Materiałem ilustracyjnym uzupełnił Karol Estreicher. Warszawa, Trzaska, Evert i Michalski [c1939]. 2 v. illus., ports., plans, facsims. 29 cm.

A well-illustrated Polish encyclopedia of the arts based on Zygmunt Glozer's *Encyklopedia staropolska ilustrowana* (published in 1900–03) but entirely rewritten by Aleksander Brückner.

209

Vollmer, Hans. Kunstgeschichtliches Wörterbuch. Leipzig und Berlin, Teubner, 1928. 272 p. 18 cm. (Teubners kleine Fachwörterbücher, 13)

Contains entries for artists, terms, movements, places, and gives bibliographical references at end of more important entries.

Bibliography p. 268–70.

210

Watelet, Claude Henri de, and Levesque, P. C. Dictionnaire des arts de peinture, sculpture et gravure. Paris, Prault, 1792. 5 v. 21 cm.

Translated into German and elaborated as *Aesthetisches Wörterbuch über die bildenden Künste* by C. H. Heydenreich (Leipzig, 1793–95).

A dictionary of terms rather than one dealing with individual artists. In the article devoted to painting a list of outstanding contemporary artists is mentioned. The work gives a summary of the aesthetic views and opinions of late 18th-century classicism.

211

Weber, Victor Frédéric. "Ko-ji hô-ten"; dictionnaire à l'usage des amateurs et collectionneurs d'objets d'art japonais et chinois: on y trouvera: l'explication des noms usuels et des noms propres qui se rencontrent dans les ouvrages traitant de l'art et des religions de l'Extrême-Orient; des renseignements sur les lieux célèbres de la Chine et du Japon, ainsi que sur les nombreux personnages et héros historiques et légendaires; la description des jeux, des moeurs et coutumes, des fêtes et des pratiques religieuses ou laïques; les biographies, les signatures et autres signes particuliers, des peintres, sculpteurs, ciseleurs, céramistes et autres artistes et artisans; et enfin le résumé des contes et légendes de la Chine et du Japon qui ont inspiré les artistes de ces deux pays dans l'illustration des ouvrages et l'ornementation de leurs meubles et objets usuels. Le dictionnaire est illustré de plus de 2100 gravures et dessins intercalés dans le texte et sur 75 planches dont 5 en couleurs. Paris, L'Auteur, 1923. 2 v. illus., plates (part col.) 41 cm.

Limited ed. of 585 copies. Useful for students of Chinese and Japanese art for signatures and seals of Japanese print makers, family crests, and mythological and historical subjects.

212
Wolf, Martin L. Dictionary of the arts; with an introd. by Eric Partridge. N.Y., Philosophical Library [1951]. 797 p. 24 cm.

Attempts to cover all of the arts of the entire civilized and uncivilized world, both ancient and modern. "Emphasis rightly placed upon practice rather than upon theory."

No sources given, and the work is uneven despite an impressive list of acknowledgments p. ix–xiii. No illustrations.

213
Zani, Pietro. Enciclopedia metodica critico-ragionata delle belle arti. . . . Parma, Tipografia Ducale, 1817–24. 2 pts. in 28 v. 21 cm.

First published Parma, 1794, in eight volumes.

In the first 19 volumes an encyclopedia of about 400 artists with their specialities, nationalities, dates, and a classification according to their fame and merit. The second part (nine volumes) covers graphic arts and contains a wealth of material on subjects and characteristics of engravings of all schools and periods.

SEE ALSO: Baldinucci. Vocabolario toscano dell'arte del disegno (1987).

CHAPTER 7 | # Biography

THIS CHAPTER BRINGS TOGETHER THE MOST important and widely used biographical encyclopedias and collections of artists' lives. In addition, it includes some older and less-well-known compilations, mainly of a regional nature. The earliest collections of biographical material (prior to 1800), i.e., Vasari, Passeri, Orlandi, etc., are listed in the chapter on "Documents and Sources" because they are not the type used in daily reference work but are of interest primarily to scholars and historians. Cross references to these works are given in the appropriate entries within this chapter. Many of the general histories and handbooks listed in Chapter 10, "Histories and Handbooks of Art," also contain biographical material. Whenever such books have sections devoted to biography, that fact has been noted in the annotations to individual items.

For biographical material on artists in one field, e.g., painters, sculptors, etc., the reader is referred to the subdivision "Biography" in these specific chapters.

General

214
Bénézit, Emmanuel. Dictionnaire critique et documentaire des peintres, sculpteurs, dessinateurs et graveurs. . . . [Paris] Gründ, 1948–1955. 8 v. plates. 25 cm.

A completely rev. ed. which supplants that of 1910–20. A reprint of this ed. issued Paris, 1957.

Covers the field of art, both Eastern and Western, from 5 B.C. to 1947 A.D. Includes a directory of the more important art museums and galleries and frequently indicates

auction prices realized. Length of entry varies from a few lines to lengthy articles that include prizes received and museums where works are to be found. Gives signatures of artists; monogrammists are treated at the end of each letter of the alphabet. Illustrated by rotogravure plates, with a list at end of each volume. Volume 8 contains an alphabetical list of authors and a bibliography of works consulted.

215
[Bonafons, Louis Abel de] *known as* Abbé de Fontenay. Dictionnaire des artistes; ou, Notice historique et raisonnée des architectes, peintres, graveurs, sculpteurs, musiciens, acteurs et danseurs; imprimeurs, horlogers et mechaniciens. . . . Paris, Vincent, 1776. 2 v. 17 cm.

Arranged in dictionary form and covers subjects (academies, acrobats, etc.) as well as artists. Sources listed in the Preface.

216
Dohme, Robert. Kunst und Künstler des Mittelalters und der Neuzeit. Biographien und Charakteristiken. Unter Mitwirkung von Fachgenossen hrsg. von Dr. Robert Dohme. . . . Leipzig, Seemann, 1877–86. 4 v. in 8. illus., plates. 29 cm.

A collection of biographical and critical essays written by various specialists and illustrated by line drawings.

Contents: Abt. 1, Bd. 1–2, Kunst und Künstler Deutschlands und der Niederlande bis gegen die Mitte des achtzehnten Jahrhunderts (1877–78); Abt. 2, Bd. 1–3, Kunst und Künstler Italiens bis um die Mitte des achtzehnten Jahrhunderts (1878–79); Abt. 3, Kunst und Künstler Spaniens, Frankreichs und Englands bis gegen das Ende des achtzehnten Jahrhunderts (1880); Abt. 4, Bd. 1–2, Kunst und Künstler der ersten Hälfte des neunzehnten Jahrhunderts (1886).

217

Édouard-Joseph, René. . . . Dictionnaire biographique des artistes contemporains, 1910–1930, avec nombreux portraits, signatures et reproductions. Paris, Art et édition, 1930–34. 3 v. illus. (incl. ports.), plates. 24 cm.

―――. Supplément. Paris, 1936. 162 p. illus. 24 cm.

Publisher varies. Mostly includes artists who lived or exhibited in France between 1910–30, but also some earlier ones who influenced this group. Usually gives place and date of birth (dates omitted if there is doubt about them), where and when the artist exhibited, his awards, and his medium. Longer articles include list of important works. Many illustrations.

Errata list and Index of monograms at end of v. 3.

218

Füessli, Johann Rudolf. Allgemeines Künstlerlexicon; oder, Kurze Nachricht von dem Leben und den Werken der Mahler, Bildhauer, Baumeister, Kupferstecher, Kunstgiesser, Stahlschneider u.a., nebst angehängsten Verzeichnissen der Lehrmeister und Schüler; auch der Bildnisse, der in diesem Lexicon enthaltenen Künstler. Zürich, Orell, 1779–1821. 2 v. in 4. 37 cm.

Original ed. published in Zurich, 1763, in one volume (folio) with bibliography. An expanded ed. with supplement 1767–77. The first German dictionary of artists, the most noteworthy until Nagler (223), and still a useful reference work.

219

Marchese, Vincenzo [Fortunato]. Lives of the most eminent painters, sculptors and architects of the order of S. Dominic; tr. from the Italian of Father Marchese . . . with notes etc., by C. P. Meehan. Dublin, Duffy, 1852. 2 v. 19 cm.

First published in Florence 1845; 4th Italian ed., Bologna, 1878–79. Arranged more like a history of art than a dictionary or encyclopedia. Some documents included at end of each volume.

220

Mariette, Pierre Jean. Abecedario de P. J. Mariette et autres notes inédites de cet amateur sur les arts et les artistes. Ouvrage publié d'après les manuscrits autographes conservés au Cabinet des estampes de la Bibliothèque impériale, et annoté par M. M. Ph. de Chennevières et A. de Montaiglon.

Paris, Dumoulin, 1851/53–1859/60. 6 v. 22 cm. (Archives de l'art français, t. 2, 4, 6, 8, 10, 12)

Begun as an attempt to correct the errors of P. A. Orlandi's *Abcedario pittorico* (1704) (2023). Contains notes on artists of various schools and covers numerous media. Contents: t. 1, A-Col; t. 2, Col-Isac; t. 3, Jabach-Mingozzi; t. 4, Mocchi-Roberti; t. 5, Robusti-van Oye; t. 6, van Santen-Zumbo, Appendices p. 169–291, Supplément p. 293–343, Avertissement des éditeurs p. 345–54.

221

Meyer, Julius, ed. Allgemeines Künstler-Lexikon. Unter Mitwirkung der namenhaftesten Fachgelehrten des In- und Auslandes hrsg. von Dr. Julius Meyer. 2. gänzlich neubearb. Aufl. von Nagler's Künstler-Lexikon. . . . Leipzig, Engelmann, 1872–85. 3 v. 25 cm.

No more published. All articles are long and scholarly and signed. List of collaborators at beginning of v. 1.

Contents: v. 1, Aa–Andreani; v. 2, Andreas–Domenico del Barbiere; v. 3, Giambattista Barbiere–Giuseppe Bezzuoli.

222

Müller, Hermann Alexander, and Singer, Hans Wolfgang. Allgemeines Künstler-Lexikon. Leben und Werke der berühmtesten bildenden Künstler. 3. umbearb. und bis auf die neueste Zeit ergänzte Aufl. . . . Frankfurt a. M., Rütten, 1895–1901. 5 v. 24 cm.

Bd. 1, "Vorbereitet von H. A. Müller, hrsg. von H. W. Singer"; Bd. 2, "Hrsg. von H. W. Singer."

―――. Nachträge und Berichtigungen. Frankfurt a. M., Literarische Anstalt, Rütten & Loening, 1906. 295 p. 24 cm.

A 5th ed. (unrev.) issued in 1921–22 in six volumes. The sixth volume contains a second supplement with corrections. Gives short biographical information about each artist and his work. No bibliographies. Articles not signed.

223

Nagler, Georg Kaspar. Neues allgemeines Künstler-Lexicon . . . unveränderter Abdruck der ersten Auflage 1835–1852. Leipzig, Schwarzenberg & Schumann [1924]. 25 v. 23 cm.

Contains entries on life and works of painters, sculptors, architects, engravers, lithographers, medalists, ivory carvers, and some patrons, arranged alphabetically. No bibliographies or list of sources.

224

Spooner, Shearjashub. A biographical history of the fine arts; or, Memoirs of the lives and works of eminent painters, engravers, sculptors, and architects. From the earliest ages to the present time. Alphabetically arranged and condensed from the best authorities. N.Y., Bouton, 1865. 2 v. plates. 27 cm.

Originally published as *A biographical and critical dictionary of painters and engravers* (N.Y., Putnam, 1853). Preface claims 2000 more names included than in Bryan (1144). Contents: Introduction, consisting of articles on painting, engraving, etc.; A brief explanation of the principal terms used by writers on the fine arts; Table of Christian names in English, French, German, Italian, Dutch, and Spanish; Alphabetical list of the names acquired by distinguished artists; Alphabetical list of copyists and imitators of great masters, listed under master whose work they copied. Includes portraits of some artists and 24 plates of monograms. Alphabetical list of authorities p. [lxi]–lxii.

225

Thieme, Ulrich, and Becker, Felix. Allgemeines Lexikon der bildenden Künstler von der Antike bis zur Gegenwart; unter Mitwirkung von 300 Fachgelehrten des In- und Auslandes. . . . Leipzig, Seemann, 1907–50. v. 1–37. 28 cm.

Volumes 1 and 4 have imprint: Leipzig, Engelmann. This is the most complete and scholarly biographical dictionary in the field. It includes, as nearly as possible, all known painters, sculptors, engravers, architects, and minor artists. Signed articles by international contributors, with long bibliographies, drawing on sources from all countries. Locations of works of art are frequently given. Names with umlauts are alphabetized as if the *e* were inserted, and I and J are interfiled. Numerous cross references.

226

Vollmer, Hans. Allgemeines Lexikon der bildenden Künstler des XX. Jahrhunderts. Unter Mitwirkung von Fachgelehrten des In- und Auslandes, bearb., redigiert und hrsg. von Hans Vollmer. Leipzig, Seemann, 1953–58. v. 1–4. 27 cm. (In progress)

Half-title: Künstlerlexikon des XX. Jahrhunderts. A 20th-century supplement to Thieme-Becker (225).

Contents: v. 1, A–D; v. 2, E–J; v. 3, L–P; v. 4, Qu–U. "Verzeichnis der Abkürzungen" at beginning of each volume.

227

Waters, *Mrs.* Clara (Erskine) Clement, and Hutton, Laurence. Artists of the 19th century and their works. A handbook containing two thousand and fifty biographical sketches. 3d ed. rev. Boston, Osgood, 1885. 2 v. in 1. 20 cm.

Originally published in 1870 and again in 1884. Over 2000 brief biographical entries followed by critical quotations from authorities. Introduction discusses art academies and institutions for art education of the period. Contents: Authorities consulted; Introduction; Artists of the 19th century; Index to authorities quoted; Index of places; General index.

228

Who's who in art. Biographies of leading men and women in the world of art today—Artists, designers, craftsmen, critics, writers, teachers, collectors and curators with appendices of signatures. 9th ed. London, Art Trade Press, [1958]. 885 p. 19 cm.

1st ed. 1927; 2d ed. 1929; 3d ed. 1934; 4th ed. 1948; 5th ed. 1950; 6th ed. 1952; 7th ed. 1954; 8th ed. 1956. Over 4000 names are included. Appendices I–VI contain 600 monograms and signatures; Appendix VII, Obituaries, p. 864–74.

SEE ALSO: Baglione. Le vite de' pittori, scultori, architetti (1984); Baldinucci. Cominciamento e progresso dell'arte dell'intagliare in rame (1985); Bellori. Le vite de' pittori, scvltori, ed architetti moderni (1989); Bie. Het gulden cabinet (1990); Descamps. La vie des peintres (2000); Knorr. Allgemeine Künstler-Historie (2011); Orlandi. Abcedario pittorico (2023).

National

France

229

Audin, Marius, and Vial, Eugène. Dictionnaire des artistes et ouvriers d'art de la France. Lyonnais. Paris, Bibliothèque d'art et archéologie, 1918/19. 2 v. 26 cm.

800 copies printed. Limited to artists who died before 1900, or if date of death is not ascertainable, who began working before 1850. Artists born in Lyons but working elsewhere not included; also excluded are the silk industry and printing. Introduction contains material on statutes of the city concerning art and a list of professions contained in

this dictionary, as well as notes on corporations of Lyons. Bibliography v. 2, p. [325]–46.

230
Bellier de La Chavignerie, Émile. Dictionnaire général des artistes de l'école française depuis l'origine des arts du dessin jusqu'à nos jours. Architectes, peintres, sculpteurs, graveurs et lithographes. Ouvrage commencé par Émile Bellier de La Chavignerie, continué par Louis Auvray.... Paris, Renouard, 1882–85. 2 v. 27 cm.
————. Supplément et table topographique. Paris, Renouard, 1887. 266 p. 27 cm.

Contains all artists whose works, given to a jury, have been admitted three times to the Salon. Lists pictures and tells in which Salons they were exhibited. Contents: v. 1, A–L; v. 2, M–Z; and *Supplément* that brings work up to 1882. "Table topographique des artistes français" lists artists by province and under province by city.

231
Bérard, André. Dictionnaire biographique des artistes français du XIe au XVIIe siècle, suivi d'une table chronologique et alphabétique comprenant en vingt classes les arts mentionnés dans l'ouvrage. . . . Paris, Dumoulin, 1872. 864 columns. 22 cm.
"Ouvrage tiré à 300 exemplaires."

Includes painters, sculptors, musicians, miniaturists, calligraphers, engravers, goldsmiths, ironworkers, clockmakers, bookbinders, embroiderers, tapestry weavers (of haute lisse), and other artisans. Numbers following name of artist refer to the book from which the information was taken (with a list of 206 at the beginning). Artists are listed chronologically by their classification at the end of the volume.

232
Bonnaffé, Edmond. Dictionnaire des amateurs français au XVII siècle. Paris, Quantin, 1884. 353 p. 25 cm.

Encyclopedia of early art collectors with literary references to collections and bibliographical notes. At end of volume a supplement and "tables" which are arranged by category (painting, tapestry, etc.) and then by artist and title of work. Bibliography p. [xiii]–xvi.

233
Brune, Paul. Dictionnaire des artistes et ouvriers d'art de la Franche-Comté. . . . Paris, Bibliothèque d'art et d'archéologie, 1912. 337 p. 26 cm.

Intended as first volume in a series to cover all provinces of France. Introduction gives a history of the art of the province. The dictionary contains biographical notices and a catalog of works of the artists and artisans born in the province or attached to it by family or artistic tie, who died before 1900. Under each artist, where possible, lists exhibitions of his work and museums in which his work is found. Sources of information are also given. Alphabetical list of 77 professions contained in this dictionary p. xxix. At end of volume an index of names cited in the notices. Bibliography p. xiii–xxviii gives sources of documentation.

234
Du Peloux de Saint Romain, Charles, *Vicomte.*... Répertoire biographique et bibliographique des artistes du XVIIIe siècle français . . . Accompagné de notices sur l'art du XVIIIe siècle, les expositions, les académies et manufactures royales, les amateurs d'art, les ventes publiques et d'une importante bibliographie. Paris, Champion, 1930–41. 2 v. 26 cm.

Biographical and bibliographical material on French art and artists of the 18th century. Contents: v. 1, Répertoire biographique: Peintres, dessinateurs, graveurs p. 1–160; Sculpteurs, ciseleurs, orfèvres, fondeurs, ferronniers p. 161–212; Architectes p. 213–46; Ébénistes, doreurs, décorateurs du bois p. 247–72; [Sociétés, amateurs, ventes publiques] p. 288–328; Bibliographie p. 329–449; v. 2, Notices historiques sur l'art français dans les pays scandinaves, les manufactures particulières de faïence, de porcelaine et de tapisseries; Bibliographie p. 38–97. Bibliography in v. 2 lists about 4000 titles published in France, Germany, and England since 1930, including periodical articles.

235
Dussieux, Louis Étienne. Les artistes français à l'étranger . . . 3. éd. Paris, Lecoffre, 1876. 643 p. 24 cm.

1st ed. 1852, 2d ed. 1856. Contains "Histoire générale des arts en France" p. [3]–146; and "Les artistes français à l'étranger" p. 147–615, arranged alphabetically by country, then by province or state within each country, and within these subdivisions by individual artists.

"Table alphabétique des artistes français qui ont travaillé à l'étranger" p. 623–37 gives for each artist the medium in which he worked. "Table alphabétique des artistes français dont les oeuvres se trouvent dans les musées et quelques grands collections particulières à l'étranger" p. 639–43.

236

Gabet, Charles Henri Joseph. Dictionnaire des artistes de l'école française au XIXe siècle. Peinture, sculpture, architecture, gravure, dessin, lithographie et composition musicale. . . . Orné de vignettes gravées par M. Deschamps. Paris, Vergne, 1831. 709 p. illus. 21 cm.

Covers painters, sculptors, architects, engravers, designers, lithographers, and composers in France up to the 19th century. List of abbreviations used, opposite p. 1.

237

Gérard, Charles. Les artistes de l'Alsace pendant le moyen âge. Paris, Nancy, Berger-Levrault, 1872–73. 2 v. 24 cm.

Covers art and artists in Alsace from the 7th to the 16th century, arranged by centuries and then by individual artists.

Indexes in v. 2: (1) Les artistes de l'Alsace dans l'ordre de leur apparition chronologique p. 443–56; (2) Les artistes de l'Alsace par groupes professionnels p. 457–68; (3) Monuments religieux qui ont une série plus ou moins complète de maîtres de l'oeuvre p. 469–71; (4) Indication de tous les personnages nommés dans l'ouvrage p. 472–91.

238

Giraudet, Eugène. Les artistes tourangeaux: architectes, armuriers, brodeurs, émailleurs, graveurs, orfèvres, peintres, sculpteurs, tapissiers de haute lisse. Notes et documents inédits. . . . Tours, Rouillé-Ladevèze, 1885. 419 p. illus. (facsims.) 27 cm.

A long introduction (104 pages) discusses architecture, sculpture, and painting in the Tours region, followed by a dictionary of artists, for which documents and sources are given in footnotes. Indexes of artists and objects referred to.

239

Leblond, Victor. Les artistes de Beauvais et du Beauvaisis au XVIe siècle et leurs oeuvres. Beauvais, Imprimerie Départementale de l'Oise, 1922. 56 p. 25 cm.

Contents: Brief descriptions of cathedrals and churches of Beauvais and the architects and masons who built them, followed by a chapter on sculptors and a chapter on glassworkers. "Les familles d'artistes" treated briefly p. 49–51. "Contracts d'apprentissage" p. 51–56.

240

Lespinasse, Pierre Eugène de. Les artistes français en Scandinavie. . . . Paris, La Renaissance du Livre [1929]. 193 p. plates. 21 cm. (L'art français à l'étranger)

Contains material on French artists who worked in Scandinavia. "Résumé chronologique" p. 181–82. Bibliography p. 183–85. List of the principal paintings painted in France by Swedish painters of the 19th century and exhibited in large museums of Sweden and Finland p. 186–89.

241

Port, Célestin. . . . Les artistes angevins, peintres, sculpteurs, maîtres d'oeuvre, architectes, graveurs, musiciens, d'après les archives angevines. . . Paris, Baur [etc.] 1881. 334 p. 24 cm. (Société de l'Histoire de l'Art Français)

Artists are listed in alphabetical order and under each name is given whatever information has been gleaned from archives of the Anjou region. Sources of special interest are given in footnotes.

242

Portal, Charles. Dictionnaire des artistes et ouvriers d'art du Tarn du XIIIe au XXe siècle. Albi, Chez l'Auteur, 1925. 332 p. 25 cm.

A biographical dictionary covering artists of the Tarn district from the 13th to the 20th centuries, which includes entries for 1200 persons. All types of artists and artisans are included.

Sources on which the work is based are listed in the introduction p. xiv–xviii. "Table alphabétique des principaux noms de personnes, lieux et matières" p. 319–32.

243

Varille, Mathieu. Les peintres primitifs de Provence. Paris, Rapilly, 1946. 230 p. 17 cm.

Covers not only primitive painters but also illuminators, embroiderers, and glassmakers, working in Provence from 1250–1550.

244

Vial, Henri; Marcel, Adrian; and Girodie, André. Les artistes decorateurs du bois, répertoire alphabétique des ébenistes, menuisiers, sculpteurs, doreurs sur bois, etc., ayant travaillé en France au XVIIe et XVIIIe siècles. Paris, Bibliothèque d'Art et d'Archéologie, 1912–22. 2 v. 27 cm. (Publications pour faciliter les études d'art en France)

An edition of 600 copies. Arranged alphabetically by name of artist. Gives for each any facts which have been ascertainable, and bibliographical references. Contents: v. 1, A–L; v. 2, M–Z and Supplement. Bibliography p. xxvi–xxvii.

SEE ALSO: Piles. Abrégé de la vie des peintres, etc. (2031).

Germany and Austria

245

Merlo, Johann Jakob. Kölnische Künstler in alter und neuer Zeit; Johann Jakob Merlos neu bearb. und erweiterte Nachrichten von dem Leben und den Werken Kölnischer Künstler, hrsg. von Eduard Firmenich-Richartz unter Mitwirkung von Hermann Keussen; mit zahlreichen bildlichen Beilagen. Düsseldorf, Schwann, 1895. 1206 columns. illus., 52 plates (incl. ports.) 29 cm. (Publikationen der Gesellschaft für Rheinische Geschichtskunde, IX)

First published in Cologne, 1850. Contains painters, sculptors, architects, engravers, etc., of Cologne in a dictionary arrangement. Based mostly on archival material. For more important artists, lists their works and gives bibliographies. List of members, laws, and publications of the Gesellschaft für Rheinische Geschichtskunde p. [v]–x.

246

Mithoff, H. Wilhelm H. Mittelalterliche Künstler und Werkmeister Niedersachsens und Westfalens, lexikalisch dargestellt; zweite umgearbeitete und vermehrte Ausgabe. Hannover, Helwing, 1885. 462 p. 21 cm.

A dictionary of medieval artists and foremen of Lower Saxony and Westphalia. 1st ed. 1866. Contents: Alphabetisches Verzeichnis der Künstler und Werkmeister p. 5–356; Anhang: (1) Gruppierungen der Künstler und Werkmeister; (2) Rolle des Maler- und Glaseramts zu Lüneburg; (3) Das Künstlerwappen; (4) Urkundliche Verhandlungen mit Künstlern und Werkmeistern; (5) Die Morgensprache; (6) Schutzheilige von Künstlern und Werkleuten; (7) Glossar niederdeutscher Wörter aus mittelalterlichen Aufzeichnungen p. 439–62.

247

Tirolisches Künstlerlexikon, oder kurze Lebensbeschreibung jener Künstler, welche geborne Tiroler waren, oder eine längere Zeit in Tirol sich aufgehalten haben. Von einem Verehrer der Künste. Innsbruck, Rauch, 1830, 288 p. 20 cm.

A dictionary of artists who were born in the Tirol or who had lived and worked there for a long time. Bibliography of sources consulted p. 3–6.

248

Wastler, Josef. Steirisches Künstler-Lexicon. Graz, "Leykam," 1883. 198 p. 23 cm.

Includes architects, painters, and sculptors from Styria. Arranged in dictionary form. List of sources and abbreviations p. ix. Index of places p. 192–97.

249

Zülch, Walther Karl. Frankfurter Künstler, 1223–1700. Frankfurt am Main, Diesterweg, 1935. 670 p. 28 cm.

A study of Frankfort artists in which entries are arranged chronologically, with bibliographical and archival references for each artist, p. 1–600. List of artists arranged by their media p. 601–29. Alphabetical list of artists p. 629–54. Index of places and persons other than artists p. 654–70.

SEE ALSO: Doppelmayer. Historische Nachricht von dem Nürnbergischen . . . Künstlern (2004); Hüsgen. Nachrichten von Frankfurter Künstlern und Kunst-Sachen (2009).

Great Britain

250

Cunningham, Allan. The lives of the most eminent British painters, sculptors, and architects. . . . London, Murray, 1830–33. 6 v. plates. 16 cm.

A series of essays on 47 important British artists, preceded by "The early painters." Each essay is headed by an engraved portrait of the artist. No index, but each volume lists at the beginning the artists treated in it.

251

Hall, Henry C. Artists and sculptors of Nottingham and Nottinghamshire, 1750–1950; a biographical dictionary, containing the names and dates of over 170 artists and sculptors of the past and present, with biographical notes of each. Nottingham, H. Jones, 1953. 95 p. 21 cm.

Contents: pt. 1, Artists of the past p. 11–67; pt. 2, Contemporary artists p. 71–85; pt. 3, Sculptors p. 89–95. Arranged in dictionary form under these three sections.

252

Redgrave, Samuel. A dictionary of artists of the English school: painters, sculptors, architects, engravers and ornamentists; with notices of their lives and work. . . . 2d ed. London, Bell, 1878. 497 p. 22 cm.

First published by Longmans, 1874. "New edition revised to the present date."—*Pref.* Covers artists born in England as well as those foreigners who worked there in connection with art institutions. For each artist gives medium, short biographical facts, and important works if he is well known.

253

Rees, Thomas Mardy. Welsh painters, engravers, sculptors (1527–1911) arranged alphabetically, with thirty portraits. . . . Carnarvon, Welsh Pub. Co. [191?]. 188 p. ports. 22 cm.

Brief notices for each artist with authorities and dates.

254

Strickland, Walter G. A dictionary of Irish artists. . . . Dublin, Maunsel, 1913. 2 v. illus., plates (incl. ports.) 26 cm.

Covers the lives and works of Irish artists from earliest times to the present day. Includes "every artist of any note who has worked in Ireland and those of Irish birth . . . who have followed their profession in England." Index v. 2, p. 665–728. Appendix v. 2, p. 579–664, gives an account of various societies of artists and art institutions in Ireland.

SEE ALSO: Vertue. . . . Vertue notebooks (2044).

Italy

255

Alizeri, Federigo. Notizie dei professori del disegno in Liguria dalla Fondazione dell'Accademia. Genova, Tip. Luigi Sambolino, 1864–66. 3 v. plates. 28 cm.

Three introductory chapters followed by a list of artists arranged by the medium in which they worked, covering the 18th and 19th century artists of Genoa and its vicinity. Each volume has its own index, and v. 3 has a subject index to the three volumes, p. 516–39.

256

Bolognini Amorini, Antonio. Vite dei pittori ed artefici bolognesi. Bologna, Tipi Gover-

nativi alla Volpe, 1848. 5 v. in 2. plates. 24 cm.

An attempt to bring *Felsina pittrice* (2016) up to date by enlarging and correcting it.

Includes painters, sculptors, and architects of Bologna, devoting an essay to each artist. A life of Malvasia is at the beginning of v. 1, and a long article on the Carracci is also included. At end of each volume is a list of the artists covered.

257

Campori, Giuseppe, ed. Gli artisti italiani e stranieri negli stati Estensi. . . . Modena, Camera, 1855. 537 p. 23 cm.

An edition of 250 copies. Covers Italian and foreign artists working in the d'Este states, arranged in dictionary form. Index of cities and lands (of the d'Este states) mentioned in the work p. 503–06. Artists index p. 507–37.

258

Campori, Giuseppe. Memorie biografiche degli scultori, architetti, pittori, ec. nativi di Carrara e di altri luoghi della provincia di Massa, con cenni relativi agli artisti italiani ed esteri che in essa dimorarono ed operarono, e un saggio bibliografico. Modena, Vincenzi, 1873. 466 p. 21 cm.

Well-documented notes, arranged in alphabetical order, on artists who worked in Carrara and others who came to select Carrara marble for their sculptures. Contents: (1) Artisti nativi della provincia p. 1–260; (2) Artisti estranei alla provincia p. 261–373; (3) Saggio bibliografico artistico p. 375–430. Appendice p. 431–40. Indexes to each of the first two sections, and index of places.

259

Corna, Andrea. . . . Dizionario della storia dell'arte in Italia con duecento illustrazioni. . . . 2. ed. Piacenza, Tarantola [1930]. 2 v. illus. 28 cm.

1st ed. 1916; 2d ed. corrected and augmented. A biographical dictionary including Italian painters, sculptors, architects, potters, goldsmiths, and engravers. Contents: v. 1, Abacco-Gavasetti; v. 2, Gavasetti-Zurlengo.

260

Fenaroli, Stefano. Dizionario degli artisti bresciani. Brescia, Tip. Editrice del Pio Istituto Pavoni, 1877. 317 p. 20 cm.

In general, covers painters, sculptors, and architects of Brescia, but some outstanding goldsmiths, engravers, and metalworkers are included. Contents: Dizionario p. 1–262;

Documenti p. 263–89; Indice degli artisti nominati nel dizionario p. 291–300 (with dates). Appendice: Nomi di artisti bresciani dei quali non si conoscono opere p. 303–17.

261
Gubernatis, Angelo de, *Conte.* Dizionario degli artisti italiani viventi, pittori, scultori e architetti. . . . Firenze, Le Monnier, 1889. 640 p. 25 cm.
A dictionary of Italian painters, sculptors, and architects living about 1888. List of 29 artists who died since work went to press p. 637.

262
Padovano, Ettore. Dizionario degli artisti contemporanei. [Milano] Istituto Tip. Editoriale [1951]. 403 p. illus., col. plates. 25 cm.
An attempt to include all 20th century artists (painters, sculptors, architects, etc.) working in Italy. As information was obtained by questionnaire it is uneven in coverage. Index of names p. 385–99 lists artists included and medium in which they work. Index of illustrations p. 400–03.

263
Valgimigli, Gian Marcello. Dei pittori e degli artisti Faentini de'secoli XV e XVI. Faenza, Conti, 1869. 180 p. 26 cm.
2d ed. 1870. A collection of notes on the artists of Faenza. "Indice" is a table of contents listing artists treated.

264
Zannandreis, Diego. Le vite dei pittori, scultori e architetti veronese. . . . Giuseppe Biadego, ed. Verona, Franchini, 1891. 559 p. 26 cm.
1st ed. of a work written early in the 19th century dealing with the lives of artists of Verona. Index to the lives p. 535–43. Index of places p. 545–59. Bibliography p. [xxvii–xxxv].

SEE ALSO: Baruffaldi. Vite de' pittori e scultori ferraresi . . . (1988); Boschini. Le minere della pittura (1992); Dominici. Vite de' pittori, scultori, ed architetti napoletani . . . (2003); Malvasia. Felsina pittrice (2016); L'Opera del genio italiano all'estero (2458); Pascoli. Vite de' pittori, scultori, ed architetti moderni (2029); Passeri. Vite de' pittori, scultori ed architetti (2030); Pozzo. Le vite de' pittori, degli scultori ed architetti veronesi (2035); Soprani. Le vite de' pittori, scoltori, et architetti genovesi (2040); Vasari. Le vite de' piv eccellenti architetti, pittori et scvltori

italiani (2041) and Le vite de' piv eccellenti pittori, scvltori e architettori (2042); Verci. Notizie intorno alla vita e alle opere de' pittori, scultori e intagliatori (2043).

Latin America

265
Merlino, Adrián. Diccionario de artistas plásticos de la Argentina, siglos XVIII-XIX-XX. [Buenos Aires, 1954] 433 p. illus. 23 cm.
For each artist gives the places where he has exhibited, the museums containing his works, and the prizes he has received. Bibliography p. 408–14. "Instituciones de la Argentina vinculadas a las artes plasticas" p. 416–28.

266
Vargas Ugarte, Ruben. Ensayo de un diccionario de artifices coloniales de la America meridional. [Lima?] Baiocco, 1947. 391 p. 24 cm.
A dictionary of Spanish American artists with a separate section for each of the four centuries covered. Each section arranged alphabetically by name of artist. "Indice" p. 381–91 is just a listing (grouped by centuries) of the names included in the dictionary.
———. Apendice. [Lima?] Baiocco, 1955. 118 p.

Low Countries

267
Duverger, Jozef. De Brusselsche steenbikkeleren: beeldhouwers, bouwmeesters, metselaars enz. der XIVe en XVe eeuw met een aanhangsel over Klaas Sluter en zijn Brusselsche medewerkers te Dijon. Gent, Vyncke, 1933. 134 p. 25 cm.
Covers sculptors, architects, stonemasons, etc., of Brussels in the 14th and 15th centuries. Contents: Voorrede. (1) Het handschrift; (2) Het steenbikkeleren-ambacht te Brussel; (3) De beteekenis van het handschrift; (4) Aanhangsel: Klaas Sluter en zijn Brusselsche medewerkers; (5) Ledenlijst van het steenbikkeleren-ambacht. Index of names p. 77–130.

268
Immerzeel, Johannes, *Jr.* De levens en werken der Hollandsche en Vlaamsche kunstschilders, beeldhouwers, graveurs en bouwmeesters, van het begin der vijftiende eeuw tot heden . . . uit. door Mr. C. H. Immerzeel en

C. Immerzeel. . . . Amsterdam, van Kestern, 1842–43. 3 v. illus. 25 cm.

2d ed. 1855, Amsterdam, Diederichs. A dictionary covering the lives and works of Dutch and Flemish painters, sculptors, engravers, and architects from the beginning of the 15th century to 1840.

Arranged in dictionary form, with some entries under names of museums as well as artists, and numerous portraits of artists in the text. "Monogrammen" v. 3, p. [263]–307.

269

Kramm, Christiaan. De levens en werken der Hollandsche en Vlaamsche kunst-schilders, beeldhouwers, graveurs en bouwmeesters, van den vroegsten tot op onzen tijd. . . . Amsterdam, Diederichs, 1857–64. 6 pts. and supp. in 4 v. 25 cm.

A biographical dictionary of Dutch and Flemish artists from the beginning of time until the present day, based partly on Immerzeel (268). Supplement contains biography of the author.

270

Lerius, Théodore François Xavier van. Biographies d'artistes anversois. Publ. par P. Génard. Antwerpen, Kockx, 1880–81. 2 v. 24 cm. (Maatschappij der Antwerpsche Bibliophilen, uitgave 8, 11)

Sources given throughout. Volume 1 contains biographies of 27 Antwerp artists on 265 pages; v. 2 contains biographies of 20 artists on 395 pages.

271

Willigen, Adriaan van der. Les artistes de Haarlem; notices historiques avec un précis sur la gilde de St. Luc. Éd. rev. et augm. Haarlem, Bohn, 1870. 366 p. geneal. tables, facsims. 24 cm.

Translated from the Dutch. First part is on the Guild of St. Luc p. 1–57. Notes on various Haarlem artists, arranged alphabetically, p. 66–351. "Revue chronologique des personnes mentionnées dans la deuxième partie" p. 61–65. Appendix, "Faienciers et potiers de Haarlem," p. 353–59. Index of names p. 360–66. Genealogical tables of various families of artists and four pages of facsimiles of signatures.

272

Wurzbach, Alfred, Ritter von Tannenberg. Niederländisches Künstler Lexikon, auf Grund archivalischer Forschungen. Wien, Halm, 1906–11. 3 v. facsims. 28 cm.

A valuable biographical dictionary covering Dutch and Flemish artists, including some of the 19th century. Contains biographical information, lists of important works, and bibliographies, with many facsimiles of signatures. Letters C and K, and I, J, and Y, are filed together. Volume 3 is a supplement and includes anonymous masters and monogrammists.

SEE ALSO: Gool. De nieuwe schouburg der Nederlantsche kunstschilders en schilderessen (2007); Mander. Het schilder-boeck (2018); Weyerman. De levens-beschryvingen der Nederlandsche konst-schilders en konstschilderessen (2048).

Oriental Countries

273

Beale, Thomas William. An Oriental biographical dictionary, founded on materials collected by the late Thomas William Beale. . . . New ed., rev. and enl. by Henry George Keene. . . . London, Allen, 1894. 431 p. 25 cm.

The emphasis is on Persia. Names are printed in Persian following the English form.

274

Giles, Herbert Allen. A Chinese biographical dictionary. London, Quaritch; Shanghai, Kelly & Walsh, 1898. 1022 p. 25 cm.

"Index to literary names, sobriquets, canonisation and persons whose names are only mentioned in the body of the work" p. 981–1018. Corrigenda et addenda p. 1019–22.

SEE ALSO: British Museum. Department of Prints and Drawings. Index of Chinese artists . . . (93).

Russia and Slavic Countries

275

Dlabač, Jan Bohumir. Allgemeines historisches Künstler-Lexikon für Böhmen und zum Theil auch für Mähren und Schlesien. Gesammelt und bearb. von Gottfried Johann Dlabacž . . . Auf Kosten der hochlöblichen Herrenstände Böhmens herausgegeben. Prag, Hasse, 1815. 3 v. in 1. 22 cm.

Includes musicians as well as artists of Bohemia, Moravia, and Silesia, with sources for the majority of entries.

276

Neumann, Wilhelm. Lexikon baltischer Künstler. . . . Riga, Jonck & Poliewsky, 1908. 171 p. 22 cm.

Covers painters, sculptors, architects, engravers, etc., who were born in the Baltic area or who worked there and assimilated the style of these provinces. Arranged in dictionary form with bibliographies for many of the artists included.

277
Rastawiecki, Edward, *Baron*. Słownik malarzów polskich. . . . Warszawa, Nakł autora, 1850–57. 3 v. ports. 23 cm.
A Polish biographical dictionary covering Polish painters and foreign artists working in Poland. Includes statutes of the following guilds: glaziers, gilders, and apothecaries.

278
Sobko, Nikolai Petrovich. Slovar' russkikh khudozhnikov. . . . (XI–XIX vv.) S. Petersburg, Stasulevich, 1883–99. 3 v. illus. 30 cm.
A dictionary of Russian artists covering from the 11th through the 19th century. Gives biographical information and bibliographies for the individual artists.

279
Toman, Prokop. Nový slovník československých výtvarných umělců. Praha, Ryšavý, 1936. 792 p. 27 cm.
A Czech biographical dictionary arranged alphabetically. Some bibliographies given at end of articles. Bibliography of sources p. 3–4.

Scandinavia

280
Gelsted, Otto. Kunstner leksikon, med 1100 biografier af Danske billed-huggere, malere, grafikere og dekorative kunstnere fra 1900–1942. København, Jensen, 1942. 197 p. 24 cm.
A dictionary of contemporary Danish artists including sculptors, painters, engravers, and decorative artists, arranged alphabetically, with a paragraph of information for each artist.

281
Samlerens kunstnerleksikon. Redaktion: Hans Werner . . . I–II. København, Samleren, 1929–32. 2 v. illus. 19 cm.
Includes contemporary artists. Arranged in dictionary form, giving a few lines for each artist.

282
Svenska konstnärer; biografisk handbok. 5. uppl. Malmö, Skånetryckeriets [1955]. 438 p. 20 cm.

Includes 4000 names of architects, painters, sculptors, engravers, and dealers of Swedish nationality. Arranged in dictionary form with a short paragraph for each artist, including in some cases where reproductions of his works can be found. "Verket och mastaren" p. 429–38 arranged geographically.

283
Svenskt Konstnärslexikon; tiotusen svenska konstnärers liv och verk. [Redaktion: Gösta Lilja, Bror Olsson, S. Artur Svensson] Malmö, Allhem, 1952–(57). v. 1–(3). illus., plates (part col.), ports. 29 cm.
To be completed in five volumes and a supplement. It will contain 10,000 biographies of Swedish artists living and dead. Covers painting, sculpture, graphic arts, folk art, decorative arts and church decoration, stage and costume design, etc. Majority of the articles are signed and give the usual biographical information and bibliographies of important artists. Profusely illustrated in both black and white and color, including many portraits of artists. Contents: v. 1–3, Abbe-Lunderberg.

284
Weilbach, Philip. Kunstnerleksikon; udgivet af en komité med støtte af Carlsbergfondet, Redaktion: Merete Bodelsen og Povl Engelstoft. [København] Aschehoug, 1947–52. 3 v. illus., plates, ports. 27 cm.
3d ed. 1st ed. published in 1877–78 under title *Dansk kunstnerlexikon;* 2d ed. in 1896–97 under title *Nyt dansk kunstnerlexikon.* A Danish art dictionary of signed articles with bibliographies at end of entries and illustrations in the text. Contents: v. 1, A–H; v. 2, I–P; v. 3, Q–Ø and supplement. Bibliography v. 3, Supp. p. [52]–53. "Rettelser og tilføjelser" v. 3, Supp. p. 57–86. "Arkitektur Index" v. 3, Supp. p. 89–135.

285
Weinwich, Neils Heinrich. Dansk, Norsk og Svensk kunstnerlexicon. Kjøbenhavn, Seidelin, 1829. 197 p. 23 cm.
A dictionary of Danish, Norwegian, and Swedish artists, listed alphabetically, with a short paragraph for each artist. No bibliographies or sources are given, nor are artists' works mentioned.

Spain and Portugal

286
Baquero Almansa, Andrés. Catálogo de los profesores de las bellas artes murcianos. . . . Murcia, Nogués, 1913. 500 p. 23 cm.

150 copies printed. An account of artists in the province of Murcia preceded by a historical introduction of 28 pages. Biographies arranged by centuries. Chronological tables p. 497–500. A nine-page alphabetical index of artists at end of volume.

287

Ceán Bermúdez, Juan Agustín. Diccionario histórico de los más ilustres profesores de las bellas artes en España. . . . Madrid, Ibarra, 1800. 6 v. 16 cm.

Dictionary arrangement of Spanish artists and others working in Spain. Includes architects, painters, sculptors, miniature painters, engravers, silversmiths, glassworkers, embroiderers, and metalworkers.

Volume 6 contains: "Suplemento" p. 55–91; "Tablas cronológicas de los profesores de las bellas artes en España" p. 95–184, arranged by medium; "Tablas geográficas de los profesores de las bellas artes en España" p. 187–376.

288

Elías de Molíns, Antonio. Diccionario biográfico y bibliográfico de escritores y artistas catalanes del siglo XIX (apuntes y datos). . . . Barcelona, Administración, 1889–[95]. 2 v. illus., plates. 28 cm.

A dictionary of Catalan artists of the 19th century. Includes bibliographies.

289

Furió, Antonio. Diccionario histórico de los ilustres profesores de las bellas artes en Mallorca. Palma, Mallorquina, 1946 [i.e., 1947]. 337 p. 16 cm. (Biblioteca balear, 10)

A dictionary of artists in Majorca. Contents: Chronological chart of artists arranged by centuries and medium in which they worked p. 9–12; Introduction p. 13–84; Dictionary p. 85–306.

290

Gestoso y Pérez, José. Ensayo de un diccionario de los artífices que florecieron en Sevilla desde el siglo XIII al XVIII inclusive. . . . Sevilla, Oficina de la Andalucía Moderna, 1899–1909. 3 v. facsims. 25 cm.

A dictionary of artists of Seville from the 13th through the 18th centuries. Contents: v. 1, A–O; v. 2, P–Y; v. 3, Apendices a los tomos 1 y 2. Volume 3 is illustrated with 20 facsimiles of signatures. Index at end of each volume.

291

Machado, Cyrillo Volkmar. Collecção de memorias relativas ás vidas dos pintores, e escultores, architetos, e gravadores portugueses, e dos estrangeiros, que estiverão em Portugal, recolhidas e ordenadas por Cyrillo Volkmar Machado, seguidas de notas pelos Dr. J. M. Teixeira de Carvalho e Dr. Vergílio Correia. Coimbra, Imprensa da Universidade, 1922. 295 p. facsim. 22 cm. (Subsidios para a historia da arte portuguesa [v.] 5)

Facsimile of title page of 1st ed., Lisbon, 1823. Covers Portuguese painters, sculptors, architects, and engravers. "Memorias concernentes a vida e algumas obras de Cyrillo Volkmar Machado, escriptas por elle mesmo" p. [243]–60.

292

Ossorio y Bernard, Manuel. Galleria biográfica de artistas españoles del siglo XIX. . . . Madrid, Moreno y Rojas, 1883–84. 749 p. illus., ports. 28 cm.

1st ed. 1868. A biographical dictionary of 19th century Spanish artists which mentions their works. No sources given. "Indice de los artistas contenidos en esta obra" p. 717–49.

293

Peréz-Costanti, Pablo. Diccionario de artistas que florecieron en Galicia durante los siglos XVI y XVII. . . . Santiago, Seminario c. Central, 1930. 610 p. 25 cm.

A dictionary of Galician artists of the 16th and 17th centuries. Arranged in dictionary form with bibliographical references to archival material given at end of articles. Some signatures given in the text. "Indice alfabetico de Pueblos" p. 595–609.

294

Raczyński, Atanazy, *Hrabia*. Dictionnaire historico-artistique du Portugal, pour faire suite à l'ouvrage ayant pour titre: Les arts en Portugal, lettres adressées à la Société artistique et scientifique de Berlin et accompagnées de documens. . . . Paris, Renouard, 1847. 306 p. plates. 23 cm.

Intended as a sequel to the author's *Les arts en Portugal* (748). Arranged in dictionary form with a few lines for each artist. Sources are usually given.

Numerous cross references from variant forms of names. Chronological list of kings of Portugal p. x–xii.

295

Ráfols, José F., ed. Diccionario biográfico de artistas de Cataluña desde la epoca romana hasta nuestros dias. . . . Barcelona, Millá, 1951–54. 3 v. illus. 25 cm.

A dictionary of artists of Catalonia, both

the native-born and those who worked there. Includes painters, sculptors, engravers, architects, ceramic workers, goldsmiths, glassworkers, armorers, etc., arranged alphabetically with a short paragraph for each. Each volume has indexes, and v. 3 has an artist index arranged by centuries p. 366–622.

296
Ramiréz de Arellano, Rafael. Diccionario biográfico de artistas de la provincia de Córdoba. Madrid, Perales y Martinez, 1893. 535 p. 23 cm. (Colección de documentos inéditos para la historia España . . . t. CVII)
Biographies are arranged alphabetically p. 63–282. "Cronologica," which is divided according to media, lists artists in chronological order p. 295–303. This is followed by documents pertaining to various aspects of art and a study of goldsmithing in Cordoba.

297
Saltillo, Miguel Lasso de la Vega y López de Tejada, *Marqués* del. Artistas y artífices sorianos de los siglos XVI y XVII (1509–1699). 1. ed. Madrid, Editorial Maestre, 1948. 476 p. illus., 30 plates. 26 cm.
Includes painters, sculptors, architects, and musicians from the province of Soria. General index p. [467]–76.

298
Stirling-Maxwell, *Sir* William, *Bart*. Annals of the artists of Spain . . . a new edition, incorporating the author's own notes, additions and emendations with portraits and 24 steel and mezzotint engravings, also numerous engravings on wood. . . . 2d ed. London, Nimmo, 1891. 4 v. illus., plates (incl. ports.) 24 cm.
Edited by Robert Guy. Preface to 1st ed. (published 1848) discusses previous works covering this field. Bibliographical footnotes. "Velazquez and his works" v. 4, p. [1551]–65. "Catalogues of the works of Velazquez and Murillo" v. 4, p. [1567]–1641. Monograms of artists v. 4, p. [1642]. Index p. 1645–70.

299
Viñaza, Cipriano Muñoz y Manzano, *Conde* de la. Adiciones al Diccionario histórico de los más ilustres profesores de las bellas artes en España de D. Juan Agustín Ceán Bermúdez. . . . Madrid, Tip. de los Huérfanos, 1889–94. 4 v. in 2. 20 cm.
A dictionary of Spanish artists forming a supplement to Ceán Bermúdez (287). In addition to alphabetical entries under name of artist there are tables, arranged chronologi-

cally, under medium, and geographical indexes. Sources for information are frequently given. Contents: t. 1, Edad media . . . ; t. 2–4, Siglos XVI, XVII y XVIII.

SEE ALSO: Cumberland. Anecdotes of eminent painters in Spain (1998); Palomino de Castro. An account of the lives and works of the most eminent Spanish painters, sculptors and architects (2026) and Las vidas de los pintores y estatuarios eminentes españoles (2028).

Switzerland

300
Brun, Carl. Schweizerisches Künstler Lexikon; dictionnaire des artistes suisses. Hrsg. vom Schweizerischen Kunstverein. . . . Frauenfeld, Huber, 1905–17. 4 v. 26 cm.
A dictionary of Swiss artists which includes painters, sculptors, architects, as well as glasspainters, enamelers, medalists, goldsmiths, cabinetworkers, etc., who were born in Switzerland, and foreigners who worked there. Each entry signed and at beginning of each volume a list of contributors. Longer articles contain bibliographies. Volume 4, Supplement.

United States

301
Fielding, Mantle. Dictionary of American painters, sculptors and engravers. . . . N.Y., Struck, 1945. 433 p. illus., plates. 27 cm.
Originally published in 1926 and reprinted in this edition of 1500 copies. Contains biographies and records of nearly 8000 artists. In the case of living artists, addresses are given. Bibliography p. 424–33.

302
Groce, George Cuthbert, and Wallace, David H. The New-York Historical Society's Dictionary of artists in America, 1564–1860. New Haven, Yale Univ. Press; London, Oxford Univ. Press, 1957. 759 p. 24 cm.
"A documented biographical dictionary of painters, draftsmen, sculptors, engravers, lithographers and allied artists, either amateur or professional, native or foreign-born, who worked within the present continental limits of the United States between the years 1564 and 1860, inclusive."—*Introd.* Between ten and eleven thousand entries arranged alphabetically by name of artist. For each artist gives "full names, dates and places of

birth and death, media and subject matter of his work, chronology of residences and exhibitions, pupils and in some instances locations and reproductions of representative works." "Key to sources" p. 713–59.

303

Smith, Ralph Clifton. A biographical index of American artists. . . . Baltimore, Williams & Wilkins, 1930. 102 p. 24 cm.

Names of about 4700 artists in alphabetical order, each followed by a brief statement of place and date of birth and death, media in which artist worked, and abbreviations indicating one or more reference works in which further information may be found. List of works to which references are made p. ix.

304

Tuckerman, Henry Theodore. Book of the artists; American artist life, comprising biographical and critical sketches of American artists: preceded by an historical account of the rise and progress of art in America. N.Y., Putnam, 1867. 639 p. 28 ports. 24 cm.

Contents: Introduction p. 7–39; Early portrait painters (biographies of important artists) p. 71–397; Portraiture, genre and historical painters p. 398–505; Landscape painters p. 506–69; Sculptors p. 570–619. Appendix contains list of American pictures in public and private collections (arranged geographically by collection). Index p. 635–39. This edition contains some photographic portraits. Later impressions (1870, 1882) include appendices containing an account of notable pictures and private collections.

305

Who's who in American art; a biographical directory of contemporary artists, editors, critics, executives, etc. v. 1–(6), 1936/37–(1956). N.Y., Bowker [c1935]–(56). 23–26 cm. Biennial (irregular)

Subtitle varies slightly. Formerly published in the *American art annual* (106). Volumes 1–4, 1936/37–1940/47 were issued as pt. 2 of the *Annual*, v. 33–36, 1936–1940/47. Editors: 1936/37–   A. C. McGlauflin; Dorothy B. Gilbert. Issued 1936/37–   by the American Federation of Arts. Includes entries for painters, sculptors, graphic artists, book illustrators, craftsmen, cartoonists, textile designers, art historians and writers, critics and editors, museum personnel, educators and lecturers. Volume 4 includes a bibliography of American art by Elizabeth McCausland p. 611–57, 1947 (1130).

SEE ALSO: Appleton. Who's who in Northwest art (107); Index of 20th century artists (96).

| # Iconography

AMONG THE MOST RECURRENT REFERENCE questions in an art reference library are those dealing with iconographical problems. Here are listed some of the books which are most useful in answering questions of this type, including a number of books which are not art reference books in the strictest sense. In keeping with the policy of not listing monographs on individual artists and sites, books dealing with a single subject or theme have been omitted. Enough general works, however, have been listed to lead the reader to the specific topics.

General

306
Bailey, Henry Turner, and Pool, Ethel. Symbolism for artists, creative and appreciative. Worcester, Mass., Davis Press, 1925. 247 p. illus., 46 plates on 22 l. 18 cm.

1st printing 1925; 2d printing 1928. Contents: Abbreviations; Illustrations (46 plates); Elements and meanings (arranged alphabetically) p. 55–221; Appendix A: College and university colors; Appendix B: Bibliography p. 236–38; Appendix C: Plate and figure references.

307
Behling, Lottlisa. Die Pflanze in der mittelalterlichen Tafelmalerei. Weimar, Hermann Böhlaus Nachfolger, 1957. 221 p. 48 illus., 130 plates (1 col.) 30 cm.

A scholarly study of representations of botanical allegory in medieval German and Netherlandish panel pictures. "Literaturverzeichnis" p. 186–90. "Pflanzenregister" p. 192–210. "Personen- und Schriftenregister" p. 211–21.

308
Bulfinch, Thomas. Bulfinch's Mythology: The age of fable, The age of chivalry, Legends of Charlemagne; with dictionary index. Illus. by Elinore Blaisdell. N.Y., Crowell [1947]. 957 p. col. plates, map. 22 cm.

A standard collection of myths and legends originally published 1855 and frequently reprinted. Contents: Stories of gods and heroes; King Arthur and his knights; The Mabinogeon; Hero myths of the British race; Legends of Charlemagne. "Dictionary and index" p. 877–957 lists characters in the text, indicates pronunciation, and gives a few identifying sentences.

309
Droulers, Eug. Dictionnaire des attributs, allégories, emblèmes, et symboles. Turnhout, Belgique, Brepols [c1948?]. 281 p. illus. 28 cm.

Alphabetically arranged, with a short entry under each heading. Includes names of people, attributes, and allegorical figures. Numerous small line drawings and other illustrations. Bibliography p. [276]–81.

310
Edwardes, Marian, and Spence, Lewis. A dictionary of non-classical mythology. London, Dent; N.Y., Dutton [1912]. 214 p. plates. 18 cm. (Everyman's Library)

Contains short articles on names and myths of Assyrian, Babylonian, Celtic, Chinese, Egyptian, Hindu, Japanese, Mexican, North and South American Indian, Persian, Scandinavian, and Teutonic cultures. Some bibliographical references are included. "Chief authorities" p. ix–xii.

311
Ehrenstein, Theodor. Das alte Testament im Bilde, ein Illustrationswerk mit über 2000 Abbildungen von altchristlichen, mittelalterlichen und neuzeitlichen Kunstwerken.

Wien, Kende, 1923. 943 p. plates. 35 cm.

A collection of pictorial representations of various iconographical themes, arranged according to subjects represented. Index of places and artists p. 925–39. "Quellennachweis" p. 940–44.

312

Errera, *Mme.* Isabelle. Répertoire abrégé d'iconographie. . . . Wetteren, de Meester, 1929–38. 3 v. 25 cm.

Includes only A to C; no more published. Attempts to give in alphabetical order the names of people and episodes in the Bible and historical and mythological figures appearing in painting, sculpture, etc., from the Middle Ages to the present. Abbreviations v. 1, p. viii; bibliography v. 1, p. ix–xxiv.

313

Frazer, *Sir* James George. The golden bough; a study in magic and religion. 3d ed. London, N.Y., Macmillan, 1953. 13 v. 22 cm.

This is the 3d printing of the 3d ed., first published in 1907–15. A one-volume abridgment was published in 1922. While not essentially a work on iconography it is useful for the study of primitive art. Includes bibliographical footnotes.

Contents: v. 1–2, The magic art and the evolution of kings; v. 3, Taboo and the perils of the soul; v. 4, The dying god; v. 5–6, Adonis, Attis, Osiris, studies in the history of Oriental religion; v. 7–8, Spirits of the corn and of the world; v. 9, The scapegoat; v. 10–11, Balder the Beautiful, the fire festivals of Europe and the doctrine of the external soul; v. 12, Bibliography and a general index; v. 13, Supplement (originally published 1936 under title: *Aftermath; a supplement to The golden bough*).

314

Gayley, Charles Mills. The classic myths in English literature and in art, based originally on Bulfinch's "Age of fable" (1855); accompanied by an interpretative and illustrative commentary . . . new ed., rev. and enl. Boston & N.Y., Ginn [c1911]. 597 p. illus., plates, maps, geneal. tables. 20 cm.

A general one-volume handbook including the most important myths. Reprinted in 1939.

315

Goldsmith, Elizabeth E. Ancient pagan symbols. N.Y., London, Putnam, 1929. 220 p. illus., plates. 17 cm.

"A companion volume to *Sacred Symbols in Art* [355]. Much of the material used here has been derived from a previous and larger volume, *Life Symbols* . . ." (N.Y., Putnam, 1924). Arranged alphabetically under these chapter headings: Elements, Lotus, Tree of Life, The dual principle, The Cross, The serpent, Chinese trigrams, The four supernatural creatures of the Chinese, Animal symbolism in Chinese art, The sun, The moon, The wheel, The swastika, The trisula, Sacred birds, Sacred animals, Ancient gods and goddesses, Twice-born gods, Triads and the triangle, Some general symbols and symbolic figures in early art.

Not a scholarly work but a useful reference tool. Index p. 213–20.

316

Goodenough, Erwin Ramsdell. Jewish symbols in the Greco-Roman period. [N.Y.] Pantheon [1953–(58)] v. 1–(8). illus. 32 cm. (Bollingen series, 37)

A scholarly study, to be completed in ten volumes, which attempts to evaluate the archaeological material from the Judaism of the early Christian centuries, which became the symbols of Christian art.

Contents: v. 1, The archeological evidence from Palestine; v. 2, The archeological evidence from the Diaspora; v. 3, Illustrations; v. 4, The problem of method; symbols from cult; v. 5–6, Fish, bread, and wine; v. 7–8, Pagan symbols in Judaism. Bibliographical footnotes.

317

Hall, Adelaide Susan. A glossary of important symbols in their Hebrew, pagan, and Christian forms. Boston, Bates & Guild, 1912. 103 p. 19 cm.

A concise and easy to use compilation, arranged by type or form. Bibliography on fourth preliminary leaf. Index p. 98–103.

318

Leach, Maria, ed. Funk and Wagnalls' Standard dictionary of folklore, mythology, and legend. Maria Leach, editor, Jerome Fried, associate editor. N.Y., Funk & Wagnalls, 1949–50. 2 v. 26 cm.

Treats of gods, heroes, customs, tales, motifs, beliefs, games, and dances of various cultures of the world. No illustrations. Contains bibliographies. Longer articles are signed.

319

Lehner, Ernst. Symbols, signs, and signets. Cleveland, World Pub. Co. [1950]. 221 p. (chiefly illus.) 32 cm.

Reproduces signs under the following headings: Symbolic gods and deities; Astronomy and astrology; Alchemy; Magic and mystic; Church and religion; Heraldry; Monsters and imaginary figures; Japanese crests; Marks and signets; Watermarks; Primitive marks; Cattle brands; Hobo signs. Some sections have indexes but no general one. Makes no claim to being complete. Bibliography p. 217–21.

320

Mackenzie, Donald Alexander. The migration of symbols and their relations to beliefs and customs. . . . London, Paul, Trench, Trubner; N.Y., Knopf, 1926. 219 p. 24 cm. (The history of civilization)

Half-title: [Pre-history and antiquity]. Contents: (1) The swastika; (2) The spiral; (3) Ear symbols; (4) Tree symbols. Index p. 184–219.

321

Marle, Raimond van. Iconographie de l'art profane au moyen-âge et à la Renaissance, et la décoration des demeures. . . . La Haye, Nijhoff, 1931–32. 2 v. illus., plates. 34 cm.

A valuable work for secular iconography of the Middle Ages and Renaissance. Volume 1, La vie quotidienne; v. 2, Allégories et symboles. Profusely illustrated. No index.

Contents: v. 1, Le noble, les agréments de la vie du noble, les passe-temps, la nature, la chasse et la pêche, la guerre, l'enseignement et le savant, la vie rurale, les rapports entre les deux sexes; v. 2, L'allégorie éthique, les allégories philosophiques, les sciences et les arts, allégories diverses, la mort, l'amour.

322

Montfaucon, Bernard de. L'antiquité expliquée et représentée en figures. . . . Paris, Delaulne, 1719. 5 v. in 10. plates. 44 cm.
———. Supplément. . . . Paris, Delaulne, 1724. 5 v. plates. 45 cm.

2d ed., rev. and corrected, 1722. English translation: London, Tonson & Watts, 1721–22 (Supplement, 1725).

An early attempt at an iconography of ancient art, with scholarly text and engraved plates. Indexes at end of v. 5.

323

The Mythology of all races. . . . Louis Herbert Gray, ed., George Foot Moore, consulting ed. Boston, Marshall Jones Co., 1916–32. 13 v. illus., plates (part col.), maps. 25 cm.

Volumes 2, 4–5, 7–8, 13 edited by J. A. Macculloch and G. F. Moore, with imprint: Boston, Archaeological Institute of America, Marshall Jones Company. Each volume contains bibliographies, footnotes, and illustrations of the art of the various peoples.

Contents: v. 1, Greek and Roman, by W. S. Fox; v. 2, Eddic, by J. A. Macculloch; v. 3, Celtic, by J. A. Macculloch; Slavic, by Jan Machal; v. 4, Finno-Ugric Siberian, by Uno Holmberg; v. 5, Semitic, by S. H. Langdon; v. 6, Indian, by A. B. Keith; Iranian, by A. J. Carnoy; v. 7, Armenian, by M. H. Ananikian; African, by Alice Werner; v. 8, Chinese, by J. C. Ferguson; Japanese, by Masaharu Anesaki; v. 9, Oceanic, by R. B. Dixon; v. 10, North American, by H. B. Alexander; v. 11, Latin American, by H. B. Alexander; v. 12, Egyptian, by W. M. Müller; Indo-Chinese, by J. G. Scott; v. 13, Index.

324

Nissen, Claus. Die botanische Buchillustration, ihre Geschichte und Bibliographie. Stuttgart, Hiersemann, 1951. 2 v. in 1. 31 cm.

Contents: Bd. 1, Geschichte p. 1–254, Allgemeines Schrifttum p. 255–64; Bd. 2, Bibliographie, 234 p. Indexes: of artists p. 239–74; of plants p. 275–92; of countries p. 293–302; of authors p. 303–16.

325

Petity, Jean Raymond de. Le manuel des artistes et des amateurs ou dictionnaire historique et mythologique des emblêmes, allégories, énigmes, devises, attributs et symboles, relativement au costume, aux moeurs, aux usages & aux cérémonies. . . . Paris, Costard, 1770. 4 v. 17 cm.

An early iconographical dictionary. "Catalogue raisonné des auteurs qu'on a consultés pour la composition de cet ouvrage" v. 4, p. 549–655. "Discours sur la connaissance des tableaux" v. 4, p. 656–764.

326

Pigler, A. Barockthemen; eine Auswahl von Verzeichnissen zur Ikonographie des 17. und 18. Jahrhunderts. [Budapest] Verlag der Ungarischen Akademie der Wissenschaften, 1956. 2 v. illus. 24 cm.

A selective inventory of iconographic themes used in 17th and 18th century art with some examples from their previous development, listed chronologically by artists, with frequent indication of where reproductions may be found. Effectively illustrated. Volume 1 contains religious representations in the Old and New Testaments, and saints. Volume 2 contains secular representations in Greek and Roman history, legends and folk tales, general history, allegories, and subject pictures. Index to both volumes in v. 2, p. 609–21.

327
Poot, Hubert Korneliszoon. Het groot natuur-en zedekundigh werelttoneel; of, Woordenboek, van meer dan 1200 aeloude Egiptische, Grieksche en Romeinsche zinnebeelden of beeldenspraek. . . . Delft, Reiner Boitet, 1743. 3 v. illus. 34 cm.

With engraved frontispiece and headpieces. An early work on iconography based on Cesare Ripa, Zaratino Kastellini, Pierus Valerianus, Horus Apollo.

328
Praz, Mario. . . . Studies in seventeenth-century imagery . . . London, The Warburg Institute, 1939–47. 2 v. illus. 25 cm. [Studies of the Warburg Institute, ed. by Fritz Saxl, v. 3]

Volume 2 has subtitle: "A bibliography of emblem books." An important study of emblems and devices in the 17th century.

Volume 1 has index of names p. 209–16; of emblems p. 217–21. Volume 2 has index of artists p. 203–09.

329
Reallexikon für Antike und Christentum; Sachwörterbuch zur Auseinandersetzung des Christentums mit der Antiken Welt. . . . hrsg. von Theodor Klauser. Bd. 1–(Lfg. 23). Stuttgart, Hiersemann, 1950–(57). Illus., diagrs. 28 cm.

A scholarly dictionary of antiquity and Christianity. Contains bibliographies. Contents: Bd. 1–(Lfg. 23), A–(Dionysius Aeropagita). List of abbreviations at beginning of v. 1.

330
Ronchetti, Giuseppe. Dizionario illustrato dei simboli, emblemi, attributi, allegorie, immagini degli dei ecc. Milan, Hoepli, 1922. 1009 p. 91 plates. 16 cm.

A useful handbook arranged in dictionary form which identifies people and abstract qualities as represented in art. Illustrated by 91 plates consisting of line drawings of the various people and concepts as they have been depicted. Arranged alphabetically, with only one illustration for each subject.

331
Schlesinger, Max. Geschichte des Symbols; ein Versuch. . . . Berlin, Simion, 1912. 474 p. 27 cm.

A scholarly treatise on symbolism covering its many aspects as well as its manifestations in the art of various cultures and periods. No illustrations. Long bibliographies at the end of chapters. Index of names and subjects p. 457–74.

332
Schramm, Percy Ernst. Herrschaftszeichen und Staatssymbolik; Beiträge zu ihrer Geschichte vom dritten bis zum sechzehnten Jahrhundert. . . . Stuttgart, Hiersemann, 1954–56. 3 v. plates. 25 cm. (Schriften der Monumenta Germaniae Historica, Bd. 13 $^{1-3}$)

A scholarly work on governmental symbols. Indexes to cover all three volumes: of names and subjects v. 3, p. 1111–54; of monuments arranged according to place of preservation v. 3, p. 1155–65.

333
Volkmann, Ludwig. Bilderschriften der Renaissance, Hieroglyphik und Emblematik in ihren Beziehungen und Fortwirkungen. Leipzig, Hiersemann, 1923. 132 p. illus. 32 cm. (Veröffentlichungen des Deutschen Vereins für Buchwesen und Schrifttum)

Standard work on the emblems and hieroglyphics of the Renaissance. Index of names and subjects p. 125–29. Index of hieroglyphics and emblems p. 130–32.

334
Vries, Anne Gerard Christiaan de. De Nederlandsche emblemata; Geschiedenis en bibliographie tot de 18e eeuw. Amsterdam, Ten Brink & de Vries, 1899. 152 p. plates. 25 cm.

A doctoral dissertation written under C. Bellaar Spruyt. The standard book on Dutch emblems.

335
Waters, *Mrs.* Clara (Erskine) Clement. A handbook of legendary and mythological art . . . Boston and N.Y., Houghton, Mifflin, 1892. 23d ed. 575 p. illus. 20 cm.

1st ed. published 1871; 13th ed. 1881. Contents: Symbolism in art; Legends and stories illustrated in art; Legends of place; Ancient myths which have been illustrated in art. "Catalogue of pictures" p. [529]–62.

SEE ALSO: Junius. De pictura (2010).

Classical

336
Ladendorf, Heinz. Antikenstudium und Antikenkopie; Vorarbeiten zu einer Darstellung ihrer Bedeutung in der mittel-

alterlichen und neueren Zeit. Berlin, Akademie-Verlag, 1953. 190 p. 50 plates. 30 cm. (Abhandlung der Sächsischen Akademie der Wissenschaften zu Leipzig. Philologisch-historische Klasse, Bd. 46, Heft 2)

A stimulating discussion of copies of Greek and Roman works of art, from medieval times to the present, with a section of notes, p. 81–120, and a valuable classed bibliography of the subject, p. 121–61. Index to authors listed in the bibliography, p. 162–67.

A supplement, p. 168–75, lists by city and then by collection, ancient works of art, with mention of copies or studies made of them and pertinent references to be found in the bibliography, notes, or plates section. An index of the copyists, referring back to the city wherein the original art work is located, is on p. 175.

The plates are composite groupings of various treatments of the same theme. Index to the plates, p. 176–81. General index, p. 182–90.

336A

Roscher, Wilhelm Heinrich. Ausführliches Lexikon der griechischen und römischen Mythologie. Leipzig, Teubner, 1884–1927. 6 v. and 3 supp. in 5 v. illus., geneal. tables. 25 cm.

Scholarly signed articles and bibliographies, which make it important for iconography, as each personage or myth is considered with reference to its appearance in art. Contents: v. 1–6, A–Z; Supplements: Epitheta deorum, ed. by C. F. H. Bruchmann and I. B. Carter (1893–1902, 2 v.); Mythische Kosmographie der Griechen, by E. H. Berger (1904, 2 v.); Geschichte der klassischen Mythologie und Religionsgeschichte, by Otto Grupp, 1921.

337

Schwab, Gustav Benjamin. Gods & heroes, myths & epics of ancient Greece. [N.Y.] Pantheon [1946]. 764 p. illus. 24 cm.

"Translated from the German text and its Greek sources by Olga Marx and Ernst Moritz."—*p. 5.* A good collection of the stories of the ancient myths and epics of Greece. Index p. 745–64.

338

Seyffert, Oskar. A dictionary of classical antiquities, mythology, religion, literature [and] art. Rev. and ed. by Henry Nettleship and J. E. Sandys. N.Y., Meridian Books, 1956. 716 p. illus. 21 cm. (The Meridian library, ML2)

1st ed. 1891; 2d ed. 1891; 3d ed. 1894. Contains articles on Greek and Roman divinities, lives and works of philosophers, historians, orators, poets, and artists of Greece and Rome. Also treats general subjects: i.e., religion, architecture, painting, sculpture, music, drama, etc. General index p. 709–14. Index to illustrations p. 715–16.

339

Smith, *Sir* William. A classical dictionary of Greek and Roman biography, mythology and geography . . . rev. throughout and in part rewritten by E. E. Marindin. . . . London, Murray, 1919. 1018 p. illus., map. 23 cm.

1st ed. 1848; 4th ed. (rev.) 1894. The historical articles contain all the names of any importance which occur in Greek and Roman writers from the earliest times to 476, with a few added from later periods. Appendix p. 1019 contains bibliographical references.

340

Smith, *Sir* William. A concise dictionary of Greek and Roman antiquities; based on Sir William Smith's larger dictionary, and incorporating the results of modern research, ed. by F. Warre Cornish . . . with over 1100 illustrations taken from the best examples of ancient art. N.Y., Holt, 1898. 829 p. illus. 24 cm.

Tables of Greek and Roman measures, weights, and money p. 753–75. Greek index p. 776–96; Latin index p. 797–823; English index p. 824–29.

341

Smith, *Sir* William; Wayte, William; and Marindin, G. E. A dictionary of Greek and Roman antiquities. . . . 3d ed., rev. and enl. London, Murray, 1890–91. 2 v. illus. 25 cm.

1st ed. published 1842– ; 2d ed. 1849. Scholarly work with many signed articles and a bibliography.

SEE ALSO: Bernoulli. Griechische Ikonographie (961) and Römische Ikonographie (962); Müller. Handbuch der klassischen Altertums-Wissenschaft (196); Pauly. Pauly's Real-Encyclopädie der classischen Altertumswissenschaft (199).

Christian

342

Barbier de Montault, Xavier. Traité d'iconographie chrétienne. . . . Paris, Vivès, 1890. 2 v. 39 plates. 24 cm.

Drawings by M. Henri Nodet. Divided into 19 books with a "Sommaire" of the work indicating its plans, p. 7–29. "Table alphabétique": v. 1, p. 363–407; v. 2, p. 459–512.

343

Baring-Gould, Sabine. Lives of the saints, with introduction and additional lives of English martyrs, Cornish, Scottish, and Welsh saints, and a full index to the entire work. New and rev. ed. Illus. by 473 engravings. Edinburgh, Grant, 1914. 16 v. illus., plates, 4 maps, geneal. tables, plan. 22 cm.

First published 1872–82. Biographies of individual saints are given according to their day; thus the index must be used if day is not known. Volume 16 contains an index to saints whose lives are given (p. 333–63), and an index to subjects. Contents: v. 1–15, January–December (July, Oct., and Nov., each 2 v.); v. 16, Appendia, Indices.

344

Bles, Arthur de. How to distinguish the saints in art by their costumes, symbols and attributes. . . . N.Y., Art Culture Pubs., Inc., 1925. 168 p. illus. 31 cm.

Consists of 12 chapters devoted to symbolism in general and the symbolism of a specific category, e.g., Virgin Mary, Heavenly Hosts, Evangelists, Monastic Orders, etc. Appendices: Alphabetical table of martyrdoms; Tables of 320 saints, classified by habitual costume; Alphabetical table of saints classified by their diverse categories; Alphabetical tables of the symbols and attributes of the saints, with those who bear them.

General index divided into: Saints, Artists, Museums and galleries, Cathedrals, Churches, Institutions, Private collectors and dealers. List of illustrations, classed alphabetically. Bibliography p. 163.

345

Bond, Francis. Dedications and patron saints of English churches; ecclesiastical symbolism; saints and their emblems. . . . London and N.Y., Milford, Oxford Univ. Press, 1914. 343 p. 252 illus. 23 cm.

Contents: pt. 1 consists of dedications to various saints; pt. 2 is devoted to explanation of the symbolism; pt. 3 consists of an alphabetical list of emblems of the saints, and an alphabetical list of saints followed by their emblems. Bibliography p. xi–xvi. Index of proper names p. 333–40. General index p. 341–43.

346

Braun, Joseph. Tracht und Attribute der Heiligen in der deutschen Kunst . . . mit 428 Abbildungen. Stuttgart, Metzler, 1943. 4 p., 854 columns. illus. 28 cm.

Covers German painting, sculpture, and engraving from the Middle Ages through the 18th century. A well-illustrated, scholarly work, printed with two columns to the page. Part 1 is an alphabetical listing of the saints, their costumes and attributes, p. 17–764. Part 2 is devoted to the costumes and attributes of the saints, p. 777–803, and an index of attributes p. 843–52. Bibliography: col. 1–8.

347

Butler, Alban. Butler's Lives of the saints; complete edition, edited, revised and supplemented by Herbert Thurston, S.J., and Donald Attwater. N.Y., Kenedy [1956]. 4 v. 24 cm.

1st ed. published in London between 1756 and 1759 with title: *The lives of the fathers, martyrs, and other principal saints,* and contained 1486 entries. The 1956 ed. has 2565 entries, arranged according to the saint's day.

Contents: v. 1, Jan., Feb., March; v. 2, Apr., May, June; v. 3, July, Aug., Sept.; v. 4, Oct., Nov., Dec. Each volume has its own index, and v. 4 a general index of names, p. 681–707.

348

Cabrol, Fernand. Dictionnaire d'archéologie chrétienne et de liturgie, publié par le R.P. dom Fernand Cabrol . . . avec le concours d'un grand nombre de collaborateurs. Paris, Letouzey et Ané, 1907–53. v. 1–15 [4]. (fascs. 1–176) illus., plates (part col.), plans, facsims. 28 cm.

Issued in parts, 1903–53. Volumes 3–14 [1] "publié par le Rme. dom Fernand Cabrol . . . et le R.P. dom Henri Leclercq." Contains scholarly signed articles with full bibliographies and excellent illustrations. Covers Christian art, iconography, and symbols as well as liturgy, rites, ceremonies, and manners and customs of the early church up to the time of Charlemagne.

349

Cahier, Charles. Caractéristiques des saints dans l'art populaire enumerées et expliquées. . . . Paris, Poussielgue, 1867. 2 v. illus. 36 cm.

Arranged alphabetically by the attributes, under each a list of saints or biblical characters to whom they pertain, and a discussion of the symbol. Articles on apostles, evangelists, etc., are included in the same alphabet. Under "patrons divers" is a list of saints with the cities or groups of which they are patrons, followed by a list (p. 635) arranged by object of patronage.

Contents: v. 1, A–F; v. 2, G–Z. At end of v. 2, a "Répertoire général des saints par ordre alphabétique" (p. 797–865), and a "Supplément provisoire aux caractéristiques des saints."

350

Didron, Adolphe Napoléon. Christian iconography; or, The history of Christian art in the Middle Ages . . . Trans. from the French by E. J. Millington and completed with additions and appendices by Margaret Stokes. . . . London, Bell, 1886. 2 v. illus. 19 cm. (Bohn's Illustrated library)

Original French ed. published with title: *Iconographie chrétienne* (Paris, Imprimerie Royale, 1843). A standard book on this subject. Contents: v. 1, The history of the nimbus, the aureole and the glory, representations of the persons of the Trinity; v. 2, The Trinity: angels, devils, death, the soul, the Christian scheme; Appendices: (1) Short descriptions of various scenes from Old and New Testament as represented in art; (2) Byzantine guide to painting; (3) Text of the Biblia Pauperum. General index v. 2, p. 440–52.

351

Doyé, Franz von Sales. Heilige und Selige der römische-katholischen Kirche, deren Erkennungszeichen, Patronate und lebensgeschichtliche Bemerkungen. Leipzig, Vier Quellen Verlag [1929]. 2 v. 160 color plates. 24 cm.

Arranged alphabetically by name of saint with a few lines of identification and references to sources. Contents: Bd. 1, Aaron bis Martyres; Bd. 2, Martyres bis Zwölf Brüder; Anhang: (1) Deutsche Heilige; (2) Die alten Trachten der männlichen und weiblichen Orden sowie der geistlichen Mitglieder der ritterlichen Orden. "Register der Erkennungszeichen" v. 2, p. 855–89. "Register der Patronate" v. 2, p. 890–905.

352

Drake, Maurice, and Drake, Wilfred. Saints and their emblems. . . . Illustrated by xii plates from the photographs and drawings by Wilfred Drake, with a foreword by Aymer Vallance. London, Laurie, 1916. 235 p. 12 plates (3 col.) 35 cm.

A very useful work. Three plates show medieval ecclesiastical vestments and identify their various parts. Contents: (1) Dictionary

of saints; (2) Dictionary of emblems; (3) Appendices: Patriarchs and prophets, Sibyls, Patron saints of arts, trades, and professions, Other patron saints.

353

Evans, Edward Payson. Animal symbolism in ecclesiastical architecture. . . . N.Y., Holt; London, Heinemann, 1896. 375 p. illus. 20 cm.

Illustrated with 78 line drawings. Bibliography p. [343]–49. Index p. 351–75.

354

Ferguson, George Wells. Signs and symbols in Christian art, with illustrations from paintings of the Renaissance. N.Y., Oxford Univ. Press [1954]. 346 p. illus., plates (part col.) 29 cm.

Contains sections on animals; birds and insects; flowers, trees and plants; earth and sky; the human body; the Old Testament; St. John the Baptist; the Virgin Mary; Jesus Christ; The Trinity; Madonna and Angels; the Saints; radiances, letters, colors and numbers; religious dress; religious objects; artifacts. Each section arranged alphabetically. Line drawings usually accompany discussion of the objects. Illustrations are from paintings in the Kress collection, but they can be found only by using the index, as there are no references to them in the text. Index p. 329–41. Bibliography p. 343–46.

355

Goldsmith, Elizabeth Edwards. Sacred symbols in art. 2d ed. N.Y., London, Putnam, 1912. 296 p. 53 illus. 17 cm.

1st ed. 1911. Based on Jameson, Didron, Lindsay's *Sketches of Christian art,* and the *Golden legend.* Contents: (1) Symbols of the saints (alphabetically arranged); (2) Saints and symbols (alphabetically arranged); (3) Historical and devotional subjects and how these may be distinguished in art; (4) General symbols; (5) Colours as emblems; (6) Symbols of God the Father, the Son, the Holy Ghost and the Trinity; (7) The seven archangels, The three archangels; (8) Symbols and attributes of the Virgin; (9) Legends of the Madonna as represented in the historical series; (10) Devotional representation of the Virgin Mary; (11) St. John the Baptist; (12) The four evangelists; (13) The twelve apostles; (14) St. Mary Magdalene; (15) The Last Supper; (16) The four Latin Fathers; (17) Patron saints of Christendom; (18) Four great virgins of the Latin church; (19) Legends of the saints most frequently found in art; (20) Monastic orders and the habits by which they may be distinguished; Appendix; Index p. 293–96.

356

Grabar, André. L'Empereur dans l'art byzantin; recherches sur l'art officiel de l'empire d'Orient. Paris, Les Belles Lettres, 1936. 296 p. 40 plates. 25 cm. (Publications de la Faculté des Lettres de l'Université de Strasbourg, fasc. 75)

A study of the iconography of the Byzantine emperors that goes beyond the narrow confines of the title. Bibliographical footnotes. Index of names and subjects p. 273–83. Iconographic index p. 285–89.

357

Grabar, André. Martyrium; recherches sur le culte des reliques et l'art chrétien antique. [Paris] Collège de France, 1943–46. 2 v. and portfolio of 70 plates (incl. plans). 25 cm.

At head of title: Collège de France. Fondation Schlumberger pour les études byzantines. An important book on the iconography of early Christian art. Contents: v. 1, Architecture; v. 2, Iconography. Index for both volumes at end of v. 2, p. 375–400.

358

Guénebault, Louis Jean. Dictionnaire iconographique des figures, légendes et actes des saints, tant de l'ancienne que de la nouvelle loi, et répertoire alphabétique des attributs. . . . Paris, Chez l'Éditeur, 1850. 1232 columns. 27 cm.

Volume 45 of *Encyclopédie théologique* of l'Abbé Migne. Contents: pt. 1, Dictionnaire iconographique des figures, et actes des saints . . . Suppléments, additions & corrections; pt. 2, Répertoire générale et alphabétique des attributs des saints p. 764–872, Additions et corrections à la 1 & 2 parties p. 872–902.

"Table bibliographique des auteurs et des ouvrages cités dans ce volume" p. 1070–1220. "Indicule alphabétique des matières contenues dans les notes" p. 1221–28.

359

Guénebault, Louis Jean. Dictionnaire iconographique des monuments de l'antiquité chrétienne et du moyen âge, depuis le Bas-empire jusqu'à la fin du seizième siècle, indiquant l'état de l'art et de la civilisation à ces diverses époques. . . . Paris, Leleux, 1843–45. 2 v. 24 cm.

An early iconographical dictionary.

360

Hirn, Yrjö. The sacred shrine; a study of the poetry and art of the Catholic church. . . . London, Macmillan, 1912. 574 p. 23 cm.

A new ed. London, Faber, 1958. 432 p. with additions to the bibliography and notes by Dr. C. H. Talbot.

"A Swedish edition of this work was published in 1909." Contents: (1) Catholic Art, The Altar, The Relics, The Reliquary, The Mass, The Holy of Holies, The Host, The Monstrance, The Tabernacle; (2) The Dogma of Mary, The Gospel of Mary, Mary's Conception, The Incarnation, The Visitation, The Virginal Birth, The Holy Manger, The Sorrowing Mother, Mary's Death and Assumption, The Symbols of the Virgin, The Sacred Shrine. Index of authorities quoted p. 555–70. Index of subjects p. 571–74.

361

Holweck, Frederick George. A biographical dictionary of the saints, with a general introduction on hagiology. . . . St. Louis, Herder, 1924. 1053 p. 24 cm.

A useful and comprehensive one-volume dictionary which includes all the saints recognized in any Christian church. For each saint a short biography and some bibliographical references.

362

Hulme, Frederick Edward. The history, principles and practice of symbolism in Christian art. 6th ed. N.Y., Macmillan; London, Sonnenschein, 1910. 234 p. illus. 20 cm. (The antiquarian library, 2)

1st ed. 1891. Illustrated with line drawings. Index p. 229–34.

363

Husenbeth, Frederick Charles. Emblems of saints: by which they are distinguished in works of art. . . . 3d ed. edited by Augustus Jessopp. . . . Norwich, Norfolk and Norwich Archaeological Soc., 1882. 426 p. col. illus. (coats of arms), plates. 23 cm.

A useful compendium. The only illustrations are in the section on sacred heraldry. Contents: pt. 1, Saints with their emblems, Patriarchs and prophets with their emblems; pt. 2, Emblems with their saints, Patrons of arts, trades, and professions, Patrons of countries and cities, Calendars.

Appendices: (1) On the treatment of the sibyls in art, by W. Marsh; (2) On sacred heraldry, by E. L. Blackburne. "Principal works consulted or referred to" p. ix–xi. Page xii gives some quaint spellings of saints' names.

364

Jacobus *de Varagine*. The golden legend of Jacobus de Voragine, translated and adapted from the Latin by Granger Ryan and Helmut Ripperger. . . . London, N.Y., Longmans, Green, 1941. 2 v. facsims. 22 cm.

"Based on the Latin edition of Graesse, published in Leipzig in 1850."—*Foreword.* Legends of the saints are arranged according to the calendar or days on which their feasts are celebrated. Index at end of v. 1 for that volume only. Index at end of v. 2 includes material in both volumes.

365

Jameson, *Mrs.* Anna Brownell (Murphy). The history of Our Lord as exemplified in works of art: with that of His types; St. John the Baptist; and other persons of the Old and New Testament, commenced by the late Mrs. Jameson. Continued and completed by Lady Eastlake. . . . 2d ed. London, Longmans, Green, 1865. 2 v. illus., plates. 22 cm.

A 4th ed. was published by Longmans, London, 1881. Indexes at end of v. 2: (1) Names of artists; (2) Galleries, churches, museums and other depositories of art; (3) General index.

366

Jameson, *Mrs.* Anna Brownell (Murphy). Legends of the Madonna as represented in the fine arts. . . . Cor. and enl. ed. Boston, Houghton Mifflin, 1891. 483 p. illus. 17 cm.

A 2d ed. 1857; 3d ed. 1864; 5th ed. 1872. Frequently reprinted. "Forms third series of Sacred and Legendary Art." Old but still useful. Illustrated with line drawings. Index of artists, galleries, churches, museums, and a general index.

367

Jameson, *Mrs.* Anna Brownell (Murphy). Legends of the monastic orders as represented in the fine arts; forming the second series of Sacred and legendary art. London, Longmans, Green, 1872. 461 p. illus., plates. 22 cm.

1st ed. 1850. Gives a description of the founders, habits, and attributes of the different orders, the principal churches and edifices of each order, and legends of various saints connected with monastic life. General index p. 451–61.

368

Jameson, *Mrs.* Anna Brownell (Murphy). Sacred and legendary art. . . . Ed. with additional notes by Estelle M. Hurll. . . . Boston

and N.Y., Houghton Mifflin, 1896. 2 v. illus., plates. 21 cm.

Originally written in 1848 and frequently published until 1911. Contents: (1) Introduction; (2) Of angels and archangels; (3) The four evangelists; (4) The twelve apostles; (5) The doctors of the church; (6) St. Mary Magdalene, St. Martha, St. Lazarus, St. Maximin, St. Marcella, St. Mary of Egypt and the beautiful penitents; (7) The patron saints of Christendom; (8) The virgin patronesses; (9) The early martyrs; (10) The Greek martyrs; (11) The Latin martyrs; (12) The Roman martyrs; (13) Martyrs of Tuscany, Lombardy, Spain, and France; (14) The early bishops; (15) French bishops; (16) The hermit saints; (17) Warrior saints of Christendom. Index of places p. 783–87. General index p. 788–800.

369

Kaftal, George. Iconography of the saints in Tuscan painting. Florence, Sansoni [1952]. 1274 numb. columns. 1185 illus., 8 col. plates. 32 cm.

"Limited to schools of panel fresco painting of Florence, Siena, Arezzo, Lucca and Pisa from the 14th to the end of the 15th century." Under each saint's name gives short biography, relics, type, images, cycles, scenes in which he or she is depicted, then an art bibliography, literary sources of scenes, and a hagiographical bibliography. Contents: (1) Saints and blessed, Unidentified saints and blessed; (2) Index of attributes and distinctive signs, Index of painters, Topographical index of paintings, Bibliographical index, Index of saints and blessed, Calendar, Addenda.

370

Knipping, John Baptist. De iconografie van de contra-reformatie in de Nederlanden. . . . Hilversum, Brand, 1939–40. 2 v. illus., diagr. 29 cm.

Covers iconography of the Counter Reformation in the Netherlands. A French résumé of 20 pages is laid in v. 1. At end of each volume a list of illustrations, a detailed index, and a table of contents. Bibliography: v. 1, p. [305]–10; v. 2, p. 317–18.

371

Künstle, Karl. Ikonographie der christlichen Kunst. . . . Freiburg im Breisgau, Herder, 1926–28. [v. 1, 1928] 2 v. illus. 27 cm.

Volume 2 has individual title page reading: *Ikonographie der Heiligen*. A standard work on Christian iconography. Many illustrations. Bibliography at the beginning of each chapter. Each volume has its own index. Volume 1 covers history of iconography, animal symbolism in the Middle Ages, angels, subjects from Old and New Testaments, etc. Volume 2 is a dictionary of the saints.

372
Mâle, Émile. . . . L'art religieux de la fin du moyen âge en France; étude sur l'iconographie du moyen âge et sur ses sources d'inspiration; 250 gravures. Paris, Colin, 1908. 558 p. illus. 29 cm.
A 4th ed., rev. and enl., published Paris, 1941; 5th ed., 1949, is not a revision but contains the same material with a different arrangement of pagination. "Index des oeuvres d'art citées dans cet ouvrage" p. 543–54.

373
Mâle, Émile. L'art religieux de la fin du XVIe siècle, du XVIIe siècle et du XVIIIe siècle; étude sur l'iconographie après le concile de Trente. Italie, France, Espagne, Flandres. 2. éd., rev. et corr., illustrée de 294 gravures. Paris, Colin, 1951. 532 p. 294 illus. 29 cm.
1st ed. published as *L'art religieux après le concile de Trente*, 1932. A history of religious iconography in the greater part of Catholic Europe at the time of the Counter Reformation and for two centuries thereafter. "Index des oeuvres d'art citées dans cet ouvrage" p. 513–26, classified alphabetically by place.

374
Mâle, Émile. . . . L'art religieux du XIIe siècle en France; étude sur les origines de l'iconographie du moyen âge. . . . Paris, Colin, 1922. 459 p. illus. 29 cm.
A 5th ed. published by Colin, Paris, 1947. A standard work on the iconography of the Middle Ages in France. "Index des oeuvres d'art citées dans cet ouvrage" p. 443–54.

375
Mâle, Émile. . . . L'art religieux du XIIIe siècle en France; étude sur l'iconographie du moyen âge et sur ses sources d'inspiration. . . 4. éd. rev. et corr. . . . Paris, Colin, 1919. 490 p. illus. 29 cm.
1st ed. Paris, Leroux, 1898, 534 p.; 2d ed. Paris, Colin, 1902, 468 p.; 8th ed. Paris, Colin, 1948, 420 p. A standard work on French iconography of the 13th century. "Index des oeuvres d'art citées dans cet ouvrage" p. 477–83.

376
Mâle, Émile. Religious art from the twelfth to the eighteenth century. [N.Y.] Pantheon; London, Routledge & Paul [1949]. 208 p. 48 plates. 24 cm.
Paperback ed. issued by Noonday Press. Originally published in French, 1945(?); 2d ed. 1946. A usable collection of passages from the four standard works, selected by the author himself.

377
Mâle, Émile. Religious art in France, XIII century; a study in medieval iconography and its sources of inspiration. . . . Tr. from the 3d ed. (rev. and enl.) by Dora Nussey, with 190 illus. London, Dent; N.Y., Dutton, 1913. 414 p. illus. 29 cm.
A translation of number 375.
Appendix: List of the principal works devoted to the life of Christ (end of the 12th, and 13th and 14th centuries) p. 401–06. Bibliography p. 407–10. Index of works of art p. 411–15, arranged alphabetically by place.

378
Menzies, Lucy. The saints in Italy; a book of reference to the saints in Italian art and dedication. . . . London, The Medici Society [1924]. 496 p. 18 cm.
Intended as a pocket guide for tourists in Italy. Sources are not listed, although Mrs. Jameson, Baring-Gould, and *Acta Sanctorum* are mentioned in the preface. The majority of the saints covered are Italian but some others who are depicted in Italian art are included. "Emblems of the saints" gives the emblem and its denotation. "Instances of how the saints are often represented in art" lists attributes and the saints bearing them. Contents: Lives and legends of saints p. 1–463; Emblems of the saints; Note on the monastic orders.

379
Millet, Gabriel. Recherches sur l'iconographie de l'évangile aux XIVe, XVe et XVIe siècles, d'après les monuments de Mistra, de la Macédoine et du Mont-Athos. . . . Paris, Fontemoing, 1916. 809 p. illus., plates. 24 cm.
A standard work for early Christian iconography. Well illustrated with 670 illustrations. Arranged according to the themes portrayed, with a very detailed "Sommaire" p. xxxvii–lxiv. Bibliography p. xvii–xxxvi. "Répertoire des monuments" p. 715–73. "Noms d'artistes" p. 774–76. "Répertoire de l'iconographie" p. 777–87. "Répertoire générale" p. 788–98.

380

Molsdorf, Wilhelm. Christliche Symbolik der mittelalterlichen Kunst . . . Zweite, wesentlich veränderte und erweiterte Auflage des "Führers durch den symbolischen und typologischen Bilderkreis der christlichen Kunst des Mittelalters. . . ." Leipzig, Hiersemann, 1926. 294 p. 11 plates. 24 cm.

Considerably enlarged and revised since the 1917 ed. A standard German work on the symbolism of medieval art with the material systematically arranged under 1153 categories. Bibliography p. [ix]–xiii. Index p. 265–93.

381

Réau, Louis. Iconographie de l'art chrétien . . . Paris, Presses Universitaires de France, 1955–59. 3 v. in 6. illus. 24 cm. *Caveat!*

Covers Western medieval art as well as Byzantine and after the Council of Trent. Examples chosen from painting, sculpture, tapestries, glass, and enamels, illustrated by good rotogravure plates. Contents: v. 1, Introduction générale; v. 2, L'iconographie de la Bible, Ancien et Nouveau Testament; v. 3, L'iconographie des saints suivie d'un répertoire de leurs patronages et de leurs attributs, pt. 1, A–F; pt. 2, G–O; pt. 3, P–Z and Répertoire. Bibliographies at the end of each chapter and general ones v. 1, p. 21–26, and v. 3, p. 1382–84.

382

Ricci, *Signora* Elisa. Mille santi nell'arte . . . prefazione di Corrado Ricci; 700 illustrazioni. Milan, Hoepli, 1931. 734 p. illus., plates. 22 cm.

A dictionary of saints in art. For each saint it gives a few lines of identification and a list of works of art where the saint appears, usually with a reference to a reproduction in the book. Bibliography p. xiii–xiv. Calendar p. xv–xx. Index of attributes p. 687–99. Index of protectors p. 701–15. Index of artists p. 717–34.

383

Roeder, Helen. Saints and their attributes; with a guide to localities and patronage. London, Longmans, Green [1955]. 391 p. illus. 17 cm.

Also published by Regnery, Chicago [1956, c1955]. Arranged alphabetically by attributes, under each a list of saints who are thus represented. For each saint the dates of his death and his day. Bibliography p. xiv. "Index of saints" p. 355–78. "Index of localities" p. 379–91.

384

Rohault de Fleury, Charles. Archéologie chrétienne. Les saints de la messe et leurs monuments . . . études continuées par son fils. . . . Paris, Librairies-Imprimeries Réunies, 1893–1900. 10 v. illus., 1064 plates (incl. plans). 33 cm.

"Tirés à 150 exemplaires." Issued in portfolios.

For each saint gives a short biography and then lists the monuments of his cult beginning with Rome or the city of martyrdom, covering Italian, French, German, English, and other countries. For each monument gives its history, description, and chronology. Illustrated with line drawings, and plates which contain plans, elevations, and line drawings.

Contents: (1) Les vierges; (2) Vierges et martyrs; (3) Papes; (4) Ministres sacrés; (5) Diacres, Médecins; (6) Saint Pierre; (7) Saint Pierre, Saint Paul, Saint Philippe, Saint Jacques Mineur; (8) Saint Jean Évangéliste, Saint Jacques-le-Majeur; (9) Saint Barthélemy, Saint Matthieu, Saint Thomas; (10) Saint André, Saint Simon et Saint Jude, Saint Mathias, Saint Barnabé, Saint Jean-Baptiste, Agneau de Dieu.

Bibliographical footnotes.

385

Rohault de Fleury, Charles. L'évangile; études iconographiques et archéologiques. . . . Tours, Mame, 1874. 2 v. illus., map. 34 cm.

A rudimentary work on the iconography and archaeology of the Gospels. Consists of an inventory describing images or texts, classed according to their exterior character, e.g., mosaics, frescoes, miniatures, and the minor arts.

386

Rohault de Fleury, Charles. La messe; études archéologiques sur ses monuments continuées par son fils. . . . Paris, Morel, 1883–89. 8 v. illus., 680 plates. 33 cm.

Volumes 4–8 have imprint: Paris, Librairie des imprimeries réunies (in portfolios). A monumental work on the Mass and its iconography, covering developments during various periods from the early Christian era. Illustrated by plates of line drawings. Each volume has its own table of contents.

387

Rohault de Fleury, Charles. La Sainte Vierge; études archéologiques et iconographiques. . . . Paris, Poussielgue, 1878. 2 v. illus., 157 plates. 34 cm.

An important early work on the iconography of the Virgin Mary. Contents: (1) Vie terrestre de Marie, Vie glorieuse et culte de Marie; (2) Sanctuaires et images (treated by countries), Tableau des principaux types de Madones p. 613–17. List of plates at end of each volume.

388

Smith, Earl Baldwin. Early Christian iconography and A school of ivory carvers in Provence. Princeton, Princeton Univ. Press, 1918. 276 p. illus., tables. 28 cm. (Princeton monographs in art and archaeology VI)

Arranged by subject treated. Contains bibliographical footnotes. Index p. 255–76.

389

Smits, Carolus. De iconografie van de Nederlandsche primitieven. Amsterdam, "De Spieghel," 1933. 267 p. 80 plates on 40 l. 26 x 21 cm.

A Dutch study of the iconography of early Dutch and Flemish painting. Bibliography p. 239–50. Iconographical index p. 255–67.

390

Stange, Alfred. Das frühchristliche Kirchenbäude als Bild des Himmels. Köln, Comel, 1950. 162 p. illus., plates, plans. 22 cm.

A study of the iconography of church buildings.

391

Tabor, Margaret Emma. The saints in art, with their attributes and symbols alphabetically arranged. . . . London, Methuen [1908]. 208 p. 20 plates. 18 cm.

1st ed. "An epitome of Mrs. Jameson and Lord Lindsay for the traveler." "Biblical characters are only included in so far as they are the subjects of traditions or legends beyond the Bible narrative and well known historical personages . . . are very shortly treated."—*Pref.* Date of feast of the saint is given. If a representation of the saint is especially famous, the name of the artist and the church or gallery where it is located are mentioned. Illustrated by 20 plates reproducing well-known works of art. Index of symbols and attributes p. xxv–xxxi. General index p. 201–08.

392

Timmers, J. J. M. Symboliek en iconographie der Christelijke kunst, met 138 illustraties. Roermond-Maaseik, Romen & Zonen, 1947. 1125 p. 137 illus. on 69 l. 17 cm.

Introduction gives the history of Christian symbolism. Parallel texts are given in Dutch and Latin for biblical passages as sources for representation, and examples are frequently cited. Contains short biographies of saints and a table of their attributes. Also covers the virtues and vices, the world about us, animals, plants, etc.

Contents: (1) De godheid; (2) De openbaring; (3) De H. Kerk en genademiddelen; (4) Maria, moeder des Heren; (5) De deugden en de zonden; (6) De tijd; (7) Het kerkgebow; (8) De mens; (9) De zichtbare wereld; (10) De heiligen en hun attributen. Bibliography p. 1015–30. Index of subjects, people, and places p. 1033–1116.

393

Twining, Louisa. Symbols and emblems of early and mediaeval Christian art. London, Longman, Brown, Green & Longmans, 1852. 190 p. 93 plates. 29 cm.

Purpose is "to collect and arrange in chronological order the principal forms that have been used symbolically in different periods of art."—*Pref.* It does not pretend to be a complete survey. Whenever possible English examples are used. Emblems and attributes of saints are not included.

Subjects treated: The persons of the Trinity, Evangelists, Old Testament subjects, Apostles, the Church, Baptism, Death, Soul, Evil spirit, Hell, Animals, Birds, Trees, Flowers. For each subject various representations are given. Many plates of line drawings. List of authorities p. 189–90 with two pages of references to manuscripts.

394

Waters, *Mrs.* Clara (Erskine) Clement. Handbook of Christian symbols and stories of the saints as illustrated in art. . . . Ed. by Katherine E. Conway. . . . Boston, Ticknor, 1886. 349 p. illus. (31 plates). 21 cm.

Copyright 1871, 1881, and 1896. An old work but still useful. Contents: (1) Symbolism in art p. 1–36; (2) Legends and stories illustrated in art p. 37–324, arranged alphabetically. General index p. 325.

395

Webber, Frederick Roth. Church symbolism; an explanation of the more important symbols of the Old and New Testament, the primitive, the mediaeval and the modern church. . . . Introduction by Ralph Adams Cram. 2d ed., rev. Cleveland, Jansen, 1938. 413 p. illus., plates. 27 cm.

Originally published 1927. "The more important saints of church art" p. 265–98.

"Examples of old and modern symbolism" p. 301–56 (plates). "A glossary of the more common symbols" p. 357–86. Bibliography p. 389–94. Index to the text p. 395–413.

Oriental

396

Akiyama, Aisaburo. Buddhist hand-symbol. . . . Yokohama, Yoshikawa Book Store, 1939. 86 p. illus., plates (part col.) 26 cm.

Text in English and Japanese. Each symbol is illustrated by a drawing or illustration. No index, but a table of contents (p. i–iii) lists the gestures discussed.

397

Asiatic mythology, a detailed description and explanation of the mythologies of all the great nations of Asia, by J. Hackin. . . . London, Harrap [1932]. 459 p. illus., col. plates. 32 cm.

Contains articles on the mythology of Persia, the Kāfirs, Buddhism in India, Brahmanic mythology, mythology of Lamaism, of Indo-China and Java, Buddhist mythology in Central Asia, mythology of modern China, and of Japan. Each article written by a specialist and profusely illustrated. Index at end of volume includes both subjects and names.

398

Banerjea, Jitendra Nathan. The development of Hindu iconography. [2d ed. rev. and enl. Calcutta] Univ. of Calcutta, 1956. 653 p. 48 plates. 25 cm.

1st ed. 1941, 459 p., issued as thesis, University of Calcutta. Contents: (1) Study of Hindu iconography; (2) The antiquity of image-worship in India; (3) The origin and development of image-worship in India; (4) Brahmanical divinities and their emblems on early Indian coins; (5) Deities and their emblems on early Indian seals; (6) Iconoplastic art in India—Factors contributing to its development; (7) Iconographic terminology; (8) Canons of iconometry; (9) Cult icons—Vyantara Devatas; (10) Cult icons—Visnu and Surya; (11) Cult icons—Siva and Sakti; (12) Miscellaneous and syncretistic icons. List of abbreviations p. xix–xx. Select bibliography p. [627–32]. General index 633–53.

399

Bhattacharyya, Benoytosh. The Indian Buddhist iconography, mainly based on the Sādhanamālā and other cognate Tāntric texts of rituals. . . . London, N.Y., Milford, Oxford Univ. Press, 1924. 220 p. 69 plates. 26 cm.

A 2d rev. ed. Calcutta, Mukhopadhyay, 1958. 478 p. 357 illus.

"An attempt to write a comprehensive work on the Buddhist iconography of India." —Pref. The text is illustrated by pictures representing works of art and by line drawings. Glossary p. 189–99. Bibliography p. [201]–03. Index p. 205–20.

400

Dowson, John. A classical dictionary of Hindu mythology and religion, geography, history, and literature. 8th ed. London, Routledge & Paul, 1953. 411 p. (Trubner's Oriental series)

Originally published 1879. "This work is derived entirely from the publications of European scholars."—Pref. Unfortunately not illustrated and no bibliography. Sanskrit index p. 385–406. General index p. 407–11.

401

Edmunds, William H. Pointers and clues to the subjects of Chinese and Japanese art, as shown in drawings, prints, carvings and the decoration of porcelain and lacquer. With brief notices of the related subjects. London, Low, Marston [1934]. 706 p. 26 cm.

1000 copies printed. Contents: Pointers and clues (consists of a list of subjects or attributes given in English, with their equivalent given under the vernacular); Chinese chronological table with Japanese readings; Chinese subjects; Buddhist subjects; Japanese chronological table; Japanese subjects; Glossary of Japanese words p. 697–706.

402

Fergusson, James. Tree and serpent worship; or, Illustrations of mythology and art in India in the first and fourth centuries after Christ; from the sculptures of the Buddhist topes at Sanchi and Amravati . . . 2d ed. rev., corrected, and in great part re-written. London, India Museum, 1873. 274 p. illus., 100 plates (part double, incl. photos, map, plans). 35 cm.

1st ed. 1868. A useful early work which covers the architecture of India as well as the theme of tree and serpent worship in both the Eastern and Western world. Illustrated by woodcuts in the text and mounted photographs as plates. Chronological table of dynasties and rulers p. 264–65. Index p. 271–74.

403

Getty, Alice. The gods of northern Buddhism, their history, iconography and progressive evolution through the northern Buddhist countries. . . . Oxford, Clarendon Press, 1928. 220 p. plates (part col.), diagr. 29 cm.

First printed 1914; 2d ed. rev., 1928. The introduction contains a "general survey of Buddhism and its evolution and a short survey of Buddhist art." Each chapter is devoted to one important god and his various manifestations. "Explanation of Sanskrit, Tibetan, Chinese, Mongolian and Japanese words used in the text" p. 183–203. Bibliography p. 203–07. Index p. 207–20.

404

Gopinātha Rāu, T. A. Elements of Hindu iconography. . . . Madras, Law Printing House, 1914–16. 2 v. in 4. plates, tables. 26 cm.

Contains texts in Sanskrit as well as English. Each volume has an index of 30 to 35 pages and many plates. Bibliography, v. 1, p. xxvii, xxix–xxx.

405

Gordon, *Mrs.* Antoinette K. The iconography of Tibetan Lamaism. . . . N.Y., Columbia Univ. Press, 1939. 129 p. illus., plates (part col.) 31 cm.

A new rev. ed. published by Tuttle, Rutland, Vt., 1959.

The object of this book and its charts is "to give a descriptive outline of the principal gods of the Tibetan pantheon, those which are commonly encountered in sculpture and painting."—*Pref.* Also included are rules of Sanskrit pronunciation, a glossary of Sanskrit terms in general use, and a short account of the development of Buddhism into Lamaism. Many charts, illustrations, and diagrams. Excellent charts of the various mudras p. 20–24, with descriptions. Bibliography p. 109–16. General index p. 117–29.

406

Mayers, William Frederick. Chinese reader's manual; a handbook of biographical, historical, mythological, and general literary reference. Reprinted from the edition of 1874. Shanghai, American Presbyterian Mission Press, 1910. 444 p. 22 cm.

A useful compendium of information covering subjects of Chinese art as well as literature. Contents: pt. 1, Index of proper names, p. 1–312, is an encyclopedia of names, with Chinese characters given and information

identifying subject or place; pt. 2, Numerical categories p. 313–80; pt. 3, Chronological tables of the Chinese dynasties p. 381–410; pt. 4, Index of Chinese characters p. 411–44.

407

Mensching, Gustav. Buddhistische Symbolik. . . . Gotha, Klotz, 1929. 52 p. 68 plates. 29 cm.

An illustrated treatment of Buddhist symbolism which covers architecture as well as cult and animal symbols. Index p. 47–48. Index of illustrations p. 51–52. Bibliography p. 49–50.

408

Thomas, P. Epics, myths and legends of India; a comprehensive survey of the sacred lore of the Hindus and Buddhists. Bombay, Taraporevala [194?]. 132 p. plates. 28 cm.

"An attempt . . . to give the reader a faithful representation of the mythological systems of the Hindus and Buddhists."—*Pref.* Bibliography p. 124. Glossary and index (in one alphabet) p. 125–32.

409

Toki, Hôryû. Si-do-in-dzou; gestes de l'officiant dans les cérémonies mystiques des sectes Tendaï et Singon. . . . Paris, Leroux, 1899. 234 p. illus., plates. 25 cm. (Musée Guimet. Annales, Bibliothèque d'études, t. 8)

Translated from the Japanese under the direction of S. Kawamoura. Introduction and annotations by L. de Milloué. The gestures are well illustrated by line drawings. Index of Japanese names and terms p. 203–10. Index of Chinese names and terms p. 211–14. Index of Sanskrit names and terms p. 219–22. Table of contents p. 223–34.

410

Waterbury, Florence. Early Chinese symbols and literature: Vestiges and speculations, with particular reference to the ritual bronzes of the Shang dynasty. N.Y., Weyhe, 1942. 164 p. 77 plates. 32 cm.

Good illustrations. Bibliography p. 139–46. Index p. 147–53.

411

Werner, Edward Theodore Chalmers. A dictionary of Chinese mythology. . . . Shanghai, Kelly & Walsh, 1932. 627 p. 26 cm.

Contents: Preface; Pronunciation of Chinese words p. xv–xvii; Dictionary of Chinese mythology p. 1–612; Index to myths p. 612–22; Table of Chinese dynasties p. 623–24. Bibliography p. 625–27.

412

Werner, Edward Theodore Chalmers. . . . Myths and legends of China . . . with 32 illustrations in colours by Chinese artists. London, Harrap [1922]. 453 p. col. plates. 25 cm.

A popular type of book which recounts Chinese legends and myths.

413

Williams, Charles Alfred Speed. Outlines of Chinese symbolism and art motives; an alphabetical compendium of antique legends and beliefs, as reflected in the manners and customs of the Chinese. . . . 3d rev. ed. Shanghai, Kelly & Walsh, 1941. 472 p. illus., col. plates. 25 cm.

1st ed. 1931; 2d ed. 1932. An extremely useful reference book, with bibliographies at the end of longer articles. Gives Chinese characters following the English entry. Index p. 459–69.

CHAPTER 9

Methodology

THIS CHAPTER IS CONFINED TO BOOKS ON the methods of art history and art research rather than on the methods employed by the creative artist himself. In conformance with the policy stated in the Preface, books on the methodology of aesthetics are not included.

414

Bendinelli, Goffredo. . . . Dottrina dell'archeologia e della storia dell'arte (storia, metodo, bibliografia). Milano [etc.] Società Anonima Editrice Dante Alighieri (Albrighi, Segati & c.), 1938. 495 p. 21 cm.

Bibliography at end of each chapter. A list of periodicals in the fields of archaeology and history of art, p. 489–95, is compiled by country of issue.

415

Chambers, Frank Pentland. The history of taste; an account of the revolutions of art criticism and theory in Europe. N.Y., Columbia Univ. Press, 1932. 342 p. plates, facsim. 25 cm.

A survey of the development of artistic theories from the Middle Ages through the 19th century, with some remarks on antiquity.

Bibliography p. 307–12. "Notes" p. 315–24. Index p. 327–42.

416

Clark, *Sir* Kenneth McKenzie. The study of art history, an address delivered at the Jubilee meeting of the Historical Association in the Senate House, University of London on Wednesday, 4th January 1956. [London, 1956] 16 p. 22 cm.

Reprinted from the *Universities quarterly*, v. X, no. 3, May 1956. A short critical survey of the most important European art historians and their work.

417

Collingwood, Robin George. The principles of art. Oxford, Clarendon Press, 1938. 347 p. 23 cm.

Issued in paperback ed. by Oxford, Galaxy. Originally published 1938 and reprinted 1950. Attempts to answer the question, "What is art?"

418

Dresdener, Albert. Die Kunstkritik, ihre Geschichte und Theories. München, Bruckmann, 1915. 1 v. 23 cm.

No more published. A history of the gradual development of art criticism up to the 18th century, particularly in France. Index p. 351–59.

419

Frankl, Paul. Das System der Kunstwissenschaft; mit 58 Abbildungen. Brünn, Rohrer, 1938. 1063 p. illus. 25 cm.

An attempt to approach the meaning ("Sinn") of art through a scientific system. Index p. 1047–63.

420

Grassi, Luigi. Costruzione della critica d'arte. Roma, Edizioni dell'Ateneo [1955]. 229 p. plates, diagr. 22 cm. (Collana "Nuovi saggi" 10)

A study of the development of criticism of art history from Greek and Roman times to the present. Bibliography p. 210–22. Index p. 223–29.

421

Hedicke, Robert. Methodenlehre der Kunstgeschichte, ein Handbuch für Studierende. . . . Strassburg, Heitz, 1924. 301 p. 22 cm.

A complex, theoretical guide for art historians on the foundations and research methods of their field. "Schriftenverzeichnis" p. 277–92. Index p. 293–301.

422

Kallen, Horace Meyer. Art and freedom; a historical and biographical interpretation of the relations between the ideas of beauty, use and freedom in western civilization from the Greeks to the present day. . . . N.Y., Duell, Sloan & Pearce [c1942]. 2 v. 24 cm.

"A study of beauty and use as freedom brings them to event in the works of man and as themes of philosophical disputation. Although the procedure is historical and biographical, the outcome is not a history of esthetics."—*Pref.*

Bibliographical references included in "Notes" v. 2, p. 965–78. Index v. 2, p. 979–1006.

423

Ladendorf, Heinz. Kunstwissenschaft (in Universitas Litterarum, Handbuch der Wissenschaftskunde. Berlin, De Gruyter, 1953–55. Lfg. 8, p. [605]–634)

A definition of art history in all its ramifications with a well-subdivided bibliography, which consists predominantly of German books.

424

Lavalleye, Jacques. Introduction aux études d'archéologie et d'histoire de l'art. Tournai, Casterman, 1946. 210 p. 20 cm.

A 2d ed. published Louvain, Nauwelaerts, 1958, 274 p. A methodological essay with a selective bibliography. Index of names and people p. 183–91; of places p. 193–206.

425

Lessing, Gotthold Ephraim. Laocoon; an essay upon the limits of painting and poetry. With remarks illustrative of various points in the history of ancient art. Tr. by Ellen Frothingham. Boston, Roberts, 1877. 250 p. 18 cm.

One of the classic studies defining the limits and basic rules of art. Index p. 247–50.

426

Modigliani, Ettore. Mentore, guida allo studio dell'arte italiana. 2d ed. Milano, Hoepli [1946]. 685 p. 128 plates on 64 l. 21 cm.

Original edition published 1940 under the name of Fernanda Wittgens, for political reasons.

Contents: I, Nozioni generali storiche e techniche—Nomenclatura; Appendice: I, No-

mi degli artisti; II, Panorama della storia dell'arte italiana; III, Bibliografia p. 193–272; IV, Il patrimonio artistico; V, Il metodo; VI, La tutela del patrimonio artistico.

Good bibliographical section, in part annotated. Indexes of illustrations, technical terms, places, artists, works, and things p. 627–85.

427

Panofsky, Erwin. The history of art as a humanistic discipline. (*In his* Meaning in the visual arts. Garden City, Doubleday, 1955, p. 1–25) 18 cm. (Anchor books A59)

Originally published in Greene, T. M., ed. *The meaning of the humanities* (Princeton, Princeton Univ. Press, 1940, p. 89–118). An excellent brief introduction to the methodology of art history.

428

Pepper, Stephen Coburn. Principles of art appreciation. N.Y., Harcourt, Brace [1949]. 326 p. illus., 20 plates (part col.) 24 cm.

Aesthetic standards applied to the appreciation and analysis of specific works of art. Index p. 313–26.

429

Schapiro, Meyer. Style. (*In* Anthropology today, an encyclopedic inventory. . . . A. L. Kroeber, ed. Chicago, Univ. of Chicago Press, 1953, p. 287–312)

An important analysis of the problems of style. Bibliography p. 311–12.

430

Tietze, Hans. Die Methode der Kunstgeschichte, ein Versuch. Leipzig, Seemann, 1913. 489 p. 26 cm.

A thoroughgoing description of the methods and the various branches of art historical research.

Bibliographical footnotes. Author index p. 481–89.

431

Timmling, Walter. Kunstgeschichte und Kunstwissenschaft. . . . mit einer Abhandlung: Meinungen über Herkunft und Wesen der Gotik von Dr. Paul Frankl. . . . Leipzig, Koehler & Volckmar, 1923. 303 p. 20 cm. (Kleine Literaturführer, Bd. 6)

A classed and well-annotated bibliography of German literature in the field of fine arts, covering all periods of general art, architecture, sculpture, painting, and the applied arts.

Subject and author index p. 282–303.

432

Venturi, Lionello. . . . History of art criticism; tr. from the Italian by Charles Marriott. N.Y., Dutton, 1936. 345 p. 22 cm.

A historical survey of critical approaches to art history, which also discusses briefly some of the earlier sources for art history.

Bibliography p. 325–45. No index.

433

Waetzoldt, Wilhelm. Deutsche Kunsthistoriker. . . . Leipzig, Seemann, 1921–24. 2 v. 24 cm.

A history of art history and theory in Germany. Contents: v. 1, Von Sandrart bis Rumohr; v. 2, Von Passavant bis Justi.

"Zeittafel der Quellenschriften" v. 1, p. 319–23 and v. 2, p. 279–84. "Literatur" v. 1, p. 325–32 and v. 2, p. 285–96. Index v. 2, p. 299–311.

434

Wölfflin, Heinrich. . . . Das Erklären von Kunstwerken. Mit einem Nachwort des Verfassers. Leipzig, Seemann [1943]. 52 p. 19 cm. [Kleine Bücherei zur Geistesgeschichte, Bd. 1]

"Die erste Auflage dieser . . . Schrift erschien im Jahre 1921 als erstes Heft der von dem Verlag E. A. Seemann herausgegebenen 'Bibliothek der Kunstgeschichte.' "—*p.* [5].

An introduction to the comprehension of the individual work of art as such, by one of the great critics.

435

Wölfflin, Heinrich. . . . Gedanken zur Kunstgeschichte, Gedrucktes und Ungedrucktes; mit 24 Abbildungen. 2. Aufl. Basel, Schwabe [1941]. 165 p. illus. 26 cm.

Essays on the subject of art history itself. Contents: Grundbegriffe; Das Klassische; Kritische Kunstgeschichte; Nationale Charaktere; Jacob Burckhardt; Verzeichnis der Abbildungen.

CHAPTER 10 | # Histories and Handbooks of Art

General

436

Bazin, Germain. Histoire de l'art de la préhistoire à nos jours. Paris, Garamond [1953]. 461 p. illus. (part col.), map. 23 cm.

A one-volume French survey of the history of art—East and West—with small illustrations in the text. Bibliography p. [443]–49. Index p. 450–59. Sources of photographs p. 460–61.

437

Cheney, Sheldon. A new world history of art. N.Y., Viking, 1956. 676 p. illus., col. plates. 26 cm.

Maps on lining papers.

A completely rev. ed. with additional text of the author's *World history of art,* first published in 1937, with an 8th printing in 1952. A popular one-volume history of art with rather poor illustrations.

"Table of dates" p. 656–57. "Descriptive bibliography" p. 660–64. "Index and glossary" p. 665–76.

438

Cossío, Manuel Bartolomé, and Pijoán y Soteras, José. Summa artis, historia general del arte. . . . 1. ed. Bilbao, Madrid, Espasa-Calpe, s.a., 1931–(52). v. 1–(15). illus., plates (part col.) 28 cm.

Profusely illustrated, including some color plates. Bibliographies, usually at end of volumes, but sometimes at end of sections or chapters.

Contents: v. 1, Arte de los pueblos aborígenes; v. 2, Arte del Asia occidental; v. 3, El arte egipcio hasta la conquista romana; v. 4, El arte griego hasta la toma de Corinto por los Romanos (146 a. J.C.); v. 5, El arte romano hasta la muerte de Diocleciano; Arte etrusco y arte helenístico después de la toma de Corinto; v. 6, El arte prehistórico

europeo; v. 7, Arte cristiano primitivo; Arte bizantino, hasta la saqueo de Constantinopla por los cruzados el año 1204; v. 8, Arte bárbaro y prerrománico, desde el siglo IV hasta el año 1000; v. 9, El arte románico, siglos XI y XII; v. 10, Arte precolombiano, mexicano y maya; v. 11, Arte gótico de la Europa occidental, siglos XIII, XIV y XV; v. 12, Arte islámico; v. 13, Arte del período humanistico, trecento y cuatrocento; v. 14, Renacimiento romano y veneciano, siglo XVI; v. 15, El arte del renacimiento en el norte y el centro de Europa.

439

Faure, Elie. History of art. . . . Tr. from the French by Walter Pach. . . . N.Y., Harper, 1921–30. 5 v. illus., fold. tables. 22 cm.

Reprinted in two volumes (N.Y., Dover, 1948). First published in French in 1909. A standard French history of art.

Contents: [1] Ancient art; [2] Mediaeval art; [3] Renaissance art; [4] Modern art; [5] The spirit of the forms. Synoptic tables at end of each of the first four volumes.

440

Gardner, Helen. Art through the ages. 3d ed. N.Y., Harcourt, Brace [1948]. 851 p. illus., maps. 25 cm.

Originally published 1926; 2d ed. 1936; 4th rev. ed. 1959 under the editorship of Sumner McK. Crosby. 840 p.

A one-volume survey of art history covering both Western and Eastern art of all ages. Bibliographies at end of each chapter and a short general one in the appendix, limited mostly to English and readily available works. Glossary p. 793–99. Index p. 801–51 indicates pronunciation of some foreign names.

441

Gombrich, Ernst Hans Josef. The story of art. With 370 illus. 8th ed., rev. N.Y., Lon-

don, Phaidon, 1956. 462 p. illus. (part col.)
26 cm.

Aims "to tell the old story of art once more in simple language, and to enable the reader to see how it hangs together."—*Pref.* Not strictly a reference book, but a good one-volume history of art for beginners in the field, written by a recognized authority. More emphasis on painting than on sculpture and architecture. Only the works illustrated are discussed in the text.

"A note on art books" p. [447]–50. Index and glossary p. 459–62.

442

Hamann, Richard. Geschichte der Kunst von der altchristlichen Zeit bis zur Gegenwart. . . . Berlin, Knaur, 1933. 968 p. 1110 illus. (incl. plans), 11 plates (part col.) 25 cm.

An offset ed. was reprinted by Mary Rosenberg (N.Y., 194?). A good general one-volume history of art from early Christian times to the present, in German. Well illustrated with good color plates. A similar volume (443) covers ancient art.

"Chronologische Gesamtübersicht" p. 894–97; "Verzeichnis der wichtigsten Künstler und Werke" p. 898–950; Erklärung kunstgeschichtlicher Fachausdrücke" (Glossary) p. 951–56; "Quellennachweis der Vorlagen" (Sources of photos) p. 957–58; "Register" p. 959–68.

443

Hamann, Richard. Geschichte der Kunst von der Vorgeschichte bis zur Spätantike. . . . München, Droemer, 1952. 980 p. 966 illus., 18 col. plates. 25 cm.

Together with (442) forms a good two-volume history of art. This volume covers prehistoric to late antique art.

Glossary p. 888–94. Bibliography p. [958]–67. Register p. 968–78. Index of important works and artists p. 895–957.

444

Handbuch der Kunstwissenschaft. Berlin-Neubabelsberg, Wildpark-Potsdam, Athenaion, ca. 1913–30. illus., plates. 29 cm.

One of the most scholarly series (as far as text is concerned), consisting of 27 works covering both Eastern and Western art and thus forming a general history of art. Written by recognized authorities and containing bibliographies. Amply illustrated, unfortunately on poor paper.

Contents: Baum, Julius. *Die Malerei und Plastik des Mittelalters, II: Deutschland, Frankreich und Britannien,* 1930; Bercken,

Erich von der. *Malerei der Renaissance in Italien,* 1927; Brinckmann, A. E. *Barockskulptur,* 1919; Brinckmann, A. E. *Die Baukunst des 17. und 18. Jahrhunderts,* 1915–19; Brinckmann, A. E. *Stadtbaukunst,* 1920; Burger, Fritz. *Die deutsche Malerei vom ausgehenden Mittelalter bis zum Ende der Renaissance,* 1913–19, 3 v.; Burger, Fritz. *Die Kunst des 19. und 20. Jahrhunderts,* 1917; Clasen, K. H. *Baukunst des Mittelalters: Die gotische Baukunst,* 1930; Curtius, Ludwig. *Die antike Kunst,* 1923–39, 2 v. in 3; Diez, Ernst. *Die Kunst der islamischen Völker,* 1917; Diez, Ernst. *Die Kunst Indiens,* 1925; Drost, Willi. *Barockmalerei in den germanischen Ländern,* 1926; Dülberg, Franz. *Niederländische Malerei der Spätgotik und Renaissance,* 1929; Escher, Konrad. *Malerei der Renaissance in Italien,* 1922, v. 1 [1–2]; Feulner, Adolf. *Skulptur und Malerei des 18. Jahrhunderts in Deutschland,* 1929; Frankl, Paul. *Die frühmittelalterliche und romanische Baukunst,* 1926; Haupt, Albrecht. *Baukunst der Renaissance in Frankreich und Deutschland,* 1923; Hildebrandt, Edmund. *Malerei und Plastik des 18. Jahrhunderts in Frankreich,* 1924; Hildebrandt, Hans. *Kunst des 19. und 20. Jahrhunderts,* 1924; Kummel, Otto. *Die Kunst Chinas, Japans und Koreas,* 1929; Pevsner, Nikolaus. *Barockmalerei in den romanischen Ländern,* 1928; Pinder, Wilhelm. *Die deutsche Plastik vom ausgehenden Mittelalters bis zum Ende der Renaissance,* 1924–29, 2 v.; Schubring, Paul. *Die italienische Plastik des Quattrocento,* 1924; Vitzthum von Eckstädt, Georg. *Die Malerei und Plastik des Mittelalters in Italien,* 1924; Weese, Arthur. *Skulptur und Malerei in Frankreich im XV. und XVI. Jahrhundert,* 1927; Willich, Hans. *Die Baukunst der Renaissance in Italien bis zum Tode Michelangelos,* 1914–28, 4 v.; Wulff, Oskar. *Altchristliche und byzantinische Kunst,* 1918–39, 3 v.

445

Hauser, Arnold. The social history of art. [Tr. in collaboration with the author by Stanley Godman] N.Y., Knopf; [London] Routledge & Paul [1951]. 2 v. illus. 25 cm.

A paperback ed. published by Vintage, 1957.

Paged continuously. Bibliographical references included in "Notes" p. 961–77. Indexes of subjects and names p. 979–1022.

446

Histoire générale de l'art. Préf. par Émile Mâle; textes de Eugène Pittard [et al.] [Paris]

Flammarion [1950–51]. 2 v. illus., col. plates, maps. 30 cm.

Covers Eastern and Western art, including primitive. Many good rotogravure illustrations. Each section is by a different author, a specialist in the field.

Includes bibliographies at ends of chapters. Index of places v. 2, p. 381–87; of artists v. 2, p. 389–94.

447

Historia del arte Labor. Barcelona, Labor, 1931–(53). 16 v. illus., plates (part col. mounted). 28 cm.

A Spanish edition of the Propyläen series (454) in which the parts dealing with Spain are rewritten and enlarged by Spanish art historians.

Contents: (1) Sydow, Eckart von. *Arte de los pueblos naturales y prehistoricos* [193?]; (2) Schäfer, Heinrich. *Arte del antiguo Oriente*, 1933; (3) Rodenwaldt, Gerhart. *Arte clásico* (*Greco y Roma*), 1931; (4) Fischer, Otto. *Arte de India, China y Japon*, 1933; (5) Glück, Heinrich. *Arte del Islam*, 1932; (6) Hauttman, Max. *Arte de la alta edad media*, 1934; (7) Karlinger, Hans. *Arte gótico*, 1932; (8) Bode, Wilhelm von. *Arte del protorenacimiento en Italia* [193?]; (9) Schubring, Paul. *Arte del renacimiento en Italia*, 1936; (10) Glück, Gustav. *Arte del renacimiento fuera de Italia*, 1936; (11) Weisbach, Werner. *Arte barocco en Italia, Francia, Alemania y España*, 1934; (12) Friedländer, Max J., and Lafuente Ferrari, M. J. F. *El realismo en la pintura del siglo XVII*, 1934 (2d ed. 1945); (13) Brinckmann, Albert Erich, and Lozoya, J. C., marqués de. *Arte rococó*, 1953; (14) Pauli, Gustav. *Arte del clasicismo y del romanticismo*, 1948; (15) Waldmann, Emil, and Jiménez-Placer, Fernando. *Arte del realismo & impresionismo en el siglo XIX*, 1944; (16) Rudolph, Alfred. *Arte del siglo XX* [195?].

448

Huisman, Georges, ed. Histoire générale de l'art. Paris, Quillet, 1938. 4 v. illus., plates. 31 cm.

Written by a group of nine specialists: Luc Benoist, Louis Bréhier, J. G. Goulinat, Charles Kunstler, Elie Lambert, Mme. Lion-Goldschmidt, Henri Martinie, Robert Rey, and Charles Terrasse.

Attempts to cover the art of East and West simultaneously. Each volume has synchronized tables which relate Eastern to Western art for the periods covered. Well illustrated

by rotogravures, illustrations, and a few good color plates.

Contents: v. 1, Des origines à moyen-âge; v. 2, L'art médiéval; v. 3, L'art classique XV-XVIIe siècles, L'art extrême orient; v. 4, XVIII-XIX-XXe siècles. Contents of the four volumes are listed at beginning of each volume.

A fairly detailed table of contents at end of each volume. No bibliographies or general indexes.

449

Lavedan, Pierre. Histoire de l'art . . . Paris, Presses Universitaires de France, 1949–50. 2 v. 19 cm. (Clio, introduction aux études historiques, 10 & 12)

Volume 1 published 1949; v. 2 originally published 1944, 2d ed. rev. 1950. A general history of art confined to the area of Europe and the Mediterranean, excluding India, the Far East, the Pacific, and Negro Africa. No illustrations.

Contents: v. 1, Antiquité. Avec la collaboration de Simone Besques; v. 2, Moyen âge et temps modernes.

Particularly valuable for the extensive bibliography v. 1, p. ix–xxxv, with short annotations. Additional bibliographies at ends of chapters. Essay on "Méthodologie" v. 1, p. xxxviii–xliii. List of abbreviations at beginning of each volume. Index at end of each volume and a detailed "Table des matières."

450

Lübke, Wilhelm. Grundriss der Kunstgeschichte . . . 15 Aufl. Esslingen a.N., Neff, 1920–25. 6 v. illus., plates (part col.) 26 cm.

First published 1860. A two-volume English translation, illustrated by engravings, was published from the 7th German ed. (N.Y., Dodd Mead, 1878).

A standard German history of art which has been revised many times. Well illustrated with halftones in the text and some color plates.

Contents: v. 1, Die Kunst des Altertums . . . bearb. von Dr. Erich Pernice, 15. Aufl., 1921; v. 2, Die Kunst des Mittelalters . . . bearb. von Dr. Max Semrau, 1923; v. 3, Die Kunst der Renaissance in Italien und in Norden, von Dr. Max Semrau, 4. Aufl., 1920; v. 4, Die Kunst der Barockzeit und der Rokoko, von Dr. Max Semrau, 4. Aufl., 1921; v. 5–6, Die Kunst des XIX. Jahrhunderts und der Gegenwart, von Dr. Friedrich Haack, 6. Aufl., 1922–25 (2 v.).

Only the last two volumes contain bibliographies. Index at end of each volume.

451

Michel, André. Histoire de l'art depuis les premiers temps chrétiens jusqu'à nos jours, pub. sous la direction de André Michel . . . Paris, Colin, 1905–[29]. 8 v. in 17. illus., plates. 29 cm.

——. Index d'ensemble; noms d'artistes, noms de lieux, sujets et table générale par Louise Lefrançois-Pillon. Paris, Colin [1929]. 279 p. 29 cm.

An important scholarly work which covers art from the early Christian period to the present. Each section written by a specialist in his field, and bibliography at end of each chapter. Volume 8, pt. 3 has a section on Latin America by Louis Gillet, which is considered the best attempt to show the development of Latin American art from the time of the European conquest to the present.

Contents: (1) Des débuts de l'art chrétien à la fin de la période romane (2 v.); (2) Formation, expansion et évolution de l'art gothique (2 v.); (3) Le réalisme: les débuts de la Renaissance (2 v.); (4) La Renaissance (2 v.); (5) La Renaissance dans les pays du Nord, Formation de l'art classique moderne (2 v.); (6) L'art en Europe au XVIIe siècle (2 v.); (7) L'art en Europe au XVIIIe siècle (2 v.); (8) L'art en Europe et en Amérique au XIXe siècle et au début du XXe (3 v.).

At end of index volume is also an index of collaborators and a general table of contents for the whole work. A list of collaborators for that specific volume appears at beginning of each volume.

452

Pelican history of art, ed. by Nikolaus Pevsner. London, Baltimore, Penguin Books, 1953–(58). v. 1–(16). illus., plates, maps, plans. 27 cm.

As projected, this series will consist of 50 volumes, each written by a specialist in his field. They are well illustrated with halftones and contain bibliographies. Some volumes also have glossaries and maps.

Contents: (1) Waterhouse, Ellis. *Painting in Britain 1530–1790*, 1953; (2) Rowland, Benjamin. *The art and architecture of India: Buddhist, Hindu, Jain*, 1953; (3) Summerson, John. *Architecture in Britain, 1530–1830*, 1954; (4) Blunt, Anthony. *Art and architecture in France, 1500–1700*, 1954; (5) Rickert, Margaret. *Painting in Britain: the Middle Ages*, 1954; (6) Hamilton, George Heard. *The art and architecture of Russia*, 1954; (7) Frankfort, Henri. *The art and architecture of the ancient Orient*, 1955; (8) Paine, Rob-

ert Treat, and Soper, Alexander. *The art and architecture of Japan*, 1955; (9) Stone, Lawrence. *Sculpture in Britain: the Middle Ages*, 1955; (10) Sickman, Laurence, and Soper, Alexander. *The art and architecture of China*, 1956; (11) Lawrence, Arnold Walter. *Greek architecture*, 1957; (12) Webb, Geoffrey. *Architecture in Britain: the Middle Ages*, 1956; (13) Not yet published; (14) Smith, William Stevenson. *The art and architecture of ancient Egypt*, 1958; (15) Hitchcock, Henry-Russell. *Architecture: Nineteenth and twentieth centuries*, 1958; (16) Wittkower, Rudolf. *Art and architecture in Italy, 1600–1750*, 1958.

453

Pijper, Fredrik. Handboek tot de geschiedenis der christelijke kunst . . . 's Gravenhage, Nijhoff, 1917. 284 p. 55 plates (incl. plans). 25 cm.

A good Dutch survey of Christian art from its inception through the rococo-baroque period. Bibliography at end of each chapter. Alphabetical index p. 261–84.

✓**454**

Propyläen-Kunstgeschichte. Berlin, Propyläen Verlag, 1923–[33]. 24 v. illus. (part col.) 27 cm.

The strength of this series lies not in the text but in the lavish illustrations—some in color—which form a unique body of visual material. At end of each volume is found a list of plates and for each artist represented his dates of birth, death, and activity as well as his working place and medium.

Contents: (1) Sydow, Eckart von. *Die Kunst der Naturvölker und der Vorzeit*, 1923; (2) Schäfer, H. *Die Kunst des alten Orients*, 1925; (3) Rodenwaldt, G. *Die Kunst der Antike*, 1927; (4) Fischer, Otto. *Die Kunst Indiens, Chinas und Japans*, 1928; (5) Glück, H. *Die Kunst des Islam*, 1925; (6) Hauttmann, Max. *Die Kunst des frühen Mittelalters*, 1929; (7) Karlinger, Hans. *Die Kunst der Gotik*, 1927; (8) Bode, W. *Die Kunst der Frührenaissance in Italien*, 1926; (9) Schubring, Paul. *Die Kunst der Hochrenaissance in Italien*, 1926; (10) Glück, G. *Die Kunst der Renaissance in Deutschland*, 1928; (11) Weisbach, W. *Die Kunst des Barock in Italien, Frankreich und Spanien*, 1924; (12) Friedländer, M. J. *Die niederländischen Maler des 17. Jahrhunderts*, 1923; (13) Osborn, Max. *Die Kunst des Rokoko*, 1929; (14) Pauli, G. *Die Kunst des Klassizismus und der Romantik*, 1925; (15) Waldmann, E. *Die Kunst des Realismus und des*

Impressionismus im 19. Jahrhundert, 1927; (16) Einstein, Carl. *Die Kunst des 20. Jahrhunderts,* 1926.

Ergänzungsband: Bock, E. *Geschichte der graphischen Kunst,* 1930; Feulner, A. *Kunstgeschichte des Möbels,* 1927; Horst, Carl. *Die Architektur der deutschen Renaissance,* 1928; Kühn, Herbert. *Die vorgeschichtliche Kunst Deutschlands,* 1935; Platz, G. A. *Die Baukunst der neuesten Zeit,* 1930; Platz, G. A. *Wohnräume der Gegenwart,* 1933; Karlinger, H. *Deutsche Volkskunst,* 1928; Schmidt, Max. *Kunst und Kultur von Peru,* 1929.

455

Reinach, Salomon. Apollo; an illustrated manual of the history of art throughout the ages, from the French, by Florence Simmonds; with 600 illustrations. Completely rev. and new chapter by the author. N.Y., Scribner, 1935. 378 p. illus. 19 cm.

First published 1904. A much used handbook with numerous very small illustrations. General bibliography p. 353, with bibliography at end of each chapter. Index.

456

Robb, David Metheny, and Garrison, Jesse Janes. Art in the western world. 3d ed. N.Y., Harper [1953]. 1050 p. illus., col. map. 24 cm.

1st ed. 1935; 2d ed. 1942. "Material of the first edition has been rewritten, amplified and brought up to date by inclusions of later monuments. In addition to this, a section on the minor arts has been added. . . . A discussion, in relatively nontechnical terms, of the artistic traditions of the Occident."—*Pref.*

"Selected critical bibliography" p. 980–1003. Glossary p. 1005–18. "Chronological table" p. 1019–39. Index p. 1041–50.

457

Seroux d'Agincourt, Jean Baptiste Louis Georges. Histoire de l'art par les monumens, depuis sa décadence au IVe siècle jusqu'à son renouvellement au XVIe . . . Paris, Treuttel et Würtz, 1823. 6 v. in 3. 325 plates (incl. plans). 52 cm.

Translation by Ticozzi, Prato, 1826–29; English ed. published 1847 by Quaritch. An early general history of art issued in 24 pts., 1810–23.

Contents: v. 1, Architecture; v. 2, Sculpture, painting; v. 3, Text and description of plates; v. 4, Plates; v. 5, Plates of painting. "Notice sur la vie et les travaux de J. L. G. Seroux d'Agincourt" by A. E. Gigault de La Salle v. 1, p. 1–10.

458

Springer, Anton. Handbuch der Kunstgeschichte . . . Elfte Aufl. . . . Leipzig, Kröner, 1918–29. 6 v. illus., col. plates. 28 cm.

1st ed. 1875; 2d ed. 1881; 12th ed. 1923. Each volume has a special title page. A standard German history of art which has had many editions and revisions. Well illustrated with halftones in text and color plates.

Contents: v. 1, Die Kunst des Altertums, 11. Aufl. nach Adolf Michaelis bearb. von Paul Wolters, 1920; v. 2, Frühchristliche Kunst und Mittelalter, 10. umgearb. Aufl., bearb. von Joseph Neuwirth, 1919; v. 3, Die Kunst der Renaissance in Italien, 10. erweiterte Aufl. bearb. von Adolf Philippi, 1918; v. 4, Die Kunst der Renaissance im Norden: Barock und Rokoko, 10. verb. und erweiterte Aufl., bearb. von Paul Schubring, 1920; v. 5, Die Kunst von 1800 bis zur Gegenwart, 7. verb. und erweiterte Aufl. bearb. von Max Osborn, 1920; v. 6, Die aussereuropäische Kunst . . . von Curt Glaser, Stella Kramrisch, Ernst Kühnel . . . [und anderen] 1929.

Each volume has its own index at end. Only v. 6 contains bibliographies.

459

Thienen, Frithjof Willem Sophi van, ed. Algemeene kunstgeschiedenis, de kunst der menschheid van de oudste tijden tot heden . . . Utrecht, de Haan, 1941–51. 6 v. illus. (incl. maps, plans), plates (part col.) 27 cm.

A general Dutch history of art with various sections written by specialists. Eastern art and primitive art are included. Good clear illustrations and plates.

Bibliography at end of each volume. Index of the complete work at end of v. 6, p. 365–84.

460

Upjohn, Everard Miller; Wingert, Paul S.; and Mahler, Jane Gaston. History of world art. 2d ed. rev. and enl. N.Y., Oxford Univ. Press, 1958. 876 p. 671 illus., 17 col. plates, maps (on lining papers). 24 cm.

1st ed. 1949. A useful one-volume survey of the field written by recognized scholars. The entire book has been revised and new chapters added covering prehistoric art, art of the American Indian, and primitive art, as well as an expanded discussion of the art of the 20th century. The illustrations are placed throughout the text, in contrast to the 1st ed., where they formed a pictorial survey at the beginning of the book.

Captions give size of works of art. Glossary p. 831–39; "Suggested reading" p. 841–50; Index p. 851–76.

461

Woermann, Karl. Geschichte der Kunst aller Zeiten und Völker . . . Leipzig und Wien, Bibliographisches Institut, 1905–22. 6 v. illus., plates (part col.) 26 cm.

A standard, well-illustrated history of art. Contents: Bd. 1, Die Kunst der Vor- und ausserchristlichen Völker; Bd. 2, Die Kunst der christlichen Völker bis zum Ende des 15. Jahrhunderts; Bd. 3, Die Kunst der christlichen Völker vom 16. bis zum Ende des 19. Jahrhunderts; Bd. 4, Die Kunst der alteren Neuzeit vom 1400 bis 1550; Bd. 5, Die Kunst der mittleren Neuzeit von 1550 bis 1750; Bd. 6, Die Kunst der jüngeren Neuzeit von 1750 bis zur Gegenwart (1922).

Bibliography, listed alphabetically: v. 1, p. [607]–21; v. 2, p. [661]–85; v. 3, p. [696]–717; v. 4, p. [582]–606; v. 5, p. [474]–90; v. 6, p. 512–29. Each volume has its own index.

Ancient

General

462

Byvanck, Alexander Willem. De kunst der oudheid . . . Leiden, Brill, 1946–(57). v. 1–(3) illus., incl. maps, plans, plates. 25 cm.

A modern Dutch history of ancient art. Volume 1 covers Egypt, Mesopotamia, Syria, Babylonia; v. 2 covers Crete, Mycenae, and early Greek art; v. 3 covers Greek art from 480 to 300 B.C.

"Literatuur": v. 1, p. [444]–61; v. 2, p. [512]–29; v. 3, p. [364]–86. Each volume has its own index.

463

Déchelette, Joseph. Manuel d'archéologie préhistorique, celtique et gallo-romaine. Paris, Picard, 1908–(34). v. 1–(6). illus., plates, maps. 23 cm.

A useful manual of prehistoric, Celtic, and Gallo-Roman archaeology. Contents: v. 1, Archéologie préhistorique; v. 2, Archéologie protohistorique ou celtique: Age du bronze; v. 3, Premier âge du fer ou époque de Hallstatt; v. 4, Second âge du fer ou époque de La Tène; v. 5–6, Manuel d'archéologie gallo-romaine, par Albert Grenier: pt. 1, Généralités, Travaux militaires; pt. 2, L'archéologie du sol, Routes, Navigation, Occupation du sol.

Each volume contains bibliographies and a general index.

464

Handbuch der Archäologie, im Rahmen des Handbuchs der Altertumswissenschaft; in Verbindung mit E. Walter Andrae . . . Helmut Arntz . . . Friedrich Wilh. Freiherr von Bissing . . . hrsg. von Walter Otto . . . München, Beck, 1939–(53). (4) v. illus., plates. 26 cm. (Müller, Ivan Philipp Edvard, Ritter von. Handbuch der Altertumswissenschaft, 6. Abt.)

Published in parts 1937–(53). Volume 1 contains: General introduction; List of abbreviations; The Stone Age and the ancient Orient (Babylonia, Syria, Egypt, Assyria, etc.). Volume 2 covers the Stone and Bronze Ages in Europe and adjoining territory before 1000 B.C. Volumes 3 and 4 deal with ancient Greece and Rome. Volume 3 ¹, *Die Griechische Plastik* by Georg Lippold, is one of the best treatements of Greek sculpture. Volume 4 ¹, *Malerei und Zeichnung* by Andreas Rumpf, is probably the best and most up-to-date account of Greek painting.

Each volume has its own indexes.

465

Perrot, Georges, and Chipiez, Charles. Histoire de l'art dans l'antiquité: Égypte, Assyrie, Perse, Asie Mineure, Grèce, Étrurie, Rome . . . Paris, Hachette, 1882–1914. 10 v. illus., plates (part col.) 28 cm.

An old standard history of ancient art. Contents: v. 1, L'Égypte; v. 2, Chaldée et Assyrie; v. 3, Phénicie, Cypre; v. 4, Judée, Sardaigne, Syrie, Cappadoce; v. 5, Perse, Phrygie, Lydie et Carie, Lycie; v. 6, La Grèce primitive: l'art mycénien; v. 7, La Grèce de l'épopée, la Grèce archaïque (le temple); v. 8, La Grèce archaïque, la sculpture; v. 9, La Grèce archaïque, la glyptique, la numismatique, la peinture, la céramique; v. 10, La Grèce archaïque, la céramique d'Athènes.

Index at end of each volume.

466

Winckelmann, Johann Joachim. Johann Winckelmanns . . . Geschichte der Kunst des Altertums. Dresden, Walther, 1764. 2 v. in 1. 431 p. illus. 26 cm.

Paged continuously. Title vignettes, head and tail pieces. Schlosser lists it as Lehrgebäude der Geschichte . . . . An English translation by G. Henry Lodge published 1872–73 (Boston, Osgood).

This is an important book in the history of art, for it marks the beginning of modern interest in ancient art, besides being the first book to bear the title of a history of art.

Index of 16 pages at end of volume.

SEE ALSO: Hamann. Geschichte der Kunst von der Vorgeschichte bis zur Spätantike (443).

Assyria, Babylonia, Egypt, Mesopotamia

467

Aldred, Cyril. Middle Kingdom art in ancient Egypt, 2300–1590 B.C. London, Tiranti, 1950. 56 p. plates, map. 19 cm.

A concise treatment of the art of this period, with emphasis on sculpture. Bibliography p. 32.

468

Aldred, Cyril. New Kingdom art in ancient Egypt during the eighteenth dynasty, 1590 to 1315 B.C. London, Tiranti, 1951. 98 p. plates, map. 19 cm.

Similar in treatment to the other two volumes by this author. Bibliography p. 40.

469

Aldred, Cyril. Old Kingdom art in ancient Egypt. London, Tiranti, 1949. 40 p. plates, map. 19 cm.

A useful short survey of Egyptian art of this period, with an outline of Egyptian history to 2134 B.C. Emphasis on sculpture. Bibliography p. 26.

470

Barrois, Augustin Georges. Manuel d'archéologie biblique. Paris, Picard, 1939–53. 2 v. illus. (incl. plans), map, diagrs. 23 cm.

A useful manual covering the various aspects of ancient civilization in Palestine, including art, architecture, and iconography.

"Bibliographie générale" v. 2, p. 469–77. "Index général" v. 2, p. 479–93. "Index des mots hébreux et araméens" v. 2, p. 494–502.

471

Capart, Jean. Documents pour servir à l'étude de l'art égyptien, publiés par Jean Capart . . . Paris, Les Éditions du Pégase, 1927–31. 2 v. 200 plates (part col.) 41 cm.

Edition of 612 copies. A collection of collotype plates reproducing important works of Egyptian art from various museums and collections, with accompanying text. Size indicated on guard sheets.

Bibliography: v. 1, p. 75–81; v. 2, p. 95–106. "Liste des musées, monuments et collections": v. 1, p. 83–84; v. 2, p. 107–08. "Index général": v. 1, p. 85–89; v. 2, p. 109–14.

472

Capart, Jean. Egyptian art; introductory studies . . . . Translated from the French by Warren R. Dawson. N.Y., Stokes; London, Allen & Unwin [1923]. 179 p. 64 plates on 32 l. 25 cm.

"A translation of the introductory chapters of . . . *Leçons sur l'art égyptien.*"—*Translator's Pref.* A standard work on Egyptian art.

Contains bibliographies. Index p. 177–79.

473

Christian, Viktor. Altertumskunde des Zweistromlandes von der Vorzeit bis zum Ende der Achämenidenherrschaft . . . Leipzig, Hiersemann, 1940– . v. 1. plates, plans, maps. 25 cm.

Issued in parts 1938– . Each volume will appear in two parts: pt. 1, Text; pt. 2, Tafeln. Covers the antiquities of the valleys of the Tigris and Euphrates rivers. Supersedes Handcock's *Mesopotamian archaeology* (475). Well illustrated; includes many plans and diagrams of pottery shapes.

Includes bibliographies.

474

Frankfort, Henri. The art and architecture of the ancient Orient. [Harmondsworth, Middlesex] Penguin Books [1954]. 279 p. illus., 192 plates, map, plans. 27 cm. (The Pelican history of art, Z7)

A very useful recent survey of the field, incorporating the results of modern scholarship. Well illustrated. Bibliography p. 269–70. Index p. 273–79.

475

Handcock, Percy Stuart Peache. Mesopotamian archaeology; an introduction to the archaeology of Babylonia and Assyria . . . London, Macmillan, 1912. 423 p. illus., 33 plates, map. 23 cm. (Handbooks to ancient civilization series)

Bibliography p. 406–07. "List of more important kings & rulers and a brief chronological summary" p. 408–10. Index p. 411–23.

476

Harcourt-Smith, Simon. Babylonian art. London, Benn, 1928. 50 p. 76 plates. 23 cm. (Kai Khosru monographs on eastern art)

Short text with no index.

477

Hayes, William Christopher. The scepter of Egypt; a background for the study of the Egyptian antiquities in the Metropolitan Museum of Art. N.Y., Harper in co-operation with the Metropolitan Museum of Art, 1953. v. 1. illus., map. 26 cm.

To be completed in two volumes. A very useful work, incorporating the most recent scholarship in the field. Contents: pt. 1, From the earliest times to the end of the Middle Kingdom.

Chronological table p. 2. Bibliography p. [353]–74. Indexes of proper names: (A) Egyptian kings p. 377–79; (B) Egyptian personal names p. 379–82; (C) Divinities p. 382; (D) Geographic and ethnic names p. 383–85. General index p. 389–99.

478

Maspero, *Sir* Gaston Camille Charles. Manual of Egyptian archaeology and guide to the study of antiquities in Egypt. For the use of students and travellers . . . tr. and enl. by Agnes S. Johns. 6th English ed. With three hundred and forty-two illustrations. N.Y., Putnam, 1926. 385 p. illus. 19 cm.

1st English ed. 1887; 6th English ed. 1914 (London, Grevel; N.Y., Putnam), reprinted in 1926. A useful standard handbook. Index p. 371–85.

479

Smith, William Stevenson. Ancient Egypt as represented in the Museum of Fine Arts . . . 3d ed. fully rev. Boston, Museum of Fine Arts, 1952. 187 p. illus. 23 cm.

This book "is really a short history of the development of Egyptian culture and art, well illustrated with pieces in the Museum collections."—*Pref.*

Egyptian chronology p. 169–77. Introduction (Bibliographical) p. [7]–9. Index p. 178–79.

480

Vandier, Jacques. Manuel d'archéologie égyptienne. Paris, Picard, 1952–(55). v. 1–(2) in (4). illus., maps. 23 cm.

A useful modern compendium of Egyptian archaeology by a leading authority. To be complete in four volumes.

Contents: t. 1, Les époques de formation: [ptie.] 1, La préhistoire; [ptie.] 2, Les trois premières dynasties; t. 2, Les grandes époques: [ptie.] 1, Architecture funéraire; [ptie.] 2, Architecture religieuse et civile.

Bibliography: t. 1, p. 991–95; t. 2, p. 1025–

41; also bibliographical footnotes. Indexes: t. 1, p. 996–1024; t. 2, p. 1042–78.

481

Woolley, *Sir* Charles Leonard. The development of Sumerian art . . . London, Faber [1935]. 3 p., 90–140 p. incl. plates (part col.) 29 cm.

Good illustrations, with some color plates. Index p. 137–40.

482

Zervos, Christian. L'art de la Mésopotamie de la fin du quatrième millénaire au XVe siècle avant notre ère . . . Elam, Sumer, Akkad. Paris, "Cahiers d'Art" [c1935]. 264 p. illus., plates, map. 33 cm.

Primarily a picture book, with a slight text including some poems based on the literary sources of the period.

Crete, Etruria, Greece, Rome

483

Beazley, John Davidson, and Ashmole, Bernard. Greek sculpture & painting to the end of the Hellenistic period . . . Cambridge, Univ. Press, 1932. 107 p. plates. 21 cm.

"This book is a reprint of the chapters on Greek art in *The Cambridge Ancient History*. No substantial alterations have been made, but the text has been revised, a number of new pictures . . . added, and the bibliography remodelled."—*Pref.*

An excellent short handbook. Bibliography p. [103]–07.

484

Bossert, Helmuth Theodor. The art of ancient Crete, from the earliest times to the iron age . . . 3d ed. London, Zwemmer, 1937. 44 p. illus. (incl. plans), 304 plates. 25 cm. (The earliest cultures of the Mediterranean countries, I)

Mostly a picture book. Text consists of: Notes on Aegean chronology & terminology, Survey of Aegean chronology from the iron age to the bronze age (in tabular form), and Notes on the illustrations p. 14–44.

Bibliography p. 13–14.

485

Ducati, Pericle. . . . L'arte classica, con 12 tavole in rotocalco e 949 riproduzioni d'arte nel testo. Ristampa corr. della 3. ed. interamente riveduta. Torino, Unione Tipografico-Editrice Torinese, 1944. 829 p. illus. (incl.

plan), plates. 27 cm. (Storia dell'arte classica e italiana, v. 1)

A well-illustrated survey of classical art covering ancient Greek and Roman art.

"Cronistoria archeologica" p. [763]–82. "Musei e collezioni" p. [783]–88. "Bibliografia" p. [789]–802. Indexes: of artists p. 803–05; alphabetical index p. 806–18; of illustrations p. [819]–29.

486

Ducati, Pericle. L'arte in Roma dalle origini al sec. VIII . . . Bologna, Cappelli [c1938]. 500 p. illus., 303 plates, plans, diagrs. 25 cm. ([Istituto di Studi Romani] Storia di Roma, v. XXVI)

Well-illustrated history of Roman art to the 8th century.

Bibliography p. [421]–36, with annotations. Indexes of places, names, and things.

487

Ducati, Pericle. Storia dell'arte etrusca . . . Firenze, Rinascimento del Libro, 1927. 2 v. 284 plates (incl. plans). 29 cm.

Edition of 1050 copies. A standard history of Etruscan art.

Contents: v. 1, Text; v. 2, Plates. Bibliography at end of each chapter. Index at end of v. 1.

488

Evans, *Sir* Arthur John. The palace of Minos; a comparative account of the successive stages of the early Cretan civilization as illustrated by the discoveries at Knossos . . . London, Macmillan, 1921–35. 4 v. in 6. illus., plates (part col.), maps, plans, facsims. 26 cm.

A standard work.

Contents: v. 1, The neolithic and early and middle Minoan ages; v. 2, pt. 1, Fresh lights on origins and external relations: the restoration in town and palace after seismic catastrophe towards close of M. M. III, and the beginnings of the new era; v. 2, pt. 2, Town houses in Knossos of the new era and restored west palace section, with its state approach; v. 3, The great transitional age in the northern and eastern sections of the palace: the most brilliant records of Minoan art and evidences of an advanced religion; v. 4, pt. 1, Emergence of outer western enceinte, with new illustrations, artistic and religious, of the middle Minoan phase; chryselephantine "lady of sports," "snake room" and full story of cult; late Minoan ceramic evolution and "palace style"; v. 4,

pt. 2, "Camp-stool fresco"—long-robed priests and beneficent genii; chryselephantine boygod and ritual hair-offering; intaglio types, M. M. III–L. M. II; late hoards of sealings; deposits of inscribed tablets and the palace stores; linear script B and its mainland extension; closing palatial phase—"room of throne"—and final catastrophe with epilogue on the discovery of "ring of Minos" and "temple tomb."

————. Index to the Palace of Minos, by Joan Evans . . . London, Macmillan, 1936. 221 p. 26 cm.

489

Fowler, Harold North, and Wheeler, James Rignall. A handbook of Greek archaeology . . . with the collaboration of Gorham Phillips Stevens. N.Y., Cincinnati [etc.] American Book Co. [c1909]. 559 p. 19 cm. (Greek series for colleges and schools; ed. under the supervision of H. W. Smyth)

Mostly out of date, but the chapter on technique of archaeology has not been replaced. A chapter is devoted to each medium, i.e., architecture, sculpture, coins, etc.

Bibliography p. 542–50. Detailed index p. 551–59.

490

Giglioli, Giulio Quirino. L'arte etrusca. Milano, Treves, 1935. 7 p., xvii–lxxii, 95 p. plates (part col.) 35 cm.

A good pictorial survey of Etruscan art covering architecture, sculpture, painting, and the minor arts. "Descrizione e bibliografia dei monumenti" p. 5–78.

491

Hall, Harry Reginald Holland. Aegean archaeology; an introduction to the archaeology of prehistoric Greece . . . London, Warner, 1915. 270 p. illus., 33 plates, map. 23 cm. (Handbooks to ancient civilizations series)

Out of date but still useful. Short bibliography p. 261–63. Index p. 265–70.

492

Koch, Herbert. Römische Kunst. 2. erweiterte Aufl. Weimar, Böhlaus, 1949. 160 p. illus., 61 plates (part col.) 21 cm.

1st ed. (1925) was in "Jedermanns Bücherei" series. A good short survey of Roman art.

Bibliography p. [145]–50. Chronological outline p. 151–54. Author and subject index p. 158–60.

493

Lübke, Wilhelm, and Pernice, Erich. Die Kunst der Griechen ... 17. Aufl., vollständig neubearb. von Berta Sarne. Wien, Neff, 1948. 464 p. illus., col. plates, plans. 27 cm.

Part of the author's *Kunst des Altertums* (v. 1 of his *Grundriss der Kunstgeschichte*). An excellent one-volume history of Greek art, profusely illustrated. Bibliography p. 464.

494

Matz, Friedrich. Geschichte der griechischen Kunst. Frankfurt am Main, Klostermann [c1950]. v. 1. illus., plates, plans. 25 cm.

The first volume to appear of an important history of Greek art which reflects developments of recent scholarship in this field. Volume 1 covers the geometric and early archaic styles.

Contents: Bd. 1, Die geometrische und die früharchaische Form, 2 v. (text and plates). Bibliography: v. 1 (Textband), p. 511–38.

495

Mau, August. Pompeii, its life and art ... tr. into English by Francis W. Kelsey ... with numerous illustrations from original drawings and photographs. New ed., rev. and cor. N.Y., London, Macmillan, 1904. 557 p. illus., plates, plans. 21 cm.

1st ed. 1899; new rev. ed. 1902. A standard work, old but still useful. "Key to the plan of Pompeii" p. 559–[60]. "Bibliographical appendix" p. 513–50. Index p. 551–57.

496

Pausanias. Pausanias's Description of Greece, tr. with a commentary by J. G. Frazer ... London and N.Y., Macmillan, 1898. 6 v. illus., plates, maps, plans. 26 cm.

2d ed. 1913. A description of Greece as it was in the 2d century A.D., translated from the original Greek, with a commentary.

Contents: v. 1, Translation; v. 2, Commentary on Book I: Attica; Appendix: The pre-Persian temple on the Acropolis; v. 3, Commentary on Books II–V: Corinth, Laconia, Messenia, Elis; v. 4, Commentary on Books VI–VIII: Elis, Archaia, Arcadia; v. 5, Commentary on Books IX, X: Boeotia, Phocis, addenda; v. 6, Indices, maps.

497

Pendlebury, John Devitt Stringfellow. The archaeology of Crete; an introduction ... London, Methuen [1939]. 400 p. 53 illus., 50 plates, plans, 24 maps. 23 cm. (Methuen's handbooks of archaeology)

Covers the culture of Crete from the earliest times down to the Roman age. "List of abbreviations" p. xxi–xxii. "Select bibliography" p. 381–83. Index p. 387–400.

498

Richter, Gisela Marie Augusta. Archaic Greek art against its historical background; a survey. N.Y., Oxford Univ. Press, 1949. 226 p. 107 plates, map (on lining papers). 27 cm. (The Mary Flexner lectures, 9)

A well-illustrated survey of archaic Greek art, covering c. 650–480 B.C., written by a recognized scholar. "Abbreviations and bibliography" p. xiii–xviii. General index p. 211–20. Index of museums and collections p. 221–26.

499

Riis, Poul Jørgen. An introduction to Etruscan art. Copenhagen, Munksgaard, 1953. 144 p. 82 plates. 25 cm.

"A collection of archaeological essays" (*Pref.*) which gives a good picture of Etruscan art in the light of modern scholarship. Includes bibliographies. Index p. 137–44.

500

Rizzo, Giulio Emanuele. Storia dell'arte greca. Torino, Tipografico-Editorice Torinese, 1913. illus. 27 cm. (Storia dell'arte classica e italiana [by Rizzo and Toesca] v. 1)

Incomplete work; only pts. 1–11 published. Issued serially in fascicles. Few illustrations. "Prolegomeni alla storia dell'arte greca; appendice critica e bibliografica all'Introduzione," p. 13–49, contains the bibliography. No index.

501

Rumpf, Andreas, and Mingazzini, Paolo. Manuale di storia dell'arte classica. Firenze, La "Nuova Italia," 1936. 197 p. 65 plates. 25 cm.

Based on a work first published under the auspices of Gercke.

Bibliography at end of each section.

502

Salis, Arnold von. Die Kunst der Griechen ... 2. Aufl. ... Leipzig, Hirzel, 1922. 303 p. illus. 25 cm.

1st ed. 1919. A good German history of Greek art.

503

Seta, Alessandro della. Italica antica dalla caverna prehistorica al palazzo imperiale. 2. ed. Bergamo, Istituto Italiano d'Arti Grafiche, 1928. 509 p. illus. 27 cm. (Collezione di monografie illustrate. Serie: Storia della civiltà, 3)

Covers ancient Italian civilization from prehistoric caves to the imperial palace. Classed bibliography p. [435–76]. General index p. 477–98.

504

Strong, Eugénie (Sellers). . . . Art in ancient Rome . . . N.Y., Scribner, 1928. 2 v. illus. (incl. plans). 19 cm. (Ars una: species mille. General history of art)

A standard handbook on Roman art. Contents: v. 1, From the earliest times to the principate of Nero; v. 2, From the Flavian dynasty to Justinian, with chapters on painting and the minor arts in the first century, A.D.

Bibliography at end of most of the chapters; "General bibliography" v. 1, p. xii. Index v. 2, p. 209–20.

505

Wace, Alan John Bayard. Mycenae, an archaeological history and guide. Princeton, Princeton Univ. Press, 1949. 150 p. 110 plates, maps. 29 cm.

A standard modern work on Mycenae. Illustrated by good plates and many plans and diagrams. Bibliography p. 139–41. Index p. 143–50.

506

Walters, Henry Beauchamp. The art of the Romans . . . N.Y., Macmillan, 1911. 185 p. illus., 71 plates. 26 cm.

Old but still useful. Bibliography p. xv–xvi. Chronological table (to 324 A.D.) p. 176–77.

Alois Riegl. Römanisch kunst Industrie

507

Wickhoff, Franz. Roman art; some of its principles and their application to early Christian painting . . . tr. and ed. by Mrs. S. Arthur Strong . . . London, Heinemann; N.Y., Macmillan, 1900. 198 p. illus., 14 plates. 32 cm.

First published in Vienna in 1895 with title: *Die Wiener Genesis*, ed. by Wilhelm von Härtel and Franz Wickhoff. Index p. 191–98.

508

Zervos, Christian. L'art de la Crète néolithique et minoenne. Paris, Éditions "Cahiers d'Art" [1956]. 523 p. (p. 59–488 illus.) 8 col. plates, map. 39 cm.

Although in format primarily a picture book with excellent illustrations, it also includes much material not published else-

where on neolithic and Minoan art in Crete. "La chronologie minoenne" p. 509–12. "Notes tenant lieu aussi d'indications bibliographiques" p. 512–16. "Bibliographie complémentaire" p. 516. "Index alphabétique des noms" p. 517–18; "Index alphabétique par matière" p. 519–21.

509

Zervos, Christian. L'art des Cyclades du début à la fin de l'âge du bronze, 2500–1100 avant notre ère. Paris, Éditions "Cahiers d'Art" [1957]. [278] p. illus., plates (part col.), maps. 39 cm.

A well-illustrated work on the civilization of the Cyclades islands, covering the civilization, history, and religion of this region. Bibliography p. 271. Subject index p. 273–74. Index of names p. 274–[75].

510

Zervos, Christian. La civilisation de la Sardaigne du début de l'énéolithique à la fin de la période nouragique, II. millénaire—V. siècle avant notre ère. Paris, Éditions "Cahiers d'Art" [1954]. 380 p. illus., map. 39 cm.

Covers geography, history, architecture, costume, industry, armament, religion, life, and funerary rites of Sardinia; illustrated by excellent plates. Includes bibliographical references. "Index des lieux Sardes cités dans l'ouvrage" p. 377–80.

Early Christian—Gothic

511

Allen, John Romilly. Celtic art in pagan and Christian times. London, Methuen [1904]. 315 p. illus., 44 plates. 23 cm. (The antiquary's books. General ed., J. C. Cox)

Covers Celtic art from the Bronze Age through the Christian period. Well illustrated with drawings in the text and plates. Index p. 305–15.

512

Bréhier, Louis. L'art byzantin . . . Paris, Laurens [c1924]. 203 p. 106 illus. 21 cm. (Les patries de l'art)

A short, readable history of the subject. Includes bibliographies.

"Dates principales de l'histoire de l'art byzantin" p. 181–82; "Développement historique de l'empire byzantin" p. 183–85; "Principaux artistes connus de l'art byzantin" p. 186–87; "Centres d'art byzantin" p. 188–200.

513

Bréhier, Louis. L'art chrétien, son développement iconographique des origines à nos jours . . . 2. éd., rev. et complétée. Paris, Laurens, 1928. 480 p. illus., 16 plates. 29 cm.

A history of Christian art to the present day.

Bibliography p. [450]–54. "Index iconographique" p. 455–61; "Index des artistes" p. 462–63; "Index géographique" p. 464–69.

514

Dalton, Ormonde Maddock. Byzantine art and archaeology . . . Oxford, Clarendon Press, 1911. 727 p. 457 illus. 26 cm.

Covers period between 4th century and the close of the 15th century. Does not include architecture.

Contains: General introduction; discussion of geographical areas of Byzantine art; nine chapters divided by medium, i.e., sculpture, painting, enamels, etc.; chapter on iconography; chapter on ornament.

Indexes: (1) General, p. 715–20; (2) Iconography, p. 721–23; (3) Museums, libraries, treasuries, and collections, p. 723–25; (4) Authorities, p. 725–27.

515

Dalton, Ormonde Maddock. East Christian art, a survey of the monuments . . . Oxford, Clarendon Press, 1925. 396 p. 1 illus., 69 plates. 30 cm.

"The arrangement of the present book is similar to that of *Byzantine art and archaeology* (514), but apart from some of the purely descriptive matter, the chapters are all new, and written from a somewhat different standpoint."—*Pref.*

A less inclusive and more popular treatment than the preceding title. Architecture is included, as well as painting, sculpture, minor arts, and ornament.

Bibliographical footnotes. General index p. 387–93. Index of authors p. 394–96.

516

Diehl, Charles. L'art chrétien primitif et l'art byzantin. Paris et Bruxelles, van Oest, 1928. 61 p. 64 plates. 26 cm. (Bibliothèque d'histoire de l'art)

A short summary of the subject. Bibliography p. 57–58. No index.

517

Diehl, Charles. Manuel d'art byzantin . . . 2. éd. rev. et augm. Paris, Picard, 1925–26. 2 v. illus. 23 cm.

Originally published in 1910. Arranged chronologically. Includes architecture, painting, sculpture, and the minor arts.

Bibliographical notes and abbreviations p. [xiii]–xv. Also bibliographical footnotes. General index p. 911–33. Iconographical index p. 934–40.

518

Dumbarton Oaks papers. no. 1–(12). [Cambridge, Harvard Univ. Press, 1941–(58)] (11) v. illus., plates. 30 cm.

"Devoted primarily to late classical, early medieval, and Byzantine art." Issued by the Dumbarton Oaks research library and collection of Harvard University. Indexed in *B. d. f. Z.*

519

Garrucci, Raffaele. Storia della arte cristiana nei primi otto secoli della chiesa . . . e corredata della collezione di tutti i monumenti di pittura e scultura, incisi in rame su cinquecento tavole ed illustrati. Prato, Guasti, 1872–81. 6 v. illus., 500 plates. 48 cm.

A great compendium of material, illustrated by line drawings. Contents: v. 1, Teorica, Annali; v. 2, Pitture cimiteriali; v. 3, Pitture non cimiteriali; v. 4, Musaici cimiteriali e non cimiteriali; v. 5, Sarcofagi ossia sculture cimiteriali; v. 6, Sculture non cimiteriali.

520

Gayet, Albert Jean. L'art copte; école d'Alexandrie—architecture monastique—sculpture—peinture—art somptuaire; illustrations de l'auteur. Paris, Leroux, 1902. 334 p. illus., 6 plates. 29 cm.

A standard work on Coptic art. Illustrated with line drawings. No index.

521

Grüneisen, Wladimir de. Les caractéristiques de l'art copte. Florence, Alinari, 1922. 193 p. illus., 66 plates. 33 cm.

Profusely illustrated with plates. Bibliographical footnotes.

"Matériel documentaire et bibliographie" p. 27–29; "Table générale des matières" p. 163–74; "Table des noms de ville et de pays" p. 175–79; "Table hagyographique et des personnages bibliques et ecclésiastiques" p. 181–82; "Table des sources et des auteurs" p. [183]–87; "Table des figures contenues dans le texte" p. [189]–90; "Table des planches" p. [191]–93.

522
Hinks, Roger Packman. Carolingian art. London, Sidgwick & Jackson, 1935. 224 p. 24 plates (incl. facsims.) 23 cm.
Bibliography p. 215–18.

523
Jacobsthal, Paul. Early Celtic art. Oxford, Clarendon Press, 1944. 2 v. illus., plates. 32 cm.
"Covers the 4th and 3d centuries B.C. and part of the 2d and 5th of the art of the Gauls."—*Pref*. Not a corpus of all specimens preserved but a selection of works chosen for their style and technique. Glass and Celtic art in Spain are omitted. Excellent clear plates.
Volume 1, text; v. 2, plates. Contents: (1) The image of man; (2) Animals; (3) Grammar of Celtic ornament; (4) A survey of implements and some remarks on their technique; (5) Chronology; (6) Celtic crafts, their origin and connexions; Epilogue; Catalogue p. 165–205.
Indexes p. 214–42: (1) References to the catalogue; (2) Key to plates p. 216–60; (3) References to the pages where patterns decorating objects other than those illustrated are explicitly or implicitly mentioned or discussed; (4) Proveniences; (5) Ancient writers and inscriptions; (6) Arts and styles (other than early Celtic); (7) Some matters of interest; (8) Concordance to some books especially familiar to students of the subject.

524
Jantzen, Hans. Ottonische Kunst. Mit 182 Abbildungen und 31 Zeichnungen. [München] Münchner Verlag [1947]. 180 p. illus., plates. 27 cm.
A sound and well-illustrated treatment of Ottonian art. Bibliographical references included in "Anmerkungen" p. 163–71. Place index p. 176–78.

525
Kaufmann, Carl Maria. Handbuch der christlichen Archäologie, Einführung in die Denkmälerwelt und Kunst des Urchristentums. Dritte, vermehrte und verbesserte Auflage . . . Paderborn, Schöningh, 1922. 683 p. illus., plans. 23 cm.
A German treatment of early Christian art and archaeology. Index p. 637–83.

526
Kleinschmidt, Beda. Geschichte der christlichen Kunst. Paderborn, Schöningh, 1926. 637 p. 388 illus. 22 cm. (Wissenschaftliche

Handbibliothek, 3. Lehrbücher verschiedener Wissenschaften, 7)
2d ed. A history of Christian art, by a noted Franciscan scholar, which includes architecture, painting, sculpture, church decoration, and iconography.
Contents: Verzeichnis der abgekürzt zitierten Bücher (Bibliography) p. xxi–xxviii; Verzeichnis der benutzten Kunstdenkmäler-Inventari p. xxix; Abkürzungen p. xxx; Text p. 1–600; Alphabetisches Verzeichnis kunsttechnischer Ausdrücke p. 601–05; Sinnbilder, Attribute und Darstellungsformen der bekannteren-Heiligen p. 606–11; Register der Namen, Sachen und Abbildungen p. 612–37.

527
Kondakov, Nikodim Pavlovich. Histoire de l'art byzantin considéré principalement dans les miniatures. Éd. française originale, publiée par l'auteur, sur la traduction de M. Trawinski, et précédée d'une préface de M. A. Springer . . . Paris, Librairie de l'Art, 1886–91. 2 v. illus., plates. 32 cm. (Bibliothéque internationale de l'art)
Edition of 300 copies printed. Volume 1 contains 29 engravings; v. 2, 13. List of manuscripts cited in the text v. 2, p. [181]–84.

528
Kraus, Franz Xaver, and Sauer, Joseph. Geschichte der christlichen Kunst. Freiburg im Breisgau [etc.] Herder, 1896–1908. 2 v. in 3. illus., plates. 28 cm.
Covers the history of Christian art from its beginning through the Italian Renaissance. Especially useful for its section on early Christian art.
Contents: v. 1, Hellenistic, Roman, early Christian and Byzantine, and the early beginnings of the art of the northern people; v. 2, pt. 1, Middle Ages; v. 2, pt. 2, Italian Renaissance. Index for the whole work v. 2, pt. 2, p. 805–56.

529
Leclercq, Henri. Manuel d'archéologie chrétienne depuis les origines jusqu'au VIIIe siècle. Paris, Letouzey et Ane, 1907. 2 v. illus. 25 cm.
Illustrated with some line drawings. Contents: I, Les influences, Les catacombes et les cimetières, Les édifices chrétiens avant la Paix de l'Église, L'art et les cimetières juifs (Appendix); II, Méthodes de construction, L'architecture, La peinture, La mosaïque, Statuaire et polychromie, Le bas-relief, Les ivoires, La glyptique, Orfèvrerie et émaillerie, La verrerie, La terre cuite, La fonte,

La numismatique, Les tissages, Les miniatures, Artes minores.

Bibliography at end of each chapter. Glossary v. 1, p. 79–100. "Abbréviations employées dans le classement des monuments" v. 1, p. 432–33; "Essai de classement des fresques des catacombes de Rome et de Naples" v. 1, p. 529–88. General tables of contents v. 2, p. 657–75.

530

Lethaby, William Richard. Medieval art, from the peace of the church to the eve of the Renaissance, 312–1350. Rev. by D. Talbot Rice. London, N.Y., Nelson [1949]. 223 p. illus. 25 cm.

Lethaby's original work of 1904, rev. and brought up to date by D. Talbot Rice. A standard survey of the subject with many plans and diagrams in the text. Index p. 215–23.

531

Lowrie, Walter. Art in the early church. [N.Y.] Pantheon [1947]. 268 p. plates, plans. 27 cm.

Based on the author's earlier work, *Monuments of the early church*, 1901 (532), but does not entirely supersede the first work and lacks some of its merit.

"Select bibliography" p. 233–43. Index p. 247–58; Chronological table p. 259–68.

532

Lowrie, Walter. Monuments of the early church . . . London, N.Y., Macmillan, 1923. 432 p. illus. 21 cm. (Handbooks of archaeology and antiquities)

Published also under title: *Christian art and archaeology*. Originally published 1901 and reprinted 1923.

Contents: (1) Introduction; (2) Christian cemeteries; (3) Christian architecture; (4) Pictorial art (painting, sculpture, mosaics, and miniatures); (5) The minor arts; (6) Civil and ecclesiastical dress. "Select bibliography," p. 415–26, is annotated. Index p. 427–32.

533

Marucchi, Orazio. . . . Éléments d'archéologie chrétienne . . . Paris, Rome, Desclee, Lefebvre, 1899–1903. 3 v. illus., maps, plans. 23 cm.

Old but still useful. Contents: v. 1, Notions générales; v. 2, Itinéraire des catacombs; v. 3, Basiliques et églises de Rome. Appendice: Catalogue alphabétique de toutes les églises de Rome, v. 3, p. [499]–521.

"Auteurs à consulter" v. 1, p. [xiii]–xiv. Volume 1 has an alphabetical index (p. 349–92); other two volumes have only tables of contents.

534

Marucchi, Orazio. Manual of Christian archaeology . . . 4th Italian ed., rev. by Giulio Belvederi . . . Roma, 1933; translated and adapted by Hubert Vecchierello. Paterson, N.J., St. Anthony Guild Press, Franciscan Monastery, 1935. 448 p. illus. (incl. plans, facsims.) 24 cm.

1st Italian ed. 1905. "This manual was composed particularly for classroom use."—*Pref.*

Contents: Foundations of Christian archaeology—A brief synopsis of the history of the persecutions; Preliminary ideas on the ancient Christian cemeteries; Christian epigraphy; Ancient Christian art; Christian basilicas. "Footnotes" p. 391–431; "Principal works to be consulted in a study of Christian archaeology" p. 434–37. Index p. 438–48.

535

Monuments de l'art byzantin. Paris, Leroux, 1899–(1927). plates. 40 cm.

Five volumes issued 1899–1927. Useful for large plates. Examples: (4) Diehl, Charles. *Les monuments chrétiens de Salonique,* 1918; (5) Millet, Gabriel. *Les monuments de l'Athos,* 1927.

536

Morey, Charles Rufus. Early Christian art; an outline of the evolution of style and iconography in sculpture and painting from antiquity to the eighth century. [2d ed.] Princeton, Princeton Univ. Press, 1953. 296 p. illus. 31 cm.

A standard work, first published 1941. The second edition includes a discussion of the frescoes of S. Maria di Castelseprio, as well as minor corrections and alterations of the original text; the notes and bibliography are brought up to date. Architecture and textiles are not included. Illustrated with collotype plates.

Bibliographical abbreviations p. 200; Bibliographical references included in "Notes" p. 201–32. Index p. 235–58; Description of the illustrations p. 261–96.

537

Morey, Charles Rufus. Medieval art . . . N.Y., Norton [1942]. 412 p. illus., plates. 26 cm.

A general treatment by a recognized scholar. Contents: (1) Introduction; (2) Early

Christian art; (3) Byzantine art; (4) Romanesque art; (5) High Gothic art; (6) Late Gothic art. "Reading list" p. [393]–96. Index p. 399–412.

538
Peirce, Hayford, and Tyler, Royall. L'art byzantin . . . Paris, Librairie de France, 1932–34. 2 v. illus., 408 plates. 33 cm.
Covers the Roman Empire from the beginning of the 4th century A.D. through the 6th century. Does not include architecture. Each volume has a summary text covering the various techniques, scholarly notes describing the plates, a chronological resumé of the period, and a historical map.
"Liste des ouvrages consultés pour le présent volume": v. 1, p. 112–[113]; v. 2, p. 144–47.

539
Rice, David Talbot. Byzantine art. Oxford, Clarendon Press, 1935. 255 p. illus., 48 plates, 5 maps, plans. 21 cm.
"Aims to give a general outline of Byzantine art, of all that it stood for, of all that it led to, and of what it was derived from."—*Pref.* Intended for the general reader and the student. Illustrated by line drawings as well as plates and maps.
Bibliography at end of each chapter. "Table of dates" p. [239]–42. Index p. [245]–55.

540
Rossi, Giovanni Battista de. La Roma sotterranea cristiana, descritta ed illustrata dal cav. G. B. de Rossi, pub. per ordine della sanità di n.s. papa Pio Nono . . . Roma, Cromolitografia Pontificia, 1864–77. 3 v. illus., plates (part col.), fold. plans and atlas. 37 cm.
A large pioneer work on the catacombs and early Christian activities of Rome, amply illustrated. "Analise geologica ed architettonic diciarata da Michele Stefano de Rossi" at end of each volume.

541
Rostovt͡sev, Mīkhaīl Īvanovīch. Dura-Europos and its art. Oxford, Clarendon Press, 1938. 162 p. illus., plates, map, plan. 25 cm.
A short survey of the history and topography of Dura-Europos and its art. General bibliography p. [135]. Index p. [153]–62.

542
Strzygowski, Josef. L'ancien art chrétien de Syrie, son caractère et son évolution d'après les découvertes de Vogüé et de l'expédition de Princeton; la façade de Mschatta et le calice d'Antioche; étude préliminaire de Gabriel Millet; ouvrage honoré d'une subvention du Ministère de l'Éducation Nationale et illustré de 24 planches phototypiques et de 122 gravures. Paris, Boccard, 1936. lii, 215 p. illus. (incl. maps), 42 plates on 25 l., fold. plan. 33 cm.
Translated by Christian Sénéchal. A discussion of early Christian art in Syria by a recognized scholar; now somewhat out of date.
"Répertoire des monuments par Henri Stern" p. [203]–05 serves as a subject index. "Table des figures" p. [209]–11 and "Table des matières" p. [213]–15.

543
Swarzenski, Hanns. Monuments of Romanesque art; the art of church treasures in north-western Europe. Chicago, Univ. of Chicago Press [1954]. v. 1. 102 p. 238 plates. 32 cm.
A collection of excellent illustrations of important monuments in ivory, gold, bronze, enamel, and manuscript painting in north-western Europe from 800 to 1200, with a short introduction and a catalog of the plates, by a recognized scholar.
Bibliographies included in "Notes on the plates" p. 37–85. Indexes: Iconography p. 86–91; Names p. 92–93; Places of origin p. 94–96; Present locations p. 97–100; Materials and techniques p. 101.

544
Wulff, Oskar K. Altchristliche und byzantinische Kunst von ihren Anfängen bis zur Mitte des ersten Jahrtausends. Berlin-Neubabelsberg, Akademische Verlagsgesellschaft Athenaion [c1918]. 2 v. illus., plates (part col.) 29 cm.
Continuous pagination. A standard reference work. Contents: v. 1, Die altchristlicher Kunst von ihren Anfängen bis zur Mitte des ersten Jahrhunderts; v. 2, Die byzantinische Kunst von der ersten Blüte bis zu ihren Ausgang.
Includes bibliographies. Index of subjects p. 617–25; Index of historical names p. 625–26; Geographical index p. 626–29; Index of plates p. [631]–32.
———. Bibliographisch-kritischer Nachtrag zu Altchristliche und byzantinische Kunst von Dr. Oskar Wulff . . . Potsdam, Akademische Verlagsgesellschaft Athenaion [1939]. 88 p. illus. (incl. plans). 29 cm.
Index of subjects and names p. 86–87; Geographical index p. 87–88.

Renaissance—Modern

545
Alvard, Julien. Témoignages pour l'art abstrait, 1952. Paris, Éditions d'Aujourd'hui, 1952. 295 p. 208 illus., 30 plates (27 col.) 24 cm.

"Introduction de Léon Degand. Propos recueillis par Julien Alvard et R. V. Gindertael."—*Title Page*. A compendium of photographs and color reproductions of the works of 34 abstract artists, arranged alphabetically by name. Includes short biographies, theoretical writings, and portraits.

546
Benesch, Otto. The art of the Renaissance in northern Europe; its relation to the contemporary spiritual and intellectual movements . . . Cambridge, Harvard Univ. Press, 1945. 174 p. plates, facsims., diagrs. 24 cm.

Reprinted 1947. "First presented to the public in a series of lectures delivered at the Lowell Institute in Boston in March 1944."—*Pref.*

A good survey of Northern painting. Bibliographical references in "Notes" p. 145–61. Index p. 165–74.

547
Cheney, Sheldon. Expressionism in art. Rev. ed. N.Y., Tudor [1948]. 415 p. illus. 25 cm.

1st ed. 1934. Rev. ed. has "20 new illustrations along with numerous text corrections and added footnotes."—*Verso of Title Page*. Attempts to analyze the characteristic elements of expressionist art. Index p. 413–15.

548
Cheney, Sheldon. A primer of modern art; with 179 illustrations. 7th ed. rev. and enl., with 44 new illustrations and an added bibliography. N.Y., Liveright [1932]. 383 p. illus. 24 cm.

1st ed. 1924. A popular attempt to explain modern art and some of its schools. Now somewhat out of date. Bibliography p. 369–70. Index p. 379–83.

549
Cheney, Sheldon. The story of modern art. N.Y., Viking, 1945. 643 p. illus. 25 cm.

First published 1941. "This book is a narrative account of the development of the art that is in the mid-twentieth century called modern."—*Foreword.*

A popular treatment, which covers only painting. Index p. 631–43.

550
Pevsner, Nikolaus. Pioneers of modern design from William Morris to Walter Gropius. [2d ed.] N.Y., Museum of Modern Art [1949]. 151 p. illus. 26 cm.

1st ed. published in 1936; has title: *Pioneers of the modern movement from William Morris to Walter Gropius.*

A basic attempt to chronicle the founders and foundations of modern architecture and art in the 19th century. Bibliographical references included in "Notes" p. 136–45.

551
Read, Herbert Edward. Surrealism . . . edited with an introduction by Herbert Read, contributions by André Breton, Hugh Sykes Davies, Paul Éluard, George Hugnet. N.Y., Harcourt, Brace, 1936. 251 p. illus. 21 cm.

Contents: Introduction, by Herbert Read; Limits not frontiers of surrealism, by André Breton; Surrealism at this time and place, by Hugh S. Davies; Poetic evidence, by Paul Éluard; 1870 to 1936, by George Hugnet.

552
Wölfflin, Heinrich. Principles of art history; the problem of the development of style in later art. Trans. by M. D. Hottinger. London, Bell, 1932. 237 p. incl. illus. plates. 26 cm.

1st German ed. 1915. "English translation made from the 7th German edition of *Kunstgeschichtlichen Grundbegriffe.*" A reprint edition was issued about 1950 (N.Y., Dover), and the book is now available in a paperback edition.

Although this is not strictly speaking a reference book, it has become a milestone in art historical writing and is primarily important for the understanding of the baroque.

Contents: (1) Linear and painterly; (2) Plane and recession; (3) Closed and open form; (4) Multiplicity and unity; (5) Clearness and unclearness.

SEE ALSO: Documents of modern art (2409); N.Y. Museum of Modern Art. Publications (2456).

Primitive

553
Adam, Leonhard. Primitive art. Rev. and enl. ed. Harmondsworth, Middlesex, Penguin Books [1949]. 271 p. illus., 32 plates on 16 l. 19 cm. (Pelican books, A67)

A general survey extending into questionably related fields, such as prehistoric, art of children, and of the insane. Illustrated by line drawings in the text and small illustrations on rotogravure plates.

Bibliography included in "Notes" p. 248–60. Index p. 261–71.

554

Appleton, LeRoy H. Indian art of the Americas. N.Y., Scribner [1950]. 279 p. 79 col. plates, maps. 32 cm.

Bibliography p. 265–70. Index to stories p. 271–74; to plates p. 275–77. Sources of the plates p. 278–79.

555

Basler, Adolphe. L'art chez les peuples primitifs: Afrique—Océanie—Archipel Malais—Amérique et terres arctiques. Styles et civilisations. Paris, Librairie de France, 1929. 83 p. 106 plates on 53 l. 28 cm.

An early general survey of primitive art. Good clear plates. Bibliography p. 79–83, arranged by geographical location.

556

Boas, Franz. Primitive art . . . Cambridge, Harvard Univ. Press, 1927. 376 p. illus., 15 plates. 24 cm.

Reprinted in paperback edition 1955 (N.Y., Dover). A basic book on the subject with major emphasis on the Northwest coast.

Contents: (1) Introduction; (2) The formal elements in art; (3) Representative art; (4) Symbolism; (5) Style; (6) The art of the Northwest coast of North America; (7) Primitive literature, music and dance. No index but a list of illustrations and plates and a table of contents.

557

Brown, Gerard Baldwin. The art of the cave dweller; a study of the earliest artistic activities of man . . . London, Murray, 1928. 280 p. illus., plates (1 col.), maps. 24 cm.

1st ed. 1928; a cheaper ed. 1932. Particular emphasis on the art rather than on prehistoric archaeology. Index p. 275–80.

558

Buck, Peter Henry. Arts and crafts of Hawaii. [Honolulu] Bishop Museum Press, 1957. 606 p. illus., 7 tables. 27 cm. (Bernice P. Bishop Museum, Special publication 45)

The first comprehensive publication on the arts and crafts of Hawaii, by the eminent Polynesian scholar Te Rangi Hiroa. Bibliography p. 581–85. Index p. 587–606.

559

Chauvet, Stephen. Les arts indigènes en Nouvelle-Guinée. Paris, Société d'Éditions Géographiques, Maritimes et Coloniales, 1930. 350 p. illus., 114 plates on 57 l., map. 33 cm.

A standard and generally comprehensive work on New Guinea, illustrated by good collotypes. Bibliography p. [314]–16.

560

Drucker, Philip. Indians of the Northwest coast. [N.Y.] Published for the American Museum of Natural History [by] McGraw-Hill [c1955]. 208 p. illus., map. 24 cm. ([American Museum of Natural History, N.Y.] Anthropological handbook, no. 10)

Covers economy, material culture, society, religion, ceremonials, cycle of life, art, sub-areas, and cultural relationships. Well illustrated.

Bibliography p. 197–99. Index p. 201–08.

561

Firth, Raymond William. Art and life in New Guinea . . . London & N.Y., Studio [1936]. 126 p. incl. illus., plates. 26 cm.

A nontechnical book but extremely useful for its numerous magnificent plates. "Select bibliography" p. 126.

562

Kidder, Alfred Vincent. An introduction to the study of southwestern archaeology with a preliminary account of the excavations at Pecos. New Haven, Yale Univ. Press, 1924. 151 p. illus. (incl. maps), 50 plates. 29 cm. (Papers of the Southwestern expedition, no. 1)

At head of title: Dept. of Archaeology, Phillips Academy, Andover, Mass. A standard, though old, work with good illustrations. Bibliography p. [137]–51.

563

Kühn, Herbert. Die Kunst der Primitiven . . . mit zweihundert-fünfzehn Abbildungen. München. Delphin, 1920. 240 p. illus., 215 plates (part col.) 27 cm.

Gives a short account of paleolithic art, the rock pictures in northwestern America and of the Neolithic and Bronze Ages in Europe, the art of Negro Africa, and of Benin. An attempt to theorize on primitive art on the basis of two types of economy, that of the food gatherer and that of the sedentary agrarian. The art is often forced to fit into the theory.

Bibliography p. 178–222. Index of illustrations p. 223–43; of names p. 244–46.

564

Lowie, Robert Harry. Indians of the plains. N.Y., Published for the American Museum of Natural History [by] McGraw-Hill [1954]. 222 p. illus., map. 24 cm. ([American Museum of Natural History, N.Y.] Anthropological handbook, no. 1)

Well illustrated. Contents: (1) Introduction; (2) Material culture; (3) Social organization; (4) Recreation; (5) Art; (6) Supernaturalism; (7) Prehistory and history; (8) Acculturation; (9) Conclusion.

Bibliography p. 205–07. Index p. 209–22.

565

Luquiens, Huc Mazelet. Hawaiian art . . . Honolulu, Hawaii, The Museum, 1931. 59 p. illus., plates. 24 cm. (Bernice P. Bishop Museum, Special publication 18)

An account of Hawaiian art written by an American painter-etcher after a prolonged residence in the islands. Although it is not strictly a reference book it is the only volume covering this field.

566

Osborn, Henry Fairfield. Men of the old stone age, their environment, life and art . . . illustrations by upper palaeolithic artists and Charles R. Knight, Erwin S. Christman and others. 3d ed. N.Y., Scribner, 1934. 559 p. 2 plates, maps. 24 cm.

Originally published 1915; 3d ed. 1918, often reprinted. A standard book on the subject but now rather out of date. Bibliography p. 527–46. Index p. 549–59.

567

Spearing, Herbert Green. The childhood of art; or, The ascent of man; a sketch of the vicissitudes of his upward struggle, based chiefly on the relics of his artistic work in prehistoric times . . . [2d and rev. ed.] London, Benn [1930]. 2 v. illus., plates (part col.), map, tab. 26 cm.

First published 1912. Continuous pagination. A now obsolete book on the subject, whose chief value lies in its drawings and illustrations. Covers palaeolithic cave art, early Egyptian, early Chaldean, Cretan, and Greek art.

Bibliography v. 2, p. 537–40. Index v. 2, p. 541–48.

568

Sydow, Eckhart von. Die Kunst der Naturvölker und der Vorzeit . . . Berlin, Propyläen-Verlag, 1923. 569 p. illus. (part col.), 24 plates (part col.) 29 cm.

The earliest one-volume publication on primitive art and still a very useful general book. Contents: (1) Die Kunst der Naturvölker; (2) Die altamerikanischen Kulturvölker; (3) Europäische Vorgeschichte; (4) Die nordgermanische Kunst der Völkerwanderungs- und Wikinger-Zeit.

List of illustrations, p. 493–550, gives size. "Literatur- und Quellenverzeichnis" p. 551–58. Index p. 559–69.

569

Tischner, Herbert. Oceanic art. 96 photos by Friedrich Hewicker. [N.Y.] Pantheon [1954]. 32 p. 96 plates. 31 cm.

Map on lining paper. Mostly a picture book with 11 pages of text and 10 pages of notes on the plates, giving size. Excellent clear, full-page plates of superb examples of Oceanic art.

Bibliography p. 17–20.

570

Vaillant, George C. Indian arts in North America . . . N.Y. and London, Harper, 1939. 63 p. 96 plates (incl. map). 27 cm.

Although limited in scope and brief in treatment, this remains one of the solid books on American Indian art. Contains 52 pages of general introductory text and then for each plate gives name of object, region from which it came, culture, period, size, location, and museum number.

Selected bibliography p. 55–63, arranged by chapters.

571

Wingert, Paul Stover. Art of the South Pacific islands. London, Thames and Hudson; N.Y., Beechhurst Press [1953]. 64 p. illus., 50 plates, maps. 26 cm.

A general summary of the field by a recognized authority. The material first appeared in the catalog of the loan exhibition of the art of the South Pacific islands, held at the De Young Memorial Museum, San Francisco, Sept. 18–Nov. 15, 1953.

Bibliography p. 46.

572

Wingert, Paul Stover. An outline guide to the art of the South Pacific. N.Y., Columbia Univ. Press, 1946. 61 p. plates, maps. 24 cm.

"Brief sections give as an introduction to each major area and island group historical and geographical data, a description of the natives and the distinctive elements of the culture. These are followed by a comprehensive listing of the art forms, for which physical facts, meaning and function are included. In some cases where beliefs and customs have a direct bearing on the character of the art these are also briefly discussed or defined."—*Pref.*

Plates give size of objects. "Selected bibliography" p. [45]–57. "South Pacific art in American museums" p. [59]–60. "Sources for reproductions" p. 60–61.

573

Wissler, Clark. The American Indian, an introduction to the anthropology of the New World. 3d ed. N.Y., Smith, 1950. 466 p. illus., plates, maps, diagrs. 21 cm.

1st ed. 1917; 3d ed. 1938. "Linguistic tables and bibliography" p. [389]–439.

National

Australia

574

Moore, William. The story of Australian art, from the earliest known art of the continent to the art of today. Sydney, Australia, Angus & Robertson, 1934. 2 v. illus., plates (part col.) 26 cm.

A general history of Australian art. "Dictionary of Australian artists, including the names of benefactors" v. 2, p. 155–234. Index to both volumes at end of v. 2.

Canada

575

Colgate, William G. Canadian art, its origin and development. Toronto, Ryerson [c1943]. 278 p. illus., col. plate. 26 cm.

Running title: *Canadian art 1820–1940.* Foreword by Charles W. Jeffery. A general survey of the development of art in Canada.

List of "Canadian, British, and French contemporaries" with their dates p. 263–65. Bibliography p. 267–70. Index p. 271–78.

576

McInnes, Graham. Canadian art. Toronto, Macmillan, 1950. 140 p. illus. (part col.) 27 cm.

Rev. and expanded ed.; 1st ed. 1939 titled *A short history of Canadian art.* It "attempts to be brief and general rather than detailed and diffuse."—*Foreword.* Includes painting, sculpture, and the allied arts.

Appendices: A, Art institutions and public art collections (arranged geographically) p. 115–16; B, Chronology p. 117–19; C, Select list of Canadian artists with dates p. 120–25. Select bibliography p. 126–31. Index p. 133–40.

577

MacTavish, Newton. The fine arts in Canada . . . Toronto, Macmillan, 1925. 181 p. illus., plates (part col.) 26 cm.

A general treatment of the subject, with ten of the 24 chapters devoted to individual artists. List of illustrations p. xi–xiii, arranged alphabetically by artist. No index.

France

578

Bréhier, Louis. L'art en France des invasions barbares à l'époque romane . . . Paris, La Renaissance du Livre [1930]. 210 p. plates, facsims. 20 cm. (À travers l'art français)

A general study covering early French art—Merovingian and Carolingian—including architecture, sculpture, mosaics, illuminated manuscripts, metalwork, etc.

"Bibliographie sommaire" p. [207]–08. No index.

580

Enlart, Camille. Manuel d'archéologie française depuis les temps mérovingiens jusqu'à la renaissance. 2d ed. rev. Paris, Picard, 1919–32. 3 v. in 5. illus., plates, plans. 23 cm.

A manual of French archaeology from Merovingian times to the Renaissance. Contents: t. 1, Architecture religieuse: pt. 1, Périodes mérovingienne, carolingienne et romane (1919); pt. 2, Période française, dite gothique, style flamboyant, renaissance (3d ed. rev., 1929); pt. 3, Table alphabétique et analytique des matières; t. 2, Architecture civile et militaire (1929): pt. 1, Architecture civile; pt. 2, Architecture militaire et navale, par Jean Verrier (2d ed. rev. & augm., 1932). Bibliography with each chapter.

"Répertoire d'églises romanes" v. 1, p. 434–54, arranged alphabetically by department. "Répertoire archéologique de l'architecture monastique, civile et militaire des départements" v. 2, pt. 3, p. [713]–870. "Glossaire des termes spéciaux à l'architecture militaire et à l'architecture navale" v. 2, pt. 2, p. 871–80.

Volume 1, pt. 3 contains: Table alphabétique et analytique des matières p. 3–40; Répertoire alphabétique et analytique des localités et monuments p. [41–164]; Erratum à la 2e éd. p. 165–80. Volume 2, pt. 1 contains: Index alphabétique p. 881–923.

581

Evans, Joan. Art in medieval France, 987–1498. London, N.Y., Oxford Univ. Press, 1948. 317 p. [281] plates, fold. map, plans. 28 cm.

2d impression [1952]. A scholarly treatment of this general subject, well-illustrated with halftones of excellent quality. Map inside back end papers shows location of all the cities mentioned.

"List of books consulted" p. [293]–300. Index p. 303–17.

582

Fontainas, André; Vauxcelles, Louis; and Mourey, Gabriel. Histoire générale de l'art français de la révolution à nos jours. Paris, Librairie de France [1922]. 3 v. illus., plates (part col.) 33 cm.

Volume 2 also by Georges Gromort; v. 3 by Gabriel Mourey. A general history of French art from the Revolution to our times.

Volume 1 covers painting, engraving, and drawing; v. 2, architecture and sculpture; v. 3, decorative art. Table of contents at end of each volume. No bibliographies or indexes.

583

Réau, Louis. Histoire de l'expansion de l'art français . . . Paris, Laurens, 1924–33. [v. 1, 1933] 3 v. in 4. plates. 25 cm.

Covers French art in other countries, from the Renaissance to the present day. Mentions that Dussieux (235) is full of inaccuracies. Each volume contains a section called "Documents" which includes names of foreign artists belonging to the Academy, as well as other documents.

Contents: v. 1, Le monde latin—Italie, Espagne, Portugal, Roumanie, Amérique du Sud; v. 2, pt. 1, Belgique et Hollande, Suisse, Allemagne et Autriche, Bohème et Hongrie (1928); v. 2, pt. 2, Pays scandinaves, Angleterre, Amérique du Nord (1931); v. 3, Le monde slave et l'Orient (1924).

Includes bibliographies. Each volume contains an alphabetical index.

584

Roy, Maurice. Artistes et monuments de la renaissance en France; recherches nouvelles et documents inédits. Paris, Champion, 1929–34. 2 v. illus., plates. 29 cm.

At head of title: Ouvrage publié sous le patronage de la Société de l'Histoire de l'Art

Français. Volume 2 was published after the death of the author and edited by Adrien Blanchet (Paris, Picard). Continuously paged.

A scholarly work attempting to correct previous errors and throw new light on the art history of the period by means of original and unpublished documents from the national and departmental archives.

"Bibliographie des travaux de M. Maurice Roy" v. 2, p. [577]–82. "Index général" v. 2, p. 583–624.

585

Schneider, René. L'art français . . . Paris, Laurens, 1925–30. 6 v. illus., plans, diagrs. 22 cm. (Les patries de l'art)

Popular rather than scholarly. Contents: v. 1, Moyen âge: origines—art roman—art gothique du XIIIe siècle; v. 2, Fin du moyen âge—renaissance; v. 3, XVIIe siècle (1610–1690); v. 4, XVIIIe siècle (1690–1789); v. 5, XIXe siècle: du classicisme Davidien au romantisme; v. 6, XIXe et XXe siècles: du réalisme à notre temps.

Extensive bibliography and table of contents at end of each volume. Indexes of artists at ends of v. 3 and 4.

SEE ALSO: Dussieux. Les artistes français à l'étranger (235).

Germany and Austria

586

Dehio, Georg Gottfried. Geschichte der deutschen Kunst . . . Berlin und Leipzig, 1923–34. 3. Aufl. 4 v. *and* atlas of plates. Plans. 28 cm.

A standard German history of German art covering from the beginnings through the 19th and 20th centuries. Comprises four volumes of text and four plate volumes. Each of the eight volumes has its separate index. The fourth volume, covering the 19th and 20th centuries, is by Gustav Pauli.

587

Dehio, Georg Gottfried. Handbuch der deutschen Kunstdenkmäler, begründet vom Tag für Denkmalpflege. Berlin, Deutscher Kunstverlag, 1925–28. 5 v. 19 cm.

At head of title: Deutscher Verein für Kunstwissenschaft, Georg Dehio. An important topographical series. Each volume contains a place index and an index of artists.

Contents: Bd. 1, Mitteldeutschland, 3.

Aufl., 1927; Bd. 2, Nordostdeutschland, 3. Aufl., 1926; Bd. 3, Süddeutschland, 3. Aufl., 1925; Bd. 4, Südwestdeutschland im Anhang Elsass-Lothringen und die deutsche Schweiz, 2. Aufl., 1926; Bd. 5, Nordwestdeutschland, 2. Aufl., 1928.

588

Dehio, Georg Gottfried. Handbuch der deutschen Kunstdenkmäler, begründet vom Tag für Denkmalpflege. 2. Abteilung: Österreich . . . Berlin, Deutscher Kunstverlag, 1933–(35). v. 1–(2). maps, plans. 19 cm.

At head of title: Deutscher Verein für Kunstwissenschaft, Georg Dehio. The second section of the important Dehio topographical handbook, dealing with Austria.

Contents: Bd. 1, Die Kunstdenkmäler in Kärnten, Salzburg, Steiermark, Tirol und Vorarlberg, hrsg. von Dagobert Frey und Karl Ginhart. Bd. 2, Wien, Niederösterreich, Oberösterreich und Burgenland, hrsg. von Dagobert Frey und Karl Ginhart.

589

Dehio, Georg Gottfried. Handbuch der deutschen Kunstdenkmäler, Neu bearb. von Ernst Gall. München, Deutscher Kunstverlag, 1954–(56). v. 1–(3). illus., maps, plans. 19 cm.

A postwar edition of this important topographical work, including monuments damaged in the war.

Contents: Bd. [1] Östliches Schwaben, von Ernst Gall; Bd. [2] Südliches Hessen, 2. verb. Aufl. Bearb. unter Mitwirkung von M. Herchenröder, O. Müller, G. Tiemann, H. Walbe, H. K. Zimmermann; Bd. [3] Westliches Schwaben, von Ernst Gall.

590

Deutsche Kunstgeschichte. München, Bruckmann, 1942–(56). 6 v. illus., col. plates. 27 cm.

A well-illustrated modern history of German art, also known as "Bruckmanns Deutsche Kunstgeschichte." Each volume has its own index.

Contents: (1) Hempel, Eberhard. Geschichte der deutschen Baukunst, 1949, 2d ed., 1956; (2) Müller, Theodor. Geschichte der deutschen Plastik, 1952; (3) Fischer, Otto, and Feulner, A. Geschichte der deutschen Malerei, 3d ed., 1956; (4) Fischer, Otto. Geschichte des deutschen Zeichnung und Graphik, 1951; (5) Kohlhaussen, Heinrich. Geschichte des deutschen Kunsthandwerkes, 1955; (6) Roh, Franz. Die Kunst des 20. Jahrhunderts, 1958.

591

Geschichte der deutschen Kunst . . . Berlin, Grote, 1887–91. 5 v. plates, plans. 29 cm.

A standard history of German art, now somewhat old. Each volume has its own indexes.

Contents: Bd. 1, Geschichte der deutschen Baukunst von Robert Dohme; Bd. 2, Geschichte der deutschen Plastik von W. Bode; Bd. 3, Geschichte der deutschen Malerei von H. Janitschek; Bd. 4, Geschichte des deutschen Kupferstiches und Holzschnittes von Carl von Lützow; Bd. 5, Geschichte des deutschen Kunstgewerbes von Jakob von Falke.

592

Österreichische Kunsttopographie. [n.s.] Bd. 1–(31). Wien, In Kommission bei A. Schroll, 1907–(51). illus., plates, maps, plans. 28–32 cm.

Published by Institut für Österreichische Kunstforschung des Bundesdenkmalamtes (varies). Editors: Max Dvorak and Dagobert Frey. Each volume has a special title page and bibliography.

A great monographic inventory, by region and monument, of Austrian architectural and art treasures. Thoroughly illustrated and indexed.

593

Picton, Harold W. Early German art and its origins, from the beginnings to about 1050 . . . London, Batsford [1939]. 148 p. illus. (incl. plans), plates. 27 cm.

With a foreword by Prof. Josef Strzygowski. The material is treated by medium, i.e., building, ornament, painting, bone, ivory, goldsmithing, etc.

Bibliographical footnotes. Index p. 148.

594

Pinder, Wilhelm. Vom Wesen und Werden deutscher Formen; geschichtliche Betrachtungen . . . Leipzig, Seemann [c1937–51]. v. 1–4 in 5. illus., plates, plans. 23 cm.

A new edition, edited by Georg Scheja, was published in 1957, with four volumes of text and three volumes of plates (Frankfort, Hans F. Menck Verlag).

Each volume has also a special title page. Volume 1 has a separate volume of plates. A sound, well-illustrated history of German art.

Contents: Bd. 1, Die Kunst der deutschen Kaiserzeit bis zum Ende der staufischen Klassik, 2 v.; Bd. 2, Die Kunst der ersten Bürgerzeit bis zur Mitte des 15. Jahrhunderts; Bd.

3, Die deutsche Kunst der Dürerzeit; Bd. 4, Holbein der Jüngere und das Ende der altdeutschen Kunst. No indexes.

595
Weigert, Hans. Geschichte der deutschen Kunst von der Vorzeit bis zur Gegenwart . . . Berlin, Propyläen-Verlag [1942]. 1010 p. illus. (incl. maps, plans, facsims.), 16 col. plates, diagrs. 27 cm.

A one-volume history of German art from its early beginnings to the present day. Bibliography p. 951–[58]. Index of names and subjects p. 959–1008.

Great Britain

596
Brown, Gerard Baldwin. The arts in early England . . . London, Murray, 1903–37. 6 v. in 7. illus., plates, maps, plans, tables. 24 cm.

Reprinted in part from *The Builder*. Contents: v. 1, The life of Saxon England in its relation to the arts; v. 2, Ecclesiastical architecture in England from the conversion of the Saxons to the Norman conquest; Appendix, Index list, and map of Saxon churches; v. 3–4, Saxon art and industry in the pagan period (2 v.); v. 5, The Ruthwell and Bewcastle crosses, the Gospels of Lindisfarne and other Christian monuments of Northumbria; v. 6, pt. 1, Completion of the study of the monuments of the great period of the art of Anglican Northumbria; v. 6, pt. 2, Anglo-Saxon sculpture, prepared for press by E. H. L. Sexton.

Each volume has its own index.

597
Finlay, Ian. Art in Scotland. London, Oxford Univ. Press, 1948. 180 p. plates (1 col.) 22 cm.

"My purpose in this book has been to piece together the significant trends, the Scottish trends, of art in Scotland."—*Pref.* A general survey, from the "Celtic ascendancy" to the contemporary movement. Index p. 175–80.

598
Graves, Algernon. Summary of and index to Waagen. London, Pub. by A. Graves, 1912. 366 p. 29 cm.

125 copies printed. An index to Waagen, *Treasures of art in Great Britain* (606). An "easy reference to the page on which the picture is described or criticised and to those who have not got the work it will be useful in giving the titles of the pictures and owners' names at the time when Dr. Waagen

wrote."—*Pref.* All of the pictures mentioned in Waagen (over 9000), including the collections of King Charles I and the Orleans Gallery, are included in the summary. Part 2 is a list of those pictures mentioned by Waagen in his tour of 1835 and not repeated in the later work, p. 277–94. Part 3 is a special index of all the 1130 portraits mentioned by Waagen, p. 295–352, followed by an index of owners, p. 353–66.

Summary is arranged alphabetically by artist, under which are listed titles of the paintings, page references to Waagen, and the owners.

599
Henry, Françoise. Irish art in the early Christian period. . . . With 80 collotype plates and numerous text illustrations. London, Methuen [1940]. 220 p. 55 illus., 80 plates. 23 cm.

"This book is not a history of art in Ireland but a study of Irish art wherever it flourished."—*Pref.* A scholarly work, similar in format to Kendrick's *Anglo-Saxon art* (600).

Bibliographical footnotes; "Index of bibliographical abbreviations" p. 205–08. General index p. 209–20.

600
Kendrick, Thomas Downing. Anglo-Saxon art to A.D. 900 . . . London, Methuen [1938]. 227 p. illus., 104 plates. 23 cm.

A historical survey of early art in Britain by a recognized scholar. Based on lectures given at the Courtauld Institute. Index p. 223–27.

601
Kendrick, Thomas Downing. Late Saxon and Viking art. London, Methuen [1949]. 152 p. 21 illus., 96 plates. 22 cm.

A continuation of his work, *Anglo-Saxon art* (600), the two books together "forming a fairly complete account of the foundations of the English Medieval style."—*Pref.* of *Anglo-Saxon art*. Index p. 149–52.

602
Mahr, Adolf. Christian art in ancient Ireland . . . Dublin, Stationery Office, 1932–(41). 2 v. 130 plates. 37 cm.

Does not "aim at an exhaustive treatment of its subject" (*Introd.*), but consists of 130 plates which are a representative selection of material in various museums.

Chronological framework: (1) Vernacular Keltic Style from the 7th century to the end of the 8th century; (2) The Hiberno-Viking

Style from 850–1000; (3) The last Animal Style in Ireland, 1000–1125; (4) Hiberno-Romanesque Style, 1125 till Anglo-Norman conquest.

Volume 1 contains List of plates, Introduction, and 80 plates; v. 2 contains 3 chapters of text by A. Mahr and Harold G. Leash, Notes on sculptural and architectural plates, Description and chronological notes by Joseph Raftery, Plates 81–130.

Bibliography v. 2, p. [169]–76. Chronological list v. 2, p. 177. Index v. 2, p. 179–84.

603

The Oxford history of English art, ed. by T. S. R. Boase. [Oxford, Clarendon Press, 1949–(57)] illus., plates, plans. 25 cm.

To be completed in 11 volumes, each written by a specialist in the field. Contains bibliography and index.

Now published: v. 2, D. T. Rice, *English art, 871–1100*, 1952; v. 3, T. S. R. Boase, *English art, 1100–1216*, 1953; v. 4, P. Brieger, *English art, 1216–1307*, 1957; v. 5, J. Evans, *English art, 1307–1461*, 1949; v. 8, M. Whinney and O. Millar, *English art, 1625–1714*, 1957.

604

Saunders, O. Elfrida. History of English art in the Middle Ages . . . Oxford, Clarendon Press, 1932. 272 p. plates. 21 cm.

Preface by Tancred Borenius. The author's attention is limited "to those branches of art which include figure-representation and . . . leave out . . . purely decorative work."—*Foreword*. Covers wall painting, sculpture, illumination, and embroidery. Architecture is omitted.

Contents: (1) Art before the conquest; (2) The Romanesque period; (3) The Gothic period. Includes bibliographies p. 260–62, and at ends of chapters. "Places containing works of art mentioned (arranged according to locality)" p. 263–64. Subject index p. 265–67. General index p. 268–72.

605

Stokes, Margaret MacNair. Early Christian art in Ireland . . . Dublin, Stationery Office, 1928. 2 v. in 1. illus., plates. 22 cm.

1st ed. 1887 as a "South Kensington Museum art handbook." This is a reprint. A general treatise covering illumination, metalwork, sculpture, and architecture.

"Chronological table of examples of Irish art, the date of which can be approximately fixed" p. 70. Includes bibliographies. Indexes: v. 1, p. 97–101; v. 2, p. 71–75.

606

Waagen, Gustav Friedrich. Treasures of art in Great Britain: being an account of the chief collections of paintings, drawings, sculptures, illuminated mss. . . . London, Murray, 1854. 3 v. 22 cm.

Translated from the German by Lady Eastlake. A supplementary volume published 1857 with title: *Galleries and cabinets of art in Great Britain*. Both volumes are indexed in Graves's *Summary of and index to Waagen* (598).

Written in the form of a travel diary. Valuable for locating works of art in private collections. Index v. 1, p. xiii–ix, lists all works mentioned in the text.

607

Whitley, William Thomas. Art in England, 1800–1820 . . . N.Y., Macmillan; Cambridge, Univ. Press, 1928. 344 p. 16 plates. 26 cm.

"Contemporary opinions have been gathered from newspapers and other sources on the principal pictures shown year by year at the Academy exhibitions . . . Reports of interesting actions at law connected with the arts are given, with occasional references to picture sales of importance, and an account of the hitherto unrecorded return to art criticism of the notorious Anthony Pasquin."—*Pref.*

The purpose was to add new information to what had already been published. The material is arranged by date. Index p. 321–45.

608

Whitley, William Thomas. Art in England, 1821–1837. Cambridge, Univ. Press, 1930. 371 p. plates. 26 cm.

"The present volume is intended as a continuation of my *Artists and their friends in England 1700–1799* and *Art in England 1800–1820*. Its object is to give information, additional to that already published in books on the subject, concerning the history of art in England from 1821–1837."—*Pref.*

Covers early history of the National Gallery and the efforts to found it, inner history of the Royal Academy, and comments from newspapers and magazines on pictures shown in various exhibitions. Some letters are included; also notes on some of the important art sales of the period. Arranged chronologically.

Appendix: The National Gallery—the early days in Trafalgar Square p. 345–48. Index p. 349–72.

609

Whitley, William Thomas. Artists and their friends in England 1700–1799 . . . London, The Medici Society [1928]. 2 v. plates, facsims. 26 cm.

A discussion of the history and surroundings of artists working in England between 1700 and 1799, in which the progress of the early art schools and the societies of artists arising from them are traced. Also contains material on American painters.

The information was culled from letters, anecdotes, contemporary criticisms, facts and figures, and records of all kinds concerning 18th century artists. It has been collected from many sources among which are records of the Royal Society, the Society of Arts, the old Incorporated and Free Societies of Artists, the notebooks of George Vertue, letters and manuscripts at the British Museum and the Record Office, and newspapers.

Appendix of "Identified pictures, 1760–91" v. 2, p. 367–96. Index at end of v. 2.

Italy

610

Ancona, Paolo d'. Umanesimo e rinascimento, con 16 tavole in rotocalco e 716 figure. 3. ed. riveduta e aggiornata, con la collaborazione di Maria Luisa Gengaro. Torino, Unione Tipografico-Editrice Torinese, 1948. 726 p. illus., plates. 27 cm. (Storia dell'arte classica e italiana, v. 3)

An Italian survey of humanism and Renaissance art, well-illustrated. Bibliography p. 653–82. Index of artists p. 683–90; of places and monuments p. 691–726.

611

Arslan, Edoardo. La pittura e la scultura veronese dal secolo VIII al secolo XIII, con un'appendice sull'architettura romanica veronese. Milano, Bocca, 1942. 232 p. 281 plates, plans. 23 cm. (Pubblicazioni della Facoltà di Lettere e Filosofia della R. Università di Pavia, 2)

Intended as a companion piece to the author's *Architettura romanica veronese*, 1940.

Appendix: "Nuove osservazione e aggiunto sull'architettura romanica veronese" p. 189–223. Bibliographical footnotes. Index of artists p. 225–26; of places p. 227–32.

612

Barbaroux, Vittorio E., and Giani, Giampiero. Arte italiana contemporanea . . . Prefazione di Massimo Bontempelli. Milano,

Grafico [1940]. [27] p. 150 plates (part col.), facsims. 39 cm.

2d ed. of 700 copies. A collection of very good plates, many of which are in color.

"Indice e dati biografici" (at end of volume) lists artists alphabetically, giving for each artist birth date and number of plates devoted to him. "Firma e tavolozza" gives facsimile of each artist's signature, list of colors in his palette, or (if he is a sculptor) the word *scultore*.

613

Blunt, Anthony. Artistic theory in Italy, 1450–1600. Oxford, Clarendon Press, 1940. 168 p. plates. 21 cm.

2d impression, 1957, is a reprint of the 1st ed. except for minor corrections and a few additions to the bibliography.

This book deals with artistic theory of the Italian Renaissance in its fully developed form and is thus primarily concerned with the 16th century. The theory of Alberti is the starting point, and the last three chapters discuss the Mannerist theory.

Bibliographic footnotes; Bibliography p. 160–63. Index p. 165–68.

614

Burckhardt, Jakob Christoph. Civilization of the Renaissance in Italy; an essay. [Translation by S. G. C. Middlemore] 3d ed., rev. London, N.Y., Phaidon; distributed by Oxford Univ. Press [1950]. 462 p. illus., plates. 19 cm.

Originally published 1860; many subsequent editions. A standard work on the Renaissance. Index p. 455–62.

615

Cairola, Stefano, ed. Arte italiana del nostro tempo . . . Saggi critice di Luciano Anceschi [et al.] Bergamo, Istituto Italiano d'Arti Grafiche [1946]. 119 p. 304 plates (part col.) 35 cm.

Largely a collection of plates (some colored) with a few lines of descriptive text or commentary for each plate. Text, p. 1–106, consists of a few biographical lines and a signed critical commentary, usually with a portrait of the artist. Index of plates p. 109–19.

616

Constantini, Vicenzo. Storia dell'arte italiana. Milano, Ceschina, 1945–49. 4 v. illus., plates, plans. 25 cm.

A general history of Italian art of the popular type. Small illustrations in the text.

Contents: v. 1, Arte antica; v. 2, Dalle catacombe al Gotico; v. 3, Il Rinascimento; v. 4, Dal Seicento alla contemporaneità. No footnotes, no bibliography.

All indexes are at end of v. 4 and included in the pagination, although they are divided by volume instead of being in one alphabet. First is the table of contents of v. 4 (the others are at ends of the individual volumes), followed by the indexes of artists' names and locations of the works for v. 1, then by these indexes for v. 2, 3, and 4.

617

Dvořák, Max. Geschichte der italienischen Kunst im Zeitalter der Renaissance . . . München, Piper, 1927–28. 2 v. plates, plans. 26 cm.

Edited by Johannes Wilde and Karl M. Swoboda. A standard German work on Italian Renaissance art.

Contents: Bd. 1, Das 14. und 15. Jahrhundert; Bd. 2, Das 16. Jahrhundert. Bd. 1 has 79 illustrations; Bd. 2 has 104. At end of v. 2: "Personnenregister zu Band I und II" p. 211–14; "Ortsregister zu Band I und II" p. 215–23.

618

Fokker, Timon Henricus. Roman baroque art, the history of a style . . . London, Oxford Univ. Press, Milford, 1938. 2 v. plates, plans. 30 cm.

Divided into Early, Full, and Late Baroque, then subdivided into church interiors, church facades, palaces, town planning and fountains, painting, and sculpture. Contents: v. 1, Text; v. 2, Plates (278 excellent illustrations).

Bibliography v. 1, p. [xvii]–xxii. Index of artists v. 1, p. 359–61; of popes, prelates, and other persons v. 1, p. 362–64; of works of art and localities v. 1, p. 365–68.

619

Golzio, Vincenzo. Il Seicento e il Settecento, con 14 tavole in rotocalco e 955 figure nel testo. [Torino] Unione Tipografico-Editorice Torinese [1950]. 979 p. illus. 27 cm. (Storia dell'arte classica e italiana, v. 4)

A 2-v. ed. (1292 p.) published 1955 ([Torino] U.T.E.T.). According to the preface, this is not a work of erudition but a compilation of the critical precepts of others, showing the art of the 17th and 18th centuries in its fundamental aspects.

Bibliographical appendix p. 919–26. Index of artists p. 927–39; of places and monuments p. 940–77.

620

Lavagnino, Emilio. L'arte moderna dai neoclassici ai contemporanei. [Torino] Unione Tipografico-Editrice Torinese [1956]. 2 v. illus., plates. 27 cm. (Storia dell'arte classica e italiana, v. 5 [1-2])

Paged continuously. A well-illustrated survey of 19th and 20th century Italian art. "Bibliografia essenziale" p. 1263–78. Indexes: of artists p. 1279–95; of places and monuments p. 1297–1344.

621

Lavagnino, Emilio. . . . Storia dell'arte medioevale italiana . . . Con 12 tavole in rotocalco e 898 figure nel testo. Torino, Unione Tipografico-Editrice Torinese, 1936. 803 p. illus. (incl. plans), 12 plates. 27 cm.

A well-illustrated survey of medieval Italian art. Contents: L'età paleocristiana e l'alto medioevo; L'arte romanica; Il gotico e il trecento.

"Annotazione bibliografica" p. [770]–79. Indexes: of artists p. 781–84; of places and monuments p. 785–803.

622

Ricci, Corrado. Art in northern Italy . . . London, Heinemann; N.Y., Scribner, 1911. 372 p. illus., col. plates. 19 cm. (Ars una: species mille. General history of art)

A general handbook. Illustrations (in the text) are very small. Bibliography at end of each chapter. Index p. 351–72.

623

Symonds, John Addington. Renaissance in Italy . . . N.Y., B. A. Cerf, D. S. Klopfer, Modern Library [1935]. 2 v. 21 cm. (The modern library of the world's best books)

A standard history of the Renaissance, originally published in the late 19th century. Contents: v. 1, Age of the despots: The revival of learning; The fine arts; Italian literature (chap. I–III); v. 2, Italian literature (chap. IV–XVII); The Catholic reaction.

624

Toesca, Pietro. Storia dell'arte italiana. Torino, Unione Tipografico-Editrice Torinese, 1927–[51]. 2 v. in 3. illus., plates (part col.) 28 cm. (Storia dell'arte classica e italiana [by Rizzo and Toesca] 3)

A scholarly work, well illustrated. Contains architectural plans. Contents: v. 1 (in 2 pts.), Il medioevo; v. 2, Il trecento.

Bibliographical references in notes at ends of chapters and in footnotes. At end of each volume are indexes of artists, places, and things.

625

Venturi, Adolfo. A short history of Italian art . . . translated by Edward Hutton . . . N.Y., Macmillan, 1926. 376 p. 300 illus. 21 cm.

A good, basic one-volume history of Italian art by the author of the monumental work *Storia dell'arte italiana* (626). Index p. 355–76.

626

Venturi, Adolfo. Storia dell'arte italiana . . . Milano, Hoepli, 1901–40. 11 v. in 25 pts. illus., plates. 25 cm.

The definitive history of Italian art.

Contents: v. 1, Dai primordi dell'arte cristiana al tempo di Giustiniano; v. 2, Dall'arte barbarica alla romanica; v. 3, L'arte romanica; v. 4, La scultura del trecento e le sue origini; v. 5, La pittura del trecento e le sue origini; v. 6, La scultura del quattrocento; v. 7, La pittura del quattrocento, pt. I–IV; v. 8, L'architettura del quattrocento, pt. I–II; v. 9, La pittura del cinquecento, pt. I–VII; v. 10, La scultura del cinquecento, pt. I–III; v. 11, L'architettura del cinquecento, pt. I–III.

Each volume contains a table of contents, called "Indice," a place index, and, beginning with v. 4, an index of artists. These indexes, however, refer only to the single volumes.

627

Willard, Ashton Rollins. History of modern Italian art . . . 2d ed., with a supplement to the text and additional illustrations. London, N.Y., Longmans, Green, 1900. 713 p. 40 plates. 24 cm.

Covers sculpture, painting, and architecture from the time of Canova to the end of the 19th century. Index p. 703–13.

628

Wölfflin, Heinrich. Classic art, an introduction to the Italian Renaissance. [2d ed.] With 200 illus. N.Y., Phaidon, 1953. 296 p. illus. (part mounted col.) 26 cm.

"Translated by Peter and Linda Murray from the 8th German edition." Originally published in German in 1899; a well-known English edition, issued by Putnam in 1913, was translated by Walter Armstrong and called *The art of the Italian Renaissance*. 1st ed. of *Classic art* 1952.

Introduction by Herbert Read. All notes have been translated in full. Some illustrations have been added to this edition.

Latin America

629

Angulo Iñiguez, Diego. Historia del arte hispano-americano . . . Barcelona-Buenos Aires, Salvat Editores, s.a., 1945–56. v. 1–3. illus. (incl. plans), plates (part col.) 26 cm.

A useful work on Spanish-American art.

Volume 1 written by Enrique Marco Dorta; bibliographies at end of chapters; no index. Volume 2 by Dorta, Angulo, and M. J. Buschiazzo; extensive bibliographies according to chapters and subjects treated. Volume 3 by Dorta, Angulo, and M. J. Buschiazzo.

630

Duque-Estrada, Luiz Gonzaga. A arte brasileira; pintura e esculptura. Rio de Janeiro, Lombaerts, 1888. 254 p. 19 cm.

An unillustrated history of painting and sculpture in Brazil, with emphasis on the founding of the Academy and the artists trained there.

631

Feuchtwanger, Franz, and Groth-Kimball, Irmgard. The art of ancient Mexico. 109 photographs by Irmgard Groth-Kimball; text and notes by Franz Feuchtwanger. London, Thames & Hudson [1954]. 125 p. (p. [31–110] plates) 4 col. plates. 31 cm.

A collection of excellent rotogravure plates with explanatory notes p. 113–24 giving size of objects, and a 29-page summary of the art. A chart showing overlapping cultures and their periods p. 30.

632

Guido, Angel. Redescubrimiento de América en el arte . . . Buenos Aires, "El Ateneo," 1944. 769 p. illus., plates (part col.), plans, facsims., diagrs. 30 cm.

3d ed., corregida y aumentada; 1st ed. 1941. A general survey, with many rather poor illustrations.

Alphabetical index of proper names p. 749–54; of geographical and ethnological names p. 755–58.

633

Joyce, Thomas Athol. Central American and West Indian archaeology; being an introduction to the archaeology of the states of Nicaragua, Costa Rica, Panama and the West Indies . . . N.Y., Putnam; London, Warner, 1916. 270 p. illus., 28 plates, maps. 23 cm. (Handbooks to ancient civilizations series)

Now obsolete but still useful. Deals with the life and customs of the inhabitants of this region. Bibliography p. 258–63.

634
Joyce, Thomas Athol. Maya & Mexican art . . . London, "The Studio," 1927. 191 p. incl. illus., plates. 22 cm.

Map on lining paper. A good short summary, well illustrated with clear halftones. Covers architecture, sculpture, pottery, painting and draughtsmanship, metalwork, clothing and personal adornment, stone-flaking, mosaic, and leatherwork.

"Select bibliography" p. 187–91.

635
Joyce, Thomas Athol. Mexican archaeology, an introduction to the archaeology of the Mexican and Mayan civilizations of pre-Spanish America . . . London, Warner, 1920. 384 p. illus., 30 plates, map. 23 cm. (Handbooks to ancient civilizations series)

First published 1914; 2d impression 1920. A standard work on the subject.

Appendices: I, Names of the days in the Mexican and Maya calendars; II, Names of the months in the Mexican and Maya calendars. Index p. 375–84.

636
Joyce, Thomas Athol. South American archaeology; an introduction to the archaeology of the South American continent with special reference to the early history of Peru . . . N.Y., Putnam; London, Macmillan, 1912. 292 p. illus., 26 plates, map. 23 cm. (Handbooks to ancient civilizations series)

Now obsolete but still useful. Bibliography contained in Appendix p. 277–82. Index p. 283–92.

637
Keleman, Pál. Baroque and rococo in Latin America . . . N.Y., Macmillan, 1951. 302 p. 192 plates, map. 29 cm.

Covers the art of Latin America in the 17th and 18th centuries. Illustrated by many halftones on 192 plates. Chapter 13 contains special material on colonial organs.

Bibliography p. 279–94. Index p. 295–302.

638
Kelemen, Pál. Medieval American art, a survey in two volumes. N.Y., Macmillan, 1946. 2 v. plates. 29 cm.

First published 1943; reissued 1946. Rev. ed. in 1 v. 1956 (N.Y., Macmillan, 414 p., 308 plates).

Covers all aspects of art and media up to the conquest. Contents: v. 1, Text; v. 2, Plates.

Chronological chart v. 1, p. 383. Bibliography v. 1, p. 385–405. Index v. 1, p. 407–14, refers to text and plates.

639
Lehmann, Walter, and Ubbelohde-Doering, Heinrich. The art of old Peru . . . N.Y., Weyhe; London, Benn, 1924. 67 p. illus. (incl. map), 140 plates. 34 cm. (Publication of the Ethnological Institute of the Ethnographical Museum, Berlin)

A standard work, though now out of date. Excellent collotype plates, many in color, accompanied by notes which form a chronological basis for the arrangement.

Table of plates p. 56–65 gives size of objects. "List of recent and important publications" p. 66–68.

640
Morley, Sylvanus Griswold. The ancient Maya, 3d ed. rev. by George W. Brainerd. Stanford, Stanford Univ. Press, 1956. 494 p. illus., maps, diagrs., tables. 24 cm.

1st ed. 1946; 2d ed. 1947. Includes a description of the region where the Mayas lived; history; ancient and modern Maya manners, customs, and art; and an appraisal of the Maya civilization.

Appendix: Correlation of Maya and Christian chronologies p. 443–48. Bibliography p. 467–81. Index p. 483–94.

641
Navarro, José Gabriel. Summary of ten lectures on Ecuadorian art. [Panama, 1935] 45 p. illus., plates. 31 cm. (Centro de Estudios Pedagógicos e Hispanoamericanos de Panamá [Publicaciones no. 1])

A resumé of material previously published by the author which gives the English reader a useful outline of colonial art. Illustrations are poor.

642
Nuceté-Sardi, José. Notas sobre la pintura y la escultura en Venezuela. Caracas, Artes Gráficas, 1940. 62 p. 24 illus., plates. 24 cm.

Contains brief remarks on the principal Venezuelan artists from colonial times to the present, frequently citing specific works. Fairly good illustrations.

Contents: Signos iniciales; Cifras de afirmacion; Contemporaneidad y futuro. Bibliography p. [62].

643

Pagano, José León. . . . El arte de los argentinos . . . Buenos Aires, Edición del autor, 1937–40. 3 v. illus. (incl. plans), 33 col. plates. 33 cm.

A general reference work on Argentine art, with most emphasis on modern painting. Volume 1 includes a chapter on the art of the Jesuit foundation p. 69–93, and a section on architecture up to the present p. 19–65; while the concluding section (v. 3, p. 379–580) deals with contemporary sculpture.

Contents: t. 1, Desde los aborígenes hasta el período de los organizadores; t. 2, Desde la acción innovadora del "nexus" hasta nuestros días; t. 3, Desde la pintura en Córdoba hasta las expresiones mas recientes; pintura, escultura, grabado. Indexes at end of each volume.

644

Rubens, Carlos. Pequena historia das artes plasticas no Brasil . . . São Paulo, Nacional, 1941. 388 p. 6 plates. 19 cm. (Biblioteca pedagogica brasileira, ser. 5a, Brasiliana v. 198)

The most complete treatment of Brazilian art but unfortunately not well illustrated. Bibliography p. [385]–86. No index (only table of contents).

645

Schiaffino, Eduardo. La pintura y la escultura en Argentina; 1783–1894 . . . Buenos Aires, Edición del autor, 1933. 418 p. 144 illus., plates. 32 cm.

Introduction gives a survey of colonial art throughout Latin America, followed by a discussion of 19th century native and visiting artists. The book is valuable for personal recollections and anecdotes of the writer, a late 19th century painter.

Index of illustrations p. [407]–13. Table of contents p. 415–18.

646

Solá, Miguel. Historia del arte hispanoamericano: arquitectura, escultura, pintura y artes menores en la America española durante los siglos XVI, XVII, XVIII. Barcelona, Labor [1935]. 341 p. illus. (incl. map, plan), 51 plates. 19 cm.

The only general book on Latin American colonial art. While sections devoted to different regions are brief they contain much information.

Bibliography p. 331–34. Alphabetical index p. 335–41.

647

Spinden, Herbert Joseph. . . . Ancient civilizations of Mexico and Central America . . . N.Y., 1928. illus., plates, map, diagrs. 20 cm. (American Museum of Natural History. Handbook series no. 3, 3d and rev. ed.)

"Publication of the Anthropological handbook fund." 1st ed. 1917; 2d rev. ed. 1922. "This little book is intended as a general commentary and explanation of the Indians of Mexico and Central America, and especially of their history."—*Pref.*

Bibliography p. 255–58. Index p. 259–70.

648

Spinden, Herbert Joseph. A study of Maya art; its subject matter and historical development . . . Cambridge, Peabody Museum, 1913. 285 p. illus., 30 plates. 36 cm. (Peabody Museum of American Archaeology and Ethnology, Harvard Univ. Memoirs, v. VI)

A rev. and enl. ed. pub. under title, *Maya art and civilization*, Indian Hills, Colo., Falcon's Wing Press, 1957. 432 p. 26 cm.

An important work on this subject despite its age. "Table of nomenclature" p. [249]–61. Bibliography p. [263]–76. Index p. 277–85.

649

Toor, Frances. Mexican popular arts. Mexico, Toor Studios, 1939. 107 p. illus., col. plates. 24 cm.

A popular type of book, but quite inclusive, treating toys and fireworks as well as textiles, metalwork, leather, etc. A map shows areas where various crafts are practiced. No index.

650

Toscano, Salvador. Arte precolombino de México y de la América Central . . . [México] Instituto de Investigaciones Estéticas, Universidad Nacional Autónoma de México, 1944. 556 p. illus. (incl. plans), col. plates, map. 34 cm.

Covers architecture, sculpture, painting, ceramics, mosaics, metalwork, and feathers in Mexico and Central America. Bibliography at end of each section. Name index p. 543–57.

651

Toussaint, Manuel. Arte colonial en México. México, Universidad Autónoma de México, Instituto de Investigaciones Estéticas, 1948 [i.e., 1949]. 501 p. illus., 3 col. plates. 34 cm.

Covers roughly 1590 to 1821 in Mexico. Bibliography p. [xxvii]–xxxi. Index p. 473–99,

652

Toussaint, Manuel. Arte mudejar en América. México, Porrúa [1946]. 143 p. 108 plates (3 col.) 29 cm.

Covers the flowering of this art in the Dominican Republic, Cuba, Mexico, Central America, Venezuela, Colombia, Ecuador, Peru, Bolivia, Chile, Argentina, Uruguay, Brazil, and the United States.

"Bibliografia general" p. 13 and "Bibliografia" at end of each article. "Apendice de documentos" p. 119–27. "Vocabulario de terminos mudejares" p. 129–31.

653

Ubbelohde-Doering, Heinrich. The art of ancient Peru. N.Y., Praeger [1952]. 55 p. illus., 244 plates (part col.), map. 28 cm. (Books that matter)

Excellent halftone plates, with 18 pages of introduction, and notes on the plates p. 19–51. Bibliography p. 53–55.

654

Vaillant, George Clapp. Aztecs of Mexico; origin, rise and fall of the Aztec nation. Garden City, N.Y., Doubleday, 1941. 340 p. 64 plates. 24 cm. (The American Museum of Natural History. Science series)

Map on lining papers. There is also a Pelican paperback edition.

An important and useful book although outdated in several respects. Bibliography p. 299–325. Index p. 327–40.

SEE ALSO: Pan American Institute of Geography and History. Commission on History. Publications (2461).

Low Countries

655

Gelder, Hendrik Enno van. Kunstgeschiedenis der Nederlanden; samenvattende kunstgeschiedenis van Nederland en Vlaanderen van begin tot heden . . . Utrecht, de Haan [1936]. 568 p. illus., 12 col. plates. 25 cm.

A general Dutch history of Netherlands art (Dutch and Flemish) from the medieval period to the present time. Many illustrations which are not very clear. Chapters written by various specialists.

Bibliography at end of some of the chapters. Index p. 561–68.

656

Gelder, Hendrik Enno van, and Duverger, J. Kunstgeschiedenis der Nederlanden van

de middeleeuwen tot onze tijd . . . Utrecht, de Haan, 1954–55. 2 v. illus., col. plates. 27 cm.

A general history of Netherlands art with various sections written by different scholars. Halftone illustrations in text and color plates.

Contents: v. 1, De Middeleeuwen de zestiende eeuw; v. 2, Van het einde van de zestiende eeuw tot onze tijd en Noord-Nederland.

657

Hymans, Henri Simon. Belgische Kunst des 19. Jahrhunderts . . . mit 200 Abbildungen. Leipzig, Seemann, 1906. 253 p. illus. 28 cm. (Geschichte der modernen Kunst, vi)

A general survey of 19th century Belgian art with illustrations in the text. List of illustrations p. xi–xiii. Index of artists p. 250–53.

658

Kunstreisboek voor Nederland. Amsterdam, van Kampen & Zoon, 1954– . v. 1–4. 18 cm.

1st ed. 1940. An abridgment of the *Voorloopige lijst* in 11 volumes; considered a Dutch equivalent of Dehio (587).

Contents: v. 1, Noord-Holland, Zuid-Holland; v. 2, Friesland, Groningen-Drente; v. 3, Overijssel, Gelderland, Utrecht; v. 4, Zeeland, Nord-Brabant, Limburg.

659

Leurs, Stan, ed. Geschiedenis van de Vlaamsche kunst, met de medewerking van prof. dr. Arthur H. Cornette, dr. Marthe Crick-Kuntziger [en anderen] . . . onder leiding van prof. dr. ir. Stan Leurs . . . Antwerpen, Uitgeverij "De Sikkel," 1936–39. 2 v. illus. (incl. plans), col. plates. 29 cm.

A general history of Flemish art covering architecture, sculpture, and painting. Well illustrated.

Bibliographies at ends of chapters. Index at end of v. 2 is divided into names p. 954–61, and buildings p. 962–70. List of illustrations at end of each volume.

660

Weissman, Adriaan Willem. Documents classés de l'art dans les Pays-Bas, du Xme au XIXme siècle . . . formant suite à l'oeuvre de feu J. J. van Ysendyck. Utrecht, Oosthoek, [1914]. 2 p. 120 plates. 43 cm.

Issued in 20 parts, 1905–14?; the first 17 parts in Haarlem by H. Kleinmann & Co. A collection of reproductions of the art of the Low Countries, forming a supplement to Ysendyck (661).

661

Ysendyck, Jules Jacques van, ed. Documents classés de l'art dans les Pays-Bas du Xième au XVIIIième siècle . . . Anvers, Maes, 1880–89. 20 pts. in 5 v. 720 plates. 44 cm.

A corpus of reproductions of examples of the art of the Low Countries, covering architecture, sculpture, and the minor arts. Each volume has a "Table générale et alphabétique."

Oriental Countries

662

Bachhofer, Ludwig. A short history of Chinese art. [N.Y.] Pantheon [1946]. 139 p. illus., plates. 31 cm.

A brief survey covering pottery, bronzes, sculpture, and painting from the neolithic age through the 18th century. Dimensions are given in "List of illustrations" p. 11–14. "Chinese dynasties" p. 15.

Bibliographical references included in "Notes" p. 129–31. Index p. 133–39.

663

Borovka, Grigoriĭ Iosifovich. Scythian art. . . . Trans. from the German by . . . V. G. Childe . . . N.Y., Stokes; London, Benn, 1928. 111 p. 74 plates on 37 l. 23 cm. (Kai-Khosru monographs on eastern art)

A standard book on this subject. Bibliographical note p. 11–14.

664

Buhot, Jean. Histoire des arts du Japon. Paris, van Oest, 1949– . v. 1. illus. 33 cm. (Annales du Musée Guimet. Bibliothèque d'art. Nouv. série, 5)

The first volume of a projected history of Japanese art by a recognized scholar. Only one volume published to date. Contents: v. 1, Des origines à 1350. Includes bibliographies. "Index des caractères" p. 255–67. "Index complémentaire" p. 268–70.

665

Contenau, Georges. Manuel d'archéologie orientale depuis les origines jusqu'à l'époque d'Alexandre . . . Paris, Picard, 1927–47. 4 v. illus., maps. 23 cm.

Continuous paging. Covers ancient Persia, Mesopotamia, Syria (Upper Syria), Palestine, and Asia Minor (Assyria, Babylonia, Sumeria, Phoenicia, and Arabia). Volume 4 is a supplement attempting to cover recent excavations and to bring the work up to date.

General bibliography at end of each volume is followed by separate ones for each chapter: v. 1, p. 491–521; v. 2, p. 1073–86; v. 3, p. 1603–10. Volume 2 has recent additions to the general bibliography. "Bibliographie depuis 1930" v. 4, p. 2307–43.

General index v. 3, p. 1621–60. Index to v. 4 p. 2345–57.

666

Coomaraswamy, Ananda Kentish. History of Indian and Indonesian art . . . N.Y., Weyhe; Leipzig, Hiersemann; London, Goldston, 1927. 295 p. incl. maps. 128 plates. 29 cm.

The standard history of the art of this area by a recognized authority. Contains maps showing the locations mentioned in the text p. 255–62. Bibliography p. 214–28 includes journals and serials as well as books.

667

Coral Rémusat, Gilberte de, Comtesse. L'art khmer, les grandes étapes de son évolution. Avec un préface de Georges Coedès . . . 2. éd. Paris, van Oest, 1951. 128 p. 159 illus., 44 plates, maps. 28 cm. (Études d'art et d'ethnologie asiatiques, 1)

Originally published 1940. A recent scholarly publication on Khmer art, taking into account the developments of recent scholarship in the field and showing the evolution of this art.

"Tableau des principaux monuments groupés par styles" p. 120–22. Bibliographical footnotes.

668

Eckardt, Andreas. A history of Korean art, trans. by J. M. Kindersley . . . London, Goldston, 1929. 225 p. illus., plates, maps, plans, diagrs. 30 cm.

A well-illustrated history of Korean art. "Remarks on the pronunciation of Korean, Japanese and Chinese words" p. xi. Comparative table of Far Eastern history, Plate A.

Bibliography on p. 3 and at beginning of each section. General index p. 204–16. Index of names with Chinese characters p. 217–25.

669

Fenollosa, Ernest Francisco. Epochs of Chinese and Japanese art; an outline history of East Asiatic design. New & revised ed., with copious notes by Professor Petrucci . . . London, Heinemann [1921]. 2 v. illus., plates (part col.), diagrs. 26 cm.

Originally published 1912. A general survey of Chinese and Japanese art from the earliest times to the present, by a pioneer in the field. The preface includes a biography of the author.

Notes v. 2, p. 207–16. Glossary of proper names v. 2, p. 217–28. Index v. 2, p. 229–35.

670
Foucher, Alfred. L'art gréco-bouddhique du Gandhâra; étude sur les origines de l'influence classique dans l'art bouddhique de l'Inde et de l'Extrême-Orient. Paris, Leroux, 1905–51. 2 v. in 4. illus., map. 28 cm. (Publication de l'École Française d'Extrême-Orient, v. V–VI)

A standard work on the Greco-Buddhist art of Gandhara. Contents: (1) Introduction —Les édifices, Les bas-reliefs; (2 ¹⁻²) Les images—L'histoire—Conclusions; (2 ³) Additions et corrections—Index.

Index of contributors v. 2,³ p. 889–94; of collections v. 2,³ p. 895–96. General index v. 2,³ p. 897–920.

671
Freer Gallery of Art, Washington, D.C. Annotated outlines of the history of Chinese arts [by] Grace Dunham Guest, assistant director, with revisions and additions by Archibald G. Wenley, director. Washington, D.C., Freer Gallery of Art, Smithsonian Institution, 1945. v. 1. 6 plates, map. 27 cm.

Cover title: Outline for the study of Far Eastern Arts. Chinese.

Leaves variously numbered; reproduced from typewritten copy. A useful outline of the periods and the salient characteristics of each.

Supplements: I, Brief list of Buddhist terms (3 p.); II, List of Chinese and Japanese characters and equivalents (15 p.); III, Bibliography compiled by A. G. Wenley (22 p.).

672
Freer Gallery of Art, Washington, D.C. Annotated outlines of the history of Japanese arts. Washington, D.C., 1950. [55] l. map. 27 cm.

Various pagings. On cover: Outline for the study of Far Eastern arts. Japan.

A useful outline of the periods and characteristics of this art. Supplements: I, Brief list of Buddhist terms; II, List of Chinese and Japanese characters and equivalents, comp. by A. G. Wenley; III, Bibliography.

673
Groslier, Bernard Philippe, and Arthaud, Jacques. The arts and civilization of Angkor, 6 plates in colour, 112 illustrations in photo-gravure. N.Y., Praeger [1957]. 230 p. (incl. plates). 6 col. plates. 28 cm.

Photographs by Jacques Arthaud. Text by a recognized authority. "This book aims at providing a succinct visual conspectus of the civilization of ancient Cambodia."—*Introd.*

"Notes on proper names and their pronunciation" p. 215. "Synoptic table" p. 218–19. "Notes on the inscriptions and photographs" p. 221–29. Bibliography p. 216–17. Index of maps and figures p. 230.

674
Grousset, René. The civilizations of the East, trans. from the French by Catherine Alison Phillips . . . N.Y., Knopf [1931–35]. 4 v. illus. 24 cm.

A well-illustrated general introductory survey of the field of Oriental art written by a competent scholar. Covers the arts of Persia (v. 1); India and Greater India (v. 2); China (v. 3); and Japan, Bengal, Nepal, and Tibet (v. 4). General index to all four volumes at end of v. 4.

675
Havell, Ernest Binfield. A handbook of Indian art . . . N.Y., Dutton, 1920. 222 p. 79 plates on 71 l. 23 cm.

A concise survey of architecture, sculpture, and painting in India, which is now somewhat out of date. Index p. 213–22.

676
Havell, Ernest Binfield. Indian sculpture and painting, illustrated by typical masterpieces, with an explanation of their motives and ideals. 2d ed. London, Murray [1928]. 288 p. 78 plates (part col.) 26 cm.

1st ed. 1908; 2d ed. rev. in both text and illustrations. A good early work on the subject. Contents: pt. 1, Sculpture; pt. 2, Painting. Appendix: The Indian process of fresco buono p. 278–86. Index p. 287–88.

677
Herzfeld, Ernst Emil. Iran in the ancient East; archaeological studies presented in the Lowell lectures at Boston. London, N.Y., Oxford Univ. Press, 1941. 363 p. illus., 131 plates (part col.) on 72 l. 33 cm.

A well-illustrated treatment of the subject. Contents: (1) The prehistoric period; (2) The dawn of history; (3) The Achaemenian period; (4) The Arsacidan and Sasanian periods.

Names of places p. 355–57; of people p. 359. Index p. 361–63.

678

LeCoq, Albert von. Die buddhistische Spät-antike in Mittelasien. Berlin, Reimer, 1922–33. 7 v. illus. (incl. maps, plans), 205 plates (part col.) 45 cm. (atlas, 61 cm.)

At head of title: Ergebnisse der Kgl. preus-sischen Turfan-expeditionen. A fundamental work on Central Asia. Excellent collotype plates reproducing material, much of which was destroyed in the last world war.

Contents: v. 1, Die Plastik; v. 2, Die ma-nichaeischen Miniaturen; v. 3, Die Wand-malereien; v. 4, Atlas zu den Wandmalereien; Beschreibender Text zum Atlas der Wand-malereien (laid in); v. 5, Neue Bildwerke; v. 6, Neue Bildwerke II; v. 7, Neue Bildwerke III.

"Chronologische Tabelle" v. 1, p. 17–18. "Verzeichnis der Tafeln" v. 1, p. 19–29, gives size of objects portrayed. "Verzeichnis der erhaltenen Malereien Indo-Iranischen Stils aus den wichtigsten Fundstätten der Oase von Kutscha" v. 7, p. 69–78. "Schlagwort-verzeichnis zu Text und Tafeln von Bd. I–VII" v. 7, p. 78–80.

679

LeMay, Reginald Stuart. A concise history of Buddhist art in Siam . . . Cambridge, Univ. Press, 1938. 165 p. 180 plates, maps. 29 cm.

Aims "to give a connected history of the different forms of Buddhist art which have flourished in Siam from the early years of the Christian era up to the end of the 16th century."—*Pref.*

Bibliography p. 151–55. Index p. 159–65.

680

Mackay, Ernest John Henry. Early Indus civilizations. 2d ed. rev. London, Luzac, 1948. 169 p. plates, maps, plans. 22 cm.

First published 1935 as *The Indus civiliza-tion;* 2d ed. rev. and enl. by Dorothy Mackay. A readable account of archaeological excava-tions in this area.

"Chronology and connections with other countries" p. 146–58. Bibliography at end of "Addendum" p. 159–60; Bibliography p. 161–62. Index p. 165–69.

681

Manuel d'art musulman. 2e éd. Paris, Picard, 1926–27. 2 v. in 4. 968 illus. 23 cm. (Manuels d'archéologie et d'histoire de l'art)

1st ed. 1907. Contents: (1) Marçais, Georges. L'architecture: Tunisie, Algérie, Maroc, Es-pagne, Sicilie (2 v.); (2) Migeon, Gaston. Arts plastiques et industriels (2 v.).

Bibliographies. Index at end of each vol-ume.

682

Minamoto, Hoshu. An illustrated history of Japanese art . . . trans. from the Japanese by Harold G. Henderson. Kyoto, Hoshino, 1935. 264 p. 220 plates (part col.) 27 cm.

An introductory book, consisting of photo-graphs of characteristic works of art arranged chronologically, and descriptive text for each item. Translated from a work intended for students. The translator has added short in-troductory paragraphs before each period. Glossary p. 258–64.

683

Minns, Ellis Hovell. Scythians and Greeks; a survey of ancient history and archaeology of the north coast of the Euxine from the Danube to the Caucasus . . . Cambridge, Univ. Press, 1913. 720 p. illus., 9 plates, 9 maps. 30 cm.

An important, scholarly work covering the civilization and art in this region. "General Russian bibliography" p. xxiv–xxxiii, and bibliographies at ends of chapters. "Muse-ums" p. xxxvi gives a list, with descriptions, of Russian museums in this field. Index p. 681–720.

684

Mulk-Rāj, Ānand. The Hindu view of art, with an Introductory essay on art and reality by Eric Gill. London, Allen & Unwin [1933]. 245 p. illus., plates. 19 cm.

A very useful book which includes a list and description of the most frequently rep-resented mudras. Contents: (1) The religio-philosophical hypothesis; (2) The aesthetic hypothesis; (3) The principles of artistic prac-tice. Chronology p. 224–31. Bibliography p. [233]–40. Index p. 241–45.

685

Parmentier, Henri. L'art khmèr classique; monuments du quadrant nord-est . . . Paris, Les Éditions d'Art et d'Histoire, 1939. 2 v. illus., plates, plans. 28 cm. (Publications de l'École Française d'Extrême-Orient [v. XXIX bis])

Covers Khmer art from about the 9th to the 15th century. Contents: v. 1, Text; v. 2, Plates, plans and drawings.

"Lexique des termes étrangers" v. 1, p. 343–47. "Table alphabétique des points ar-chéologiques et géographiques mentionnés dans ce volume" v. 1, p. 349–53.

686

Parmentier, Henri. L'art khmèr primitif . . .
Paris, van Oest, 1927. 2 v. plates, maps, plans.
28 cm. (Publications de l'École Française
d'Extrême-Orient [XXI])

Covers roughly Khmer art from the 7th
to the 9th century. Contents: v. 1, Text; v. 2,
Plates.

"Lexique des termes étrangers" v. 1, p. 377–
78. "Table générale des monuments" p. 379–
97 gives in columns: (1) Names; (2, 3) References; (4, 5) Inscriptions; (6, 7, 8) Situation;
(9, 10, 11) References to this volume (text,
illus., or plate). Index p. 399–402.

687

Pope, Arthur Upham, ed. A survey of Persian art from prehistoric times to the present . . . London and N.Y., Oxford Univ.
Press, 1938–39. 6 v. illus. (incl. maps, plans),
plates (part col.), diagrs. 39 cm.

"Published under the auspices of the
American Institute for Iranian Art and Archaeology." A collection of signed articles by
specialists on various aspects of Persian art.
The handsomest series issued on the subject,
with excellent illustrations. Volumes 1–3,
Text; v. 4–6, Plates.

Contents: v. 1, Pre-Islamic (prehistoric,
Achaemenid, Parthian, Sasanian); v. 2, Islamic (architecture, pottery, calligraphy); v.
3, Islamic (painting, textiles, carpets, metalwork, minor arts); v. 4, Plates 1–510, Pre-Islamic; v. 5, Plates 511–980, Islamic; v. 6,
Plates 981–1482, Islamic.

Index volume compiled by Theodore Besterman. London, New York, Oxford University Press, 1958. 136 p. 22 cm.

688

Rostovt͡sev, Mīkhaīl Ivanovīch. The animal
style in South Russia and China . . . Princeton, Princeton Univ. Press; London, Milford,
Oxford Univ. Press, 1929. 112 p. 33 plates. 28
cm. (Princeton monographs in art and archaeology, XIV)

An important early work in the field. Contents: (1) The Scythian period; (2) The Sarmatian period; (3) Origin of the Scythian
animal style and the animal style in China
of the Chou Dynasty; (4) Animal style in
China in the time of the Han Dynasty.

689

Rostovt͡sev, Mīkhaīl Ivanovīch. Iranians &
Greeks in South Russia. Oxford, Clarendon
Press, 1922. 260 p. illus. (incl. plans), plates,
map. 30 cm.

The author has "tried to give a history of
the South Russian lands in the prehistoric,
the protohistoric, and the classical periods
down to the epoch of the migration"—*Pref.*

Contents: The prehistoric civilization; The
Cimmerians and the Scythians in South
Russia (8th to 5th centuries B.C.); The Greeks
on the shores of the Black Sea down to the
Roman period; The Scythians at the end of
the 4th and in the 3d century B.C.; The Sarmatians; The Greek cities of South Russia in
the Roman period; The polychrome style
and the animal style; The origin of the Russian state on the Dnieper.

Bibliography p. 223–38. Index p. 239–60.

690

Sirén, Osvald. . . . Histoire des arts anciens
de la Chine . . . Paris et Bruxelles, van Oest,
1929–35. 6 v. illus., plates. 33 cm. (Annales du
Musée Guimet. Bibliothèque d'art. n.s. III–
IV)

The first four volumes have been translated into English (London, Benn, 1929–30).
A general history of early Chinese art. Volume 4 is one of the very few works on Chinese architecture.

Contents: (1) La période préhistorique,
L'époque Tcheou, L'époque Tch'ou et Ts'in;
(2) L'époque Han et les six dynasties; (3) La
sculpture de l'époque Han à l'époque Ming;
(4) L'architecture; (5) Histoire de la peinture
chinoise: I, Des origines à l'époque Song; (6)
Histoire de la peinture chinoise: II, L'époque
Song et l'époque Yuan.

Each volume has its own index and lists of
illustrations.

691

Smith, Vincent Arthur. A history of fine art
in India and Ceylon. 2d ed. rev. by K. de
B. Codrington. Oxford, Clarendon Press,
1930. 238 p. illus., plates (part col.) 29 cm.

1st ed. 1911. An important early work in
the field. Covers from the 3d century B.C. to
the present, and is well illustrated with halftone plates and a few text figures.

"Short bibliography" p. 230. Index p. 231–
38.

692

Stein, *Sir* Mark Aurel. Innermost Asia; detailed report of explorations in Central Asia,
Kan-su and eastern Īrān, carried out and described under the orders of H.M. Indian government . . . Oxford, Clarendon Press, 1928.
4 v. illus., plates (part col.), plans, facsims.,
maps. 34 cm.

Volumes 1–2 paged continuously. "With descriptive lists of antiques by F. H. Andrews and F. M. G. Lorimer; and appendices by J. Allan, E. Benveniste, A. H. Francke, L. Giles, R. L. Hobson, T. A. Joyce, S. Konow, A. von LeCoq, W. Lentz, S. Lévi, H. Maspero, F. E. Pargiter, R. Smith, W. J. Sollas, R. C. Spiller, F. W. Thomas, V. Thomsen."

A well-illustrated, monumental work on the trade route countries of Central Asia. Contents: v. 1–2, Text; v. 3, Plates and plans; v. 4, Maps (in portfolio). "List of abbreviated titles" v. 1, p. [xxiii]–xxvi.

693

Stein, *Sir* Mark Aurel. Serindia; detailed report of explorations in Central Asia and westernmost China carried out and described under the orders of H.M. Indian government . . . Oxford, Clarendon Press, 1921. 5 v. illus., plates (part col.), 94 (i.e., 96) maps, 59 plans, facsims. 35 cm.

Volumes 1–3 paged continuously. "With descriptive lists of antiques by F. H. Andrews, F. M. G. Lorimer, C. L. Woolley, and others; and appendices by J. Allan, L. D. Barnett, L. Binyon, E. Chavannes, A. H. Church, A. H. Francke, A. F. R. Hoernle, T. A. Joyce, R. Petrucci, K. Schlesinger, F. W. Thomas."

"A full record of the explorations, archaeological in the first place but to a large extent also geographical . . . of my second Central-Asian expedition . . . 1906–8 . . ."— *Introd.*

A monumental work on Central Asia and China. Contents: v. I–III, Text; v. IV, Plates; v. V, Maps (in portfolio). Bibliography v. 1, p. [xxv]–xxviii.

694

Tokyo. National Museum. Pageant of Japanese art. Tokyo, Toto Bunka [1952–54]. 6 v. illus. (part col.), plates. 37 cm.

A popular ed. issued in 1958. Contents the same but size reduced to 19 cm.

Good plates with text written by the staff of the National Museum in Tokyo. Contents: v. 1–2, Painting; v. 3, Sculpture; v. 4, Ceramics and metalwork; v. 5, Textiles and lacquer; v. 6, Architecture and gardens.

Each volume contains 75–100 pages of historical text; a glossary of terms; list of plates and one of illustrations, giving the size of objects; and index of artists.

695

Tsuda, Noritake. Handbook of Japanese art . . . with 345 illustrations and 10 color

plates. Tokyo, Sanseido, 1935. 527 p. illus., plates (part col.), map. 23 cm.

A well-illustrated survey. "List of museums, temple treasures and private collections" p. 499–508 is arranged geographically and gives location and contents of each collection.

"A short bibliography" p. 505–09 lists books written in English. Index p. 509–25.

696

Vogel, Jean Philippe. Buddhist art in India, Ceylon and Java . . . trans. from the Dutch by A. J. Barnouw . . . Oxford, Clarendon Press, 1936. 115 p. illus., plates. 20 cm.

A good short survey. Bibliography p. [107]–10.

697

Yamanaka & Company. A brief history of the glyptic art and architecture of Japan, together with a brief description of temples and shrines and a biography of eminent architects and sculptors. N.Y., Yamanaka & Co., 1902. 91 p. 19 cm.

"Shinto shrines and Buddhist temples," p. 37–73, lists them alphabetically and gives a few descriptive sentences about each. "Biography of eminent architects and sculptors" p. 74–91.

698

Zimmer, Heinrich Robert. The art of Indian Asia, its mythology and transformations. Completed and edited by Joseph Campbell, with photos by Eliot Elisofon and others. [N.Y.] Pantheon [1955]. 2 v. illus., plates, maps. 32 cm. (Bollingen series, 39)

A work of major importance. Covers the architecture, painting, and sculpture of India and Indian Asia, and contains very good illustrations. Contents: v. 1, Text; v. 2, Plates.

Appendices: A, Some notes on the art of painting; B, Maps and chronological charts. Bibliographical footnotes. Description of plates v. 1, p. 399–427. Index of picture sources v. 1, p. 431–32. General index v. 1, p. 433–65.

SEE ALSO: Ars Asiatica (2380); Frankfort. The art and architecture of the ancient Orient (474); Paine and Soper. The art and architecture of Japan (452); Rowland. The Harvard outline and reading lists for Oriental art (76) and The art and architecture of India (452); Sickman and Soper. The art and architecture of China (452).

Russia and Slavic Countries

699
Akademiiā Nauk SSSR. Institut Istorii
Iskusstv. Istoriiā russkogo iskusstva. Pod
obshchei red. I. E. Grabaria, V. N. Lazareva,
V. S. Kemenova. Moskva, Akademii Nauk
SSSR, 1953–(55). v. 1–(3). illus., plates (part
col.) 30 cm.
A comprehensive work, edited by I. E.
Grabar', which is planned to be completed
in 12 volumes and to cover the history of
Russian art. To date only three volumes
have been published. Some monographs on
specific topics of art, recently issued as independent works, will be included later in this
history. Profusely illustrated.
Contents: v. 1, Drevneishee iskusstvo vos-
tochnoi evropy; v. 2, Iskusstvo novgoroda; v.
3, Iskusstvo srednerusskikh kniazhestv XIII–
XV vekov.
Good bibliographies and indexes at ends
of volumes.

700
Alexy, Janko. Osudy slovenských výtvarní-
kov. V Bratislave, Štátne Nakladatel'stvo,
1948. 426 p. illus. 29 cm.
Contains material on 74 contemporary
Slovak artists, with illustrations of their
works. Bibliography p. [427]. Contents p.
[429–30].

701
Alpatov, Mīkhail Vladimīrovich, and Bru-
nov, Nikolai. Geschichte der altrussischen
Kunst. Augsburg, Filser, 1932. 2 v. illus. (incl.
plans), plates. 28 cm.
A scholarly German work on Russian art
covering architecture, painting, and sculpture. Contents: v. 1, Text; v. 2, Plates.
Bibliography at end of each chapter. Index of names, places, and subjects p. 414–23.

702
Bunt, Cyril George Edward. Russian art,
from Scyths to Soviets. London, N.Y., The
Studio [1946]. 272 p. plates (part col.) 26 cm.
A short history of Russian art in its en-
tirety, covering architecture, painting, enamels, miniatures, sculpture and ceramics,
woodcarving, and embroideries.
Bibliography p. 268. Index p. 269–72.

703
Conway, *Sir* William Martin. Art treasures
in Soviet Russia. London, Arnold, 1925. 284
p. plates. 23 cm.

"A description of works of art in Russia
and the manner and prospects of their preservation."–*Pref.* Index p. 279–84.

704
Filov, Bogdan Dīmītrov. Early Bulgarian art.
Berne, Haupt, 1919. 86 p. illus., 58 plates (10
col.) 33 cm.
Contents: (1) The first kingdom of Bulgaria; (2) The second kingdom of Bulgaria;
(3) The Turkish period.
Index p. 81–82. List of illustrations p. 83–
84; of plates p. 85–86.

705
Filov, Bogdan Dīmītrov. Geschichte der altbulgarischen Kunst bis zur Eroberung des
bulgarischen Reiches durch die Türken . . .
Berlin, Gruyter, 1932. 100 p. incl. plans. 48
plates on 24 l. 25 cm. (Grundriss der slavischen Philologie und Kulturgeschichte
[10])
This volume covers the period 679 to 1393
in Bulgarian art. Bibliographies at ends of
chapters. "Register" p. 96–100.

706
Filov, Bogdan Dīmītrov. Geschichte der bul-
garischen Kunst unter der türkischen Herr-
schaft und in der neueren Zeit . . . Berlin,
Leipzig, Gruyter, 1933. 94 p. 64 plates. 24 cm.
(Grundriss der slavischen Philologie und
Kulturgeschichte [10])
Covers Bulgarian art in the period from
1393 to 1930. Bibliography at end of each
chapter.

707
Geschichte der russischen Kunst. Dresden,
Verlag der Kunst. Bd. 1, 1957. 388 p. illus.
col. plates. 32 cm. (In progress)
A German translation of the Russian work
(699). Bibliographie p. 346–60. Verzeichnis
des Abbildung p. 361–68. Register p. 369–84.

708
Grabar', Igór' Emmanuīlovīch. Istoriiā russ-
kago iskusstva. Moskva, Knebel' [1909]. 6 v.
illus., plates (part col.) 31 cm.
A fundamental history of Russian art from
the 14th to the end of the 19th century. Some
volumes written by specialists, edited by
Grabar. Good illustrations.
Contents: v. 1–4, Architecture; v. 5, Sculpture; v. 6, Painting (to the 17th century).
Table of contents at end of each volume.

709
Holme, Geoffrey, ed. Art in the U.S.S.R.: architecture, sculpture, painting, graphic arts,

theatre, film, crafts . . . London, N.Y., The Studio, 1935. 137 p. 84 plates (5 col.) 30 cm.

A popular survey of art today (1935) in the Soviet Union, with articles on the various aspects of the arts written by specialists. Articles vary in length, from two to five pages.

710

London, Kurt. The seven Soviet arts . . . London, Faber [1937]. 381 p. illus., plates, diagrs. 23 cm.

"Trans. by Eric S. Bensinger."

"Covers music, literature, theatre, ballet, painting, plastic arts, architecture, film, radio, gramophone, as well as artists' organizations, the system of artistic training, and the cultural principles of the Soviets."—*Pref.* Index p. 367–81.

711

Matthey, Werner von. Russische Kunst. Einsiedeln, Benziger [1948]. 115 p. 48 plates, plans. 21 cm.

A short survey of Russian art from early times until today. Bibliography p. [110]. Index p. [111]–15.

712

Petrov, Petr Nikolaevich, ed. Sbornik materialov dlîa istorii I. S.-Peterburgskoĭ akademii khudozhestv za 100 let. S.-Peterburg, 1864–66. 3 v. tables. 29 cm.

A history of the Russian Academy over 100 years.

713

Réau, Louis. L'art roumain; 48 planches hors texte en héliogravure. Paris, Larousse [1946]. 107 p. 48 plates. 18 cm. (Arts, styles et techniques)

A short survey, almost in outline form, of Roumanian art from its beginnings until the present day.

Bibliography p. 102–05. "Notices biographiques des principaux artistes cités" p. 100–01.

714

Réau, Louis. L'art russe . . . Paris, Laurens, 1921–22. 2 v. illus., plates. 26 cm.

A standard French work on Russian art. Contents: v. 1, Des origines à Pierre le Grand; v. 2, De Pierre le Grand à nos jours.

"Bibliographie de l'art russe ancien" v. 1, p. [365]–71; "Bibliographie de l'art russe moderne" v. 2, p. [271]–77.

"Index des noms propres" v. 1, p. [372]; "Lexique d'archéologie et d'iconographie russes" v. 1, p. 373–87; "Vocabulaire de l'art russe moderne" v. 2, p. 278–86; L'art russe dans les musées français" v. 2, p. 287; "Index alphabétique" v. 2, p. 289–91.

715

Réau, Louis. L'art russe . . . Paris, Larousse [1945]. 138 p. 64 plates. 17 cm. (Arts, styles et techniques)

A general survey in outline form. Very poor paper. Biographical descriptions of the principal artists cited p. 126–31. Bibliography p. 132–35.

716

Rice, David Talbot, ed. Russian art; an introduction. London, Gurney and Jackson, 1935. 136 p. illus., 12 plates. 19 cm.

"Published in connection with the exhibition of Russian art, Belgrave Square, London, 1935." Intended as a short introduction to Russian art in English.

Contents: Russian art—an appreciation, by T. Borenius; An historical survey, by A. Polovtsoff; The periods and schools of early Russian painting, by P. Muratoff; Art in the 18th century, by A. Benois; Early 19th century painting, by S. Ernst; Decorative art—theatre and ballet, by T. T. Rice; Textiles, by A. Kendrick; Metalwork and enamels, by L. Grinberg; The art of the book, by P. Apostol; Porcelain, by A. Popoff; Table of emperors and dates.

717

Rice, Tamara (Abelson) Talbot. Russian art. West Drayton, Middlesex, Penguin Books [1949]. 276 p. illus., map. 18 cm. (Pelican books, A182)

A good short survey of Russian architecture, painting, sculpture, and peasant arts from the 10th century to the present.

"Relevant dates in Russian history" p. 11–12. "A short bibliography" p. 13. Index p. 268–76.

718

Rubissow, Helen. The art of Russia. N.Y., Philosophical Library, 1946. 32 p. illus., 164 plates. 28 cm.

A popular type of picture book with a short introductory text. Bibliography p. 27. Index of illustrations p. 28–31. List of artists (with dates), p. 31–32, is not an index.

719

Wulff, Oskar K. Die neurussische Kunst im Rahmen der Kulturentwicklung Russlands von Peter dem Grossen bis zur Revolution. Augsburg, Filser [c1932]. 2 v. plates. 28 cm.

A standard German work covering art in Russia from the time of Peter the Great to the Revolution. Contents: Bd. 1, Textband; Bd. 2, Tafelband.

"Literaturverzeichnis" v. 1, p. [350]. "Quellennachweis der entlehnten Abbildungen" v. 1, p. [351]–55. "Namenregister" v. 1, p. [356]–61.

SEE ALSO: Hamilton. The art and architecture of Russia (452); Rostovt͡sev. The animal style in South Russia and China (688) and Iranians & Greeks in South Russia (689).

Scandinavia

720

Adama van Scheltema, F. Die altnordische Kunst; Grundprobleme vorhistorischer Kunstentwicklung. Berlin, Mauritius, 1924. 252 p. illus., plates. 26 cm.

A scholarly study of early Nordic art forms —pottery, metals, etc. No index; no bibliography.

721

Alfons, Sven, and Lindwall, Bo. Svensk konstkrönika under 100 år . . . redaktion och inledning: Ragnar Josephson. Stockholm, Natur och Kultur [1944]. [427], 19 p. illus., col. plates. 33 cm.

An unusually well-illustrated survey of Swedish art in the past hundred years.

"Person-och illustrationsregister" of 8 p. at end; "Generationsregister" of 3 p. is a chronology; "Motivregister" of 8 p.; "Kallfirteckning" p. 19 (at end).

722

Beckett, Francis. Danmarks kunst. København, Koppel, 1924–26. 2 v. illus. 27 cm.

A general history of Danish art from its earliest beginnings through the Gothic period. Contents: v. 1, Oldtiden og den aeldre middelalder; v. 2, Gotiken.

Each volume contains "Henvisninger" (notes with bibliographical references), and an index of names.

723

Cornell, Henrik. Den svenska konstens historia från hedenhös till omkring 1800 . . . Stockholm, Bonnier [1944]. 469 p. illus. (incl. plans), 348 plates (16 col.) 23 cm.

A general history of Swedish art from its beginning to about 1800. Covers architecture, painting, and sculpture, with a supplementary chapter on graphic arts from 1600–1700.

Bibliography is arranged by chapters. "Litteraturanvesningar" p. 421–32. Index of names p. 433–40; of places and monuments p. 441–69. "Rättelse" slip mounted on p. 150.

724

Hannover, Emil. Dänische Kunst des 19. Jahrhunderts . . . mit 120 Abbildungen. Leipzig, Seemann, 1907. 168 p. illus. 28 cm. (Geschichte der modernen Kunst, VII)

A general survey of the subject, covering architecture, sculpture, and painting. Index of artists p. 167–68.

725

Holme, Charles. Peasant art in Sweden, Lapland and Iceland . . . London, The Studio, 1910. 48 p. 88 plates (12 col.) 29 cm.

Primarily a picture book. Contents: Sweden, by Sten Granlund (tr. by E. Adams-Roy); Lapland, Iceland, by Jarno Jessen.

726

Lexow, Einar Jacob. Norges kunst. Oslo, Steenske [1926]. 342 p. illus., plates (11 col.) 21 cm.

A well-illustrated history of Norwegian art from its beginnings until the 20th century, covering architecture, painting, and sculpture. Bibliography p. 340–42. No index.

727

Lindblom, Andreas Adolf Fredrik. Sveriges konsthistoria från forntid till nutid . . . Stockholm, Nordisk Rotogravyr [1944]–(46). v. 1–(3). illus. (incl. plans), col. plates. 26 cm.

A very well-illustrated general history of Swedish art. Contents: v. 1, Från stenåldern till Gustav Vasa; v. 2, Från Gustav Vasa till Gustav III; v. 3, Från Gustav III till Våra Dagar.

Each volume contains: Afterword; Notes on paintings; Glossary of terms; Place index to works of art and artist index.

728

Nordensvan, Georg Gustaf. Schwedische Kunst des 19. Jahrhunderts. Leipzig, Seemann, 1904. 140 p. illus., 2 plates. 26 cm. (Geschichte der modernen Kunst, V)

A general survey of Swedish 19th century art, illustrated in the text. Index of artists.

729

Nordensvan, Georg Gustaf. Svensk konst och svenska konstnärer i nittonde århundradet . . . ny . . . uppl. Stockholm, Bonnier [1925–28]. 2 v. illus. 26 cm.

Includes art from the late 18th through the

19th century in Sweden. Contents: v. 1, Från Gustav III till Karl XV; v. 2, Från Karl XV till sekelslutel.

Bibliography v. 2, p. [511]–13. Index of names v. 2, p. 514–26.

730

Okkonen, Onni. Finnish art. 208 plates. [Tr. from the Finnish by Helen Goldthwait-Väänänen] Porvoo, Söderström [1946]. 41 p. plates. 30 cm.

A pictorial survey of Finnish art, with particular emphasis on modern painting and sculpture. Short explanatory text giving the division into periods and mentioning some of the most outstanding artists. No index.

731

Okkonen, Onni. Suomen taiteen historia . . . Porvoo, Söderström [1945]. 2 v. 637 illus., 8 col. plates. 26 cm.

Covers architecture, painting, and sculpture in Finland from early times to the present day. Contents: v. 1, Edellinen osa. Muinaisuudesta 1800-luvun realismiin; v. 2, Jälkimmäinen osa. 1800-luvulta nykypäiviin. Index v. 2, p. 427–37.

732

Romdahl, Axel Ludvig, and Roosval, Johnny August Emanuel. Svensk konsthistoria, utgifven af A. L. Romdahl och Johnny Roosval, under medverkan of Sigurd Curman, Axel Gauffin, Georg Göthe . . . Stockholm, Aktiebolaget Ljus, 1913. 612 p. 428 illus., 16 col. plates. 27 cm.

A basic history of art in Sweden, covering architecture, painting, and sculpture. The section on the 18th century was written by Axel Gauffin, Georg Göthe, and Sigurd Curman; sections in other subject areas written by specialists.

Bibliography at end of each chapter. Index of artists p. 603–06; of places p. 607–12. Table of contents p. [613].

733

Roosval, Johnny August Emanuel. Swedish art, being the Kahn lectures for 1929 . . . Princeton, Princeton Univ. Press, 1932. 77 p. illus. (incl. plans), 39 plates. 27 cm. (Princeton monographs in art and archaeology, XVIII)

Not a complete history, as the rococo and classic periods are omitted. Bibliographical footnotes.

734

Scandinavian art; illustrated. [By] Carl Laurin, Emil Hannover, Jens Thiis. N.Y.,

The American-Scandinavian Foundation, 1922. 662 p. illus. 24 cm. (Scandinavian monographs, V)

Introduction by Christian Brinton. A useful, adequately illustrated survey of this field by well-known scholars.

Contents: A survey of Swedish art, by C. Laurin; Danish art in the 19th century, by Emil Hannover; Modern Norwegian art, by J. Thiis. Index to artists (with their dates) p. 647–62.

735

Shetelig, Haakon, and Falk, Hjalmar. Scandinavian archaeology . . . translated by E. V. Gordon. Oxford, Clarendon Press, 1937. 458 p. illus., 62 plates, diagrs. 23 cm.

Covers art, religion, customs, etc., from the earliest settlements through the Viking and Iron Ages.

Abbreviations p. xx, "Note on terminology" p. xviii–xix. Bibliographical footnotes. Index p. 437–58.

736

Strömböm, Sixten Georg Mauritz. Konstnärsförbundets historia. Med företal av Prins Eugen. Stockholm, Bonnier, 1945– . v. 1– . illus., plates, facsims. 30 cm. (In progress)

A scholarly history of Swedish painting and sculpture, with particular emphasis on the 19th century. Contents: v. 1, Till och med 1890.

Bibliographical references in "Noter" v. 1, p. 327–70. Index of artists p. 371–77; of illustrations p. 378–80. Chronological table p. 382–87.

737

Tikkanen, Johann Jakob. Modern art in Finland. Helsinki, Government Printing Office [1926]. 59 p. illus. 23 cm.

A rather popular account of painting and sculpture in Finland by a professor of art history, perhaps written for the tourist trade.

738

Tirranen, Hertta. Suomen taiteilijoita Juho Rissasesta Jussi Mäntyseen; elämäkertoja . . . Porvoo, Helsinki, Söderström [1950]. 494 p. illus. 26 cm.

Contains material on 47 20th-century Finnish artists, with illustrations and portraits of the artists. Index p. 489–94.

739

Wennervirta, Ludvig. Suomen taide; esihistoriallisesta ajasta meidän päiviimme; avustaja; Aarne Europaeus, U. T. Sirelius, K. K.

Meinander, Carolus Lindberg, Rafael Blomstedt . . . Helsingissä, Kustannusosakeyhtiö Otava [1927]. 652 p. 546 illus., 6 col. plates. 26 cm.

Swedish ed. 1926. A general history of Finnish art from the earliest times to the present day, covering architecture, painting, and sculpture.

Contents: Esihistoriallinen taide [by] Aarne Europaeus; Kansantaide [by] U. T. Sirelius; Vanhempi kuvaamataide [by] K. K. Meinander; Rakennustaide [by] Carolus Lindberg; Uudempi kuvaamataide [by] L. Wennervirta; Taideteollisuus [by] Rafael Blomstedt. Index of artists p. 645–52.

Spain and Portugal

√ **740**

Ars Hispaniae. Historia universal del arte hispánico. Madrid, Editorial Plus-Ultra [c1947]–(56). v. 1–(12). illus., plates. 28 cm.

To be complete in 20 volumes. A well-illustrated history of Spanish art written by specialists. Each volume has detailed bibliography and indexes by subjects, places, and persons.

Contents: (1) Arte prehistórico, Colonizaciones púnica y griega, Arte ibérico, El arte de las tribus célticas; (2) Arte romano, Arte paleochristiano, Arte visigodo, Arte asturiano; (3) Arte califal hispano-arabe, Arte mozerabe; (4) Arte almohades, Arte nazarí, Arte mudéjar, Arte morisco; (5) Arquitectura y escultura romanicas; (6) Pintura e imagineria románicas; (7) Arquitectura gótica; (8) Escultura gótica; (9) Pintura gótica; (10) Cerámica y vidrio; (11) Arquitectura del siglo XVI; (12) Pintura del renacimiento; (13) Pintura del renacimiento; (14) Arte barroco; (15) Pintura del siglo XVII; (16) Arte neoclasico; (17) Artes aplicadas de los siglos XVI y XVIII; (18) Arte del siglo XIX; (19) Arte del siglo XIX, por el Dr. Javier de Salas Bosch; (20) Arte del siglo XX, por Juan Eduardo Cirlot.

741

Camón Aznar, José. Las artes y los pueblos de la España primitiva. Madrid, Espasa-Calpe, 1954. 935 p. illus. (part col.), maps, diagrs. 28 cm.

A well-illustrated, comprehensive treatment of primitive art in Spain. Bibliography p. 861–74.

"Indice geográfico y onomástico" p. 875–903. "Indice de figuras" p. 905–27. "Indice de materias" p. 929–34.

742

Gaya Nuño, Juan Antonio. Historia del arte español, con 300 reproduciones fuera de texto. Madrid, Editorial Plus-Ultra [1946]. 478 p. plates. 20 cm. (La historia para todos)

A short survey of Spanish art from its beginnings to the present day. Chronological tables p. 438–[48]. Bibliography p. [448]–50. Index of names p. 451–65.

743

Hagen, Oskar. Patterns and principles of Spanish art. 2d ed. Madison, Univ. of Wis. Press, 1943. 279 p. illus. 24 cm.

"A completely rewritten edition"; 1st ed. 1936. An outline or summary of Spanish art in English by a competent scholar.

Some bibliographical footnotes. Index of personal names p. 265–72; of place names p. 275–79.

744

Jiménez-Placer, Fernando, and Cirici Pellicer, Alejandro. Historia del arte español. Barcelona, Labor, 1955. 2 v. illus., plates (part col.) 28 cm.

A well-illustrated history of Spanish art. Contents: v. 1, Del paleolitico al renacimiento (Arquitectura); v. 2, Del renacimiento (Escultura) hasta el siglo XX.

Subject index p. 1043–64; index of places p. 1065–80.

745

Laforge, Edouard. Des arts et des artistes en Espagne jusqu'à la fin du dix-huitième siècle. Lyon, Perrin, 1859. 370 p. 23 cm.

A rather general history of Spanish art. Table of contents listing chapters p. 361–62. "Table analytique" p. 363–70.

746

Lambert, Elie. L'art gothique en Espagne aux XIIe et XIIIe siècles . . . Paris, Laurens, 1931. 314 p. illus. (incl. plans), 48 plates. 27 cm.

A standard treatment of Gothic art in Spain of the 12th and 13th centuries, well illustrated with many plans and diagrams.

Annotated bibliography p. [291]–98. "Abbayes cisterciennes d'Espagne" p. 299. Alphabetical index p. 301–05. List of figures p. 307–08; of plates p. 309–10.

747

Lozoya, Juan Contreras y López de Ayala, *Marqués* de. Historia del arte hispánico . . . Barcelona, Salvat Editores, s.a., 1931–49. 5 v. illus. (part col.) 26 cm.

An important history of Spanish art from prehistory to the present. Well illustrated but almost no color plates.

Bibliographies at end of each chapter. Volume 5 has also a supplementary bibliography to the entire work, p. 671–83, arranged by volume and chapter. Each volume has its own index, divided into a geographical index, one of artists, one of others mentioned in the volume; and a listing of plates and illustrations as well.

748

Raczyński, Atanazy, *Hrabia*. Les arts en Portugal; lettres adressées à la Société artistique et scientifique de Berlin, et accompagnées de documens. Paris, Renouard, 1846. 548 p. 21 cm.

Contains excerpts from various manuscripts of François de Hollande, as well as letters by the author and others on art in Portugal.

"Table des matières" p. 525–28 lists in some detail just what is included. Index of artists and writers mentioned, as well as the principal buildings mentioned, p. 529–46.

749

Santos, Reynaldo dos. L'art portugais: architecture, sculpture et peinture. Préf. de Marcel Aubert. Paris, Plon [1953]. 98 p. plates (4 col.) 26 cm. (Collection "Messages," 4)

"Éditions d'histoire et d'art." A modern survey of Portuguese architecture, sculpture, and painting by a recognized authority, with good illustrations.

List of illustrations p. 93–95. Table of contents p. 97–98.

SEE ALSO: Monumenta Cataloniae (2451).

Switzerland

750

Gantner, Joseph. Kunstgeschichte der Schweiz von den Anfängen bis zum Beginn des 20. Jahrhunderts. Frauenfeld und Leipzig, Huber [1936]–(56). 3 v. illus. 30 cm.

A scholarly work on Swiss art from its beginnings to the beginning of the 20th century. Contents: Bd. 1, Von den helvetisch-römischen Anfängen bis zum Ende des romanischen Stiles; Bd. 2, Die gotische Kunst; Bd. 3, Die Kunst der Renaissance, des Barock und des Klassizismus [von] Adolf Reinle.

"Übersicht über die wichtigste Literatur": v. 1, p. [xiii]–xvi; v. 2, p. [ix–xi]; v. 3, p. [xiii]–xiv. Also includes bibliographies in the text.

"Orts- und Künstlerregister," v. 2, p. [379]–88, covers v. 1–2; v. 3, p. [423]–35, covers v. 3.

751

Die Kunstdenkmäler der Schweiz. Basel, Birkhäuser, 1927–(57). Bd. 1–(38). illus., plates, maps. 26 cm.

Series title page reads: Herausgegeben von der Schweizerischen Gesellschaft für Erhaltung historischer Kunstdenkmäler, mit eidgenössischen, kantonalen und privaten Subventionen. Some few volumes are in French and bear a series title: Les monuments d'art et d'histoire de la Suisse.

A systematic publication of the art of Switzerland, of which 38 volumes have appeared to date. Written by various specialists and treating of the art monuments of the cantons of Switzerland. Emphasis is placed on the period from early Middle Ages to the mid-19th century, with prehistoric and Roman periods treated as an introduction.

Each volume is well illustrated and contains bibliographies and indexes of places and names; some also contain tables of metalworkers' marks, etc. The series is divided by cantons, then by districts. Cantons included so far: Schwyz, Basel, Zug, Zürich, Graubünden, Aargau, Liechtenstein, St. Gall, Schaffhausen, Bern, Luzern, Neuchâtel, Bribourg, and the cathedral of Lausanne.

752

Nicolas, Raoul. Die schöne alte Schweiz; die Kunst der schweizer Kleinmeister. Stuttgart, Montana-Verlag [c1926]. 102 p. 73 plates (part col.) 30 cm.

Published in seven parts. A brief survey of minor Swiss artists, including painters, draughtsmen, engravers, and publishers.

"Inhaltsverzeichnis" is a table of contents. "Verzeichnis der Tafeln" and "Verzeichnis der in diesem Werke erwähnten schweizerischen Kleinmeister (Maler, Zeichner, Radierer und Verleger)" give dates for the artists listed.

United States

753

Baur, John Ireland Howe. Revolution and tradition in modern American art. Cambridge, Harvard Univ. Press, 1951. 170 p. plates. 25 cm. (The Library of Congress series in American civilization)

"An attempt to define and trace the development of the chief movements in our painting and sculpture during the last fifty years, with occasional excursions into architecture and the graphic arts when these could help to clarify the central subject . . . does consider certain problems related to the position of the artist and his work in our present-day society."—*Pref.*

Bibliographical references included in "Notes" p. 157–60. Index p. 163–70.

754

Cahill, Holger, and Barr, Alfred H., eds. Art in America; a complete survey . . . N.Y., Reynal & Hitchcock [c1935]. 162 p. illus. (incl. plan), col. plates. 32 cm.

Originally published in two parts in 1934 as text for a series of radio broadcasts.

A short summary of the arts in America, covering painting, sculpture, architecture, stage design, photography, and the motion picture. Written by various authorities and well illustrated. Lists and bibliographies p. 153–62. No index.

755

Cowdrey, Mary Bartlett. American Academy of Fine Arts and American Art-Union, 1816–1852 . . . N.Y., N.Y. Historical Society, 1953. 2 v. illus. 24 cm.

Contents: v. 1, Foreword, by James Thomas Flexner; The American Academy of Fine Arts, by Theodore Sizer; The American Art-Union, by Charles E. Baker; Publications of the Art-Union, by Mary Bartlett Cowdrey; Sale of Art-Union holdings, 1852, by Malcolm Stearns, Jr.; v. 2, Exhibition record p. 3–427; Index p. 429–504.

Also contains list of members, honorary members, academicians, and associates of the American Academy, as well as a chronology of its activities from 1801–43. For the Art-Union it gives the following information: Officers and managers (1839–51); plan, charter, constitution; bylaws of the committee on management; relations with other art unions; relations with artists; relations with The National Academy of Design.

Bibliographical references.

756

Dunlap, William. A history of the rise and progress of the arts of design in the United States. . . . New ed., illustrated, edited, with additions, by Frank W. Bayley and Charles E. Goodspeed . . . Boston, Goodspeed, 1918. 3 v. plates (1 col.), facsims. 24 cm.

1st ed. 1834. A standard early work on American art.

Addenda: "List of painters, sculptors, architects, and engravers working in this country before 1835 and not previously mentioned in this work," arranged alphabetically, with brief information about each artist. Bibliography v. 3, p. 346–77, supplied by the editors.

757

Kelby, William, comp. Notes on American artists, 1754–1820, copied from advertisements appearing in the newspapers of the day . . . N.Y., New York Historical Society, 1922. 80 p. ports. 25 cm. (The New York Historical Society. The John Divine Jones Fund series . . . v)

Edition of 300 copies. "It is not claimed that every advertisement has been copied." Mostly from New York newspapers, with some from Philadelphia. Artists included are waxworkers, stone and seal cutters, engravers, painters, dancers, etc.

Complete list of portraits and sculpture in the New York Historical Society p. 59–76. Index p. 77–80.

758

Larkin, Oliver W. Art and life in America. N.Y., Rinehart [1949]. 547 p. illus. 29 cm.

Undoubtedly the best one-volume history of American art. Well illustrated. "Bibliographical notes" p. 483–514. Index p. 515–47.

759

Mather, Frank Jewett; Morey, Charles Rufus; and Henderson, William James. The American spirit in art. New Haven, Yale Univ. Press, 1927. 354 p. illus., 3 plates. 26 cm. (Pageant of America [v. 12])

A well-illustrated survey of the field, covering painting, sculpture, graphic arts, and music. Index p. 345–54.

760

Modern artists in America. no. 1 [1949–50]. N. Y., Wittenborn Schultz, Inc. [1951–]. illus. 26 cm.

Edited by Robert Motherwell, Ad Reinhardt, and Bernard Karpel; Photography, Aaron Siskind; Sec., Sally Lorin. Intended to be a biennial publication; only one volume published.

This "First series is devoted to the events of the previous two seasons." It contains: Artists' sessions at Studio 35; The Western Round Table of Modern Art; A sequence of paintings and sculpture 1949–50; Exhibitions of artists in N.Y. galleries 1949–50; Paris-New York 1951, by Michel Seuphor; The Louise and Walter Arensberg Collection; Museum acquisitions; Art in the world of events; A calendar of excerpts; Painters and poets in Barcelona; Art publications, an international section.

Index to bibliography p. 193–96; to text p. 197–98.

761
Neuhaus, Eugen. The history & ideals of American art . . . Stanford University, Calif., Stanford Univ. Press; London, Oxford Univ. Press, 1931. 444 p. plates. 27 cm.

It is an "historical and aesthetic analysis of American art and of the outside influences which shaped its course from its . . . beginnings to . . . the present day."—*Pref.*

Names of artists (with dates) are given in boldface type. Short biographical notes on artists at end of each chapter. Bibliography p. 427–38. Index p. 439–44.

SEE ALSO: Lancour. American art auction catalogues (144).

Techniques

762
Plenderleith, Harold James. The conservation of antiquities and works of art; treatment, repair, and restoration. London, N.Y., Oxford Univ. Press, 1956. 373 p. illus., tables. 25 cm.

Written by a recognized authority for the nonscholar and "intended as a handbook for the collector, the archaeologist, and the museum curator, and as a workshop guide for the technician."—*Pref.* Well illustrated with pictures of equipment and objects from the British Museum.

Contents: pt. 1, Organic materials; pt. 2, Metals; pt. 3, Siliceous and related materials. Appendixes p. 343–60 give various formulae and technical details of many processes. Bibliographical footnotes. Index p. 361–73.

763
Vasari, Giorgio. Vasari on technique; being the introduction to the three arts of design, architecture, sculpture and painting, prefixed to the Lives of the most excellent painters, sculptors and architects . . . now for the first time tr. into English by Louisa S. Maclehose; ed. with introduction and notes by Professor G. Baldwin Brown. N.Y., Dutton; London, Dent, 1907. 328 p. illus., 17 plates (1 col.) 22 cm.

An English translation of the description of technique and practical directions about materials and processes, which were published as the preface to the 1568 ed. (2042) with commentary added. Index p. 315–28.

| # Architecture

Bibliography

764

Hitchcock, Henry-Russell. American architectural books; a list of books, portfolios, and pamphlets on architecture and related subjects published in America before 1895. 3d rev. ed. Minneapolis, Univ. of Minn. Press, 1946. 130 p. 26 cm.

Originally issued 1938–39 as a preliminary mimeographed bibliography. Sheets of addenda and corrigenda issued in 1940.

Arranged alphabetically by author. Location of copies in important libraries is indicated.

765

Roos, Frank John. Writings on early American architecture; an annotated list of books and articles on architecture constructed before 1860 in the eastern half of the United States. Columbus, Ohio State Univ. Press, 1943. 271 p. 23 cm. (Ohio State Univ., Columbus. Graduate school studies. Contribution in fine arts, no. 2)

Contents: General references, Colonial, Early Republican, New England, Middle Atlantic States, Southern States, North Atlantic States, Architects.

Bibliographies p. 237–39.

Index p. 243–71.

766

Zamora Lucas, Florentino, and Ponce de Leon, Eduardo. Bibliografía española de arquitectura (1526–1850) . . . Madrid, Asoc. de Libreros y Amigos del Libro, 1947. 205 p. illus., facsim. 26 cm. (Publicaciones de la Asoc. de Libreros y Amigos del Libro, 3)

Arranged chronologically by the four centuries.

Index of authors, collaborators, and anonymous works p. 195–202.

SEE ALSO: Columbia University. Libraries. Avery Architectural Library. Catalog (12); Royal Institute of British Architects. Library. Catalogue (22).

Dictionaries and Encyclopedias

767

Architectural Publication Society. Dictionary of architecture . . . London, Richards, 1852–92. 6 v. illus., plates (part col.), plans. 37 cm.

Still a most important work despite its age. Covers architectural forms and subjects, biographies of architects, terminology, and place names with a description of architectural features of the locality. Includes bibliographical references.

768

Bodson, Fern. Dictionnaire des termes récents, symboles & abbréviations; architecture, art de construire, génie civil. Bruxelles, Editec S.P.R.L. [1948]. 244 p. 19 cm.

Gives definition and description as well as etymology for the terms included, and frequently references to usage or sources.

Bibliography p. 233–44.

"Table polyglotte" p. 210–15 gives equivalents in 21 languages.

769

Britton, John. A dictionary of the architecture and archaeology of the Middle Ages; including words used by ancient and modern authors in treating of architectural and other antiquities . . . also, biographical notices of ancient architects. . . . Illustrated by numerous engravings by J. Le Keux . . . London, Longman, Orme, Brown, Green, and Longmans, 1838. 498 p. 39 plates (incl. plans). 25 cm.

"Titles of books and other authorities consulted and referred to" p. xiii–xviii.

"A tabular chronological epitome of the history of architecture in England" by George Godwin, Jr., 2 p. at end of volume.

770

Corkhill, Thomas. A concise building encyclopaedia; an explanation of words, terms, and abbreviations used in building and constructional work, and a work of reference for architects, surveyors, civil and structural engineers, and the various craftsmen engaged in building. 3d ed. London, Pitman, 1951. 365 p. illus. 20 cm.

1st ed. (1932) of 237 pages contains 7000 terms.

The terms defined are those used in Great Britain rather than in the United States.

771

Gwilt, Joseph. An encyclopedia of architecture, historical, theoretical, & practical . . . illustrated with about seventeen hundred engravings on wood. Revised, portions rewritten, and with additions (in 1888) by Wyatt Papworth. . . . New impression. London, N.Y., Longmans Green, 1899. 1443 p. illus., diagr. 23 cm.

1st ed. 1851; 2d ed. 1872; 3d ed. 1881.

"A brief synoptical list of the principal architects, ancient and modern, with their chief works" p. 1129–59.

"A catalogue of the principal and most useful publications relating to architecture" p. [1160]–1220.

"A glossary of terms used in architecture and in building" p. 1201–1393.

Index p. 1395–1443.

772

Isham, Norman Morrison. A glossary of colonial architectural terms, with illustrations. [N.Y.] Walpole Society, 1939. 37 p. illus. 24 cm.

250 copies printed.

Many drawings illustrate the terms.

773

Osborne, Arthur Leslie. A dictionary of English domestic architecture. London, Country Life Limited [1954]. 111 p. illus., plans. 26 cm.

A useful dictionary of terms used in and relating to English domestic architecture, with numerous cross references, line drawings, and plans.

774

Parker, John Henry. A concise glossary of terms used in Grecian, Roman, Italian and

Gothic architecture . . . 5th ed., rev. Oxford and London, J. Parker & Co., 1879. 355 p. illus. 18 cm.

Originally published in an 1869 ed. of 323 pages.

Usually indicates language from which each term is derived.

775

Prasanna-Kumāra, Āchārya. A dictionary of Hindu architecture, treating of Sanskrit architectural terms, with illustrative quotations from Silpasastras, general literature and archaeological records . . . London, N.Y., Oxford Univ. Press [1927]. 861 p. 25 cm.

"A full dictionary of all architectural terms used in the Manasara, with illustrations in English and illustrative quotations from cognate literature where available for the purpose."—*Pref.*

Appendix I, A sketch of Sanskrit treatises on architecture p. 749–804; Appendix II, A list of historical architects with short notes on their works p. 805–24.

Index p. 825–61.

776

Runge, Ilse Dorothea. Dictionnaire technique de l'architecture et de la construction . . . Baden-Baden, Wervereis, 1954. 477 p. 22 cm.

A German-French and French-German dictionary of terms used in architecture and city planning. Includes terms of materials, work, methods, utensils, geometry, drawing, markets, and a few fine arts terms useful to architects. No definitions given. Gender of words is always indicated in each language.

777

Saylor, Henry Hodgman. Dictionary of architecture. N.Y., Wiley [1952]. 221 p. illus. 18 cm.

"Attempts to give spelling, pronunciation (if unusual), and concise definition of the terms met in the study, historical reading and practice of architecture. . . . Illustrations have been restricted to objects that are difficult or impossible to describe in words alone." A most useful, small American dictionary of recent years.

778

Sturgis, Russell, ed. A dictionary of architecture and building, biographical, historical, and descriptive, by Russell Sturgis . . . and many architects, painters, engineers and other expert writers, American and foreign . . . N.Y., Macmillan, 1901–02. 3 v. illus., plates. 27 cm.

Standard dictionary in this field, although old.

Entries are under specific rather than broad, general headings. Longer articles and biographies are signed. Preface states authority responsible for each section. Illustrated by line drawings.

Complete bibliography of sources consulted at end of v. 3, p. 1141–1212, arranged alphabetically by author.

779

Viollet-le-Duc, Eugène Emmanuel. Dictionnaire raisonné de l'architecture française du XIe au XVIe siècle. Paris, Bance, 1854–68. 10 v. illus. 24 cm.

Volumes 7–10 have imprint: Paris, Morel.

————. Table analytique et synthétique du Dictionnaire raisonné de l'architecture française du XIe au XVIe siècle, avec table alphabétique des noms de lieux par départements pour la France et par contrées pour l'étranger [par Henri Sabine]. Paris, Librairie des Imprimeries Réunies, 1889. 387 p. 24 cm.

A basic dictionary with long articles, including sculpture and applied arts as well as architecture.

780

Ware, Dora, and Beatty, Betty. A short dictionary of architecture, including some common building terms. . . . With an introduction on the study of architecture by John Gloag . . . N.Y., Philosophical Library [c1945]. 109 p. illus., diagr. 21 cm.

Short, terse definitions of terms commonly used in architecture, both classical and present day. Many line drawings and diagrams.

Short bibliography p. 108–09 including only English works.

781

Wasmuths Lexikon der Baukunst. Berlin, Wasmuth [c1929–37]. 5 v. illus., plates (part col.), ports., maps, plans (part col.), diagr. 30 cm.

"Unter Mitwirkung zahlreicher Fachleute herausgegeben von Günther Wasmuth; Schriftleitung: Dr.-Ing Leo Adler; Bildredaktion: Georg Kowalczyk."

Covers artistic, social, legal, and historical aspects of architecture and includes terms and biographies. Excellent illustrations, with many diagrams and plans. Longer articles are signed. Short bibliographies given.

Contents: Bd. 1–4, A–Z; Bd. 5, Nachtrag A–Z.

Biography

782

American architects directory. 1st ed. 1956. N.Y., Pub. under the sponsorship of American Inst. of Architects by R. R. Bowker, 1955. 723 p. 29 cm.

Editor, George S. Koyl. Gives list of officers, past and present, of the Institute, honorary members, fellows, and medals and awards p. xviii–xxxvii. Biographical dictionary p. 1–632 gives brief biographical information and affiliations. Geographical index p. 635–99. List of publications and documents of the AIA p. 711–13. "Council of architectural registration boards (NCARB)" p. 714–16. "Association of collegiate schools of architecture" p. 717–20. "Selected list of journals on architecture" p. 721–23.

783

Bauchal, Charles. Noveau dictionnaire biographique et critique des architectes français . . . Paris, André, Daly, 1887. 842 p. 28 cm.

Part 1 covers French architects from earliest times to the end of the 18th century; pt. 2 deals with architects who died between 1801 and 1885. Index to monuments cited in the dictionary p. 735–822; arranged according to Departments and then cities, under which are names of the architects. Monuments built in foreign countries by French architects p. 822–26. Bibliography p. 827–37.

784

Colvin, Howard Montagu. A biographical dictionary of English architects 1660–1840. London, Murray; Cambridge, Mass., Harvard Univ. Press [1954]. 821 p. 23 cm.

Aims "to include every architect (whether amateur, tradesman or professional, who habitually made architectural designs) . . . the major part of whose career falls within the limiting dates."—Pref. Does not include Scottish architects. List of buildings is as full and accurate as possible and usually in chronological order. Sources of information are given in brackets immediately following. Also contains articles on The practice of architecture 1660–1840, The building trades, and The architectural profession. Index of persons p. 769–71, and of places p. 783–821.

785

Mayer, Leo Ary. Islamic architects and their works. Genève, A. Kundig, 1956. 183 p. 26 cm.

Covers "the Muslim world from Morocco to Baloochistan . . . [with] Pakistan, India, Indonesia and other Islamic or part-Islamic

states of the Far East . . . excluded."—*Pref.*
Includes only architects whose buildings still
exist, wholly or in part, or whose works were
adequately described before their destruc-
tion. For each architect gives brief biographical information and a detailed bibliography.
Contents: Introduction p. [15]–29; Roll of
architects p. [31]–135; Topographical index
p. [137]–47; Bibliography p. [149]–83.

786
Royal Institute of British Architects. Library. Index of architects of several countries and many periods (except English
medieval) in nearly 60 old and new selected
indexes . . . London, The Institute. 66 p.
Typewritten script. In progress and
expected to appear in 1959, in a limited
edition.

787
Withey, Henry F., and Rathbun, Elise. Biographical dictionary of American architects (deceased). Los Angeles, New Age Pub.
Co. [1956]. 678 p. 23 cm.
Gives material concerning the lives of
nearly 2000 men and women who carried on
work from *ca.* 1740–1952. Includes bibliographies.

SEE ALSO: Baert. Mémoires sur les sculpteurs
et architectes des Pays-Bas (944); Bessone-
Aurelj. Dizionario degli scultori ed architetti italiani (945); Dézallier d'Argenville.
Vies des fameux architectes (2002).

Histories and Handbooks

788
Benoit, François. . . . L'architecture . . .
Paris, Laurens, 1911–34. 4 v. illus. (incl. maps,
plans), plates, diagrs. 25 cm. (Manuels d'histoire de l'art)
A thoroughly organized handbook of archaeology and architecture. Contents: v. 1,
Antiquité; v. 2, L'Orient, médiéval et moderne; v. 3, L'Occident médiéval du romain
au roman; v. 4, L'Occident médiéval romano-
gothique et gothique.
"Chronologie monumentale" v. 4, p. 413–
45. "Tableau synoptique de l'activité archi-
tecturale et de la concurrence des styles en
occident du début du IVe siècle à la fin du
XIIIe siècle" v. 4, p. 447–57. Indexes of monuments, of architects, of artistic references,
and of history and geography in each volume.

789
Burckhardt, Jakob, and Lübke, Wilhelm.
Geschichte der neueren Baukunst. Stuttgart,
Ebner, 1882–(1927). 10 v. illus. (incl. plans).
25 cm.
Volumes 8–9 have imprint: Esslingen, Neff;
v. 10 has imprint: Stuttgart, Neff. A classic
German work.
Contents: Bd. 1, J. Burckhardt. Geschichte
der Renaissance in Italien, 3. Aufl., 1891; Bd.
2–3, W. Lübke. Geschichte der Renaissance
in Deutschland, 2. verb. & verm. Aufl., 1882;
Bd. 4, W. Lübke. Geschichte der Renaissance
in Frankreich, 2. verb. & verm. Aufl., 1885;
Bd. 5, C. Gurlitt. Geschichte des Barockstiles
in Italien, 1887; Bd. 6, C. Gurlitt. Geschichte
des Barockstiles, des Rococo und des Klas-
sicismus in Belgien, Holland, Frankreich,
England, 1888; Bd. 7, C. Gurlitt. Geschichte
des Barockstiles und des Rococo in Deutschland, 1889; Bd. 8, O. Schubert. Geschichte
des Barock in Spanien, 1908; Bd. 9, P. Klopfer. Von Palladio bis Schinkel, 1911; Bd. 10,
A. Haupt. Geschichte der Renaissance in
Spanien und Portugal, 1927.
Each volume has index of artists and
places.

790
Choisy, Auguste. Histoire de l'architecture.
Paris, Vincent, Fréal, 1954. 2 v. illus., plans.
24 cm.
Originally published in 1899. A general
history of architecture by a recognized authority. Illustrated by drawings in the text.
No bibliographies. No index, but the tables
of contents at end of each volume are fairly
detailed.

791
Fergusson, James. A history of architecture in
all countries from the earliest times to the
present day. London, Murray, 1891–99. 5 v.
illus., plans, maps. 23 cm.
Rev., expanded, and rearranged ed. of his
The Illustrated handbook of architecture,
first published in 1855, and frequently reprinted and revised. Volumes 1–2, 3d ed. edited by R. Phené Spiers; v. 4–5, 3d. ed.
edited by Robert Kerr.
Contents: v. 1–2, History of ancient and
medieval architecture; v. 3, History of Indian and Eastern architecture; v. 4–5, History of modern styles of architecture. Index
to the entire work v. 5, p. 439–53.

792
Fletcher, *Sir* Banister Flight. A history of architecture on the comparative method, for

students, craftsmen & amateurs . . . 16th ed. London, Batsford, 1954. 1033 p. illus., maps, plans. 25 cm.

1st ed. 1896. A standard reference work, profusely illustrated with many drawings, plans, cross sections, etc.

According to the preface each style is considered under five sections: (1) Geographical, geological, climatic, religious, social, historical; (2) Architectural character; (3) Examples; (4) Comparative analysis (Plans, walls, openings, roofs, columns, mouldings, and ornament); (5) Reference books. Bibliographies at end of each chapter. Glossary of terms.

793

Gloag, John. Guide to Western architecture. With 279 illus. in the text of which 161 were drawn by Hilton Wright. N.Y., Macmillan; London, Allen and Unwin [1958]. 407 p. illus., 32 plates, maps. 25 cm.

A useful but summary outline of the architecture of Western civilization from the 6th century B.C. to the present. Illustrated with line drawings in the text, and plates.

"Sources of reference in the text" p. 347–56. "Some books on architecture" p. 357–60 (annotated). "The principal architects and their works, from the seventh century B.C. to the end of the Renaissance" p. 361–92. Index p. 395–407.

794

Guadet, Julien. Éléments et théorie de l'architecture; cours professé à l'École Nationale et Spéciale des Beaux-Arts . . . Paris, Librairie de la Construction Moderne [1902]. 4 v. illus., 47 plates, plans. 29 cm.

Treated in the manner of the courses given at the École des Beaux-Arts. Each volume has its own table of contents. Volume 3 contains "Table alphabétique des matières contenues dans l'ouvrage" p. [535]–64 and "Table alphabétique des figures contenues dans l'ouvrage" p. 565–601. Volume 4, "Additions," has its own table of contents and the same indexes of subjects and illustrations as v. 3.

795

Hamlin, Alfred Dwight Foster. A text-book of the history of architecture . . . 5th ed. N.Y., London, Longmans, Green, 1904. 453 p. illus., plate. 19 cm. (College histories of art)

Numerous editions and printings; new ed., rev. 1928 (N.Y., Longmans, Green). An old work but still useful. Attempts to "sketch

the various periods and styles of architecture with broadest possible strokes and to mention . . . the most important works of each period or style."—*Pref.*

Bibliography p. xix–xx. "Glossary of terms not defined in the text" p. 429–30. Index of architects p. 431–34. Index p. 435–53.

796

Hamlin, Talbot Faulkner. Architecture through the ages . . . [Rev. ed.] N.Y., Putnam [1953]. 684 p. illus., plates, plans. 24 cm.

Originally published in 1940. A good one-volume history of architecture. Bibliography (mostly background books) included in the Foreword. Index p. 659–84.

797

Handbuch der Architektur, unter Mitwirkung von Fachgenossen hrsg. von Josef Durm, Hermann Ende, Eduard Schmitt und Heinrich Wagner . . . Darmstadt, Diehl, 1883–(1943). 79 v. illus., plates, plans, diagrs. 28 cm.

The volumes of 4. Teil are called "Halbbände." By 1943 79 volumes (1st–4th eds.) had appeared. Continued by *Fortschritte auf dem Gebiete der Architektur.*

A monumental work on architecture, much of which is of merely historical value. Divided into four sections covering: (1) General building; (2) Historical styles; (3) Building construction; (4) Design, building and equipment. Contains bibliographies.

798

Kimball, Sidney Fiske, and Edgell, George Harold. A history of architecture . . . N.Y., London, Harper [1918]. 621 p. illus., plans. 21 cm. (Harper's fine arts series)

A useful one-volume handbook. "Bibliographical note" and "Chronological list of monuments" at end of each chapter. Glossary p. 589–602. Index p. 605–21.

799

Kugler, Franz Theodor. Geschichte der Baukunst . . . Mit Illustrationen und andern artistischen Beilagen . . . Stuttgart, Ebner & Seubert, 1856–59. 3 v. illus., plans. 23 cm.

A standard German history of architecture illustrated by drawings in the text. Each volume contains its own indexes of places, artists, and illustrations.

800

Lübke, Wilhelm. Geschichte der Architektur von den ältesten Zeiten bis zur Gegenwart . . . 6. Aufl. . . . Leipzig, Seeman, 1884–86. 2 v. illus., plans. 25 cm.

A standard German history of architecture covering both Oriental and Western art. "Register der technischen Ausdrücke" v. 2, p. 553–54. "Verzeichnis der Baumeister" v. 2, p. 554–58. "Ortsregister" v. 2, p. 558–72.

801
Lundberg, Erik. Arkitekturens formspråk; studier över arkitekturens konstnärliga värden i deras historiska utvekling. Stockholm, Nordisk Rotogravyr [1945]–(56). v. 1–(6). illus., plates (part col.), maps, plans. 26 cm.

An extensive, clearly illustrated history of architectural development. Contents: (1) Den aldre antiken; (2) Den yngre antiken 300 f.Kr.–600 (300 B.C.–600 A.D.); (3) Västerlandets medeltid, 600–1200; (4) Västerlandets medeltid 1200–1450; (5) Renässansen i Italien 1420–1620; (6) Sengotiken samt Renässansen utanför Italien 1420–1540. Includes bibliographies.

802
Pevsner, Nikolaus. An outline of European architecture. [1st American ed.] N.Y., Scribner [1948]. 242 p. illus., 72 plates, plans. 23 cm.

A terse history of architecture confining itself to the main trends of post-Roman Europe. "Some technical terms explained" p. 223–24. "American postscript" p. 227–34. Bibliography p. 217–22. Index p. 235–42.

803
Simpson, Frederick Moore. A history of architectural development . . . London, N.Y., Longmans, Green, 1921–22. 3 v. illus. (incl. plans), plates. 24 cm. (Half-title: The Architects' library. Editor: F. M. Simpson)

Originally published 1905–11; 1921–22 ed. is called "New Impression." Illustrated with many drawings, plans, and diagrams.

Contents: v. 1, Ancient, Early Christian, and Byzantine; v. 2, Medieval; v. 3, The Renaissance in Italy, France, and England. Each volume has separate index at end. Volume 1 has appendix giving "approximate superficial areas of typical buildings or portions of buildings . . . and the percentages of their voids and solids" p. 259; v. 2 has appendix of "Table of dimensions of typical churches" p. 373–77. Bibliography v. 1, p. xv–xvi.

804
Simpson, Frederick Moore. Simpson's history of architectural development. [new ed.] London, N.Y., Longmans, Green [1954]–(56). v. 1–(2). illus., maps, plans. 22 cm.

An entirely new ed. to be completed in five volumes. Only the method and technique of the original work are retained.

Contents: v. 1, Hugh Plommer. Ancient and classical architecture, 1956; v. 2, Cecil Stewart. Early Christian, Byzantine and Romanesque architecture, 1954; v. 3, Cecil Stewart. Medieval architecture (not yet published); v. 4, J. Quentin Hughes and Robert Lynton. Renaissance architecture (not yet published); v. 5, Thomas Howarth. Nineteenth and twentieth century architecture (not yet published).

Bibliographies, glossaries, and indexes of buildings and plans.

805
Sturgis, Russell. A history of architecture . . . N.Y., Baker & Taylor [c1906]–15. 4 v. illus., plates, plans. 27 cm.

Volumes 3–4 are by A. L. Frothingham and have imprint: Garden City, N.Y., Doubleday, Page, 1915.

Contents: I, Antiquity; II, Romanesque and Oriental; III, Gothic in Italy, France, and Northern Europe; IV, Gothic in Great Britain, Renaissance, modern architecture. Index to all four volumes at end of v. 4, p. 335–57.

Ancient

806
Anderson, William James. The architecture of ancient Greece: an account of its historic development, being the first part of the Architecture of Greece and Rome, by William J. Anderson . . . and R. Phené Spiers . . . rev. and rewritten by William Bell Dinsmoor . . . London, Batsford [1927]. 241 p. illus., plates, plans, map. 24 cm.

An old standard work. See Dinsmoor, W. B. (813) for latest ed. Bibliography p. [201]–11.

807
Anderson, William James. The architecture of ancient Rome: an account of its historic development; being the second part of the Architecture of Greece and Rome, by William J. Anderson . . . and R. Phené Spiers . . . rev. and rewritten by Thomas Ashby . . . London, Batsford [1927]. 202 p. illus., plates, plans, map. 24 cm.

A standard work. "Chronological memoranda" p. xii. Selective bibliography p. [175]–79. Glossary p. [180]–92.

808
Canina, Luigi. Gli edifizj di Roma antica cogniti per alcune reliquie, descritti e dimostrati nell'intera loro architettura dal commendatore Luigi Canina. Roma, Canina, 1848–56. 6 v. 517 plates. 59 cm.

Imprint of v. III–VI: Stab. Tip. di G. A. Bertinelli. A corpus of beautiful plans and drawings of the ancient buildings of Rome.

Volumes 1, 3, 5 contain text; v. 2, 4, 6 are plates. Arranged by form: v. 1, walls and doors, temples, forums, basilicas, and porticos; v. 3, theaters, amphitheaters, circuses, baths, aqueducts, bridges, triumphal arches, and commemorative monuments; v. 5, text with map of Campagna. List of plates at beginning of each plate volume.

809
Choisy, Auguste. L'art de bâtir chez les Égyptiens. Paris, Rouveyre, 1904. 155 p. illus., 24 plates. 29 cm.

A standard work on Egyptian construction, illustrated with line drawings in the text and plates.

810
Choisy, Auguste. L'art de bâtir chez les Romains . . . Paris, Ducher, 1873. 216 p. illus., 24 plates. 42 cm.

A standard work on Roman construction.

811
Clarke, Somers. Ancient Egyptian masonry: the building craft by . . . Somers Clarke . . . and R. Engelbach . . . London, Oxford Univ. Press, Milford, 1930. 242 p. illus., plates, map, diagrs. 26 cm.

A detailed treatment of "problems incident to the construction of a stone building in Ancient Egypt."—*Pref.* Well illustrated.

Appendix I, Ancient Egyptian tools; Appendix II, "List of localities in Egypt and Lower Nubia mentioned in the volume" p. 225–26; Appendix III, Chronology p. 227–29. Bibliography p. [230]–32. Index p. 233–42.

812
Desgodetz, Antoine B. Les édifices antiques de Rome, mésurés et dessinés très-exactement sur les lieux . . . Rome, Poggioli, 1822. 116 p. 137 plates, plans. 41 cm.

Originally published 1682; several later editions; English translation 1848 (London, Weale). Title page and text in French and Italian. Very detailed, measured drawings and elevations of the important ancient monuments in Rome.

———. Supplemento all'opera sugli edifizi antichi di Roma . . . Roma, Dai Tipi della Rev. Cam. Apostolica, 1843. 2 v. in 1. 93 plates, plans. 41 cm.

813
Dinsmoor, William Bell. The architecture of ancient Greece; an account of its historic development . . . 3d ed. rev. London, Batsford [1950]. 424 p. illus., maps. 24 cm.

"Revised and enlarged edition based on the first part of the *Architecture of Greece and Rome* by William J. Anderson and R. Phené Spiers."—*Title Page.* A standard work.

Appendix of "Metric measurements of temples" p. 337–40 (with measurements in feet). Chronological list of Greek temples (chart). Selected, classed bibliography p. 341–86; list of periodicals p. 386; glossary p. 387–97; detailed index p. 398–424.

814
Espouy, Hector d'. Fragments d'architecture antique d'après les relevés & restaurations des anciens pensionnaires de l'Académie de France à Rome . . . Paris, Massin [1896]–1905. 2 pts. 200 plates. 44 x 33 cm.

Careful renderings of details and ornament from ancient monuments.

815
Fyfe, Theodore. Hellenistic architecture; an introductory study . . . Cambridge, The Univ. Press, 1936. 247 p. illus., 29 plates. 24 cm.

Contents: (1) Rise and development of Hellenistic architecture; (2) The temple; (3) Tombs and monuments; (4) The orders, scenic and Barock tendencies; (5) Detail and decoration; (6) Materials, construction and technique; (7) The house; (8) Civic design; (9) Aftermath of Hellenism.

Glossary p. 197–206. Index p. 239–47.

816
Platner, Samuel Ball. A topographical dictionary of ancient Rome . . . completed and revised by Thomas Ashby. London, Oxford Univ. Press, 1929. 608 p. illus., plates, maps, plans. 25 cm.

A standard work for Roman architecture. "List of abbreviations" p. xix–xxiii. "Chronological index to dateable monuments" p. 587–600. "Addenda & corrigenda" p. 601–08.

817
Plommer, Hugh. Ancient and classical architecture. London, N.Y., Longmans Green [1956]. 384 p. illus., plates, plans. 22 cm. (Simpson's History of architectural development, 1)

The most up-to-date volume in this field. Bibliographical footnotes. "Architectural glossary" p. 367–71. "Chief authorities used, with abbreviations" p. xxi–xxii. Index p. 372–84.

818

Rivoira, Giovanni Teresio. Roman architecture and its principles of construction under the empire, with an appendix on the evolution of the dome up to the XVIIth century . . . translated from the Italian by G. McN. Rushforth. Oxford, Clarendon Press, 1925. 310 p. illus. (incl. plans). 30 cm.

Bibliography (of the author) p. [xvii]. General index p. 309–10. Index of places p. 303–08; of coins p. 311.

819

Robertson, Donald Struan. A handbook of Greek & Roman architecture . . . 2d ed. Cambridge, Univ. Press, 1943. 407 p. illus. (incl. plans), 24 plates. 24 cm.

1st ed. 1929. The aim of the book is "to state briefly but clearly the main facts in the history of Greek, Etruscan, and Roman architecture from the earliest times to the foundation of Constantinople."

Appendixes: I, "Select chronological tables of Greek, Etruscan, and Roman buildings from 1000 B.C. to 330 A.D." p. 332–46; II, "Select bibliography (up to 1928) of prehistoric, Greek, Etruscan, and Roman architecture from the earliest times to 330 A.D." p. [347]–78; III, "Select glossary of architectural terms" p. 379–90 and "Reference list of Greek terms mentioned in this book."

820

Seure, Georges. Monuments antiques relevés et restaurés par les architectes pensionnaires de l'Académie de France à Rome; notices archéologiques par Georges Seure . . . Paris, Massin [1910–12]. 3 v. illus., 280 plates (incl. plans) on 208 l. 46 cm.

Beautiful plans, drawings, and restorations of ancient monuments. Contents: v. 1, Monuments antiques de la Grèce et des pays grecs; v. 2, Monuments antiques de Rome; v. 3, Monuments antiques de l'Italie et des provinces romaines.

———. Supplément. [Notices archéologiques par Victor Chapot] Paris, Massin [192?]. 9 p. 53 plates (incl. plans). 46 cm.

821

Smith, Earl Baldwin. Egyptian architecture as cultural expression . . . N.Y., London, Appleton-Century, 1938. 264 p. illus. (incl. plans). 28 cm.

A sound work on Egyptian architecture, well illustrated with line drawings and plans. Index p. 257–64.

822

Stuart, James, and Revett, Nicholas. The antiquities of Athens, measured and delineated by James Stuart . . . and Nicholas Revett . . . London, Haberkorn, 1762–1830. 5 v. illus., plates, maps. 56 cm.

Several later editions. Measured drawings of outstanding Greek monuments. Important as an inspiration of the Classic Revival movement.

Volume 5 is a supplement: *Antiquities of Athens and other places in Greece, Sicily, etc.* (London, Priestly and Weale, 1830).

SEE ALSO: Lafreri. Speculum Romanae magnificentiae (2012); Lawrence. Greek architecture (452); Vitruvius Pollio. De architectura (2046).

Early Christian—Gothic

823

Butler, Howard Crosby. Early churches in Syria, fourth to seventh centuries. . . . Ed. and completed by E. Baldwin Smith . . . [Princeton] Pub. for the Department of Art and Archaeology of Princeton Univ., 1929. 274 p. illus., plans. 39 cm. (Princeton monographs in art and archaeology)

A standard work on this phase of early Christian architecture. Index p. 265–74.

824

Choisy, Auguste. L'art de bâtir chez les Byzantines . . . Paris, Société Anonyme, 1883. 187 p. illus., 25 plates. 42 cm.

A standard work on Byzantine methods of construction, illustrated by many diagrams and plates.

825

Cottineau, L. H. Répertoire topo-bibliographique des abbayes et prieurés . . . Mâcon, Protat, 1935–38. 2 v. Fasc. 1–11. 29 cm.

An alphabetical listing of religious houses officially bearing the title of abbey or priory. For each gives a brief history and bibliography.

826

Dehio, Georg Gottfried. Die kirchliche Baukunst des Abendlandes, historisch und systematisch dargestellt von G. Dehio und G. von Bezold. Stuttgart, Cotta, 1887–1901. 2 v.

illus. 25 cm. *and* atlas of 601 plates in 5 v. 41 cm.

A standard reference work on Christian architecture. Plates consist of drawings and renderings.

Contents: Bd. 1, Der christlich-antike Stil, Der romanische Stil; Bd. 2, Der gotische Stil. Extensive bibliographies at the beginning of the chapters. Index to both volumes in v. 2, p. 600–23.

827

Golzio, Vincenzo. Architettura bizantina e romanica. Milano, Società Editrice Libreria, 1939. 233 p. illus. (incl plans). 30 cm.

A well-illustrated survey of Byzantine and Romanesque architecture. Bibliography p. 228. Index of artists and places p. 229–33.

828

Hamann, Richard. Deutsche und französische Kunst im Mittelalter . . . Marburg, Kunstgeschichtliches Seminar, 1922–23. 2 v. illus. 29 cm.

Covers some aspects of German and French medieval architecture. Good illustrations.

Contents: v. 1, Südfranzösische Protorenaissance und ihre Ausbreitung in Deutschland auf dem Wege durch Italien und die Schweiz; v. 2, Die Baugeschichte der Klosterkirche zu Lehnin und die normannische Invasion in der deutschen Architektur des 13. Jahrhunderts.

829

Hamilton, John Arnott. Byzantine architecture and decoration, with a foreword by Professor D. Talbot Rice. London, Batsford [1956]. [302] p. illus., plates. 23 cm.

"The whole book has been revised and re-written."—*Pref.* 1st ed. 1933.

The standard work on Byzantine architecture, well illustrated. Bibliography p. 281–94. Index p. 297–[302].

830

Jackson, *Sir* Thomas Graham. Byzantine and Romanesque architecture. 2d. ed. Cambridge, Univ. Press, 1920. 2 v. illus., plates (part col.), plans. 25 cm.

A general survey of the field. Many illustrations, with details, sketches, and plans. "Chronological table of architectural examples" p. [269]–77. Index at end of v. 2, p. 278–85.

831

Jackson, *Sir* Thomas Graham. Gothic architecture in France, England and Italy . . .

Cambridge, The Univ. Press, 1915. 2 v. illus., 191 plates (part col.), plans, diagrs. 25 cm.

A continuation of the author's *Byzantine and Romanesque architecture* (830).

Illustrated by drawings, halftones, and numerous plans. "Chronological table of dates" v. 2, p. 321–30. Index v. 2, p. 331–39.

832

Porter, Arthur Kingsley. Medieval architecture, its origins and development, with lists of monuments and bibliographies. New Haven, Yale Univ. Press, 1912. 2 v. illus., plates, plans, diagrs. 28 cm.

First published 1909 (N.Y., Baker & Taylor). Written for the beginner rather than the specialist. Well illustrated with many plates, diagrams, and plans.

Volume 1 is subtitled: The origins; v. 2: Normandy and the Ile de France. Covers Roman, Early Christian, Byzantine, Lombard, Norman, Romanesque in the Ile de France, Transition, Culmination, and Flamboyant Gothic. England is not included.

Each chapter has lists of monuments with descriptions classed according to importance. A general index at end of each volume. Bibliographies (v. 1, p. 333–467; v. 2, p. 417–79) are classed and annotated and contain bibliographical indexes.

833

Villard de Honnecourt. Facsimile of the sketch-book of Wilars de Honecort, an architect of the thirteenth century; with commentaries and descriptions by M. J. B. A. Lassus . . . and by M. J. Quicherat . . . translated and edited with many additional articles and notes, by the Rev. Robert Willis . . . London, Parker, 1859. 243 p. 73 plates (incl. facsims.), plan. 32 cm.

The original work is no. 19093 of the French manuscripts in the Bibliothèque Nationale, Paris. There is another facsimile edition, in French, with title: *Album de Villard de Honnecourt* (Paris, Berthaud [1906]).

Contents: List of engravings; Essay on Wilars de Honecort and his sketch-book, by M. Jules Quicherat; Description of the manuscript and its contents; Tabular view of the various pagings, quires and subjects of the ms.; Classified list of the subjects of the drawings; Explanation of the plates; Addenda and corrigenda. Glossarial index p. 241–43.

834

Villard de Honnecourt. Kritische Gesamtausgabe des Bauhüttenbuches ms. fr. 19093 der Pariser Nationalbibliotek. Hrsg. von H.

R. Hahnloser. Wien, Schroll, 1935. 342 p. illus., plates, 66 facsims. 31 cm.

A scholarly German commentary on the manuscript of Villard de Honnecourt. Excellent collotype plates.

Bibliography p. 280–81; Glossary p. 288–97. "Personen- Orts- und Sachregister, zusammengestellt von Dr. Otto Reicher" p. 298–340.

SEE ALSO: Simpson's History of architectural development, v. 2 (804).

Renaissance—Modern

835

Briggs, Martin Shaw. Baroque architecture . . . with 109 illustrations. London, Unwin [1913]. 238 p. illus., 71 plates. 26 cm.

One of the first of the limited number of books on this subject in English. Bibliography at end of each chapter except the last.

836

Encyclopédie de l'architecture . . . Constructions modernes . . . [Paris] Morancé [193?–(40?)]. v. 1–(12). plates, plans. 28 cm.

A corpus of excellent plates containing reproductions and plans of modern buildings, mostly French, although some are from other countries. At beginning of each volume is a general table of contents, an analytical table arranged by subjects, and an alphabetical list of architects and builders.

837

Giedion, Siegfried. Space, time and architecture; the growth of a new tradition. 3d ed. enl. Cambridge, Mass., Harvard Univ. Press, 1954. 778 p. illus., maps, plans. 25 cm. (The Charles Eliot Norton lectures for 1938–39)

1st ed. 1941; 2d ed. 1949. A pioneer treatise on the spiritual and technological foundations of modern architecture. Bibliographical footnotes. Index p. 768–78.

838

Hamlin, Talbot Faulkner. Forms and functions of twentieth-century architecture . . . N.Y., Columbia Univ. Press, 1952. 4 v. illus., plans. 26 cm.

"Prepared under the auspices of the School of Architecture of Columbia University" and compiled by specialists. "A new work to succeed Guadet's Éléments et théorie de l'architecture [794]."—Pref.

Contents: v. 1, The elements of building; v. 2, The principles of composition; v. 3–4,

Building types. Each chapter contains suggested readings. General index to the four volumes in v. 4, p. 843–906. "Index of architectural works" v. 4, p. 907–46.

839

Hitchcock, Henry-Russell. Modern architecture, romanticism and reintegration. N.Y., Payson & Clarke, 1929. 252 p. plates. 29 cm.

A standard work on modern architecture. "Bibliographical note" p. [237]–41. Index p. 245–52.

840

Jackson, *Sir* Thomas Graham. The Renaissance of Roman architecture . . . Cambridge, The Univ. Press, 1921–23. 3 v. illus., plates (part col.), plans. 25 cm.

Contents: v. 1, Italy; v. 2, England; v. 3, France. Each volume has a chronological table of dates and an index.

841

Whittick, Arnold. European architecture in the twentieth century. London, Lockwood, 1950–53. 2 v. illus. 26 cm.

Contents: v. 1, Historical background and the early years of the century. Transition from war to peace 1919–1924; v. 2, The era of functionalism, 1924–1933. To be completed by a third volume covering the period between 1933 and 1950.

Bibliography: v. 1, p. 219–23; v. 2, p. 244–48. Each volume has its own index.

842

Zevi, Bruno. Storia dell'architettura moderna. [Torino] Einaudi, 1950. 786 p. illus., plates, plans, map, diagrs. 22 cm. (Saggi, 136)

2d rev. ed. of 795 pages published 1953. A good one-volume Italian account of modern architecture which covers the United States as well as Europe.

Chronological tables p. 689–715. Bibliography p. [559]–685. Index of names p. 717–39; of places and monuments p. 741–52; of illustrations in the text p. 753–60; of plates p. 761–79.

SEE ALSO: Hitchcock, H.-R. Architecture: Nineteenth and twentieth centuries (452).

National

France

843

Androuet du Cerceau, Jacques. Les plus excellents bastiments de France; gravés en fac-similé par Faure Dujarric . . . Nouvelle éd. augmentée de planches inédites de Du Cerceau . . . Paris, Levy, 1868–70. 2 v. 136 plates (incl. plans). 46 cm.

Originally published 1576–79; 2d ed. 1607; 3d ed. under title *Livre d'architecture* (Paris, Marcette, 1648). All are identical.

A collection of engravings of façades, plans, and details of important French buildings rendered by an eminent French architect.

844

Aubert, Marcel. L'art français à l'époque romane, architecture et sculpture . . . [Paris] Morancé [1929–51]. 4 v. illus., 180 plates, plans. 53 cm.

This series completes the material found in *L'art roman en France, l'architecture et la décoration* by Camille Martin (858). A collection of excellent collotypes of French Romanesque architecture, including plans, with a short text.

Contents: (1) Ile-de-France, Champagne, Alsace, Normandie, Vallée de la Loire; (2) Poitou, Saintonge, Angoumois, Périgord, Nivernais, Auvergne, Velay; (3) Bourgogne; (4) Provence, Languedoc.

Includes bibliographies.

845

Blomfield, *Sir* Reginald Theodore. A history of French architecture from the death of Mazarin till the death of Louis XV, 1661–1774 . . . London, Bell, 1921. 2 v. 200 plates (incl. plans). 29 cm.

A standard work. Bibliography v. 1, p. [xxiii]–xxviii; "A list of surintendants des bâtiments and of directeurs de l'Académie de France à Rome" v. 1, p. xxix–xxx; Appendix "on the flat vaulting of the Roussillon" v. 1, p. 221–24.

Appendix "Soufflot and the dome of the Pantheon" v. 2, p. 201–02; Index v. 2, p. 203–33.

846

Blomfield, *Sir* Reginald Theodore. A history of French architecture, from the reign of Charles VIII till the death of Mazarin . . . London, Bell, 1911. 2 v. 178 plates (incl. plans, facsims.) 29 cm.

A standard work covering French Neo-Classic architecture from its tentative beginnings c.1494 to its mature development in 1661. Illustrated by the author's drawings and halftones.

Bibliography v. 1, p. xxvii–xxxii. Index v. 2, p. 153–76.

847

Daly, César. Motifs historiques d'architecture et de sculpture d'ornement (première série). Décorations extérieures empruntées à des monuments français du commencement de la renaissance à la fin de Louis XVI. Paris, Daly, 1881. 2 v. 198 plates. 45 cm.

Beautifully drawn details of drawings, moldings, cornices, consoles, etc.

848

Daly, César. Motifs historiques d'architecture et de sculpture d'ornement (2. série). Décorations intérieures empruntées à des édifices français du commencement de la renaissance à la fin de Louis XVI (XVIe, XVIIe, XVIIIe siècles) . . . Paris, Ducher, 1880. 2 v. 164 plates (17 col.) 46 cm.

Carefully rendered details of ornament from interior decoration in France from the 16th to the 18th century.

849

Flipo, Vincent. Mémento pratique d'archéologie française; illustré de 700 gravures dans le texte et de 18 hors-texte, tirés en héliogravure. [Paris] Firmin-Didot [c1930]. 372 p. illus. (incl. plans), plates. 27 cm.

Covers 8th to 16th centuries. Particularly valuable for the diagrams of architectural details which are superimposed, on transparent paper, on top of reproductions of church interiors.

Contents: (1) L'architecture p. 9–268; (2) La décoration p. 268–331; (3) L'iconographie p. 332–45. "Bibliographie sommaire" p. [349]; "Glossaire" p. 351–59 includes many drawings and diagrams. "Table onomastique des illustrations" p. 361–68; "Table des planches hors-texte" p. 369.

Appendices include "Conseils techniques" p. 346–48.

850

France. Commission des Monuments Historiques. Archives de la Commission des monuments historiques; pub. par ordre de . . . M. Achille Fould . . . 1855–72. Paris, Gide et Baudry [1855–72]. 4 v. illus., 235 plates (part col.) 64 x 47 cm.

A series of beautifully executed plates of plans, elevations, and sections, begun under the second Empire, of French architectural monuments arranged by type, with descriptive text. Decorative arts are included.

Contents: v. 1, Architecture antique, Moyen âge: Architecture religieuse; v. 2, Moyen âge: Architecture religieuse, Architecture épiscopale et monastique; v. 3, Moyen âge: Architecture militaire; v. 4, Renaissance: Architecture civile.

851
France. Commission des Monuments Historiques. Archives de la Commission des monuments historiques pub. sous le patronage de l'Administration des Beaux-Arts par . . . A. de Baudot . . . [et] A. Perrault-Dabot . . . assistés d'une délégation de la Commission . . . Paris, Laurens [etc., 1898–1903]. 5 v. 500 plates (incl. plans). 47 cm.

Not to be confused with "Archives" of an earlier Commission, published 1856–73, edition of 350 copies, not for sale. An architectural survey on good plates of elevations, sections, plans, views, and details of French architectural monuments, including some minor monuments. No text, no index.

Contents: t. 1, Ile de France, Picardie; t. 2, Normandie, Bretagne, Anjou, Poitou; t. 3, Champagne, Lorraine, Bourgogne, Franche-Comté, Nivernais, Orléanais, Touraine; t. 4, Lyonnais, Berri, Bourbonnais, Auvergne, Dauphiné, Angoumois, Aunis, Saintonge; t. 5, Périgord, Languedoc, Provence, Guyenne, Gascogne.

852
Hautecoeur, Louis. Histoire de l'architecture classique en France. Paris, Picard, 1943–57. 7 v. in 9. illus., plans. 30 cm.

The most ambitious work of recent times on French architecture.

Contents: t. 1, La formation de l'idéal classique: la renaissance. La formation de l'idéal classique: l'architecture sous Henri IV et Louis XIII; t. 2, La règne de Louis XIV; t. 3, Première moitié du XVIIIe siècle: le style Louis XV; t. 4, Seconde moitié du XVIIIe siècle: le style Louis XVI, 1750–1792; t. 5, Revolution et empire, 1792–1815; t. 6, Le restauration et le gouvernement de juillet, 1815–1848; t. 7, La fin de l'architecture classique 1848–1900.

Each volume (except one) has its own index and appendices listing various items, such as organs and convents, built during the period covered.

853
Hubert, Jean. L'art pré-roman . . . dessins de Joséphine Hubert. Paris, Éditions d'Art et d'Histoire, 1938. 202 p. illus. (incl. maps), 40 plates, plans, diagrs. 28 cm. (Les monuments datés de la France, collection pub. sous la direction de M. Louis Hautecoeur)

With this collection of plates the author traces the art of France from the 5th to the 10th century, covering architecture and decoration.

Bibliographical footnotes. Index p. 179–90. List of figures in the text p. [191]–94; List of plates p. [195]–200. Table of contents p. [201]–02 lists the monuments with their dates.

854
Inventaire général des richesses d'art de la France . . . Paris, Plon, 1876–1913. 22 v. in 24. plans. 29 cm.

At head of title: Ministère de L'Instruction Publique et des Beaux-Arts . . .

A detailed and extensive inventory of French architectural monuments and their decorative arts, issued in fascicles, each covering an individual structure, combined in volumes which are analytically indexed.

The inventory, which was never quite finished, comprises 5 series: (1) Paris. Monuments religieux, 1876–1901, 3 v. in 5; (2) Paris. Monuments civils, 1879–1913, 4 v.; (3) Province. Monuments religieux, 1886–1907, 4 v.; (4) Province. Monuments civils, 1877–1911, 8 v.; (5) Archives du Musée des monuments français, 1883–97, 3 v., which contain historical museum papers relating to the organization of French museums.

855
Lasteyrie du Saillant, Robert Charles, *Comte* de. L'architecture religieuse en France à l'époque gothique, ouvrage posthume publié par les soins de M. Marcel Aubert. Paris, Picard, 1926–27. 2 v. illus. (incl. plans). 31 cm.

A standard work on French Gothic religious architecture. "Table alphabétique" v. 2, p. 577–602.

856
Lasteyrie du Saillant, Robert Charles, *Comte* de. L'architecture religieuse en France à l'époque romane. 2. éd. rev. et augm. d'une bibliographie critique, par M. Marcel Aubert. Paris, Picard, 1929. 857 p. illus. (incl. plans). 31 cm.

1st ed. 1911. A standard work on French Romanesque religious architecture. "Bibliographie critique des ouvrages parus depuis la première édition" p. 726–828. Index p. 829–51.

857
Martin, Camille. L'art gothique en France; l'architecture et la décoration. Paris, Eggimann [c1913–25]. 146 plates. 52 cm.

[Sér. 1] by Camille Martin; sér. 2 by Camille Enlart. Ser. 2 has imprint: Paris, Morancé.

Excellent collotype reproductions of important Gothic monuments in France, preceded in each volume by 16 pages of explanatory text.

858

Martin, Camille. L'art roman en France; l'architecture et la décoration . . . Paris, Eggimann [c1910–14]. 2 v. (Sér. 1, 3) illus., 160 plates. 52 cm.

Excellent collotype plates of Romanesque architecture and decoration in France. Each volume has 12–16 pages of text with descriptive notes and plans.

859

Ward, William Henry. The architecture of the Renaissance in France: a history of the evolution of the arts of building, decoration and garden design under classical influence from 1495 to 1830. 2d ed. rev. N.Y., Scribner [1926]. 2 v. illus., plates, plans. 24 cm.

1st ed. 1911. Paged continuously. A well-illustrated basic work. Contents: v. 1, The early Renaissance (1495–1640); v. 2, The later Renaissance (1640–1820).

Bibliography and index: v. 1, p. 266a–266f; duplicated in v. 2, p. 502–33. Each volume has index to text and index to illustrations.

SEE ALSO: Blondel. Architecture françoise (1991); Delorme. Le premier tome de l'architecture (1999); Mariette. L'architecture françoise (2019); Marot. L'architecture française (2020) and Recueil des plans, profils et eleuations (2021).

Germany and Austria

860

Koepf, Hans. Deutsche Baukunst von der Römerzeit bis zur Gegenwart; mit einer Einfuhrung von Julius Baum. Stuttgart, Deutscher Fachzeitschriften- und Fachbuch-Verlag [1956]. 2 v. in 1 illus., plans. 30 cm.

A survey of German architecture from its origins to the present day, richly illustrated with plans and diagrams in the text. Arranged by building but with no coherent text.

Index of buildings p. 255–63; of architects p. 264–67; of illustrations p. 268–70; of plates p. 623–24.

861

Sedlmayr, Hans. Österreichische Barockarchitektur, 1690–1740. Wien, Filser, 1930. 86 p. illus. (plans), plates. 28 cm.

A well-illustrated, detailed treatment of the baroque phase of Austrian architecture. "Literatur" p. 61. "Register zu den Abbildungen" p. 83–84.

Great Britain

862

Bond, Francis. Gothic architecture in England; an analysis of the origin & development of English church architecture from the Norman conquest to the dissolution of the monasteries . . . London, Batsford, 1905. 782 p. illus., plates, plans, diagrs. 27 cm.

"Titles of authorities quoted" p. viii–xii; "Chronology of English churches" p. [638]–57. Index to illustrations p. [709]–38; to places p. [739]–72; of subject matter and glossary p. [773]–82.

863

Bond, Francis. An introduction to English church architecture from the 11th to the 16th century . . . London, N.Y., Milford, 1913. 2 v. 1400 illus. 30 cm.

Paged continuously. Bibliography included in Preface. English and French glossaries p. xix–xxxv. Place index p. 961–80; Subject index p. 981–86.

864

Britton, John. The architectural antiquities of Great Britain, represented and illustrated in a series of views, elevations, plans, sections, and details of various ancient English edifices, with historical and descriptive accounts of each. London, Longman, Hurst, Rees, & Orme, 1807–26. 5 v. illus., 356 plates (incl. plans). 29 cm.

The various monuments are treated separately. Volume 5 contains a "Chronological history of Christian architecture in England" and an appendix containing: (1) Alphabetical list of architects and founders of buildings; (2) Chronological list of ecclesiastical edifices in Great Britain; (3) Chronological list of architectural monuments; (4) List of pulpits; (5) List of fonts; (6) The stone crosses; (7) Glossary of terms, Index of references to architectural members and subjects comprised in the plates and letter press of the five volumes, and an Alphabetical index of names of persons, places, terms, etc. to the fifth volume.

Each volume has its own index.

865

Britton, John. Cathedral antiquities. Historical and descriptive accounts, with 311 illustrations of the following English cathedrals. Viz. Canterbury, York, Salisbury, Norwich, Oxford, Winchester, Lichfield, Hereford, Wells, Exeter, Worcester, Peterborough, Gloucester, and Bristol. The engravings mostly by J. Le Keux, esq. from drawings by E. Blore . . . [and others]. London, Nattali, 1836. 5 v. illus., plates, plans. 30 cm.

For each church gives bibliography, lists of archbishops, priors, deans, etc. and a chronological table of different parts of the cathedral, as well as an index.

866

Clapham, Alfred William. English Romanesque architecture after the conquest . . . Oxford, Clarendon Press, 1934. 180 p. illus., plates, plans, diagrs. 25 cm.

"This book is concerned with Ecclesiastical architecture and touches only on secular buildings of the same age when they throw some light on the evolution of mouldings and detail."—*Pref.* Bibliographical footnotes. Index p. 163–80.

867

Clapham, Alfred William. English Romanesque architecture before the conquest . . . Oxford, Clarendon Press, 1930. 168 p. illus., plates, plans. 25 cm.

"The first two periods of this English Romanesque are alone dealt with in the present volume, bringing the story down to the Norman Conquest."—*Pref.* Index. p. 159–68.

868

Dugdale, *Sir* William. Monasticon anglicanum: a history of the abbies and other monasteries, hospitals, frieries, and cathedral and collegiate churches, with their dependencies, in England and Wales; also of all such Scotch, Irish, and French monasteries, as were in any manner connected with religious houses in England . . . Originally pub. in Latin. New ed., enriched with a large accession of materials now first printed from leiger books, chartularies, rolls and other documents preserved in the national archives, public libraries, and other repositories; the history of each religious foundation in English being prefixed to its respective series of Latin charters. By John Caley . . . Henry Ellis . . . and the Rev. Bulkeley Bandinel . . . London, Longman, Hurst, Rees, Orme & Browne [etc.], 1817–30. 6 v. in 8. illus., plates, plans. 37 cm.

Originally published in three volumes, London, 1655–73.

An ancient and vast record of monastic es-

tablishments in England. General index in last volume p. 1665–1870.

869

Georgian Society, Dublin. Records of eighteenth-century domestic architecture and decoration in Dublin . . . [Dublin] Printed for the Society at the Dublin Univ. Press by Ponsonby & Gibbs, 1909–13. 5 v. illus., plates plans. 31 cm.

A collection of reproductions of details and drawings of architecture and decoration in Dublin, with short explanatory text. Good halftone illustrations.

"Catalogue of Georgian houses in Ireland" v. 5, p. [81]–107. General index to the five volumes in v. 5, p. 109–29, divided into persons, places, and subjects.

870

Gotch, John Alfred, and Brown, W. Talbot. Architecture of the Renaissance in England . . . London, Batsford, 1894. 2 v. illus., 145 plates (incl. plans, diagrs.) 49 cm.

". . . illustrated by a series of views and details from buildings erected between the years 1560–1635, with historical and critical text . . ."—*Title Page.* Collotype plates and measured plans and drawings.

"Topographical list of subjects illustrated," "Chronological list of subjects illustrated," and "Index to illustrations and descriptive text" at beginning of v. 1.

871

Gotch, John Alfred. Early Renaissance architecture in England; a historical & descriptive account of the Tudor, Elizabethan & Jacobean periods. 1500–1625 . . . 2d ed. rev. London, Batsford; N.Y., Scribner, 1914. 319 p. illus., 18 plates. 23 cm.

1st ed. 1901. "A list of selected works on early Renaissance architecture in England" p. 305–08. Index p. 309–19.

872

Gotch, John Alfred. The growth of the English house from early feudal times to the close of the 18th century. 2d ed. rev. and enl. N.Y., Scribner, 1928. 214 p. illus. (incl. plans), 94 plates on 47 l. 22 cm.

1st ed. 1909. A general survey of the field. Illustrated by halftones and numerous plans and diagrams. "Index to text and illustrations" p. 202–14.

873

Great Britain. Royal Commission on the Ancient and **Historical Monuments** and Constructions of England. An inventory of the historical monuments in [various counties of England], 1911–(52). illus., plates, maps. 28 cm.

There are also comparable publications for Scotland and Wales. Scholarly work, well illustrated. Counties included: Buckinghamshire, 2 v.; Dorset, 1 v.; Essex, 4 v.; Herefordshire, 3 v.; Hertfordshire, 1 v.; Huntingdonshire, 1 v.; London, 5 v.; Oxford, 1 v.; Westmorland, 1 v.; Middlesex, 1 v.

Indexes, glossaries.

874

Hitchcock, Henry-Russell. Early Victorian architecture in Britain. New Haven, Yale Univ. Press, 1954. 2 v. illus., maps, plans. 28 cm. (Yale historical publications. History of art, 9)

A definitive history of architecture in England from about 1825 to 1852. Contents: v. 1, Text; v. 2, Illustrations. Index v. 1, p. 615–35.

875

Lloyd, Nathaniel. A history of the English house from primitive times to the Victorian period. London, Architectural Press; N. Y., Helburn, 1931. 487 p. illus., plates, plans, diagrs. 33 cm.

Contains 167 pages of text, divided by centuries; p. 170–469 consists of halftone illustrations and plans arranged according to type: exteriors, entrances, windows, chimneys, staircases, etc., with descriptive text. Index p. 477–87.

876

MacGibbon, David, and Ross, Thomas. The castellated and domestic architecture of Scotland from the twelfth to the eighteenth century . . . Edinburgh, Douglas, 1887–92. 5 v. illus. (incl. plans). 26 cm.

Illustrated by numerous plans and line drawings in the text. "Scottish sundials" v. 5, p. 357–514; "Early Scottish masters of works, master masons, and architects" v. 5, p. [515]–69.

Index at end of each volume and a "General index to the whole work" v. 5, p. 571–95. "Topographical index of buildings described in the whole work" v. 5, p. 597–603.

877

Moore, Charles Herbert. The medieval church architecture of England . . . N.Y., Macmillan, 1912. 237 p. illus., 23 plates. 23 cm.

"Its purpose is to set forth the character of medieval church architecture in England in the light of structural analysis and comparison with the French Gothic art, and of the conditions and influences under which it was produced."—*Pref.* Index p. 229–37.

878

Nash, Joseph. Mansions of England in the olden time . . . London, M'Lean, 1839–49. 4 v. col. plates. 55 cm.

Volumes 2, 3, and 4 are called 2d, 3d, and 4th series. A smaller ed. (29 cm.), edited by Charles Holme with an introduction by C. Harrison Townsend, was published by "The Studio" in 1906; another ed., London, Heinemann, 1912.

A collection of tinted lithographs of famous Tudor and Elizabethan mansions, with representations of contemporary figures.

879

Pugin, Augustus Charles. Examples of Gothic architecture; selected from various ancient edifices in England: consisting of plans, elevations, sections, and parts at large . . . accompanied by historical and descriptive accounts. By A. Pugin . . . the literary part by E. J. Willson . . . London, Printed for the author, Augustus Pugin, 1831–36. 3 v. plates, geneal. tables. 30 cm.

Volume 2 by A. Pugin and A. W. Pugin; text of v. 3 by Thomas Larkins Walker. Volume 3 in 3 pts. with individual title page: The history and antiquities of the Vicars' Close, Wells, [the Manor house and church at Great Chalfield, the Manor house at South Wraxhall and the church of Saint Peter at Biddestone] forming Part I–[III] of "Pugin's Examples of Gothic architecture," third series.

Carefully rendered drawings and plans.

880

Tipping, Henry Avery. English homes . . . London, Country Life, 1921–37. 9 v. illus. (incl. plans). 40 cm. (Country Life library)

A new ed. of this work, covering material down to 1840, has been issued by Christopher Hussey in three volumes, 1955–1958, 32 cm.

Each volume contains a descriptive text and excellent halftone plates of exterior and interior views of about 24 famous English country houses of the period. Each volume contains its own index.

Contents: Period 1, Norman and Plantagenet, 1066–1485; Period 2, Early Tudor, 1485–1558; Periods 1 & 2, Medieval and Early Tudor, 1066–1558; Period 3, Late Tudor and Early Stuart, 1558–1649, in 2 v.; Period 4,

125

Late Stuart, 1649–1714, in 2 v.; Period 5, Early Georgian, 1714–1760; Period 6, Late Georgian, 1760–1820.

881
The Victoria history of the counties of England. London, Constable [etc.] 1900–(55). illus., plates (part col.), maps. 32 cm.

Editors of the series: H. Arthur Doubleday and William Page.

A series which consists of the history of each county in England treated as a monograph. Some counties run to several volumes and have separate index volumes. Well illustrated, with much information regarding the architecture of the various regions.

SEE ALSO: Campbell. Vitruvius Britannicus (1994); Chambers. A treatise on civil architecture (1997).

Italy

882
Anderson, William James. The architecture of the Renaissance in Italy; a general view for the use of students and others . . . 5th ed., rev. and enl. by Arthur Stratton . . . London, Batsford [1927]. 316 p. 150 illus., 90 plates, diagrs., plans. 24 cm.

A standard history of the Renaissance in Italy, first published in 1896. "A chart of the chief buildings of the Italian Renaissance, arranged in localities and in chronological order" p. 288–99.

Bibliography p. 300–03. Index to text p. 305–12; to illustrations p. 313–16.

883
Cummings, Charles Amos. A history of architecture in Italy from the time of Constantine to the dawn of the Renaissance. New ed. . . . Boston, Houghton Mifflin, 1927. 2 v. illus. (incl. plans). 24 cm.

Introduction by Ralph Adams Cram. A standard work originally published in 1901. "List of authorities consulted" v. 1, p. [xiii]–xv. Index v. 2, p. 313–25.

884
Letarouilly, Paul Marie. Édifices de Rome moderne; ou, Recueil des palais, maisons, églises, couvents et autres monuments . . . Paris, Morel, 1868–74. 770 p. illus., plates. 30 cm. *and* 3 atlases of 354 plates (incl. plans, diagrs.) 58 cm.

Detailed, measured drawings of plans and details of famous monuments. Gives in tabular form: Principal events in the history of Rome; List of Popes since the 15th century; Chronological list of architects who have practiced in Rome since the 15th century; List of principal buildings of modern Rome, according to the date of their construction.

Historical and critical notices concerning the plates p. 137–733. "Table analytique générale des planches et du texte" p. 735–70, arranged by types, i.e., palaces, orders, mosaics, etc.

885
Martin, Camille. L'art roman en Italie; l'architecture et la décoration . . . Paris, Eggimann [c1912–24]. 2 v. illus. 160 plates. 53 cm.

Volume 2 by Camille Enlart (Paris, Morancé [1924]). A collection of excellent collotype plates illustrating Romanesque architecture in Italy, with descriptive text. List of plates at beginning of each volume. Bibliography v. 2, p. [6].

886
Porter, Arthur Kingsley. Lombard architecture . . . New Haven, Yale Univ. Press, 1915–17. 4 v. 244 plates (incl. plans). 28–39 cm.

Edition of 750 copies printed. An important work. Volume 1 covers structure, ornament, accessory arts, iconography, and contains "Chronological chart" p. xxi–xxxvii; v. 2, Monuments: Abbazia di Albino–Milan; v. 3, Monuments: Mizzole–Voltorre; v. 4 is atlas of plates.

Bibliography v. 1, p. [441]–83. Index v. 3, p. 585–611.

887
Ricci, Corrado. Baroque architecture and sculpture in Italy. London, Heinemann; N.Y., Dutton, 1912. 280 p. of illus. 30 cm.

Primarily a picture book with excellent halftone plates. Text p. v–xiii. Index of illustrations (by place) p. 275–78; of artists p. 279–80.

888
Rivoira, Giovanni Teresio. Lombardic architecture, its origin, development and derivations . . . trans. by G. McN. Rushforth. Re-edited with additional notes. Oxford, Clarendon Press, 1933. 2 v. illus. (incl. plans). 30 cm.

Earlier English ed. (London, Heinemann, 1910); original Italian ed. (Roma, Loescher, 1901–07). A standard work.

Bibliographical footnotes. "Index of places" v. 2, p. 383–97. "General index" v. 2, p. 398–401.

889

Stegmann, Carl Martin, and Geymueller, Heinrich von. The architecture of the Renaissance in Tuscany, illustrating the most important churches, palaces, villas and monuments . . . with a preface by Guy Lowell. N.Y., Architectural Pub. Co. [1924]. 2 v. illus., plates, plans. 41 cm.

Originally issued in German (Munich, Bruckmann, 1885–1908. 11 v. in 46 pts. 64 cm.).

A collection of photographs, plans, and measured drawings of important monuments in Tuscany.

890

Tuckerman, Arthur Lyman. A selection of works of architecture and sculpture belonging chiefly to the period of the Renaissance in Italy . . . N.Y., Comstock, 1891. 90 plates. 45 cm.

A collection of 90 good collotype plates without text. List of plates at the beginning.

SEE ALSO: Palladio. I quattro libri dell'architettvra (2025); Piranesi. Le antichità romane (2033); Scamozzi. Idea dell'architettura universale (2038); Serlio. Il primo [–quinto] libro d'architettura (2039); Vignola. Regola delli cinqve ordini d'architettvra (2045).

Latin America

891

Kubler, George. Mexican architecture of the sixteenth century. New Haven, Yale Univ. Press, 1948. 2 v. (574 p.) illus., maps, diagrs., facsims., plans. 28 cm. (Yale historical publications. History of art, 5)

Continuously paged. A scholarly treatment of the whole cultural development of the time.

Appendix: Documents for mendicant buildings v. 2, p. 450–535. "Bibliographical note" v. 2, p. [432]–49. Index v. 2, p. 537–74.

892

Mindlin, Henrique E. Modern architecture in Brazil. N.Y., Reinhold [1956]. 256 p. (chiefly illus.) plans. 30 cm.

Preface by Prof. S. Giedion. Primarily a picture book with many plans. Gives a good survey of contemporary architecture in Brazil.

Bibliographical references to material dealing with separate monuments in periodicals p. 245–54. Bibliography p. 255.

893

Palm, Erwin Walter. Los monumentos arquitectónicos de la Española, con una introducción a América. Ciudad Trujillo, República Dominicana, 1955. 2 v. plates, plans. 28 cm. (Publicaciones de la Universidad de Santo Domingo. Año del benefactor de la patria)

A thorough survey of architecture of San Domingo. Bibliography v. 2, p. 159–90. Index v. 2, p. 191–217.

894

Sanford, Trent Elwood. The story of architecture in Mexico, including the work of the ancient Indian civilizations and that of the Spanish colonial empire which succeeded them, together with an account of the background in Spain and a glimpse at the modern trend. N.Y., Norton [1947]. 363 p. illus. (incl. maps), plates, diagrs. 25 cm.

"First edition." Contents: (1) Anahuac; (2) Spain; (3) New Spain; (4) Mexico. List of "Cathedral cities of Mexico" p. 329–31. Glossary p. 332–46, which includes pronunciation of Mexican place names.

Bibliography p. 347–50. Index p. 351–63.

895

Totten, George Oakley. Maya architecture. Washington, D.C., Maya Press [c1926]. 250 p. illus., plates (part col.), map, plans. 42 cm.

The standard work on the subject. Gives outline history and summary of events according to three chronologies (p. 17–23). Bibliography p. 249–50.

896

Wethey, Harold Edwin. Colonial architecture and sculpture in Peru. Cambridge, Harvard Univ. Press, 1949. 330 p. 367 plates. 27 cm.

A well-illustrated study of the 16th and 17th century architecture and sculpture within the boundaries of modern Peru. "Catalogue of monuments in Lima" p. 246–78. Bibliography p. [279]–86. Index p. 321–30.

Low Countries

897

Godefroy, J. Geschiedenis van de bouwkunst in Nederland; met 277 illustraties en kaarten tusschen den tekst. Amsterdam, "Kosmos" [1920]. 219 p. illus. (incl. plans). 21 cm.

A history of Dutch architecture which is more or less a textbook, with diagrams, plans, sketches, etc.

898

Vermeulen, Frans. . . . Handboek tot de geschiedenis der Nederlandsche bouwkunst . . . 's Gravenhage, Nijhoff, 1923–41. 3 v. in 6. illus. (incl. plans), plates. 26 cm. (Nijhoff's handboeken)

A general history of Dutch architecture. Contents: v. 1, Voorgeschiedenis en middel-eeuwen; v. 2, Kentering en renaissance; v. 3, Barok und klassicisme.

Includes bibliographies. Indexes in v. 3: of places p. 467–79; of persons p. 480–96; of subjects p. 496–506.

899

Weissman, Adriaan Willem. Geschiedenis der Nederlandsche bouwkunst. Met 185 af-beeldingen naar schilderijen, teekeningen, prenten en fotografiën. Amsterdam, van Looy, 1912. 457 p. illus. 27 cm.

A scholarly, detailed history of Dutch ar-chitecture. Glossary p. 447–57.

Oriental Countries

900

Boerschmann, Ernst. Chinesische Architek-tur . . . Berlin, Wasmuth [c1925]. 2 v. illus. (incl. map), plates (part col.), plans. 35 cm.

A collection of 340 good collotype plates arranged by building types or forms, e.g., pagodas, tombstones, etc., with short intro-ductory text. Geographical key v. 2, p. 64–66. Bibliography v. 2, p. 68.

901

Briggs, Martin Shaw. Muhammadan archi-tecture in Egypt and Palestine . . . Oxford, Clarendon Press, 1924. 255 p. illus. (incl. plans), 78 plates. 30 cm.

An important and scholarly book. Bibliog-raphy at end of each chapter and one on p. 18–19 covering the field in general. Glossary p. 245–46. Index p. 247–55.

902

Brown, Percy. Indian architecture (Buddhist and Hindu periods). Bombay, Taraporevala [1942]. 210 p. 118 plates (incl. maps, plans) on 63 l. 29 cm.

A standard work (with plans, dimensions, elevations, and good illustrations) covering the period from about 3000 B.C. through the 17th century.

"Chronology of the principal Ellora cave temples" p. 194. Glossary of terms p. 195–203. Bibliography p. [204]; "References" at end of each chapter. Index p. 205–10.

903

Brown, Percy. Indian architecture (the Is-lamic period). Bombay, Taraporevala [1942]. 140 p. 100 plates (incl. map, plans) on 50 l. 29 cm.

A 2d rev. and enl. ed. of 146 pages has been issued with no date. A standard work (with plans, elevations, dimensions, and good illustrations) covering the era from about 1200 A.D. to modern times.

Glossary of terms p. 132–36. Bibliography p. [137]; "References" at end of some chap-ters. Index p. 138–40.

904

Creswell, Keppel Archibald Cameron. Early Muslim architecture, Umayyads, early 'Ab-bāsids & Tūlūnids. Oxford, Clarendon Press, 1932–40. 2 v. illus., plates, plans, diagrs. 46 cm.

A monumental work covering the first three centuries of Islamic architecture in all countries, including Egypt. Arranged strictly chronologically. For each monument gives a description of the original structure, an analysis, and its architectural origins.

Contents: v. 1, A.D. 622–750; v. 2, A.D. 750–905. Includes bibliographies.

905

Creswell, Keppel Archibald Cameron. The Muslim architecture of Egypt. Oxford, Clarendon Press, 1952– . v. 1– . illus., plates, maps, plans. 46 cm.

A monumental work. Contents: v. 1, Ikh-shīds and Fātimids, A.D. 939–1171. "List of monuments described" p. 291. Includes bib-liographies.

906

Fergusson, James. History of Indian and Eastern architecture. Rev. and ed. with addi-tions; Indian architecture by James Burgess, and Eastern architecture by R. P. Spiers . . . London, Murray, 1910. 2 v. illus., plates, maps, plans, diagrs. 24 cm.

1st ed. 1876; 2d ed. 1899. One of the earliest treatments of the subject.

Contents: v. I: (1) Buddhist architecture; (2) Architecture in the Himalayas; (3) Dra-vidian style; (4) Chalukyan style; v. II: (5) Jaina architecture; (6) Northern or Indo-Aryan style; (7) Indian Saracenic architec-ture. Index v. II, p. 503–21, covers both vol-umes.

907

Marcais, Georges. L'architecture musulmane d'occident: Tunisie, Algérie, Maroc, Espagne et Sicile. Paris, Arts et Métiers Graphiques [c1954]. 541 p. illus., plans. 27 cm.

Edition of 3000 copies. Arranged the same as its predecessor which had title *L'architecture* . . . (Paris, Picard, 1926–27, 2 v.) and series title "Manuel d'art musulman [I]." Many plans and diagrams.

Bibliography p. 497–[513]. "Index des termes techniques" p. 515–18; "Index des noms de personnes" p. 519–23; "Index des noms de lieux" p. 525–[30].

908

Rivoira, Giovanni Teresio. Moslem architecture; its origins and development. Tr. from the Italian by G. McN. Rushforth. London, N.Y., Milford, Oxford Univ. Press, 1918. 383 p. incl. plates, illus. (incl. plans). 27 cm.

"This book does not pretend to be a history of Moslem architecture"—*Pref.* Instead it describes some of the chief stages in the development of the mosque from its birth to the XIIth century and discusses the "theory according to which the origin and development of the systematic use of the horseshoe arch belongs to the Iberian peninsula." Treats mosques in Medina, Mecca, Kufa, Jerusalem, Cairo, Kairawan, Damascus, Armenia, and Spain.

Index of places p. 373–80. General index p. 381–83.

909

Soper, Alexander Coburn. The evolution of Buddhist architecture in Japan. Princeton, Princeton Univ. Press; London, Milford, Oxford Univ. Press, 1942. 330 p. plates, plans. 30 cm. (Princeton monographs in art and archaeology, 22)

A concise and scholarly treatment. "Outline chronology" p. xv–xvi. Bibliography p. 307–17. Index p. 319–30.

910

Wilber, Donald Newton. The architecture of Islamic Iran; the Il Khānid period. Princeton, Princeton Univ. Press, 1955. 208 p. illus., maps, plans. 31 cm. (Princeton monographs in art and archaeology, 29)

Oriental studies, 17. An important work covering the architecture of the 13th and 14th centuries A.D. in Iran, composed of a historical sketch and a catalog of the surviving monuments (p. 100–189), which includes individual bibliographies.

"Architectural monuments known only through literary references" p. 190–91. Bibliography p. 192–200. Index p. 201–08.

SEE ALSO: Sirén. Histoire des arts anciens de la Chine, v. 4 (690).

Russia and Slavic Countries

911

Bošković, Durde. Medieval art in Serbia and Macedonia: church architecture and sculpture. Beograd, Jugoslovenska Knjiga [1951?]. 116 p. plates. 17 cm.

The best short introductory work in English, comprising a collection of plates representing views or details of the monastery churches. Includes a short essay by a well-known Serbian architect, giving an outline of the history of medieval Serbian architecture p. 7–19.

Table of contents; no index.

912

Buxton, David Roden. Russian mediaeval architecture; with an account of the Transcaucasian styles and their influence in the West . . . Cambridge, Univ. Press, 1934. 112 p. illus. (incl. plans), 109 plates, map. 25 cm.

A scholarly book well illustrated by halftones. Contents: (1) Russia; (2) Transcaucasia. Bibliography p. 105–07 is divided by languages and annotated. Index p. 109–12.

913

Deroko, Alexander. Monumentalna i dekorativna arkitektura u srednjevekovnoj Srbiji. Monumental and decorative architecture in medieval Serbia. Beograd [Serbian Academy of Sciences], 1953. 359 p. illus., maps, plans. 32 cm.

In Serbian with French and English summaries. The first comprehensive survey of Serbian ecclesiastical architecture in the Middle Ages since Millet (915). Covers 263 monuments. An up-to-date bibliography p. 326–27.

914

[Eliasberg, Alexander]. Russische Baukunst. München, Müller, 1922. [176] p. illus. 29 cm.

A short introductory text (33 p.) followed by quite good halftone plates, the majority of which come from Grabar, representing Russian architecture from ancient to modern times.

Bibliography p. 34. Index of illustrations p. 171–74; of places p. 175; of artists p. [176].

915

Millet, Gabriel. L'ancien art serbe; les églises . . . Paris, Boccard, 1919. 208 p. 249 illus., plans. 33 cm.

Published by L'Académie des Inscriptions et Belles Lettres (Fondation Piot). A scholarly work on ancient Serbian churches.

Contents: Introduction; (1) L'école de Rascie; (2) L'école de la Serbie byzantine; (3) L'école de la Morava. Bibliography p. [202]. Index of monuments p. [203]–04. Table of contents p. 205–08.

916

Voyce, Arthur. Russian architecture, trends in nationalism and modernism. N.Y., Philosophical Library [1948]. 282 p. illus., maps. 24 cm.

A brief survey of Russian architecture from its beginnings up to the present day. Numerous but poor illustrations. "References" p. xxi.

Scandinavia

917

Langberg, Harald. Danmarks bygningskultur, en historisk oversight. Udgivet med støtte af Grundejernes Hypothekforening i anledning af foreningens jubilaeum 18. februar 1955. København, Nordisk Forlag, 1955. 2 v. illus., plans. 28 cm.

A well-illustrated history of Danish architecture. Contents: v. 1, Tiden indtil 1754; v. 2, Tiden fra 1754–1930.

Bibliography included in "Kommentar" v. 2, p. 239–66. Index v. 2, 283–304.

918

Lundberg, Erik. Byggnadskonsten i Sverige. [Stockholm] Nordisk Rotogravyr [c1940–48]. 2 v. illus., plates, plans. 30 cm.

A well-illustrated history of Swedish architecture with many plans. Each volume has its own indexes. Contents: v. 1, Under medeltiden 1000–1400; v. 2, Sengotik och renässans, 1400–1650.

Spain and Portugal

919

Azcárate, José Maria de. Monumentos españoles; catálogo de los declarados histórico-artisticos. 2. ed., revisada y ampliada. Madrid, Consejo Superior de Investigaciones Científicas, 1953–54. 3 v. illus., plans. 17 cm.

A catalog of historical architectural monuments in Spain arranged alphabetically by place. For each monument gives a descriptive and historical paragraph, a photograph, usually a plan, and an extensive bibliography.

List of abbreviations, v. 3, p. 497–99. Name index, v. 3, p. 501–13; Topographical index, v. 3, p. 515–33.

920

Bevan, Bernard. History of Spanish architecture . . . London, Batsford [1938]. 199 p. illus., 94 plates. 24 cm. (Historical architecture library)

First published 1938. A standard text in English on Spanish architecture. Well illustrated. Bibliography p. 173–79. Index p. 181–99.

921

Byne, Arthur, and Byne, *Mrs.* Mildred (Stapley). Spanish architecture of the sixteenth century; general view of the plateresque and Herrera styles . . . N.Y., London, Putnam, 1917. 436 p. incl. 80 plates, 140 illus., plans. 27 cm. (Publications of the Hispanic Society of America, no. 109)

A standard work on the architecture of this period in Spain. Index p. 431–36.

922

Camón Aznar, José. La arquitectura plateresca . . . Madrid [Aguirre] 1945. 2 v. plates. 25 cm.

A standard work on plateresque architecture. Contents: v. 1, text; v. 2, plates. Bibliography, v. 1, p. 405–25. Index of names v. 1, p. 427–39; Geographical index v. 1, p. 441–55.

923

Guérinet, Armand. L'Espagne monumentale: architecture & sculpture, ensembles & détails. Paris, Guérinet [190–?]. 120 plates. 32 cm.

Issued in portfolio. A collection of plates illustrating important Spanish monuments of architecture and sculpture. The paper is poor and the illustrations are not clear. No text, only a line or two of descriptive matter in the list of photographs.

924

Haupt, Albrecht. Die Baukunst der Renaissance in Portugal von den Zeiten Emmanuel's des Glücklichen bis zu dem Schlusse der spanischen Herrschaft . . . Frankfurt, Keller, 1890–95. 2 v. illus., plates, plan. 26 cm.

A standard work on Portuguese Renaissance architecture. Contents: Bd. 1, Lissabon und Umgegend; Bd. 2, Das Land. "Benutzte Litteratur über die Geschichte Portugals und seiner Kunst" v. 1, p. [vi]; "Litteratur-Nachtrag zum 1. Bande" v. 2, p. [v]. Each volume also contains a place and name index.

925

Lampérez y Romea, Vicente. Arquitectura civil española de los siglos I al XVIII . . . Madrid, "Saturnino Calleja," 1922. 2 v. illus., plates, plans. 29 cm.

A standard work on Spanish civil architecture from the 1st to the 18th century. Numerous small illustrations and plans.

Contents: t. 1, Arquitectura privada; t. 2, Arquitecture pública. "Indice bibliográfico" v. 2, p. [561]–83. "Indice geográfico de monumentes Tomo I y Tomo II" v. 2, p. 587–619.

926

Lampérez y Romea, Vicente. Historia de la arquitectura cristiana española en la edad media según el estudio de los elementos y los monumentos . . . 2. ed. Madrid, Espasa-Calpe, 1930. 3 v. plates, maps, plans. 28 cm.

A standard work on medieval Christian Spanish architecture. Illustrated by halftones which are not very clear. Each volume has its own index and list of the monuments discussed. "Bibliografia española moderna" at end of several chapters.

927

Monumentos arquitectónicos de España, publicados á expensas del Estado, bajo la dirección de una comisión especial, creada por il Ministerio de fomento . . . Madrid, Impr. y Calcografía Nacional, 1859–80. 8 v. illus., plates, plans. 76 cm.

Edited by José Gil Dorregaray. Published in parts, v. 1–3 without text; v. 4–8 with Spanish and French text in parallel columns. Plates partly in colors and gold. Vignettes and initials in letter-press, partly in colors and gold.

A collection of plates dealing with the most important architectural monuments of Spain, elaborately produced and including plans, sections, and details, with descriptive text.

928

Watson, Walter Crum. Portuguese architecture. London, Constable, 1908. 280 p. illus., 55 plates. 28 cm.

A standard work on Portuguese architecture. "Books consulted" p. 272. Index p. 273–80.

929

Weise, Georg. Studien zur spanischen Architektur der Spätgotik. Reutlingen, Gryphius-Verlag [1933]. 132 p. illus., plans. 27 cm. (Tübinger Forschungen zur Archäologie und Kunstgeschichte, Bd. XIV)

A discussion of late Gothic architecture in Spain.

930

Whitehill, Walter Muir. Spanish Romanesque architecture of the eleventh century. [London] Oxford Univ. Press, 1941. 307 p. illus., plates, maps, plans. 25 cm.

A scholarly and important book. Contents: (1) The historical setting of eleventh century architecture in Spain; (2) Catalonia; (3) Castille, León, Navarre, Aragón and Galicia. Bibliography p. [285]–99. Index p. 301–07.

SEE ALSO: Ponz. Viage de España (2034).

United States

931

Andrews, Wayne. Architectural photographs, series one–(13), nos. 1–(1703). N.Y. [194–]–(57). photos. 28 cm.

A corpus of excellent photographs mainly of American architecture which are issued by the author in series, and form a prime source for architectural illustration.

932

Andrews, Wayne. Architecture, ambition and Americans; a history of American architecture, from the beginning to the present, telling the story of the outstanding buildings, the men who designed them and the people for whom they were built. N.Y., Harper [1955]. 315 p. illus. 24 cm.

A history of American architecture emphasizing the cultural and social background, with a valuable bibliography. Bibliography p. 289–303. Index p. 307–15.

933

Edgell, George Harold. The American architecture of today . . . N.Y., London, Scribner, 1928. 401 p. illus., plans. 24 cm.

A well-illustrated book, written by a well-known art historian for the layman. Bibliography p. 379–401. "Classified list of monuments" p. xxiii–xxxi.

934

Fitch, James Marston. American building; the forces that shape it. Boston, Houghton Mifflin, 1948. 382 p. illus. 24 cm.

"Attempts to trace the main forces which have shaped American building."—*Pref.* Bibliographical footnotes. Index p. 375–82.

935

The Georgian period; being photographs and measured drawings of colonial work with text, by William Rotch Ware. 1923 ed., with new classifications and indexes . . . N.Y., U.P.C. Book Co. [1923]. 6 pts. in 3 v. illus., (incl. plans), 454 plates. 37 cm.

Originally published 1899–1904. A basic work on 18th century American colonial architecture. Contents: v. 1, text and indexes; v. 2, plates 1–228; v. 3, plates 229–454.

"Books used by the early architects" v. 1, p. 253. Volume 1 also contains: Numerical chronology p. xi–xiii; Alphabetical chronology p. xv–xvii; Alphabetical list of plates p. xix–xxv; Geographical index p. xxvii–xxxv; Subject index of plates p. xxxvii–xliv; Text on various sections of the country, written by various authors p. 1–272; Alphabetical, geographical and historical index of text p. 273–99; Subject index of text p. 301–06.

936

Hamlin, Talbot Faulkner. Greek revival architecture in America . . . London, N.Y., Oxford Univ. Press, 1944. 439 p. illus., 94 plates. 24 cm.

An important book on the architecture of the Classic Revival in the United States from 1820 to 1860.

"The American development of Greek inspired forms" p. 339–55; "Some articles of architectural interest published in American periodicals prior to 1851" p. 356–82. Bibliography p. 383–409. Index p. 411–39.

937

Historic American Buildings Survey. Historic American buildings survey catalog of the measured drawings and photographs of the Survey in the Library of Congress, March 1, 1941. Washington, U.S. Government Printing Office, 1941. 470 p. illus. (incl. plans). 24 cm.

1st ed. 1938. An index to the collection of blueprints and photographs of historic American buildings, housed in the Library of Congress and duplicated in other libraries. Arranged alphabetically by state and community.

This second edition also gives a short de-

scription of each building. Index p. 431–70.

938

Kimball, Sidney Fiske. Domestic architecture of the American colonies and of the early republic . . . N.Y., Scribner, 1922. 314 p. illus., plans. 29 cm.

Reprinted in 1927. Based on a course of lectures delivered at the Metropolitan Museum of Art in 1920. Well illustrated.

"Chronological chart of houses" p. 265–69; "Notes on individual houses—date, authorship, and original form" p. 273–300, alphabetically arranged by name of the original owner. Bibliographical footnotes. Index p. 303–14.

939

Millar, Donald. Measured drawings of some colonial and Georgian houses . . . N.Y., Architectural Book Pub. Co., 1916–30. 3 v. 121 plates, plans. 43 cm.

The collection includes measured drawings of façades and exterior and interior details of important early American houses. List of plates at beginning of each volume. No index.

940

Morrison, Hugh Sinclair. Early American architecture, from the first colonial settlements to the national period. N.Y., Oxford Univ. Press, 1952. 619 p. illus., maps, plans. 24 cm.

An excellent general history of American colonial architecture, including all types of buildings in all of the colonies.

Includes bibliographies. "Reference notes" p. 581–91. "Index of sources of illustrations" p. 593–95. Index p. 597–619.

941

Tallmadge, Thomas Eddy. The story of architecture in America. N.Y., Norton [c1927]. 311 p. plates. 24 cm.

A general history of architecture in the United States from 1630 to the present date. Index p. 305–11.

SEE ALSO: The Monograph series recording the architecture of the American colonies (2450).

| # Sculpture

Indexes

942

Reinach, Salomon. Répertoire de la statuaire grecque et romaine . . . Paris, Leroux, 1897–(1930). v. 1–(6) in (8). illus. 20 cm.

A collection of line drawings of ancient statues, arranged roughly by subjects. Contents: t. 1, Clarac de poche, contenant les bas-reliefs de l'ancien fonds du Louvre et les statues antiques du Musée de Sculpture de Clarac . . . ; t. 2, 7000 statues antiques, réunies pour la première fois . . . 2 v.; t. 3, 2640 statues antiques; t. 4, 4000 statues antiques; t. 5, 2380 statues . . . 2 v.; t. 6, 1350 statues antiques.

Each of these six volumes contains an index, and v. 5 a general index for the five volumes. Volume 1 includes a biography of the Comte de Clarac. Each volume has a list of the publications in which the works are found.

943

Reinach, Salomon. Répertoire de reliefs grecs et romains . . . Paris, Leroux, 1909–12. 3 v. illus. 28 cm.

Line drawings in each volume. Volume 1 is arranged alphabetically by place of origin; v. 2 and 3 by place of conservation. In each section the reliefs are classed as follows: (1) Gods and heroes; (2) Historic scenes, legends of Rome, iconography; (3) Religious life; (4) Military life; (5) Civil life, occupations; (6) Theater, games, dancing; (7) Funerary reliefs; (8) Banquets; (9) Horsemen, horses, other animals; (10) Landscape, inanimate objects, ornaments; (11) Miscellaneous.

Contents: t. 1, Les ensembles; t. 2, Afrique, Iles brittaniques; t. 3, Italie, Suisse.

Errata and addenda and a general index for the three volumes appear at the end of v. 3.

Biography

944

Baert, Philippe. Mémoires sur les sculpteurs et architectes des Pays-Bas . . . publiés par M. le baron de Reiffenberg. Bruxelles, Hayez, 1848. 160 p. 22 cm. (Extrait des Bulletins de la Commission Royale d'Histoire en Belgique)

Covers sculptors and architects of the Low Countries from the beginning of the 15th century, continuing chronologically to the mid-19th century. For every artist it tries to give the year and place of birth, nationality, date of their reception into academies of painting, names of their masters and pupils, epitaphs, and most important works.

"Table alphabétique des auteurs," p. 149–54, is really a bibliography of sources. Index of artists p. 155–60.

945

Bessone-Aurelj, Antonietta Maria. Dizionario degli scultori ed architetti italiani. Genova, Editrice Dante Alighieri, 1947. 523 p. 23 cm.

A dictionary of Italian sculptors and architects, intended as a complement to her *Dizionario dei pittori italiani* (1161). Very short notices in general with no sources or bibliographies given. Adequate cross references.

946

Grant, Maurice Harold. A dictionary of British sculptors from the XIIIth century to the XXth century. London, Rockliff [1953]. 317 p. 23 cm.

Makes no claim to being exhaustive. Mostly gives short entries with name of artist, dates, or century in which he worked. No sources given, nor bibliography. "Appendix of 'Some later sculptors'" p. 278–81. "Index to sitters and titles of sculptural works" p. 282–317.

947

Gunnis, Rupert. Dictionary of British sculptors 1660–1851. London, Odhams [1953]. 514 p. 26 cm.

Contains more than 1700 individual entries for sculptors working in Great Britain in this period. Under each artist gives dates, short biography, list of signed or documented works, and references to authorities. More stress is laid on artists whose biographies have not been published before. For more important artists a fairly complete list of their works is given, but with minor craftsmen only their best productions are mentioned. Preface indicates sources consulted. Index of places p. 453–75; Index of names p. 477–514.

948

Lami, Stanislas. Dictionnaire des sculpteurs de l'école française. Paris, Champion, 1898–1921. 8 v. 29 cm.

Arranged alphabetically by name of artist. For each a detailed list of his works arranged chronologically. Whenever possible it includes for each work the date of completion, its whereabouts, price paid for it, early engravings which reproduce it, and museums which contain casts of it. Contents: From middle ages to the reign of Louis XIV (1 v., 1898); Sculptors under the reign of Louis XIV (1 v., 1906); Eighteenth century (2 v., 1910–11); Nineteenth century (4 v., 1914–21). Contains bibliographies.

SEE ALSO: Alcahalí y de Mosquera. Diccionario biográfico de artistas valencianos (1172); Claretie. Peintres & sculpteurs contemporains (1156); Laroche. Algunos pintores y escultores (1165); Mak van Waay. Lexicon van Nederlandsche schilders en beeldhouwers (1168); Pamplona. Dicionário de pintores e escultores portugueses (1176); Westecker. Künstler des Ruhrlandes (1158).

Histories and Handbooks

950

Chase, George Henry, and Post, Chandler Rathfon. A history of sculpture . . . N.Y., London, Harper [c1924]. 582 p. illus. 21 cm. (Harper's Fine arts series)

A useful handbook. One chapter is devoted to Oriental sculpture. "Bibliographical note" at end of each chapter. Glossary p. 549–50. Index of sculptors p. 551–56; of monuments and places p. 557–82.

951

Lübke, Wilhelm. Geschichte der Plastik, von den ältesten Zeiten bis zur Gegenwart. 3. verm. und verb. Aufl. . . . Leipzig, Seemann, 1880. 2 v. illus., plates. 26 cm.

1st ed. 1863. An English ed., *History of sculpture,* translated by F. E. Bunnett (London, Smith, Elder and Co., 1872).

An early German history of sculpture which covers Oriental as well as Western. Indexes of artists and places.

952

Maskell, Alfred. Ivories . . . London, Methuen; N.Y., Putnam [1905]. 443 p. 88 plates. 27 cm. (The connoisseur's library)

Covers ivory carvings from prehistoric times to the present day. "A list of ivories to which reference is made," giving size, p. 416–30. Bibliography p. 431–37. Index p. 438–43.

953

Maskell, Alfred. Wood sculpture . . . London, Methuen; N.Y., Putnam [1911]. 425 p. 59 plates. 26 cm. (The connoisseur's library)

In general covers only figure sculpture and certain decorative work in relief. Omits Russia and the Orient. Treats only to end of Gothic period. Bibliography p. xv–xxxii. Index p. 417–26.

954

Pelka, Otto. Elfenbein. 2. Aufl. mit 316 Abbildungen im Text. Berlin, Schmidt, 1923. 419 p. illus. 23 cm. (Bibliothek für Kunst- und Antiquitäten-Sammler, Bd. XVII)

1st ed. 1920. A survey of ivories from the antique through the 18th century, with a chapter on forgeries. Bibliography p. 404–05. "Künstlerverzeichnis" p. 406–07. "Ortsverzeichnis" p. 408–19.

955

Post, Chandler Rathfon. A history of European and American sculpture from the early Christian period to the present day . . . Cambridge, Harvard Univ. Press, 1921. 2 v. plates. 27 cm.

A standard work. Bibliography v. 2, p. 271–89. "Index to names of sculptors" v. 2, p. 291–99; "Index to plates mentioned in Parts I and II" v. 2, p. 301–12, includes only early Christian, medieval, and anonymous works.

956

Rindge, Agnes Millicent. Sculpture . . . N.Y., Payson and Clarke, 1929. 186 p. 40 plates. 24 cm.

"The contemporary point of view about

the art of sculpture . . . an analysis of those elements which constitute a work of art in sculpture."—*Introd.* Poor illustrations, many to the page.

Contents: (1) Nature and function of sculpture; (2) Requirements of sculpture as an art form; (3) Origin—purpose of sculpture; (4) Analysis of grand periods of sculpture; (5) Realism in sculpture; (6) The contemporary creed. Index of artists p. 185–86.

957

Schottmüller, Frida. Bronze Statuetten und Geräte. 2. Aufl. Berlin, Schmidt, 1921. 204 p. illus. 24 cm. (Bibliothek für Kunst- und Antiquitäten-Sammler, Bd. XII)

1st ed. 1917. A good treatment of bronze statues and vessels, covering both the historical and technical aspects.

Contents: pt. 1, Künstlerische Voraussetzungen; pt. 2, Material und Technik; pt. 3, Geschichte der Kleinkunst in Bronze; pt. 4, Kunstsammlungen (p. 179–91). Bibliography p. [192]–201. Index of artists p. 202–04.

958

Les sculpteurs célèbres. [Publié sous la direction de Pierre Francastel avec la collaboration de Jean Alazard, et al.] [Paris] Mazenod [1954]. 421 p. plates (part col.) 30 cm. (La Galerie des hommes célèbres, collection dirigée et présentée par Lucien Mazenod, 8)

A collection of rotogravure plates and some colored halftones of works of sculpture, with an accompanying text written by specialists, thus forming a sort of history of sculpture.

"Essai d'un répertoire historique des sculpteurs célèbres," p. 321–401, lists under periods and countries the names of important artists and gives a few sentences about each one. "Table des planches" gives sizes of the sculpture. "Sculpteurs cités dans l'ouvrage" p. 416–21.

Ancient

959

Die antiken Sarkophagreliefs; im Auftrage des Kaiserlich Deutschen Archäologischen Instituts, mit Benutzung der Vorarbeiten von Friedrich Matz, hrsg. und bearb. von Carl Robert und Gerhart Rodenwaldt . . . Berlin, Grote, 1890–(1952). v. 2–3 [1–3], 5 [1], 7. illus. plates. 45 cm. (v. 7, 34 cm.)

Volumes 1 and 6 never published; v. 4 to appear next. Imprint varies: v. 7, Berlin, Gebr. Mann. A monumental corpus of ancient reliefs on sarcophagi.

Contents: v. 2, Mythologische Cyklen; v. 3, Einzelmythen—pt. 1, Actaeon-Hercules; pt. 2, Hippolytos-Meleagros; pt. 3, Niobiden-Tryptolemos ungedeutet; v. 5, Die Meerwesen auf den antiken Sarkophagreliefs, von Andreas Rumpf; v. 7, Die jüngeretruskischen Steinsarkophage, bearb. von Reinhard Herbig.

960

Arndt, Paul. Photographische Einzelaufnahmen antiker Sculpturen, nach Auswahl und mit Text von Paul Arndt. München, Verlagsanstalt für Kunst und Wissenschaft, 1893–(1947). v. 1–(17 B). 5100 photos. 39 x 58 cm. (Text 26 cm.)

——. Register zu Serie I–V bearb. von Georg Lippold. München, Bruckmann, 1911. 105 p.

——. Register zu Serie VI–X bearb. von O. Brendel. München, Bruckmann, 1929. 94 numb. col.

Title and imprint vary slightly. Editors: Serie 2–7, Paul Arndt and Walther Amelung; Serie 8–9, Georg Lippold, Paul Arndt and Walther Amelung; Serie 11–15, Paul Arndt and Georg Lippold; Serie 15B– , Georg Lippold.

A numbered series of photographs of single objects of ancient art with accompanying text by specialists. A valuable corpus of often inaccessible and hitherto unpublished Greek and Roman works which are scattered in various museums and in private collections. The photographs are issued unmounted.

961

Bernoulli, Johann Jakob. Griechische Ikonographie mit Ausschluss Alexanders und der Diadochen . . . München, Bruckmann, 1901. 2 v. illus., plates. 26 cm.

A standard work on Greek portraiture, arranged by subject. Contents: v. 1, Die Bildnisse berühmter Griechen von der Vorzeit bis an das Ende des V. Jahrhunderts v. Chr.; v. 2, Die Bildnisse berühmter Griechen vom IV. Jahrhundert v. Chr. bis an die römische Zeit.

Bibliography v. 1, p. [xii]–xv. Index of subjects and names v. 2, p. 227–30; of places v. 2, p. 231–41.

962

Bernoulli, Johann Jakob. Römische Ikonographie . . . Stuttgart, Spemann, 1882–94. 2 v. in 4. illus., plates. 26 cm.

A standard work on Roman portraiture, arranged by subject. Contents: I, Die Bildnisse berühmter Römer mit Ausschluss der

Kaiser und ihrer Angehörigen (1882); II, Die Bildnisse der römischen Kaiser und ihrer Angehörigen—pt. 1, Das Julisch-Claudische Kaiserhaus (1886); pt. 2, Von Galba bis Commodus (1891); pt. 3, Von Pertinax bis Theodosius (1894).

Each volume has place index and subject index at end.

963
Bieber, Margarete. The sculpture of the Hellenistic Age. N.Y., Columbia Univ. Press, 1955. 232 p. 713 illus. 31 cm. (Columbia bicentennial editions and studies)

A scholarly treatment by a recognized authority, covering the period from the beginning of the 4th century to c. 30 B.C.

Selected bibliography p. [177]–85. Chronology p. 171–73. Index p. 189–202. List of plates p. 205–32.

964
Brunn, Heinrich von. Denkmäler griechischer und römischer Sculptur . . . München, Bruckmann, 1888–(1939?). 785 plates. text 46 cm. plates 64 cm.

The first series of 500 plates appeared 1888–1900. A *Register* to these 500 plates was prepared by Paul Arndt and published in 1897. A second series of plates (Nos. 501–550) with text and index by P. Arndt published 1902; plates 551–600 with text by P. Arndt, pub. 1906; plates 601–650 with text by P. Arndt, pub. 1912; plates 651–700 with text by P. Arndt and G. Lippold, pub. 1926; plates 701–750 with text by P. Arndt and G. Lippold, pub. 1932; plates 751–785 with text by P. Arndt and G. Lippold, pub. 1934.

An important corpus of Greek and Roman sculpture, consisting of excellent, large collotype plates with accompanying text. Frequently referred to as "Brunn-Bruckmann."

Register (to plates 1–500) at end of text volume contains: (1) list of plates in order issued, indicating where previously published and where now located; (2) index of plates arranged by present location; (3) chronological list of plates arranged by period, then subdivided by type.

965
Brunn, Heinrich von. Griechische und römische Porträts, nach Auswahl und Anordnung von Heinrich Brunn und Paul Arndt, hrsg. von Friedrich Bruckmann. München, Bruckmann, 1891–(1939). 1210 plates. 50 cm.

———. Register zu Tafel 1–760. München, Bruckmann, 1909. 53 p. 26 cm.

———. Texte zu den Tafeln 1–840 (1891–1912). München, Bruckmann [1929]. 59 p. 46 cm.

Plates from 1011– also bear name of Georg Lippold. A valuable corpus of Greek and Roman portraits, with accompanying text, similar to "Brunn-Bruckmann" (964). Frequently referred to as "Brunn-Arndt."

Register lists plates in order of issue, by place, and in chronological order.

966
Collignon, Maxime. Histoire de la sculpture grecque . . . Paris, Firmin-Didot, 1892–97. 2 v. illus., plates (part col.) 30 cm.

An early work now largely superseded. Contents: t. 1, Les origines, Les primitifs, L'archaïsme avancé, L'époque des grands maîtres du cinquième siècle; t. 2, L'influence des grands maîtres du cinquième siècle, Le quatrième siècle, L'époque hellénistique, L'art grec après la conquête romaine.

Bibliographical notes v. 1, p. xi–xii; v. 2, p. 262. Alphabetical index of artists' names v. 2, p. 693–96. General alphabetical index v. 2, p. 697–704.

967
Conze, Alexander Christian Leopold, ed. Die attischen Grabreliefs, hrsg. im Auftrage der Kaiserlichen Akademie der Wissenschaften zu Wien von Alexander Conze unter Mitwirkung von Adolf Michaelis, Achilleus Postolakkas, Robert von Schneider, Emanuel Loewy, Alfred Brueckner [und] Paul Wolters . . . Berlin, Spemann, 1893–1922. 4 v. *and* atlas of plates (4 v. in 6). 40 cm.

Imprint varies: v. 3, Berlin, Reimer, 1906; v. 4, Berlin und Leipzig, Vereinigung Wissenschaftlicher Verleger, 1911–22. A corpus of excellent collotype plates of Attic grave reliefs, arranged by periods.

"Nachträge und Berichtigungen zu Band I–IV" v. 4, p. 112–26. "Register" to the four volumes v. 4, p. 127–45, is divided into: (1) Orte der Aufbewahrung; (2) Namen; (3) Anfänge der Epigramme; (4) Sachregister.

968
Dickins, Guy. Hellenistic sculpture . . . with a preface by Percy Gardner . . . Oxford, Clarendon Press, 1920.

A brief sketch, unfinished, as the author was killed in World War I. "Published works of the author" p. [89]–94.

969
Furtwängler, Adolf. Masterpieces of Greek sculpture; a series of essays on the history of art . . . ed. by Eugénie Sellers. N.Y., Scribner, 1895. 487 p. illus., 18 plates. 32 cm.

Attempts to attribute well-known master-pieces to well-known artists. Index is divided: I, Historical; II, Museums; III, General.

970

Gardner, Ernest Arthur. A handbook of Greek sculpture . . . [2d ed.] London, Macmillan, 1920. 605 p. 20 cm. (Handbooks of archaeology and antiquities)

Originally published 1896–97. "2d ed. (complete in one volume, thoroughly revised 1915. Reprinted 1920, 1924)."—*Verso* of *Title Page.*

A useful handbook, now somewhat out of date. "Select bibliography" p. xxi–xxiv. General index p. 571–602. Index of sculptors p. 603–05.

971

Kekule von Stradonitz, Reinhard. Die antiken Terrakotten, im Auftrag des Archäologischen Instituts des Deutschen Reichs hrsg. von Reinhard Kekule von Stradonitz . . . Berlin und Stuttgart, Spemann, 1880–1911. 4 v. in 6. 254 plates (5 col.) 41 cm.

A monumental work on ancient terracottas, particularly valuable for volume 3.

Contents: Bd. 1, Die Terracotten von Pompei, bearb. von H. von Rohden, nach Zeichnungen von L. Otto u.a.; Bd. 2, Die Terracotten von Sicilien, bearb. von R. Kekule, mit LXI Tafeln, gezeichnet und radirt von L. Otto und mit vielen Abbildungen im Text; Bd. 3, Die Typen der figürlichen Terrakotten, bearb. von F. Winter, 2 v.; Bd. 4, Architektonische römische Tonreliefs der Kaiserzeit, bearb. von Hermann von Rohden, unter Mitwirkung von Hermann Winnefeld, 2 v.

972

Lamb, Winifred. Greek and Roman bronzes . . . Lincoln, MacVeagh; N.Y., Dial Press, 1929. 261 p. illus., 96 plates. 23 cm. (The illustrated library of archaeology: general editor, Arthur Bernard Cook)

Subject index p. 247–56; Museum index p. 257–61.

973

Lawrence, Arnold Walter. Classical sculpture . . . London, Cape [1929]. 419 p. illus., 160 plates. 21 cm.

Covers Greek sculpture through the Roman period. Bibliography p. 401–05. Index p. 407–19.

974

Lawrence, Arnold Walter. Later Greek sculpture and its influence on East and West . . .

N.Y., Harcourt, 1927. 158 p. 112 plates. 26 cm.

Covers period between the beginning of Alexander's conquests and the foundation of the Roman Empire.

Bibliography p. 91–92. Appendix gives list of the important works of sculpture arranged according to their probable dates; Subject index p. 137–44; Index of places and museums p. 145–58.

975

Lullies, Reinhard. Greek sculpture. Text and notes by Reinhard Lullies. Photographs by Max Hirmer. [Translated from the German by Michael Bullock] N.Y., Abrams [1957]. 88 p. illus., 264 plates (part col.) 31 cm.

German ed. pub. 1956 (Munich, Hirmer). Primarily a picture book with excellent illustrations but contains a sound text and much useful information with bibliographies in the notes on the plates, thus making it a good survey of Greek sculpture.

Includes bibliography. "List of published works on Greek sculpture selected for their bearing on the works of art reproduced in this book" p. 85–86. "Alphabetical list of present locations of works illustrated" p. 87–88.

976

Murray, Margaret Alice. Egyptian sculpture . . . with a preface by Ernest A. Gardner. London, Duckworth [1930]. 217 p. illus., 55 plates. 23 cm.

Contents: Methods of the artist; Protodynastic period: Old Kingdom, Middle Kingdom, New Kingdom; Tell El Amarna; Late period; Ptolemaic period. Index p. 195–207.

977

Picard, Charles. La sculpture . . . Paris, Picard, 1935–(54). (4) v. in (6). illus. (incl. maps, plans), plates (part col.) 23 cm.

A standard modern work on Greek sculpture. Contents: v. 1, Période archaïque; v. 2, Période classique—Ve siècle; v. 3–4, Période classique—IVe siècle, 2 pts.

Names of artists appear in bold type. Chapter on "Muséographie" lists important museum catalogs and bulletins which indicate recent acquisitions. At beginning of v. 1 is a list of abbreviations. Chronological charts and general index at end of each volume (not part of volume). Bibliography at end of each chapter.

978

Richter, Gisela Marie Augusta. The sculpture and sculptors of the Greeks . . . New rev. ed. New Haven, Yale Univ. Press; London, Oxford Univ. Press, 1950. 625 p. illus., plates, maps. 25 cm.

1st ed. 1929; 2d ed. 1930. At head of title: The Metropolitan Museum of Art. A very useful volume with numerous well-chosen illustrations.

The first part is a systematic description of the different objects of art, i.e., the nude statue, the draped figure, the metope, animals, etc. The second part is a short history of the most important sculptors. Bibliography p. [309]–18. Index p. 319–37.

979

Smith, William Stevenson. A history of Egyptian sculpture and painting in the Old Kingdom. [Oxford] Pub. on behalf of the Museum of Fine Arts, Boston, U.S.A. by the Oxford Univ. Press, 1946. 422 p. illus., 60 (i.e., 64) plates (2 col.) 35 cm.

An important work on one period of Egyptian art.

Appendix: "The colouring of Old Kingdom hieroglyphs" p. 366–82. General index p. 395–410. "Index of personal names" p. 411–16. Transliterations p. 421–22.

980

Strong, Eugénie Sellers. Roman sculpture from Augustus to Constantine . . . London, Duckworth; N.Y., Scribner, 1907. 408 p. 130 plates, tables. 20 cm.

Comparative chronological tables of the first three centuries (arranged by centuries) at the beginning. Index: pt. 1, Museums and localities containing works of art p. 397–401; pt. 2, Principal subjects and authorities p. 402–08.

981

Strong, Eugénie Sellers. La scultura romana da Augusto a Costantino; traduzione italiana di Giulio Giannelli dall'opera intieramente rifatta dall'autrice . . . Firenze, Alinari, 1923–26. 2 v. illus., plates. 29 cm.

A translation of an entirely rev. ed. of her *Roman sculpture*, 1911. The illustrations are larger and inserted in the text. Paged continuously.

Contents: v. 1, Da Augusto a Traiano; v. 2, pt. 1, Da Traiano a Costantino; pt. 2, L'arte del ritratto in Roma. Indexes: (1) Museums and places v. 2, p. 423–27; (2) Names and subjects v. 2, p. 427–31.

SEE ALSO: Lippold. Die Griechische Plastik (464); Reinach. Répertoire de la statuaire grecque et romaine (942) and Répertoire de reliefs grecs et romains (943).

Early Christian—Gothic

982

Bréhier, Louis. La sculpture et les arts mineurs byzantins . . . Paris, Éditions d'Art et d'Histoire, 1936. 109 p. 96 plates. 33 cm. (Histoire de l'art byzantin; pub. sous la direction de M. C. Diehl)

Mostly a picutre book of 96 collotype plates; 50 pages of introductory text and description of plates (p. 59–103) covering Byzantine sculpture and the minor arts. Bibliography p. [104].

983

Cust, Anna Maria. The ivory workers of the Middle Ages . . . London, Bell, 1902. 169 p. illus. 20 cm. (Handbooks of the great craftsmen. Ed. by G. C. Williamson)

Contents: (1) Consular and other secular diptychs; (2) Latin and Byzantine ivories; (3) Lombardic, Anglo-Saxon, Carlovingian and German ivories; (4) Romanesque and Gothic ivories.

"List of diptychs from Molinier" p. 157–63. "List of museums . . . richest in medieval ivory carving" p. 165–66. Bibliography p. xvii–xix. Index p. 167–70.

984

Goldschmidt, Adolph, and Weitzmann, Kurt. Die byzantinischen Elfenbeinskulpturen des X.–XIII. Jahrhunderts. Berlin, Cassirer, 1930–34. 2 v. illus., 156 plates, diagrs. 50 cm. "Hrsg. vom Deutschen Verein für Kunstwissenschaft." A scholarly corpus of reproductions of Byzantine ivories with bibliographies and indication of size.

Contents: v. 1, Kästen; v. 2, Reliefs. "Auflösung der Literaturabkürzungen" at beginning of each volume. Indexes of personal names, iconography, place of origin and preservation, private collections, and illustrations.

985

Goldschmidt, Adolph. Die Elfenbeinskulpturen . . . Berlin, Cassirer, 1914–26. 4 v. illus., plates. 49 cm. (Denkmäler der deutschen Kunst, hrsg. vom Deutschen Verein für Kunstwissenschaft [II. Sektion: Plastik. 4. Abt.])

Volumes 1–2 "bearb. von Adolph Goldschmidt unter Mitwirkung von P. G. Hübner und O. Homburger." A monumental corpus of reproductions of ivories from the 8th through the 13th centuries, with bibliographies and indication of size.

Contents: Bd. 1–2, Aus der Zeit der karolingischen und sächsischen Kaiser, VIII.-XI. Jahrhundert (1914–18); Bd. 3–4, Aus der romanischen Zeit XI.-XIII. Jahrhundert (1923–26). Each volume contains indexes of personal names, iconography, places of origin and preservation, private collections, and illustrations.

986
Koechlin, Raymond. Les ivoires gothiques français. Paris, Picard. 1924. 2 v. *and* atlas of 231 (i.e., 234) plates. 26 cm.

Tries to give as complete as possible a picture of French ivories of the 13th to 15th centuries. Volume 1, Text; v. 2, Catalog.

Contents: Les ivoires religieux; Les ivoires profanes. Appendices: (1) Ivoiriers nommés dans les comptes p. 531–40; (2) Ivoires gothiques français datés, ou signalés antérieurement au XIXe siècle p. 541–42; (3) Catalogues: I, De collections privées; II, De ventes p. 543–44. Bibliographical footnotes.

987
Porter, Arthur Kingsley. Romanesque sculpture of the pilgrimage roads. Boston, Marshall Jones, 1923. 10 v. 1527 plates. 24 cm.

A large and valuable compendium of collotype reproductions of unequal quality. The text is a study of the influence of Cluny and of the Pilgrimage to Compostella upon the formation of Romanesque and Gothic sculpture.

Contents: v. 1, Text and index; v. 2–10, plates: v. 2, Burgundy; v. 3, Tuscany and Apulia; v. 4, Aquitaine; v. 5, Catalonia and Aragon; v. 6, Castile, Asturias, Galicia; v. 7, Western France; v. 8, Auvergne and Dauphine; v. 9, Provence; v. 10, Ile de France. Volume 1 begins with a chronological chart in which are placed, side by side, the documented dates of Romanesque sculpture in all parts of Europe. Selected bibliography p. 343–56 and a comprehensive index p. 361–85, at end of text volume.

988
Wilpert, Josef. I sarcofagi cristiani antichi. Roma, Pontificio Istituto di Archeologia Cristiana, 1929–32. 4 v. (2 of text and illus. and 2 of plates). 49 cm. (Monumenti dell'antichità cristiana, I)

———. Volume terzo. Supplemento. 1936.

An extremely important corpus of material on early Christian sarcophagi, with excellent collotype plates.

Contents: (1) Il precetto del Signore: Docete omnes gentes baptizantes eos; (2) Il buon pastore; (3) San Pietro; (4) Le rappresent-

azioni del Vecchio Testamenti; (5) Le rappresentazioni del Nuovo Testamento.

Bibliographical footnotes. "Indice analitico" v. 2, p. 363–81: (1) Nomi; (2) Luoghi; (3) Cosi più notevoli. "Indice topografico" v. 3, p. 63–72. Volume 3 also has an index of its plates and text illustrations. "Indice delle tavole" at beginning of the two plate volumes.

Renaissance—Modern

989
Agard, Walter Raymond. The new architectural sculpture . . . N.Y., Oxford Univ. Press, 1935. 90 p. plates. 24 cm.

". . . only sculpture directly related to buildings has been included, an exception has been made with regard to memorials, many of which are architectural in construction."—*Pref.* Bibliography p. 85. Index of artists p. 87–88; of plates p. 89–90.

990
Brinckmann, Albert Erich. Barock-Bozzetti. English-German edition. Frankfurt am Main, Frankfurter Verlags-Anstalt [1923–25]. 4 v. illus., plates. 35 cm.

English-German text in parallel columns. A well-illustrated collection of baroque sculpture sketches. Sizes of the "bozzetti" are given.

Contents: v. 1–2, Italian sculptors; v. 3, Netherlandish and French sculptors; v. 4, German sculptors. Indexes of plates, figures, and places at end of each volume.

991
Brinckmann, Albert Erich. Barockskulptur; Entwicklungsgeschichte der Skulptur in den romanischen und germanischen Ländern seit Michelangelo bis zum 18. Jahrhundert . . . Berlin-Neubabelsberg, Akademische Verlagsgesellschaft Athenaion m.b.H. [c1919]. 2 v. illus., mounted plates. 29 cm. (Handbuch der Kunstwissenschaft, III. Abt., 2. Bd.)

A history of baroque sculpture from Michelangelo to the 18th century in the Latin and Germanic countries.

Bibliography: v. 1, p. 212; v. 2, p. 405. Indexes: of works of art v. 2, p. 407–15; of names v. 2, p. 415–25.

992
Giedion-Welcker, Carola. Contemporary sculpture; an evolution in volume and space. N.Y., Wittenborn [1955]. 327 p. illus. 26 cm. (Documents of modern art, v. 12)

A greatly enl. and rev. ed. of *Modern plastic art* (Zurich, 1937). Contains the original text essay (p. xi–xxii) and an additional one (p. xxiii–xxx) bringing it up to date.

Includes 248 pages of illustrations (table of illustrations p. 251–55); Biographies p. 257–83, which include portraits of sculptors; "Modern art and sculpture, a selective bibliography" by Bernard Karpel p. 285–324; Index p. 325–26; Photograph credits p. 327.

993

Kuhn, Alfred. Die neuere Plastik von Achtzehnhundert bis zur Gegenwart . . . 2. Aufl. München, Delphin [1922]. 134 p. illus., 71 plates. 28 cm.

1st ed. 1921. A standard survey of sculpture from the 18th century to the present day.

Index of plates p. 129–33; of names p. 133–34.

994

Maryon, Herbert. Modern sculpture, its methods and ideals . . . London, Pitman, 1933. 259 p. illus., 181 plates. 28 cm.

"The aims of modern sculpture are discussed from the point of view of the sculptors themselves."—*Pref.* Covers modern sculpture in various countries. General index p. 243–53. Index to illustrations p. 254–60.

995

Ritchie, Andrew Carnduff. Sculpture of the twentieth century . . . N.Y., Museum of Modern Art [1952]. 238 p. illus. (p. 49–224). 27 cm.

"An anthology of sculpture in the past 50 years."—*Pref.* The text outlines general stylistic currents. "Sculptors on sculpture" p. 38–47. Biographical notes by Margaret Miller p. 225–32. Bibliography by Bernard Karpel p. 233–37.

Primitive

996

African folktales and sculpture. [Folktales selected and edited by Paul Radin, with the collaboration of Elinore Marvel. Introd. to the tales by Paul Radin. Sculpture selected with an introd. by James Johnson Sweeney. N.Y.] Pantheon [1952]. 355 p. plates, map. 32 cm. (Bollingen series, 32)

Contents: Native African folktales: (1) The universe and its beginnings; (2) The animal and his world; (3) The realm of man; (4) Man and his fate; African Negro sculpture; Introd. by James Johnson Sweeney p. 323–

36, 165 illus. on collotype plates of high grade.

Index p. 353–55.

997

Guillaume, Paul, and Munro, Thomas. Primitive Negro sculpture . . . with illustrations from the collection of the Barnes Foundation at Merion, Pennsylvania. London, Cape; N.Y., Harcourt, Brace [1926]. 134 p. illus., map. 26 cm.

One of the early analyses of African Negro sculpture from the aesthetic point of view with little or no regard for its cultural background. The choice of objects is poor, and the chronological suggestions have been rendered invalid by later knowledge.

998

Kjersmeier, Carl. Centres de style de la sculpture nègre africaine . . . Paris, Morancé, 1935–38. 4 v. plates. 29 cm.

Bears dual imprint of Paris and Copenhagen. Sponsored by Ny Carlsberg Glyptotek. The first comprehensive coverage of African Negro sculpture as a whole. Very good plates.

Contents: (1) Afrique Occidentale Française; (2) Guinée Portugaise, Sierra-Leone, Libéria, Côte d'Or, Togo, Dahomey et Nigéria; (3) Congo Belge; (4) Cameroun, Afrique Equitoriale Française, Angola, Tanganyika, Rhodésie.

Notes and bibliography in each volume. List of tribes whose sculpture is discussed, at end of v. 4. List of museums whose collections of African Negro sculpture have been visited and studied by the author v. 2, p. 82.

999

Segy, Ladislas. African sculpture speaks. N.Y., Wyn [1952]. 254 p. 277 illus., maps. 29 cm.

Covers "so-called Negro art of West Africa that flourished up to a generation ago, as distinguished from contemporary West African art, and from North, East and South African art."—*Author's Note.* Its chief value lies in its numerous illustrations, for which size is given.

Appendix: Style regions p. 157–230. Bibliography p. 231–36. List of illustrations p. 237–48. Index p. 249–54.

1000

Sydow, Eckart von. Afrikanische Plastik. Aus dem Nachlass hrsg. von Gerdt Kutscher. N.Y., Wittenborn [1954]. 176 p., 144 p. of illus., maps, 29 cm.

Originally planned as v. 2 of the author's

Handbuch der afrikanischen Plastik (1001). An invaluable book on African sculpture. Even though its textual material is rather old, it is a corpus of superbly selected illustrations.

Contents: (1) Allgemeine Betrachtung; (2) Die Plastik in Sudan, Nord-Kongo, Ost- und Südzentral-Afrika; (3) Nachträge zur westafrikanischen Plastik.

Includes bibliographies, mostly at end of chapters. "Erläuterungen zum Tafelteil" p. 157–73 gives size. "Verzeichnis der Schriften von Eckart von Sydow" p. 174–77.

1001
Sydow, Eckart von. Handbuch der afrikanischen Plastik. v. 1 Die westafrikanischen Plastik. Berlin, Reimer und Vohsen, 1930. 494 p. 10 plates. 24 cm.

A systematic account which deals with Senegambia, Sierra Leone, Liberia, Ivory Coast, Gold Coast, South Togo, Southern Nigeria, the Cameroons, French Equatorial Africa, the Lower Congo, South Belgian Congo, and Northern Angola. A first volume which was completed posthumously by Gerdt Kutscher with publication of *Afrikanische Plastik* (1000) in 1954.

List of abbreviations p. x–xi. Index p. 490–94.

1002
Trowell, Margaret. Classical African sculpture. London, Faber [1954]. 103 p. 48 plates, maps. 26 cm.

A stimulating, perceptive book on the subject. Contents: (1) The appreciation of African art; (2) The function of the craftsman and his art; (3) Geography, history and social pattern; (4) A brief critique of African sculpture.

Bibliographical footnotes and "Other books of reference not directly quoted in text" p. 99.

1003
Vatter, Ernst. Religiöse Plastik der Naturvölker. Frankfurt am Main, Frankfurter Verlags-Anstalt, 1926. 192 p. illus. 25 cm.

Covers primitive religious sculpture. Illustrated with halftones in text. "Erläuterungen zu den Abbildungen" p. 175–87 gives size of objects. Bibliography p. 188–93.

1004
Wingert, Paul Stover. American Indian sculpture; a study of the Northwest coast. By special arrangement with the American Ethnological Society. N.Y., Augustin [1949]. 144 p. illus., 76 plates, maps. 25 cm.

A scholarly work which is the only book devoted to the art of the Salish Indians of the southern part of the Northwest coast.

Contents: (1) The sculptures and their significance; (2) Classification and analysis of styles; (3) Tribal and regional distribution; (4) Characteristics of Salish sculpture. Catalog of illustrations gives size. Bibliography p. [124]–29.

1005
Wingert, Paul Stover. The sculpture of Negro Africa. N.Y., Columbia Univ. Press, 1950. 96 p. illus., plates, map. 24 cm.

"Text is divided under the headings of the four art-producing geographical regions: West Africa, Cameroon, Central Africa and East Africa. Within each of these regions the various major art areas are defined and important tribal styles are characterized."— Pref. Good clear halftone illustrations.

"African Negro sculpture in American collections," p. 79–81, lists museums with collections and gives a few sentences describing each collection. Bibliography p. [83]–96.

National

France

1006
Aubert, Marcel. Le Bourgogne, la sculpture ... Paris, van Oest, 1930. 3 v. 204 plates. 38 cm. (Les richesses d'art de la France ...)

Issued in 18 parts, 1927–30. A collection of plates, with notes, covering sculpture in Bourgogne. A few pages of introductory text.

"Tables des noms de personnes" p. 75–77. "Table des noms de lieux" p. 78–80. "Table chronologique des édifices" p. 81–83. "Table des planches," p. 84–88, is a numerical listing which amounts to a geographical arrangement.

1007
Devigne, Marguerite. La sculpture mosane du XIIe au XVIe siècle; contribution à l'étude de l'art dans la région de la Meuse moyenne. Paris et Bruxelles, van Oest, 1932. 284 p. 72 plates. 33 cm.

A sound treatment of the sculpture of the Meuse valley from the 11th to the 16th century. Bibliography p. [219]–34. List of plates p. 235–58; Addenda p. 259–76.

1008
Gardner, Arthur. Medieval sculpture in France. N.Y., Macmillan, 1931. 490 p. illus., 113 plates. 26 cm.

The standard work on this subject. Covers both Romanesque and Gothic sculpture. "Note on Saint-Denis statues" p. 478–80. "Index of subjects of illustrations" p. 481–83. "Index of persons, masons and sculptors etc." p. 484–86. "Index of places" p. 486–91.

1009

Gonse, Louis. La sculpture française depuis le XIVe siècle. Paris, Libraires Imprimeries Réunies, 1895. 360 p. illus., 31 plates. 39 cm.

A general history of French sculpture. Illustrated by engravings in the text and rotogravure plates. "Index des noms de lieux, personnages representés, oeuvres d'art et artistes" p. 330–52.

1010

Paris. Musée de Sculpture Comparée. Album du Musée de Sculpture Comparée (Palais du Trocadero) pub. sous la direction de P. Frantz Marcou . . . Paris, Massin [1897]. 5 v. 357 plates. 46 cm.

A collection of good collotype reproductions of the casts of French sculpture which comprise the Musée de Sculpture Comparée, thus giving a pictorial survey of French sculpture. Dimensions are given.

Contents: Sér 1, Époque gallo-romaine XIIe siècle; Sér. 2, XIIIe siècle; Sér. 3, XIVe-XVe siècle; Sér. 4, XVIe siècle; Sér. 5, XVIIe, XVIIIe et XIXe siècles.

1011

Roussel, Jules. La sculpture français . . . [Paris] Morancé [1927–32?]. 5 v. 260 plates. 29 cm. (Documents d'architecture)

Issued in portfolios. Based on the collection of the Musée de Sculpture Comparée.

Contents: [v. 1], Époque romane; [v. 2–4], Époque gothique, 3 v.; [v. 5] Époque de la renaissance. Size of the works of art is indicated on the plates. For each plate is given the catalog number, a descriptive text, and a bibliography.

Each volume contains a bibliography and a "table analytique" which is a subject or iconographical index not only to the monuments reproduced, but also to everything on exhibit in the museum as well. Each volume contains an alphabetical index. Volume 5 has an index of "Personnages historiques."

1012

Vitry, Paul. Documents de sculpture française . . . publiés sous la direction de Paul Vitry . . . et Gaston Brière . . . recueil de . . . planches, contenant . . . documents de statuaire et de décoration. Paris, Longuet [1906–11]. 2 v. in 3. 332 plates. 42 cm.

Title varies. 1st ed. 1904; 2d ed. 1906. A collection of reproductions of French sculpture from the 12th through the 16th century, made mostly from originals rather than from casts. Arranged chronologically by period and then classified geographically or by subject. The three volumes include 332 plates which contain 2055 documents "de statuaire et de décoration."

Contents: v. 1, Moyen age; v. 2, Renaissance, 2 v. Each volume contains a "table des planches" which lists the plates and gives sources of the photographs, and an index of place names. Each part of v. 2 has an index of artists.

SEE ALSO: Aubert. L'art français à l'époque romane (844).

Germany and Austria

1013

Bange, Ernst Friedrich. Die deutschen Bronzestatuetten des 16. Jahrhunderts. Berlin, Deutscher Verein für Kunstwissenschaft, 1949. 165 p. plates. 32 cm. (Denkmäler deutscher Kunst)

A profusely illustrated, scholarly work on German bronze statuettes of the 16th century, which covers the Netherlands and Austria as well as Germany.

"Beschreibender Katalog der Statuetten" p. 113–50 includes bibliographical references. Indexes: of artists p. 157; of people, places, and subjects p. 158–60; of owners and places of preservation of the works included p. 160–[66].

1014

Bange, Ernst Friedrich. . . . Die Kleinplastik der deutschen Renaissance in Holz und Stein. Firenze, Pantheon; Leipzig, Schmidt & Günther [1928]. 113 p. 109 plates. 32 cm.

"Printed in Germany"; "Pantheon edition." A collection of good collotype plates with scholarly notes and brief text.

"Beschreibendes Verzeichnis der Tafeln," p. 15–100, includes bibliography. Indexes: of artists p. 103; of persons mentioned p. 104; of subjects p. 105–08; of owners and places of preservation p. 109–13.

1015

Burger, Willy. Altdeutsche Holzplastik . . . Berlin, Schmidt, 1926. 202 p. 113 illus. 25 cm. (Bibliothek für Kunst und Antiquitätensammler, Bd. 29)

A survey by a well-known author, which covers German Romanesque and Gothic wood sculpture, techniques, and forgeries. Small illustrations in the text. Bibliography p. [196]–292.

1016
Dehio, Georg Gottfried, and Bezold, Gust. von. Die Denkmäler der deutschen Bildhauerkunst ... Berlin, Wasmuth [1905–192?]. v. 1–4. plates. 49 cm.

A collection of collotype plates, each containing one or more reproductions of German sculpture from the 11th to the 18th century. At beginning of each volume a list of the plate numbers arranged by centuries. No text.

1017
Feulner, Adolf. ... Die deutsche Plastik des sechzehnten Jahrhunderts. Firenze, Pantheon; München, Wolff [1926]. 61 p. 91 plates. 32 cm.

A good pictorial survey of 16th century German sculpture with short introductory text. Size of works of art indicated on guard sheets. "Verzeichnis der Künstler" p. 55–[62] contains brief biographies of the artists represented.

1018
Feulner, Adolf. ... Die deutsche Plastik des siebzehnten Jahrhunderts. Florenz, Pantheon; München, Wolff [1926]. 65 p. 63 plates. 32 cm.

A collection of good collotype reproductions of German sculpture of the 17th century with introductory text. The guard sheets occasionally contain indication of size. Bibliography p. 62–[63].

1019
Halm, Philipp Maria. Studien zur süddeutschen Plastik, Altbayern und Schwaben, Tirol und Salzburg. Augsburg, Filser, 1926–28. 3 v. 464 illus., 96 plates. 32 cm.

A discussion of south German sculpture which includes the Bavarian Highlands, Swabia, the Tirol, and Salzburg. Volume 3 lacks subtitle and has second title page with title: Erasmus Grasser; its text is a monograph on this artist. Bibliography v. 2, p. 272.

1020
Jantzen, Hans. Deutsche Bildhauer des dreizehnten Jahrhunderts, mit 147 Abbildungen. Leipzig, Insel Verlag, 1925. 287 p. 147 illus. 28 cm. (Deutsche Meister, hrsg. von Karl Scheffler und Curt Glaser)

A treatment of 13th century German sculpture which covers Strassburg, Bamberg, Mainz, Magdeburg, and Naumburg. "Anmerkungen" p. 271 contains bibliography. Index of illustrations p. 283–86.

1021
Karlinger, Hans. Die romanische Steinplastik in Altbayern und Salzburg, 1050–1260. Augsburg, Filser, 1924. 149 p. plates. 32 cm. (Denkmäler deutscher Kunst, hrsg. vom Deutschen Verein für Kunstwissenschaft)

A well-illustrated treatment of Romanesque sculpture in stone from Upper Bavaria and Salzburg between 1050 and 1260. "Register der Aufnahmen und Abbildungen Sachangaben" p. 118–23 gives size. "Statistik der Denkmäler romanischer Steinplastik in Altbayern" p. 124–29. "Anmerkung zum Text" p. 130–47. Index of names and places p. 148–[50].

1022
Lübbecke, Fried. Die Plastik des deutschen Mittelalters ... München, Piper [1922?]. 2 v. plates. 32 cm.

A history of German medieval sculpture with 169 pages of text. Volume 1 contains plates 1–63 and v. 2, plates 64–164. Index v. 1, p. 171–75. Index of plates v. 1, p. 176–80.

1023
Lüthgen, Eugen. Romanische Plastik in Deutschland. Bonn und Leipzig, Schroeder, 1923. 180 p. 178 plates. 31 cm.

Covers German sculpture from the 11th century through the end of the Romanesque style. Contents: I, Einleitung; II, Die Kunst des 11. Jahrhunderts; III, Die Kunst des romanischen Stiles; IV, Die Frühstufe des romanischen Stiles; V, Die Stilvollendung; VI, Der spätromanische Stil.

Notes p. 141–42; Catalog p. 143–67. Index of plates p. 168–78; Index of subjects and names p. 179–80.

1024
Meller, Simon. ... Die deutschen Bronzestatuetten der Renaissance. Florenz, Pantheon; München, Wolff [c1926]. 49 p. 90 plates. 32 cm.

"Printed in Germany." A pictorial survey of German Renaissance bronze statues with a short introductory text. Plates of high quality.

"Verzeichnis der abgebildeten Bronzestatuetten" gives dates for artists and works.

1025

Panofsky, Erwin. . . . Die deutsche Plastik des elften bis dreizehnten Jahrhunderts. Muenchen, Wolff [c1924]. 2 v. illus., plates. 32 cm.

A basic book on German sculpture of the 11th to the 13th century with excellent collotype illustrations. Contents: v. 1, Text; v. 2, Plates.

"Allgemeinere Literatur": [v. 1] p. [71] and bibliography in notes. Place index v. 1, p. 179–81.

1026

Pinder, Wilhelm. . . . Die deutsche Plastik des fuenfzehnten Jahrhunderts. Muenchen, Wolff [c1924]. 41 p. 105 plates. 32 cm.

A collection of good collotype plates representing German sculpture of the 15th century, with a brief introductory text. Size of works of art is indicated on guard sheets.

1027

Pinder, Wilhelm. . . . Die deutsche Plastik des vierzehnten Jahrhunderts. Muenchen, Wolff [c1925]. 85 p. 104 plates. 32 cm.

A collection of collotype plates representing 14th century German sculpture, with introductory text. "Verzeichnis der Bildtafeln" p. 83–[86] is a listing of plates in numerical order.

1028

Sauerlandt, Max. . . . Die deutsche Plastik des achtzehnten Jahrhunderts. Firenze, Pantheon; München, Wolff [1926]. 46 p. 108 plates. 32 cm.

A collection of good collotype plates representing German 18th century sculpture, with a brief introductory text. Bibliography p. 43–[44]. "Verzeichnis der Bildtafeln," p. 45–[47], includes dates of artists, which are also given on guard sheets.

1029

Sitwell, Sacheverell. German baroque sculpture . . . with 48 photographs by Anthony Ayscough, and descriptive notes by Nikolaus Pevsner. London, Duckworth [1938]. 95 p. plates. 26 cm.

Contents: Introduction; The brothers Asam, by Sitwell; Descriptive notes, by Pevsner, p. 49–84; Table of names and dates p. 92–93. Bibliography p. 85–90, by Nikolaus Pevsner.

1030

Wilm, Hubert. Die gotische Holzfigur, ihr Wesen und ihre Entstehung. 4. Aufl., mit 178 Abbildungen. Stuttgart, Metzler, 1944. 171 p. illus., plates. 27 cm.

Originally published 1923. A well-illustrated treatment of the Gothic figure sculpture in wood.

Bibliographical references included in "Anmerkungen" p. 130–38. "Katalog der Abbildungen," p. 138–58, gives size of sculpture. Place index p. 159–61; index of persons and subjects p. 162–71.

1031

Wilm, Hubert. Gotische Tonplastik in Deutschland; mit 12 Abbildungen im Text und 207 Einzelabbildungen auf 120 Tafeln. Augsburg, Filser, 1929. 122 p. illus., 120 plates. 29 cm.

A scholarly work on Gothic clay sculpture in Germany. Well illustrated. Bibliography p. [101]–05. Indexes: Of names p. 109–10; of artists and names of people p. 111; of subjects p. 112–13; of illustrations p. 117–22.

Great Britain

1032

Chancellor, Edwin Beresford. The lives of the British sculptors, and those who have worked in England from the earliest days to Sir Francis Chantrey . . . London, Chapman & Hall, 1911. 329 p. 23 plates. 23 cm.

A discussion of the lives and works of the most promising sculptors, rather than a dictionary or mere listing. Index p. 299–329.

1033

Crossley, Frederick Herbert. English church monuments A.D. 1150–1550; an introduction to the study of tombs & effigies of the medieval period. N.Y., Scribner [1921]. 274 p. illus. 27 cm.

Contents: County index of illustrations; (1) General introduction: materials, provenance and makers of tombs and effigies, Medieval contracts for tombs, Colour decoration; (2) Architectural decoration of tombs and chantry-chapels; (3) Effigies and costume: Chronological series of illustrated effigies; Costume, civil; Costume, military; Brasses.

Index and glossary of terms p. 257–74.

1034

Esdaile, Katherine Ada McDowall. English church monuments, 1510 to 1840 . . . London, Batsford [1946]. 144 p. illus., plates. 23 cm.

"A sequel to Mr. Crossley's *English church monuments* [1033]."—*Pref.*

Contents: (1) Men and materials, etc.,

Patrons and portraits; (2) Types and influences; (3) Design and the craftsman; (4) The types portrayed, with notes on costume; (5) Epitaphs, and some contrasted verdicts. Index p. 140–44.

1035
Esdaile, Katherine Ada McDowall. English monumental sculpture since the Renaissance. N.Y. and Toronto, Macmillan [1927]. 179 p. plates. 23 cm.
Includes statues, tombs, and mural tablets; covers symbolism, costume, and historical development. "Some representative sculptors" p. 117–57. Index p. 169–79.

1036
Gardner, Arthur. English medieval sculpture . . . Cambridge, Univ. Press, 1951. 351 p. illus. 28 cm.
"The original handbook revised and enlarged with 283 photos." First published in 1935 with title: *A handbook of English medieval sculpture.*
Covers English sculpture from the preconquest period to 1540, treated historically. Bibliography p. 345–46. Index p. 347–52.

1037
Henry, Françoise. La sculpture irlandaise pendant les douze premiers siècles de l'ère chrétienne . . . 145 figures, 171 planches hors texte . . . Paris, Leroux, 1933. 2 v. illus., plates, map. 33 cm. (Études d'art et d'archéologie sous la direction d'Henri Focillon)
A scholarly work on Irish sculpture of the first 12 centuries of the Christian era. Contents: v. 1, Texte; v. 2, Planches.
"Répertoire bibliographique, comprenant l'index des croix et des sculptures d'églises" v. 1, p. [199]–213. "Index des motifs ornementaux et thèmes iconographiques" v. 1, p. [215]–216. "Index général" v. 1, p. [217]–21. "Liste des abréviations bibliographiques" v. 1, p. [223]–29.

1038
Longhurst, Margaret Helen. English ivories . . . London, Putnam [1926]. 171 p. incl. illus., plates (6 col.) 29 cm.
Contents: Preface; Historical introduction p. 1–61; Ascriptions; Catalogue p. 65–116 (indicating size). Bibliography p. 117. Index of collections of English ivories p. 119–20. General index p. 121–23.

1039
Prior, Edward Schroder, and Gardner, Arthur. An account of medieval figure-sculpture in England, with 855 photographs . . .

Cambridge, Univ. Press, 1912. 734 p. illus. 28 cm.
Book 1 covers iconography and materials of the medieval sculptor; Book 2 covers the historical development from 650 to 1520; Book 3 treats of the sepulchral effigy.
"Bibliography of English medieval sculpture" p. [105]–08. Index p. [723]–34.

Italy

1040
Bode, Wilhelm von. Denkmäler der Renaissance-Sculptur Toscanas . . . München, Bruckmann, 1892–1905. 12 v. 233 p. 34 cm. 11 v. of 557 plates (mounted photos). 64 cm.
———. Sonderdruck der Register, bearbeitet von Frida Schottmüller. München, Bruckmann, 1905. 53 p. 23 cm.
A corpus of 557 plates covering Renaissance sculpture in Tuscany, similar to the Brunn-Bruckmann *Denkmäler* (964), with a short descriptive text. One volume of text, 11 of plates.

1041
Bode, Wilhelm von. Florentine sculptors of the Renaissance. 2d ed. rev. . . . N.Y., Scribner, 1928. 258 p. 104 plates. 26 cm.
1st German ed. 1902; 1st English ed. [1908]. Translated by Jessie Haynes. A basic history of this field, old but not superseded. Index p. 245–58.

1042
Bode, Wilhelm von. The Italian bronze statuettes of the Renaissance . . . by Wilhelm Bode . . . assisted by Murray Marks . . . Translated from the German by William Grétor. London, Grevel, 1908–12. 3 v. 101 illus., 266 plates. 51 cm.
1st German ed. 1907; rev. German ed. 1922.
"As complete as possible account of all Italian Renaissance bronze statuettes and utensils of real artistic value . . . scattered among museums and private collections . . . grouped by schools and artists."—*Pref.* Excellent plates.
Contents: v. 1, Florentine bronze artists of the fifteenth century; v. 2, Copies of ancient works of art in bronze statuettes by unknown masters chiefly of the Paduan school; v. 3, Masters of the late Renaissance. Each volume contains text (about 20 pages), list of illustrations in the text, and list of plates.

1043
Cicognara, Leopoldo, *conte*. Storia della scultura dal suo risorgimento in Italia fino al

secolo di Canova . . . per servire di continu-
azione alle opere di Winckelmann e di
d'Agincourt. Venezia, Picotti, 1813–18. 3 v.
181 plates. 44 cm.

Edition of 500 copies. 2d ed., rev. and enl.
by the author, 7 v. and atlas (Prato, Gia-
chetti, 1823–25). An early history of sculpture from its revival to the time of Canova,
illustrated with line drawings.

At end of v. 3: "Indice degli scultori, architetti, fonditori, intagliatori, e coniatore
nominati nell'opera" and "Indice generale
delle materie" (for the three volumes).

1044

Crawford, David Alexander Edward Lindsay.
Evolution of Italian sculpture, by Lord Bal-
carres . . . London, Murray, 1909. 348 p. 53
plates. 26 cm.

A general history of the field, beginning
with Benedetto Antelami. Index p. 343–48.

1045

Davies, Gerald Stanley. Renascence; the
sculptured tombs of the fifteenth century in
Rome, with chapters on the previous centuries from 1100 . . . London, Murray, 1910.
381 p. plates. 26 cm.

Contents: pt. 1, General discussion; pt. 2,
(a) Alphabetical list of Roman churches
mentioned in this book p. 181–82, (b) Chronological list of the most important tombs of
Rome p. 182–90, (c) Principal sculptured
tombs of Rome (1100–1500) arranged under
churches, with brief biographical notices p.
190–369.

"Books of reference" p. xiii–xiv. "Index of
tombs and artists—General index" p. 371–81.

1046

Ferrari, Giulio. . . . Il legno nell'arte italiana;
riproduzioni in parte inedite di saggi dal
periodo romanico al neo-classico . . . Milano,
Hoepli [1911?]. 24 p. 277 plates. 31 cm. (Collezioni artistica Hoepli)

A collection of reproductions of Italian
woodwork covering sculpture, choir stalls,
and carvings, from the Romanesque period
through the 18th century, with brief introductory text.

1047

Haseloff, Arthur E. Pre-Romanesque sculpture in Italy . . . Firenze, Pantheon; N.Y.,
Harcourt Brace, 1930. 85 p. 80 plates. 32 cm.

Translated from the German by Ronald
Boothroyd. Bibliography p. 73–77. Geographical index p. 79–82; General index p.
83–[86].

1048

Maclagan, Eric Robert Dalrymple. Italian
sculpture of the Renaissance; the Charles
Eliot Norton lectures for the years 1927–
1928 . . . Cambridge, Harvard Univ. Press,
1935. 277 p. illus. 25 cm.

A rather general survey. Index of artists
p. 277–[78].

1049

Mayer, August Liebmann. Mittelalterliche
Plastik in Italien. München, Delphin [c1923].
27 p. 40 plates. 34 cm.

Covers medieval sculpture in Italy. Excellent plates. No index.

1050

Perkins, Charles Callahan. Historical handbook of Italian sculpture . . . N.Y., Scribner,
1883. 432 p. illus. 24 cm.

Includes work up to 1600. Appendix contains long documentary notes. Index to
towns p. 405–22; Index of artists' names p.
423–32.

1051

Perkins, Charles Callahan. Tuscan sculptors;
their lives, works and times . . . London,
Longman, Green, Roberts, 1864. 2 v. 43
plates. 29 cm.

Illustrated by line drawings. A chronology
at end of each chapter. Index at end of v. 2,
p. 237–67.

1052

Planiscig, Leo. Piccoli bronzi italiani del
rinascimento. Milano, Treves, 1930. 65 p. 226
plates. 31 cm. (Arti minori; collezione diretta
da Ardvino Colasanti)

A standard work on small Italian Renaissance bronzes. Good illustrations.

Bibliographical index p. 51–[52]. Index of
plates according to artist p. 55–64; of plates
according to location of the work p. 65–[66].

1053

Planiscig, Leo. Venezianische Bildhauer der
Renaissance . . . Wien, Schroll, 1921. 652 p.
illus. 32 cm.

A standard work on Venetian sculpture of
the Renaissance with 711 illustrations.

"Register" and "Künstlerverzeichnis" p.
643–46. "Ortsverzeichnis" p. 647–[55].

1054

Reymond, Marcel. La sculpture florentine . . .
Florence, Alinari, 1897–1900. 4 v. 40 illus.,
39 plates. 37 cm.

A standard French work on Florentine

sculpture. Contents: (1) Les prédécesseurs de l'école florentine et la sculpture florentine au XIVe siècle; (2) Première moitié du XVe siècle; (3) Seconde moitié du XVe siècle; (4) Le XVIe siècle et les successeurs de l'école florentine.

Each volume is treated as an entity. Volume 1 has "Essai de classification chronologique" p. 215–16. Each volume has a "Table des graveurs" which lists the illustrations first by broad period and then by artist. Volume 4 has a "Table par ordre alphabétique" covering all four volumes.

1055

Salmi, Mario. Romanesque sculpture in Tuscany. Firenze, Rinascimento del Libro, 1928. 153 p. 80 plates. 29 cm. (Studies of ancient and modern art, directed by Antonio Maraini)

Rather poor illustrations. Index of artists p. 143; of monuments p. 145–52.

1056

Schubring, Paul. Die italienische Plastik des Quattrocento . . . Wildpark-Potsdam, Athenaion [c1924]. 282 p. illus. 29 cm. (Handbuch der Kunstwissenschaft)

A standard work on Italian sculpture of the 15th century. Bibliography at end of each division. Name index p. 273–78; Place index p. 278–81.

1057

Waters, William George. Italian sculptors . . . 2d ed. enl. London, Methuen; N.Y., Doran, 1926. 285 p. 78 illus., 51 plates. 20 cm.

1st ed. 1911. A handbook consisting of entries for individual artists (arranged alphabetically) which covers 1150 to 1690.

Catalog of anonymous sculpture p. 237–44. Index p. 245–85 which is really an index by place.

1058

Wiles, Bertha Harris. The fountains of Florentine sculptors and their followers, from Donatello to Bernini. Cambridge, Harvard Univ. Press, 1933. 163 p. illus., plates. 30 cm.

Most of the fountains included in the discussion are late Renaissance and early baroque.

"Sources and bibliography" p. [109]–35. "Lost fountains" p. [136]–39. "Key to abbreviations" p. 140–44. Index p. 147–63.

SEE ALSO: Tuckerman. A selection of works of architecture and sculpture (890).

Latin America

1059

Navarro, José Gabriel. La escultura en el Ecuador (siglos XVI al XVIII) . . . Madrid, Marzo, 1929. 195 p. illus., 28 plates. 25 cm.

At head of title: Real Academia de Bellas Artes de San Fernando. "Prologo de José Francis." A basic book in the field of South American sculpture, which shows the influence of Europe and the Orient upon the native element in the school of Quito. Well illustrated.

"Indice" is only a table of contents, at the end.

1060

Weismann, Elizabeth (Wilder). Mexico in sculpture, 1521–1821. Cambridge, Harvard Univ. Press, 1950. 224 p. illus. 27 cm.

More of a picture book than a reference work, but done in a scholarly manner with extremely valuable notes, which are up to date.

"Notes" p. 189–219. Bibliography p. 220–22. Index p. 223–24.

SEE ALSO: Wethey. Colonial architecture and sculpture in Peru (896).

Low Countries

1061

Konrad, Martin. Meisterwerke der Skulptur in Flandern und Brabant. Berlin, Imago [c1928]. 80 plates. 35 cm.

Issued in ten "Lieferungen." A collection of 80 gravure plates of sculpture in Flanders and Brabant, with 41 pages of text and scholarly notes on the individual plates. Notes include the size of the object reproduced and an elaborate bibliography of the work.

1062

Rousseau, Henry. La sculpture aux XVIIe et XVIIIe siècles . . . Brussels, van Oest, 1911. 163 p. 31 plates. 22 cm. (Collection des grands artistes des Pays-Bas)

A summary sketch of sculpture in the Low Countries in the 17th and 18th centuries. Chapters treat of various forms, i.e., rood screens, tombs, altars, etc.

Bibliography p. [158]–60. "Table alphabétique des noms d'artistes" p. 153–57.

SEE ALSO: Fokker. Werke niederländischer Meister in den Kirchen Italiens (1353).

Oriental Countries

1063

Bachhofer, Ludwig. Early Indian sculpture . . . Paris, Pegasus Press; N.Y., Harcourt, Brace [1929]. 2 v. 161 plates. 32 cm.

Also published in German. A collection of excellent plates illustrating this sculpture, with 124 pages of introductory text. Size of objects is sometimes given. Bibliography v. 1, p. 125–28. Index v. 1, p. 129–37.

1064

Khandalavala, Karl. Indian sculpture and painting; an introductory study. Bombay, Taraporevala, 1938. 84 p. plates (part col.), map. 38 cm.

Primarily a picture book with fairly good color and black and white plates, and a short introductory text, providing a survey of Indian art.

1065

Kramrisch, Stella. . . . Indian sculpture; 116 illustrations and 1 map. London, N.Y., Oxford Univ. Press; Calcutta, Y.M.C.A. Pub. House, 1933. 240 p. 50 plates, map. 19 cm. (The heritage of India series)

"Not an outline of the history of Indian sculpture but rather 'stylistical investigations' of Indian sculpture as conditioned by the Indian craftsman."—*Pref.*

Contents: (1) Ancient Indian sculpture; (2) Classical sculpture; (3) Medieval sculpture; (4) Essential qualities of Indian plastic art; (5) Explanation of plates. Bibliography p. 225–28. Index of names and subjects p. 231–40.

1066

Sirén, Osvald. Chinese sculpture from the fifth to the fourteenth century; over 900 specimens in stone, bronze, lacquer and wood, principally from northern China. With descriptions and an introductory essay. London, Benn; N.Y., Scribner, 1925. 4 v. illus. (incl. plans), 623 plates. 34 cm.

A major work with emphasis on Buddhist sculpture. The plates are arranged chronologically and divided into provincial groups within the chronological framework. Size of objects is usually indicated in notes on the plates. There are 124 pages of text and 168 pages of description of the plates.

Contents: v. 1, Text; v. 2–4, Plates. Index v. 1, p. cxlix–clii.

1067

Warner, Langdon. The craft of the Japanese sculptor. N.Y., McFarlane, and Japan Society of N.Y., 1936. 55 p., 86 l. 85 plates. 29 cm.

A collection of good plates illustrating Japanese sculpture from about A.D. 552–1867, with 55 pages of introductory text tracing the development of technique in this sculpture.

1068

With, Karl. Buddhistische Plastik in Japan bis in den Beginn des 8. Jahrhunderts n. Chr. 3. Aufl. . . . Wien, Schroll, 1922. 64 p. 222 p. of illus. 31 cm.

A collection of good clear plates with introductory text. "Verzeichnis der Tafeln" p. 9–10.

Russia and Slavic Countries

SEE: Bŏsković. Medieval art in Serbia and Macedonia (911).

Scandinavia

1069

Fett, Henry Per. Billedhuggerkunsten i Norge under Sverreaetten. Kristiania, Cammermeyer, 1908. 122 p. illus. 30 cm.

Edition of 800 copies printed. A study of Norwegian sculpture in the Sverre dynasty (12th century). French summary p. 119–22. Bibliography p. 117–18 contains many titles from other languages.

1070

Thorlacius-Ussing, Viggo, ed. Danmarks billedhuggerkunst fra oldtid til nutid, ved Johannes Brøndsted [et al.] København, Hirschsprung, 1950. 499 p. illus. 27 cm.

A history of Danish sculpture, with each chapter written by a specialist. Bibliography p. 479–85. "Register over bildende kunstnere" p. 487–90. "Person-og stedregister" p. 491–99.

Spain

1071

Araujo y Gómez, Fernando. Historia de la escultura en España, desde principios del siglo XVI hasta fines del XVIII, y causas de su decadencia . . . Madrid, Tello, 1885. 640 p. 27 cm.

An alphabetical and synoptical index of Spanish sculptors and foreigners who worked in Spain from the 16th to the end of the 17th centuries. Bibliography p. [623]–30.

1072

Pardo Canalís, Enrique. Escultores del siglo XIX. Madrid, Consejo Superior de Investigaciones Científicas, Institute Diego Velázquez de Arte, 1951. 396 p. illus., 103 plates. 25 cm.

Contents: Text, which consists of 15 chapters, each devoted to one sculptor, p. 3–146; Documentation p. 147–362; Bibliographical sources p. 363–73, which are divided into manuscripts and printed books.

Index of names p. 379–93; of illustrations p. 394–96.

1073

Pillement, Georges. La sculpture baroque espagnole . . . Biographies et bibliographie par Nadine Daniloff. Paris, Michel [1945]. 174 p. 80 plates. 21 cm.

A survey of Spanish baroque sculpture. "Notices biographiques," p. 127–62, give a page or so to each artist. Bibliography p. [163]–67.

1074

Proske, Beatrice Irene (Gilman). Castilian sculpture, Gothic to Renaissance. Printed by order of the Trustees. N.Y. [Hispanic Society of America] 1951. 525 p. illus. 27 cm. (Hispanic notes & monographs; essays, studies, and brief biographies. Peninsular series)

A well-illustrated, scholarly treatment of Castilian sculpture. "References" p. 499–509. Index p. 511–25.

1075

Weise, Georg. Die Plastik der Renaissance und des Frühbarock im nördlichen Spanien; Aragón, Navarra, die Baskischen Provinzen und die Rioja, unter Mitwirkung von Dr. Ingrid Kreuzer, Geb. Ossmann. Tübingen, Hopfer [1957]. v. 1. plates. 24 cm. (In progress)

A well-illustrated treatment of Renaissance and early baroque sculpture in northern Spain, by a recognized authority. Contents: v. 1, Die Plastik der ersten Hälfte des 16. Jahrhunderts. Includes bibliographies. Indexes of artists, places, and illustrations p. 96–100.

1076

Weise, Georg. Spanische Plastik aus sieben Jahrhunderten . . . Reutlingen, Gryphius, 1925–[39]. 4 v. in 6. illus., plates. 27 cm. (Tübinger Forschungen zur Archäologie und Kunstgeschichte, Bd. 3, 6, 9, 17)

The definitive work on Spanish sculpture, intended to cover the 12th to 18th centuries. Profusely illustrated. Another volume soon

to be issued on early baroque in northern Spain.

Bd. II: Unter Mitwirkung von Hannschubert Mahn und Berthold Conrades. Bd. III has individual title page: Renaissance und Frühbarock in Altkastilien: 1. Halbbd., Die Spätgotik in Altkastilien und die Renaissanceplastik der Schule von Burgos; 2. Halbbd., Die Renaissanceplastik der Schulen von Palencia und Valladolid. Bd. IV, Die Plastik der Renaissance und des Frühbarock in Toledo und dem übrigen Neukastilien.

Volume 2, pt. 1 (Text), v. 3, pt. 2, and v. 4 each have an index by place and artist.

SEE ALSO: Guérinet. L'Espagne monumentale (923).

Switzerland

1077

Deonna, Waldemar. La sculpture suisse des origines à la fin du XVIe siècle. Bâle, Birkhaeuser, 1946. 131 p. 78 illus. (part col.) 27 cm. (Art suisse, 1)

A short survey of Swiss sculpture by a recognized authority. Bibliography p. 127. List of photographs and figures p. 128–29.

United States

1078

Gardner, Albert Ten Eyck. Yankee stonecutters; the first American school of sculpture, 1800–1850. N.Y., Pub. for the Metropolitan Museum of Art by Columbia Univ. Press, 1945. 84 p. 12 plates on 6 l. 31 cm.

Appendices: I, The precursors; sculptors, stonecutters, carvers, and modelers in America before 1800, p. 59; II, A biographical dictionary; American sculptors born between 1800 and 1830, p. [60]–73; III, The successors; some American sculptors born between 1830 and 1850, p. 74 (with their dates). Early nineteenth-century American sculpture in the collection of the Metropolitan Museum p. 75. Bibliography p. [76]–80.

1079

Lipman, Jean Herzberg. American folk art in wood, metal and stone, 183 illus., 4 color plates. [N.Y.] Pantheon [1948]. 193 p. illus. (part mounted col.) 29 cm.

Based on the *Index of American design.* Contents: Ship figureheads and ornaments; Weathervanes; Cigar store figures and other traditional signs; Circus and carrousel carvings; Toys; Decoys; Sculpture for house and garden; Portraits.

List of illustrations p. 12–22 gives dimensions. Bibliography p. [187]–93.

1080

Pinckney, Pauline A. American figureheads and their carvers . . . N.Y., Norton [c1940]. 223 p. illus. (incl. facsims.), 32 plates. 26 cm.

An attempt at a chronological record of American ship carving.

Appendix: (1) List of figureheads p. 169–75; (2) Contemporary descriptions of figureheads p. 176–85; (3) List of carvers p. 186–203; (4) Bibliography (arranged by chapters) p. 204–10. Index p. 211–23.

1081

Schnier, Jacques Preston. Sculpture in modern America. Berkeley, Univ. of Calif. Press, 1948. 224 p. illus. (p. [69–220]). 29 cm.

"Object of book is to present a comprehensive survey of present day American sculpture."—*Pref.* Intended as a reference book. Good, clear illustrations, grouped by subject.

Bibliography p. 65–67. Index to plates p. 221–22; to text p. 223–24.

1082

Taft, Lorado. The history of American sculpture. New ed. with a supplementary chapter by Adeline Adams. N.Y., Macmillan, 1930. 622 p. illus., 15 plates. 26 cm.

First published 1903; 2d ed., 1924. Supplementary chapter by Adeline Adams with title "Certainties and hopes" p. 591–605; also a "Supplementary chapter: 1923" for 1924 ed. included. The standard history of the subject.

"General bibliography" p. 607–18 includes section of periodical articles p. 611–18. "Index of sculptors' names" p. 619–20. "Index to supplementary chapters" p. 621–22.

Techniques

1083

Casson, Stanley. The technique of early Greek sculpture . . . Oxford, Clarendon Press, 1933. 246 p. illus., plates. 26 cm.

Covers Greek sculpture up to 450 B.C. Examines in detail "The various technical methods used by the Greeks in the making of stone and bronze statues in order that the reactions of style upon technique and of technique upon style may be established and analysed."—*Pref.* Contents: (1) The development of techniques historically considered;

(2) The tools and methods used in antiquity. Bibliography p. xv. Index of museums p. 239–41. General index p. 242–46.

1084

Hoffman, Malvina. Sculpture inside and out. N.Y., Norton [c1939]. 330 p. incl. illus., plates, diagrs. 26 cm.

"First edition." A well-illustrated description of various techniques of sculpture, written by a practicing artist. Index p. 319–30.

1085

Putnam, Brenda. The sculptor's way; a guide to modelling and sculpture . . . fully illustrated with plates and diagrams. N.Y., Toronto, Farrar & Rinehart [c1939]. 357 p. illus., diagrs. 28 cm.

The book "aims to sum up the single and personal experience of the author's 30 years of practicing and teaching sculpture and also the 'time tested experience of the vast army of creative artists of the past.' " Well illustrated with halftones and diagrams.

Covers copying plaster casts, modeling in relief, modeling and casting, with a chapter on human anatomy. Also contains chapters on Ceramic sculpture by Carl Waters, Stone and marble carving by Robert A. Baillie, Wood carving by Gleb Derujinsky, and Bronze casting by Anton Baiky. Index p. 347–57.

1086

Rich, Jack C. The materials and methods of sculpture. N.Y., Oxford Univ. Press, 1947. 416 p. illus. 25 cm.

Contents: (1) The anatomy of sculpture; (2) The plastic earths; (3) Plastic wax; (4) Plaster of Paris; (5) Casting; (6) Metal; (7) Surface treatment of metals; (8) Stone; (9) Sculpture in stone; (10) Wood; (11) Other sculptural materials. Appendix contains tables of various useful information. Bibliography p. 369–74. Glossary p. 375–80. Index p. 381–416.

1087

Slobodkin, Louis. Sculpture; principles and practice. Cleveland, World Pub. Co. [1949]. 255 p. illus. 29 cm.

A well-illustrated book on the techniques of sculpture, written by a practicing sculptor.

Contents: (1) First sculpture; (2) Modeling; (3) Modeling a figure from life; (4) Permanent materials; (5) Plaster—an intermediate material; (6) Composition in sculpture; (7) Carved mediums of sculpture; (8) Terra cotta; (9) **Cast stone**; (10) Cast metals; (11)

Reliefs—high and low; (12) Architectural sculpture; (13) Conclusion. A gallery of great sculpture p. 210–49. Index p. 251–55.

1088
Toft, Albert. Modelling and sculpture; a full account of the various methods and processes employed in these arts. Rev. ed. N.Y., Macmillan, 1950. 348 p. 21 cm.

A standard work on the subject, containing a glossary. Earlier editions published 1922 and 1929.

1089
Zorach, William. Zorach explains sculpture, what it means and how it is made. N.Y., American Artists Group [1947]. 302 p. illus. 27 cm.

A description of the technical aspects of sculpture given by a practicing artist. Includes many drawings and diagrams. Appendix: Supply houses where you can buy clay, marble, etc., with addresses p. 299–300. Index of artists, countries, and periods p. 301–02.

CHAPTER 13

Drawings

Histories and Handbooks

1090

British Museum. Dept. of Prints and Drawings. A handbook to the drawings and watercolours in the Department of Prints and Drawings, British Museum, by A. E. Popham. . . . With eight plates. London, Printed by order of the Trustees, 1939. 144 p. 8 plates. 22 cm.

The British section was written by Edward Croft Murray and part of the Netherlands section by A. M. Hind (cf. *Pref.*). Considered to be the best of the modern handbooks in English on the subject of drawings.

Appendices: (1) The growth of the British Museum collection; (2) Collections of drawings; (3) Reproductions of drawings. Bibliographical footnotes. Index of artists p. 135–44.

1091

Degenhart, Bernhard. Europäische Handzeichnungen aus fünf Jahrhunderten. Berlin, Atlantis-Verlag [1943]. xxxviii, 193 p. (p. [1–160] plates) 32 cm.

A well-illustrated survey of European drawings from Villard d'Honnecourt to the late 19th century, with 38 pages of text.

"Bilderläuterungen" p. 163–[94] includes bibliographical references. No index.

1092

Delacre, Maurice, and Lavallée, Pierre. Dessins de maîtres anciens. Réunis et publiés par M. Delacre . . . et P. Lavallée . . . Paris, van Oest, 1927. 100 p. 48 plates. 39 cm.

A collection of collotype plates, with descriptive text, of drawings from little-known or inaccessible collections. "Table alphabétique des artistes" p. [97].

1093

De Tolnay, Charles. History and technique of old master drawings, a handbook. N.Y., Bittner [1943]. 155 p. plates. 31 cm.

On spine: Old master drawings. "The present work may be conceived as in some respects a complement to Meder [1126]. . . . In the selection of plates, the attempt was made to illustrate by means of characteristic and qualitatively outstanding examples the development of European drawing."—*Pref.*

Period covered is roughly from the late 14th to the late 19th centuries. Contents: (1) Survey of the theories of drawing; (2) Methods of construction; (3) Creative processes and categories of drawing; (4) The origins of Renaissance and modern drawing; (5) Principal methods of treatment; (6) Survey of the development of drawing; (7) Materials and techniques; (8) Survey of the development of great public and private collections.

Bibliographical references included in "Notes" p. 87–100; Bibliographical abbreviations p. 101–02. Catalogue p. 103–49 usually gives dimensions. Index of names p. 151–55 includes persons, collections, codices, and reproductions.

1094

Dodgson, Campbell. Modern drawings. London, The Studio; N.Y., The Studio Publications, 1933. 176 p. incl. illus., plates (part mounted). 30 cm.

A collection of reproductions of modern drawings in many countries of the Western world, with short text. "List of illustrations" p. 6–8 is arranged alphabetically, thus forming an index.

1095

Geiger, Benno. Handzeichnungen alter Meister. Zürich, Amalthea-Verlag [c1948]. 142 p. (p. 31–142, plates) 44 cm.

Edition of 330 copies. A collection of 112 fine reproductions of old master drawings, with "Verzeichnis" p. 17–27 which gives medium, size, and collection from which the drawing comes.

1096

Leporini, Heinrich. Die Künstlerzeichnung; ein Handbuch für Liebhaber und Sammler ... mit 169 Abbildungen im Text. Berlin, Schmidt, 1928. 405 p. 169 illus. 25 cm. (Bibliothek für Kunst- und Antiquitäten-Sammler, Bd. XXX)

A useful one-volume survey of the field of drawings. Contents: (1) Einführung; (2) Die Entwicklung der Handzeichen; (3) Der Sammler. "Literatur und Reproduktionen" p. [390]–98.

1097

Leporini, Heinrich. Die Stilentwicklung der Handzeichnung, XIV. bis XVIII. Jahrhundert. Mit 304 Tafeln in Kupfertiefdruck. Wien, Manz [1925]. 79 p. 304 plates. 32 cm.

Good reproductions of drawings with an introductory text (p. 5–43) which traces the development of drawings from the 14th to the 19th centuries in various European countries. "Literatur und Reproduktionswerke" p. [46]. "Verzeichnis der Bildtafeln" p. 46–77 describes briefly the plates and indicates size of the drawings. "Register der Abbildungen," p. 78–79, is a list of artists' names.

1098

Mongan, Agnes, ed. One hundred master drawings. Cambridge, Harvard Univ. Press, 1949. 208 p. illus. 29 cm.

Presented in honor of Paul J. Sachs. "Seventy master drawings," a loan exhibition at the Fogg Museum of Art, Nov. 1948–Jan. 1949, held on the occasion of the 70th birthday of Paul J. Sachs, and 30 additional drawings from the museum's collections.

A collection of collotype reproductions of drawings, with descriptive text written by various authors, and bibliographical indications for each plate. An introduction, "Drawing and the man of letters" by Jean J. Seznec, p. xii–xv.

"Books frequently cited" p. 203–04; also text includes bibliographies. "Glossary of materials" p. 205–07. "List of artists" forms an index p. 208.

1099

Reitlinger, Henry Scipio. Old master drawings, a handbook for amateurs and collectors ... London, Constable, 1922. 188 p. 72 plates. 29 cm.

Treats of materials, forgeries, care and arrangement of drawings, mending and restoration; also includes chapters on various national schools, i.e., Italian, Dutch, French, etc. Index p. 183–88.

1100

Reynolds, Graham. Nineteenth century drawings, 1850–1900. London, Pleiades Books, 1949. 52 p. 73 plates. 29 cm. (Pleiades art books)

The text covers French, English, and German schools. "Illustrations" p. 8–12 includes size. Index of artists p. 52.

1101

Reynolds, Graham. Twentieth century drawings ... London, Pleiades Books, 1946. 44 p. 67 plates (part mounted col.) 29 cm. (Pleiades art books, Gen. ed., James Laver)

First published 1946. A collection of halftones reproducing artists of the 20th century, with introductory text. "Index of artists," p. 44, gives their dates.

1102

Tietze, Hans. European master drawings in the United States. N.Y., Augustin [1947]. 326 p. illus. 31 cm.

A collection of collotype reproductions of drawings with descriptive text for each drawing, including bibliography. "List of reference books" p. [1]. Index of places p. 323–24.

SEE ALSO: Florence. R. Galleria degli Uffizi. I disegni della R. Galleria degli Uffizi in Firenze (2417); Marées Gesellschaft (2441); Prestel-Bücher (2466); Prestel Gesellschaft (2467); Sachs. Modern prints & drawings (1552); Vasari Society for the reproduction of drawings (2487).

National

France

1103

George, Waldemar. Le dessin français de David à Cézanne et l'esprit de la tradition baroque. Paris, Éditions Chroniques du Jour, 1929. v–lxxxix p. incl. illus. (97 illus. on 32 l.) 2 plates. 30 cm.

Edition of 1000 copies. A good survey which attempts to fix the character of a century from its plastic handwriting.

1104

Hugelshofer, Walter. Dessins et aquarelles de maîtres français du XIXe siècle ... [tr. par S. et S. Stelling-Michaud]. Bâle, Éditions Holbein, 1947. 11 p. 28 plates (part col.) 53 cm. (Société Holbein. Publication, 1)

Issued in portfolio. Edition of 400 copies. A de luxe publication of excellent collotype reproductions of French 19th century drawings and water colors belonging to Swiss public and private collections.

Notes on the plates indicate where the drawings have been exhibited and give bibliography.

1105

Huyghe, René. Le dessin français au XIXe siècle. Notices biographiques de Philippe Jaccottet. Lausanne, Mermod [1948]. xliii, 183 p. (p. 1–[138], plates) 2 illus. 29 cm.

An edition of 6500, of which 1500 are in Swedish. A pictorial survey of French 18th century drawings with 33 pages of text by a recognized authority.

"Notes biographiques" p. 141–72 contains bibliographical references. "Catalogue" p. 173–[76].

1106

Lavallée, Pierre. Le dessin français du XIIIe au XVIe siècle . . . Paris, van Oest, 1930. 151 p. 80 plates. 39 cm.

A collection of good collotypes illustrating French engravings from the 13th to the 16th centuries, with 49 pages of introductory text and a description of the drawings reproduced.

"Marques de collections relevées sur les dessins reproduits" p. [129]–30. "Bibliographie sommaire" p. [131]–38. "Index alphabétique des noms d'artistes" p. [139]–41. "Table alphabétique des planches" p. [143]–45. "Tables des planches" p. [147]–51.

1107

Shoolman, Regina Lenore, and Slatkin, Charles Eli. Six centuries of French master drawings in America. N.Y., Oxford Univ. Press, 1950. 256 p. illus. 29 cm.

A popular survey of French drawings, more valuable for the illustrations than the text. Includes bibliographies.

Germany and Austria

1108

Dörries, Bernhard. Deutsche Zeichnungen des 18. Jahrhunderts. München, Bruckmann [1943]. 159 p. incl. illus., plates. 29 cm.

Pages 42–155 are plates. A pictorial survey of German drawings of the 18th century, with short text.

"Verzeichnis der Abbildungen" gives dates of artist, where drawing is located, and size.

1109

Friedländer, Max J., and Bock, Elfried. Handzeichnungen deutscher Meister des 15. und 16. Jahrhunderts. Berlin, Propyläen Verlag [1921]. 65 p. illus., 100 plates (part col.) 37 cm.

A collection of fine plates with 32 pages of text. "Beschreibendes Verzeichnis nach Meistern geordnet" p. [41]–61.

1110

Garzarolli-Thurnlackh, Karl. Die barocke Handzeichnung in Österreich . . . Zürich, Amalthea-Verlag [c1928]. 98 p. 118 plates on 59 l. 28 cm.

A survey of Austrian drawings of the baroque period, containing 65 pages of text and halftone illustrations. Bibliographical footnotes. Index of artists p. 76–94 gives a descriptive paragraph or two for each artist.

Italy

1111

Benesch, Otto. . . . Venetian drawings of the eighteenth century in America. N.Y., Bittner, 1947. 41 p. plates. 32 cm. [Bittner art monographs]

A collection of good collotype plates with introductory text and notes on the plates. Bibliographical footnotes.

1112

Berenson, Bernhard. The drawings of the Florentine painters, amplified ed. . . . Chicago, Univ. of Chicago Press, 1938. 3 v. plates. 34 cm. (Univ. of Chicago publications in art)

Originally published 1903 by Murray, London, and Dutton, N.Y. (2 v., 47 cm.). A monumental work.

Contents: v. 1, Text; v. 2, Catalogue; v. 3, Illustrations. "Signs and abbreviations" v. 2, p. v–xii, includes bibliographical references.

Indexes at end of v. 2: General index p. 365–73; General place index p. 375–84; Place index of drawings p. 385–88.

1113

Fischel, Oskar. Die Zeichnungen der Umbrer; mit neun Tafeln in Lichtdruck, einer Tafel in Kornätzung und mit 343 Textabbildungen. Berlin, Grote, 1917. 280 p. illus., 10 plates. 35 cm.

"Sonderdruck aus dem Jahrbuch der Kgl. preuss. Kunstsammlungen, 1917, Heft 1 und 2 und Beiheft." A scholarly treatment of Umbrian drawings with a critical catalog of drawings of this school and numerous illustrations. Index p. 261–80.

1114

Hadeln, Detlev, *Freiherr* von. Venezianische Zeichnungen der Hochrenaissance. Berlin, Cassirer, 1925. 39 p. 65 plates. 35 cm.

Covers Venetian drawings of the Renaissance, with same format as number 1115 below.

1115

Hadeln, Detlev, *Freiherr* von. Venezianische Zeichnungen des Quattrocento. Berlin, Cassirer, 1925. 66 p. 91 plates. 35 cm.

A collection of good reproductions of 15th century Venetian drawings with about 25 pages of text and a descriptive catalog arranged alphabetically by artist.

1116

Hadeln, Detlev, *Freiherr* von. Venezianische Zeichnungen der Spätrenaissance. Berlin, Cassirer, 1926. 31 p. 104 plates. 35 cm.

Covers Venetian drawings of the late Renaissance, with same format as number 1115 above.

1117

Tietze, Hans, and Tietze-Conrat, Erica. The drawings of the Venetian painters in the 15th and 16th centuries. N.Y., Augustin [1944]. 398 p. 200 plates on 100 l. 29 cm.

"A companion piece to Bernhard Berenson's book on the drawings of the Florentine painters."—*Introd.* A scholarly corpus of Venetian drawings, arranged alphabetically by artist.

Contents: Catalogue proper p. 31–365; General index p. 369–77; General place index p. 378–88; Place index of drawings p. 389–96; List of illustrations p. 397–98; Acknowledgment of copyright p. [399]; Illustrations p. [401] ff. Bibliographical references in "Signs and abbreviations" p. xiii–xvi.

Low Countries

1118

Bernt, Walther. Die niederländischen Zeichner des 17. Jahrhunderts. Zwei Bände mit 705 Abbildungen. Mit einem Geleitwort von J. Q. van Regteren Altena. München, Bruckmann [1957–58]. 2 v. illus. 29 cm.

A corpus of 17th century Netherlands drawings, arranged alphabetically by name of artist, which forms a companion piece to the author's work on Dutch painters (1337).

Gives biographical information and bibliography for each artist. For each drawing reproduced, gives size, technique, and location.

1119

Henkel, Max Ditmar. Le dessin hollandais des origines au XVIIe siècle . . . Paris, van Oest, 1931. 139 p. 76 plates. 39 cm.

Translated by Mlle. Louise Ibels. A collection of good collotypes taken from museums and private collections in Holland, showing the history of Dutch drawings from the 15th century to Rembrandt, with good text and short descriptions of the plates.

"Table alphabétique des artistes" p. [134]–36. "Table des planches" p. [137]–39.

Spain

1120

Mayer, August Liebmann. Dibujos originales de maestros españoles. 150 apuntes y estudios de artistas del siglo XVI hasta el siglo XIX, escogidos y publicados por August L. Mayer . . . N.Y., Hispanic Society of America; Leipzig, Hiersemann, 1920. 2 v. 150 mounted plates. 51 cm.

Seal of the Hispanic Society of America on title page. Printed in Germany.

A collection of excellent collotype plates of Spanish drawings from the 16th to the 19th centuries, with a list of the plates at beginning of v. 1.

Switzerland

1121

Ganz, Paul. Handzeichnungen schweizerischer Meister des XV.–XVIII. Jahrhunderts. Im Auftrage der Kunstcomission unter Mitwirkung v. Prof. D. Burckhardt & Prof. H. A. Schmid, hrsg. von Dr. Paul Ganz . . . 1.–3. Serie. Basel, Helbing & Lichtenhahn [1904–08]. 3 v. 180 plates (part col.) 39 cm.

Issued in 12 parts, each part containing 15 plates with descriptive text (29 cm.). Volume 3: . . . unter Mitwirkung v. verschiedenen Fachgenossen.

A collection of very good reproductions of Swiss drawings with descriptive text for each plate. Contains the work of 81 masters on 180 plates.

At end of each volume an "Übersicht der Tafeln . . . nach Meistern geordnet" which is an artist index. Volume 3 also has a similar index covering all three volumes. "Übersicht der Tafeln in chronologischer Reihenfolge" v. 3, two unnumbered plates.

United States

1122

Bolton, Theodore. Early American portrait draughtsmen in crayons . . . N.Y., Sherman, 1923. 111 p. ports. 25 cm.

Edition of 325 copies printed. Lists artists up to 1860, including foreign painters working in America. Portraits drawn in black crayon, colored crayons or pastels, and black lead pencil, and several outline portraits in ink are listed. A companion volume to *Early American portrait painters in miniature* (1179).

"Index—Names of the artists" p. 101–02; "Index—Names of the sitters" p. 103–11.

1123

Slatkin, Charles Eli, and Shoolman, Regina Lenore. A treasury of American drawings . . . N.Y., Oxford Univ. Press, 1947. 35 p. plates. 32 cm.

Useful as a survey of American drawings. Consists of 32 pages of text followed by good plates. Bibliographical footnotes.

Techniques

1124

Blake, Vernon. The art and craft of drawing; a study both of the practice of drawing and of its aesthetic theory as understood among different peoples and at different epochs; especial reference being made to the construction of the human form from the practical draughtsman's point of view. London, Oxford Univ. Press, Milford, 1927. 414 p. illus., plates, diagrs. 23 cm.

A standard work. Contents: (1) Introduction; (2) Relations between composition and drawing; (3) Technical methods; (4) Mass equilibrium; (5) Perspective; (6) The main masses of the human body; (7) Values; (8) Anatomy and form; (9) Construction of the human frame; (10) Landscape drawing; (11) "Primitive" drawing; (12) Conclusion.

Index p. 405–11. Anatomical index p. 413–[15].

1125

Lavallée, Pierre. Les techniques du dessin, leur évolution dans les différentes écoles de l'Europe. 2. éd. revue et corrigée. Paris, Van Oest, Éditions d'Art et d'Histoire, 1949. 110 p. plates. 23 cm.

A useful book by a recognized authority. Poor paper and as a result fuzzy illustrations.

Contents: (1) La plume; (2) Le pinceau; (3) Les pointes de métal; (4) Le fusain; (5) Les pierres; (6) Le pastel; (7) Le crayon de graphite ou mine de plomb; (8) Les supports du dessin; (9) Les techniques dans l'histoire du dessin. Bibliography p. 99–103, and bibliographical footnotes.

1126

Meder, Joseph. Die Handzeichnung; ihre Technik und Entwicklung. 2. verb. Aufl. Wien, Schroll, 1923. 738 p. illus. (part col.), plates (part col.) 30 cm.

A standard work on drawings, particularly useful for the description of various techniques. "Abkürzungen und Verzeichnis der häufig verwendeten Literatur und Tafelwerke" p. [711]–14. "Namen und Sachregister" p. 715–38.

1127

Nicolaïdes, Kimon. The natural way to draw; a working plan for art study. Boston, Houghton Mifflin, 1941. 221 p. illus., plates, tables. 26 cm.

A well-known book on the technique of drawing written by a long-time instructor at the Art Students League, which embodies his methods of teaching the subject.

1128

Watrous, James. The craft of old-master drawings. Madison, Univ. of Wisconsin Press, 1957. 170 p. illus. 27 cm.

A well-illustrated technical description of drawing techniques covering metalpoint, chiaroscuro, and pen drawing; inks for drawing; chalks, pastels, crayons, charcoal, and graphite. Appendix contains "Commercial and noncommercial sources of materials" and a list of masterworks cited. Bibliography p. 154–56. Index p. 164–70.

SEE ALSO: Plenderleith. The conservation of prints, drawings, and manuscripts (1601).

CHAPTER 14 | # Painting

Bibliography

1129
Creswell, Keppel Archibald Cameron. A bibliography of painting in Islam. Le Caire, L'Institut Français d'Archéologie Orientale, 1953. 100 p. 28 cm. (Publications de l'Inst. Français d'Arch. Orientale du Caire. Art islamique, 1.)

"This bibliography, which contains 1008 items, forms part of *A Bibliography of the Architecture, Arts and Crafts of Islam,* begun in 1912 which at the present moment runs to about 9200 items under Authors and about 11,000 under Subjects."—(*Pref.*)

A classed bibliography with short annotations on some items.

1130
McCausland, Elizabeth. A selected bibliography on American painting and sculpture from Colonial times to the present. (In *American art annual,* v. 36, pt. 2 *Who's who in American art,* p. 611–53, 1947.) 23 cm.

An expanded edition of the same bibliography which was originally published in *Magazine of art,* v. 39, Nov. 1946, p. 329–49.

"Has been compiled to show the scope of American art history."

Titles in "General Works" section are listed chronologically. In section on Painters and Sculptors, entries are made under name of artists and then chronologically.

1131
McColvin, Eric Raymond. Painting, a guide to the best books with special reference to the requirements of public libraries . . . London, Grafton, 1934. 216 p. 23 cm.

An annotated, classed bibliography of books, with prices and indication of books that are out of print.

Covers painting and such related fields as aesthetics, drawing, anatomy, color, mate-

rials, and technique; special classes of painting: landscape, marine, etc.; history of painting in different periods and countries; and guides to and catalogs of important public and private collections.

1132
Someren, Jan Frederik van. Essai d'une bibliographie de l'histoire spéciale de la peinture et de la gravure en Hollande et en Belgique (1500–1875). Amsterdam, Muller, 1882. 207 p. 24 cm.

Limited edition of 350 copies.

A classed bibliography, attempting to list all works published in Europe up to 1875 which deal with Dutch and Flemish painting and engraving. Annotations confined to bibliographical notes or peculiarities.

Author index p. i–viii, following p. 207.

Indexes

1133
Davies, Randall, ed. Black's dictionary of pictures . . . London, Black, 1921. 190 p. 23 cm.

A listing of about 1000 paintings in England and on the Continent, arranged alphabetically by name of artist and then by gallery. For each picture gives size, description, and the number in the official catalog of the gallery in which it was hanging in 1914. Usually gives date of the picture, date of acquisition, and occasionally quotes a few sentences from Crowe and Cavalcaselle. Not of great reference value because of limitation of scope and currency.

1134
Errera, Isabelle. Dictionnaire répertoire des peintres depuis l'antiquité jusqu'à nos jours. Paris, Hachette, 1913. 716 p. 19 cm.

———. Supplément. Paris, Hachette, 1924. 245 p. 19 cm.

An alphabetical listing of names of painters from antiquity to 1882 (any artist who died since 1882 is not included), with information in tabular form to cover: (1) country of origin; (2) date of birth; (3) where artist worked; (4) date of death. Includes Chinese and Japanese painters. Names are entered in the vernacular except that Dutch names with *ij* are under *y*. Sources from which information was obtained are indicated and a list of such sources is given p. 7–15.

1135

Errera, Isabelle. Répertoire des peintures datées. Bruxelles, van Oest, 1920–21. 2 v. 32 cm.

An attempt to list paintings dated between 1081 and 1875; 40,700 paintings are included. The paintings are listed chronologically. Volume 2 begins with 1776. Information given for each painting: (1) year when the picture was made, begun, or finished; (2) country of origin of the painter; (3) name of painter; (4) subject of the painting; (5) location of painting; (6) source of this information.

List of abbreviations and bibliography at beginning of work, v. 1, p. [9]–26. Alphabetical index of artists at end of v. 2, p. [868]–920.

1136

Morse, John D. Old masters in America, a comprehensive guide; more than two-thousand paintings in United States and Canada by forty famous artists. Chicago, Rand McNally [1955]. 192 p. illus. 20 cm.

"A complete listing of every picture now on display in America by 40 of Europe's old masters."—*Pref.* Arranged alphabetically by artist. Under each artist a thumbnail biography and a commentary, followed by a list of works in the United States and Canada (arranged alphabetically by states, cities, and museums), with size of paintings and one illustration for each artist. Geographical index to museums p. 181–92, listed alphabetically by state and city.

1137

Reinach, Salomon. Répertoire de peintures du moyen âge et de la renaissance (1280–1580) . . . Paris, Leroux, 1905–23. 6 v. illus. 20 cm.

A compilation of 6224 line drawings of paintings, arranged by subject; for each painting gives artist, title, and location in gallery or private collection. General arrangement: Old Testament, Lives of Jesus and Mary, Angels, Saints, Allegories, Mythol-

ogy and profane history, Genre subjects, Portraits. If a work has already appeared in the *Klassische Bilderschatz* (Munich, Bruckmann, 1889–[1900] 12 v.) this is indicated. Each volume (except v. 5) has "Index topographique et muséographique," "Index des sujets," and "Index des noms d'artistes." Volume 6 contains corrections and additions, and indexes covering all six volumes.

1138

Reinach, Salomon. Répertoire des vases peints grecs et étrusques . . . Paris, Leroux, 1899–1900. 2 v. in 1. illus. 19 cm.

Compiled from various other publications, with the arrangement by the names of the publications from which the illustrations are derived. Bibliography v. 2, p. 366–87. General alphabetical index v. 2, p. 388–421.

Dictionaries and Encyclopedias

1139

Berckelaers, Ferdinand Louis. A dictionary of abstract painting, preceded by a history of abstract painting [by] Michel Seuphor [pseud.] [Tr. from the French by Lionel Izod, John Montague and Francis Scarfe] N.Y., Tudor [1957]; London, Methuen [1958]. [305] p. illus. (chiefly col.) 22 cm.

Originally published in French as *Dictionnaire de la peinture abstraite* (Paris, Hazan, 1957). Contains short biographical entries for more than 500 artists and 200 small color illustrations. Although the coverage is supposed to be international, the emphasis is on the French school.

Contents: pt. 1, History of abstract painting p. 1–[88]; Appendices (containing manifestos by Severini, Malevitch, and Mondrian) p. 91–[104]; Chronological table of abstract art p. [106–13]; pt. 2, Dictionary of abstract painting p. 117–[294].

Bibliography p. 297–[305]; and some entries contain bibliographical references.

1140

Dictionnaire de la peinture moderne. [Publié avec la collaboration de Raymond Cogniat, et. al., et avec le concours de Robert Maillard] Paris, Hazan [1954]. 328 p. illus. (part col.) 22 cm.

Translated into English as the *Dictionary of modern painting* . . . (General editors: Carlton Lake and Robert Maillard. N.Y., Paris Book Center, 1955. 328 p. illus.); and into German as *Knaurs Lexikon moderner Kunst* (Munich, Knaur, 1955. 336 p. illus.).

Covers the period from the Impressionists to around 1940 (the only living painters included flourished before World War II).

Contains 240 articles arranged alphabetically, covering individual artists, art movements, schools of painting, places, etc. Longer articles are signed with initials, with a list of contributors appearing at the front of the work.

Small color reproductions illustrate the text.

1141
Encyclopedia of painting; painters and painting of the world from prehistoric times to the present day. Bernard S. Myers, editor. Contributing associates: Milton W. Brown [and others]. N.Y., Crown, 1955. 511 p. illus. (part col.) 29 cm.

An attempt to cover in an inexpensive volume the outstanding painters, movements, styles, and techniques from ancient times to the present. In one alphabet contains entries for individual artists, famous galleries and museums, schools of painting, catch titles of works of art, terminology. Numerous cross references.

Oriental art is treated under broad headings, i.e., Chinese, Persian, Indian, Japanese, with cross references from well-known artists.

Profusely illustrated in color and black and white but quality of color is not too good.

Contributors listed on title page; sections covered by each are indicated in Preface. No bibliography.

Biography

General

1142
Aeschlimann, Erardo, and Ancona, Paolo d'. Dictionnaire des miniaturistes du moyen âge et de la renaissance dans les différentes contrées de l'Europe. Avec 155 planches dont 7 en couleurs. 2. éd. rev. et augm. contenant un index ordonné par époques, régions, écoles. Milan, Hoepli, 1949. 239 p. plates (part col.) 31 cm.

Originally published in 1940 under name of Aeschlimann only, but since the war is over d'Ancona's name may be added. New edition has more entries and contains later sources and more plates, but the illustrations are not as good as in the first edition. A dictionary of miniature painters of the Middle Ages and Renaissance in Europe, confined to biographies of true and proper artists, omitting copyists, calligraphers, patrons, amateurs, and others linked with the field. Bibliographical references. Index by epochs, subdivided by countries, p. [221]–39.

1143
Bradley, John William. A dictionary of miniaturists, illuminators, calligraphers, and copyists, with references to their works and notices of their patrons, from the establishment of Christianity to the eighteenth century. Comp. from various sources, many hitherto inedited . . . London, Quaritch, 1887–89. 3 v. 24 cm.

Reprinted 1958 by Burt Franklin, N.Y.

Gives name of artist and his century; indicates whether he was a copyist, calligrapher, illuminator, or miniaturist; and then summarizes what is known of his work. Sources of information are usually given. Appendix, p. 425–40, gives list of supplementary names.

1144
Bryan, Michael. Bryan's Dictionary of painters and engravers. New ed. rev. and enl. under the supervision of George C. Williamson. London, Bell, 1926–34. [v.1, 1930] 5 v. plates, ports. 27 cm.

First published in 1816. Rev. in 1849 by J. Stanley, and in 1876 a supplement was prepared by Ottley. New ed. (2 v., 1884–89) under R. E. Graves and Walter Armstrong as editors. A 4th ed. of five volumes, revised by Williamson, first printed in 1903–04 and reprinted many times. Last ed. greatly expanded (72 biographies added in one volume and over 600 corrections and nearly 600 new biographies in v. 5).

A standard work. Longer articles are signed by specialists and give lists of the artists' works. Illustrated by halftone plates.

1145
Champlin, John Denison, and Perkins, Charles C., eds. Cyclopedia of painters and paintings. . . . With more than two thousand illustrations . . . N.Y., Empire State Book Co., 1927. 4 v. illus. 30 cm.

Originally published by Scribner, 1885–87.

In one alphabet gives articles on painters which include biographical information; lists of paintings with locations in museums; and descriptions of each painting, with its history, whether it has been engraved, and by whom. Biographical references are given. Entries are made under "best known English appellation."

Bibliography v. 1, p. xix–xxxvi.

1146

Clouzot, Henri. Dictionnaire des miniaturistes sur émail . . . [Paris] Morancé [c1924]. 241 p. 12 plates (incl. ports.) 24 cm. (Archives de l'amateur)

Treats only of artists who make miniatures on enamel, with special emphasis on French and Swiss artists. Contains about 600 entries giving birth and death dates, where the artist worked, and museums and collections containing his works. Bibliography p. xiii–[xx].

1147

Darmon, J. E. Dictionnaire des peintres miniaturistes sur vélin, parchemin, ivoire et écaille . . . Paris, Morancé [1927]. 123 p. 8 plates. 24 cm. (Aide-mémoire de l'amateur et du professionnel)

Dictionary preceded by a description of the process of miniature painting. Usually gives dates of the artist with a few lines of biography, but in the case of important artists their works are listed chronologically. Numerous entries under "Anonymes."

1148

Foster, Joshua James. A dictionary of painters of miniatures (1525–1850) with some account of exhibitions, collections, sales, etc., pertaining to them . . . edited by Ethel M. Foster . . . London, Allan, 1926. 330 p. ports. 26 cm.

"This book is an amplification of the list of artists . . . in my work entitled *Miniature painters, British and foreign,* published several years ago [1903]."—*Author's Pref.* Aims to give: (1) Biographical and critical details relating to artists who worked as portrait miniaturists; (2) Information as to the provenance and ownership of works by the same, where ascertainable; (3) Particulars of auction sales or other distributions of examples. Sources mentioned in Preface p. xii–xiii. List of abbreviations p. xv.

1149

Guédy, Théodore. Dictionnaire universel des peintres anciens, modernes et contemporains . . . Paris, L'auteur, Imprimerie typographique La publicité générale, 1892. 450 p. incl. facsims. 26 cm.

First published 1882. Arranged according to school (or country) and then alphabetically by artist. For each artist a short biography, list of pupils and imitators and chief characteristics, as well as prices brought at sales, and signatures or monograms. Includes Russian, Swedish, Norwegian, and Danish artists. Also includes a résumé of the origins

of painting and an historical account of various schools. "Table alphabétique" p. 237–69.

1150

James, Ralph N. Painters and their works; a dictionary of great artists who are not now alive, giving their names, lives, and the prices paid for their works at auction. London, Gill, 1896–97. 3 v. plates. 19 cm.

Contents: v. 1, Aalst to Hyre; v. 2, Ibbetson to Rysbregts; v. 3, Sabbateni to Zyl and Appendix.

Appendix I, Additions and corrections; II, Imitators and copyists; III, Signatures and marks (84 plates at end of v. 3); IV, List of subscribers.

1151

Pilkington, Matthew. A general dictionary of painters; containing memoirs of the lives and works of the most eminent professors of the art of painting, from its revival by Cimabue, in the year 1250, to the present time. . . . A new ed. revised and corrected throughout, with numerous additions . . . London, M'Lean, 1824. 2 v. 22 cm.

At the beginning of v. 1 a list of 202 works in six languages from which it has been compiled. "An explanation of terms used in painting" p. xxix–xxxvi. Supplement at end of v. 2 contains additional lives, anecdotes, and corrections.

1152

Seguier, Frederick Peter. A critical and commercial dictionary of the works of painters comprising 8,850 sale notes of 980 original notes on . . . artists . . . between 1250 and 1850. London, Longmans, 1870. 241 p. 26 cm.

Intended as a kind of appendix to biographical dictionaries such as Pilkington (1151) and Bryan (1144). For each painter gives dates of birth and death, prices obtained in the London market, and "descriptive notes on the subjects and styles of all the principal masters whose names have not appeared in former dictionaries."

1153

Siret, Adolphe. Dictionnaire historique et raisonné des peintres de toutes les écoles, depuis l'origine de la peinture jusqu'à nos jours . . . 3. éd. originale (considérablement augm.) Berlin, Altmann, 1924. 2 v. plates, ports. 27 cm.

Originally issued in 1848; 2d ed. 1866; 3d ed. 1883, reprinted 1924. Under each name gives: name of artist, school, dates of birth and death, place of birth, medium in which he worked, historical account of his life, principal works and where found (mostly in public museums), characteristics of his style, and mention of famous sales where works of the artist have been sold, with name of buyer and seller and price paid. Gives monograms affixed to canvases when known. Alphabetical tables arranged by school and century at end of v. 2. Swedish and Norwegian schools listed under German, Swiss under French and German, and American under English. Contents: v. 1, A-Lotyn; v. 2, Lotz-Z. Supplement in v. 2 contains addenda and corrigenda.

1154
Ticozzi, Stefano. Dizionario dei pittori dal rinnovamento delle belle arti fino al 1800 . . . Milano, Ferrario, 1818. 2 v. plates. 21 cm.

Includes painters from other countries besides Italy. Contains 2 plates of monograms (40 in all). No bibliographies. At end of v. 2 an index of ancient Greek and Roman painters.

SEE ALSO: Dézallier d'Argenville. Abrégé de la vie des plus fameux peintres (2001); Félibien. Entretiens sur les vies et les ouvrages des plus excellens peintres (2006); Grant. Flower paintings through four centuries (1189).

National

France

1155
Chennevières-Pointel, Philippe, i.e., Charles Philippe, *marquis* de. Recherches sur la vie et les ouvrages de quelques peintres provinciaux de l'ancienne France. Paris, Dumoulin, 1847–62. 4 v. 4 plates. 22 cm.

Author's name appears on title page of v. 1 as Ph. de Pointel. Besides biographical material it covers artistic theory, the publication of early works, and material on provincial academies. Each volume has its own "Index" which is a table of contents. Volume 4 is a monograph on Hilaire Pader of Toulouse.

1156
Claretie, Jules. . . . Peintres & sculpteurs contemporains; portraits gravés par L. Massard . . . Paris, Librairie des Bibliophiles, 1882–84. 2 v. illus., 32 ports. 25 cm.

Contents: sér. 1, Artistes décédés de 1870–

1880; sér. 2, Artistes vivants en janvier 1881. An engraved portrait of each of the 32 artists treated.

SEE ALSO: Félibien. Entretiens sur les vies et les ouvrages des plus excellens peintres (2006).

Germany and Austria

1157
Schultz, Alwin. Untersuchungen zur Geschichte der schlesischen Maler (1500–1800). Breslau, Korn, 1882. 173 p. 24 cm.

A dictionary of painters of Silesia, giving usually just a few sentences for each artist.

1158
Westecker, Wilhelm. Künstler des Ruhrlandes. Essen, Hellweg [1954]. 107 p. illus. 27 cm.

Covers contemporary painting and sculpture in the Ruhr. For each artist (arranged alphabetically) gives a full-page illustration of his work and a page or more of biographical and critical information. Index of names p. 106–07.

Great Britain

1159
Grant, Maurice Harold. A dictionary of British landscape painters, from the 16th century to the early 20th century. Leigh-on-Sea, Lewis [1952]. 233 p. 26 cm.

Includes names of all landscape painters who worked in Great Britain, whether of British or foreign birth, and others who surrounded their subjects with landscape. Very brief entries; no sources and no bibliography.

1160
Long, Basil Somerset. British miniaturists. London, Bles, 1929. 475 p. ports., facsims. 32 cm.

"Attempts to give as complete a list as possible of the miniaturists, chiefly portrait painters, who worked in Great Britain and Ireland between 1520 and 1860. Foreigners who worked in England and miniaturists who were born in Great Britain and Ireland, but worked elsewhere, are included if their period of activity falls between the above dates. . . . A considerable number of American miniaturists are thus included. . . . I have attempted to quote the salient known facts about each miniaturist and to mention those of his miniatures which can be seen in public galleries."—*Pref.* Also mentions some miniatures, paintings, and drawings in private collections.

Under each name (arranged alphabetically) is a short biographical sketch and a list of works. References to reproductions are also given. Plates at end of book.

Contains: Notes on British miniature painting; List of abbreviations; List of illustrations; Lists of artists represented by illustrations; List of provincial towns and miniaturists who worked there; List of British miniaturists.

SEE ALSO: Auerbach. Tudor artists (1278); Edwards. Anecdotes of painters . . . in England (1283); Walpole. Anecdotes of painting in England (2047) and Anecdotes of painting in England; 1760–1795 (2058).

Italy

1161

Bessone-Aurelj, Antonietta Maria. Dizionario dei pittori italiani, con una lettera di Corrado Ricci. 2. ed. ampliata. Milano, Albrighi, 1928. 678 p. 23 cm.

1st ed. 1915. A dictionary of Italian painters with short entries for individual artists. Miniaturists are marked by an asterisk. "Libri letti o consultati" p. 675–78. Appendix carries additions for 2d ed.

1162

Colnaghi, *Sir* Dominic Ellis. A dictionary of Florentine painters from the 13th to the 17th centuries . . . ed. by P. G. Konody and Selwyn Brinton . . . London, Lane [1928]. 286 p. 29 cm.

Based mainly on Florentine guild records. Short bibliographies given in parentheses at end of articles and some principal works listed.

1163

Comanducci, Agostino Mario. Dizionario illustrato dei pittori e incisori italiani moderni (1800–1900). 2. ed. riveduta da L. Pelandi. Milano, S. A. Grafitaliagia Pizzi & Pizio, 1945. 2 v. illus., col. plates. 31 cm.

1st ed. 1934.

An illustrated dictionary of Italian painters and engravers of the 19th century with more than 3000 artists included. Some illustrations added and others dropped from the 1st ed., and 70 colored plates added. Bibliography v. 1, p. [v–xii].

1164

Gnoli, Umberto. Pittori e miniatori nell'Umbria. Spoleto, Argentieri [1923–25]. 411 p. plates. 30 cm.

1000 copies printed. A biographical dictionary of Umbrian painters, miniaturists, and glassworkers up to 1600, which also includes Italian, German, and Flemish artists working in Umbria. Long scholarly articles with bibliographies for each artist. Bibliography p. 9–10. Topographical index p. 357–411.

SEE ALSO: Ridolfi. Le maraviglie dell'arte (2036).

Latin America

1165

Laroche, Ernesto. Algunos pintores y escultores. [Montevideo] Ministerio de instrucción publica y prevision social, República oriental del Uruguay, 1939. 214 p. illus., plates, ports. 25 cm.

3d ed. of 1000 copies. Covers about 20 Uruguayan artists of the 19th century. Gives portrait of the artist as well as poor reproductions of some works and biographical and critical information.

1166

Lira, Pedro. Diccionario biográfico de pintores. Santiago de Chile, Esmeralda, 1902. 552 p. 24 cm.

While it covers artists of all countries and schools it is particularly valuable for the coverage of Chilean artists. "Primero apéndice: Los pintores vivos" p. [453–539]. "Segundo apéndice: Pintores Chilenos vivos en 1901" p. [541]–51.

Low Countries

1167

Bautier, Pierre [et al.] Dictionnaire des peintres. . . . Préface de Paul Fierens. Bruxelles, Maison Larcier [1950?]. 694 p. 17 cm. (Petits dictionnaires des lettres et des arts en Belgique, 4)

Contains Belgian painters born before 1900 and artists born in Belgium, i.e., Philippe de Champaigne. For each artist gives full name, dates, description of types of paintings, and list of most important works and bibliography. Signed entries for some of the more important artists. An effort is made to include the latest sources.

1168

Mak van Waay, S. J. Lexicon van Nederlandsche schilders en beeldhouwers 1870–1940 . . . Amsterdam, N. V. Wereldbibliotheek, 1944. 136 p. 28 cm.

"Dit werk moet beschouwd worden als een

vervolg op het werk van Albert Plasschaert *De Hollandsche schilderkunst."—Voorwoord.* A biographical dictionary of Dutch painters and sculptors with short entries giving pertinent facts. No bibliographies.

1169
Scheen, P. A. Honderd jaren Nederlandsche schilder-en teekenkunst. De romantiek met voor- en natijd (1750–1850) . . . Den Haag, Uitgevers-Bureau "Boek en Periodiek," 1946. 381 p. 417 plates on 209 l. 25 cm.

A biographical dictionary containing entries for about 3000 Dutch painters, illustrated by good clear plates reproducing material not usually published, and including bibliographical references. Bibliography p. 359–62. Indexes: Monogrammen en signaturen van in dit handboek behandelde schilders en schilderessen p. 364–76; Opgave van de in dit handboek opgenomen monogrammen, signaturen en afbeeldingen p. 377–80; Aanvullingen en wijzigingen p. i–xxxix.

1170
Seyn, Eug. M. H. de. Dessinateurs, graveurs et peintres des anciens Pays-Bas; écoles flamande et hollandaise. Turnhout (Belgique), Brepols [1949?]. 302 p. ports. 28 cm.

Short entries of a few lines for each artist give dates of birth and death, with whom he studied, and the type of subjects he portrayed. Illustrated by some plates of portraits. Bibliography p. [299]–302.

SEE ALSO: Crowe. Lives of the early Flemish painters (1344); Houbraken. De groote schouburgh der nederlantsche konstschilders en schilderessen (2008).

Oriental Countries

1171
Tokyo. Institute of Art Research. Index of Japanese painters. Tōkyō, The Society of Friends of Eastern Art, 1941. 156 p. table. 19 cm.

"The Index contains about 600 names, with short biographies of painters who are familiar in the reproductions and the articles which have been published for the past several years in important publications of the country. . . ."—*Pref.* Names given in Japanese characters after the English forms. At end of volume: (1) List of albums of reproductions (no place, date, or publisher given); (2) List of names of places (giving pre-Meiji and modern form in alphabetical order according to pre-Meiji names); (3) Explanation of schools; (4) Table of schools (a chart).

Spain and Portugal

1172
Alcahalí y de Mosquera, José Maria Ruiz de Lihori y Pardnes, *Barón* de. Diccionario biográfico de artistas valencianos; obra premiada en los Juegos florales de lo Ratpenat el año 1894. Valencia, Domenech, 1897. 443 p. 26 cm.

Covers painters and sculptors of Valencia. No index or bibliography.

1173
Ballesteros de Martos. . . . Artistas españoles contemporáneos, el arte España, prólogo de José Frances. Madrid, Tipografia Gagües [19–]. 242 p. 32 plates on 16 l. 20 cm.

A few general remarks on contemporary Spanish painting and then treatment of 17 separate artists. Index at end of book, following p. 242 and plates.

1174
Huard, Étienne. Vie complète des peintres espagnols et histoire de la peinture espagnole. Paris, Bureau du Journal des Artistes, 1839–41. 2 v. 23 cm.

A standard early history of Spanish painting and painters. At end of each volume an alphabetical list of the artists treated therein.

1175
O'Neil, A. A dictionary of Spanish painters . . . from the fourteenth century to the eighteenth. London, C. O'Neil, 1833–34. 2 v. 25 cm.

Short articles, arranged alphabetically by name of artist. At the beginning a short list of artists by schools, and at end of v. 2 a short list of some of the most important Spanish paintings and where found.

1176
Pamplona, Fernando de. Dicionário de pintores e escultores portugueses ou que trabalharam em Portugal. Edicão dirigida e prefaciada por Ricardo do Espírito Santo Silva. [Lisboa, 1954– . v. 1– . plates (part col.), facsims. 26 cm. (In progress)

A dictionary of Portuguese painters and sculptors. Includes signatures and bibliographies for more important artists. Volume 1 covers A–L.

1177
Quilliet, Frédéric. Dictionnaire des peintres espagnols . . . Paris, L'auteur, 1816. 407 p. 22 cm.

Based on Ceán Bermúdez (287), Palomino Velasco (2028), and other sources.

Introduction p. xv–xxxvii contains a summary account of Spanish painting. The main text lists a great number of works by the painters treated, many with long descriptions.

1178

Viardot, Louis. Notices sur les principaux peintres de l'Espagne; ouvrage servant de texte aux gravures de la Galerie Aguado. Paris, Gavard, 1839. 355 p. 27 cm.

Based on Pacheco's *Arte de la pintura* (2024), Palomino's *El museo pictórico* (2027), Ponz's *Viage de España* (2034), and Ceán Bermúdez' *Diccionario histórico* (287).

Consists of individual treatment for outstanding artists and the artists who headed various schools; then under the title of a school or movement are brought together various artists and their works. Also includes a chapter "Étrangers peintres en Espagne" which treats of Luca Giordano, Raphael Mengs, Pedro Campaña, Antonie Moro, etc.

Table of contents p. 349–51 and alphabetical index p. 353–55.

United States

1179

Bolton, Theodore. Early American portrait painters in miniature . . . N.Y., Sherman, 1921. 180 p. ports. 25 cm.

"The present volume lists as many of the portrait painters in miniature, both native Americans and foreign painters working in America, from the earliest times until 1850, as it has been possible to enumerate. It includes not only ivory miniatures but small portraits in oil and water color as well."–*Pref.*

An alphabetical listing of artists working in the medium, giving biographical information as well as a listing of some of their works. Index p. 177–80.

1180

Park, Esther Ailleen. Mural painters in America. Part I. A biographical index . . . Pittsburg, Kansas State Teachers College, 1949– . 27 cm.

"Period covered is from 1800 through June 1947, with references to some 259 books, to 178 magazine titles (over 500 volumes) and to 1,544 artists."–*Pref.* In order to be included an artist had only to be credited with one or more mural works in the United States.

"Biographical index," p. 19–182, is ar-

ranged alphabetically by artist. Under name of artist gives dates of birth and death (if not living), references to his work in periodicals, references in books, and reproductions in magazines. The form of entry is like that of the *Art index.* Part II is to be a geographical index which will indicate location of the murals. "Key to symbols" p. 9–18.

Histories and Handbooks

1181

Abbot, Edith R. The great painters in relation to the European tradition . . . N.Y., Harcourt, Brace [c1927]. 478 p. 94 plates. 23 cm.

A basic one-volume survey of painting from the beginning of Christian painting in Italy to the present day. "Books for reference" at end of some chapters. "Brief biographies," p. 418–46, gives a few sentences of data about the most important painters. "Supplementary list of paintings" p. 447–64. Index p. 465–78.

1182

Bazin, Germain, ed. History of painting. Published under the supervision of Germain Bazin. Translated from the French by Rosamund Frost. [Ed. by André Gloeckner] Text, research, biographies, bibliographies by Marc Logé, André Leclerc, M. de Gesne, Frederick Moss, S. Béguin. N.Y., Hyperion [1951]. 2 v. illus. (part col.) 19 cm.

Primarily a pictorial history (with generally poor reproductions) including a small amount of text. Covers only Western art. Contents: v. 1, Classic painting (begins with early Christian art); v. 2, Modern painting (19th and 20th centuries).

Biographical paragraphs of important artists are arranged alphabetically at end of each volume: v. 1, p. 323–56; v. 2, p. 349–91. Bibliographies: v. 1, p. 309–19; v. 2, p. 341–46.

1183

Blanc, Charles, ed. Histoire des peintres de toutes les écoles . . . Paris, Renouard, 1861–70. 14 v. illus. 36 cm.

Issued in 631 parts, 1849–76. A standard work of the 19th century, now out of date. The text is by various scholars.

For each school usually gives a short historical summary, followed by chapters devoted to the principal artists, with their portraits and signatures, and reproductions of their works. Minor masters are sometimes in the appendix. In most cases alphabetical and chronological lists of artists are at end of volume.

Contents: v. 1, École allemande, 1875; v. 2, École anglaise, 1863; v. 3, École bolonaise, 1874; v. 4, École espagnole, 1869; v. 5, École flamande, 1868; v. 6, École florentine, 1870; v. 7–9, École française, 3 v., 1862–65; v. 10–11, École hollandaise, 2 v., 1861; v. 12, Écoles milanaise, lombarde, ferraraise, genoise et napolitaine [1875]–76; v. 13, École ombrienne et romaine, 1870; v. 14, École venitienne, 1868.

1184
Boehn, Max von. Miniaturen und Silhouetten, ein Kapitel aus Kulturgeschichte und Kunst . . . 3. Aufl. München, Bruckmann [1919]. 207 p. illus., col. plates. 20 cm.
A general survey of the field of miniatures and silhouettes, partly in color. Contents: (1) Die Miniatur und ihre Geschichte; (2) Die Miniatur und ihre Verwendung; (3) Die Silhouette. Alphabetical index of names and locations p. 203–07.

1185
Byron, Robert. The birth of western painting: a history of colour, form, and iconography, illustrated from the paintings of Mistra and Mount Athos, of Giotto and Duccio, and of El Greco . . . London, Routledge, 1930. 236 p. 94 plates. 29 cm.
"The text and notes are by Robert Byron. The bulk of the illustrations is the work of David Talbot Rice." The verso of each plate contains letterpress description of the following plate.
List of illustrations p. xi–xvi. "Classification of plates showing dates, schools, and artists" p. [237]. Bibliography p. 220–26. Index p. 227–36.

1186
Clark, *Sir* Kenneth McKenzie. Landscape painting. N.Y., Scribner, 1950. 147 p. 104 plates. 24 cm.
English ed. titled *Landscape into art* (London, Sedgwick, 1950). "Based on lectures given during . . . [the author's] first year as Slade Professor to the University of Oxford."
Contents: I, The landscape of symbols; II, The landscape of fact; III, Landscape of fantasy; IV, Ideal landscape; V, The natural vision; VI, The northern lights; VII, The return to order; Epilogue. Index p. 145–[48].

1187
Cogniat, Raymond. Histoire de la peinture. [Paris] Nathan [c1954–55]. 2 v. col. illus. 32 cm. (Grandes encyclopédies Fernand Nathan)
A popular survey, illustrated entirely by color plates of uneven quality.

1188
Davenport, Cyril James Humphries. Miniatures, ancient and modern. Chicago, McClurg, 1908. 174 p. illus., 33 plates. 16 cm. (Little books on art)
"First published in 1907" (London, Methuen). A rather general treatment of miniatures with emphasis on portraits rather than illuminated manuscripts.
Contents: (1) Introductory; (2) English miniatures of the 16th century; (3) English miniatures of the 17th century; (4) English miniatures of the 18th and 19th centuries; (5) Foreign miniatures; (6) Enamels; (7) Wax miniatures.
Bibliography p. 165–66. Index p. 167–74.

1189
Grant, Maurice Harold. Flower paintings through four centuries, including a dictionary of flower painters from the XVI to the XIX century . . . A descriptive catalogue of the collection formed by Mayor the Honourable Henry Rogers Broughton. Leigh-on-Sea, Lewis [1952]. 85 p. 40 plates (9 col.) 29 cm.
Edition of 500 copies.
Contents: Sources consulted p. 13; pt. 1, A sketch history of flower painting through four centuries p. 21–27; pt. 2, A dictionary of flower painters from the XVI to the XIX century p. 31–47 (a mere listing by century of the painters, giving dates of birth and death and country of origin); pt. 3, Catalogue of the collection of flower paintings p. 51–85 (gives a short biographical paragraph about each artist and lists his paintings in the Broughton collection).

1190
Heath, Dudley. Miniatures . . . London, Methuen; N.Y., Putnam [1905]. 40, 319 p. illus., 42 plates (part col.) 27 cm. (The connoisseur's library)
"The object is to give a historical account of the art of miniature which shall be suggestive and stimulating to further study and appreciation rather than an exhaustive catalogue or an authoritative guide for the specialist."—*Pref.*
Appendix: Collections and collectors p. 293–302. Bibliography p. xxxv–xl is annotated. Index to plates p. xiii–xxxiv gives line drawings of contents of plates as well as a description. Index p. 303–20.

1191

Propert, John Lumsden. A history of miniature art. With notes on collectors and collections ... London, N.Y., Macmillan, 1887. 285 p. 22 plates. 36 cm.

Emphasis is on English work from the 16th through the 19th centuries. One chapter each on illuminated manuscripts and foreign schools. Good collotype plates. A section devoted to collectors and collections, p. 191–257, discusses them from Greece and Rome through the 19th century.

"List of works consulted" p. [xv]–xvi. Index p. 259–85.

1192

Réau, Louis. La miniature. Melun, Librairie d'Argences, 1946. 256 p. 104 plates (8 col.) 28 cm. (His Histoire de la peinture au moyen-âge, v. 1)

A general survey of miniature painting in illuminated manuscripts which covers Byzantine, Occidental (monastic and laic), and Islamic miniatures. At end of each chapter is given a list of the principal manuscripts discussed with their dates. An alphabetical list of the principal illuminated manuscripts, arranged by place of preservation, p. 26–27.

General bibliography p. 28–30 and further bibliographies at the end of each chapter. Index p. 241–46.

1193

Robb, David Metheny. The Harper history of painting; the Occidental Tradition. N.Y., Harper [c1951]. 1006 p. illus., col. plates. 27 cm.

A good one-volume survey including painting from the Pre-Classic period (cave paintings) to the present day. "Glossary: Identifications and definitions" p. 945–63. "Selected bibliography" p. 965–83. Index p. 985–1006.

1194

Williamson, George Charles. The history of portrait miniatures. London, Bell, 1904. 2 v. 104 (i.e., 107) plates. 40 cm.

Edition of 520 copies printed. "The object of the author has been to compile a comprehensive account of the art of miniature portrait painting as exhibited in the great collections of England and the Continent, and to narrate the history of the chief exponents of the art."—*Pref.*

The standard work on portrait miniatures covering 1531–1860. Appendices: (1) Extracts from Norgate's manuscript in the Bodleian Library; (2) Extracts from King's manuscript

in the British Museum entitled "Miniatura. "Notable collectors and the chief collections" v. 2, p. 123–47. "The literature of the subject" v. 2, p. 148–60. Index v. 2, p. 183–211. Index of artists whose works are illustrated v. 1, p. xxi–xxii; of collections from which the illustrations are taken v. 1, p. xxiii–xxiv; of portraits illustrated v. 1, p. xxv–xxix.

Ancient

1195

Beazley, John Davidson. Attic black-figure vase-painters. Oxford, Clarendon Press, 1956. 851 p. 24 cm.

Arrangement of the painters is roughly chronological, but the book is divided into two sections: painters of large vases p. 1–417, and of small vases p. 418–663. "Principal shapes" p. xi–xii. "Abbreviations" p. xiii–xvi.

Includes bibliographical references. Indexes of: Proveniences p. 717–22; Mythological subjects p. 723–28; Collections p. 729–97; Publications p. 798–846; Painters, potters, groups, classes p. 847–51.

1196

Beazley, John Davidson. Attic red-figure vase-painters. Oxford, Clarendon Press, 1942. 1186 p. 24 cm.

1st ed., 1925, contained 10,000 items. This edition has more than 15,000. "The painters are arranged, roughly speaking, in chronological order; but groups of painters are kept together."—*Introd.* Includes bibliographies.

Abbreviations p. x–xii; Shapes p. viii–x. Indexes: (1) Proveniences p. 969–77; (2) Mythological subjects p. 978–86; (3) Collections p. 987–1093; (4) Publications p. 1094–1179; (5) Artists p. 1180–86.

1197

Beazley, John Davidson, and Jacobsthal, Paul, eds. Bilder griechischer Vasen ... Berlin-Wilmersdorf, Keller, 1930–39. v. 1–13. 390 plates. 30 cm.

Each volume contains scholarly text, excellent collotype reproductions, and bibliographies.

Contents: Hft. 1, Hahland, W. Vasen um Meidias, 1930; Hft. 2, Beazley, J. D. Der Berliner Maler, 1930; Hft. 3, Schefold, K. Kertscher Vasen, 1930; Hft. 4, Beazley, J. D. Der Pan-Maler, 1931; Hft. 5, Ducati, P. Pontische Vasen, 1932; Hft. 6, Beazley, J. D. Der Kleophrades-Maler, 1933; Hft. 7, Payne, H. G. G. Protokorinthische Vasenmalerei, 1933; Hft. 8, Webster, T. B. L. Die Niobidenmaler, 1935; Hft. 9, Technau, W. Exekias, 1936; Hft. 10, Diepolder, H. Der Penthesilea-Maler, 1936; Hft. 11, Rumpf, A. Sakonides, 1937; Hft. 12, Trendall, A. D. Frühitaliotische Vasen, 1938; Hft. 13, Smith, H. R. W. Der Lewismaler (Polygnotos II), 1939.

1198

Beazley, John Davidson. Etruscan vase-painting. Oxford, Clarendon Press, 1947. 351 p. 42 plates. 30 cm. (Oxford monographs on classical archaeology [v. 1])

A scholarly work. "List of abbreviations" p. xiii–xvi. Bibliographical footnotes. General index p. 311–16. Index of collections p. 317–38; of publications p. 339–51.

1199

Buschor, Ernst. Greek vase-painting . . . with CLX illustrations; tr. by G. C. Richards . . . & with a preface by Percy Gardner . . . London, Chatto & Windus, 1921. 179 p. 96 plates. 26 cm.

Index of names p. 174–80.

1200

Buschor, Ernst. Griechische Vasen; mit 282 Abbildungen. München, Piper [1940]. 272 p. illus. 26 cm.

The latest edition of this basic work. Well illustrated. No bibliographies or index.

√1201

Corpvs vasorvm antiqvorvm . . . Paris, Champion [etc.] 1922–(58). illus., plates (part col.) 33 cm.

At head of title: Union Académique Internationale. Issued in portfolio form. The majority of fascicles are published by Champion in Paris, but the series for Germany, Spain, Italy, and Poland have native imprints.

Each fascicle is dedicated to the vases in a specific museum and is written by a specialist. A series each for Belgium, Denmark, Germany, Spain, France, Great Britain, Greece, Italy, Low Countries, Poland, United States, and Yugoslavia.

———. Konkordanz zum Corpvs vasorvm antiqvrvm by Jan W. Crous. Rome, Bretschneider, 1942. 244 p. 33 cm.

Contains concordances, covering only the first 74 fascicles, up to 1942, arranged by countries, museums, collections, and especially, groups of vases, i.e., Attic black figure, Italo red figure, etc.

1202

Davies, *Mrs.* Nina M. (Cummings). Ancient Egyptian paintings selected, copied, and described by Nina M. Davies, with the editorial assistance of Alvan H. Gardiner . . . Chicago, Univ. of Chicago Press, 1936. 3 v. illus., 104 col. plates (part double) 60 cm. (v. 3, 26 cm.)

Special publication of the Oriental Institute of the University of Chicago; James Henry Breasted, editor. A de luxe publication with fine color collotype reproductions covering Egyptian painting from about 2700 B.C. to about 1100 B.C. Includes bibliographies, and dimensions are given in the text volume.

Contents: v. 1–2, Plates; v. 3, Descriptive text. General index, v. 3, p. 201–06; Index of localities p. 207; Index of personal names p. 207–09.

1203

Denkmäler der Malerei des Altertums. München, Bruckmann, 1904–(44). v. 1–2$^{1\text{-}4}$. illus. 38 cm. and 2 atlases of plates (part col.) 50–51 cm.

Editors: 1904–34, Paul Herrmann; 1939– , Reinhard Herbig. Issued in parts, in portfolios.

A corpus of collotype reproductions (a few in color: 6 in Seriè 1) with a scholarly textual description and bibliographical notes. Seriè 1 consists of 194 plates and bears the imprint 1909–31; Seriè 2 has 213 plates and bears the imprint 1939.

Text, v. 1, contains "Alphabetisches Verzeichnis der Tafeln," "Verzeichnis der Textabbildungen," "Standort-Verzeichnis," and "Text zu Tafeln," 1–194.

1204

Pfuhl, Ernst. Malerei und Zeichnung der Griechen. München, Bruckmann, 1923. 3 v. plates (part col.) 29 cm.

The definitive scholarly work on Greek painting and drawing. Contents: Bd. 1–2, Text; Bd. 3, Verzeichnisse und Abbildungen.

Indexes in v. 3: (1) Inhaltsverzeichnis (a detailed breakdown of subjects) p. [921]–27; (2) Verzeichnis der wichtigsten Abkürzungen p. 928–29; (3) Verzeichnis der Namen und Sachen, Inschriften und Literaturangeben:

A. Namen (in 4 classes) p. 929–37;

B. Sachen—1) Antiquaria 2) Einflusse und Beziehungen 3) Farbe 4) Gefässformen 5) Geistesleben 6) Komposition 7) Licht und Schatten 8) Mythologie, Götter, Heroen 9) Ornament 10) Stile, Gattungen, Schulen, Epochen 11) Technik 12) Tiere und Fabelwesen 13) Verzierungs**weise,** Tektonik 14) Zeichnung, p. 937–76; C. Inschriften p. 976–78; D. Antike Autoren p. 978–81; (4) Verzeichnis der Reproduktionserlebnisse p. 981.

1205

Pfuhl, Ernst. Masterpieces of Greek drawing and painting . . . Tr. by J. D. Beazley . . . N.Y., Macmillan [1955]. 151 p. 126 p. of illus. (part col.) 29 cm.

Originally published in 1926. The 1955 ed. contains an appendix by John D. Beazley listing the attributions of the vases illustrated, p. 146–47.

[This book] "is intended neither as a guide to the study of vases nor as a history of Greek painting. It is . . . a collection, though not an arbitrary one, of masterpieces of Greek painting and drawing. . . . The plates contain a selection from the 800 reproductions in my three-volume work *Malerei und Zeichnung der Griechen* [1204]."—*Pref.*

Bibliography p. 144–45. Index p. 148–52. "List of artists of the Attic vases illustrated" by J. D. Beazley p. 146–47.

1206

Swindler, Mary Hamilton. Ancient painting, from the earliest times to the period of Christian art . . . New Haven, Yale Univ. Press, 1929. 488 p. illus., plates (part col.), maps. 28 cm.

A standard work in this field. Discusses prehistoric, Egyptian, Oriental, Cretan, Greek, Etruscan, Pompeian, Graeco-Roman, and Roman painting. Includes chronological tables and a tentative chronology of some of the most important vase-painters.

Detailed and classed bibliography p. [433]– 70. Glossary p. 471–72. Index p. 473–88.

1207

Weege, Fritz. . . . Etruskische Malerei, mit 89 Textabbildungen und 101 Tafeln. Halle (Saale), Niemeyer, 1921. 120 p. illus., plates. 32 cm.

The standard work on Etruscan painting.

SEE ALSO: Monumenti della pittura antica scoperti in Italia (2452); Rumpf. Malerei und Zeichnung (464); Smith. A history of Egyptian sculpture and painting (979).

Early Christian—Gothic

1208

Anthony, Edgar Waterman. Romanesque frescoes. Princeton, Princeton Univ. Press, 1951. 208 p. 500 plates. 31 cm.

"This book is an attempt to write a concise history of mural painting in western Europe from the end of the Early Christian period until Gothic times."—*Pref.*

An outline of the early styles and iconography from antiquity to the 9th century and a summary of general characteristics of Romanesque frescoes are given in the introduction. Covers Italy, Germany, France, Belgium, Spain, Switzerland, England, Denmark, and South Sweden.

Bibliographical footnotes. Bibliographical abbreviations p. 204. Index of places p. 205– 08.

1209

Beissel, Stephan. Geschichte der Evangelienbücher in der ersten Hälfte des Mittelalters. Freiburg im Breisgau, Herder, 1906. 365 p. illus. 23 cm. (Ergänzungshefte zu den "Stimmen aus Maria-Laach" 92–93)

A standard work on the books of the Evangelists. Few illustrations. Appendices: (1) Vorreden der Evangelienbücher; (2) Kapiteleinteilungen; (3) Lebensskizzen der Evangelisten; (4) In Evangelienbüchern dargestellte Szenen.

Index of manuscripts p. 346–54; of persons and subjects p. 355–65.

1210

Beissel, Stephan, ed. Vaticanische Miniaturen . . . Quellen zur Geschichte der Miniaturmalerei. Mit XXX Tafeln in Lichtdruck. Miniatures choisies de la Bibliothèque du Vatican . . . Freiburg im Breisgau, St. Louis, Mo., Herder, 1893. 59 p. 30 plates. 35 cm.

A selection of manuscripts from the Vatican Library with scholarly descriptive notes and good reproductions. German and French text in parallel columns.

Bibliographical footnotes. List of manuscripts discussed p. 53–56. Index of principal subjects and names p. 57–59.

1211

Birch, Walter de Gray, and Jenner, Henry. Early drawing and illuminations. An introduction to the study of illustrated manuscripts; with a dictionary of subjects in the British Museum . . . London, Bagster, 1879. 310 p. 12 plates. 23 cm.

Introduction gives a short description of various collections in the British Museum, explains the numbering of manuscripts, and describes the various types of services for which the books were intended, and the contents of the manuscripts.

"Index of illustrated manuscripts" p. 1–26 lists the manuscripts indexed in this work, arranged by languages. "Reference table to numerical order of manuscripts earlier than the 15th century" p. 27–30 lists the manuscripts according to number. "Dictionary of principal subjects" p. 31–300 is an alphabetical listing which gives under each subject the various manuscripts, with exact pages, in which it is represented. Earliest representations are listed first.

1212

Boeckler, Albert. Abendländische Miniaturen bis zum Ausgang der romanischen Zeit. Berlin und Leipzig, de Gruyter, 1930. 133 p. 106 plates (incl. facsims.) 30 cm. (Tabvlae in vsvm scholarvm, ed. svb cvra Iohannis Lietzmann, 10)

An account of Romanesque illuminated manuscript paintings from Carolingian times to the middle of the 13th century. It includes more manuscripts in American libraries than does any other European (including British) work. Bibliography p. [124]–27. Index of manuscripts p. 128–33; of plates p. 105–23.

1213

Boinet, Amédée. La miniature carolingienne; ses origines, son développement. Ouvrage pub. avec le concours de l'Académie des Inscriptions et Belles-lettres . . . Paris, Picard, 1913. 6 p. 160 plates. 38 cm.

Published in portfolio. A collection of good collotype plates illustrating Carolingian miniatures, with a listing of the plates. The text volume has never been published.

1214

Breasted, James Henry. Oriental forerunners of Byzantine painting; first century wall paintings from the fortress of Dura on the Middle Euphrates . . . Chicago, Univ. of Chicago Press [1924]. 105 p. illus. (incl. plans), plates (part col.), maps. 31 cm. (The University of Chicago Oriental Institute publications, v. 1)

Introduction by Franz Cumont. Index p. 103–05.

1215

Diehl, Charles. La peinture byzantine . . . Paris, van Oest, 1933. 109 p. 96 plates. 33 cm. (Histoire de l'art byzantin, pub. sous la direction de M. Charles Diehl)

"Ouvrage publié avec le concours de l'Académie des Inscriptions et Belles-Lettres (Fondation E. Piot)."—*Title Page.* The text

covers mosaics, frescoes, miniatures, and icons from the 5th to the 15th centuries. Collotype plates.

"Description des planches" p. 61–99. "Table des planches" p. 101–07.

1216

Ebersolt, Jean. . . . La miniature byzantine, ouvrage accompagné de la reproduction de 140 miniatures. Paris et Bruxelles, van Oest, 1926. 110 p. 72 plates. 36 cm.

A standard work on Byzantine miniatures with good collotype plates. Includes art from the 5th to the 15th centuries. Very short bibliography p. 83. General index p. 85–91; Index of manuscripts arranged alphabetically by place p. 93–98; Index of plates p. [99]–107.

1217

Gerstinger, Hans. Die griechische Buchmalerei, mit 22 Abbildungen in Textband und 28 Tafeln nach Originalen der Nationalbibliothek in Wien . . . Wien, Österreichischen Staatsdruckerei, 1926. 2 v. 52 p. plates and portfolio of 28 plates (part col.) 51 cm.

An important work on Greek illuminated manuscripts illustrated by very good reproductions of originals housed in the Nationalbibliothek in Vienna.

"Literatur" p. 42. A very detailed index covering names, manuscripts, and subjects p. 49–52.

1218

Herbert, John Alexander. Illuminated manuscripts. London, Methuen; N.Y., Putnam, 1911. 355 p. 51 plates. 26 cm. (The connoisseur's library)

Reprinted 1958 by Burt Franklin, N.Y.

Out of date but still the only volume in English on the general subject of the history of illuminated manuscripts. "Notes on the various kinds of liturgical illuminated manuscripts" p. 324–29 describes various types of manuscripts, what they contain, and what they were used for.

Select bibliography p. 331–40. Index is divided into: Manuscripts, which are listed by location; Scribes and illuminators p. 341–46; and General p. 347–[56].

1219

Köhler, Wilhelm Reinhold Walter. Die karolingischen Miniaturen, im Auftrage des Deutschen Vereins für Kunstwissenschaft. Berlin, Cassirer, 1930–58. v. 1–2 in 3. plates, tables. 27 cm. *and* 2 v. of 240 plates. 50 cm. (Deutscher Verein für Kunstwissenschaft. Denkmäler deutscher Kunst)

A standard work on Carolingian miniatures.

Contents: Bd. 1, Die Schule von Tours: Teil 1, Die Ornamentik; Teil 2, Die Bilder. Includes bibliographies throughout the catalog and "Neue Literatur über die Schule von Tours," v. 1², p. 339–40. At end of v. 1², an index of names and subjects p. 342–49, and an index of manuscripts, arranged alphabetically by city where they are located, p. 426–33. Bd. 2, Die Hochschule Karls des Grossen.

1220

Leroquais, Victor. . . . Les breviaires manuscrits des bibliothèques publiques de France. Paris [Mâcon, Protat] 1934. 5 v. and atlas of xiii p., 140 plates (facsims.) 33 cm.

Consists of 133 pages of introductory text relating to breviaries in general and their development, followed by 914 manuscripts arranged by place where they are located.

Volume 4 also contains: (1) Additions and corrections (nos. 915–1034), descriptions of manuscripts erroneously listed as breviaries in the *Catalogue général des manuscrits des bibliothèques de France;* (2) Supplement to missal manuscripts (nos. 1035–45) adding to the author's *Les sacramentaires* . . . (1224); (3) List of breviary manuscripts arranged alphabetically by the libraries and archives where they are located; (4) List of churches and abbeys to which they are attributed.

Volume 5 consists of a general index, and errata and addenda.

1221

Leroquais, Victor. . . . Les livres d'heures, manuscrits de la Bibliothèque nationale . . . Paris [Mâcon, Protat] 1927. 2 v. 33 cm. and atlas of 130 plates. 35 cm.

―――. Supplément aux Livres d'heures, manuscrits de la Bibliothèque nationale (acquisitions récentes et donation Smith-Lesouïf). Mâcon, Protat, 1943. 72 p. 40 plates. 33 cm.

Consists of 85 pages of introductory text on books of hours, followed by a description of 313 books of hours and 24 in the supplement, arranged by manuscript number.

Volume 2 contains: "Quelques prières des livres d'heures" p. 305–50; "Additions et corrections" p. 351–52; "Table des livres d'heures manuscrits de la Bibliothèque nationale par ordre numérique" p. 355–70; "Table par ordre chronologique des livres d'heures manuscrits auxquels sont empruntées des planches du tome III" p. 371–72. "Table générale" p. 373–403.

1222

Leroquais, Victor. . . . Les pontificaux manuscrits des bibliothèques publiques de France . . . Paris [Mâcon, Protat] 1937. 3 v. and portfolio of xiii p., 140 facsims. 33 cm.

A general introduction of 154 pages covering pontifical manuscripts in general, followed by a description of 233 manuscripts, arranged according to place of location. Additions and corrections (nos. 234–50) and manuscripts which are not pontificals but sacramentaries, breviaries and missals, etc., v. 2, p. 429–62.

Volume 3 contains: (1) List of pontifical manuscripts arranged alphabetically by the public libraries where they are located; (2) List of churches or abbeys to which they are attributed; (3) General index; (4) Errata and addenda.

1223

Leroquais, Victor. Les psautiers, manuscrits latins des bibliothèques publiques de France. Mâcon, Protat, 1940–41. 2 v. 33 cm. and portfolio atlas of xiii p., 140 plates. 34 cm.

An introductory text of 136 pages dealing with psalters, followed by a description of 472 psalters arranged alphabetically by their location.

Additions and corrections (nos. 473–493) v. 2, p. 275–91. A list of psalters arranged alphabetically by the libraries and archives where they are preserved v. 2, p. 293–322. Additions v. 2, p. 323–29. Errata and addenda v. 2, p. 517–18. General index v. 2, p. 331–515.

1224

Leroquais, Victor. Les sacramentaires et les missels, manuscrits des bibliothèques publiques de France. Paris, 1924. 3 v. and atlas of xii p., 125 plates (facsims.) 35 cm.

A general introduction of 47 pages and a description of 914 sacramentaries and missals, arranged chronologically.

Volume 3 contains: Additions and corrections p. 284–88; List of manuscripts arranged alphabetically by libraries and archives where they are preserved p. 289–310; List of sacramentaries and missals alphabetically listed by the churches and abbeys with which they are associated p. 311–32; List of manuscripts from which are drawn the plates in v. 4, p. 333–34.

General index v. 3, p. 335–425.

1225

Martin, Henry. Les joyaux de l'enluminure à la Bibliothèque Nationale . . . Paris, van Oest, 1928. 134 p. 102 plates (2 col.) 36 cm.

Contains 94 pages of text forming a résumé of the various periods represented, from the Byzantine era through its decadence, until after the 14th century; followed by plates representing treasures of illumination in the Bibliothèque Nationale.

"Notices des manuscrits dont sont tirées les miniatures" p. 95–117, with bibliography. "Table des planches" p. 119–34. "Bibliographie de l'oeuvre de Henry Martin" p. [ix]–xii.

1226

Mély, Fernand de. Les primitifs et leurs signatures . . . Paris, Geuthner, 1913. v. 1. illus., plates. 36 cm.

Edition of 400 copies printed. A well-illustrated, documented work on the signatures of miniaturists.

Contents: v. 1, Les miniaturistes. Chapter 1 covers 817–1260; 2, 1260–1391 (Les corporations laïques); 3, 1391–16th century. Index p. 409–23.

1227

Omont, Henri. Miniatures des plus anciens manuscrits grecs de la Bibliothèque Nationale du VIe au XIVe siècle . . . Paris, Champion, 1929. 66 p. 136 plates. 46 cm.

At head of title: Paris. Bibliothèque Nationale. Département des Manuscrits.

A collection of 136 collotype plates representing ten important Greek manuscripts in the Bibliothèque Nationale, with scholarly text describing the plates. "Répertoire alphabétique des principaux personnages mentionnés et des principales matières contenues dans les notices des planches" p. 61–62.

1228

Warner, George Frederic. Illuminated manuscripts in the British Museum. Miniatures, borders and initials, reproduced in gold and colours. With descriptive text by George F. Warner. Series I–IV. London, Printed by order of the Trustees, 1903. 146 p. 60 col. plates. 39 cm.

Edition of 500 copies printed. Good chromolithographs with a page or two of text for each plate.

1229

Weitzmann, Kurt. . . . Die armenische Buchmalerei des 10. und beginnenden 11. Jahrhunderts. Bamberg [Reindl] 1933. 25 p. 17 plates. 26 cm. (Istanbuler Forschungen . . . Bd. 4)

A short scholarly survey by a recognized authority on Armenian illumination. Bibliographical footnotes.

1230

Weitzmann, Kurt. . . . Die byzantinische Buchmalerei des 9. und 10. Jahrhunderts mit 94 Abbildungen in Text und 93 Lichtdrucktafeln. Berlin, Mann, 1935. 93 p. illus., 93 plates. 32 cm.

At head of title: Archäologisches Institut des Deutschen Reiches. Abteilung Istanbul.

A scholarly work on Byzantine illumination. Bibliographical footnotes. "Verzeichnis der griechischen Handschriften" p. 89–91. "Verzeichnis der datierten und sicher datierbaren Handschriften" p. 92. "Verzeichnis der zum Vergleich herangezogenen Kunstdenkmäler" p. 93.

1231

Westwood, John Obadiah. Facsimiles of the miniatures & ornaments in Anglo-Saxon & Irish manuscripts . . . drawn on stone by W. R. Tymms, chromolithographed by Day and sons, limited. London, Quaritch, 1868. 155 p. 53 col. facsims. 59 cm.

Edition of 200 copies printed. An old book but still useful, containing a collection of 53 chromolithographs representing pages from various manuscripts with accompanying text. List of plates p. xi–xii. List of manuscripts arranged alphabetically by location p. xii–xv.

1232

Wickhoff, Franz, ed. . . . Beschreibendes Verzeichnis der illuminierten Handschriften in Österreich . . . Bd. 1–8[7, pt. 3]. Leipzig, Hiersemann, 1905–38. 8 v. in 21 pts. illus. (incl. facsims.), plates (part col.) 36 cm. (Publikationen des K.K. Instituts für österreichische Geschichtsforschung)

A monumental, scholarly work dealing with the manuscripts in various Austrian libraries. Well illustrated with collotypes.

Contents: Bd. 1, Die illuminierten Handschriften in Tirol, von H. J. Hermann; Bd. 2, Die illuminierten Handschriften in Salzburg, von H. Tietze; Bd. 3, Die illuminierten Handschriften in Kärnten, von R. Eisler; Bd. 4, Die illuminierten Handschriften in Steiermark: T. 1, Die Stiftsbibliotheken zu Admont und Vorau, von P. Buberl; Bd. 5, Die illuminierten Handschriften der Rossiana in Wien-Lainz, von H. Tietze; Bd. 6, Die illuminierten Handschriften in Dalmatien, von H. Folnesics; Bd. 7, Die illuminierten Handschriften im österreichischen Küstenlande, in Istrien und der Stadt Triest, von

H. Folnesics; Bd. 8, (Neue Folge I–VII), Die illuminierten Handschriften und Inkunabeln der Nationalbibliothek in Wien: [T. I] Die frühmittelalterlichen Handschriften des Abendlandes, von H. J. Hermann; T. II (N. F. Bd. 2), Die deutschen romanischen Handschriften, von H. J. Hermann; T. III (N. F. Bd. 3), Die romanischen Handschriften des Abendlandes, mit Ausnahme der deutschen Handschriften, von H. J. Hermann; T. IV (N. F. Bd. 4), Die byzantinischen Handschriften, von Paul Buberl und Hans Gerstinger, 2 v.; T. V (N.F. Bd. 5), Die italienischen Handschriften des dugento und trecento, von H. J. Hermann, 3 v.; T. VI (N.F. Bd. 6), Die Handschriften und Inkunabeln der italienischen Renaissance, von H. J. Hermann, 4 v.; T. VII (N.F. Bd. 7), Die westeuropäischen Handschriften und Inkunabeln der Gotik und der Renaissance, mit Ausnahme der niederländischen Handschriften, von H. J. Hermann, 3 v.

Neue Folge, Bd. I–VII: Publikationen des zweiten Kunsthistorischen Instituts der Universität Wien, in Verbindung mit dem Österreichischen Institut für Geschichtsforschung.

Contains bibliographies. Each volume has elaborate indexes.

1233

Wilpert, Josef. Die Malereien der Katakomben Roms. Freiburg im Breisgau, Herder, 1903. 596 p. illus. and atlas of 267 plates. 40 cm.

The definitive work on the frescoes in the catacombs. The plates are excellent halftones, many in color.

Beilage: (1) Die mit Malereien geschmückten Grabstätten den einzelnen Katakomben in chronologischer Reihenfolge p. 541–66; (2) Chronologische Reihenfolge sämmtlicher mit Malereien geschmückter Grabstätten in den Katakomben Roms p. 567–74.

Bibliographical footnotes. "Verzeichnis der Tafeln mit Angabe der Masse" p. 575–80 gives size. "Namen und Sachregister" p. 581–96.

1234

Wilpert, Josef. Die römischen Mosaiken und Malereien der kirchlichen Bauten vom IV. bis XIII. Jahrhundert . . . 2. Aufl. Freiburg im Breisgau, Herder, 1917. 4 v. 542 illus., 300 col. plates. 44 cm.

1st ed. 1916. A monumental work with a text which is probably the best discussion of early Christian art. Volume 3 is mostly halftone plates; v. 4 has excellent collotypes.

Contents of v. 1–2: Bk. 1, Allgemeine Untersuchungen zur konstantinischen, nachkonstantinischen und mittelalterlichen Monumentalkunst Roms; Bk. 2, Die hervorragendsten kirchlichen Denkmäler mit Bilderzyklen; Bk. 3, Untersuchungen über einzelne Darstellungen; Bk. 4, Tafelgemälde; Bk. 5, Schlussbetrachtungen.

Bibliographical footnotes. "Verzeichnis der Textbilder" v. 1, p. xxxiv–xlviii. "Namen und Sachregister zu den Textbänden" v. 2, p. 1207–21. "Topographisches Verzeichnis der Tafeln und Textbilder" v. 2, p. 1223–25. "Verzeichnis der Tafeln" at the beginning of each plate volume.

1235

Zimmermann, Ernst Heinrich. Vorkarolingische Miniaturen. Berlin, Deutscher Verein für Kunstwissenschaft, 1916. 329 p. plates. 26 cm. and 4 portfolios of plates. 34 x 45 cm. (Deutscher Verein für Kunstwissenschaft. Denkmäler deutscher Kunst. III. Sektion. Malerei. 1. Abt.)

A scholarly work on pre-Carolingian manuscripts, with a corpus of reproductions. The text volume gives a detailed description, with bibliography, for each plate included in the atlases.

Bibliography p. [328]–29. Index of manuscripts, arranged alphabetically by location, p. 311–21. Index of scribes, writers, and collections p. 324–26.

SEE ALSO: Société Française de Reproductions de Manuscrits à Peintures. Bulletin (2473); Studies in manuscript illumination (2479).

Renaissance—Modern

1236

Haftmann, Werner. Malerei im 20. Jahrhundert. München, Prestel-Verlag [c1954]. 550 p. illus., plates. 22 cm. and Tafelband. 517 p. 24 cm.

A good German treatment of 20th century painting. "Anhang- Biographische Übersichten, Namen- und Sachregister" p. 482–533, consists of short biographical paragraphs with bibliographical references. Index of names p. 534–43; of subjects p. 544–49.

1237

Huyghe, René. Les contemporains. Nouv. éd. Notices biographiques par Germain Bazin. Paris, Tisné, 1949. 122 p. 164 plates (part col.) 34 cm. (La peinture française)

1st ed. translated into English by Paul C.

Blum (N.Y., French and European Publications, 1939).

"Tracé directeur de la peinture moderne," 2 p. following plates; "Note bibliographique," 2 unnumbered p.; "Notices biographiques," 2 unnumbered p.; Notices biographiques sur les artistes figurants dans l'album," 25 unnumbered p.; "Index alphabétique des peintres modernes et contemporains cités dans le texte," 4 p. at end of volume.

1238
Kahnweiler, Daniel Henry. The rise of cubism. Trans. by Henry Aronson. N.Y., Wittenborn, Schultz [1949]. 35 p. illus. 26 cm. (The documents of modern art, 9)

"This is the first translation into any language of the original German text, written in 1915 and published under the title *Der Weg zum Kubismis.*"

A short survey of cubism by a man who was a friend and advocate of the artists in the movement. "Writings of Daniel Henry Kahnweiler, compiled by Bernard Karpel" p. ix–xi.

1239
Mather, Frank Jewett. Western European painting of the Renaissance. N.Y., Tudor, 1948. 873 p. plates. 24 cm.

First published in 1939 by Holt. A general survey which supplements the author's *History of Italian painting* (1317). Appendix contains "Historical illustrations" (excerpts from documents and sources). "Bibliography and notes" p. 785–99. Index p. 849–73.

1240
Meier-Graefe, Julius. Modern art; being a contribution to a new system of aesthetics; from the German by Florence Simmonds and George W. Chrystal. London, Heinemann; N.Y., Putnam, 1908. 2 v. illus., 209 plates. 30 cm.

A well-known history of painting and some sculpture, covering from the time of Hogarth and Poussin to the beginning of the 20th century, with introductory chapters on earlier painting. Written by a pioneer in the modern field, this work may be somewhat dated but is still valid for its basic insight. Index v. 2, p. 327–37.

1241
Muther, Richard. The history of modern painting. . . . Rev. ed. continued by the author to the end of the XIX century. London,

Dent; N.Y., Dutton, 1907. 4 v. illus., plates (part col.) 26 cm.

A rather detailed history of 19th century painting (a few artists from the 18th century are included), which is particularly valuable for its treatment of Germany, Norway, Denmark, Russia, and Sweden, since many histories do not include these countries. Well illustrated with some color plates. Locations of paintings are not given.

Bibliographies (at end of each volume) are long and detailed. "Index of artists" gives birth date, birthplace, and death date of each artist, as well as references to the bibliographical sections.

1242
Myers, Bernard S. Modern art in the making. N.Y., McGraw-Hill, 1950. 457 p. illus. 26 cm.

A survey of modern painting from the time of the French revolution to the present day, stressing its relationship to contemporary history and social development. A few illustrations in the text. Bibliography, "What to read," is arranged by chapters and is confined to works in English. Index p. 447–57.

1243
Raynal, Maurice. History of modern painting. Geneva, Skira [1949–50]. 3 v. mounted col. illus. 35 cm. (Painting, colour, history)

A one-volume abridgment of 339 pages called *Modern painting* published 1953.

The text to each volume is by M. Raynal and others; v. 1–2 translated by Stuart Gilbert; v. 3 translated by Douglas Cooper; Historical and biographical notes by Jean Leymaire and others.

Not really a reference book but has popular appeal. More useful for the illustrations than the text. All illustrations are in color. The size of each painting is given. Contents: v. 1, From Baudelaire to Bonnard; v. 2, Matisse, Munch, Rouault; v. 3, From Picasso to surrealism.

Each volume contains "Biographical and bibliographical notices" which are chronological outlines of the artists' lives, with a bibliography of writings by and about each artist, and a list of his exhibitions. Each volume also has a general "Selected bibliography" and a general index. "Pictures mentioned in the text" and "Writers and critics" in v. 1.

1244
Rewald, John. The history of impressionism. N.Y., Museum of Modern Art [1946]. 474 p. illus., col. plates. 26 cm.

A French ed. published by Albin, Paris, 1955.

Maps on lining-papers. The definitive work on this subject, covering the years from 1855–1886. Good illustrations, many in color. Bibliography p. 446–63 is classed and annotated. Sources of illustrations p. 434; List of participants in the various group shows p. 435; Biographical chart p. 436–45. Index p. 464–74.

1245

Rewald, John. Post-impressionism from Van Gogh to Gauguin . . . N.Y., Museum of Modern Art [1956]. 614 p. illus., col. plates. 26 cm.

Maps on end-papers. Bibliography p. 551–94. Biographical chart p. 540–49. Participants in the Exhibition of Independents—1884–1893, p. 530. Index p. 595–611.

1246

Schmidt, Paul Ferdinand. Geschichte der modernen Malerei. Stuttgart, Kohlhammer [1952]. 279 p. illus. (part col.) 28 cm.

A history of modern painting with many color plates. Part 1 covers the second half of the 19th century; pt. 2 covers the 20th century. Index of names and subjects p. 273–78. Bibliography p. 279 (all German publications).

1247

Soby, James Thrall. After Picasso. Hartford, Mitchell; N.Y., Dodd, Mead, 1935. 114 p. 60 plates. 27 cm.

"It is the purpose of this book to document briefly several aspects of this reaction [against the hypothesis of "painting as architecture" for which Picasso primarily stands] as it has manifested itself in the work of two groups of artists, the Neo-Romantics and the Surrealists."—*Pref.* Index p. 113–14.

National

Canada

1248

Buchanan, Donald W. The growth of Canadian painting. With a foreword by Eric Newton. London, Collins, 1950. 112 p. 80 plates (part col.) 25 cm.

"Tries to give a chart of 20th century painting in Canada."—*Pref.* Not an orthodox history of Canadian art. Includes an "introductory chapter on the earlier developments in which landmarks of the 19th century are given." Covers the work of 27 artists who are discussed in the text. Index p. 111–12.

France

1249

Barnes, Albert Coombs, and De Mazia, Violette. The French primitives and their forms from their origin to the end of the fifteenth century . . . Merion, Pa., Barnes Foundation [c1931]. 551 p. incl. plates. 24 cm.

"The body of the book contains the definition of the French form, a statement of its principal sources, and an account of the more important types of painting included in it. Between the text of the book proper and the Appendix is a list of Addenda which comprises matters of detail relating to various main types treated in the preceding text. The Appendix contains additional analyses of particular paintings and schools, supplementary to the text. . . . In the last section of the book, the usual catalogue attributions of the pictures discussed and mentioned are listed in order to facilitate their identification."—*Pref.*

Contains 156 illustrations. "Catalogue data on pictures mentioned" p. 517–44 is arranged geographically by the location of the painting. Index p. 545–51.

1250

Blum, André, and Lauer, Philippe. La miniature française aux XVe et XVIe siècles, avec un avant-propos du comte A. de Laborde . . . ouvrage accompagné de la reproduction de 173 miniatures dont une planche en couleurs. Paris, van Oest, 1930. 128 p. 100 plates. 37 cm.

Contains 54 pages of text with an explanation and commentary (by P. Lauer) on the plates of French manuscripts of the 15th and 16th centuries. Bibliographical references.

List of manuscripts, classed by cities and libraries, p. 107–08. List of plates p. 109–22. Alphabetical index to the commentary p. 123–28.

1251

Dimier, Louis. Histoire de la peinture de portrait en France au XVIe siècle accompagnée d'un catalogue de tous les ouvrages subsistant en ce genre, de crayon, de peinture à l'huile, de miniature, d'émail, de tapisserie et de cire en médaillons. Paris et Bruxelles, van Oest, 1924–26. 3 v. plates. 29 cm.

Volume 1 is a history of portrait painting in France in the 16th century, illustrated by 64 plates. Volume 2 contains the catalog, which lists all the works of portraiture painted in France in the 16th century, arranged as follows: (1) Original pencil sketches; (2) Copies in crayon; (3) Original paintings; (4) Painted copies; (5) Miniatures; (6) Prints when they bear witness of a lost work.

Volume 3 consists of a "Catalogue des ouvrages de second main," "Additions et corrections" p. 273–78, and "Errata" p. 279. Bibliography p. 281–89. "Table analytique de la première partie" p. 291–310. "Table des musées, cabinets etc. ainsi que les publications auxquelles on renvoie dans cet ouvrage" p. 311–30. "Table alphabétique des portraits catalogués dans cet ouvrage" p. 331–57. "Table des matières" at end of each volume.

1252

Dimier, Louis, and Réau, Louis. Histoire de la peinture française depuis les origines jusqu'à David. Paris, van Oest, 1925–27. 5 v. plates. 33 cm.

Contents: v. 1, L. Dimier, Histoire de la peinture française des origines au retour de Vouet, 1300 à 1627 (1925); v. 2–3, L. Dimier, Histoire de la peinture française du retour de Vouet à la mort de Lebrun, 1627 à 1690 (1926–27); v. 4–5, L. Réau, Histoire de la peinture française au XVIIIe siècle (1925–26).

Each of the three works contains a bibliography and a table of plates, but no index. The whole forms a history of French painting from its origin to the beginning of the 19th century.

1253

Dimier, Louis. Les peintres français du XVIIIe siècle; histoire des vies et catalogue des oeuvres; ouvrage publié sous la direction de M. Louis Dimier, avec la collaboration de nombreux savants et spécialistes. Paris et Bruxelles, van Oest, 1928–30. 2 v. 128 plates. 29 cm.

The two volumes contain chapters on 35 individual artists of the 18th century, written by various authors. For each artist gives a biography, a catalog of his works (including paintings, drawings and engravings, and tapestries), and a bibliography. Dimensions of the works are given in the catalog.

"Additions au tome première" p. 393–96, at end of v. 2.

1254

Dorival, Bernard. Les étapes de la peinture française contemporaine. Paris. Gallimard, 1943–(46). v. 1–(3). 21 cm.

A fourth volume of illustrations is projected. A good survey of modern French painting.

Contents: v. 1, De l'impressionisme, au fauvisme, 1883–1905; v. 2, Le fauvisme et le cubisme, 1905–1911; v. 3, Depuis le cubisme, 1911–1944.

Bibliographical notes: v. 1, p. [275]–84; v. 2, p. [347]–61; v. 3, p. [325]–38. List of names of artists v. 3, p. 339–51, covers all three volumes.

1255

Guiffrey, Jean, and Marcel, Pierre. La peinture française; les primitifs. Paris, Eggimann [1913–c1925]. 2 v. 120 plates. 46 cm.

In portfolio. "2. série, par Jean Guiffrey, Pierre Marcel et Charles Terrasse" (Paris, Morancé [c1925]).

A collection of collotype reproductions of French painting prior to the 16th century, including mural painting, altar pieces, paintings of civil or religious subjects, and portraits of French origin. For each plate there is the equivalent of about one page of descriptive text.

1256

Martin, Henry. La miniature française du XIIIe au XVe siècle. . . . Ouvrage accompagné de 134 reproductions de miniatures, dont 4 planches en couleurs. Paris et Bruxelles, van Oest, 1923. 118 p. 104 plates (4 col.) 37 cm.

A general survey of French illuminated manuscripts from the 13th to the 15th century, with 84 pages of text, and description of the plates p. 85–105. Includes bibliographical references.

1257

Sloane, Joseph C. French painting between the past and the present; artists, critics, and traditions, from 1848 to 1870. Princeton, Princeton Univ. Press, 1951. 241 p. plates. 31 cm. (Princeton monographs in art and archaeology, 27)

A study of French painting of the Second Empire in the light of the criticism of the time. The appendix contains paragraphs identifying critics and other important figures of the time mentioned in the text.

Bibliography p. 227–35. Index p. 237–241.

1258

Sterling, Charles. La peinture française: Les peintres du moyen âge. Paris, Bibliothèque Française des Arts [c1942]. 85, 76 p. 150 plates (22 mounted col.) 34 cm.

Part 1 consists of 76 pages of text by a recognized authority describing the various schools and trends of medieval painting; notes p. 77–85; and a list of important exhibitions; followed by 150 plates, several in color. Part 2 consists of "Répertoire de tableaux français du moyen âge" p. 3–66, in which the works of the 14th and 15th centuries are treated separately, each divided into (1) pictures legitimately considered as French, and (2) those whose French character is spurious or questionable. This section also contains individual commentaries on the plates reproduced. Sizes of the paintings are given.

Bibliography p. 71–[77] at end.

1259

Wilenski, Reginald Howard. French painting. [Rev. ed.] London, The Medici Society [1949]. 310 p. 140 plates (part col.) 24 cm.

1st ed. 1931. In the second edition the earlier chapters and epilogue have been rewritten. A general survey of French painting from the time of St. Louis to the present. Index p. 295–310.

1260

Wilenski, Reginald Howard. . . . Modern French painters. 3d ed. London, Faber, 1954. 424 p. 106 plates. 28 cm.

1st ed. 1940; 2d ed. 1949. A rather popular account of French painting in the late 19th and early 20th centuries, from the impressionist movement to surrealism.

Appendix I: "Bibliographical and catalogue notes" suggests bibliography for individual artists and lists paintings, indicating where they are hung. Index p. 379–424.

Germany and Austria

1261

Deusch, Werner Richard. Deutsche Malerei des dreizehnten und vierzehnten Jahrhunderts, die Frühzeit der Tafelmalerei. Berlin, Genius [1940]. 29 p. 96 plates. 32 cm.

A pictorial survey of German painting of the 13th and 14th centuries with an extensive bibliography and brief textual survey.

"Katalog der Kunstwerke und Abbildungen" p. 21–29 gives information regarding the paintings reproduced, including size and approximate dates. Bibliography p. 18–20.

1262

Deusch, Werner Richard. . . . Deutsche Malerei des fünfzehnten Jahrhunderts, die Ma-

lerei der Spätgotik. Berlin, Wolff [c1936]. 31 p. 104 plates. 32 cm. [Geschichte der Malerei]

A pictorial survey with brief text covering German 15th century painting. "Katalog der Künstler und Abbildungen" p. 20–31 gives brief information about artists and pictures reproduced, including size. "Schrifttum" p. 17–19. "Alphabetisches Künstlerverzeichnis" p. 31.

1263

Deusch, Werner Richard. . . . Deutsche Malerei des sechzehnten Jahrhunderts, die Malerei der Dürerzeit. Mit einem Vorwort von F. Winkler . . . Berlin, Wolff [c1935]. 30 p. 104 plates. 32 cm. [Geschichte der Malerei]

A pictorial survey of German painting of the 16th century with brief introductory text. "Katalog der Künstler und Abbildungen" p. 22–30 contains information regarding artists and pictures reproduced, wtih indication of size. Bibliography p. 21.

1264

Deusch, Werner Richard. . . . Malerei der deutschen Romantiker und ihrer Zeitgenossen. Berlin, Wolff [c1937]. 31 p. 100 plates (part col.) 32 cm. [Geschichte der Malerei. Sonderband]

A pictorial survey of German romantic painting, covering roughly 1800–1840, with brief introductory text and extensive bibliography.

"Katalog der Künstler und Abbildungen" p. 20–31 lists artists with brief information regarding them and their painting reproduced, including size of the works. "Schrifttum" p. 15–19.

1265

Dickinson, *Mrs.* Helena Adell (Snyder). German masters of art, with four illustrations in colour and one hundred and ten in monotone. N.Y., Stokes [c1914]. 286 p. illus., plates (4 col.) 27 cm.

Somewhat out of date but still the only one-volume history of German painting in English. Covers painters through the middle of the 16th century. Index of painters' names p. 285–86.

1266

Glaser, Curt. Die altdeutsche Malerei . . . München; Bruckmann, 1924. 510 p. illus., plate. 27 cm.

Covers from the latter 14th century through the 18th. Illustrated with halftones in the text.

Bibliography in "Anmerkungen" p. 499–500. Index of artists p. 501–02; of places p. 503–10.

1267

Glaser, Curt. Les peintres primitifs allemands du milieu du XIVe siècle à la fin du XVe . . . Paris, van Oest, 1931. 138 p. 104 plates. 33 cm.

Covers German painting from the middle of the 14th century to the end of the 15th. Text written by the director of the Staatliche Kunstbibliothek in Berlin, illustrated by excellent collotype plates. Index of plates p. 131–35; of subjects p. 137–38.

1268

Goering, Max. Deutsche Malerei des siebzehnten und achtzehnten Jahrhunderts, von dem Manieristen bis zum Klassizismus. Berlin, Genius Verlag [1940]. 31 p. 96 plates. 32 cm.

Same format as volumes on previous centuries by W. R. Deusch (1261–1263). Covers 17th and 18th century German painting. "Anmerkungen zu den Künstlern und Bildern" p. 19–32 gives size of paintings reproduced. Bibliography p. 16–18.

1269

Goldschmidt, Adolph. German illumination. Firenze, Pantheon [1928?]. 2 v. 200 plates. 32 cm. (The Pantheon series)

Each volume has about 25 pages of text, an index, and good collotype plates. Contents: v. 1, Carolingian period; v. 2, Ottonian period. Bibliographies: v. 1, p. xv–xvii; v. 2, p. xv–xvii.

1270

Hamann, Richard. Die deutsche Malerei vom Rokoko bis zum Expressionismus . . . Leipzig und Berlin, Teubner [c1925]. 472 p. 362 illus., 10 col. plates. 26 cm.

A general history of German painting from before 1800 to the present. Well illustrated. Index p. 468–72.

1271

Heise, Carl Georg. Norddeutsche Malerei; Studien zu ihrer Entwicklungsgeschichte im 15. Jahrhundert von Köln bis Hamburg . . . Leipzig, Wolff, 1918. 192 p. 100 plates. 28 cm.

Covers north German painting from Cologne to Hamburg in the 15th century. Contents: Köln, Westfalen, Niedersachsen, Hamburg. Index of artists p. 169–71; of works of art p. 172–79. List of plates p. 183–92.

1272

Röthel, Hans Konrad. Moderne deutsche Malerei, mit 50 Farbtafeln und 28 Graphiken. Wiesbaden, Vollmer, 1957. 103 p. illus. (part col.) 33 cm.

A well-illustrated account of modern German painting. An English ed. published 1957 by Reynal, N.Y.

"Dokumente" p. 73–80. "Biographien und Literatur über die Künstler" p. 81–95. "Schrifttum" p. 97–101. List of important exhibitions p. 101. Index of illustrations p. 102.

1273

Stange, Alfred. Deutsche Malerei der Gotik. Berlin, Deutscher Kunstverlag, 1934–(58). 9 v. plates. 26 cm.

The definitive work on the painting of this period, treated by regions. Covers panel and wall painting, and book illustration. Each volume contains an index and is illustrated by collotype plates.

Contents: (1) Die Zeit von 1250 bis 1350; (2) Die Zeit von 1350 bis 1400; (3) Norddeutschland in der Zeit von 1400 bis 1450; (4) Südwestdeutschland in der Zeit von 1400 bis 1450; (5) Köln in der Zeit von 1450 bis 1515; (6) Nordwestdeutschland von 1450 bis 1515; (7) Oberrhein, Bodensee, Schweiz und Mittelrhein von 1400 bis 1450; (8) Schwaben in der Zeit von 1450 bis 1500; (9) Franken, Böhmen und Thüringen-Sachsen in der Zeit von 1400 bis 1500.

1274

Swarzenski, Georg. Die Regensburger Buchmalerei des X. und XI. Jahrhunderts . . . Leipzig, Hiersemann, 1901. 228 p. 35 plates, 101 facsims., reduced. 35 cm. (Denkmäler der süddeutschen Malerei des frühen Mittelalters, Teil 1)

Covers illuminated manuscripts of the Regensburg school. Index p. 219–28.

1275

Swarzenski, Georg. Die Salzburger Malerei von den ersten Anfängen bis zur Blütezeit des romanischen Stils; Studien zur Geschichte der deutschen Malerei und Handschriftenkunde des Mittelalters . . . Leipzig, Hiersemann, 1908–13. 219 p. and atlas of 135 plates. 35 cm. (Denkmäler der süddeutschen Malerei des frühen Mittelalters, Teil 2)

Scholarly treatment of the medieval manuscripts of the Salzburg school. Volume 2 contains the plates and a place index to them.

"Register" p. 207–19 divided into: (1)

Handschriftliche Denkmäler; (2) Kunstdenkmäler mit Ausschluss der Handschriften; (3)
Namen und Persönlichkeiten; (4) Ortsverzeichnis; (5) Sachregister.

1276

Tintelnot, Hans. Die barocke Freskomalerei
in Deutschland, ihre Entwicklung und europäische Wirkung. München, Bruckmann
[1951]. 336 p. illus., 8 col. plates, maps. 27 cm.
A study of the development of baroque
painting in Germany and its results throughout Europe. Bibliographical references included in "Anmerkungen" p. 307–32.
"Künstlerverzeichnis" p. 333–35. "Bilder-
nachweis" p. 336.

1277

Worringer, Wilhelm. Die Anfänge der Tafelmalerei; mit 126 Abbildungen. Leipzig,
Insel-Verlag, 1924. 349 p. illus. 27 cm.
(Deutsche Meister)
A sound treatment of German painting of
the 14th and 15th centuries. List of plates p.
348–50 and table of contents, but no index.

Great Britain

1278

Auerbach, Erna. Tudor artists; a study of
painters in the royal service and of portraiture on illuminated documents from the accession of Henry VIII to the death of Elizabeth I. [London] Univ. of London, Athlone
Press, 1954. 222 p. 52 plates (part col.) 26 cm.
Appendices: (1) Warrants and other documents p. 140–43; (2a) Biographical notes on
serjeant painters p. 144–49; (2b) Biographical
notes on other painters p. 150–94; (3) Analytical table of decorations on plea rolls p.
195–203. Bibliography p. 204–11. Index p.
212–22.

1279

Baker, Charles Henry Collins. British painting . . . with a chapter on primitive painting by Montague R. James . . . London, The
Medici Society [1933]. 319 p. 152 plates. (12
col.) 24 cm.
A general history of British painting from
the medieval period to 1900, by a recognized
scholar.
Appendices: (1) List of some characteristic
works p. 231–69 (arranged alphabetically by
artist); (2) List of miniatures in principal
collections by N. Hilliard, Isaac and Peter
Oliver, the two Hoskins, and Samuel Cooper

p. 270–75; (3) List of principal British paintings in American collections p. 276–88.
Bibliography p. xxxv–xxxvi. Index p. 289–
319. List of illustrations p. ix–xxiii.

1280

Caw, *Sir* James Lewis. Scottish painting, past
and present, 1620–1908 . . . Edinburgh, Jack,
1908. 503 p. 76 plates. 27 cm.
A standard work on the subject. Contents:
I, The past, 1620–1860; II, The present,
1860–1908. Résumé and conclusion: the sub-
jective, emotional and technical characteristics of Scottish painting. Index p. 497–503.

1281

Cundall, Herbert Minton. A history of British water-colour painting, with a biographical list of painters . . . London, Murray, 1908.
279 p. 58 col. plates. 24 cm.
Appendices: (1) Chronological list of the
members and associates of the Royal Society
of Painters in Water Colours p. 153–61; (2)
List of the members of the Associated Artists
in Water Colours p. 163–64; (3) List of the
members and associates of the Royal Institute of Painters in Water-Colours p. 165–75;
(4) A biographical list of British water colour
painters p. 177–272 (alphabetically arranged
with a few lines about each artist). Index p.
273–79.

1282

Cursiter, Stanley. Scottish art to the close of
the nineteenth century. London, Harrap
[1949]. 134 p. plates (part col.) 26 cm.
In spite of title, the book covers only painting, from its origin to the end of the 19th
century. Bibliography p. 129–30. Index of
artists p. 131–35.

1283

Edwards, Edward. Anecdotes of painters who
have resided or been born in England; with
critical remarks on their productions . . . intended as a continuation to the Anecdotes
of painting, by the late Horace, earl of Orford. London, Leigh and Sotheby, 1808. 327
p. plates. 30 cm.
Continues Walpole (2047). Index p.
321–27.

1284

Foster, Joshua James. British miniature
painters and their works. London, Low,
Marston, 1898. 146 p. plates. 32 cm.
Edition of 425 copies printed. A well-illustrated history of British miniature painting.

Appendices contain lists of miniatures exhibited in important exhibitions. List of works of reference p. xi–xii. Index p. 147–51.

1285
Gilbey, *Sir* Walter. Animal painters of England from the year 1650; a brief history of their lives and works . . . illustrated with 28 specimens of their paintings, chiefly from wood engravings by F. Babbage. London, Vinton, 1900–1911. 3 v. plates. 27 cm.

Volumes 1–2 contain chapters on 51 painters (in alphabetical order) with an "Index to paintings and engravings" at the end of each volume. Volume 3 contains material on 46 additional painters and has its index to the paintings and engravings. The indexes are arranged alphabetically by title of the work. At the end of the discussion of each artist is a list of his works.

1286
Grant, Maurice Harold. A chronological history of the old English landscape painters (in oil) from the XVIth century to the XIXth century (describing more than 500 painters) . . . with 585 illustrations . . . London, Author [1926?]. 2 v. illus., plates. 38 cm.

"These volumes make small pretence to biographical discovery, or even to much biography; though both one and the other are effected, the first often by accident, the latter from the plan of the work. Their intention is to assist the art collector and connoisseur rather than the art historian, and in consequence the canvases of the more than 500 painters described are objects of more particular attention than their careers."

Well illustrated, including many signatures. Continuous pagination. Artists are arranged chronologically. Appendices list the artists according to various categories, viz., by countries, Scottish, Welsh, London-born, amateurs, women, water colourists, and portrait painters who did landscapes.

A new revised and greatly augmented edition is being published, which will comprise eight volumes and include the lives and works of about 900 English landscape painters from 1545–1880, with about 800 illustrations. Volume 1 covering 1545–1670 and v. 2 covering 1670–1780 appeared in 1957.

1287
Johnson, Charles. English painting from the seventh century to the present day. London, Bell, 1932. 350 p. 48 plates. 23 cm.

A general survey of the subject by a lecturer in the National Gallery. More emphasis on landscape than on portraiture. "First book on English painting that deals with the whole period from the 7th century to the present."—*Pref.*

Bibliography p. 335–38. "Chronological list I (some early medieval paintings mentioned in the text)" p. xii; "Chronological list II (British painters and others who worked in England)" p. xiii–xiv. "Abbreviations and references used in the text" p. xv–xvi. Index p. 339–50.

1288
MacKay, William Darling. The Scottish school of painting. London, Duckworth; N.Y., Scribner, 1906. 369 p. plates. 20 cm. (The library of art)

A general survey of the popular type by a competent author. "Scottish painters referred to with dates and places of birth and death, and where they studied and practiced" p. [364]–69.

1289
Masai, F. Essai sur les origines de la miniature dite irlandaise. Bruxelles, Éditions "Erasme," 1947. 146 p. 64 plates. 27 cm. (Les publications de scriptorium, 1)

A scholarly study of the origins of Irish miniatures. "Tables des planches" p. 141–45. Bibliography p. 6–8.

1290
Millar, Eric George. English illuminated manuscripts from the Xth to the XIIIth century. Paris, van Oest, 1926. 145 p. 100 plates, tables. 37 cm.

"An attempt of a survey of the art of book illumination in England from the tenth century to the year 1300."—*Introd.* Contains 37 pages of text, a description of the plates p. 69–103, and a "Hand list of English illuminated manuscripts" p. 105–28.

Includes bibliographical references and footnotes. Index p. 129–35. List of plates p. 137–45.

1291
Millar, Eric George. English illuminated manuscripts of the XIVth and the XVth centuries. Paris, van Oest, 1928. 106 p. 100 plates. 37 cm.

The standard work on English illumination with 42 pages of text and a description of the plates p. 43–77. "Hand list of English illuminated manuscripts" p. 79–94. Contains bibliographical references. Index p. 95–98.

1292

Oakeshott, Walter Fraser. The sequence of English medieval art, illustrated chiefly from illuminated mss. 650–1450. London, Faber [1950]. 55 p. illus., 56 plates (part col.), chart. 28 cm.

A short general survey of English medieval painting based mainly on decorated manuscripts rather than on wall painting, beginning with Anglo-Saxon times.

Contents: A short survey of the field p. 1–29; Notes p. 30–31; Appendix I, The Book of Durrow and the Northumbrian style; Appendix II, The representation of the human figure in Northumbrian manuscripts, and in manuscripts produced in the south, 675–825; List of plates in chronological order (with detailed descriptive notes) p. 42–51.

Indexes of books, persons, and subjects represented p. 53–55.

1293

Redgrave, Richard. A century of British painters. New ed. . . . London, Phaidon, 1947. 612 p. incl. illus., plates. 19 cm.

"Largely founded upon the second edition of 1890."—*Editor's Pref.*, signed Ruthven Todd. 1st ed., 1866, was the "first popular account of British painting." This edition has been corrected and brought up to date. "Bibliographical index" p. [593]–612. "List of plates" p. 587–91. "Index to plates" p. 613.

1294

Saunders, O. Elfrida. English illumination. Firenze, Pantheon [c1928]. 2 v. 129 plates (incl. facsims.) 32 cm.

"Issued in the U.S. . . . by the David McKay company . . . Philadelphia." A standard book on English manuscript miniatures.

Volume 1 contains 120 pages of text and plates 1–50. Volume 2 contains plates 51–129. Bibliography v. 1, p. [121]–24. Index of manuscripts v. 1, p. 125–28. General index v. 1, p. 129–32.

1295

Sparrow, Walter Shaw. A book of sporting painters. A companion volume of new research to "British sporting artists" and "Angling in British art" with 136 illustrations. London, Lane; N.Y., Scribner [1931]. 240 p. plates (part col.), facsims., geneal. tab. 29 cm.

Each chapter is devoted to a single artist. Appendix contains a selection of last wills and testaments. "Index and general list of artists who have been of interest to sportsmen and country-lovers—1650–1900" p. 205–40, which Waterhouse describes as an index-dictionary at the end.

1296

Tristram, Ernest William. English medieval wall painting . . . Prepared with the assistance of the Courtauld Institute of Art and published on behalf of The Pilgrim Trust. [London] Milford, Oxford Univ. Press, 1944–50. 2 v. in 3. plates (part col.) 33 cm.

Each volume has a scholarly text discussing the paintings in various sections of the country, a chapter on technique, a chapter on iconography which lists subjects depicted and names of places where paintings are located, a detailed catalog of the paintings (with bibliography), and an index to the text chapters. Size is sometimes given in the list of plates.

Contents: v. 1, The twelfth century, with a catalogue by E. W. Tristram, compiled in collaboration with W. G. Constable; v. 2, The thirteenth century, with a catalogue by E. W. Tristram, compiled in collaboration with Monica Bardswell, [pt. 1] text, [pt. 2] plates. Includes bibliographies.

1297

Tristram, Ernest William. English wall painting of the fourteenth century. Edited by Eileen Tristram, with a catalogue by E. W. Tristram compiled in collaboration with Monica Bardswell. London, Routledge & Paul [1955]. 311 p. 64 plates. 26 cm.

A scholarly work. Contents: pt. 1, text; pt. 2, plates. Appendices: (A) List of subject-paintings of lesser interest, whether extant or recorded; (B) List of places with remains of strictly decorative painting of lesser interest, either extant or recorded; (C) Tabulation of items in accounts for the decoration of St. Stephen's Chapel, Westminster Palace; (D) List of painters working between 1300–1400 in London and elsewhere; (E) List of places which have or once had 14th century wall paintings, arranged under countries; (F) Iconographic list; (G) List of drawings by E. Tristram and Monica Bardswell in the Victoria and Albert Museum from wall paintings of the 14th century.

Includes bibliographies: p. 126–28, for Chapters 1–5; and in the catalog at the end of each entry. "Abbreviations used in the bibliography of the catalogue" p. 272–73. List of plates p. ix–xi. Index (Chapters 1–4) p. 307–11.

1298

Wilenski, Reginald Howard. English painting. London, Faber [1933]. 302 p. 160 plates. 25 cm.

A general historical survey by a well-known author. Appendix to Chapter 4 is Hogarth's "Analysis of Beauty" and the appendix to Chapter 14 is "The Burghclere Memorial Chapel" in Hampshire.

Italy

1299

Ancona, Paolo d'. . . . La miniatura fiorentina (secoli XI–XVI) . . . Florence, Olschki, 1914. 2 v. 110 plates (1 col.) 41 cm.

Printed in an edition of 300 examples. Standard work on miniatures of the Florentine school. Volume 1 contains 109 pages of text and good collotype plates, while v. 2 contains the descriptive catalog and indexes.

Bibliography v. 2, 3d preliminary leaf. Indexes: Of codexes p. 889–900; Of works p. 901–09; Of subjects (figures and scenes in the miniatures, places, and people) p. 911–30; Of miniaturists, calligraphers and copyists p. 931–34; Of plates p. 935–41.

1300

Ancona, Paolo d'. La miniature italienne du X au XVIe siècle . . . traduction de M. P. Poirier . . . Paris, van Oest, 1925. 128 p. 97 plates (part col.) 37 cm.

Consists of 93 pages of text dealing with Italian miniatures from the 10th to the 16th century, with bibliographical footnotes.

Index of manuscripts p. 97–107, arranged by place; of miniaturists p. 111–16. List of plates p. 119–28.

1301

Antal, Frederick. Florentine painting and its social background; the bourgeois republic before Cosimo de' Medici's advent to power: XIV and early XV centuries. London, Kegan Paul [1948]. 388 p. 160 plates. 25 cm.

A history of Florentine painting, rather than a reference book, with emphasis on the influences of the social life and concepts of the period. Includes bibliographies. Index of persons p. 383–88.

1302

Baroni, Costantino, and Ludovici, Sergi Samek. La pittura lombarda del quattrocento. Messina, D'Anna [1952]. 282 p. 103 plates. 22 cm.

Covers painting in Lombardy in the 15th

century. Printed on very poor paper with illustrations of poor quality.

General text p. 3–262 with bibliographical footnotes. Index of artists p. 267–70; of places p. 271–78; of illustrations p. 279–82.

1303

Berenson, Bernhard. The Italian painters of the Renaissance. [London] Phaidon [1952]. 488 p. (p. [208–478] illus.) 16 col. plates. 28 cm.

A more lavishly illustrated edition of the title published in 1930 (Oxford, Clarendon Press). Comprises the text of the four earlier volumes known as *Renaissance painters*, revised and combined into a single volume. A paperback ed. was issued by Meridian Books, 1957.

Index p. 481–88 includes plate references but is not as detailed as the one in the 1930 ed.

1304

Berenson, Bernhard. Italian pictures of the Renaissance, a list of the principal artists and their works with an index of places . . . Oxford, Clarendon Press, 1932. 723 p. 18 cm.

An Italian ed. translated by E. Cecchi was published in 1936. Arranged alphabetically by artist. This list is not only a combination of the lists in the four volumes of *Renaissance painters* but it includes many more artists and many more pictures than the earlier editions.

The original editions were: *Venetian painters* (1894, 1895, 1897); *Florentine painters* (1896, 1900, 1909); *Central Italian painters* (1897, 1909); *North Italian painters* (1907). These were published in French in 1926 and in German in 1923.

The essays from these four volumes were likewise published in one volume by Clarendon Press (Oxford, 1932) and subsequently in an illustrated edition by Phaidon Press in 1952 (1303).

For each artist gives: dates and teachers; a list of his paintings arranged alphabetically under the name of the city where they are located; dates of the pictures when known. Index of places p. 609–723.

1305

Berenson, Bernhard. Italian pictures of the Renaissance; a list of the principal artists and their works with an index of places. Venetian school in two volumes. [London] Phaidon press [1957]. 2 v. 1333 illus. 27 cm.

A new and greatly rev. ed. of the author's famous lists, which were first issued in the

1890's in four volumes, then revised in a 1932 ed. In 1936 an Italian ed. of the lists, with revisions, was issued. This edition, which incorporates the latest attributions and scholarship, also corrects errors in earlier editions and is profusely illustrated.

Bibliographical references. Topographical index v. 2, p. 1–44.

1306

Brown, Alice Van Vechten, and Rankin, William. A short history of Italian painting . . . London, Dent; N.Y., Dutton, 1921. 414 p. 31 plates. 21 cm.

Originally published in 1914. A useful handbook, but somewhat out of date.

"List of books" p. 316–36 is an annotated bibliography which includes a list of periodicals. The authors are identified in the bibliography.

"Index to artists and paintings mentioned with certain additional examples" p. 337–411 lists artists, their works, and sometimes short critical phrases describing the paintings. "An index to drawings" p. 411–12. "An index to private and less known collections" p. 412–14.

1307

Cecchi, Emilio. The Sienese painters of the trecento . . . translated from the Italian by Leonard Penlock . . . London, N.Y., Warne [1931]. 185 p. 256 plates. 28 cm.

On verso of title page: British copyright "Valori Plastici," Rome, 1931.

Contents: The Sienese painters of the trecento p. 7–140; Short bibliography p. 141–45; Notes on plates p. 146–66; List of plates p. 167–78; General index p. 179–85 (prepared by publisher of the English edition).

1308

Crowe, Sir Joseph Archer, and Cavalcaselle, Giovanni Battista. A history of painting in Italy, Umbria, Florence, and Siena, from the second to the sixteenth centuries . . . ed. by Langton Douglas . . . [2d ed.] London, Murray, 1903–14. 6 v. plates. 23 cm.

This is another edition of *A new history of painting in Italy, from the II to the XVI century,* originally published in 1864; Italian ed. published in Florence in 1875–1908. An early standard work illustrated with Alinari photographs, one to a plate.

Contents: v. 1, Early Christian art; v. 2, Giotto and the Giottesques; v. 3, The Sienese, Umbrian and north Italian schools; v. 4, Florentine masters of the XV century; v. 5, Umbrian and Sienese masters of the XV and XVI century; v. 6, Sienese and Florentine masters of the XVI century.

Volume 1 contains the biographies of Crowe and Cavalcaselle. Indexes of persons and places at the end of each volume.

1309

Crowe, Sir Joseph Archer, and Cavalcaselle, Giovanni Battista. A history of painting in north Italy, Venice, Padua, Vicenza, Verona, Ferrara, Milan, Friuli, Brescia, from the fourteenth to the sixteenth century . . . London, Murray, 1871. 2 v. plates. 23 cm.

2d ed. (N.Y., Scribner; London, Murray, 1912, 3 v.) edited by Tancred Borenius.

The 1871 ed. has one index at end of v. 2; the 1912 ed. has indexes of artists and places at end of v. 3. The 1871 ed. is illustrated with line drawings; the 1912 ed. is illustrated with Alinari photographs.

1310

Edgell, George Harold. A history of Sienese painting. N.Y., MacVeagh, Dial, 1932. 302 p. plates, facsims. 25 cm.

A well-illustrated general history of Sienese painting. Index p. 293–302.

1311

Garrison, Edward B. Italian Romanesque panel painting; an illustrated index. Florence, Olschki, 1949. 266 p. illus. 32 cm.

Covers the era from the late 11th century to the point in the late 13th or early 14th century "at which the classico-naturalistic revival connected with Cavallini and Giotto took form."—*Foreword.*

Main section is called "Preliminary notice on panels and crucifixes." Contains a list of photographers (giving information about negative collections since the war), school and painter index, list of dated panels, list of falsely attributed panels, place index.

For each panel gives: (1) place history; (2) description; (3) inscriptions; (4) measurements; (5) condition; (6) attribution and dating; (7) bibliography; (8) photographic negatives. Panels are grouped according to shape, with a short notice preceding each group. Each panel is given a serial number, and almost all are illustrated. Bibliography p. 247–53.

1312

Goering, Max. Italian painting of the sixteenth century; with a preface by Prof. Dr. Hermann Voss . . . with 104 full-page plates in photogravure. London, Zwemmer, 1936. 31 p. 104 plates. 31 cm.

Printed in Germany. A pictorial survey with short introductory text covering the painting of the late Renaissance and mannerism.

"Annotated list of artists and pictures" p. 17–31 includes brief biographical material on the various artists as well as information on the pictures reproduced, including size of the canvas. Bibliography p. 15–16.

1313

Goering, Max. . . . Italienische Malerei des siebzehnten und achtzehnten Jahrhunderts, mit einem Vorwort von Giuseppe Fiocco . . . Berlin, Wolff [c1936]. 31 p. 104 plates. 32 cm. [Geschichte der Malerei]

A pictorial survey of Italian painting in the 17th and 18th centuries, with brief introductory text.

"Anmerkung zu den Künstlern und Bildern" p. 18–[32] contains brief biographies of artists represented and information regarding the pictures reproduced, including indication of size. Bibliography p. 17.

1315

McComb, Arthur Kilgore. The baroque painters of Italy . . . Cambridge, Harvard Univ. Press [c1934]. 145 p. plates. 26 cm.

"Intention is to trace the main development, in a brief way, of Italian painting during the 17th and 18th centuries."—*Pref.* Text comprises p. 3–115.

"Bibliographical notes" p. [129]–40 is in part annotated. "List of the more important ceiling paintings and the larger decorative schemes of the 17th century in and near Rome" p. 119. "List of Italian paintings of the 17th and 18th centuries in American collections" p. 123–27.

1316

Marle, Raimond van. The development of the Italian schools of painting . . . The Hague, Nijhoff, 1923–38. 19 v. illus., plates. 25 cm.

An important and well-illustrated work on Italian Renaissance painting covering from its beginnings through the 15th century.

Contents: v. 1, From the 6th until the end of the 13th century; v. 2, The Sienese school of the 14th century; v. 3, The Florentine school of the 14th century; v. 4, The local schools of north Italy of the 14th century; v. 5, The local schools of central and southern Italy of the 14th century; v. 6, Iconographical index; v. 7, Late Gothic painting in north Italy of the 15th century; v. 8, Gen-

tile, Pisanello and late Gothic painting in central and southern Italy; v. 9, Late Gothic painting in Tuscany; v. 10, The Renaissance painters of Florence in the 15th century—1st generation; v. 11, The Renaissance painters of Florence in the 15th century—2d generation; v. 12–13, The Renaissance painters of Florence in the 15th century—3d generation; v. 14, The Renaissance painters of Umbria; v. 15, The Renaissance painters of central and southern Italy; v. 16, The Renaissance painters of Tuscany; v. 17–18, The Renaissance painters of Venice; v. 19, General index.

Volume 6 consists of Iconographical index to v. 1–5. Volume 19, General index, contains an index by place (for larger towns the material is divided into (1) Churches and monasteries, (2) Public collections, (3) Public buildings and streets, (4) Private collections); also an artist index which includes the name of the artist, his dates, and "where possible an indication of the site of his activity."

1317

Mather, Frank Jewett. A history of Italian painting . . . N.Y., Holt, 1923. 495 p. illus. 19 cm.

An introductory work consisting of a short survey of the field. "Hints for reading" p. 489–90. Index p. 491–95.

1318

Meiss, Millard. Painting in Florence and Siena after the Black Death. Princeton, Princeton Univ. Press, 1951. 194 p. 169 illus. 31 cm.

A scholarly treatment of Florentine and Sienese painting from about 1350 to 1370. The emphasis is on iconology.

Appendices: I, Chronological table p. 166–67; II, Facts about the painters p. 168–71; III, A new polyptych by Andrea da Firenze p. 175–76.

Bibliographical footnotes. Index p. 177–94.

1319

Offner, Richard. A critical and historical corpus of Florentine painting . . . [N.Y.] College of Fine Arts, New York Univ. [1930]–(58). Section III, vols. 1–(6) in (8). plates. 32 cm.

Intended to be published in 30 volumes in the following six sections: I, The origins; II, First half of the 14th century; III, First half of the 14th century; IV, Middle and late 14th century; V, 15th century; VI, 15th century.

"Every work from the origin of Florentine painting to the late 15th century will be reproduced. Reproductions on right-hand page while essential critical and historical data bearing on it are on the left. Various kinds of type faces are used to denote different kinds of information given, i.e., disputed facts, original sources, opinions of the editor, etc."—*The Arts,* v. 16, p. 639–40, 1930.

1320

Pallucchini, Rodolfo. La pittura veneziana del cinquecento. Novara, Istituto Geografico De Agostini [1944]. 2 v. plates. 25 cm. (Storia della pittura italiana)

Primarily a picture book with rotogravure illustrations, covering Venetian painting of the 16th century. Bibliography v. 2, p. xlix–lviii.

1321

Pope-Hennessy, John. Sienese quattrocento painting. Oxford, Phaidon; N.Y., Oxford Univ. Press [1947]. 33 p. 93 (i.e., 91) plates, illus. 31 cm.

A picture book with good text, rather than a reference tool. "This book is an anthology of Sienese paintings and not a history of quattrocento painting."—*Pref.* It reproduces a small number of pictures (the work of 12 artists) in detail rather than many general photographs.

Contents: Text p. 7–24; Notes on plates p. 25–33; Index of collections, 2 p. at end of volume.

1322

Schmeckebier, Laurence Eli. A handbook of Italian Renaissance painting. N.Y., Putnam [c1938]. 362 p. 21 cm.

No illustrations, but a useful handbook. Appendix contains lists of Popes at Rome and reigning princes of Italian and French states of the period covered; "Table of important historical events"; "Selected works from Italian Renaissance literature"; "Important literary sources for Italian Renaissance painting."

Bibliographies p. 317–37. Index of artists p. 341–43. Iconographical index p. 344–62.

1323

Schubring, Paul. Cassoni; Truhen und Truhenbilder der italienischen Frührenaissance, ein Beitrag zur Profanmalerei im Quattrocento . . . Leipzig, Hiersemann, 1915. 479 p. 15 plates. 27 cm. and atlas of 186 plates. 45 cm.

An important work on this aspect of Italian Renaissance painting.

Contents: Text p. 1–216; Katalog p. 219–418; Literaturverzeichnis p. [419]–28; Anhang I, Fest datierbare Cassoni, Deschi und Letti p. [429]; Anhang II, Bottega-Buch des Marco del Buono und des Apollonio di Giovanni, Florenz 1446–1463, p. [430]–37; Anhang III, Antonio Averlino Filaretes Mythologien an der Bronzetür von St. Peter in Rom und die im Sforzinda erwähnten mythologischen Stoffe p. [438]–40.

Indexes: (1) Inhalt p. [441]–45; (2) Ortsregister p. [446]–50; (3) Register der Meister und Schulen p. [451]–54; (4) Autoren-Register p. 455–59; (5) Geschlechter-Register p. 460–66; (6) Mythus, Sage und antike Historie p. 467–74; (7) Ergänzendes Sachregister p. 475–77; (8) Verzeichnis der Abbildungen des Textbandes.

———. Supplement . . . Leipzig, Hiersemann, 1923. 6 p. 59 illus., 24 plates (part col.) 45 cm.

1324

Toesca, Pietro. Florentine painting of the trecento. N.Y., Harcourt, Brace; Firenze, Pantheon [c1929]. 82 p. 119 plates. 32 cm. (The Pantheon series)

A good survey of 14th century Florentine painting. Contents: List of plates p. vii–xiii; Text p. 1–58; Notes p. 59–74 (containing bibliographies); Index of artists p. 75–76; Index of places and monuments p. 79–82.

1325

Toesca, Pietro. La pittura e la miniatura nella Lombardia, dai più antichi monumenti alla metà del quattrocento, con 481 incisioni e 35 tavole. Milano, Hoepli, 1912. 594 p. illus., 34 plates (incl. facsims.) 32 cm.

A scholarly, well-illustrated treatment of painting in Lombardy.

"Indice dei luoghi" p. 583–90. "Indice dei nomi e delle cose principali" p. 591–94. "Indice delle abbreviazioni bibliografiche meno ovvie o dubbie" p. 595.

1326

Voss, Hermann Georg August. Die Malerei der Spätrenaissance in Rom und Florenz; mit 247 Abbildungen. Berlin, Grote, 1920. 2 v. illus. 25 cm.

Paged continuously. A standard work on the painting of the late Renaissance in Florence and Rome. Well illustrated in the text.

In the bibliography v. 2, p. [599]–604, primary sources are marked ** and other important works *. Index of names and subjects v. 2, p. [605]–09; of places v. 2, p. [610]–20.

1327
Weigelt, Curt Heinrich. Sienese painting of the trecento. Florence, N.Y., Pantheon [192?]. 107 p. 120 plates. 32 cm.
Excellent plates with numerous details of paintings. Contents: Text consisting of a survey of the subject and individual treatments of Duccio, Simone Martini, and the Lorenzetti p. 1–55; Notes containing bibliographical material p. 61–92; Geographical index p. 93–106; Index of names p. 107–08.

Latin America

1328
Acquarone, Francisco, and Queiroz Vieira, A. de. Primores da pintura no Brasil com uma introdução historica e textos explicativos ... Rio de Janeiro [Edição dos Autores, 1942]. 2 v. mounted col. plates. 36 cm.
The development of 19th century painting in Brazil is shown, beginning with the "Coroaçao de Pedro I" and going up to the impressionists of the early 20th century. Each of the 20 parts consists of eight good color plates with a page of biographical material on the artist and a criticism of the painting. Size of paintings is given. No index or table of contents.

1329
Giraldo Jaramillo, Gabriel. La pintura en Colombia. [1. ed.] México, Fondo de Cultura Económica [1948]. 248 p. illus., 49 plates. 23 cm. (Colección Tierra Firme, 36)
A general survey of painting in Colombia. Covers Colonial period, Republican period, Moderns and Contemporaries. Bibliography p. 182–84. Index of names p. 237–44; of illustrations p. 245–46.

1330
Myers, Bernard S. Mexican painting in our time. N.Y., Oxford Univ. Press, 1956. 283 p. 124 illus. 29 cm.
Bibliography p. 269–76. Index p. 277–83.

1331
Reis, José Maria dos. ... História da pintura no Brasil, prefácio de Oswaldo Teixeira ... (312 ilustrações). São Paulo, Editôra LEIA, 1944. 409 p. incl. illus., plates. 33 cm.
A well-illustrated history of Brazilian painting. Bibliography p. [391]–97. Index of names p. 405–09; of illustrations p. 401–04.

1332
Romera, Antonio R. Historia de la pintura chilena. Santiago de Chile, Editorial del Pacifico [1951]. 223 p. illus. 22 cm.

A general survey of painting in Chile, not very well illustrated. Bibliography p. 199–212. Index of names p. 213–19.

1333
Romero Brest, Jorge. La pintura brasileña contemporánea ... Buenos Aires, Editorial Poseidón [1945]. 7–112 p. illus., plates (part col.) 24 cm.
A general survey of contemporary Brazilian painting with good illustrations. "Notas" p. 35–37 contains bibliography. Short biographical notices p. 39–47. Index of reproductions p. 109–12.

1334
Schmeckebier, Laurence Eli. Modern Mexican art ... Minneapolis, Univ. of Minnesota Press [c1939]. 190 p. plates (part col.) 27 cm.
Despite the title it covers only painting. Selected bibliography p. 181–83. Index p. 184–90.

1335
Soria, Martin S. La pintura del siglo XVI en Sud America. Buenos Aires, Univ. de Buenos Aires. Istituto de Arte Americano e Investigaciones Estéticas, 1956. 125 p. 82 illus. on plates. 27 cm.
A survey of 16th century painting in South America by a competent scholar. Bibliographical footnotes.

Low Countries

1336
Baker, Charles Henry Collins. Dutch painting of the seventeenth century ... London, Studio [1926]. 62 p. 69 plates (1 col.) 22 cm.
A short survey in English, treated by types of painting, i.e., genre, landscape, portraiture, etc. Bibliography p. 61–62. Index of artists p. v–x. List of illustrations p. x–xii.

1337
Bernt, Walther. Die niederländischen Maler des 17. Jahrhunderts ... 1042 Abbildungen und 516 Signaturen. Einleitung von Hans Sauermann. [München] Münchner Verlag [1948]. 3 v. plates. 30 cm.
Reproduces work of 524 Dutch and Flemish painters, excluding Rubens, Van Dyck, Frans Hals, Rembrandt, and Vermeer. Preference is given to pictures so far unpublished. Under each artist gives dates, short description of the type of work he did, and his sig-

nature. For each picture gives name, date if known, size in centimeters, and location. Biographical and bibliographical details are omitted. Contents: Bd. 1, Lucas Achtschellinck bis Willem Claesz. Heda; Bd. 2, Cornelis de Heem bis Theodor Rombouts; Bd. 3, Willem Romeyn bis Gerard Pietersz. van Zyl. At end of v. 3 a subject index (of types of paintings) and an alphabetical index of painters.

1338

Bode, Wilhelm von. Great masters of Dutch and Flemish painting. Tr. by Margaret C. Clarke. London, Duckworth; N.Y., Scribner, 1909. 358 p. 39 plates. 20 cm.

Translated from the 2d and rev. ed. of Dr. Bode's *Rembrandt und seine Zeitgenossen.* An old standard work in which each chapter is devoted to an individual artist or subject, viz., genre, landscape. Index p. 339–58.

1339

Branden, Frans Jozef van den. Geschiedenis der Antwerpsche schilderschool. Antwerpen, Buschmann, 1883. 1436 p. 26 cm.

History of painting of the Antwerp school. "Naamlijst der bijzonder vermelde schilders en schilderessen" p. 1427–34. "Inhoud" p. 1435–36.

1340

Burger, Willy. Die Malerei in den Niederlanden, 1400–1500. München, Guenther, Koch, 1925. 167 p. 289 plates. 29 cm.

Covers painting in the Netherlands in the 15th century. Excellent clear plates. Bibliography in "Schriftennachweis" p. 164–67. Artist index p. 163.

1341

Byvanck, Alexander Willem. La miniature dans les Pays-Bas septentrionaux; traduit du néerlandais par Mlle. Adrienne Haye. Paris, Les Éditions d'Art et d'Histoire, 1937. 185 p. 100 plates. 33 cm.

A history of miniature painting of the northern Low Countries. Contains 108 pages of text followed by "Notices des manuscrits dont sont tirées les miniatures" p. 117–61, which contains bibliographical references. "Liste des autres manuscrits mentionnés" p. 163–65. "Liste des miniaturistes" p. 166. Bibliography p. 167–70. Index of plates p. 171–85.

1342

Byvanck, Alexander Willem, and Hoogewerff, Godefridus Joannes. La miniature hollandaise dans les manuscrits des 14e, 15e et 16e siècles . . . La Haye, Nijhoff, 1922–26. 91 p. 112 illus. and 2 portfolios of 240 plates. 44 cm.

The text volume has general title on cover only, dated 1925, while title page bears date of 1926. A scholarly and important work printed in 300 copies.

Text volume contains: Introduction p. xv–xxv; Notes descriptives des manuscrits p. 1–74 (with bibliographical references); Liste des manuscrits étudiés p. 75–78 (arranged by location); Liste des autres manuscrits mentionnés p. 79; Principaux livres et mémoires auxquels se réfère le présent ouvrage p. 80; Index alphabétique des reproductions, d'après les sujets p. 82–84; Index alphabétique des noms etc. figurants dans l'introduction et dans les notices descriptives p. 85–88; Liste de figures p. 89.

1343

Conway, William Martin Conway, *Baron.* The Van Eycks and their followers . . . London, Murray, 1921. 529 p. 25 plates. 26 cm.

Despite the title, really a history of Flemish painting up to and including Brueghel. Several illustrations on each plate. General index p. 523–29. Index of works of art p. 509–22.

1344

Crowe, *Sir* Joseph Archer, and Cavalcaselle, Giovanni Battista. Lives of the early Flemish painters: notices of their lives and works . . . 3d ed. London, Murray, 1879. 383 p. plates. 20 cm.

1st ed. 1857; 2d ed. (London, Murray, 1872) titled *The early Flemish painters.* An early standard work.

Contents: Painting in the Dark Ages; 12 chapters, each devoted to an important artist; Progress of the art in Flanders; Its influence abroad. Index p. 369–83.

1345

Dülberg, Franz. Niederländische Malerei der Spätgotik und Renaissance. Berlin, Wildpark-Potsdam, Akademische Verlagsgesellschaft Athenaion [c1929] 177 p. illus., 11 plates (part col.) 29 cm.

Covers both Dutch and Flemish painting of the late Gothic and Renaissance periods. Illustrations in the text and 11 color plates. Bibliography at the end of each chapter. Index of names p. 172; of places p. 174–76.

1346

Durrieu, Paul, *Comte*. La miniature flamande au temps de la cour de Bourgogne (1415–1530), ouvrage publié avec le concours de l'Académie des Inscriptions et Belles-lettres (Fondation Piot) . . . Bruxelles et Paris, van Oest, 1921. 80 p. 103 plates. 37 cm.

Covers Flemish miniature painting of the 15th and 16th centuries and consists of 40 pages of text followed by commentary on the 103 plates p. 41–73. "Table des planches" p. 75–78. "Table des personnages historiques des XVe et XVIe siècles, dont des effigies contemporaines se trouvent sur les planches" p. 79–80.

1347

Elst, Joseph Julien M. Ignace van der, *Baron*. The last flowering of the Middle Ages . . . Garden City, N.Y., Doubleday, Doran, 1944. 127 p. illus., plates (part col.) 32 cm.

A well-illustrated survey in English of Flemish painting and its background. No index, no bibliography. An alphabetical list of illustrations p. 7–8.

1348

Eynden, Roeland van den. Geschiedenis der vaderlandsche schilderkunst, sedert de helft der XVIII eeuw. Door Roeland van Eijnden en Adriaan van der Willigen. . . . Met portretten . . . Te Haarlem, Loosjes, 1816–20. 3 v. plates. 24 cm.

———. Aanhangsel op de drie deelen bevattende necrologie, enz. Haarlem, Loosjes, 1840. 334 p. 24 cm.

A thorough report by a contemporary witness of the late phase of Dutch painting, with emphasis on individual artists. Index of names at end of each volume.

1349

Fierens, Paul. La peinture flamande de Bruegel au XVIIIe siècle. Paris, Éditions d'Art et d'Histoire, 1942. 77 p. 48 plates. 21 cm. (Collection de précis d'histoire de l'art)

A general summary of Flemish painting from Brueghel to the 18th century. "Bibliographie sommaire" p. 69–71. List of plates p. 73–75 and list of contents p. 77.

1350

Fierens, Paul. La peinture flamande des origines à Quentin Metsys . . . Paris, Éditions d'Art et d'Histoire, 1938. 76 p. 68 plates. 21 cm. (Collection de précis d'histoire de l'art)

A general survey of early Flemish painting illustrated with rotogravure plates. "Bibliographie sommaire" p. [70]–71. List of plates p. 73–75.

1351

Fierens-Gevaert, Hippolyte. Histoire de la peinture flamande des origines à la fin du XVe siècle . . . Paris et Bruxelles, van Oest, 1927–29. 3 v. 229 plates. 33 cm.

A history of Flemish painting from its beginnings to the end of the 15th century.

Contents: [1] Les créatures de l'art flamand; [2] Les continuateurs des Van Eyck; [3] La maturité de l'art flamand, par Fierens-Gevaert et Paul Fierens.

Bibliography v. 3, p. [111]–24. Each volume has its own list of plates and table of contents.

1352

Fierens-Gevaert, Hippolyte. . . . Les primitifs flamands. Brussels, van Oest, 1908–12. 4 v. 169 plates. 34 cm.

At head of title: La peinture en Belgique: musées, églises, collections etc.

A discussion of the Flemish primitives by a well-known authority.

Contents: (1) Les créatures de l'art flamand; (2) Maturité des écoles de Bruges et de Gand; (3) Débuts du XVI siècle, Fin de l'idéal gothique; (4) Fin du XVI siècle, Réalistes et romanisants. Bibliography at end of each volume as well as a list of plates and table of contents.

1353

Fokker, T. H. Werke niederländischer Meister in den Kirchen Italiens. Haag, Nijhoff, 1931. 156 p. 15 plates. 26 cm. (Studien van het Nederlandsch Historisch Instituut te Rome. I)

An inventory of Dutch and Flemish paintings and sculpture in Italian churches, with notes on the artists.

"Künstlerregister" p. 4–67 gives biographical material on artists arranged in dictionary form. "Inventar der Kunstwerke" p. 68–150 is a listing by place of the works of art, with bibliographical references. Bibliography p. 151–56.

1354

Friedländer, Max J. Die altniederländische Malerei. Berlin, Cassirer, 1924–37. 14 v. plates. 31 cm.

A very important scholarly work on early Netherlandish painting.

Contents: (1) Die van Eyck, Petrus Christus; (2) Roger van der Weyden und der Meister von Flémalle; (3) Dierick Boots und

Joos van Gent; (4) Hugo van der Goes; (5) Geertgen van Haarlem und Hieronymus Bosch; (6) Memling und Gerard David; (7) Quentin Massys; (8) Jan Gossart, Bernart van Orley; (9) Joos van Cleve, Jan Provost, Joachim Patenier; (10) Lucas van Leyden und andere holländische Meister seiner Zeit; (11) Die Antwerper Manieristen Adriaen Ysenbrant; (12) Pieter Coeck, Jan van Scorel; (13) Anthonis Mor und seine Zeitgenossen; (14) Pieter Bruegel und Nachträge zu den früheren Banden.

Volume 14 contains an index of the artists included in the 14 volumes p. 138–48, and an index of masters p. 149–53.

1355

Friedländer, Max J. Die niederländischen Maler des 17. Jahrhunderts. Berlin, Propyläen-Verlag, 1923. 355 p. incl. illus., plates (col. mounted). 27 cm. (Propyläen-Kunstgeschichte, 12)

A history of Netherlandish painting in the 17th century. One chapter of text devoted to Flemish masters and one to Dutch. For each artist it gives dates of birth and death, names of masters with whom he studied, and a list of his paintings reproduced, with sizes and locations.

Index of illustrations p. 319–32, divided into Dutch and Flemish. General index p. 333–36.

1356

Fromentin, Eugène. Masters of past time; Dutch and Flemish painting from Van Eyck to Rembrandt [ed. by H. Gerson]. N.Y., Phaidon, 1948. 389 p. 96 plates. 19 cm.

Translated by Andrew Boyle and first published in English in 1913. A classic of art criticism rather than a reference book. Selected bibliography p. 381–83. Index of names p. 385–87; of collections p. 388–89.

1357

Heidrich, Ernst. Alt-niederländische Malerei; 200 Nachbildungen, mit geschichtlicher Einführung und Erläuterungen . . . Jena, Diederichs, 1924. 277 p. illus. 27 cm. (Die Kunst in Bildern [Bd. III])

There is also a 1910 ed. A pictorial survey of early Netherlandish painting. For each picture gives the title in German, French, and English, its location and size.

Text comprises p. 1–63. "Übersicht der Künstler" p. 64 is a chart of artists by period and city. Notes on plates p. 265–77.

1358

Heidrich, Ernst. Vlaemische Malerei; 200 Nachbildungen mit geschichtlicher Einführung und Erläuterungen . . . 1–10 Tausend. Jena, Diederichs, 1913. 287 p. illus. 27 cm. (Die Kunst in Bildern [Bd. V])

A pictorial survey of Flemish painting. Text comprises p. 1–80. For each illustration gives the title in German, French, and English, its location and dimensions. Explanation of plates p. 281–88. "Alphabetische Übersicht" p. 288.

1359

Hofstede de Groot, Cornelis. A catalogue raisonné of the works of the most eminent Dutch painters of the seventeenth century based on the work of John Smith . . . translated and edited by Edward G. Hawke. London, Macmillan, 1908–27. 8 v. 25 cm.

Also published in German as Beschreibendes und kritisches Verzeichnis der Werke des hervorragendsten holländischen Maler des XVII. Jahrhunderts . . . (Esslingen, Neff, 1907–28, 10 v.).

The last two volumes of the German ed. have not been included in the English ed., thus excluding ten artists treated in the former.

An important work for research in Dutch painting. Covers the works of 40 painters in the German ed. and 30 in English (33 treated by Smith [1370] and seven additional).

The title of each picture is followed by a description and details as to signature, material on which painted, and size. A history of each picture is given, where recorded in books, where exhibited, sales in which it appeared, and its last-known home. Pictures are numbered throughout and Smith's numbers added. "Pictures are cataloged under the names given them by their owners. . . . Pictures falsely attributed to masters have been deliberately omitted."—Pref. At end of each volume is an index of public and private collections and owners.

1360

Hoogewerff, Godefridus Joannes. De Noord-Nederlandsche schilderkunst . . . 's Gravenhage, Nijhoff, 1936–47. 5 v. illus. (incl. facsims.) 25 cm.

An important Dutch work giving the history of painting in the northern part of the Netherlands up to the end of the 16th century. Bibliographical footnotes.

Volume 5 is an index volume containing synopses of previous volumes, a list of works of artists mentioned, iconographical index, topographical index, and index of personal names.

1361

Hotho, Heinrich Gustav. Die Malerschule Huberts Van Eyck, nebst deutschen Vorgängern und Zeitgenossen. Öffentliche Vorlesung gehalten von H. G. Hotho. Berlin, Veit, 1855–58. 2 v. 20 cm.

An early work on Dutch and Flemish painting of the 15th century. Contents: v. 1, Geschichte der deutschen Malerei bis 1450; v. 2, Die flandrische Malerei des fünfzehnten Jahrhunderts. Fairly detailed table of contents but no indexes.

1362

Lemonnier, Camille. L'école belge de peinture, 1830–1905. Brussels, van Oest, 1906. 239 p. 100 plates. 29 cm.

Edition of 50 copies printed. A general survey of Belgian painting of the 19th century. Index of names of artists p. 231–36.

1363

Löhneysen, Hans-Wolfgang von. Die ältere niederländische Malerei; Künstler und Kritiker. Eisenach, Röth [1956]. 556 p. plates (part col.) 25 cm. (Bücher der Brücke)

A useful work on early Netherlandish painters. For each artist (listed alphabetically) gives outline of biography, bibliography, and critical excerpts, as well as a discussion by the author.

Bibliography p. 522. "Bibliographisches Verzeichnis des Arbeitsmaterials" p. 523–36. Index of people, places and subjects p. 537–52; of illustrations p. 554–56.

1364

Michiels, Alfred. Histoire de la peinture flamande depuis ses débuts jusqu'en 1864 ... 2. éd. Paris, Librairie Internationale, 1865–76. 10 v. 23 cm.

First published in Brussels 1845–49. An early work on Flemish painting. No illustrations, no index, no bibliography.

1365

Panofsky, Erwin. Early Netherlandish painting, its origins and character. Cambridge, Harvard Univ. Press, 1953. 2 v. plates. 32 cm. (Charles Eliot Norton lectures, 1947–48)

A scholarly work. It does not attempt to cover all of early Netherlandish painting but rather the Van Eycks, the Master of Flémalle, and Roger van der Weyden, with emphasis on manuscript painting.

Contents: v. 1, Text; "Notes" p. 361–511; v. 2, Plates. Index v. 1, p. 537–73.

1366A

Les Primitifs flamands: I. Corpus de la peinture des anciens Pays-Bas méridionaux au quinzième siècle ... Anvers, De Sikkel, 1951–(52). v. 1–(2). plates (part col.) 30 cm.

An important corpus of 15th century Flemish painting which incorporates the latest research and technical methods. The entire series is divided into three sections.

Works are classified as to whether painted by artists known by name or unknown masters. Each entry includes information as to classification in the Corpus, a description of the material based on laboratory work, an iconographic description, a historical account, references to parallel documents, the opinions and conclusions of the writer, an extensive bibliography, editions of archival documents and literary sources, followed by photographs of the entire work and details.

Contents: v. 1, nos. 1–4, Le Musée Communal de Bruges by A. Janssens de Bisthoven and R. A. Parmentier; v. 2, no. 5, La Galerie Sabauda de Turin par C. Aru et Et. de Geradon, 1952.

1366B

Les Primitifs flamands: II: Répertoire des peintures flamandes des quinzième et seizième siècles. [Publications du Centre National de Recherches "Primitifs flamands"] Anvers, De Sikkel, 1953– . v. 1, pt. 1. illus., plates. 30 cm.

Includes bibliographies. Contents: [v. 1] fasc. 1, Collection d'Espagne, sous la direction de J. Lavalleye.

1366C

Les Primitifs flamands: III. Contributions à l'étude des primitifs flamands. [Publications du Centre National de Recherches "Primitifs flamands"] Anvers, De Sikkel, 1953. v. 2. illus., plates (part col.) 30 cm.

Includes bibliographies. Contents: v. 2, L'Agneau mystique au laboratoire, examen et traitement, sous la direction de Paul Coremans.

1367

Puyvelde, Leo van. La peinture flamande à Rome. Brussels, Librairie Encyclopédique, 1950. 239 p. 96 plates. 29 cm.

A treatment of Flemish painting in Rome. The text is divided by centuries and then by artists who settled in Rome and those who were there only temporarily. Under each category individual artists are treated. Illustrated by good clear halftones.

Bibliographical footnotes. Index of names and places p. 225–36; of illustrations and references p. 237–39.

1368

Roh, Franz. Holländische Malerei; 200 Nachbildungen mit geschichtlicher Einführung und Erläuterungen. Jena, Diederichs, 1921. 1–15 Tausend. 335 p. illus., plates. 28 cm. (Die Kunst in Bildern [V])

Contains 120 pages of text covering Dutch painting and 200 plates, each giving the title in French, German, and English, its location, and its size. Biographical notes on the pictures p. 321–34. Index of illustrations p. 335.

1369

Rooses, Max. Dutch painters of the nineteenth century. With biographical notes. With six etchings by Ph. Zilcken, six photogravure plates and over 200 other illustrations. Tr. by F. Knowles. London, Low, Marston, 1898–1901. 4 v. illus., plates. 32 cm.

Also published in a French ed. This work consists of a series of articles by various well-known writers on the life and works of the most celebrated Dutch painters of this century, with a summary of the whole school by Rooses.

Each volume contains the essays and reproductions for 12 painters. No index, but artists are listed on spines of volumes.

1370

Smith, John, *dealer in pictures, London*. A catalogue raisonné of the works of the most eminent Dutch, Flemish and French painters; in which is included a short biographical notice of the artists with a copious description of their principal pictures . . . a statement of the prices at which such pictures have been sold at public sales on the continent and in England; a reference to the galleries and private collections in which a large portion are at present, and the names of the artists by whom they have been engraved; to which is added a brief notice of the scholars and imitators of the great masters of the above schools . . . London, Smith, 1829–42. 9 v. plates. 27 cm.

Reprinted for Sands and Co., London and Edinburgh, 1908 in an edition of 1250 copies. Volume 9 is a supplement.

An important early work which was revised and brought up to date by Hofstede de Groot (1359). Contains a description of the works

of 33 Dutch, four Flemish, and three French artists.

Contents: v. 1, Gerard Dow, Peter van Slingelandt, Francis van Mieris, William van Mieris, Adrian Ostade, Isaac Ostade and Philip Wouwermans; v. 2, Peter Paul Rubens; v. 3, Anthony van Dyck and David Teniers; v. 4, Jan Steen, Gerard Terburg, H. E. vander Neer, Peter de Hooge, Gonzales Cocques, Gabriel Metsu, Gaspar Netscher, A. van der Werf, Nicholad Maes, Godfrey Schalcken; v. 5, Nicholas Berghem, Paul Potter, Adrian vander Velde, Karel du Jardin, Albert Cuyp, John vander Heyden; v. 6, Jacob Ruysdael, Minderhout Hobbema, John and Andrew Both, John Wynants, Adam Pynaker, John Hackaert, William vander Velde, Ludolph Backhuyzen, John van Huysum, Rachel Ruisch; v. 7, Rembrandt van Rhyn; v. 8, Nicholas Poussin, Claude Lorraine and Jean Baptiste Greuze; v. 9, Supplement.

1371

Voll, Karl. Die altniederländische Malerei von Jan van Eyck bis Memling; ein entwicklungsgeschichtlicher Versuch . . . Leipzig, Insel-Verlag, 1923. 280 p. 63 plates. 21 cm.

1st ed. 1905. A history of early Netherlandish painting from Jan van Eyck to Memling. Notes p. 227–74.

1372

Warner, Ralph. Dutch and Flemish flower and fruit painters of the XVIIth and XVIIIth centuries . . . with introduction by Thomas Rohan; comprising 280 illustrations representing 104 masters. London, Mills & Boon, 1928. 244 p. illus. 33 cm.

The standard work on the subject. Contains a corpus of photographs with very brief descriptive text p. 12–239, and a dictionary of painters illustrated p. 240–44, which merely lists alphabetically the artists and gives dates of birth and death, where they worked, and under whom they studied. Bibliography p. 11.

1373

Wilenski, Reginald Howard. Dutch painting. London, Faber; N.Y., Beechhurst [1955]. 211 p. illus., plates (part col.) 26 cm.

First published 1929 under title *An introduction to Dutch art;* 2d impression 1929; reprinted 1937. Rev. ed. 1945; reprinted 1946 and 1947. Rev. and enl. ed. 1955.

The original edition was mainly concerned with Dutch figure painting, but this edition has an added chapter on flower painting. A general survey of the subject with lists of characteristic pictures given under each major artist discussed. Index p. 207–11.

1374

Winkler, Friedrich. Die altniederländische Malerei; die Malerei in Belgien und Holland von 1400–1600. Berlin, Propyläen-Verlag, 1924. 412 p. illus. 26 cm.

A well-illustrated history of painting in Belgium and Holland in the 15th and 16th centuries. Index of paintings p. 391–404 arranged by place; of artists p. 405–07; of illustrations p. 408–13.

1375

Winkler, Friedrich. Die flämische Buchmalerei des XV. und XVI. Jahrhunderts; Künstler und Werke von den Brüdern van Eyck bis zu Simon Bening . . . Leipzig, Seemann, 1925. 210 p. incl. illus., 91 plates. 31 cm.

A standard work on Flemish miniature painting of the 15th and 16th centuries.

Contents: (1) Vorwort; (2) Einleitung; (3) Geschichtlicher Überblick; (4) Die Künstler Verzeichnis ihrer Werke p. 13–154; (5) Die Handschriften Verzeichnis nach Orten p. 155–209; (6) Verzeichnis der Künstlernamen p. 210. Includes bibliographical references.

Oriental Countries

1376

Andrews, Frederick Henry. Wall paintings from ancient shrines in Central Asia; recovered by Sir Aurel Stein; described by Fred H. Andrews. Published under the orders of the Government of India. London, Oxford Univ. Press, 1948. 128 p. illus., fold. map, plans. 39 cm. and portfolio of 32 plates (part col.) 65 cm.

An important publication with excellent illustrations. Index p. 113–28.

1377

Arnold, *Sir* Thomas Walker, and Grohmann, Adolf. The Islamic book; a contribution to its art and history from the VII–XVIII century . . . Paris, Pegasus; N.Y., Harcourt, Brace, 1929. 130 p. illus., 104 plates (part col.) 32 cm.

Edition of 375 copies. A major contribution to the field. Contents: pt. 1, The early Islamic period from the VII–XII century, by A. Grohmann; pt. 2, The period from the XIII–XVIII century, by Sir T. W. Arnold; Notes and references.

"Table of papyri, manuscripts and other pieces discussed in the text" p. 117–19. Bibliography p. 116. Index of subjects, persons, and places p. 121–31.

1378

Arnold, *Sir* Thomas Walker. Painting in Islam, a study of the place of pictorial art in Muslim culture . . . Oxford, Clarendon Press, 1928. 159 p. 64 plates (part col.) 29 cm.

"This book aims to indicate the place of painting in the culture of the Islamic world" rather than to be a history of Muslim painters. An important and valuable work.

"A chapter of biography" p. 138–49. Bibliographical footnotes. Index of manuscripts p. 153. General index p. 155–59.

1379

Binyon, *Sir* Laurence. Painting in the Far East; an introduction to the history of pictorial art in Asia, especially China and Japan . . . 4th ed. rev. throughout. London, Arnold; N.Y., Longmans, Green, 1934. 302 p. 41 plates. 27 cm.

1st ed. 1908; 2d ed. 1913; 3d ed. 1923. An early work in the field.

"Notes" p. 293–94 gives lists of the principal artists in various periods. Index p. 297–302.

1380

Binyon, *Sir* Laurence; Wilkinson, J. V. S.; and Gray, Basil. Persian miniature painting, including a critical and descriptive catalogue of the miniatures exhibited at Burlington House, January–March 1931 . . . London, Oxford Univ. Press, 1933. 212 p. 113 plates (part col.) 39 cm.

While this book is primarily a catalog of an exhibition, it is actually the best treatment of the field and covers the history of Persian miniatures in a scholarly way. Excellent illustrations.

Appendixes: (1) Dūst Muhammed's account of past and present painters; (2) Mīrzā Muhammad Haydar Dughlāt on the Herat school of painters; (3) The Album from the Gulistan Museum. Bibliography p. 193–95. Index p. 199–212.

1381

Blochet, Edgar. Musulman painting, XIIth–XVIIth century . . . translated from the French by Cicely M. Binyon, with an introduction by Sir E. Denison Ross . . . London, Methuen [1929]. 123 p. 200 plates (12 col.) 26 cm. (The connoisseur's library)

A well-illustrated history of Persian painting written by a recognized scholar. Index p. 118–24.

1382

Bowie, Henry P. On the laws of Japanese painting: an introduction to the study of the art of Japan. With prefatory remarks by Iwaya Sazanami and Hirai Kinza. [N.Y., Dover, c1951] 117 p. 66 plates. 24 cm.

Originally published 1911. Also issued in a paperback ed. by Dover. This is a useful book for the principles of both Chinese and Japanese painting.

Contents: (1) Personal experiences; (2) Art in Japan; (3) Laws for use of brush and materials; (4) Law governing conception and execution; (5) Canons of the aesthetic in painting; (6) Subjects for Japanese painting; (7) Signatures and seals, Explanation of headbands. Index p. 111–17.

1383

Brown, Percy. Indian painting. 5th ed. Calcutta, Y.M.C.A. Pub. House, 1947. 132 p. plates. 19 cm. (The Heritage of India series)

1st ed. 1917; 2d ed. 1927; 3d ed. 1930; 4th ed. 1932. A paper-backed ed. on poor paper, which is apparently a reprint of the 2d ed.

"Principal collections of Indian painting" p. 125–26. "List of India pigments" p. 123. Bibliography p. 124–25.

1384

Brown, Percy. Indian painting under the Mughals, A.D. 1550 to A.D. 1750 . . . Oxford, Clarendon Press, 1924. 204 p. 72 plates (part col.) 30 cm.

A particularly useful volume. Contents: pt. 1, Historical; pt. 2, Descriptive.

Appendices: (A) List of painters and their principal works p. 195–98; (B) List of collections of Indian pictures p. 199; (C) Bibliography p. 200–01. Index p. 202–04.

1385

Coomaraswamy, Ananda Kentish. Rajput painting; being an account of the Hindu paintings of Rajasthan and the Panjab Himalayas from the sixteenth to the nineteenth century described in their relation to contemporary thought . . . London, N.Y., Oxford Univ. Press, 1916. 2 v. illus., 77 plates (part col.) 38 cm.

A monumental work. Volume 1, Text; v. 2, Plates. Contents: (1) The Rajput schools; (2) Subject matter of Rajput paintings; (3) Allied arts and the present day. No bibliography, no index.

1386

Ferguson, John Calvin. Chinese painting. Chicago, Univ. of Chicago Press [c1927]. 199 p. 59 plates (part col.) 28 cm.

A pioneer work which is a survey of the technique and history of Chinese painting. "The Chinese dynasties" p. ix. "Sources of information" p. 14–27. "Index of Chinese names" p. 185–99 lists them alphabetically by Western form and gives also the Chinese characters.

1387

Gangoly, Ordhendra Coomar. Masterpieces of Rajput painting, selected, annotated and described in relation to original Hindi texts from religious literature. Calcutta, Manager-"Rupam" [1926?]. 104 p. 52 plates (part col.) 45 cm.

Edition limited to 210 copies. "An attempt to co-relate the subject matter of the pictures to their literary sources."—*Pref.* More a picture book than a reference work, but useful for the many illustrations representing this art. An important contribution to the field, with color plates of good quality.

1388

[Harada, Kinjiro] The pageant of Chinese painting. Tokyo, Otsuka-kogeisha, 1936. [41 p.] 1000 plates on 500 l. 31 cm.

Valuable as a pictorial survey of Chinese painting. Text in Japanese (39 pages) and English (2 pages). Index p. 1–8 lists artists' names in both English and Japanese form.

1389

Kiai-tseu-yuan houa tchouan; les enseignements de la peinture du jardin grand comme un grain de moutarde; encyclopédie de la peinture chinoise; traduction et commentaires par Raphaël Petrucci, augmentés d'une préface, d'un dictionnaire biographique . . . illustrés d'environ cinq cents gravures. Paris, Laurens, 1918. 519 p. illus. 41 cm.

Edition of 500 copies printed. A French translation of the famous Mustard Seed Garden treatise on Chinese painting, with commentaries.

"Vocabulaire des termes techniques" given in both French and Chinese characters p. 447–62. "Index des noms de peintres et des personnages historiques ou légendaires cités dans le texte ou les commentaires," p. 463–509, forms a sort of biographical dictionary of Chinese painters.

1390

Kramrisch, Stella. A survey of painting in the Deccan. London, The India Society, 1937. 234 p. 24 plates. 28 cm.

An important contribution to the field of Indian painting. The size of the paintings is indicated in the legends accompanying them.

Contents: (1) Ajanta; (2) Elura; (3) Vijayanagar; (4) The last phase. Appendix: Catalogue of paintings from Golconda and Hyderabad in the collection of Sir Akbar Hydari, on loan in the Prince of Wales Museum, Bombay, p. 189–98. Bibliographical references included in the "Notes." Index p. 231–34.

1391

Martin, Fredrik Robert. The miniature painting and painters of Persia, India and Turkey, from the 8th to 18th century . . . London, Quaritch, 1912. 2 v. illus., 275 plates (4 col.) 40 cm.

Volume 1 contains text describing various schools, techniques, etc.; a list of painters p. 111–36, arranged chronologically and listing some of their works; and a chart of synchronology giving names and dates of outstanding artists in various countries and Europe. Given in parallel columns: Europe, Egypt, Persia, Transoxiana, India, China. Volume 2 contains the black and white plates. Bibliography v. 1, p. 143–44. Index v. 1, p. [149]–56, also includes names of artists alphabetically arranged.

1392

Mehta, Nanalal Chamamlal. Studies in Indian painting, a survey of some new material ranging from the commencement of the VIIth century to circa 1870 A.D. Bombay, Taraporevala, 1926. 127 p. 44 plates (17 col.) 30 cm.

"The object of the present volume is to bring together some new material for the study of Indian painting. Most of the illustrations are published here for the first time."—*Foreword.*

Contains good plates. Size of paintings is given in the list of illustrations p. ix–xi. Index p. [129].

1393

Morrison, Arthur. The painters of Japan . . . London, Edinburgh, Jack, 1911. 2 v. 122 plates (part col.) 39 cm.

Volume 1 covers through the Kano school. The legend facing the plates includes the sizes of the works. Index v. 2, p. 115–27.

1394

Mulk-Rāj, Ānand. Persian painting. London, Faber [1930] 46 p. plate. 20 cm. (Criterion miscellany no. 25)

A summary from the first national kings of Persia, c. 212 A.D., to the present day. "List of Persian dynasties, principal reigns, and the most famous poets and artists who flourished under them" p. 41–43. "A brief bibliography" p. 45–46.

1395

Rowland, Benjamin, and Coomaraswamy, Ananda Kentish. The wall-paintings of India, Central Asia & Ceylon; a comparative study by Benjamin Rowland with an introductory essay on the nature of Buddhist art by Ananda K. Coomaraswamy, with a foreword by A. Townshend Johnson and colour plates by F. Bailey Vanderhoef, Jr. Boston, Printed at Merrymount Press, 1938. 94 p. 36 plates (30 col.) 37 cm.

Edition of 500 copies printed. Issued in a portfolio which has map on lining paper. The color plates are laid in the portfolio and the black and white ones bound in the text volume.

1396

Rowley, George. Principles of Chinese painting, with illustrations from the Du- Bois Schanck Morris Collection. Princeton, Princeton Univ. Press, 1947. 111 p. illus., 48 (i.e., 50) plates (part col.) 30 cm. (Princeton monographs in art and archaeology, XXIV)

Contents: I, Principles: (1) Subject matter and its interpretation, (2) Style; II, Catalogue of Morris Collection. List of terms p. 81; of sources p. 82. Index to pt. 1, p. 83–85.

1397

Sakisian, Armenag, *Bey.* La miniature persane du XIIe au XVIIe siècle; ouvrage accompagné de la reproduction de 193 miniatures dont deux en couleurs. Paris et Bruxelles, van Oest, 1929. 174 p. 106 plates. 36 cm.

A standard work on Persian miniatures of the 12th to the 17th century containing 145 pages of text and 106 collotype plates, with two in color. Index p. 147–58.

1398

Sirén, Osvald. Chinese painting: leading masters and principles. N.Y., Ronald [1956–58]. 7 v. plates (part col.) 28 cm.

"General aim is to represent the historical development and aesthetic significance of Chinese painting to Western art lovers."—*Pref.* Contents: pt. 1, The first millennium: v. 1, Early Chinese painting (Text); v. 2, The Sung period (Text); v. 3, Plates.—pt. 2, The later centuries: v. 4, The Yüan and early Ming masters; v. 5, The later Ming and leading Ch'ing masters; v. 6, Plates; v. 7, Annotated lists of paintings and reproductions of paintings by Chinese artists.

Annotated lists (95 pages separately numbered at end of v. 2) contain "about 1400 painters mentioned with references to historical sources to their works. The latter are listed under short descriptive titles to which often are appended letters or pointers indicating their probable degree of authenticity." —*Pref*. Bibliography for these lists p. 7–13.

Bibliography to Part 2, vols. 4 and 5, v. 4, p. 235–40.

1399
Sirén, Osvald. A history of early Chinese painting . . . London, The Medici Society [1933]. 2 v. 226 plates. 33 cm.

Limited edition of 525 copies. Contents: I, From the Han to the beginning of the Sung period; II, From the Sung to the end of the Yüan dynasty.

Bibliography, divided into Chinese books and foreign books, v. 1, p. xix–xxii. Indexes at end of v. 2 are divided into: Index of Chinese names and terms, and Index to foreign names and terms.

1400
Sirén, Osvald. A history of later Chinese painting . . . London, The Medici Society, 1938. 2 v. 242 plates. 33 cm.

Limited edition of 525 copies. Contents: I, From the end of the Yüan period to the end of the Wan Li reign, c. 1350–1620; II, From the end of the Ming period to the end of the Ch'ien Lung reign, c. 1620–1796.

Each volume contains a "List of paintings and reproductions of works by painters active mainly in that period and covered in the volume." Volume I includes an extensive bibliography in both Oriental and Western languages p. [193]–200. Volume 2 includes an index to Chinese names and terms, and an index of foreign names.

1401
Toda, Kenji. Japanese scroll painting. Chicago, Univ. of Chicago Press [1935]. 167 p. illus. (incl. map), 19 plates (part col.) 29 cm.

Part 1 is a historical discussion of Japanese scrolls. Part 2 contains: (1) Items of identification of a scroll; (2) The making of a scroll; (3) Chronological table; (4) Bibliography p. 141–42; (5) Transliteration, Measurement, Illustrations.

"List of important works of Japanese scroll painting" p. 144–49. Appendix: Titles of the scrolls p. 153–54; Biographical list p. 154–58; Eras p. 158–59; Buddhist temples and Shinto

shrines p. 159–60; Bibliographical list p. 160. Miscellaneous p. 160–64 given in Japanese and Roman letters. Index p. 167–68.

1402
Tucci, Giuseppe. Tibetan painted scrolls. Rome, Libreria dello Stato, 1949. 2 v. (798 p.) illus. 43 cm. and portfolio of 256 plates (part col.) 51 cm.

Translated from the Italian by Virginia Vacca. Contents: pt. 1, Historical, cultural and religious background; pt. 2, Evolution and character of Tibetan tankas; pt. 3, Description and explanation of the tankas; pt. 4, Sources and documents.

Genealogical tables p. 706–08. Tibetan texts p. 745–63. Index p. 765–98.

1403
Waley, Arthur. An introduction to the study of Chinese painting. London, Benn, 1923. 261 p. 49 plates (part col.) 29 cm.

Reprinted by the Grove Press, N.Y., 1958.

"This book is in the main a history of art-tradition rather than an account of Chinese painting as represented by the works that survive today . . . A series of essays rather than a general survey of early Chinese painting."—*Pref*. The size of each painting is represented in the legend opposite the reproduction. "Books" p. 253–54. Index p. 257–62.

1404
Wang, Kai. The tao of painting, a study of the ritual disposition of Chinese painting; with a translation of the Chieh tzu yuan hua chuan; or Mustard Seed Garden manual of painting, 1679–1701, by Mai-mai Sze. [N.Y.] Pantheon [1956]. 2 v. illus., plates (part col.) 27 cm. (Bollingen series, 49)

A major work in the field presented in English for the first time by Mai-mai Sze whose first volume on the ritual aspect of Chinese painting is of particular interest.

SEE ALSO: Khandalavala. Indian sculpture and painting (1064).

Russia and Slavic Countries

1405
Bakushinskiĭ, Anatoliĭ Vasil'evich. Iskusstvo Palekha [Moskva] Academia, 1934. 266 p. illus., plates. 26 cm.

A history of an old school of painting developed by the peasants in the province of Vladimir. Before the Revolution they specialized in icons; after 1917 they changed to book illustration and lacquered boxes, but kept the old style of the icon painting.

1406

Benua, Aleksandr Nikolaevich. Istoriiã russkoĭ zhivopisi v XIX veke. S.-Peterburg, Znanie, 1902. 285 p. illus., plates. 28 cm.

Issued in parts, 1901–02. A standard history of Russian painting in the 19th century, showing the development of national traditions from the earliest Russian art through the introduction of foreign influence in the time of Peter the Great, and the gradual freedom from this influence in the 19th century.

The most interesting part of the book deals with the new school of painting developed at the very end of the 19th century around the publication *Mir iskusstva,* of which the author was one of the leaders. Bibliography p. [275]–85.

1407

Benua, Aleksandr Nikolaevich. The Russian school of painting . . . with an introduction by Christian Brinton. N.Y., Knopf, 1916. 17–199 p. 32 plates. 28 cm.

Translated by A. Yarmolinsky. A popular introductory survey of Russian painting of the Western type, beginning with the 18th century. No index, bibliography, or footnotes.

1408

Farbman, Michael S., ed. Masterpieces of Russian painting . . . reproductions of Russian icons and frescoes from the XI to the XVIII centuries; text by A. I. Anisimov, Sir Martin Conway, Roger Fry, and Professor Igor Grabar . . . London, Europa [1930]. 124 p. illus., 20 col. plates. 33 cm.

A fully illustrated record of the exhibition of Russian icons at the Victoria and Albert Museum, November 1929.

Contents: (1) History of Russian icon painting, by Sir Martin Conway; (2) Russian icon painting from the west European point of view, by Roger Fry; (3) Russian icon painting: its bloom, over-refinement, and decay, by A. I. Anisimov; (4) Scientific restoration of historic works of art, by Igor Grabar; (5) Description of icons and notes on iconography and style.

"Chief places in Russia where icons are preserved" p. [125]. Bibliography (very short) p. [125].

1409

Grabar, André. La peinture religieuse en Bulgarie; préface de Gabriel Millet. Paris,

Geuthner, 1928. 396 p. illus., fold. map and portfolio of 14 p. and 64 plates. 34 cm. (Orient et Byzance, études d'art médiéval . . . I)

University of Strasbourg thesis. A scholarly work on religious painting in Bulgaria with collotype plates. Bibliography p. [vii]–xvi. "Index des monuments" p. 363–76. "Index iconographique" p. 377–84. "Index génerale" p. 385–90. "Table des gravures" p. 391–92.

The portfolio contains "Table explicative des planches," "Index des monuments," and "Index iconographique."

1410

Kondakov, Nikodim Pavlovich. The Russian icon . . . Prague, Seminarium Kondakovianum, 1928–33. 4 v. 216 plates (part col.) 43 cm. (v. 2–4, 33 cm.)

Edition of 300 copies printed. Volumes 3–4 have text in Russian with French summary. A standard work on Russian icons.

Contents: v. 1–2, plates; v. 3–4, text. Volume 1 contains 65 color plates with captions in French, German, English, Czech, and Russian; v. 2 has 136 collotypes with a descriptive text in the various languages; v. 3 has 8 halftone plates; v. 4 has 4 collotypes and 2 color plates.

Bibliography v. 3, p. [xi–xx]. Volume 4 has general and iconographical indexes in Russian only.

1411

Kondakov, Nikodim Pavlovich. The Russian icon. Trans. by Ellis H. Minns. Oxford, Clarendon Press, 1927. 226 p. illus. (incl. map), 63 (i.e., 65) plates (3 col.) on 48 l. 30 cm.

An abbreviated English ed. of the author's authoritative work on this subject (1410).

"Inscriptions and lettering, names of saints etc." p. xxi–xxiii. "Sketch map of Russia, table of Russian history" p. xxiv–xxvi. Bibliography p. xix–xx, and bibliographical footnotes. Indexes: I, General p. 205–19; II, Iconography p. 220–26.

1412

Lukomskiĭ, Georgiĭ Kreskent'evĭch. History of modern Russian painting (Russian painting of the past hundred years) (1840–1940) . . . trans. from the Russian by G. K. London, N.Y., Hutchinson [1945]. 184 p. plates. 25 cm.

A general survey. Appendices: I, Biographies: Short biographical details about the more outstanding Russian painters p. 57–63; II, List of the names of painters XVIII–XIX century (especially 1870–1920) p. 64–66; III, List of the names of painters of the XXth century (1920–1945) p. 67; IV, List of the names of painters—foreigners, who worked in Russia in the XVIIIth century until the beginning of the XIXth century p. 68.

A few bibliographical hints are given in a small note on p. 14. List of illustrations p. 12–14.

1413

Millet, Gabriel. La peinture du moyen age en Yougoslavie (Serbie, Macédoine et Monténégro) . . . Fasc. 1–2. Paris, de Boccard, 1954. 58 illus., 94 plates. 39 cm.

First volume in a series that aims to cover Yugoslav medieval mural painting from the 11th to the 15th centuries. This volume covers early paintings between the mid-11th and the mid-12th centuries in Macedonia and Rashka. It is a collection of plates in black and white of superior quality representing interiors of churches and details of their frescoes.

A list of the monuments treated is given and a short historical note on each, with bibliographical references. Index of iconographical group frescoes by subjects represented.

1414

Muratov, Pavel Pavlovich. L'ancienne peinture russe . . . Traduction du manuscrit russe, par André Caffi. Rome, Stock, 1925. 181 p. illus. 28 cm.

A discussion of Russian painting up to the beginning of the 17th century. Contents: (1) Introduction; (2) Les origines; (3) La peinture russe du XIe et du XIIe siècles; (4) Le XIIIe et le XIVe siècles; (5) De Roubliow à Denys; (6) La peinture russe au XVIe siècle; (7) La fin. Some bibliographical footnotes. No index.

1415

Muratov, Pavel Pavlovich. Les icones russes. Paris, Schriffrin [1927]. 254 p. incl. 60 plates (part col.) 28 cm.

Well illustrated, including four good color plates. List of plates. No index, no bibliography.

1416

Okunev, Nikolai Aleksandrovich. Monumenta artis serbica. Prague, Institutum Slavicum, 1928–37. 4 v. plates. 33 cm.

Volume 1 published in Zagreb. Introductory essays (in Czech) which present in a summary form a keen analysis of the characteristics of Serbian painting from the 13th to the 15th centuries.

All volumes have a short text followed by one color plate and four black and white plates. Volume 1 has parallel texts in French and German; v. 2–4 have texts in French, German, and Russian.

1417

Schweinfurth, Philipp. Geschichte der russischen Malerei im Mittelalter . . . Mit 8 Lichtdrucktafeln und 169 Abbildungen. Haag, Nijhoff, 1930. 506 p. 169 illus., 8 plates, diagr. 26 cm.

A quite thorough treatment of Russian painting in the Middle Ages as affected by Byzantine and other influences.

Some bibliographical footnotes. "Register" p. 499–506. "Verzeichnis der Abbildungen" p. 483–97 gives sources of the photographs used, and the titles and locations of the pictures reproduced.

1418

Stefănescu, I. D. Contribution à l'étude des peintures murales valaques. (Transylvanie, district de Vâlcea, Târgoviste, et région de Bucarest.) Paris, Geuthner, 1928. 90 p. 10 plates. 33 cm. (Orient et Byzance, études d'art médiéval . . . III)

Covers mural paintings from before the 17th century through the first third of the 19th century. Also a chapter on paintings restored in the 19th century and those which have been destroyed.

"Tableau chronologique des princes ayant regné en Valachie" p. 75–76. "Bibliographie" p. [77]–78. "Index des monuments" p. 79–80. "Index iconographique" p. 81–86. "Table des planches" p. 87–88.

1419

Stefănescu, I. D. L'évolution de la peinture religieuse en Bucovine et en Moldavie; depuis les origines jusqu'au XIXe siècle. Paris, Geuthner, 1928. 334 p. illus. and atlas of 8 p. and 96 plates. 33 cm. (Orient et Byzance, II)

University of Paris thesis. A scholarly work on religious painting in Bucovina. "Bibliographie" p. [309]–11. "Index des monuments" p. 313–14. "Index iconographique" p. 315–22. "Table des planches" p. 323–27. Plate volume contains "Index des monuments" and "Index iconographique."

1420

Stefănescu, I. D. L'évolution de la peinture religieuse en Bucovine et en Moldavie depuis les origines jusqu'au XIXe siècle. Nouvelles recherches, étude iconographique.

Paris, Geuthner, 1929. 192 p. illus., diagr. and atlas of 8 p. and 60 plates (2 col.) 33 cm. (Orient et Byzance, VI)

This work complements the one published the preceding year (1419) and takes account of the recent cleaning of paintings. Bibliography contains only items not included in the previous volume. "Bibliographie" p. [171]-72. "Tableau des monuments décorés de Moldavie" p. [173]. "Index des monuments" p. [175]-76. "Index iconographique" p. 177-84 contains "Les monuments décorés" and "L'iconographie." Plate volume contains "Table des planches," "Index des monuments," and "Index iconographique."

Scandinavia

1421
Been, Ch. A. Danmarks malerkunst, billeder og biografier . . . kapitlerne indledede af Emil Hannover. København, 1902-03. 2 v. in 1. illus. 32 cm.

A historical survey of three chapters on Danish painting followed by artists' biographies arranged chronologically. Covers the period from mid-18th century to the end of the 19th. Well illustrated. "Indholdsfortegnelse" at the beginning of v. 1 is an index of the artists treated.

1422
Erdmann, Domenico. Norsk dekorativ maling fra reformasjonen til romantikken. Oslo, Dybwad, 1940. 323 p. illus. 29 cm.

A history of Norwegian decorative painting from the Reformation to the romantic era. German summary p. 285-311. Bibliographical references in "Noter" p. 312-18. Index p. 319-23.

1423
Gudenrath, Eduard. Norwegische Maler von J. C. Dahl bis Edvard Munch . . . Berlin, Propyläen-Verlag [1943]. 30 p. illus., 32 col. plates. 32 cm.

A brief survey, in German, of Norwegian painting, mostly of the 19th century. "Verzeichnis der Maler" p. 29-30 gives dates and a few sentences about the training of each artist and indicates the plates of his work.

1424
Lindblom, Andreas Adolf Fredrik. La peinture gothique en Suède et en Norvège; étude sur les relations entre l'Europe occidentale et les pays scandinaves . . . Publ. par l'Académie Royale des Belles-lettres, d'Histoire et d'Archéologie de Stockholm. Stockholm, Wahlstrom & Widstrand; London, Quaritch, 1916. 252 p. illus. (incl. plans), 50 plates. 33 cm.

Translated by Mlle. C. Harel. Covers Gothic painting in Sweden and Norway. Notes p. 234-43. "Index iconographique" p. 245-48. "Index des localités des oeuvres d'art traités dans ce travail" p. 249-52.

1425
Madsen, Herman. 200 danske malere og deres vaerker. København, Pioras, 1946. 2 v. illus. 27 cm.

An important work on Danish painting, well illustrated with halftones in the text. At the beginning of each volume is an alphabetical listing of the painters discussed in the two volumes, followed by a chronological listing of the painters treated in that particular volume. "Ordforklaring" (Glossary) at end of v. 2, p. 381-88.

1426
Madsen, Karl Johan Vilhelm, ed. Kunstens historie i Danmark. [København] Jacobsen, 1901-07. 430 p. illus. 31 cm.

A history of painting in Denmark from medieval times to the 20th century. Contains seven sections, each written by a specialist. Well illustrated in the text. No index.

1427
Nordisk målarkonst; det moderna måleriets genombrott. Författare: Preben Wilmann [et. al.; Stockholm] Ehlin [1951]. 95 p. illus., 40 col. plates. 30 cm.

A well-illustrated discussion of contemporary painting in Scandinavia. Contents: Danmark, av P. Wilmann; Finland, av A. Linström; Island, av B. T. Björnsson; Norge, av L. Östby; Sverige, av C. Derkert.

"Konstnärsregister" by L. Widding gives a few sentences about each artist. "De vanligaste konsttermerna" by L. Widding is a glossary of terms. List of plates p. [5-7] gives dates for each artist, and the sizes and locations of the paintings represented.

1428
Østby, Leif. Modern Norwegian painting. Oslo, Mittet, 1949. 261 p. 1 illus. (p. 41-167, col. plates). 33 cm.

A good pictorial presentation of contemporary Norwegian painting with some explanatory text which outlines movements and influences. "Biographical notes" p. 251-[59]. Index p. 260-62.

1429

Poulsen, Vagn. Danish painting and sculpture. Copenhagen, Danska Selskab [1955]. 196 p. illus. 21 cm. (Denmark in print and pictures)

A popular account of the history of Danish art, probably written for tourists. "Note on art literature" lists four titles (p. 197). Index p. 193–97.

1430

Stenstadvold, Håkon. Norske malerier gjennom hundre år. 3 revid. utg. With an English summary. [Oslo] Dreyer [1949]. 157 p. 23 mounted col. illus., 55 col. plates. 39 cm.

1st ed. 1943. A historical survey of Norwegian painting of the past hundred years, well illustrated with color plates.

English summary p. 151–55 is followed by a "Table of illustrations" p. 156–57, which gives dates of the artists and the paintings reproduced. "Lesning om norsk kunst" p. 146–47. "Inhold" p. 148–49. "Stikkordregister" p. 149.

1431

Wennberg, Bo Göte. Svenska målare i Danmark under 1700-talet . . . Lund, Gleerup [1940]. 353 p. 76 plates on 38 l. 31 cm.

"Utgivet med anslag från Längmanska kulturfonden." A scholarly treatment of the work of Swedish artists in Denmark. Includes catalogs of the works of various artists. "Kållor och litteratur" p. 339–45. "Personregister" p. 346–52.

1432

Wennervirta, Ludvig. Goottilaista monumentaalimaalausta Länsisuomen ja Ahvenanmaan kirkoissa . . . Helsinki [Puromiehen] 1930. 279 p. illus. 26 cm. (Suomen muinaismiustoyhdistyksen aikakauskirja, XXXVIII:1)

A scholarly study of Gothic monumental painting in the churches of West Finland and Åland.

"Kirjallisuutta" p. [272]–76. "Phyimyksia" (Index) p. 277. "Die gotische Monumentalmalerei in den Kirchen von Westfinnland und Åland" p. [243]–71 is a German summary of the text.

1433

Wennervirta, Ludvig. Suomen keskiaikainen kirkkomaalaus . . . Porvoo, Söderstrom [1937]. 258 p. 135 illus., 73 plates. 26 cm.

A scholarly study of medieval church painting in Finland. "Die mittelalterliche Kirchenmalerei in Finnland, übersetzt von Rita Öhquist" p. [223]–48 is a German résumé of the text. "Chronologische Tabelle" p. 247–48. "Hakemisto" (Index) p. 249–55.

1434

Zahle, Erik, ed. Danmarks malerkunst fra middelalder til nutid . . . 3d. udg. København, Hirschsprung, 1947. 331 p. illus. (part col.) 27 cm.

1st ed. 1937. "Udgivet med tilskud fra Ny Carlsbergfondet." A general survey of painting in Denmark from the Middle Ages to the present day. Sizes of pictures are given under the reproductions.

"Litteratur om dansk malerkunst" p. [321]–24. "Danmarks offentlige malerisamlinger" p. 325–26. "Register over danske og indvandrede kunstnere" p. 327–31.

Spain

1435

Beruete y Moret, Aureliano de. Historia de la pintura española en el siglo XIX; elementos nacionales y extranjeros que han influido en ella. Madrid [Blass] 1926. 162 p. plates (part col.) 28 cm.

Contains 66 plates, four in color. Bibliography p. 149–50. Index of plates p. 152–53; of artists p. 154–62.

1436

Domínguez, Bordona, Jesús. Spanish illumination. Firenze, Pantheon [1929?] 2 v. 160 plates (incl. facsims.) 33 cm.

Volume 1 covers Visigothic through 12th century and Romanesque in Catalonia; v. 2 covers 13th century through 16th. List of manuscripts v. 2, p. 73–77, arranged by location. Bibliography v. 2, p. 78–85. Alphabetical index v. 2, p. 87–100.

1437

Gudiol i Cunill, Josep G. Els primitius. Barcelona, Babra, 1927–55. 3 v. illus., plates. 26 cm. (La pintura mig-eval catalana)

Good treatment of early medieval Catalan painting, profusely illustrated with pictures of fair quality. Contents: (1) Els pintors: la pintura mural; (2) La pintura sobra fusta; (3) Els llibres illuminats.

"Notes documentals sobre els pintors primitius" v. 1, p. 57–84. Includes bibliographies. At end of each volume an alphabetical index and an index of illustrations. Volume 3 also has an index of manuscripts.

1438

Guinard, Paul, and Baticle, Jeannine. Histoire de la peinture espagnole du XIIe au XIXe siècle . . . Paris, Tisné, 1950. 173 p. illus. (part col.) 37 cm.

Primarily a picture book with many color plates. Text by competent authors.

1439

Harris, Enriqueta. Spanish painting. Paris, Hyperion; N.Y., French and European publications [c1937]. 32 p. 104 plates (part col.) 33 cm.

Edited by André Gloeckner. Although basically a picture book it has a good short text of 17 pages. Good black and white plates but the colored ones leave much to be desired.

"The artists" p. 24–29 lists artists covered and gives a short biographical paragraph for each. Bibliography p. 30–32.

1440

Kuhn, Charles Louis. The Romanesque mural painting of Catalonia . . . Cambridge, Harvard Univ. Press, 1930. 102 p. 63 plates, map. 31 cm.

The basic work in English in this subject field. Part 1 "contains a detailed study of the monuments and an attempt to establish a definite chronology for the more important ones. Those of less significance have been relegated to a separate chapter and are arranged in alphabetic order regardless of date. The 2nd section contains a consideration of more general problems such as technique, iconography, origins of style and division of the paintings into stylistic and geographic groups."—*Pref.*

Map shows the geographic distribution of the frescoes. Bibliographical footnotes. Index p. 99–103.

1441

Lafuente Ferrari, Enrique. Breve historia de la pintura española. Cuarta edición revisada y ampliada. Con CCXL láminas que contienen 322 ilustraciones más ocho en color. Madrid, Editorial Tecnos. 1953. 657 p. 240 plates (part col.) 25 cm. (Colección Sintesis de arte)

Considered a very good one-volume history of Spanish painting. Bibliography p. 537–56 is arranged by chapters. Synoptical tables of Spanish painting p. 559–607. Index of persons p. 611–31; of places p. 633–44; of illustrations p. 645–52.

1442

Mayer, August Liebmann. Historia de la pintura española . . . 2 ed. Madrid, Espasa-Calpe, 1942. 556 p. illus., plates (part col.) 28 cm.

Originally published in German. 1st ed. 1928. Covers Spanish painting from the Romanesque through the 18th and early 19th century. Bibliography p. 541–44. Index of artists p. 545–56.

1443

Post, Chandler Rathfon. A history of Spanish painting. Cambridge, Harvard Univ. Press, 1930–(58). (12) v. in (18). illus. 25 cm.

The definitive work in the field. Contents: v. I, pt. 1, Pre-Romanesque style; pt. 2, The Romanesque style; v. II, pt. 3, The Franco-Gothic style; pt. 4, The Italo-Gothic and international styles; v. III, pt. 4 continued; v. IV, pt. 1–2, The Hispano-Flemish style in northwestern Spain; v. V, The Hispano-Flemish style in Andalusia; v. VI, pt. 1–2, The Valencian school in the late Middle Ages and early Renaissance; v. VII, pt. 1–2, The Catalan school in the late Middle Ages; v. VIII, pt. 1–2, The Aragonese school in the late Middle Ages; v. IX, pt. 1–2, The beginning of the Renaissance in Castile and Leon; v. X, The early Renaissance in Andalusia; v. XI, The Valencian school in the early Renaissance; v. XII, pt. 1–2, The Catalan school in the early Renaissance.

Includes bibliographies. General bibliography at beginning of v. 1 and additional ones before each index. Index for v. 1–3 at end of v. 3, subsequently one at end of each volume (not each part). Each index divided into names and places.

1444

Richert, Gertrud. La pintura medieval en España, pinturas murales y tablas catalanas; traducción del alemán, por José Ontañón. Barcelona, Gili, 1926. 84 p. plates. 30 cm.

At head of title: Dra. Gertrudis Richert. Edition of 1000 copies. Covers medieval painting in Spain, with 77 pages of text and 111 plates, which are fairly good halftones. No index.

1445

Sánchez-Camargo, Manuel. Pintura española contemporánea; nueva escuela, I. Madrid, Ed. Cultura Hispánica, 1954. 591 p. plates. 27 cm.

This volume covers ten contemporary painters. Gives for each artist: biographical material and commentary on his painting, ten halftone reproductions of his work, list of exhibitions, and index of paintings.

1446

Sanpere y Miquel, Salvador. Los cuatrocentistas catalanes; historia de la pintura en Cataluña en el siglo XV; obra premiada por la Junta municipal de bellas artes de Barcelona en 1902 e ilustrada con 180 fotograbados . . . Barcelona, "L'Avenc," 1906. 2 v. illus., plates. 24 cm.

A history of 15th century Catalan painting. Contents: Tomo I, Primera mitad del siglo XV; Tomo II, Segunda mitad del siglo XV.

Some bibliography given in "Literarias" v. 1, p. 14–18. Volume 2 contains indexes of: authors p. [lxxxvii]–xcv; artists p. [lxxiii–lxxxii]; places p. [lxxxiii]–lxxxvi; plates and illustrations p. [xcvii]–ci.

1447

Sanpere y Miquel, Salvador, and Gudiol i Cunill, Josep G. Els trescentistes. Barcelona, Babra [1924] 2 v. illus., plates. 24 cm. (La pintura mig-eval catalana II)

A treatment of 14th century Catalan painting with numerous illustrations, not always of high quality.

"Notes documentals sobre els escriptors i miniaturistes catalans" v. 2, p. [305]–39. Alphabetical index v. 2, p. [371]–82. List of illustrations v. 2, p. [383]–87.

1448

Sentenach y Cabañas, Narciso. Los grandes retratistas en España, obra ilustrada con 45 laminas en fototipia. Madrid, Hauser y Menet, 1914. 147 p. 2 facsims., 8 plates, 35 ports. 28 cm.

A general survey of Spanish portrait painting. "Indice de autores, citados por orden alfabético" p. 144–47. "Indice de laminas, por orden alfabético de ses autores" p. [148].

SEE ALSO: Huard. Vie complète des peintres espagnols (1174).

Switzerland

1449

Bovy, Adrien. La peinture suisse de 1600 à 1900. Bâle, Birkhaeuser, 1948. 194 p. illus. (part col.) 27 cm. (Art suisse: collection de dix monographies, t. 4)

A general treatment of Swiss painting, with each chapter covering a century. Illustrated by halftones in the text. "Bibliographie sommaire" p. 182. "Index des noms d'artistes" p. 183–89. "Table des illustrations" p. 190–93.

1450

Ganz, Paul. La peinture suisse avant la renaissance. Trans. par Paul Budry. Paris, Budry, 1925. 156 p. illus., 120 plates. 36 cm.

French ed. limited to 300 copies. Also a German ed. (Zürich, Berichthaus, 1924). Covers Swiss painting before the Renaissance. Contains excellent plates, each preceded by a sheet giving a short description of the painting, its size, and location.

Contents: Table et sommaire des chapitres p. xi–xii; Table des planches p. xiii–xvii; Table des illustrations p. xvii–xviii; Index des noms et des lieux cités p. xix–xxiii; 148 pages of text arranged geographically; Remarques et appendices p. [149]–56 which are really bibliographical footnotes.

1451

Gradmann, Erwin, and Cetto, Anna Maria. Schweizer Malerei und Zeichnung im 17. und 18. Jahrhundert. Basel, Holbein, 1944. 5–75 p. 71 plates on 39 l. 33 cm.

Swiss painting and drawing of the 17th and 18th centuries. Consists of 32 pages of descriptive text, referring in the margins to specific plates.

"Erläuterungen zu den Bildern, von Anna Maria Cetto" p. 39–[76] gives sizes and bibliography. "Künstlerverzeichnis" p. [77].

1452

Jedlicka, Gotthard. Zur schweizerischen Malerei der Gegenwart . . . Erlenbach-Zürich, Rentsch [1947] 182 p. 48 illus., 1 col. plate. 21 cm.

Various chapters cover the work of 16 contemporary Swiss painters, and one chapter gives a general survey of the painting. "Verzeichnis der Abbildungen" p. 181–82 merely lists the plates in the order in which they appear.

1453

Neuweiler, Arnold. La peinture à Genève de 1700 à 1900 . . . Genève, Jullien [1945]. 9–233 p. illus. 33 cm.

Edition of 500 copies printed. Introduction, "La peinture genevoise," by Adrien Bovy. A survey of Genevan painting from Jean Petit to the beginning of the 20th century, illustrated by rotogravures in the text.

"Répertoire général des artistes genevois ou ayant séjourné à Genève (peintres, dessinateurs, miniaturistes, peintres sur émail) nés avant 1881" p. 155–200. "L'enseignement des beaux-arts à Genève—Un résumé chronologique de l'histoire des écoles d'art à Genève depuis le XVIIIe siècle, suivi d'un liste complète des professeurs ayant enseigné dans ces écoles"; "La liste complète des lauréats des concours de la Société des Arts"; "Quelques renseignements sur les fausses attributions."

"Bibliographie sommaire" p. 230. "Index et abbréviations" p. 231. "Index des illustrations" p. 232–33.

1454
Schmidt, Georg. Schweizer Malerei und Zeichnung im 15. und 16. Jahrhundert . . . Basel, Holbein [1940]. [5]–51 p. 86 plates (14 mounted col.) on 50 l. 33 cm.

A survey of Swiss painting and drawing in the 15th and 16th centuries. "Erläuterungen zu den Bildern" p. iii–xxxviii gives sizes of paintings and bibliographies. "Künstler Verzeichnis" p. [xxxix].

1455
Wescher, Paul Reinhold. Die Romantik in der schweizer Malerei. Frauenfeld, Huber [1947]. 106 p. 71 plates. 28 cm.

A survey of romantic painting in Switzerland. Bibliography p. [109–12] following the plates. A five-page artist index at end of book which gives dates of birth and death, and a few biographical sentences.

United States

1456
Barker, Virgil. American painting, history and interpretation. N.Y., Macmillan, 1950. 717 p. illus. 26 cm.

A good modern survey of American painting. At the beginning of each chapter the artists discussed therein are listed with their dates.

Bibliographical references in "Notes" p. 669–92. Index p. 693–717 includes "Owners of the paintings mentioned in this book" (p. 714–17).

1457
Born, Wolfgang. American landscape painting; an interpretation. New Haven, Yale Univ. Press, 1948. 228 p. illus. 29 cm.

A historical survey of the subject. Bibliographical references included in "Notes" p. [217]–21. "List of illustrations" p. [vii]–xiii gives size of paintings. Index p. 223–28.

1458
Born, Wolfgang. Still-life painting in America. N.Y., Oxford Univ. Press, 1947. 54 [98] p. (p. [3–98] illus.) 32 cm.

A general history of still-life painting in America, written by a competent scholar. Good clear reproductions. "List of illustrations" p. xi–xiv gives size of pictures. No index.

1459
Brown, Milton Wolf. American painting, from the Armory Show to the depression. Princeton, Princeton Univ. Press, 1955. 243 p. illus. 29 cm.

"This study is concerned with the origins, nature and development of modern art movements in this country and their interaction with the already established tradition of realism."—*Introd.*

Covers the period between 1913 and 1929. Bibliography p. 201–37. Index p. 239–44.

1460
Burroughs, Alan. Limners and likenesses; three centuries of American painting . . . Cambridge, Harvard Univ. Press, 1936. 246 p. plates, ports. 26 cm. (Harvard-Radcliffe fine arts series)

A scholarly, critical history of American painting, with particular emphasis on portraiture.

Bibliography p. [223]–26, and in "Notes." Index p. [231]–46.

1461
Drepperd, Carl W. American pioneer arts and artists. Springfield, Mass., Pond-Ekberg, 1942. 172 p. illus. 27 cm.

A popular type of work. Discusses primitive landscapes, genre painting, portraits, miniatures, carvings, stencils, folk art, etc. One chapter is devoted to "Art instruction books to the American people" with bibliography; another to "Teachers of art to the American people," and another to "The collecting of pioneer American art."

Includes bibliographies in text and a "Source bibliography" p. 170–[77]. No index.

1462
Flexner, James Thomas. American painting. v. 1, First flowers of our wilderness (Boston, Houghton Mifflin, 1947). v. 2, The light of distant skies, 1760–1835 (N.Y., Harcourt Brace [1954]). illus., col. plates. 25 cm.

Each volume is complete in itself but together they form a "projected many-volume history of American painting as an expression of American life."—*Pref.,* v. 2. Well illustrated (v. 1 has some color plates).

Each volume contains: "Bibliography of general sources" and of "source references" (in addition, v. 2 contains "Bibliographies arranged by artists" p. 257–69); "Catalogue of illustrations"; and an index.

1463

Isham, Samuel. The history of American painting . . . with 12 full-page photogravures and 121 illustrations in the text. New ed. with supplemental chapters by Royal Cortissoz . . . N.Y., Macmillan, 1927. 608 p. incl. plates. 29 cm.

Originally published in 1905 as v. 3 of *The History of American art*, ed. by J. C. Van Dyke. Long considered the standard work in this field.

"Bibliography, compiled by Henry Meier" p. 593–600. "Index of painters' names" p. 601–05. "Index to supplementary chapters (p. 561–592)" p. 607–08.

1464

Janis, Sidney. They taught themselves; American primitive painters of the 20th century . . . foreword by Alfred H. Barr, Jr. N.Y., Dial, 1942. 236 p. illus. (incl. ports.) 26 cm.

". . . A catalogue of the lives of 30 human beings, of 54 paintings. . . . A selection of noteworthy self-taught talents in contemporary American painting, to discuss their works, to record salient experiences on the part of the artists in creating these works."—*Pref.*

For each of the artists gives a portrait and a discussion of the paintings reproduced, frequently quoting the artist's own words.

1465

Lipman, Jean. American primitive painting . . . London, N.Y., Oxford Univ. Press, 1942. 158 p. incl. illus. plates (part col.) 31 cm.

"Selected bibliography" p. 139–42 is arranged chronologically. "List of important exhibitions, 1924–1942" p. 143–45. "Primitive painters known by name" p. 147–58.

1466

Lipman, Jean, and Winchester, Alice, comps. Primitive painters in America, 1750–1950; an anthology . . . N.Y., Dodd, Mead, 1950. 182 p. illus. (part col.) 27 cm.

A compilation of 20 essays by various authors, each devoted to one artist. Well illustrated.

"Record of primitive painters" p. 168–82 gives name of painter, location, date, subject, and medium.

1467

Little, Nina Fletcher. American decorative wall painting, 1700–1850. Sturbridge, Mass.,

Old Sturbridge Village, in cooperation with Studio Publications, N.Y., 1952. 145 p. illus. (part col.) 29 cm.

Well illustrated with some color plates. Bibliography (classed and selective) p. 138–40. Index p. 141–45. "Biographical list of painters" p. 129–32. "Checklist of pictorial panels" p. 133–37.

1468

Richardson, Edgar Preston. Painting in America. The story of 450 years. N.Y., Crowell [c1956]. 447 p. plates (part col.) 26 cm. (The Growth of America series)

A sound treatment of the subject. Selected bibliography p. 417–27. Index p. 429–47.

Techniques

1469

Alston, Rowland Wright. Painter's idiom, a technical approach to painting. London, N.Y., Staples Press [1954]. 165 p. illus. 22 cm.

A rather popular volume which is "meant as an introduction to the works of such men as Sir Charles Eastlake, Max Doerner and A. P. Laurie."—*Pref.*

Part 1 is a description of methods while pt. 2 describes the techniques used by various masters, with emphasis on the 18th century. Bibliography p. 161–62. Index p. 163–65.

1470

Birren, Faber. The story of color, from ancient mysticism to modern science. Westport, Conn., The Crimson Press, 1941. 338 p. illus. (part col.) diagrs. 31 cm.

A survey of the history of theories of color by a recognized authority. Bibliography p. 328–32. Index p. 333–38.

1471

Bradley, Morton C. The treatment of pictures. Cambridge, Mass., Art Technology, 1950. 304 p. illus. 23 cm.

In loose-leaf form so that it can be corrected and improved. "Useful only as a handbook for competent conservators and curators and for students working under their direction."—*Pref.* Contains descriptions of various processes and formulae. A glossary of 7 p. and an index of 6 p.

1472

Cennini, Cennino. Il libro dell'arte . . . New Haven, Yale Univ. Press; London, Milford, Oxford Univ. Press, 1932–33. 2 v. illus., plates, facsims. 24 cm.

Volume 1 is the Italian text with an account of the prior editions of this work. Index p. 133–42.

Volume 2 is *The craftsman's handbook,* translated by D. V. Thompson. An offset of this latter title published 1954 (N.Y., Dover).

1473
Constable, William George. The painter's workshop. London, N.Y., Oxford Univ. Press, 1954. 148 p. 25 plates. 25 cm.

Written by a recognized authority and intended for laymen and art historians. Covers wax, pastel, water-color, fresco, tempera, and oil painting. Bibliography p. [137]–39. Index p. 141–48.

1474
Doerner, Max. The materials of the artist and their use in painting, with notes on the techniques of the old masters . . . translated by Eugen Neuhaus. Rev. ed. . . . N.Y., Harcourt, Brace [1949]. 435 p. plates. 22 cm.

1st ed. 1934. A standard work by a German authority which covers pigments, oil, tempera, pastel, water colors, mural painting, the techniques of the old masters, and restoring of easel pictures. Especially useful for the practicing artist.

Bibliography p. 415, with short annotations. Index p. 419–35.

1475
Eastlake, *Sir* Charles Locke. Materials for a history of oil painting . . . London, Brown, Green, and Longmans, 1847–69. 2 v. 22 cm.

A standard work. Volume 1 treats of the material relating to the Flemish method, and v. 2 of the Italian system.

1476
Gettens, Rutherford John, and Stout, George L. Painting materials, a short encyclopedia . . . with an introduction by Edward W. Forbes. N.Y., Van Nostrand, 1942. 333 p. illus., diagrs. 25 cm.

Originally published as separate sections in *Technical studies in the field of fine arts* (2349) from 1936 until 1941. Contents: (1) Mediums, adhesives and film substances; (2) Pigments and inert materials; (3) Solvents, diluents and detergents; (4) Supports; (5) Tools and equipment; (6) Glossary. Items arranged alphabetically under these six divisions.

Illustrated by some line drawings in the text. Bibliography at the end of each chapter. No general index.

1477
Hiler, Hilaire. Notes on the technique of painting, with a preface by Sir William Rothenstein. London, Faber, 1954. 346 p. facsim. 23 cm.

1st ed. 1934; reprinted 1947 and 1948. This is a new rev. ed.

Written by a practicing artist and covers: Supports and grounds, color and pigments, vehicles and media, and the conservation of paintings. Appendix: "Pigments at a glance" p. 297–302. Glossary p. 334–39. Index p. 340–46.

1478
Hours-Miedan, Madeleine. À la découverte de la peinture par les méthodes physiques. [Paris] Arts et Métiers Graphiques [1957]. 147 p. illus. 32 cm.

A collection of excellent halftones, mostly from the Département des Peintures du Musée du Louvre, with accompanying text, describing modern technical studies and methods in regard to painting. "Notes techniques" p. 134–37. "Bibliographie choisie" p. 139–44.

1479
Hubbard, Eric Hesketh. Materia pictoria. [An encyclopedia of methods in painting and the graphic arts], 2d ed. London, Pitman, 1948– . 329 p. v. 1: Oil painting. 19 cm.

1st ed. 1939. "A good deal of fresh material not printed in the first edition has been added for the second."—*Pref.* Intended to be issued in four volumes (v. 2–4 to deal with water color, fresco, tempera, encaustic, and other methods of painting, and with pigments and materials of drawing and engraving).

Arranged in dictionary form with a "List of painters, writers and others mentioned in the text" p. 327–29, and a glossary. Bibliography p. 324–26.

1480
International Museum Office. Manual on the conservation of paintings. [Paris] International museums office [c1940]. 296 p. illus., tables. 24 cm. (Publications of the International Institute of Intellectual Co-operation [League of nations])

Published also in French. A standard work.

Contents: pt. 1, Conservation; pt. 2, Restoration. Appendices: Practical recommendations p. 257–62. "Table of colours" p. 273–91 gives names of colors in English, French, German, Italian and their composition, use in painting, and alteration and restoration. Index p. 293–96.

1481
Keck, Caroline K. How to take care of your pictures, a primer of practical information. Illustrations by Ruth Sheetz Eisendrath. [N.Y.] The Museum of Modern Art & The Brooklyn Museum [1954]. 54 p. illus. 26 cm.

A useful summary of the field by a well-known restorer. Bibliography p. 54.

1482
Laurie, Arthur Pillans. Greek and Roman methods of painting: some comments on the statements made by Pliny and Vitruvius about wall and panel painting. Cambridge, Eng., Univ. Press, 1910. 124 p. 2 col. plates, diagrs. 19 cm.

A short discussion with a few color plates illustrating wax painting, etc. Index p. 120–24.

1483
Laurie, Arthur Pillans. The materials of the painter's craft in Europe and Egypt, from earliest times to the end of the XVIIth century, with some account of their preparation and use . . . Philadelphia, Lippincott, 1910. 443 p. illus., plates (part col., mounted), facsims. 20 cm.

A London ed. (The Arts and crafts of the nations; General editor, S. H. F. Capenny) published by T. N. Foulis, 1910. Gives Egyptian and classical methods, fresco painting, manuscript illumination, preparation of lakes used by old masters, and a history of the oil medium.

Bibliography p. 386–[434]. Index p. 435–[444].

1484
Laurie, Arthur Pillans. The painter's methods & materials; the handling of pigments in oil, tempera, water-colour and in mural painting, the preparation of grounds & canvas & the prevention of discolouration, together with the theories of light & colour, applied to the making of pictures, all described in a practical & non technical manner . . . Philadelphia, Lippincott, 1926. 249 p. illus., plates, diagrs. 21 cm.

Written for a craftsman painter, not a chemist.

1485
Laurie, Arthur Pillans. The technique of the great painters. London, Carroll and Nicholson, 1949. 192 p. illus., 27 plates (part col.) 26 cm.

"The object of this book is to sum up for the student of the history of art what we know about pigments, mediums, and methods of painting from Egyptian times to the present day."—*Foreword*.

Contents: Classical period (Egypt, Greece, Rome); Medieval period (rise of Christian art to 1550); Later centuries; Varnishes; Forgeries; Persian illuminated manuscripts. Some bibliographical suggestions are made in the Foreword. Index p. 191–92.

1486
Leonardo da Vinci. Treatise on painting <Codex urbinas latinus 1270> Translated and annotated by A. Philip McMahon. With an introd. by Ludwig H. Heydenreich. Princeton, Princeton Univ. Press, 1956. 2 v. illus. 23 cm.

A facsimile and scholarly modern translation of this important Renaissance treatise on the technique of painting. The facsimile reproduces the Italian text (which is a compilation by Francesco Melzi of notes from the original manuscript of Leonardo) and has caption title: *Libro di pittura* di M. Lionardo da Vinci . . .

Contents: v. 1, Translation; v. 2, Facsimile. "Table of headings" v. 1, p. 337–57. "A selective bibliography, compiled from the notes of A. Philip McMahon and supplemented by Kate Trauman Steinitz" v. 1, p. [359]–96. Concordance v. 1, p. 398–424.

1487
Luckiesch, Matthew. Color and its applications . . . N.Y., Van Nostrand, 1921. 2d ed. enl. 419 p. illus., 4 col. plates, diagrs., tables. 24 cm.

1st ed. 1915. "The aim of this book is to present a condensed treatment of the science of color . . . an attempt to cover as many phases of the subject as possible within the confines of a small volume." A standard book on the subject of color. Index to authors p. 407–09. Subject index p. 411–19.

1488
Maroger, Jacques. The secret formulas and techniques of the masters, tr. from the French by Eleanor Beckham. N.Y., Studio [1948]. 200 p. illus. 24 cm. (An American Studio book)

A description of various techniques of the old masters written by the former technical director of the laboratory of the Louvre Museum. Bibliography p. 195–96. Index of painters p. 197–200.

1489
Mayer, Ralph. The artist's handbook of materials and technique. Rev. ed. N.Y., Viking, 1957. 721 p. illus. 22 cm.

1st ed. of 561 pages published 1940; 9th printing 1953. This new edition contains some rearrangement of material, and the bibliography has been brought up to date.

"This book prepared for the purpose of giving the artist a complete and up to date account of the materials and methods of his craft . . . included [are] a few notes on matters that are not ordinarily classified with materials and methods but that bear a similar practical relation to the artist's technique."—*Pref.* Covers: Pigments, oil painting, tempera, grounds for oil and tempera, pastel, mural painting, miscellaneous materials, chemistry, conservation of pictures, and miscellaneous notes. Bibliographies p. 675–96. Index p. 697–721.

1490

Mayer, Ralph. The painter's craft; an introduction to the artists' materials. N.Y., Van Nostrand [1948]. 218 p. illus. 24 cm.

"This book is designed as a text for class or workshop instruction and as a guide for the practicing painter who wishes to acquire by independent study a systematic knowledge of the standard data relating to the craft on which his art is based. It presents the basic background knowledge that any artist must have in order to succeed as a competent professional or amateur."—*Pref.*

Contents: (1) Introduction; (2) Color; (3) Pigments; (4) Grounds; (5) Oil painting; (6) Tempera painting; (7) Aqueous paints; (8) Pastel; (9) Mural painting; (10) Studies and equipment.

Additional reading p. 211 (three titles). Index p. 213–18.

1491

Merrifield, *Mrs.* Mary Philadelphia. The art of fresco painting, as practised by the old Italian and Spanish masters, with a preliminary inquiry into the nature of the colours used in fresco painting, with observations and notes. New illustrated ed., with an introd. by A. C. Sewter. London, Tiranti, 1952. 134 p. 4 illus. 22 cm.

Also published in the United States by Transatlantic Press, 1953. First published 1846. This is a facsimile reprint of the original with a few corrections of obvious misprints and errors.

"A collection of historical texts on the techniques and materials employed by fresco painters at various dates from about the 12th to the 18th centuries and a guide and manual for the artist."—*Introd.* Index p. [129]–34.

1492

Merrifield, *Mrs.* Mary Philadelphia. Original treatises, dating from the XIIth to XVIIIth centuries on the arts of painting, in oil, miniature, mosaic, and on glass; of gilding, dyeing, and the preparation of colours and artificial gems; preceded by a general introduction; with translations, prefaces, and notes . . . London, Murray, 1849. 2 v. illus. 22 cm.

Paged continuously. An old but standard work which is still very useful. Texts arranged chronologically. Index v. 2, p. 898–918.

1493

Munsell, Albert Henry. A color notation. An illustrated system defining all colors and their relations by measured scales of hue, value, and chroma. Introduction by Royal B. Farnum. 10th ed. (edited and rearranged). Baltimore, Munsell Color Co., 1946. 74 p. illus., 3 col. plates, diagrs. 20 cm.

Contains a glossary of color terms and an index by paragraphs.

1494

Museum. The care of paintings. Le traitement des peintures. [Paris, 1951]. 161 p. illus. 31 cm. (UNESCO Publication 778)

Text in English and French. "The articles published here first appeared in *Museum* volumes III nos. 2, 3, 1950 and IV no. 1, 1951." A group of articles covering results of restoration as carried out in various countries. Index p. 153–62.

1495

Ostwald, Wilhelm. Colour science; a handbook for advanced students in schools, colleges, and the various arts, crafts, and industries depending on the use of colour . . . Authorized translation with an introduction and notes by J. Scott Taylor . . . London, Winsor & Newton [1931–33]. 2 v. illus., col. plates, diagrs. 23 cm.

A standard book on color theory written by a recognized authority. It covers color measurement, the physico-chemical aspect of color, as well as the psycho-physical.

Contents: pt. 1, Colour theory and standards of colour; pt. 2, Applied colour science.

1496

Pope, Arthur. The language of drawing and painting. Cambridge, Harvard Univ. Press [1949]. 162 p. illus., [72] plates (part col.) 24 cm.

"A revision and rearrangement of . . . [the

author's] two earlier books, *The painter's terms* and *The painter's modes of expression."—Pref.*

Contents: (1) The terms of drawing and painting; (2) Modes of representation. Appendices: (1) Design in tone relations; (2) The emotional significance of different general tonalities; (3) The question of preference for individual tones; (4) A hybrid mode of drawing an illustration in Winchester MSS. "Bibliographical note" p. 160–62.

1497

Richmond, Leonard, and Littlejohns, L. The technique of water-colour painting. N.Y., Pitman, 1944. 143 p. 47 mounted col. illus. 28 cm.

A useful discussion of water-color techniques intended for the practicing artist.

1498

Ross, Denman Waldo. On drawing and painting . . . Boston and N.Y., Houghton Mifflin, 1912. 214 p. diagrs. 26 cm.

Contents: (1) Introduction; (2) Materials and first exercises; (3) Set palettes; (4) Drawing and painting; (5) On design; (6) On pure and applied design; (7) On representation; (8) Modes of representation; (9) Representation in forms of design; (10) Conclusion; (11) Appendix—the 48 palettes of 12 colors in 12 values with black and white.

1499

Schmid, Frédéric. The practice of painting. London, Faber [1948]. 125 p. illus. 26 cm.

"The present work tries to give a historical representation of the practice of drawing and painting of the past centuries."—*Pref.* Particularly useful for the techniques of the 17th and 18th centuries and their colors and palettes. Includes bibliographies with text and Bibliography p. 119–20. Index p. 121–25.

1500

Sepeshy, Zoltan L. Tempera painting. N.Y. and London, American Studio Books [1946]. 79 p. incl. 1 illus., plates (part col.) 24 cm.

A technical description of this medium by a practicing artist.

1501

Stout, George Leslie. The care of pictures. N.Y., Columbia Univ. Press, 1948. 125 p. illus., 24 plates. 24 cm.

"An introduction to problems in the care of pictures" (*Pref.*) by a recognized authority in the field.

Appendix A: Record abstracts of repair treatment p. 93–104. Appendix B: Special means of examination p. 105–13. Bibliography p. [115]–20. Index p. 121–25.

1502

Taubes, Frederic. The technique of oil painting; a discussion of traditional oil techniques for use by the contemporary painter, with frontispiece in color and sixteen black and white plates. N.Y., Dodd, Mead, 1941. 99 p. illus., plates. 24 cm.

"State of preservation and execution of paintings from the collection of the Metropolitan Museum in New York" p. 84–91. Index p. 97–99.

1503

Theophilus, *called also* Rugerus. Theophili, qui et Rugerus, presbyteri et monachi, libri III. de diversis artibus; seu, Diversarum artium schedula. Opera et studio R. Hendrie. Londini, Murray, 1847. 447 p. 2 col. facsims. 22 cm.

Added title page: An essay upon various arts, in three books, by Theophilus, called also Rugerus, priest and monk, forming an encyclopaedia of Christian art of the eleventh century. Translated, with notes, by Robert Hendrie. London, Murray, 1847.

Latin text, with English translation, preface, and notes. An early treatise dating from the 10th or 12th century, describing the techniques in use at that time. Index p. 444–47.

1504

Thompson, Daniel Varney. The materials of medieval painting; with a foreword by Bernhard Berenson. New Haven, Yale Univ. Press, 1936. 239 p. 22 cm.

An unabridged and unaltered reprint published 1956 under title: *Materials and techniques of medieval painting* (N.Y., Dover). A paperback ed. issued by Dover, 1958.

Covers only the materials of painting in medieval Europe. Contents: (1) Carriers and grounds; (2) Binding media; (3) Pigments; (4) Metals. Index p. 231–39.

1505

Thompson, Daniel Varney. The practice of tempera painting . . . illustrated by Lewis E. York . . . New Haven, Yale Univ. Press; London, Milford, Oxford Univ. Press, 1936. 141 p. illus., plates, diagrs. 24 cm.

"The basis of the method that this book endeavors to explain is the account of Giottesque tempera painting given by Cennino d'Andrea Cennini in his 'Libro dell'arte.' "—*Pref.* A standard work on this subject.

"Appendix. Tempera practice in the Yale art school [by] Professor Lewis E. York" p. [132]–38. Index p. [139]–41.

1506
Toch, Maximilian. The chemistry and technology of paints. 3d ed. rev. and enl. N.Y., Van Nostrand, 1925. 413 p. 112 illus. 24 cm.

First published 1907, the "first book ever written on mixed paints." An extremely technical book intended for students in chemistry or paint manufacturers as a work of reference. "It is not intended for those who have no previous knowledge or training in the subject."—*Pref*. Bibliography p. 403–05.

1507
Toch, Maximilian. Paint, paintings and restoration . . . 2d ed. N.Y., Van Nostrand [1945]. 149 p. plates. 22 cm.

1st ed. 1931. "Book written for the artist, painter and manufacturer and the student." —*Pref*. Well illustrated. Bibliography p. 145–46. Index p. 147–49.

1508
Ward, James. History and methods of ancient and modern painting from the earliest times to the beginning of the Renaissance period including the methods and materials of the painter's craft of ancient and modern times. London, Chapman & Hall, 1913–21. 4 v. plates. 23 cm.

Not scholarly but useful for descriptions of techniques.

Contents: v. 1, From the earliest times to the beginning of the Renaissance period including the methods and materials of the painter's craft of ancient and modern times; v. 2, Italian painting from the beginning of the Renaissance period including the work of the principal artists from Cimabue to the Pollaiuoli; v. 3, Italian painting of the fifteenth and sixteenth centuries, including the work of the principal artists of the Florentine, Umbro-Florentine, Paduan, Muranese, and Venetian (to the Vivarini and their followers) schools; v. 4, Italian painting from the fifteenth to the eighteenth century, including the work of the principal artists and their followers of the various Italian schools not already treated in the previous volumes of this work. Each volume has its own index.

1509
Wild, Angenitus Martinus de. The scientific examination of pictures; an investigation of the pigments used by the Dutch and Flemish masters from the brothers Van Eyck to the middle of the 19th century. . . . With a foreword by Prof. Dr. F. E. C. Scheffer. Translated from the Dutch by L. C. Jackson. London, Bell, 1929. 106 p. 46 plates, diagrs. 23 cm.

A translation of *Het natuurwetenschappelijk onderzoek van schilderijen* . . . [1928].

Contents: (1) Historical and scientific investigations; (2) Blue pigments; (3) White pigments; (4) Yellow and brown pigments; (5) Red pigments; (6) Green pigments; (7) The restoration and preservation of paintings; (8) X-ray photography of paintings, Examination of paintings by means of ultraviolet light, Chronological chart of pigments. Bibliographical footnotes.

CHAPTER 15

Prints and Engravings

Bibliography

1510

Bourcard, Gustave. Graveurs et gravures, France et étranger; essai de bibliographie 1540–1910. Paris, Floury, 1910. 320 p. 25 cm.

Arranged alphabetically by subject in the case of monographs, or by author.

Includes books and periodical articles on engravers and engraving.

1511

Colin, Paul. La gravure et les graveurs. Bruxelles, van Oest, 1916–18. 2 v. 25 cm.

A classed bibliography listing 610 items in v. 1, with important items starred. Under each group or class books are listed chronologically according to language. Preference is given to the original language in which the work was published. Alphabetical author index at end of volume.

Volume 2, *Les Monographies*, contains 2659 entries listed alphabetically by name of artist and chronologically under the artist. List of periodicals with bibliographical information p. 305–25. Author index p. 327–44.

Errata and addenda to v. 1 at end of v. 2.

1512

Courboin, François, and Roux, Marcel. La gravure française; essai de bibliographie . . . Paris, Le Garrec, 1927–28. 3 v. 29 cm.

525 copies printed.

A classed bibliography including books and periodical articles.

Volume 1 covers various subjects; v. 2, biographical material on individual artists; v. 3, index.

1513

Duplessis, Georges. Essai de bibliographie contenant l'indication des ouvrages relatifs à l'histoire de la gravure et des graveurs. Paris, Rapilly, 1862. 48 p. 22 cm.

A classed bibliography begun as a catalog of his own collection.

Sources were Weigel's *Kunstcatalog* (25) and the bibliographies of M. P. Chéron in the *Gazette des beaux-arts* (2240). Table of contents, p. 45–48, is an index to the work.

1514

Levis, Howard Coppuck. A descriptive bibliography of the most important books in the English language, relating to the art & history of engraving and the collecting of prints . . . London, Ellis, 1912. 571 p. incl. illus. 30 cm.

"Only 350 copies of this book have been printed of which twenty-five have been reserved for presentation and copyright."

Intends "to describe the most important, interesting or rare books in the English language on the subject (together, of course, with some which are unimportant), and show their development and the relation between them."—*Introd.*

————. Supplement and index, by Howard C. Levis. London, Ellis, 1913. 141 p. illus. 30 cm.

SEE ALSO: Someren. Essai d'une bibliographie (1132).

Biography

1515

Basan, Pierre François. Dictionnaire des graveurs anciens et modernes, depuis l'origine de la gravure . . . 2. éd., mise par ordre alphabétique, considérablement augm. et ornée de cinquante estampes par différens artistes célèbres, ou sans aucune, au gré de l'amateur . . . Paris, L'Auteur, 1789. 2 v. 50 plates. 22 cm.

1st ed. 1767. Covers both dead and living artists, arranged in dictionary form. At end of v. 2 a list of artists found in Strutt's dictionary (1527), which are not in this one because they are unknown to the author or not considered important (p. 278–95); and a similar list for Grandinelli (p. 296–304).

1516

Beraldi, Henri. Les graveurs du XIXe siècle; guide de l'amateur d'estampes modernes . . . Paris, Conquet, 1885–92. 12 v. 24 cm.

A dictionary of engravers, arranged alphabetically, which attempts to be an inventory of prints of the 19th century. Gives short biographies of the artists, "sober appreciations," and lists of works that are as complete as possible.

1517

Bushnell, George Herbert. Scottish engravers; a biographical dictionary of Scottish engravers and of engravers who worked in Scotland to the beginning of the nineteenth century. With a chronological index. London, N.Y., Oxford Univ. Press, 1949. 60 p. 20 cm.

Contains "some details of the lives and works of 243 engravers" and is "an unofficial supplement to Bryan" (1144). Under each artist mentions whether he is in Bryan or the *Dictionary of national biography* and gives sources. List of abbreviations of sources p. xi–xii.

1518

Darmon, J. E. Dictionnaire des gravures en couleurs, en bistre et en sanguine du XVIIIe siècle, des écoles française et anglaise, en circulation dans le commerce des estampes, avec leurs prix. Nouv. éd., rev., corr. et augm. . . . Montpellier, Barral, 1929. 142 p. 26 cm.

1st ed. (Paris, 1920) appeared as the joint work of J. E. Darmon and Granger. A dictionary of French and English engravers of the 18th century.

1519

Duplessis, Georges, and Bouchot, Henri. Dictionnaire des marques et monogrammes de graveurs . . . Paris, Rouam, 1886–87. 3 v. 19 cm.

Arranged in dictionary form. Mark or monogram is identified by a few lines giving name of artists, his dates, etc.

General alphabetical index at end of v. 3.

1520

Fielding, Mantle. American engravers upon copper and steel. . . . Biographical sketches and check lists of engravings; a supplement to David McNeely Stauffer's American engravers. Philadelphia, Priv. printed, 1917. 365 p. ports. 25 cm.

Edition of 220 copies. Similar in format to Stauffer (1526). Contains notes, a check list, and a section (p. 298–316) on unknown and unsigned engravings. Index by subject of the engraving p. 321–65.

1521

Grant, Maurice Harold. A dictionary of British etchers. London, pub. for the author by Rockliff [1952]. 232 p. 23 cm.

Under each name gives dates of birth and death (or activity) and a short summary of facts about the artist or his work. No sources given. Popular rather than scholarly.

1522

Heinecken, Karl Heinrich von. Dictionnaire des artistes, dont nous avons des estampes, avec une notice détaillée de leurs ouvrages gravés. t. 1–4. Leipzig, Breitkopf, 1778–90. 4 v. 22 cm.

Volumes 1–4 cover A–Diziani. No more published.

Arranged alphabetically by artist, including painters, engravers, architects, sculptors, goldsmiths, or amateurs, after whose work engravings have been made or who have made engravings. For each artist gives his name, country, year of birth, his master, the medium in which he worked, and date of death. Bibliography of works of the artist is given and references to portraits, where possible.

The catalog of works contains: (1) portraits; (2) Bible subjects, subdivided by Old and New Testament; (3) subjects of devotion; (4) profane history; (5) mythology; (6) allegories; (7) studies.

1523

Pelliccioni, Armando. Dizionario degli artisti incisori italiani (dalle origine al XIX secolo). [Carpi (Modena), Germano, 1949]. 204 p. 22 cm.

A dictionary of Italian engravers up to the 19th century. Short entries for each artist with bibliographical references and indication as to whether or not he is included in Thieme-Becker (225). A small volume which appears to be useful. Appendix p. 201–05.

1524

Rovinskiĭ, Dmitriĭ Aleksandrovich. Podrobnyĭ slovar' russkikh graverov XVI–XIX vv. S.-Peterburg, Tipografiia Imperatorskoĭ Akademii Nauk, 1895. 2 v. illus. (part mount.), plates. 31 cm.

A dictionary of Russian engravers. Contents: t. 1, A–I; t. 2, K–F̃.

1525

Servolini, Luigi. Dizionario illustrato degli incisori italiani moderni e contemporanei. Milano, Görlich [1956]. 871 p. illus., plates (part col.) 30 cm.

A dictionary of modern and contemporary Italian engravers. Gives bibliography for each artist covered and some portraits. Well illustrated in text and with plates, 15 of which are in color.

1526

Stauffer, David McNeely. American engravers upon copper and steel. N.Y., Grolier Club, 1907. 2 v. illus., plates, ports. 25 cm.

Edition of 350 copies. Contents: pt. 1, Biographical sketches, illustrated (containing notes on about 700 American artists, arranged alphabetically), and "Index to engravings described with check-list numbers and names of engravers and artists" p. 317–91; pt. 2, Check-list of the works of the earlier engravers, covering only "the plates of men who were actually engraving in this country before 1825, though all of the work found of any man coming within this classification is covered by the lists."—*Pref.*

1527

Strutt, Joseph. A biographical dictionary; containing an historical account of all engravers, from the earliest period of the art of engraving to the present time; and a short list of their most esteemed works. With cyphers, monograms, and particular marks . . . London, Printed by J. Davis for R. Fauldner, 1785–86. 2 v. illus. 31x24 cm.

"An essay on the art of engraving with a full account of its origin and progress": v. 1, p. 1–29 and v. 2, p. 1–16. At end of each volume a table of monograms used by the engravers.

"A chronological list of the principal engravers" v. 2, p. 449–54. Corrections and additions v. 2, p. 455–58.

1528

Waller, François Gerard. . . . Biographisch woordenboek van Noord Nederlandsche graveurs, uitgegeven door beheerders van het Wallerfonds en bewerkt door W. R. Juynboll; met 61 portretten in lichtdruk. 's Gravenhage, Nijhoff, 1938. 551 p. illus., 60 ports., geneal. tables. 26 cm.

A biographical dictionary of north Dutch engravers including modern artists, some still living. For each artist indicates media in which he worked, dates, and bibliographical information. List of abbreviations in six parallel columns indicating equivalents in Dutch, French, English, German, Italian, and Spanish p. xvi–xix. Bibliography p. 498–544. Chronological list of sources p. 545–51. Appendix A, Engravers and etchers of whom no prints are known. Appendix B, Publishers of prints and maps.

SEE ALSO: Bryan. Bryan's Dictionary of painters and engravers (1144); Comanducci. Dizionario illustrato dei pittori e incisori italiani moderni (1163); Portalis and Beraldi. Les graveurs du 18. siècle (1549); Seyn. Dessinateurs, graveurs et peintres (1170).

Histories and Handbooks

1529

Bartsch, Adam von. Le peintre graveur. . . . Nouv. éd. Würzburg, Verlagsdruckerei Würzburg G.m.b.H., 1920. 21 v. in 18. plates, facsims. 23 cm.

First published 1803–21 (Vienne, Degen); reprinted 1854–76 (Leipzig, Barth). Followed by Robert-Dumesnil (1561) which includes only French engravers, Passavant (1548), and Baudi di Vesme (1573) which is limited to Italian engravers.

Dutch, Flemish, German, and Italian painter-engravers, through the 17th century, are considered; for each artist a general essay on his work, descriptions of his prints, and in some cases an alphabetical list of works discussed.

Contents: v. 1–5, [Niederlaender]; v. 6-11, Les vieux maîtres allemands; v. 12, Les clairs-obscurs des maîtres italiens; v. 13, Les vieux maîtres italiens; v. 14, Oeuvres de Marc-Antoine et de ses deux principaux élèves Augustin de Venise et Marc de Ravenne; v. 15, Estampes de différents graveurs anonymes qui semblent être de l'école de Marc-Antoine Raimondi; v. 16–18, Peintres ou dessinateurs italiens: Maîtres du seizième siècle; v. 19–21, Peintres ou dessinateurs italiens: Maîtres du dix-septième siècle.

At end of some volumes there is an alphabetical list of artists treated therein. Volume 11 is an index to v. 6–11; v. 21 contains an index to catalogs of prints mentioned in v. 1–21.

1530

Bliss, Douglas Percy. A history of wood engraving, with 120 illustrations. London, Dent; N.Y., Dutton, 1928. 263 p. illus., plates. 26 cm.

A general history, from the beginnings through the 20th century, preceded by a clear description of the technique. "Books consulted" p. 253–56. Index p. 259–63.

✓1531
Briquet, Charles Moïse. Les filigranes. Dictionnaire historique des marques du papier dès leur apparition vers 1282 jusqu'en 1600, avec 39 figures dans le texte et 16,112 facsimilés de filigranes. Deuxième édition. Leipzig, Hiersemann, 1923. 4 v. illus., plates, facsims. 32 cm.

A standard work on the history of watermarks from 1282 to 1600, arranged alphabetically by the descriptive titles of the marks. The text describes where and when each watermark was used. Bibliography v. 1, p. [viii]–x.

1532
Churchill, William Algernon. Watermarks in paper in Holland, England, France etc., in the XVII and XVIII centuries and their interconnection. Amsterdam, Hertzberger, 1935. 94, cdxxxii p. illus., facsims. 31 cm.

The text consists mostly of lists of papermakers, arranged by country; the plates reproduce 578 watermarks which correspond to numbers given in the lists.
"Some of the authorities consulted and sources of information" p. 93–94.

1533
Davenport, Cyril James Humphries. Mezzotints . . . London, Methuen, 1904. [208] p. illus., 40 plates. 26 cm. (The connoisseur's library)

Contains a technical description of the process and a historical survey. An index to the plates, preceding the text, contains small line drawings of each plate and gives dimensions, indication of date, publisher and printer, and often prices, together with brief notes on the sitters and subjects.
"List of the more important Works on Mezzotints, as well as of Books containing valuable references to them" p. xv–xviii. General index p. 201–[08].

1534
Delteil, Loys. Manuel de l'amateur d'estampes des XIXe et XXe siècles (1801–1924) avec 158 reproductions hors texte. Paris, Dorbon-Aîné [c1925]. 2 v. plates. 27 cm.

Volume 1 and part of v. 2 contain a history of 19th and 20th century engraving similar in format to Delteil (1535). Each work mentioned is noted at the bottom of the page, with indication of sales and prices.
The text is followed by "Liste des princi-

paux ouvrages relatifs à la gravure aux XIXe et XXe siècles" v. 2, p. [547]–56; "Table alphabétique des principales ventes publiques, avec noms des propriétaires, mentionnés au cours du Manuel . . ." v. 2, p. [559]–61; "Table des noms d'artistes et des titres d'estampes cités" v. 2, p. [565]–629.
———. 700 reproductions d'estampes des XIXe et XXe siècles pour servir de complément au Manuel de l'amateur d'estampes . . . Paris, Dorbon-Aîné [1925]. 2 v. plates. 27 cm.

These two volumes contain plates, chronologically arranged, to supplement the text of the *Manuel*. Each plate bears the number of the page of the text volume where it is mentioned.

1535
Delteil, Loys. Manuel de l'amateur d'estampes du XVIIIe siècle; orné de 106 reproductions hors texte. Paris, Dorbon-l'Aîné [1910]. 447 p. 105 plates. 26 cm.

A detailed consideration of engravings of the 18th century—mainly French but with some mention of other European works. Every print mentioned in the text is noted at the bottom of the page, with indication of sales and prices. Similar in format to Delteil (1534).

Bibliography p. [361]–64. "Table alphabétique des ventes publiques, avec noms de propriétaires" p. [367]–68; "Table des noms d'artistes et des estampes cités" p. [371]–442.

1536
Delteil, Loys. Le peintre-graveur illustré (XIXe et XXe siècles). Paris, Chez l'auteur, 1906–30. 31 v. illus. 33 cm.

Really a catalogue raisonné of certain graphic artists of the 19th and 20th centuries in France. Some volumes include the work of two or three artists, others are monographs; sometimes, as in the case of Daumier, three or four volumes are devoted to a single artist. For each artist there is a short biography, a portrait, and a catalog of his works. Brief descriptions of the works and identification of their various states are given; sales and prices and provenance are also indicated. Each work is illustrated.

Contents: t. 1, J. F. Millet, Th. Rousseau, Jules Dupré, J. Barthold Jongkind; t. 2, Charles Meryon; t. 3, Ingres & Delacroix; t. 4, Anders Zorn; t. 5, Corot; t. 6, Rude, Barye, Carpeaux, Rodin; t. 7, Paul Huet; t. 8, Eugène Carrière; t. 9, Edgar Degas; t. 10–11, H. de Toulouse-Lautrec; t. 12, Gustave Leheutre; t. 13, Charles-François Daubigny; t. 14–15, Francisco Goya; t. 16, Jean-François

Raffaëlli; t. 17, Camille Pissarro, Alfred Sisley, Auguste Renoir; t. 18, Théodore Géricault; t. 19, Henri Leys, Henri de Braekeleer, James Ensor; t. 20–29, Honoré Daumier (10 v.); t. 30, Albert Besnard; t. 31, Jean Frélaut.

1537
Furst, Herbert Ernest Augustus. The modern woodcut; a study of the evolution of the craft . . . with a chapter on the practice of xylography by W. Thomas Smith. With over 200 illustrations in black & white, and 16 plates in colour. London, Lane, The Bodley Head [1924]. 271 p. illus., plates (part col.) 29 cm.

A discussion of modern wood and linoleum cuts by artists of all countries, which includes a one-chapter "survey of the History of the Woodcut from the earliest known example to the commencement of the Nineteenth Century," p. 11–27.

"List of illustrations in the alphabetical order of the names of the artists" p. ix–xxiii (anonymous works listed by name of country of origin). "Bibliography of books consulted" p. 247. "Periodicals, current and defunct, containing woodcuts by modern artists" p. 248. "Hints on the practice of xylography: by W. Thomas Smith . . ." p. 251–64. "Index of woodcutters and engravers" p. 265–71.

1538
Glaser, Curt. Gotische Holzschnitte. Berlin, Propyläen [1923]. 56 p. 55 plates (part col.), facsims. 43 cm.

An introductory survey of 14th and 15th century woodcuts is followed by a catalog of the plates, giving approximate dates, collections where found, and bibliographical references. "Literatur" p. 47–48.

1539
Heller, Joseph. Handbuch für Kupferstichsammler; oder, Lexicon der Kupferstecher, Maler-Radirer und Formschneider aller Länder und Schulen nach Massgabe ihrer geschätztesten Blätter und Werke. Auf Grundlage der 2. Aufl. von Heller's Pract. Handbuch für Kupferstichsammler neu bearb. und um das Doppelte erweitert von Dr. phil. A. Andresen . . . Leipzig, Weigel, 1870–73. 2 v. 24 cm.

This handbook of engravers of all countries is arranged alphabetically by artist and lists prints with their dimensions. "Alphabetisches Verzeichnis" v. 2, p. 835–949.

———. Ergänzungsheft zu Andresen-Wessely's Handbuch für Kupferstichsammler, enthaltend die seit 1873 erschienenen hervorragenden Blätter nebst zahlreichen Nachträgen zum Hauptwerke. Bearb. von J. E. Wessely. Leipzig, Weigel, 1885. 120 p. 25 cm.

1540
Hind, Arthur Mayger. A history of engraving & etching from the 15th century to the year 1914; being the 3d and fully rev. ed. of "A short history of engraving and etching" . . . . With frontispiece in photogravure and 110 illustrations in the text. Boston, Houghton Mifflin, 1927. 487 p. illus. 26 cm.

Appendices: (1) Classified list of engravers p. 343–92; (2) General bibliography p. 393–419; (3) Index of engravers and individual bibliography p. 420–87.

1541
Hind, Arthur Mayger. An introduction to a history of woodcut, with a detailed survey of work done in the fifteenth century . . . with frontispiece and 483 illustrations in the text. London, Constable; Boston, Houghton Mifflin, 1935. 2 v. illus. 26 cm.

Paged continuously. A standard work by a well-known authority in the field. Clear and detailed, treating each subject by country. Volume 1 contains chapters on technique as well as a general historical survey and extended consideration of 15th century work.

Contents: v. 1, The primitives, single cuts and block-books; v. 2, Book-illustration and contemporary single cuts. Bibliographical references at end of each chapter and in the footnotes.

"List of illustrations" v. 1, p. xv–xl. Indexes in v. 2: I, "Designers and engravers of woodcuts" p. 760–66; II, "Printers and publishers of books" p. 767–82; III, "Books illustrated with woodcuts" p. 783–814; IV, "Prints mentioned or reproduced" p. 815–33; V, "Subjects discussed in the text" p. 834–38.

1542
Hirth, Georg, ed. Kulturgeschichtliches Bilderbuch aus drei Jahrhunderten. Bd. I–VI. Leipzig und München, Hirth [1881–90]. 6 v. illus., plates. 36 cm.

A corpus of reproductions of woodcuts, copperplates, etchings, etc. by German, French, Dutch, and other artists, illustrating the history and customs of the 16th to the 18th century. No text; introductions to v. 1–4.

1543
Ivins, William Mills. Prints and visual communication. Cambridge, Harvard Univ. Press; London, Routledge & Paul [1953]. 190 p. illus. 24 cm.

A modern account of the development of prints through the ages, written by a well-known authority. Well illustrated. Index p. 181–90.

1544

Lehrs, Max. Geschichte und kritischer Katalog des deutschen, niederländischen und französischen Kupferstichs im XV. Jahrhundert. Wien, Gesellschaft für vervielfältigende Kunst, 1908–34. 9 v. illus. 30 cm. and 9 atlases of 284 plates. 41 cm.

Edition of 140 copies printed. A scholarly work. The main text includes general information about each artist with descriptions of his works (by subject), sizes, bibliographical references, and collections where found. Text and plates are co-ordinated by number.

Each text volume contains indexes listing: (1) under the names of artists, the works reproduced, by subject; (2) subjects; (3) places; (4) bibliographical abbreviations; (5) watermarks. "Konkordanz nach Geisberg" v. 9, p. [505]–09. Artist index to the nine volumes in v. 9, p. 511–15.

1545

Leporini, Heinrich. Der Kupferstichsammler; ein Hand- und Nachschlagebuch samt Künstlerverzeichnis für den Sammler drückgraphischer Kunst. . . . Mit 105 Abbildungen im Text. Berlin, Schmidt, 1924. 305 p. illus. 25 cm. (Bibliothek für Kunst- und Antiquitäten-Sammler, Bd. XXIV)

A standard German handbook, with descriptions of work in various media for collectors of graphic art. Contains chapters on collectors' marks, the art market, papers, and watermarks.

Includes bibliographies and "Literatur" p. 301–05. The alphabetical index of artists of all times and countries, p. [164]–300, has a paragraph about each and gives dates and pertinent bibliographical references.

1546

Lippmann, Friedrich. Engravings and woodcuts by old masters (sec. XV–XIX) reproduced in facsimile under the direction of Dr. Friedrich Lippmann . . . London, Quaritch, 1889–1900 [i.e., 1904]. 5 v. plates (part col.), facsims. 57 cm.

Originally published in ten parts, 1889–1900, with provisional titles and indexes. The permanent titles and indexes were compiled under the direction of Dr. Lippmann and Dr. J. Springer. "Only eighty complete copies of the book were printed."—*Note.*

A collection of fine reproductions of engravings with a few lines about each artist in the "Contents."

Contents: v. 1, Italian and Spanish schools; v. 2, German school (engravings on metal); v. 3, Netherlandish school (engravings on metal); v. 4, German and Netherlandish schools (engravings on wood); v. 5, French and English schools.

1547

Maberly, Joseph. The print collector; an introduction to the knowledge necessary for forming a collection of ancient prints. . . . With an appendix containing Fielding's treatise on the practice of engraving. Ed., with notes, an account of contemporary etching and etchers, and a bibliography of engraving, by Robert Hoe, Jr. N.Y., Dodd, Mead, 1880. 350 p. illus., 9 plates. 24 cm.

Originally published in England (London, Saunders and Otley, 1844). An old work which contains some useful information.

"Catalogue of Durer's engravings on copper and etchings" p. 287–92; "Catalogue of Durer's wood engravings" p. 293–96; "The whole etched work of Rembrandt" p. 297–309. Annotated bibliography p. [313]–36. Index p. 341–50.

1548

Passavant, Johann David. Le peintre-graveur. Contenant l'histoire de la gravure sur bois, sur métal et au burin jusque vers la fin du XVI. siècle. L'histoire du nielle avec complément de la partie descriptive de l'Essai sur les nielles de Duchesne aîné. Et un catalogue supplémentaire aux estampes du XV. et XVI. siècle du Peintre-graveur de Adam Bartsch. Leipsic, Weigel, 1860–64. 6 v. in 3. 1 port. 23 cm.

A general history of engraving and niello work through the 16th century, in part supplementing the work of Adam von Bartsch (1529).

Contents: t. 1, Histoire de la gravure sur bois et sur métal jusque vers la fin du XVIe. siècle, Histoire de la gravure au burin jusque vers la fin du XVIe. siècle, Histoire du nielle et complément du catalogue de Duchesne Aîné; t. 2, Les maîtres allemands et néerlandais du XVe. siècle, Supplément au Peintre-graveur de Adam Bartsch, vol. VI et X, Gravures au burin allemandes du XVe. siècle, Gravures au burin néerlandaises du XVe. siècle, Table des gravures non signées des écoles allemandes et néerlandaises du XVe. siècle décrites dans ce second volume (p. [293]–99, arranged by subject); t. 3, Les maîtres néerlandais et allemands du XVIe.

siècle, Supplément au Peintre-graveur de Adam Bartsch, vol. VII–X, Catalogue des estampes néerlandaises du XVIe. siècle, Catalogue des estampes de la haute et de la basse Allemagne du XVIe. siècle; t. 4, Suite des maîtres allemands et néerlandais du XVIe. siècle, Supplément au Peintre-graveur de Adam Bartsch, vol. VII–X, Suite du catalogue des estampes allemands du XVIe. siècle; t. 5, Les maîtres italiens du XVe. et XVIe. siècle, Supplément au Peintre-graveur de Adam Bartsch, vol. XII–XVI, Gravures italiennes, Table des gravures non signées de l'école italienne avant l'époque de Marc Antoine, disposés par ordre des sujets (p. [231]–35); t. 6, Suite des maîtres italiens du XVe. et XVIe. siècle, Supplément au Peintre-graveur de Adam Bartsch, vol. XII–XVI, Gravures italiennes (suite), Table alphabétique générale des graveurs dont les estampes et les gravures sur bois ont été mentionées et cataloguées dans les six volumes, Table générale des monogrammes (p. [281]–407 [i.e., 307]).

Each volume has an alphabetical index of artists and a table of monograms therein.

1549
Portalis, Roger, *Baron,* and Beraldi, Henri. Les graveurs du dix-huitième siècle . . . Paris, Morgand et Fatout, 1880–82. 3 v. 23 cm.

Edition of 570 copies printed. An important reference tool for 18th century engraving. Arranged alphabetically by artist, and for each artist gives biographical material, a discussion of his work, and a chronological listing of his works with indication of various states, prices, and rarity. Over 400 artists treated.

Contents: v. 1, Adam-Dossier; v. 2, Drevet-Marais; v. 3, Marcenay-Zingo. Appendice v. 3, p. 715–57; Additions v. 3, p. 781–85.

Each volume has its own "Table" or alphabetical list of artists treated, and v. 3 has "Table générale des graveurs," p. 763–79.

1550
Prideaux, Sara Treverbian. Aquatint engraving: a chapter in the history of book illustration; illustrated by an original aquatint, two collotype plates, and numerous half-tone plates. London, Duckworth [1909]. 434 p. 24 plates. 25 cm.

First published 1909. Gives a brief description of the process and a history of its development and usage.

Appendices: "Books published before 1830 with aquatint plates" p. 325–57; "Biographical notices of engravers whose names appear

on the plates" p. 358–71; "Artists whose names appear on the plates" p. 372–73; "Publications by Ackermann with aquatint plates" p. 374–78; "List of books containing illustrations by T. Rowlandson, based on 'Rowlandson the caricaturist,' by J. Grego" p. 379–87; "Engravers and the books they illustrated" p. 388–405; "List of authorities" p. 406–07. Index p. 409–34.

1551
Rosenthal, Léon, and Adhémar, Jean. . . . La gravure . . . 2. éd. rev. et augm. Paris, Laurens, 1939. 488 p. illus. 25 cm. (Manuels d'histoire de l'art)

1st ed. 1909. A standard French work on engraving; this 2d ed. has been revised by M. Adhémar and brought up to date.

Bibliographies at the end of each chapter as well as a four-page general bibliography. Indexes of artists and of technical terms.

1552
Sachs, Paul Joseph. Modern prints & drawings; a guide to a better understanding of modern draughtsmanship. Selected with an explanatory text by Paul J. Sachs. N.Y., Knopf [1954]. 261 p. illus. 27 cm.

"A picture book with brief comments about prints and drawings made in modern times."—*Introd.* Chapter 10 on technical processes consists of good short descriptions of the various techniques, illustrated by four plates. Biographies p. 247–58. Bibliography p. 259–61.

1553
Schreiber, Wilhelm Ludwig. Manuel de l'amateur de la gravure sur bois et sur métal au XVe siècle. Berlin, Cohn, 1891–1911. 8 v. in 9. illus., 121 plates (part col.) on 104 l. 25 cm. (v. 6–8: 43 cm.)

Volumes 4–5: Leipzig, Harrassowitz. Volumes 1–4, 6–8, limited editions of 300 copies; v. 5, 400 copies.

A 2d rev. and enl. ed. published, in 8 v., in Leipzig, 1926–30 under the title *Handbuch der Holz- und Metallschnitte des 15. Jahrhunderts.*

A comprehensive work on 15th century wood and metal engraving, arranged by subject, with descriptions, indication of size, bibliographical references, dates, and collections.

Contents: t. 1, Catalogue des gravures xylographiques se rapportant à la Bible, l'histoire apocryphe et légendaire, la Sainte Trinité et la Sainte Vierge, 1891; t. 2, Catalogue des gravures xylographiques se rapportant aux saints et saintes, sujets religieux, mystiques et profanes, calendriers, alphabets, armoiries, portraits et suivi d'une spécification des impostures, 1892; t. 3, Catalogue des gravures sur métal et des empreintes en pâte, suivi d'un supplément provisoire, d'une clef des attributs des saints et d'une liste des marques et monogrammes, 1893; t. 4, Catalogue des livres xylographiques et xylochirographiques, indiquant les différences de toutes les éditions existantes, 1902; t. 5, Catalogue des incunables à figures imprimés en Allemagne, en Suisse, en Autriche-Hongrie et en Scandinavie, 1910–11 (2 pts.); t. 6, Atlas de fac-similés de gravures sur bois et sur métal et d'empreintes en pâte, 1893; t. 7, 8, Fac-similés des livres xylographiques, 1895, 1900.

Volumes 1–4 each contain an index of collections (by place), followed by the table of contents. Volume 5, pt. 1 has an alphabetical list (by place) of libraries containing incunabula and catalogs of same p. xiii–xx; also includes a history of the beginnings of printing (by centers of activity).

Bibliographies: v. 1, p. xiii–xvi; v. 2, p. ix–xiv; v. 3, p. x–xvi; v. 4, p. xi–xiv; v. 5, pt. 1, p. xxi–xxiv. At end of v. 5: Index des ouvrages décrits, en ordre alphabétique des villes et des imprimeurs p. 334–63; Les numéros de Hain p. 364–70; Les numéros de Copinger p. 371–3; Les numéros supplémentaires de Proctor p. 373; Initiales remarquables p. 374–78; Éditions ornées de gravures sur métal [et] . . . au burin p. 379 (by place).

1554

Slater, John Herbert. Engravings and their value; a complete guide to the collection and prices of all classes of prints. 6th ed., rev. and enl. by F. W. Maxwell-Barbour. Illustrated with 24 plates in colour and black and white, and 300 facsimile reproductions of engravers' marks. N.Y., Scribner, 1929. 707 p. plates (part col.) 30 cm.

Part I covers various types of engraving, paper, proofs and states, forgeries, technical terms, and suggestions to beginners; Part II is "A dictionary of the more important engravers and their works; giving their chief characteristics, and auction prices for representative prints" p. 87–704.

Bibliography p. 72–74. Index p. 705–07.

1555

Wedmore, *Sir* Frederick. Fine prints. New & enl. ed., with 15 illustrations. Edinburgh,

Grant, 1905. 261 p. plates. 21 cm. (The collector series)

Contains a chapter on "The task of the collector" followed by others on various masters or schools, one on mezzotints, one on lithographs, and a short appendix entitled "Certain woodcuts."

Bibliography p. 250–54. Index p. 255–61.

1556

Whitman, Alfred. Print-collector's handbook. Rev. and enl. by Malcolm C. Salaman. London, Bell, 1921. 376 p. 64 plates. 23 cm.

First published 1901; rev. 6th ed. 1912; reprinted 1918, 1921. Includes chapters devoted to various processes, frauds, and the monetary value of prints.

Bibliography p. 339–60. Index p. 361–76.

1557

Willshire, William Hughes. An introduction to the study & collection of ancient prints. 2d ed. rev. & enl. London, Ellis & White, 1877. 2 v. plates. 24 cm.

1st ed. 1874 (in 1 v.). A history of engraving beginning with Greek and Roman times, and listing various masters of the different schools.

Contains in v. 2: A chronological table of some of the more important events in the history of early engraving and typography p. 249–54; A table of monograms, marks, and cyphers p. 257–60; Water marks in paper p. 261–63; Names and marks of collectors and dealers and prints p. 264–65; Bibliography p. 279–87; Analytical table of subjects treated in the bibliography p. 288–93; Index to proper names p. 295–301; Index to subjects p. 302–05.

SEE ALSO: Monod. Aide-mémoire de l'amateur et du professionel (148).

National

France

1558

Baudicour, Prosper de. Le peintre-graveur français continué, ou Catalogue raisonné des estampes gravées par les peintres et les dessinateurs de l'école française nés dans le XVIIIe siècle, ouvrage faisant suite au Peintre-graveur français de M. Robert-Dumesnil . . . Paris, Bouchard-Huzard; Leipzig, Weigel, 1859–61. 2 v. fold. geneal. table. 22 cm.

A supplement to Robert-Dumesnil (1561), this work carries the treatment of French painter-engravers through the 18th century. Biographical sketches of the artists are followed by detailed descriptions of their works. Dimensions are given in all cases.

Each volume has both chronological and alphabetical lists of the artists included therein.

1559

Courboin, François. Histoire illustrée de la gravure en France . . . Paris, Le Garrec, 1923–26. 3 v. 32 cm. 3 portfolios of plates. 48 cm.

Edition of 775 copies printed. An illustrated history of French engraving containing an introductory historical survey, a paragraph of information on each artist, and short identification, with dimensions, of the works reproduced in the plates.

Contents: v. 1, Des origines à 1660; v. 2, De 1660 à 1800; v. 3, XIXe siècle. Each volume has its own alphabetical index of artists and titles of anonymous works.

1560

Leipnik, F. L. A history of French etching from the sixteenth century to the present day; illustrated with a frontispiece and one hundred and six reproductions in photogravure. London, Lane, The Bodley Head; N.Y., Dodd, Mead [1924]. 214 p. 106 plates. 29 cm.

"The principal aim of this book is to serve as a guide to assist collectors in the selection and classification of plates."—*Pref.* As regards the plates, the emphasis is on modern works.

Bibliography p. 193–99. Index of artists p. 201–14, with indication of current sales and prices.

1561

Robert-Dumesnil, A. P. F. Le peintre-graveur français, ou Catalogue raisonné des estampes gravées par les peintres et les dessinateurs de l'école française. Ouvrage faisant suite au Peintre-graveur de M. Bartsch . . . Paris, Warée [and Hazard], 1835–71. 11 v. plates. 21 cm.

This catalog of engravings is arranged chronologically by artist, and at the beginning of each volume is a list of artists included. Each engraving is fully described, dimensions are cited, and the various states are differentiated. Followed by Baudicour (1558), which treats of French artists born in the 18th century.

Volume 11 is a supplement by Georges Duplessis, which contains additions and corrections and a general index to the whole work (p. [353]–59). Biographical notice of the author by Georges Duplessis v. 9, p. [vii]–x; List of sales catalogs, comp. by Robert-Dumesnil, v. 9, p. xi–xv.

1562

Roger-Marx, Claude. French original engravings from Manet to the present time. London, N.Y., [etc.], Hyperion, 1939. 7–87, 130 p. incl. 128 plates on 64 l. 16 col. plates. 32 cm.

"Printed in France." "Edited by André Gloeckner." A well-illustrated survey of French prints on wood, copper, and stone from about 1862 to the present. Index of artists p. 129.

Germany and Austria

1563

Andresen, Andreas. Der deutsche peintre-graveur, oder Die deutschen Maler als Kupferstecher nach ihrem Leben und ihren Werken, von dem letzten Drittel des 16. Jahrhunderts bis zum Schluss des 18. Jahrhunderts . . . Leipzig, Danz, 1864–78. 5 v. 24 cm.

Intended as a supplement to Bartsch (1529), Robert-Dumesnil (1561), and Baudicour (1558). Biographical sketches and brief descriptions of the work of German painter-engravers, from the last third of the 16th to the end of the 18th century, are given.

At beginning of each volume is a list of the artists treated; v. 5 contains a general index to the whole work.

1564

Diederichs, Eugen, ed. Deutsches Leben der Vergangenheit in Bildern; ein Atlas mit 1760 Nachbildungen alter Kupfer- und Holzschnitte aus dem 15ten—18ten Jahrhundert. Mit Einführung von H. Kienzle. Jena, Diederichs, 1908. 2 v. illus. 41 cm.

Intended as a supplement to *Monographien zur deutschen Kulturgeschichte* (Leipzig, Diederichs, 1899–1905). A collection of engravings and woodcuts of the 15th to 18th centuries depicting German life of the times.

1565

Geisberg, Max. Bilder-Katalog zu Max Geisberg. Der deutsche Einblatt-Holzschnitt in der ersten Hälfte des XVI. Jahrhunderts: 1600 verkleinerte Wiedergaben, herausgegeben von Hugo Schmidt. München, Schmidt [c1930]. 299 p. illus. 28 cm.

A sort of summary or key to Geisberg's

Einblatt-Holzschnitt series (1566) with small reproductions of each work included in the series. The catalog is arranged alphabetically by artist and gives for each artist dates of his life and work and place of activity, works by him included in the set, sizes, and a bibliography.

1566

Geisberg, Max. . . . Der deutsche Einblatt-Holzschnitt in der ersten Hälfte des XVI. Jahrhunderts . . . München, Schmidt [c1923–29]. 43 v. 1600 mounted plates (part col.) 56 cm.

Limited edition. Volumes 33, 38, 39, 40: 81 cm. Label with descriptive letterpress mounted on verso of each plate. Issued in portfolio.

———. Übersicht über die in der ersten Hälfte des Werkes veröffentlichten Holzschnitte. München, Schmidt, 1926. 89 p. incl. plate. 22 cm.

Interleaved.

———. Die Gesamtverzeichnisse. München, Schmidt [c1930]. 52, [85] p. illus., 3 facsims. 55 cm.

"Die Titel der häufiger zitierten Bücher" p. 15.

A monumental corpus of reproductions of single German woodcuts of the first half of the 16th century, with bibliographical references for each plate.

The index volume contains "Das Verzeichnis der Schnitte," p. 16–48, which lists the plates alphabetically by artist, numbered consecutively with indication of the volume in which they are found; "Verzeichnis der Holzschnitte nach Darstellungsgegenständen geordnet," p. 49–52, which lists the plates according to broad subjects; "Inhaltsverzeichnis," p. [55–139], which is a table of contents listing the plates as they appear in the volumes; "Konkordanz," p. 10–14, which refers from the alphabetical listing to the table of contents.

1567

Hollstein, F. W. H. German engravings, etchings and woodcuts, ca. 1400–1700. Amsterdam, Hertzberger [1954–(57)]. v. 1–(5). illus. 28 cm.

Similar in format and information provided to his *Dutch and Flemish etchings . . .* (1579), it will include "some eight thousand of the more important prints of the German School, *including about five thousand which have never yet been reproduced."—Introd.* An index volume is projected.

Contents: v. 1, Aachen–Altdorfer; v. 2,

Altzenbach–B. Beham; v. 3, Hans Sebald Beham; v. 4, Beischlag–Brosamer; v. 5, Brucker–Coriolanus. Includes bibliographies for each artist.

Great Britain

1568

Goodwin, Gordon. British mezzotinters Thomas Watson, James Watson, Elizabeth Judkins . . . London, Bullen, 1904. 232 p. 6 plates. 25 cm.

Edition of 520 copies printed. For each artist there is a biography, a catalog of portraits, a catalog of subjects, and index to his prints, an index to subjects, and an index to painters.

1569

Hind, Arthur Mayger. Engraving in England in the sixteenth & seventeenth centuries; a descriptive catalogue with introductions. Cambridge, Univ. Press, 1952–(55). v. 1–(2). plates. 26 cm.

Contents: v. 1, The Tudor period; v. 2, The reign of James I. In v. 1 a general introduction to the subject precedes the "Catalogue," which is arranged by artist and gives information and bibliographical notes followed by a list of works grouped by type. Detailed descriptions and dimensions are given.

The "Catalogue" is followed by: "General bibliography"; "A note on Humphrey Dyson's collection of Elizabethan proclamations"; "A note on 'Grangers' "; "Chronological list of engravers working in England from Henry VIII (1540) to the Revolution (1689)"; "Notes on printers, printsellers and publishers"; "Notes on the most important collections available for study"; "On the arrangement of collections of engraved portraits: A note for museums and collectors"; Index p. 329–[34]; Plates (156). Volume 1 also contains "Abbreviations most frequently used in text and catalogue . . ." p. xxvii–xxx.

Volume 2 is arranged similarly but the "Catalogue" is followed by: "Anonymous engravers, including some foreign prints of English interest, by known as well as anonymous engravers"; "Corrections and additions to Part I"; Index p. 407–13; Plates (252). Each volume begins with a list of the plates included.

1570

Laver, James. A history of British and American etching . . . London, Benn, 1929. 195 p. 84 plates. 29 cm.

Size of the prints reproduced is indicated

in "List of plates" p. ix–xiv. Bibliography p. 153–86. Index p. 187–95.

1571
Russell, Charles E. English mezzotint portraits and their states from the invention of mezzotinting until the early part of the 19th century. London, Halton & Truscott Smith; N.Y., Minton, Balch, 1926. 2 v. plates. 39, 26 cm.

Volume 1 is a quarto volume of plates (39 cm.); v. 2 is the text volume with subtitle: Catalogue of corrections of and additions to Chaloner Smith's "British mezzotint portraits" (1572).

Contents (v. 2): Engravers p. 1–425; Engraver not ascertained p. 426–36; Appendix of earliest specimens p. 486–88; Errata p. 489–98; Corrections of Chaloner Smith's indices p. 499–500; Index of painters p. 501–04; Index of personages p. 505–25; Index of fancy and other names p. 526.

1572
Smith, John Chaloner. British mezzotint portraits; being a descriptive catalogue of these engravings from the introduction of the art to the early part of the present century. Arranged according to the engravers; the inscriptions given at full length; and the variations of state precisely set forth; accompanied by biographical notes . . . London, Sotheran, 1883. 4 v. in 5. illus., diagrs. and portfolio of 2 plates, 123 ports. 28 cm.

"Intends to describe all mezzotint portraits published in England, Ireland, and Scotland, down to the early part of the present century."—*Notes.*

Arrangement is alphabetical by names of engravers, then by names of personages represented. "Authors and works principally consulted" p. xiv–xvi.

Italy

1573
Baudi di Vesme, Alessandro. Le peintregraveur italien: ouvrage faisant suite au Peintre-graveur de Bartsch. Milan, Hoepli, 1906. 542 p. 26 cm.

At head of title: Alexandre de Vesme. Covers 61 Italian painter-engravers. Supplements Bartsch (1529). "Table des graveurs" p. 541–42.

1574
Hind, Arthur Mayger. Early Italian engraving, a critical catalogue with complete repro-

duction of all the prints described . . . London, Quaritch; N.Y., M. Knoedler & Co., 1938–(48). (7) v. illus., plates. 34 cm.

"This edition is limited to 375 copies for sale and 30 lettered copies not on the market. . . ." Part 2 limited to 275 copies and bears imprint: Pub. for the National Gallery, Washington, D.C.

A section of short biographical and bibliographical information on each artist is followed by a list of works with descriptions of their various states, dimensions, collections, watermarks, inscriptions, and bibliographical references. Each text volume also contains a section on watermarks, a concordance to Bartsch, Passavant, and the British Museum catalog, and an index of artists and subjects.

Contents: pt. 1, Florentine engravings and anonymous prints of other schools–v. 1, Catalogue, v. 2–4, Plates; pt. 2, Known masters other than Florentine monogrammists and anonymous–v. 5, Catalogue, v. 6–7, Plates.

"General bibliography" v. 1, p. xv–xxii. "List of collections and mode of references in the catalogue" v. 1, p. xxiii–xxvi. Additions and corrections to pt. 1 in v. 5, p. 307–13.

1575
Kristeller, Paul. Early Florentine woodcuts. With an annotated list of Florentine illustrated books. London, Paul, Trench, Trubner, 1897. 184 p. 123 plates. 30 cm.

Edition of 300 copies. The emphasis is on book illustration rather than on separate woodcuts. An introductory discussion precedes the list of illustrated Florentine books of the 15th and 16th centuries, which is arranged alphabetically (by author, subject, or form of writing), and contains descriptions of all woodcuts included.

"Books . . . which have been of special use" p. ix. "Index of printers and publishers" p. 181–84.

Latin America

1576
Haight, Anne Lyon, ed. Portrait of Latin America as seen by her print makers; Retrato de la América latina hecho por sus artistas gráficos . . . Monroe Wheeler, foreword . . . Jean Charlot, introduction. N.Y., Hastings House [c1946]. 36 p. plates. 24 cm.

While not a scholarly work, this is the only book on South American engravers currently available. A short biographical paragraph is devoted to each artist included. Text in Spanish and English.

Low Countries

1577

Burchard, Ludwig. Die holländischen Radierer vor Rembrandt, mit beschreibenden Verzeichnissen und biographischen Übersichten. 2. durch 12 Tafeln und ein alphabetisches Register verm. Ausg. Berlin, Cassirer, 1917. 183 p. 25 cm.

Biographical notes on and descriptions of the work of about 15 engravers prior to Rembrandt.

"Katalog der Radierungen" p. 121–76. "Alphabetisches Verzeichnis der zitierten Künstler und öffentlichen Sammlungen" p. 177–83.

1578

Delen, Adrien Jean Joseph. Histoire de la gravure dans les anciens Pays-Bas et dans les provinces belges, des origines jusqu'à la fin du XVIIIe siècle . . . Paris, Bruxelles, van Oest, 1924–(35). v. 1–(2⁵). 172 plates. 33 cm.

Volume 2 published Paris, Les Éditions d'Art et d'Histoire. An introductory chapter in v. 1 describes various processes of making prints; the text which follows is a chronological survey of engraving.

Contents: pt. 1, Des origines à 1500; pt. 2, Le XVIe siècle, Les graveurs-illustrateurs, Les graveurs d'estampes. A bibliography is contemplated for v. 3. Each volume has its own index of artists and titles of anonymous works, and list of plates.

1579

Hollstein, F. W. H. Dutch and Flemish etchings, engravings and woodcuts, ca. 1450–1700. Amsterdam, Hertzberger [1949–(56)]. v. 1–(14). illus. 28 cm.

The work is projected to 25 volumes and an index volume. ". . . every print of importance or of interest from the point of view of the history of art will be illustrated. . . . Great rarities and uniques of the celebrated Print Rooms are only indicated with the names of the towns. . . . The private collections are given separately. The prices of the more remarkable prints occurring in the auctions during the past fifty years, converted into dollars, are likewise indicated. . . . Between the catalogues of the works are given, also in alphabetical order, complete lists of those prints which have been engraved after paintings and drawings by well-known artists. The numbers in brackets . . . refer to Wurzbach [272]. . . ."—*Introd.*

Arranged alphabetically by names of artists. Contains brief biographical notes with

illustrations of about 10,000 (as projected) of the more important prints of the Dutch and Flemish schools, including about 7000 which have not heretofore been reproduced. Dimensions are given and all states of each work are cited.

Contents: v. 1, Abry–Berchem; v. 2, Berckheyde–Bodding; v. 3, Boekhorst–Brueghel; v. 4, Brun–Coques; v. 5, Cornelisz–Dou; v. 6, Douffet–Floris, v. 7, Fouceel–Gole; v. 8, Goltzius–Heemskerck; v. 9, Heer–Kuyl; v. 10, L'Admiral–Lucas van Leyden; v. 11, Leyster–Matteus; v. 12, Masters and monogrammists of the 15th century; v. 13, Monogrammists of the 16th and 17th century; v. 14, Meer-Ossenbeeck.

A bibliography at beginning of v. 1 and bibliographies for each artist are included.

1580

Muller, Frederik. De Nederlandsche geschiedenis in platen. Beredeneerde beschrijving van Nederlandsche historie-platen, zinneprenten en historische kaarten . . . Amsterdam, Muller, 1863–82. 4 v. illus. 24 cm.

A corpus of reproductions of prints illustrating events in Netherlandish history.

Contents: v. 1, 100 B.C.–1702 A.D.; v. 2, 1702–1795; v. 3, 1795–1879; v. 4, Supplement, aanhangsel en algemeen register.

1581

Nijhoff, Wouter. Nederlandsche houtsneden, 1500–1550, reproducties van oude Noord- en Zuid-Nederlandsche houtsneden op losse bladen met en zonder tekst in de oorspronkelijke grootte uitgegeven door Wouter Nijhoff. 's Gravenhage, Nijhoff, 1931–36. 101 p. 27 cm. and 334 plates. 67 cm.

Text dated 1933–36; plates dated 1931–35. Descriptive text to plates 1–160 was originally written in German by Hedwig Nijhoff-Selldorf and translated into Dutch by M. D. Henkel.

A collection of reproductions of Dutch woodcuts with descriptive text and bibliographical references. Pages [1]–6 of the plate volume contain a table of contents, with titles arranged by artist, and indication of location; p. 7–8, index of artists and monogrammists and titles of anonymous works.

Oriental Countries

1582

Binyon, *Sir* Laurence, and Sexton, J. J. O'Brien. Japanese colour prints. London,

Benn; N.Y., Scribner, 1923. lvi, [237] p. 46
plates (part col.), tables. 29 cm.

This standard work on Japanese prints
(Ukiyo-ye) deals with the subject according
to periods. "The body of the work is prefaced
by tables to facilitate the reading of dated
books and prints; an account of the Censor-
ship of Prints; a table of the *Mon* of the
Yedo actors during the 18th century; and a
table of publishers' trade-marks and seals."—
Pref.

"List of illustrations" p. xi–xviii. "A list of
choice colour-printed books and albums arranged in chronological order with brief descriptive details of the original issues and
the colours employed" p. 211–25.

"Select bibliography" p. l–lii. Index and
glossary p. 229–[37].

1583

Kurth, Julius. Die Geschichte des japanischen
Holzschnitts . . . Leipzig, Hiersemann, 1925–
29. 3 v. illus. (incl. plan, facsims.), plates (part
col.) 32 cm.

A standard German work on the subject
of Japanese woodcuts. Contents: Bd. 1, Einleitung; Von den Anfängen bis Harunobu;
Bd. 2, Von Harunobu bis Eishi; Bd. 3, Von
der Sekien-Schule bis zu den Hiroshige.

Bibliography v. 3, p. 221–31. Each volume
has its index of artists. "Häufig vorkom-
mende japanische Wörter" v. 1, p. 433–40, is
a listing of Japanese names and technical
terms dealing with prints, and the German
equivalents. "Signaturenregister aus allen
drei Bänden" v. 3, p. 238–39. "Die
japanischen Epochen, soweit sie für die Zeit
des Holzschnitts in Frage kommen" v. 3, p.
240–44.

1584

Michener, James A. The floating world. N.Y.,
Random [1954]. 403 p. illus. (part col.) 24
cm.

A good and accurate treatment of Japanese
prints based upon the research of recognized
authorities in the field.

Prices p. 358–59; Chronological chart p.
360; Biography p. 361–78; Bibliography p.
379–80, with annotations; Index and glossary p. 391–403.

1585

Seidlitz, Woldemar von. A history of Japanese colour-prints, with illustrations in colour and black and white. Philadelphia, Lippincott, 1910. 207 p. 75 plates (part fold.,
15 col.) 26 cm.

Translated by Anne Heard Dyer and Grace

Tripler. "Bibliography" p. 195–200. "Alphabetical list of the signs which compose the
names of the most important Japanese artists" p. 201–02. Index p. 203–07.

1586

Statler, Oliver. Modern Japanese prints, an
art reborn. With an introduction by James A.
Michener. Rutland, Vt., Charles E. Tuttle
Co. [1956]. 209 p. illus. (part col.) 27 cm.

Treats of individual modern artists arranged by schools. Appendix 1, The woods p.
183–84; Appendix 2, The prints p. 185–204.
Index p. 205–09 gives names in English and
Japanese.

1587

Stewart, Basil. Subjects portrayed in Japanese
colour-prints, a collector's guide to all the
subjects illustrated, including an exhaustive
account of the Chushingura and other famous plays, together with a causerie on the
Japanese theatre; illustrated with reproductions of over 270 prints from the author's collection and other sources: 22 in colour. London, Paul, Trench, Trubner, 1922. [382] p.
illus., plates (part col.) 39 cm.

A revision and enlargement of *Japanese
colour-prints and the subjects they illustrate,*
published 1920. The production of prints
as well as problems in the formation and
care of a collection are discussed, and the
work of the most notable artists and schools
is considered. This is followed by a detailed
survey of the various subjects illustrated.
Appendices: (1) "The dating of Japanese
prints: chronological table: Numerals" p.
331–39; (2) "Notes" p. 340–53; (3) "List of
Ukiyoye artists" (with brief identifying remarks) p. 354–63; (4) "Reproductions of artists' signatures, publishers' seals, and actors'
crests" p. 364–76; (5) Bibliography p. 377.

List of illustrations, by name of artist, p.
ix–xiv. Glossary p. xv–xvi. Index p. 379–[82].

United States

1588

Weitenkampf, Frank. American graphic
art. . . . New ed., rev. & enl. . . . N.Y., Macmillan, 1924. 328 p. illus., plates. 23 cm.

1st ed. 1912. A survey of the graphic arts
in the United States from their beginnings
to 1924, by a recognized authority. Bibliography p. 291–93. Index p. 299–328.

1589

Zigrosser, Carl. The artist in America;
twenty-four closeups of contemporary print-

makers . . . N.Y., Knopf, 1942. 207 p. plates. 26 cm.

"First edition." "The first volume of a projected two volume study of contemporary graphic art in America . . . the second volume [to be] a regional survey of American printmaking during the last thirty years."— *Introd.*

This volume covers 24 printmakers and for each gives a biographical essay, portrait, and reproduction of three works. Index of 6 p. following p. 207.

SEE ALSO: Laver. A history of British and American etching (1570).

Techniques

1590
Arms, John Taylor. Handbook of print making and print makers . . . N.Y., Macmillan, 1934. 255 p. col. plates. 20 cm.

"In it will be found a summary, but I hope, clear description of the principal methods of print making, and a condensed history of each."—*Pref.*

"Alphabetical list of artists" p. [201]–41. Index p. 245–55.

1591
Bonnardot, Alfred. Essai sur l'art de restaurer les estampes et les livres, ou Traité sur les meilleurs procédés pour blanchir, détacher, décolorier, réparer et conserver les livres, estampes et dessins. Seconde édition refondue et augmentée. Suivie d'un exposé des divers systèmes de reproduction des anciennes estampes et des livres rares. Paris, Castel, 1858. 352 p. 18 cm.

1st ed. 1846, of 400 copies. A useful French manual on the repair and preservation of prints, books, and drawings. Some passages translated into English are found in Buck, M. S. *Book repair and restoration* . . . Phila., Brown, 1918.

"Liste des ouvrages à consulter" p. 273–78. "Table analytique des matières" p. 343–49.

1592
Brown, Bolton. Lithography for artists; a complete account of how to grind, draw upon, etch, and print from the stone, together with instructions for making crayon, transferring etc. . . . Chicago, Pub. for the Art Institute of Chicago by the Univ. of Chicago Press [c1930]. 102 p. illus., plates.

30 cm. (The Scammon lectures for 1929)

Appendix: (1) Steps in making a lithograph; (2) List of materials; (3) Formulas for crayon. Index p. 97–102.

1593
Burch, Robert M. Colour printing and colour printers . . . with a chapter on modern processes by W. Gamble. N.Y., Baker & Taylor, 1911. 280 p. plates (part col.) 25 cm.

An old but still useful history of color printing from its beginnings to the early 20th century, addressed more to the historian of printing than to the art student. Contains valuable information on early color reproductions and separate color prints.

1594
Cumming, David. Handbook of lithography; a practical treatise for all who are interested in the process. London, Black, 1904. 243 p. illus. 14 plates (part col.) 20 cm.

A technical description of the process, including the materials. Glossary p. 238–39. Index p. 240–43.

1595
Hayter, Stanley William. New ways of gravure. Pref. by Herbert Read. [N.Y.,] Pantheon [1949]. 274 p. illus., col. plates. 26 cm.

A good and well-illustrated account of various techniques of prints and engravings written by a practicing artist in the field.

Contents: (1) Techniques; (2) History of the technique; (3) Implications of gravure as a specific medium.

1596
Holman, Louis Arthur. The graphic processes: intaglio, relief and planographic, with a set of actual prints illustrative of the text, selected and arranged by Louis A. Holman. Boston, Goodspeed, 1929. [116 p.] incl. plates (part col.) 43 cm.

In portfolio. For each process gives an actual example with descriptive text.

1597
Hubbard, Eric Hesketh. How to distinguish prints, written and illustrated by members of the Print Society . . . Woodgreen Common, Eng., Print Society, 1926. 127 p. illus., plates (part col.) 29 cm. (Print Society publications, no. 3)

"Glossarial index" p. 104–21. "French terms" are given opposite English equivalents p. 122–24. Also German equivalents of terms, listed alphabetically according to the English term p. 125–27. Includes bibliographies.

1598
Ivins, William Mills. How prints look; photographs with a commentary . . . N.Y., 1943. 164 p. illus. 26 cm.
Also issued in paperback by Beacon, Boston.
At head of title: The Metropolitan Museum of Art. "This book is an elementary introduction to the appearances (the outward and visible signs) of prints. It is not a history, and it contains no technical recipes or instructions for print making. Most of the time spent over it should be given to looking at pictures."—*Introd.* A useful book which contains many enlarged illustrations of details which show the difference between various processes.

1599
Leighton, Clare Veronica Hope. . . . Wood-engraving and woodcuts. London, The Studio Publications, 1932. 96 p. illus. (part mounted). 26 cm. ("How to do it" series [2])
A short, well-illustrated description of the technique of these processes with examples from various styles.

1600
Lumsden, Ernest S. The art of etching; a complete & fully illustrated description of etching, drypoint, soft-ground etching, aquatint, & their allied arts, together with technical notes upon their own work by many of the leading etchers of the present time . . . London, Seely, Service; Philadelphia, Lippincott, 1925. 376 p. illus. 21 cm. (The new art library)
Contains various types of information on equipment and techniques, and a section on some important etchers. Index p. 368–76.

1601
Plenderleith, Harold James. The conservation of prints, drawings, and manuscripts . . . [Oxford] Pub. for the Museums Association by the Oxford Univ. Press, 1937. 66 p. illus. (incl. charts), plates, diagrs. 18 cm.
"The studies which form the basis of the present work were first published in *Mouseion* [2286], official organ of the International museums office, Paris." "The present book is designed as a sequel to *The preservation of antiquities,* to which it conforms, as far as possible, in style and treatment."—*Pref.*
Contents: (1) Materials and their permanence; (2) Mounting, storage and exhibition; (3) Deterioration and reconditioning; (4) An outline of practical methods of cleaning and repair.

"Select bibliography" p. [59]–61. Index p. 63–66. Blank pages for "Notes" at end.

1602
Poortenaar, Jan. The technique of prints and art reproduction processes; a study of technical processes with 45 specimens and 90 illustrations . . . with a preface by Campbell Dodgson . . . London, Lane [1933]. 174 p. illus., plates (part col.) diagrs. 25 cm.
Useful for description of both hand, or nonmechanical, and photo-mechanical processes. Well illustrated. Index p. 172–74.

1603
Schraubstadter, Carl William. Care and repair of Japanese prints. Cornwall-on-Hudson, N.Y., Idlewild Press [1948]. 117 p. illus. 19 cm.
A useful manual on this subject. "Print sizes" p. 112–17.

1604
Singer, Hans Wolfgang, and Strang, William. Etching, engraving and the other methods of printing pictures, with ten original plates by, and four illustrations after William Strang. London, Paul, Trench, Trubner, 1897. 228 p. 14 plates. 22 cm.
A basic book on the subject. Covers various types of prints and how they are made, their limitations, etc., and mentions some important masters who have made them. Also contains chapters on "How to distinguish between different kinds of prints," "How to appreciate and enjoy prints," and "Modern photo-mechanical processes."
Bibliography p. 188–219, arranged chronologically, with a list of authors p. 219–21. Index p. 223–28.

1605
Sternberg, Harry. Silk screen color printing, presenting a new addition to the graphic arts—serigraphy. A demonstration and explanation of the process of making "multiple original" color prints . . . photographs by Bruce Edward. N.Y. and London, McGraw-Hill, 1942. 78 p. illus. (part col.) 26 cm.
"This is a technical book which attempts to give a simple and workable explanation of the medium of serigraphy."—*Colophon.* It is written by a well-known artist and is well illustrated.

1606
Wengenroth, Stow. . . . Making a lithograph. London, The Studio; N.Y., The Studio Publications, 1936. 79 p. incl. illus. (part

mounted), mounted plates. 26 cm. ("How to do it" series [11])

A well-illustrated, concise description of the lithographic process written by a practicing artist.

1607

West, Levon. Making an etching. London, The Studio; N.Y., The Studio Publications, 1932. 79 p. mounted illus. 26 cm. ("How to do it" series, 1)

A well-illustrated description of etching.

1608

Yoshida. Japanese wood-block printing. Tokyo and Osaka, The Sanseido Co. [1939]. 136 p. incl. illus., plates (part col.) 27 cm.

"Detailed in Japanese to Dr. Jiro Harada who wrote it in English."—*Pref.* An excellent and well-illustrated account of the technique of Japanese prints.

"A list of author's prints with special features and the number of blocks and impressions used," etc., p. [121]–32. Index p. 133–36.

| **Applied Arts**

General

Bibliography

1609
Debes, Dietmar. Das Ornament, Wesen und Geschichte. Ein Schriftenverzeichnis. Leipzig, Seemann [1956]. 101 p. 25 cm.

A classified bibliography of 2026 items dealing with ornamental art of all periods and civilizations, including both books and periodical articles. Indexes: of authors p. 91–97; of artists p. 97–98; of geographical names p. 98–99; of subjects p. 99–101.

SEE ALSO: Berlin. Staatliche Kunstbibliothek. . . . Katalog der Ornamentstichsammlung (10); Vienna. Österreichisches Museum für Kunst und Industrie. Bibliothek. Katalog (23).

Dictionaries and Encyclopedias

1610
The Antiques year book, encyclopaedia and directory, 1949/50–1956/57, ed. by Donald Cowie. Malvern, Tantivy Press. illus. 20 cm.

1st ed. 1949/50, edited by R. F. St. B. Pytcheley. Contains short items on a variety of subjects dealing with collecting antiques, and a directory of British antique dealers p. 267–300. Restorers' directory p. 300–06. "Round the galleries" p. 306–08. Also contains suggested tours to antique shops in various localities in England and Holland. Index to advertisers p. 608–16. Index to terms p. 616–19.

1611
Baker, Mary Gladys Steel. A dictionary of antiques, by Shelia Stuart (Mrs. Howard Baker). Edinburgh, London, Chambers [1953]. 263 p. illus. 23 cm.

Articles are alphabetically arranged under headings: Furniture, smaller antiques, pottery and china, glass, silver and Sheffield plate, and pewter. Rather popular treatment but contains numerous cross references and line drawings. Index p. 245–63.

1612
Boger, Louise Ade, and Boger, H. Batterson. The dictionary of antiques and the decorative arts; a book of reference for glass, furniture, ceramics, silver, periods, styles, technical terms etc. Illus. by I. N. Steinberg and associates. N.Y., Scribner [c1957]. 566 p. illus. 28 cm.

A useful dictionary illustrated by line drawings in the text and some halftones. "Classified list of subjects and terms" p. 535–55. Bibliography p. 559–66.

1613
Bosc, Ernest. Dictionnaire de l'art, de la curiosité et du bibelot. Paris, Firmin-Didot, 1883. 695 p. illus., plates (part col.) 28 cm.

Basically a dictionary of the minor arts, covering arms and armor, jewelry, ceramics, gold and silversmithing, fabrics, glassware, metalwork, enamel, and musical instruments.

List of the principal 19th century collectors and their collections p. 671–90.

1614
The Connoisseur. The concise encyclopedia of antiques. Editor, L. G. G. Ramsay. London and N.Y., The Connoisseur, 1954. 288 p. illus. 25 cm.

Covers furniture, English glass, ceramics, English painted enamels, British pewter, silver, jewelry, clocks and watches, arms and armor, book-collecting, needlework and embroidery, Oriental carpets and rugs, portrait miniatures, Old English drawings and prints, Old English watercolors, European painting; includes bibliographies.

"The term antique is considered to include

styles and designs used up to 1830; and where possible, an alphabetically arranged glossary of terms and styles designed to cover the whole ground of the subject is included."— *Foreword.*

List of collectors' societies and addresses p. 11. Index of names and places p. 285–88.

1615
Doane, Ethel Mary. Antiques dictionary. Brockton, Mass. [c1949]. 290 p. 24 cm.

Contains short definitions of words and terms, arranged alphabetically. Not illustrated.

Bibliography p. 283–90.

1616
Harper, George W., ed. Antique collectors guide and reference handbook. . . . Published on the occasion of the twelfth National antiques exhibition at the Commodore hotel in New York City . . . N.Y., G. W. Harper [c1939]. 87 p. illus. 28 cm.

Contents: The American wing, by Joseph Downs; A bibliography for antiques, by Alice Winchester (an annotated and recommended list of 150 books in all fields of antiques p. 15–22); Collecting societies (pertinent facts about all the collecting organizations); Why and how to collect antiques, by Thomas Hamilton Ormsbee; Antique names and terms, by G. W. Harper (A glossary for the amateur containing concise definitions and explanations of 1000 words commonly used in antique terminology p. 30–48); Exhibitors in 12th National antiques exhibition . . . ; New trends in collecting, by Charles Messer Stow.

1617
Havard, Henry. Dictionnaire de l'ameublement et de la décoration depuis le XIIIe siècle jusqu'à nos jours. . . . Nouv. éd. entièrement réfondue et considérablement augm. Paris, Quantin, Librairies-imprimeries réunies [19–]. 4 v. illus., plates (part col.) 32 cm.

Arranged as a dictionary with entries under detailed subjects as well as broad ones. Numerous cross references and many illustrations in the text.

1618
Viollet-le-Duc, Eugène Emmanuel. Dictionnaire raisonné du mobilier français de l'époque carlovingienne à la renaissance. Paris, Morel, 1868–75. 6 v. illus., 114 plates (part col.), maps. 25 cm.

A standard work but now somewhat out of date. Contents: t. 1, p. 1, Meubles; t. 2, pt. 2, Ustensiles; pt. 3, Orfèvrerie; pt. 4, Instruments de musique; pt. 5, Jeux, passe-temps; pt. 6, Outils, outillages; t. 3–4, pt. 7, Vêtements, bijoux de corps, objets de toilette; t. 5–6, pt. 8, Armes de guerre offensives et défensives. Arranged as a dictionary under these headings. Each volume has a "Table générale alphabétique" at the end, and the last volume has one for the entire work.

Histories and Handbooks

1619
Alexandre, Arsène. . . . Histoire de l'art décoratif du XVIe siècle à nos jours; préface de Roger Marx: ouvrage orné de quarante-huit planches en couleurs, douze eaux-fortes, cinq cent vingt-six dessins dans le texte . . . Paris, Laurens [1892]. 336 p. 526 illus., 60 plates (part col.) 41 cm.

Illustrated by very good chromolithographs by Lemercier and line drawings in the text. Contents: Les arts du bois, Les arts du métal, La terre et le verre, Les arts du tissu. No index but a list of plates and table of contents at end.

1620
Aloi, Roberto. L'arredamento moderno, sesta serie . . . Milano, Hoepli, 1955. 471 p. (chiefly illus., part col.) 28 cm.

1st series 1934; 2d series 1939. A collection of excellent illustrations of modern decorative arts which is international in scope. Preface by Agnoldomenico Pica.

1621
Ball, Katherine M. Decorative motives of Oriental art . . . with six hundred and seventy-three illustrations. London, Lane; N.Y., Dodd, Mead [1927]. 286 p. illus. 33 cm.

Arranged by subject. Bibliography p. [273]–81. Index p. 283–86.

1622
Batchelder, Ernest Allen. Design in theory and practice . . . N.Y., Macmillan, 1925. 271 p. illus., 66 plates. 21 cm.

"The purpose is to make the worker think in terms of design, whatever medium or technique he may choose to employ."—*Pref.* A general book on design which is widely used. Index p. 269–71.

1623
Berliner, Rudolf. Ornamentale Vorlageblätter des 15. bis 18. Jahrhunderts. Leipzig,

Klinkhardt & Biermann, 1926. 182 p. *and* atlas of 450 plates in 2 v. 32 cm.

An important corpus of decorative engravings. "Verzeichnis abgekürtzt zitierter Literatur" p. x. Indexes: of artists p. 173–75; of publishers p. 175–76; of collections from which the illustrations were reproduced p. 176–77.

1624

Bossert, Helmuth Theodore. An encyclopedia of colour decoration from the earliest times to the middle of the XIXth century, with explanatory text . . . N.Y., Weyhe, 1928. 34 p. illus., 120 col. plates. 32 cm.

A collection of color plates, mostly of mural paintings, tracing the development of designs in various periods and countries. "Catalogue" p. 14–35 consists of notes on the plates, giving sources for the illustrations.

1625

Bossert, Helmuth Theodor. Geschichte des Kunstgewerbes aller Zeiten und Völker in Verbindung mit zahlreichen Fachgelehrten herausgegeben von Dr. H. Th. Bossert. Berlin, Wasmuth [1928–35]. 6 v. illus., plates (part col.) 27 cm.

A standard work on the history of applied arts throughout the world from the ice age through the 19th century. Contains contributions by many experts. One volume is devoted to Oriental art and one to early American art. Bibliographies at end of chapters.

1626

Bossert, Helmuth Theodor, ed. Ornament in applied art, 122 color plates reproducing over 2000 decorative motives from the arts of Asia, primitive Europe, North, Central and South America, Africa, Oceania and from the peasant arts of Europe; with an introduction and catalogue by H. Th. Bossert. N.Y., Weyhe, 1924. 35 p. 122 col. plates. 40 cm.

"Main consideration has been devoted to the pre-classic, occidental, Islamic, Asiatic and ancient American cultures during the period of their higher development, as well as to those of native peoples and European folk art."—*Introd.* Plates are very good collotypes and halftones in color. "Description of plates" p. 1–24 gives location of objects. Index p. 25–26 lists plates by type of work or medium. Alphabetical list of names p. 27–33 is really an index. List of plates p. 34–35.

1627

Bossert, Helmuth Theodor. Peasant art in Europe . . . examples of peasant ornament

and handicraft taken directly from unpublished originals. London, Benn, 1927. 44 p. 132 plates (100 col.) 40 cm.

A collection of good illustrations of peasant art from various countries of Europe, arranged by country of origin. A German ed. of this work has also been published. "List of dated items" p. 30. "Table of contents" p. 21–33 is arranged alphabetically by name of object depicted. Index of names p. 34–39. Bibliography p. 40–43.

1628

Brøndsted, Johannes. Early English ornament; the sources, development and relation to foreign styles of pre-Norman ornamental art in England . . . with a preface by Reginald A. Smith. . . . Trans. from the Danish manuscript by Albany F. Major . . . London, Hachette; Copenhagen, Levin & Munksgaard, 1924. 352 p. illus. 26 cm.

"This book is based upon a treatise entitled 'Nordisk og fremmed ornamentik i vikingetiden.'" Contents: (1) From the introduction of Christianity to the encounter with the Scandinavian style c. A.D. 900; (2) The period from about A.D. 900 till the Conquest; (3) Southern Europe: oriental animal ornament in the pre-Norman period. Index p. 345–52.

1629

Christensen, Erwin Ottomar. The Index of American design. Introd. by Holger Cahill. N.Y., Macmillan, 1950. 229 p. 378 illus. (part col.) 31 cm.

A selection of about 400 illustrations of the crafts and popular and folk arts of the United States as they have been recorded in the *Index of American design,* with accompanying text. "Not only furniture, silver, glass, ceramics and textiles are included but also tavern signs, figureheads, cigar store Indians, carrousel horses, toys, pots and pans and many other items."—*Pref.*

"Subject list (p. 209–17) covers the entire collection of water-color renderings and photographs in the Index of American Design at the National Gallery of Art." Bibliography p. 219–21. Index p. 223–29.

1630

The Connoisseur. The Connoisseur period guides to the houses, decoration, furnishing, and chattels of the classic periods, edited by Ralph Edwards & L. G. G. Ramsey. New York, Reynal, 1957–58. 6 v. illus. (part col.), ports., facsims. 26 cm.

Originally published London, The Connoisseur, 1956–58.

Well-illustrated volumes containing about 175 pages of text which cover architecture, painting, sculpture, decoration, silver, glass, pottery, textiles, miniatures, jewelry, musical instruments, etc.

Contents: [1] The Tudor period, 1500–1603; [2] The Stuart period, 1603–1714; [3] The early Georgian period, 1714–1760; [4] The late Georgian period, 1760–1810; [5] The Regency period, 1810–30; [6] The early Victorian period, 1830–60. Includes bibliographical references. Indexed.

1631

Decorative art . . . the Studio year book . . . 1906–(56/57). London, The Studio Ltd. [etc.] 1906–(56/57). illus., plates (part col.) 30 cm.

Title varies: *The Studio, year book of decorative* (1921, *of applied*) *art*. Primarily pictorial, with short texts. It forms a record of 50 years of contemporary decorative arts and covers interior decoration, furniture, glass, lighting, pottery, textiles, metalwork, etc.

1632

Drepperd, Carl William. First reader for antique collectors. Garden City, Doubleday, 1946. 274 p. illus. 22 cm.

A popular type of book, covering furniture, silver, pewter, glass, toys, etc. Well illustrated. Includes bibliographies. Glossary and index p. 243–74.

1633

Evans, Joan. Pattern: a study of ornament in western Europe from 1180 to 1900. Oxford, Clarendon Press, 1931. 2 v. illus., plates. 30 cm.

A scholarly English language history of ornament. Contents: v. 1, The mistress art, Speculum naturae, The mark of the individual, Literature and decoration, The romance of distance; v. 2, The new age, The Far East, Les amateurs, The return to antiquity, The return to nature, The romance of the past, The age of theory. Bibliographical footnotes. Index v. 2, p. 201–49.

1634

Glazier, Richard. A manual of historic ornament, treating upon the evolution, tradition and development of architecture & the applied arts; prepared for the use of students and craftsmen. 6th ed. rev. and enl. with 700 illus. by the author and from photos., etc. London, N.Y., Batsford [1948]. 184 p. illus. (part col.) 25 cm.

First published 1899; 2d ed. 1906; 3d ed. 1914; 4th ed. 1926; 5th ed. 1933. A useful manual. Bibliography p. 177–81.

1635

Guilmard, Désiré. Les maîtres ornemanistes, dessinateurs, peintres, architectes, sculpteurs et graveurs; écoles française,—italienne,—allemande,—et des Pays-Bas (flamande & hollandaise). Ouvrage renfermant le répertoire général des maîtres ornemanistes avec l'indication précise des pièces d'ornement qui se trouvent dans les cabinets publics et particuliers de France, de Belgique etc. . . . Publication enrichie de 180 planches tirées à part et de nombreuses gravures dan le texte donnant environ 250 spécimens des principaux maîtres et precédée d'une introduction par M. le baron Davillier. Paris, Plon, 1880–81. 560 p. illus., facsim. *and* atlas of 180 plates. 30 cm.

A corpus of decorative designs arranged according to schools, under which masters are arranged chronologically; an index of motifs and one of artists follow each school. Old and not always complete but still useful. "Ouvrages à consulter à la Bibliothèque de Paris" p. 523–27.

"Table générale alphabétique," p. 545–58, is an author index to the whole work.

1636

Hamlin, Alfred Dwight Foster. A history of ornament. N.Y., Century [c1916]–23. 2 v. illus., 92 plates (part col.) 23 cm.

A standard and valuable work, illustrated by line drawings in the text and plates. Contents: v. [1] Ancient and medieval; v. [2] Renaissance and modern. Contains bibliographies. Index at end of each volume.

1637

Jones, Owen. The grammar of ornament. Illus. by examples from various styles of ornament . . . London, Quaritch, 1910. 157 p. illus., 111 plates (part col.) 35 cm.

An old but still standard work. With contributions by J. B. Waring, J. O. Westwood, and M. Digby Wyatt. Covers East as well as West and "savage tribes." Illustrated by chromolithography. Bibliography at end of sections. 1st ed. 1856.

1638

Labarte, Jules. Histoire des arts industriels au moyen âge et à l'époque de la renaissance . . . Paris, Morel, 1864–66. 4 v. illus. 25 cm. *and* album (2 v.) of 148 plates (part col.) 33 cm.

An old standard work. Contents: t. 1, Sculpture, orfèvrerie; t. 2, Orfèvrerie; t. 3, Peinture, émaillerie; t. 4, Émaillerie, mosaïque, peinture en matières textiles, damasquinerie, art céramique, verrerie, art de l'armurier, horlogerie, mobilier civil et religieux. "Table des matières" v. 4, p. 711–825 is an index to the whole work.

1639

Meyer, Franz Sales. A handbook of ornament, with three hundred plates, containing about three thousand illustrations of the elements, and the application of decoration to objects . . . Chicago, Wilcox & Follett, 1945. 548 p. incl. illus., plates. 22 cm.

First published in 1888 and translated into English in 1892. Foreword by Meyric R. Rogers. A standard handbook. Contents: (I) The elements of decoration; (II) Ornament applied to features; (III) Decorated objects. Index p. 543–48.

1640

Molinier, Émile. Histoire générale des arts appliqués à l'industrie du Ve à la fin du XVIIIe siècle . . . Paris, Lévy, 1896–1919. 6 v. illus., plates. 44 x 32 cm.

Volume 5 never published. An old standard work. Contents: (1) Les ivoires; (2) Les meubles du moyen âge et de la renaissance; (3) Le mobilier au XVIIe et au XVIIIe siècle; (4) L'orfèvrerie religieuse et civile au Ve à la fin du XVe siècle; (6) Les tapisseries, par Jules Guiffrey.

1641

Möller, Lieselotte. Der Wrangelschrank und die verwandten süddeutschen Intarsienmöbel des 16. Jahrhunderts. Berlin, Deutscher Verein für Kunstwissenschaft, 1956. 194 p. illus. 31 cm.

A history of intarsia and the only treatment of Mannerist decorative arts. Contains 199 illustrations on plates and 38 in the text. Catalog raisonné p. 156–76. Bibliography p. 178–83. Topographical index p. 184–85. Index p. 186–94.

1642

Racinet, Albert Charles Auguste, ed. L'ornement polychrome; deux cents vingt planches en couleur, or et argent, contenant environ 4000 motifs de tous les styles, art ancien et asiatique, moyen âge, renaissance, XVIIe et XVIIIe siècles; recueil historique et pratique publié sous la direction de M. A. Racinet . . . avec des notices explicatives et une introduction générale . . . Paris, Firmin Didot, 1888. 2 v. illus., 220 col. plates. 42 cm.

A one-volume English ed., London, Sotheran, 1873. An old standard work. Contains a general introduction and notes to each plate. "Tableau de concordance des signes et titres mis sur les planches" p. [v–vii]. "Table des motifs contenus dans les 220 planches classés par genres ou industries" at end of v. 2.

1643

Speltz, Alexander. Styles of ornament, exhibited in designs, and arranged in historical order, with descriptive text. A handbook for architects, designers, painters, sculptors, wood-carvers, chasers, modellers, cabinetmakers, and artistic locksmiths as well as for technical schools, libraries and private study. Trans. from the 2d German ed. by David O'Conor. N.Y., Grosset and Dunlap [1935]. 647 p. illus., plates. 24 cm.

"New 1936 edition, issued 1935." First German ed. published 1904; 2d ed. 1906 with 400 plates instead of 300. A very useful standard work. "The original work was undertaken with the object of representing the entire range of ornament in all its different styles from prehistoric times till the middle of the 19th century and to illustrate the different uses to which it had been applied."—*Pref.* "List of reference books" p. [627]–29. "Index of illustrations according to subject and material" p. 630–47.

1644

Strange, Edward Fairbrother. Chinese lacquer . . . London, Benn, 1926. 71 p. illus., 54 plates (part col.) 29 cm.

600 copies printed. Contents: (1) Technique; (2) History; (3) Subjects of decoration; (4) Description of the illustrations. "Marks of date" p. 65–66. "Motives of decoration" p. 67–68. Bibliography p. 69–70. Index p. 71–72.

1645

Wettergren, Erik. The modern decorative arts of Sweden . . . [Malmö] Malmö Museum; N.Y., American-Scandinavian Foundation [1926]. 240 p. illus., 142 plates (part col.) 29 cm.

Translated by Tage Palm. A comprehensive pictorial survey with 50 pages of preliminary text. "List of associations, merchants, industries, and artists who work for the decorative arts in Sweden" p. 197–204.

1646

Williamson, Scott Graham. The American craftsman . . . N.Y., Crown [c1940]. 239 p. plates, maps, facsims. 26 cm.

Covers houses and housebuilders, furniture makers, craftsmen in clay, makers of glass, silversmiths, weavers, ironmasters, pewterers, bookbinders, etc. Check list p. 191–218 of craftsmen according to their trade. Bibliographies p. 220–32.

1647

Wollin, Nils Gistaf Axelsson. Modern Swedish arts and crafts in pictures . . . N.Y., Scribner [1931]. 30 p. plates (part col.) 33 cm.

Contents: Interior decoration, Furniture, Intarsiatura, Lighting fittings, Stone, Stucco, Metals (Iron, wrought and cast; Stainless steel, Copper and bronze; Pewter; Precious metals), Glass, Ceramics, Home crafts, Modern textiles, Books, and Posters.

SEE ALSO: Allemagne. Les accessoires du costume et du mobilier (1655).

Costume

Bibliography

1648

Colas, René. Bibliographie générale du costume et de la mode; description des suites, recueils, séries, revues et livres français et étrangers relatifs au costume civil, militaire et religieux, aux modes, aux coiffures et aux divers accessoires de l'habillement . . . Paris, Colas, 1933. 2 v. 26 cm.

Limited edition of 1000 copies. 3131 items listed alphabetically by author or main entry, covering costume and fashion.

For each item gives bibliographical information, approximate size, and a description of what the work contains; also mentions its appearance in any of the important bibliographies which are listed in the preface.

Index of proper names and anonymous titles (p. 1122–1411) and a "Table méthodique" of 68 pages.

1649

Detroit. Public Library. Costume, a list of books. [Detroit] Detroit Public Library, Fine Arts Dept., 1928. 56 p. 23 cm.

Arranged alphabetically by subject or geographical division.

In general, closes with the end of the 19th century, but there are a few more recent entries on modern costume.

1650

Hiler, Hilaire, and Hiler, Meyer. Bibliography of costume, a dictionary catalog of about eight thousand books and periodicals, edited by Helen Grant Cushing, assisted by Adah V. Morris. N.Y., Wilson, 1939. 911 p. 26 cm.

Arranged in dictionary form with author, editor, engraver, illustrator, subject, and title entries in one alphabet.

Lists "approximately 8400 works on costume and adornment, including books in all languages."—*Pref.*

"Costumes and ideologies" p. xi–xxxix.

1651

Lipperheide, Franz Joseph, *Freiherr* von. Katalog der Freiherrlich von Lipperheide'-schen Kostümbibliothek . . . Berlin, Lipperheide, 1896–1905. 2 v. illus., facsim. 29 cm.

A scholarly, detailed, classed bibliography of the collection which was presented to the Prussian government and is now in the Staatliche Kunstbibliothek, Berlin (2525).

Index of names v. 2, p. 759–833, and of subjects p. 834–38.

Indexes

1652

Monro, Isabel Stevenson, and Cook, Dorothy E. Costume index; a subject index to plates and to illustrated texts . . . N.Y., Wilson, 1937. 338 p. 26 cm.

An index to plates in 615 titles, comprising 942 volumes. Detailed indexing under countries and localities and under classes of persons having special types of costume, as well as under details of costumes, with chronological subdivisions of the major classes. List of books indexed (p. 295–338) indicates location of books in a number of libraries.

————. Supplement. N.Y., Wilson, 1957. 210 p. 26 cm.

Dictionaries and Encyclopedias

1653

Leloir, Maurice. Dictionnaire du costume et de ses accessoires, des armes et des étoffes, des origines à nos jours . . . Paris, Gründ [1951]. 435 p. illus., 7 col. plates. 28 cm.

"Achevé et executé sous la direction de André Dupuis et publié sous les auspices de la Société de l'Histoire du Costume." A standard work containing more than 2000 articles, 3500 black and white illustrations, and eight colored plates. The preface by George Toudouze is devoted to Leloir, and his antecedents and relatives.

1654

Picken, Mary (Brooks). Fashion dictionary; fabric, sewing and dress as expressed in the language of fashion. Claire Valentine, editorial associate. N.Y., Funk & Wagnalls [1957] 397 p. illus., plates. 24 cm.

A rev. and expanded ed. of the author's *Language of fashion* (N.Y., Funk & Wagnalls, 1939). Includes definitions and descriptions of more than 10,000 terms, 700 illustrations of detailed drawings, and 175 photographs.

Histories and Handbooks

1655

Allemagne, Henry René d'. Les accessoires du costume et du mobilier depuis le treizième jusqu'au milieu du dix-neuvième siècle. . . . Ouvrage contenant 393 phototypies, reproduisant plus de 3000 documents. Paris, Schemit, 1928. 3 v. plates. 34 cm.

1000 copies printed. Paged continuously. Collotype illustrations. Contents: (1) Le parure et la toilette; (2) Menus objets mobiliers; (3) Outils, instruments et appareils de précision; (4) La table et la cuisine. "Table analytique" v. 3, p. 511–50. "Table méthodique" v. 3, p. [551]–63. "Bibliographie" v. 3, p. [565]–67.

1656

Argenti, Philip Pandely. The costumes of Chios, their development from the XVth to the XXth century. London, Batsford [1953]. 338 p. illus., 111 plates (part col.), map. 27 cm.

Edition of 500 copies. A well-illustrated account of Chian costume. Appendices: A–C, Original texts describing Chian costume from journals of travelers; D, Synonyms and homonyms in nomenclature of Chian costume. Bibliographical footnotes. Index p. 303–38.

1657

Bock, Fr[anz]. Geschichte der liturgischen Gewänder des Mittelalters; oder, Entstehung und Entwicklung der kirchlichen Ornate und Paramente in Rücksicht auf Stoff, Gewebe, Farbe, Zeichnung, Schnitt und rituelle Bedeutung nachgewiesen und durch 110 Abbildungen in Farbendruck. . . . Mit einem Vorworte von Dr. Georg Müller. Bonn, Henry & Cohen, 1856–71. 3 v. in 2. plates (part col.) 25 cm.

A detailed history of church vestments,

their color, design, materials, and liturgical significance. Well illustrated by many plates, some in color. Index of names v. 2, p. [363]–79.

1658

Boehn, Max von. Modes and manners . . . trans. by Joan Joshua. . . . Illustrated with reproductions of contemporary paintings . . . London, Harrap; Philadelphia, Lippincott, 1932–[36]. 4 v. illus., col. plates. 22 cm.

Attempts to describe the fashions and social manners from ancient times through the 18th century and is more a cultural history than a reference book. However, it is illustrated with art works and certain chapters deal with art. Contents: (1) From the decline of the ancient world to the Renaissance; (2) The 16th century; (3) The 17th century; (4) The 18th century. Volume 4 is illustrated with reproductions of contemporary paintings selected by Dr. Oskar Fischel.

1659

Boehn, Max von. Modes & manners of the nineteenth century as represented in the pictures and engravings of the time, translated from the German of Dr. Oskar Fischel and Max von Boehn; trans. by M. Edwardes, with an introduction by Grace Rhys . . . London, Dent; N.Y., Dutton, 1927. 4 v. illus., plates (part col.) 22 cm.

First published 1909; rev. and enl. 1927. Issued in French, German, and English. The quality of the illustrations is best in the German ed. Contents: (1) 1790–1817; (2) 1818–1842; (3) 1843–1878; (4) 1879–1914. No index.

A supplementary volume, published in 1929, covers lace, fans, gloves, walking sticks, parasols, jewelry, and trinkets.

1660

Bruhn, Wolfgang, and Tilke, Max. A pictorial history of costume; a survey of costume of all periods and peoples from antiquity to modern times including national costume in Europe and non-European countries . . . N.Y., Praeger [1955]. 74 p. 200 plates (128 col.) 35 cm. (Books that matter)

Translation of *Das Kostümwerk*. "The color plates are facsimiles from the originals colored by Max Tilke. The monochrome plates have been produced partly from Tilke's drawings and partly from engravings and photographs in the Lipperheide Kostümbibliothek."—*Pref.* Index of plates p. 73–74.

1661

Cunnington, Cecil Willett. English women's clothing in the nineteenth century. London, Faber [1948]. 460 p. illus., plates (part col.) 30 cm.

First published 1937. A detailed survey of costume and accessories of this period. "Glossary of materials" p. 429-36. "Glossary of certain technical terms" p. 437-38. "Glossary of obsolete colour names" p. 439-40. "Authorities" p. 441-42. Index p. 447-60.

1662

Cunnington, Cecil Willett. English women's clothing in the present century. London, Faber [1952]. 312 p. illus. 30 cm.

Similar to his book on the 19th century. "Glossary of textiles" p. 294-96. Index p. 297-312.

The author has also published a series of *Handbooks of English costume* . . . , covering the medieval period, the 16th, 17th, and 18th centuries (Faber, 1952-55, 23 cm.).

1663

Davenport, Millia. The book of costume. N.Y., Crown, 1948. 2 v. 958 p. illus. (part col.) 29 cm.

Paged continuously. "A chronological survey of dress through the ages. Each segment —civilization or century—has been given an historical summary and an outline of changes in its dress. These are followed by a picture section, which is subdivided by centuries and by countries, as regional differentiations become well established."—*Introd.* Illustrations are mostly from paintings, sculpture, and engravings.

"In the Index, three sorts of material will be found, names and location of biographies of artists; names of subjects shown in the illustrations; and material immediately relative to costume." Thus it is a selective index (v. 2, p. 946-58). Appendix in v. 2 contains bibliographies with annotations.

1664

Earle, Alice (Morse). Two centuries of costume in America, MDCXX–MDCCCXX. N.Y., Macmillan, 1903. 2 v. illus., plates. 21 cm.

Paged continuously. Index p. 811-24.

1665

Evans, Mary. Costume throughout the ages. [Rev. ed.] Philadelphia and N.Y., Lippincott [1950]. 360 p. illus. 22 cm.

1st ed. 1930. A short one-volume account

which resembles a textbook. Includes bibliographies at end of chapters and a general bibliography p. 318-29. Index p. 347-58.

1666

Gorsline, Douglas W. What people wore; a visual history of dress from ancient times to twentieth-century America . . . N.Y., Viking, 1952. 266 p. illus. (part col.) 31 cm.

A visual encyclopedia of historical dress from the 9th to the 20th century in Europe and from 1840 to 1925 in America, with short textual summaries and occasional historical surveys. Contents: (1) Costume of the ancient world; (2) European costume; (3) American costume. Bibliography p. 249-56, with indications of call numbers of the Metropolitan Museum of Art Library or the New York Public Library Art Reference room.

1667

Houston, Mary Galway. Ancient Egyptian, Mesopotamian & Persian costume and decoration. 2d ed., with eight plates in colour and over two hundred drawings in the text. London, Black [1954]. 190 p. illus., plates. 24 cm. (A technical history of costume, 1)

First published 1920. Emphasis on construction of the costume with diagrams. Bibliography p. 188-90.

1668

Houston, Mary Galway. Ancient Greek, Roman and Byzantine costume and decoration. 2d ed., with eight plates in colour, and over two hundred drawings in the text. London, Black, 1947. 182 p. illus., 8 col. plates. 24 cm. (A technical history of costume, 2)

First published 1931. Emphasis on techniques, patterns, and design. Bibliography p. 179-82.

1669

Houston, Mary Galway. Medieval costume in England & France; the 13th, 14th and 15th centuries. With eight plates in colour and 350 drawings in black and white. London, Black, 1939. 228 p. illus., 8 col. plates. 24 cm. (A technical history of costume, 3)

Sometimes gives patterns of costumes. Glossary of medieval terms for costume p. 219-26. Bibliography p. 227-28.

1670

Kelly, Francis Michael, and Schwabe, Randolph. Historic costume, a chronicle of fashion in Western Europe, 1490-1790 . . . London, Batsford, 1925. 284 p. illus., plates (part col.) 26 cm.

2d ed. 1929. Treats of "fashionable civil apparel" in England, France, and the Low Countries. Patterns p. 269–78. Bibliography p. 279–81. Index and glossary p. 282–84.

1671

Köhler, Karl. History of costume, edited and augmented by Emma von Sichart, trans. by Alexander K. Dallas . . . with sixteen plates in colour and about 600 other illustrations and patterns. N.Y., Watt, 1928. 463 p. illus., 16 col. plates. 22 cm.

"In editing Köhler's writings for the present work I have omitted some passages and shortened others. In particular I have discarded his introductions, which deal with the history of various periods."—*Pref.*

A handy one-volume history of costume from antiquity to 1870 with emphasis on the technical side. Patterns given. Bibliography p. 457–58. Index p. 459–64.

1672

Köhler, Karl. Praktische Kostümkunde in 600 Bildern und Schnitten, nach Carl Köhler, bearb. von Emma von Sichart. München, Bruckmann [1926]. 2 v. illus., plates (part col.) 20 cm.

Gives patterns for costumes. Contents: (1) Vom Altertum bis zur Mitte des 16. Jahrhunderts; (2) Von der Mitte des 16. Jahrhunderts bis auf die Jahre 1870. Literatur-Verzeichnis p. 545–46.

1673

Laver, James, ed. Costume of the western world. London, Harrap; N.Y., Harper, 1951. v. 3. 390 p. plates (28 col.) 28 cm.

Only v. 3: *Fashions of the Renaissance in England, France, Spain and Holland* has been published to date. The work is intended to be in six volumes and will cover ancient to modern times, with one volume on regional and specialized costume.

Volume 3 covers the years 1485 to 1650, with different sections written by various scholars. Illustrations are drawn from contemporary sources. Bibliographies.

1674

Leloir, Maurice. Histoire du costume de l'antiquité à 1914. Paris, Ernst, 1933–(49). v. 8–12. illus., plates (part col.) 33 cm.

At head of title: Ouvrage publié sous la direction de M. Maurice Leloir, et sous le patronage de la Société de l'Histoire du Costume. Préface de M. Henri Lavedan.

Each volume covers a specific period. Illustrated with line drawings in the text and color plates. Bibliographies in each volume.

1675

Lester, Katherine Morris. Historic costume; a résumé of the characteristic types of costume from the most remote times to the present day . . . illustrated by Ila McAfee and Helen Westermann. Rev. and enl. ed. Peoria, Ill., Manual Arts Press [1942]. 256 p. illus., plates. 25 cm.

1st ed. 1925; 2d ed. 1933. 1st and 2d eds. contain bibliography which is omitted in 3d. 2d and 3d eds. contain a section on American costume. A good brief survey of the field of costume. Index p. 250–56.

1676

Lester, Katherine Morris, and Oerke, Bess Viola. Illustrated history of those frills and furbelows of fashion which have come to be known as: accessories of dress; drawings by Helen Westermann. Peoria, Ill., Manual Arts Press [c1940]. 587 p. illus. 27 cm.

Cover title: Accessories of dress. Contents: (1) Accessories worn at the head; (2) Accessories worn at the neck, shoulders and waist; (3) Accessories worn on the feet and legs; (4) Accessories worn on the arm and hand; (5) Accessories carried in the hand; (6) Accessories used on the costume (embroidery, lace, fur, etc.). Bibliography p. 577–79 as well as references at end of each chapter. Index to illustrations p. 580–83; to text p. 584–87.

1677

McClellan, Elisabeth. History of American costume, 1607–1870; with an introductory chapter on dress in the Spanish and French settlements in Florida and Louisiana . . . N.Y., Tudor, 1937. 661 p. illus., plates (part col.) 28 cm.

Copyright 1904 and 1910. New ed. 1937. Contents: (1) The seventeenth century; (2) The eighteenth century. At the beginning of each of the two books a list of the rulers and periods. Glossary for 1607–1800, p. 615–30. Glossary for 1800–1870, p. 631–40. Index p. 641–54. "Authorities consulted" p. [655]–61.

1678

Norris, Herbert. Church vestments; their origin and development; illustrated with 8 pages of photographs and with 8 colour plates, and black and white drawings by the author. London, Dent [1949]. 190 p. illus., plates (part col.) 26 cm.

Arranged by types and under each type by centuries. Bibliography p. xiii–xiv. "Brief historical data" p. xv. Index p. 189–90.

1679

Norris, Herbert. Costume & fashion . . . London, Dent [1931]–(40). v. 1–3 (in 4), 6. illus., plates (part col.) 26 cm.

Volume 1 first published 1924; 2d ed. has slight revision. Volumes 4 and 5 not yet published.

Chronological data and charts are given. All illustrations are drawn by the author in black and white and color. Contents: [v. 1] Evolution of European dress through the earlier ages; v. 2, Senlac to Bosworth, 1066–1485; v. 3, The Tudors, Bk. 1, 1485–1547; Bk. 2, 1547–1603; v. 5, The Hanoverians; v. 6, The 19th century. Each volume has a general index and an index of names.

1680

Planché, James Robinson. A cyclopedia of costume or dictionary of dress; including notices of contemporary fashions on the Continent; a general chronological history of the costumes of the principal countries of Europe, from the commencement of the Christian era to the accession of George the third. London, Chatto and Windus, 1876–79. 2 v. illus., 50 plates (part col.) 20 cm.

A standard work, illustrated by engravings in the text and chromolithographs. Contents: v. 1, The dictionary; v. 2, A general history of costume in Europe. Index v. 2, p. 435–48.

1681

Racinet, Albert Charles Auguste. Le costume historique. Cinq cents planches, trois cents en couleurs, or et argent, deux cents en camaieu. Types principaux du vêtement et de la parure, rapprochés de ceux de l'intérieur de l'habitation dans tous les temps et chez tous les peuples, avec de nombreux détails sur le mobilier, les armes, les objets usuels, les moyens de transport, etc. Recueil pub. sous la direction de M. A. Racinet, avec des notices explicatives, une introduction générale, des tables et un glossaire. Paris, Firmin-Didot, 1888. 6 v. 500 plates (part col.) 41 cm.

Volume 1 is mainly explanatory text with an introduction by the author. Volumes 2–6 are plates accompanied by descriptive text and were published in 20 fascicles 1877–1886. "Bibliographie du costume" v. 1, p. 113–24. "Glossaire" v. 1, p. 125–62.

1682

Tilke, Max. Oriental costumes, their designs and colors. London, Paul, Trench, Trubner [1923]. 32 p. 128 col. plates. 30 cm.

"Printed in Germany." "Translated by L.

Hamilton." A collection of good color plates representing the most characteristic forms of the costumes of each country in the Orient, with short text. Emphasis on the construction of the costumes.

1683

Truman, Nevil. Historic costuming . . . London, Pitman, 1936. 152 p. illus., col. plates. 25 cm.

First published 1936; 3d impression 1937. An outline of costumes worn from 550 B.C. to 1910, illustrated with line drawings on which are indicated the terminology of the various parts. Appendix: Diagrams showing the evolution of styles p. 135–48. Index p. 149–52.

Furniture
Bibliography

1684

Copenhagen. Danske Kunstindustrimuseum. Bibliotek. . . . Møbler . . . [København, Petersen] 1928. 49 p. illus. 22 cm. (Its Bogfortegnelser I)

A listing, under broad subject divisions, of the holdings in the field of furniture, of this one library. Books in various languages are included. Author index p. 47–49 and series index p. [50].

1685

Detroit. Public Library. Furniture, a list of books in the Detroit Public Library. [Detroit] Detroit Public Library, Fine Arts Dept., 1929. 65 p. 23 cm.

A classed bibliography with some short annotations indicating special features.

Contents: General, Styles, Individual Pieces, Miscellaneous.

Index p. 62–65.

1686

Grand Rapids, Mich. Public Library. . . . List of books on furniture, with descriptive notes, issued in connection with the Hundredth Furniture Market in Grand Rapids, January 1928. [Grand Rapids] Library, 1927. 142 p. 24 cm.

Confined mostly to books but includes some periodicals devoted entirely to furniture.

Arranged alphabetically by author, with subject index p. 133–42.

Dictionaries and Encyclopedias

1687

Aronson, Joseph. The encyclopedia of furniture, illustrated with 1,115 photographs and many line cuts. N.Y., Crown [c1938]. 202 p. illus., plates, diagrs. 29 cm.

"The major part of this book consists of monographs of the important items of furniture knowledge, supplemented by some 2500 separate definitions and descriptions. More than half of the book is devoted to photographs."—*Pref.* A useful popular work. Numerous cross references. Bibliography p. 201–02.

1688

Bajot, Édouard. Encyclopédie du meuble du XVe siècle jusqu'à nos jours. . . . Recueil de planches contenant des meubles de style de toutes les époques et de tous les pays, depuis le XVe siècle . . . classées par ordre alphabétique . . . 2000 meubles de style reproduits à grand échelle. Paris, Schmid [1901–09]. 20 pts. in 19 v. 600 plates. 47 cm.

A corpus of illustrations of furniture containing 2000 pieces classified and arranged in alphabetical order. At the beginning of v. 1 is a "Notice" which gives a short paragraph describing the different pieces of furniture represented; and a "Table analytique des planches" which lists all of the plates arranged by type of furniture.

1689

Gloag, John. A short dictionary of furniture, containing 1764 terms used in Britain and America. With 630 illus. from original sources and by various hands of which 144 were specially drawn by Ronald Escott. London, Allen & Unwin [1952]. 565 p. illus. 22 cm.

Entries confined to "Names and terms . . . of European or Asiatic origin only when they have influenced the design, materials or use of English or American furniture."—*Pref.*

Contents: (1) Description of furniture; (2) Design of furniture; (3) Dictionary of names and terms p. 108–520; (4) Furniture makers in Britain and America p. 521–31; (5) Books and periodicals on furniture and design p. 532–36; (6) Periods, types, materials and craftsmen from 1100 to 1950 (arranged in tabular form) p. 537–65.

1690

Lockwood, Luke Vincent. The furniture collectors' glossary . . . N.Y., Walpole Society, 1913. 55 p. illus. 25 cm.

200 copies printed. A pioneer effort which is now out of focus. "The present volume is compiled with the idea of bringing together in convenient form the words used in

the cabinetmaker's art."—*Pref.* Numerous cross references and line drawings.

1691

Penderel-Brodhurst, James George Joseph, and Layton (Edwin J.). A glossary of English furniture of the historic periods . . . London, Murray [1925]. 196 p. 20 cm.

Identifies prominent cabinetmakers and authors, as well as giving definitions of terms.

SEE ALSO: Macquoid. The dictionary of English furniture (1712).

Biography

1692

Bjerkoe, Ethel Hall, and Bjerkoe, John Arthur. The cabinetmakers of America. . . . Foreword by Russell Kettell, illustrated with photographs and drawings. [1st ed.] Garden City, Doubleday, 1957. 252 p. illus., plates. 27 cm.

A biographical dictionary of American cabinetmakers. For each one gives a few sentences or paragraphs of biographical information, with references to sources. Illustrated by line drawings and halftone plates. "Cabinet making as it developed in America" p. 1–17. Glossary p. 241–46. Bibliography p. 249–52.

1693

Salverte, François de. Les ébénistes du XVIIIe siècle, leurs oeuvres et leurs marques. Ouvrage contenant un millier de notices présentées dans l'ordre alphabétique et 500 reproductions d'estampilles. 4. éd. rev. et augm. Paris, van Oest, 1953. 352 p. 71 plates. 30 cm.

First published 1923; 2d ed. 1927. This ed. contains the integral text of the 2d ed., rev. and corrected by the author and further notes added by his wife. The bibliography has been omitted but 70 new marks were added.

Appendix p. 319–26 contains a list of marks found on 18th century furniture. Index p. 327–45 does not include cabinetmakers, as they are arranged in dictionary form in the text. "Table des planches" p. [347]–52.

Histories and Handbooks

1694

Feulner, Adolf. Kunstgeschichte des Möbels seit dem Altertum . . . Berlin, Propyläen-Verlag [c1927]. 654 p. illus. 29 cm.

A basic one-volume treatment of furniture

from the Middle Ages through the Biedermeier period, with many illustrations in the text, some of which are from paintings. Bibliography p. 613–17. Index p. 635–55, and Index of illustrations p. 618.

1695

Hinckley, F. Lewis. A directory of antique furniture; the authentic classification of European and American designs for professionals and connoisseurs. N.Y., Crown [1953]. 355 p. of illus. 29 cm.

A collection of good illustrations with 34 pages of preliminary text, putting stress on the interrelation of furniture designs and the spread of French and English design influences into various countries as well as into structural methods and materials. Unfortunately the illustrations are undocumented.

1696

Johnson, Axel Petrus, and Sironen, Marta Katrina, comp. Manual of the furniture arts and crafts . . . ed. by W. J. Etten. Grand Rapids, Mich., A. P. Johnson, 1928. 899 p. illus. 17 cm.

"Furniture craftsmen, architects and artisans to the twentieth century with brief biography" p. 159–682. Contents: (1) Narrative of furniture; (2) Origin and identification of design; (3) Technical description of the furniture periods and styles; (4) Furniture woods; (5) Veneers and plywood; (6) Furniture machinery; (7) Furniture construction; (8) Furniture finished and finishing; (9) Furniture upholstery; (10) Furniture transportation; (11) Furniture as an industry; (12) Furniture museums in the U.S.; (13) Code of selling ethics; (14) Biography; (15) Bibliographies.

"Annotated bibliography of furniture books" p. 685–744. Bibliography of furniture books listed according to subject matter p. 745–80. Alphabetical index p. 841–99.

1697

Müller, Sigrid Flamand Christensen. Alte Möbel vom Mittelalter bis zum Biedermeier. 2 Aufl. München, Bruckmann [1950, c1948]. 208 p. 227 illus. 25 cm.

A one-volume survey of the history of furniture. Good clear illustrations. Bibliography p. 206. Artist index p. 207.

1698

Richter, Gisela Marie Augusta. Ancient furniture; a history of Greek, Etruscan and Ro-

man furniture . . . with an appendix by Albert W. Barker. Oxford, Clarendon Press, 1926. 191 p. illus., 100 plates. 30 cm.

The scholarly definitive work on this subject. Contains a chapter on techniques. Appendix: Scale drawings of Greek furniture, by Albert W. Barker. Bibliographical footnotes. Index p. 183–91.

1699

Schmidt, Robert. Möbel . . . Siebente verm. und verb. Aufl. Mit 239 Abbildungen. Braunschweig, Klinkhardt & Biermann [1953]. 305 p. illus. 25 cm. (Bibliothek für Kunst und Antiquitäten-Freunde, v. 5)

At head of title: Ein Handbuch für Sammler und Liebhaber. A general survey of European furniture from the early Middle Ages through the period of the Empire and Biedermeier styles. Bibliography p. 299–301. Index p. 302–04.

1700

Schmitz, Hermann. The encyclopedia of furniture; an outline history of furniture design in Egypt, Assyria, Persia, Greece, Rome, Italy, France, the Netherlands, Germany, England, Scandinavia, Spain, Russia and in the Near and Far East up to the middle of the nineteenth century, with 659 illustrations arranged on 320 plates, compiled by authorities in various countries under the general direction of Dr. Hermann Schmitz . . . and with an introduction by H. P. Shapland . . . [London] Benn [1926]. 63 p. 320 plates. 32 cm.

Also issued by Praeger, N.Y., 1957.

A collection of good clear plates with brief text.

National

France

1701

Félice, Roger de. French furniture of the Middle Ages and under Louis XIII . . . translated by F. M. Atkinson. London, Heinemann, 1923. 152 p. 65 plates (1 col.) 19 cm. (Little illustrated books on old French furniture, v. 1)

A good short account of this subject. Bibliography p. xvii. Index-glossary p. 149–52.

1702

Félice, Roger de. French furniture under Louis XIV . . . translated by F. M. Atkinson. London, Heinemann, 1922. 147 p. 65 plates (1 col.) 19 cm. (Little illustrated books on old French furniture, v. 2)

A good short account of the subject. "Principal authors" p. xxxi.

1703

Félice, Roger de. . . . French furniture under Louis XV; translated by Florence Simmonds. London, Heinemann, 1927. 132 p. 64 plates on 32 l. 19 cm. (Little illustrated books on old French furniture, 3)

"Principal authorities" p. xv.

1704

Félice, Roger de. . . . French furniture under Louis XVI and the empire, translated by F. M. Atkinson . . . London, Heinemann, 1920. 142 p. 64 plates on 32 l. 19 cm. (Little illustrated books on old French furniture, 4)

Index-glossary p. 135–42.

1705

Ledoux-Lebard, Denise. Les ébénistes parisiens, 1795–1830; leurs oeuvres et leurs marques. Ouvrage contenant 1500 notices présentées dans l'ordre alphabétique, enrichies de reproduction d'estampilles et de factures. Paris, Grund [1951]. 324 p. illus., 55 plates. 28 cm.

Arranged in dictionary form. Bibliography p. 311–18 and bibliographical references in the text.

1706

Theunissen, André. Meubles et sièges du XVIIIe siècle; menuisiers, ébénistes, marques, plans et ornementation de leurs oeuvres. Paris, Éditions "Le Document" [1934]. 194 p. illus., 64 plates (part col.), facsims., diagrs. 34 cm.

An important and useful reference book, well illustrated by plates and drawings of details, with many facsimiles of signatures included in the section devoted to artists.

Contents: Tableau synoptique donnant le classement alphabétique et chronologique des ébénistes du XVIIIe siècle, Meubles et sièges du XVIIIe siècle classés par ordre alphabétique d'auteurs p. 1–179; Fac-similé d'une facture de Chartier, ébéniste et de Morel, maître-sculpteur marbrier, en 1775, Marques d'inventaires, Marques et monogrammes de châteaux, Marques diverses p. 181–95; Listes des marbres utilisés au XVIIIe siècle; Description (Planche en couleurs).

Bibliography p. [199]–[201]. Index of 4 p. Glossary of 4 p.

Great Britain

1707

Heal, *Sir* Ambrose. The London furniture makers, from the Restoration to the Victorian era, 1660–1840; a record of 2500 cabinetmakers, upholsterers, carvers and gilders, with their addresses and working dates, illustrated by 165 reproductions of makers' trade-cards. With a chapter by R. W. Symonds on the problem of identification of the furniture they produced, illustrated by some hitherto unpublished examples of authenticated pieces. London, Batsford [1953]. 276 p. illus., facsims. 30 cm.

Contents: Sources of references p. xix; Selected list of cabinetmakers, upholsterers, carvers and gilders working in London between 1660–1840 with reproductions of a selection of the trade-cards in use during the period p. 3–212; Old English furniture and its makers, the problem of identification with examples of authenticated pieces p. 213–62; Notes on the illustrations referred to in the foregoing section p. 265–76.

1708

Jourdain, Margaret. . . . English decoration and furniture of the early Renaissance (1500–1650), an account of its development and characteristic forms. London, Batsford [1924]. 305 p. illus., plates. 35 cm. (The library of decorative art [v. 1])

Covers decoration as well as furniture, and gives both renderings and illustrations. Index to illustrations p. 297–301; to text p. 301–05.

1709

Jourdain, Margaret. . . . English decoration and furniture of the later XVIIIth century (1760–1820), an account of its development and characteristic forms. London, Batsford [1922]. 269 p. illus., plates. 36 cm. (The library of decorative art)

Good clear illustrations of furniture, decorative details, etc. Index to illustrations p. 261–66; to text p. 267–69.

1710

Lenygon, Francis. . . . Decoration in England from 1640 to 1760. 2d ed. rev. London, Batsford [1927]. 276 p. illus., plates. 36 cm. (The library of decorative art [v. 2])

Half-title: English decoration and furniture of the XVIIth–XIXth centuries II. 1st ed. 1914, impression corrected 1920; 2d ed. 1927. 1st ed. title: *Decoration in England from 1660–1770.*

A well-illustrated standard work which covers woodcarving, panelling, decorative painting, plaster work, wall hangings, lighting of rooms, etc. Index to illustrations p. 269–72; to text p. 273–76.

1711

Lenygon, Francis. Furniture in England from 1660–1760. London, Batsford; N.Y., Scribner [1914]. 300 p. illus., plates (part col.) 36 cm. (The library of decorative art, III)

A well-illustrated standard work. Index to illustrations p. 295–97; to text p. 298–300.

1712

Macquoid, Percy, and Edwards, Ralph. The dictionary of English furniture from the Middle Ages to the late Georgian period. [2d ed.] rev. and enl. by Ralph Edwards. London, Country Life [1954]. 3 v. illus. (part col.) 39 cm.

Originally published in 1904. "Mr. Edwards' revision all but amounts to a complete rewriting." Some articles are almost entirely new; most are signed and noted when revised. More emphasis on individual cabinetmakers and many new illustrations. Contents: v. 1, ACA–CHA; v. 2, CHE–MUT; v. 3, NAI–ZUC.

1713

Macquoid, Percy. A history of English furniture. With plates in colour after Shirley Slocombe, and numerous illustrations selected and arranged by the author. London, Lawrence & Bullen, 1904–08. 4 v. illus., col. plates. 39 cm.

A standard work. Contents: v. 1, The age of oak; v. 2, The age of walnut; v. 3, The age of mahogany; v. 4, The age of satinwood. Each volume has its own index.

1714

Symonds, Robert Wemyss, and Ormsbee, Thomas Hamilton. Antique furniture of the walnut period . . . N.Y., McBride, 1947. 144 p. illus. 29 cm.

Covers roughly 1660–1745. Illustrations lack clarity and paper quality is poor. Index p. 139–44.

1715

Symonds, Robert Wemyss. Furniture making in seventeenth and eighteenth century England; an outline for collectors. London, Connoisseur, 1955. 238 p. illus., 4 col. plates. 36 cm.

Includes clocks as well as furniture. Illustrated by good halftones in the text. Bibliographical footnotes. Index p. 236–38.

Italy

1716

Odom, William Macdougal. A history of Italian furniture, from the fourteenth to the early nineteenth centuries. Garden City, Doubleday, 1918–19. 2 v. illus. 39 cm.

A standard well-illustrated work. A list of plates at the beginning of each volume but no index.

1717

Schottmüller, Frida. Furniture and interior decoration of the Italian Renaissance . . . with 590 illustrations. N.Y., Brentano, 1921. 246 p. illus. 30 cm.

"Object is to illustrate the culture of the home in the time of the Italian Renaissance, the decoration of the rooms and the nature of the single objects of furniture."—*Foreword*. Primarily a picture book with 31 pages of preliminary text. "Explanatory," p. 241–46, gives brief information about the illustrations, including size. Bibliographical footnotes.

Low Countries

1718

Singleton, Esther. Dutch and Flemish furniture. N.Y., McClure, Phillips, 1907. 338 p. 57 (i.e., 62) plates. 30 cm.

The standard book on Dutch and Flemish furniture from the Middle Ages through the 19th century. Index p. 329–38.

Oriental Countries

1719

Ecke, Gustav. Chinese domestic furniture; one hundred and sixty-one plates illustrating one hundred and twenty-two pieces of which twenty-one in measured drawings. Peking, Henri Vetch, 1944. 2 v. in 1. illus., 161 plates. 38 cm.

In portfolio. "Edition limited to two hundred copies." A collection of excellent collotype plates with a short introductory text. Measurements are given in the list of plates. Contents: v. 1, Introduction; v. 2, Plates. Bibliography v. 1, p. 35–[40].

1720

Kates, George Norbert. Chinese household furniture, from examples selected and measured by Caroline F. Bieber and Beatrice M. Kates; photographs by Hedda Hammer Morrison. [1st ed.] N.Y. & London, Harper [1948]. 125 p. illus., plates. 24 cm.

Treated according to types of furniture. Bibliographical references in "Notes to the text" p. 60–63 and a "Summary working bibliography" p. 125.

Spain

1721

Byne, Arthur, and Byne, *Mrs.* Mildred (Stapley). Spanish interiors and furniture; photographs and drawings by Arthur Byne, with brief text by Mildred Stapley . . . N.Y., Helburn [1921–22]. 4 v. plates. 36 cm.

Each volume contains 100 plates representing Spanish furniture and interiors.

United States

1722

Hennessey, William James, and Hennessey, Eliza Dornin. Modern furnishings for the home. N.Y., Reinhold [c1956]. 368 p. illus. 27 cm.

A collection of good illustrations of contemporary furniture and accessories made in America. First issued in 1952 and was the first comprehensive catalog devoted exclusively to available contemporary merchandise.

1723

Kettell, Russell Hawes. The pine furniture of early New England. Illustrated. Garden City, Doubleday, Doran, 1929. [618] p. illus. 33 cm.

999 copies printed. Mostly a picture book, valuable especially for the many drawings and renderings included. "A short list of books and museums" p. [616].

1724

Miller, Edgar George. American antique furniture, a book for amateurs . . . N.Y., Barrows [c1937]. 2 v. illus. 29 cm.

Paged continuously. The book is composed of many illustrations, arranged by type of furniture (beds, chairs, etc.) with explanatory remarks showing the changes in style in successive periods. The majority of the illustrations have been chosen to represent the kind of pieces found in private homes rather than in museums. "Museums and collections in New England open to the public" p. 1065–71. Index to both volumes p. 1081–1106.

1725

Nutting, Wallace. Furniture treasury (mostly of American origin). All periods of American furniture with some foreign examples in America, also American hardware and household utensils. Five thousand illustrations with descriptions on the same page. N.Y., Macmillan, 1948. 2 v. illus. 27 cm.

Originally published 1928 in 3 v. A collection of photographs of 5000 examples of furniture (arranged by type, i.e., beds, chairs, etc.) and utensils to the end of the Empire period, in the possession of about 500 collectors from 27 states or countries. "More than 3000 examples are now shown for the first time."—*Explanatory*.

Dimensions are usually indicated, as well as the owner of the piece. A 19-page index at end of v. 2.

1726

Ormsbee, Thomas Hamilton. Early American furniture makers, a social and biographical study with 122 illustrations. N.Y., Crowell [c1930]. 183 p. illus., 67 plates (incl. facsims.) 25 cm.

Pictorial outline of American furniture p. 161–68. Chronological list of American furniture makers and clockmakers p. 171–73. Bibliography p. 177–79. Index p. 181–83.

1727

Ormsbee, Thomas Hamilton. Field guide to American Victorian furniture. Drawings by Ernst Halberstadt. Boston, Little, Brown [1952]. 428 p. illus. 19 cm.

A useful little handbook, illustrated by line drawings in the text, which covers the period of 1840–1880. Arranged by forms or types with a four-symbol code which gives comparative dollar value for any piece. "Furniture makers' language" p. xiii–xxxii. "Suggested books" p. 429.

1728

Ormsbee, Thomas Hamilton. Field guide to early American furniture. [1st ed.] Boston, Little, Brown, 1951. 464 p. illus. 19 cm.

A popular type of book, illustrated with small line drawings. "Cabinetmakers' language" p. xiii–xxxix. "Suggested books" p. 463–64.

Clocks and Watches

1729

Baillie, Granville Hugh. Clocks and watches; an historical bibliography. [1st ed.] With a foreword by Sir Harold Spencer-Jones. London, N. A. G. Press [1951]. 414 p. illus. 22 cm.

"The bibliography is confined to mechanical timepieces and to everything connected with them" (*Foreword*) and covers the subject up to the year 1800.

Annotated bibliography arranged chronologically. Name index p. 369–92; subject index p. 393–414.

1730

Baillie, Granville Hugh. Watches; their history, decoration and mechanism. London, Methuen [1929]. 383 p. 75 plates (part col.) 26 cm. (The connoisseur's library)

Bibliography p. xvi–xxiii is annotated.

"The chronology of watches" p. 349–67. Index p. 369–83.

1731

Baillie, Granville Hugh. Watchmakers and clockmakers of the world. 2d ed. London, N. A. G. Press, 1947. 388 p. 25 cm.

1st ed., published by Methuen in 1929 (Connoisseur's library), contained 25,000 names. An alphabetical list of watch and clockmakers which gives the city where each worked, his dates, type of clock or watch, etc. Lists 35,000 names of artisans to 1825, with a few of later periods.

1732

Britten, Frederick James. Old clocks and watches and their makers. A historical and descriptive account of the different styles of clocks and watches of the past in England and abroad containing a list of nearly fourteen thousand makers, by G. H. Baillie, C. Clutton, and C. A. Ilbert. 7th ed. London, Spon; N.Y., Dutton, 1956. 518 p. illus., 184 plates, 40 diagrs., facsims. 29 cm.

1st ed. 1899; 2d ed. 1904; 3d ed. 1911; 4th ed. [1920]; 5th ed. [1927?]; 6th ed. [1932]. "Much alteration and re-arrangement has gone into the present edition."–*Pref.*

Glossary of technical terms p. 297–308. Hallmarks p. 309–11. "List of former clock and watch makers" p. 319–505 gives dates and place of work. Bibliography p. 312–17. Index p. 507–18.

1733

Palmer, Brooks. The book of American clocks. N.Y., Macmillan, 1950. 318 p. 312 illus. 27 cm.

Introduction, p. 1–15, gives a short history mentioning types of clocks and also discusses American watches. "Glossary of clock terms" p. 16–19. "List of clockmakers," p. [133]–316, contains about 6000 names. Bibliography p. 317–18.

Pottery and Porcelain

Bibliography

1734

Champfleury, Jules Fleury Husson. Bibliographie céramique; nomenclature analytique

de toutes les publications faites en Europe et en Orient sur les arts et l'industrie céramiques depuis le XVIe siècle jusqu'à nos jours. Paris, Quantin, 1881. 352 p. 23 cm.

A classified bibliography which excludes Greek, Roman, and Gallo-Roman ceramics.

Part 1, "Bibliographie générale," arranged alphabetically by author. Part 2, "Bibliographie des ouvrages sur le céramique publiés chez les divers peuples," arranged by countries and then subdivided according to a scheme shown in table of contents, p. 35–52. Items in pt. 2 are annotated.

1735

Solon, Louis Marc Emmanuel. Ceramic literature: an analytical index to the works published in all languages on the history and the technology of the ceramic art; also to the catalogues of public museums, private collections, and of auction sales, in which the descriptions of ceramic objects occupy an important place; and to the most important price-lists of the ancient and modern manufactories of pottery and porcelain. London, Griffin, 1910. 660 p. 28 cm.

Contents: pt. 1, Author list with annotations; pt. 2, Classified list of the same works p. 475–649.

Bibliography p. 623–26.

Foreign titles are translated.

————. List of books on the history and technology of the ceramic art. A supplement to Ceramic literature, by M. L. Solon. (In Ceramic Society, Stoke-on-Trent, Eng. *Transactions*, v. VI, 1911–12, p. [65]–104. London, 1911. 22 cm.)

Dictionaries and Encyclopedias

1736

Barber, Edwin Atlee. The ceramic collectors' glossary . . . N.Y., Printed for the Society, 1914. 119 p. illus. 25 cm.

At head of title: The Walpole Society. "It is not claimed that the list of terms here presented is exhaustive; rather has it been considered sufficient to limit the number to those which are most likely to be needed in the work of cataloguing public and private collections."–*Pref.* Some foreign words are included, but primarily English language terms. Illustrated with line drawings in the text.

1737

Garnier, Édouard. Dictionnaire de la céramique; faïences-grès-poteries. . . . Aquarelles, marques et monogrammes d'après les dessins de l'auteur. Paris, Librairie de l'art [1893]. lxiii, 258 p. illus., col. plates. 26 cm. (Bibliothèque internationale de l'art. Guides de collectionneur)

Contents: Introduction; Dictionnaire de la céramique p. 1–222 (which includes biographical material); Table des marques et monogrammes (arranged alphabetically) p. 223–49; Marques figuratives p. 249–56.

Facsimiles of many marks are given in the text.

1738

Jervis, William Percival, comp. The encyclopedia of ceramics . . . with much original matter now first published . . . N.Y., 268–270 Canal Street [c1902]. 673 p. illus. 26 cm.

"Originally written for and published in the *Crockery and Glass Journal*, the whole of this work has now been thoroughly revised and much new information added."—*Pref.*

Marks and monograms illustrated p. 626–56.

Index, p. 657–73, lists only names mentioned in the text, not headings of entries.

Bibliography, p. 48–51, is listed in alphabetical place in main body of the work.

1739

Mankowitz, Wolf, and Haggar, Reginald G. The concise encyclopedia of English pottery and porcelain. N.Y., Hawthorn Books [1957]. 312 p. illus., plates (part col.), facsims. 26 cm.

A useful compendium of material covering factories, manufacturers, artists, processes, materials, special terminology, and potters' and artists' marks. Based on information in standard works of reference and original research. Sources are indicated at end of entries.

Contents: A selection of impressed and incised marks p. xiv–xv; The concise encyclopedia of English pottery and porcelain p. 1–249; Appendices: (1) Names of potters, pottery firms, pot-dealers, and outside decorators taken from directories p. 250–75; (2) Engravers for pottery and porcelain p. 276–89; (3) Books and articles giving lists of names of potters and pottery craftsmen etc. p. 290–92; (4) British and American museums where pottery and porcelain may be studied p. 293–96; (5) British potters on foreign soil p. 297–99; Classified bibliography p. 300–311.

SEE ALSO: Danckert. Handbuch des europäischen Porzellans (1748); Honey. European ceramic art (1754).

Biography

1740

Minghetti, Aurelio. Ceramisti. Milano, E. B. B. I., Istituto Editoriale Italiano B. C. Tosi [1939]. 451 p. illus., plates (part col.), ports., facsims. 28 cm. (Enciclopedia biografica e bibliografica "Italiana," serie XLI)

A dictionary of ceramists from the 11th century to the present. Well illustrated with inserts in the text and plates, some colored. Bibliographical references at the end of most entries.

Histories and Handbooks

1741

Burton, William. A general history of porcelain. . . . With thirty-two plates in colour and eighty in black and white. London, N.Y., Cassell, 1921. 2 v. illus., plates (part col.) 25 cm.

Covers Chinese, Japanese, Persian, Italian, Spanish, Portuguese, French, English, German, Norwegian, Swedish, and other European porcelains. Bibliography v. 2, p. 207–08. Index v. 2, p. 209–28.

1742

Burton, William, and Hobson, Robert L. Handbook of marks on pottery & porcelain. Rev. ed. London, Macmillan, 1929. 213 p. illus. 19 cm.

1st ed. 1909; reprinted with additions 1912, 1919; rev. and enl. 1928, and reprinted 1929. A useful pocket manual which is now somewhat limited. The aim is to supply "a reliable pocket volume containing the authentic and indisputable marks of the pottery and porcelain of the best 'collectors' periods.' "— *Introd.* The arrangement is geographical, but different species of ware are separately treated wherever possible.

"Works of reference consulted" p. [xii]. Indexes of names, initials, and Oriental marks p. 193–213.

1743

Chaffers, William. Collector's hand-book of marks and monograms on pottery & porcelain of the Renaissance and modern periods, with upwards of 5000 marks. Rev. and considerably augm. by Frederick Litchfield. 3d ed. London, Reeves [1952]. 367 p. illus. 20 cm.

2d ed. 1940 (London, Reeves; N.Y., Scribner), reprinted 1947 in Los Angeles by Borden Pub. Co.

A résumé of his larger work (1744).

1744

Chaffers, William. Marks and monograms on European and Oriental pottery and porcelain. . . . Ed. by Frederick Litchfield, assisted by R. L. Hobson and Justus Brinkman. 14th rev. ed. Los Angeles, Cal., Borden Pub. Co., 1946. 1095 p. illus. 26 cm.

"Notes on the current auction prices of old China, added to this present 14th ed." p. 991–92. "Quotations from auctioneers' catalogues of sales of representative specimens, which have taken place during the past 6 years" p. 993–1044. Index p. 1061–95.

1745

Chaffers, William. The new keramic gallery, containing seven hundred illustrations of rare, curious and choice examples of pottery and porcelain from early times to the beginning of the twentieth century. . . . This edition, the third, is enlarged by over 100 additional illustrations, with descriptions . . . rev. and ed. by H. M. Cundall. London, Reeves and Turner, 1926. 2 v. illus., plates (part col.) 27 cm.

1st ed. 1872; 2d ed. 1907. Paged continuously. This work forms a pictorial supplement to the author's *Marks and monograms* (1744).

1746

Cox, Warren Earle. The book of pottery and porcelain . . . N.Y., Lee and Shepard, 1944. 2 v. illus., col. plates, 3 maps. 24 cm.

Paged continuously. "This book is both a history and a description of the processes of making pottery, stoneware, soft paste, faience, 'delft,' porcelain and other wares, together with criticisms of their various appeals and defects both practically and artistically speaking, and suggestions as to methods for searching out such criticism."—*Introd.* "Definitions" p. xii–xvi. "The marks of potteries and porcelains" p. 1079–1150. Index to the two volumes p. 1151–58.

1747

Cushion, J. P., and Honey, William Bowyer. Handbook of pottery and porcelain marks. London, Faber [1956]. 476 p. illus., maps. 23 cm.

Includes 3500 factory marks and others which are of actual use in identifying the place of manufacture of a piece of pottery or porcelain. Contains many 19th and 20th century marks not previously recorded. This volume is particularly useful for English material.

Arranged by countries of origin and for each country covered, a note on the history of its pottery is given, as well as a "Historical note on the use of marks on pottery" p. 15–21. Index containing names, places, monograms, initials, and heraldic devices, in one alphabet, p. 451–76.

1748

Danckert, Ludwig. Handbuch des europäischen Porzellans. München, Prestel-Verlag [1954]. 311 p. 92 plates of facsims. 21 cm.

A fairly comprehensive book of European ceramic marks, which is very good for Continental porcelain but not English and American. Each part arranged alphabetically by names or initials. Part 1 is a dictionary arranged by names of people and places, with a few lines identifying their connection with the field of ceramics; also includes many marks.

Contents: (1) Lexikon der Stichworte (über 2000 Stichworte) p. 1–297; Anhang I, Sèvres-Künstler p. 299–304; Anhang II, China p. 305–11; (2) Katalog der Porzellan-Marken (über 3000 Marken), sep. paged section of 92 pages of plates.

"Litteratur" p. [viii]–ix.

1749

Dillon, Edward. Porcelain . . . London, Methuen [1904]. 419 p. 49 plates (part col.) 26 cm. (The connoisseur's library)

A standard work. "Marks on porcelain" p. 400–04. "Selected list of works on porcelain" p. xxvi–xxxii. "Key to bibliographical list" p. xxxiii–xxxiv. "List of works on other subjects referred to in the text" p. xxxv. Index p. 405–20.

1750

Eberlein, Harold Donaldson, and Ramsdell, Roger Wearne. The practical book of chinaware . . . with 202 halftone illustrations including 13 in full color, and numerous drawings. Rev. ed. Philadelphia, Lippincott [1948]. 320 p. illus., 120 plates (part col.) 22 cm.

1st ed. 1925. A useful introductory book, which "attempts to present the essential facts regarding china or porcelain from the beginning of its manufacture to 1840. This book deals only with such china as the person of average means can expect to have, either by way of inherited ownership or by purchase."—*Foreword.* Bibliography p. 307–10. Index p. 311–20.

1751

Grässe, Johann Georg Theodor. Graesse-Jaennicke, guide de l'amateur de porcelaines et de faïences. . . . Collection complète des marques de porcelaines et de faïences connues jusqu'à présent. Fondé par Dr. J. G. Th. Graesse . . . 9. éd. Entièrement refondue et . . . augm. . . . par F. Jaennicke. Dresden, Schoenfeld [etc.] 1901. 262 p. illus. 19 cm.

An 18th German ed., *Führer für Sammler von Porzellan und Fayencen* . . . , published in Braunschweig, Klinkhardt & Biermann, 1953. 417 p. 6000 illus.

A useful handbook of pottery and porcelain marks, arranged by country of origin. "Liste des peintres, décorateurs et doreurs de Sèvres" p. 239–43.

1752

Hannover, Emil. Pottery and porcelain, a handbook for collectors . . . edited with notes and appendices by Bernard Rackham. London, Benn, 1925. 3 v. illus. (incl. maps), col. plates. 27 cm.

A translation of *Keramish Haandbog*, 1921–24. A standard work on the subject. Contents: (1) Europe and the Near East, earthenware and stoneware [tr. by B. Rackham]; (2) The Far East [tr. by W. W. Worster]; (3) European porcelain [tr. by W. W. Worster].

Each volume contains bibliography and indexes of: (1) persons and private collections; (2) countries, places, factories, and public collections; (3) subjects, technique, and terminology.

1753

Hofmann, Friedrich Hermann. Das Porzellan der europäischen Manufakturen im XVIII Jahrhundert; eine Kunst- und Kulturgeschichte. Berlin, Propyläen-Verlag [c1932]. 537 p. illus. (incl. plans, facsims.) 24 plates (part col.) 28 cm.

A well-illustrated and complete history of European porcelain in the 18th century. A five-page section of facsimiles of marks. Index p. 519–38.

1754

Honey, William Bowyer. European ceramic art, from the end of the Middle Ages to about 1815. London, Faber [1949–52]. 2 v. illus., 220 plates (28 col.) 29 cm.

An important and useful book. Volume 1 is a collection of plates with 30 pages of introductory text. Volume 2 gives "an account [in dictionary form] of the meaning and significance of the words and names likely to be met with in the study of European ceramic art." It includes entries for factories, faïence, porcelain and other wares, artists, technical terms, collectors, and general matters. Numerous cross references and marks are given, and bibliographies are included.

Contents: (1) Illustrated historical survey; (2) A dictionary of factories, artists, technical terms, etc. General bibliography v. 2, p. 17–27. Index to marks p. 683–788.

1755

Litchfield, Frederick. Pottery and porcelain; a guide to collectors. 6th ed. rev. by Frank Tilley. Containing the marks and monograms of the important factories. London, Black [1953]. 356 p. illus. (part col.), facsims. 25 cm.

1st ed. published 1879. Well illustrated with many marks included in the text. Contents: (1) Ancient pottery; (2) Medieval and Renaissance; (3) Porcelain; (4) Hints and cautions to collectors p. 16–21; (5) Some counterfeit and misleading marks p. 22–27; (6) A short account of the different ceramic factories p. 28–319; (7) A glossary of terms used by dealers and collectors p. 320–29. Bibliography p. 331–34. Index p. 335–36.

1756

Penkala, Maria. European pottery, 5000 marks on maiolica, faience and stoneware. Hengelo, Holland, Smit [1951]. 424 p. illus., plates (part col.) 26 cm.

The work is arranged by countries and gives a description and short history of the firms represented as well as their marks, with illustrations of examples of the wares. Bibliography p. 421–24. Index to persons and factories p. 411–18; to reproductions p. 419.

1757

Savage, George. Ceramics for the collector; an introduction to pottery & porcelain. London, Rockliff; N.Y., Macmillan [1949]. 224 p. 114 illus. 22 cm.

Contents: (1) An introduction to technique; (2) Pottery and porcelain of the Far East; (3) Islam, Spain and Italy; (4) Continental faïence and stoneware; (5) Hard paste porcelain in Europe; (6) French porcelain factories; (7) English porcelain of the 18th century; (8) English pottery of the 17th and 18th centuries; (9) Valedictory. Appendix I, Notes on archaic pottery of the Near East and Mediterranean; II, European porcelain factories not included elsewhere; III, Glossary p. 215–16, of Oriental words used in the text. Bibliographies at the end of each chapter. Index p. 217–24.

1758

Savage, George. Porcelain through the ages; a survey of the main porcelain factories of Europe and Asia with 64 pages of plates, many line drawings, a bibliography, and tables of makers' marks. [Harmondsworth, Middlesex] Penguin Books [1954]. 352 p. illus., plates. 18 cm. (Pelican books, A298)

A very useful little handbook. Contents: (1) The porcelain of the Orient; (2) European porcelain. Appendices: (1) Notes on the pronunciation of Chinese words p. 307; (2) Glossary of Oriental words and Chinese words p. 308–10; (3) Chronology of Chinese porcelain p. 311–12; (4) Marks of identification found on porcelain p. 314–26. Bibliography p. 329–35. Index p. 337–52.

1759

Schmidt, Robert. Porcelain as an art and mirror of fashion . . . translated and edited with an introduction by W. A. Thorpe . . . with eight plates in colour and two hundred other illustrations. London, Harrap [1932]. 336 p. illus., col. plates. 22 cm.

"A history of porcelain in its general relation to culture."—*Pref.* Contents: (1) Far Eastern porcelain; (2) European porcelain; (3) Vessels; (4) Porcelain figures; (5) Table decorations and altar sets; (6) Sources of design in porcelain figures. "Bibliographical note" p. 311–17. Index p. 319–36.

1760

Tardy. Les poteries, les faïences et les porcelaines européennes . . . Historique, caractéristiques, décors, couleurs, et 4500 marques par Tardy. Paris, Tardy, n.d. 2 v. facsims. 20 cm.

Arranged by place. Contents: pt. 1, Allemagne, Autriche, Hongrie, Belgique, Danemark, Espagne, Estonie, Finlande, Grande Bretagne; pt. 2, Hollande, Hongrie, Italie, Luxembourg, Malte, Norvège, Pologne, Portugal, Roumanie, Russie, Suède, Suisse.

National

France

1761

Chavagnac, Xavier Roger Marie, *Comte* de and Grollier, Gaston Antoine, *Marquis* de. . . . Histoire des manufactures françaises de porcelaine, précédée d'une lettre de M. le marquis de Vogüé . . . Paris, Picard, 1906. 966 p. illus., plates. 26 cm.

Standard work on French porcelain manufacture. "Liste par ordre alphabétique des proprietaires, chefs d'atelier, décorateurs, peintres et marchands de Paris" p. 841–55. "Table alphabétique des noms" p. 859–86. "Table des marques" p. 887–966.

1762

Paris. Musée des Arts Décoratifs. Répertoire de la faïence française, publié à l'occasion de "L'Exposition retrospective de la faïence française" au Musée des Arts Décoratifs, sous la direction de Dr. Chompret . . . Jean Bloch . . . Jacques Guérin, Paul Alfassa . . . Paris, Lapina, 1933–35. 6 v. 610 plates in 5 portfolios and 1 v. of text. 39 cm.

310 copies printed. A corpus of excellent collotype plates illustrating French faïence from the 16th to the beginning of the 19th centuries, with notes on the factories, arranged alphabetically by place. Size of the examples is given on the guard sheets of the plates. Contents: v. 1–5, Plates; v. 6, Text. Bibliography p. 287–88. Index p. 289–308.

Germany and Austria

1763

Hayward, John Forrest. Viennese porcelain of the Du Paquier period. London, Rockliff [1952]. 218 p. 76 plates (4 col.) 26 cm.

The best book on Austrian porcelain of the 18th century, written by a staff member of the Victoria and Albert Museum. Gives dimensions in the captions of the plates. Includes bibliographies. Index p. 195–98.

1764

Honey, William Bowyer. Dresden china; an introduction to the study of Meissen porcelain. [new ed.] London, Faber; N.Y., Pitman [1954]. 219 p. illus., 64 plates. 23 cm.

1st ed. 1934. "This book intended to serve as an introduction to the study of Meissen porcelain of the 18th century. . . . Its purpose is to provide no more than a clear and brief account, unencumbered with confusing detail, of the history and productions of the great Saxon factory."—*Pref.* The best book in English on this subject. Marks p. 162–73. Notes p. 178–207. Bibliography p. 175–77. Index p. 209–19.

1765

Hüseler, Konrad. Deutsche Fayencen, ein Handbuch der Fabriken, ihrer Meister und Werke. Stuttgart, Hiersemann, 1956–58. 3 v. plates, tables, maps. 25 cm.

Continuous pagination. A useful handbook of German faïence. Contents: v. I, (1) Geschichte der deutschen Fayencefabriken;

(2) Vom innern Betrieb der Fayencefabriken; (3) Fayence; (4) Bilagen; v. II, (5) Die künstlerische Entwicklung der deutschen Fayence im 17. und 18. Jahrhunderts; (6) Einzelne Künstler; (7) Verschiedenes. "Abkürzungen und Zeichen" v. II, p. [183]. Biographisches Lexikon v. III, p. 371–433; Bibliographie p. 437–99; Marken p. 543–78 (with 67 plates).

1766

Ware, George Whitaker. German and Austrian porcelain. Frankfurt am Main, Woeller [1952?]. 244 p. illus., plates (part col.), facsims., maps. 26 cm.

A German ed. was also published with the translation by Mrs. Wilhelmina Woeller-Paquet. "Written by an amateur porcelain collector to help other collectors . . . prepared primarily for the information and guidance of those with limited experience."—*Pref.* Porcelain marks p. 106–16. Glossary p. 229–36. Bibliography p. 227–28.

Great Britain

1767

Phillips, John Goldsmith. China-trade porcelain; an account of its historical background, manufacture, and decoration, and a study of the Helena Woolworth McCann collection . . . Cambridge, Mass., Pub. for the Winfield Foundation and the Metropolitan Museum of Art [by] Harvard Univ. Press, 1956. 234 p. illus. (part col.), maps on end papers. 28 cm.

The best historical background for this type of porcelain. Selected bibliography p. 222–24. Index p. 229–34.

SEE ALSO: Laidacker. The standard catalogue of Anglo-American china (1781).

Greece

1768

Lane, Arthur. Greek pottery. London, Faber [1948]. 62 p. 100 plates (part col.) on 52 1. 26 cm.

A comprehensive treatment of the art of the Greek potter, with many plates illustrating the shape, plastic decoration, and painting; and an introductory essay which provides a broad survey of the subject. "Short bibliography" p. 59–60. Index p. 61–62.

Low Countries

1769

Neurdenburg, Elisabeth, and Rackham, Bernard. Old Dutch pottery and tiles; trans.

with annotations by Bernard Rackham . . . London, Benn, 1923. 155 p. 69 plates (part col.) 29 cm.

Appendix: "List of marks of Delft potters in 1764" p. 145–46. Bibliography p. 147–48. Index p. 151–55.

Oriental Countries

1770

Bowes, James Lord. Japanese marks and seals. Part I. Pottery. Part II. Illuminated mss. and printed books. Part III. Lacquer, enamels, metal, wood, ivory &c. London, Sotheran, 1882. 379 p. illus. (part col.) 29 cm.

"The zodiacal cycle and year periods" p. 341–53. Index p. 357–79.

1771

Butler, Alfred Joshua. Islamic pottery; a study mainly historical. London, Benn, 1926. 179 p. 92 plates (part col.) 39 cm.

A scholarly treatment of the pottery of the Mohammedan world, with very good plates. Bibliography p. xxi–xxiv. Index p. 177–79.

1772

Gulland, W. G. Chinese porcelain, with notes by T. J. Larkin . . . 2d ed. London, Chapman & Hall, 1902. 2 v. illus., plates. 23 cm.

Paged continuously. A useful handbook. "Chronological table" v. 2, p. [xvii]–xxiv. "Authorities" v. 1, p. [xiii]–xiv; v. 2, p. [xxxvii]–xxxviii. Index at the end of each volume.

1773

Hetherington, Arthur Lonsdale. The pottery and porcelain factories of China; their geographical distribution and periods of activity. With a folding map of China. London, Paul, Trench, Trubner; N.Y., Dutton, 1921. 15 p. fold. map. 26 cm.

Contents: (1) Factories arranged according to provinces p. 9–12; (2) Factories arranged according to dynasties p. 13–15.

1774

Hobson, Robert Lockhart. Chinese pottery and porcelain; an account of the potter's art in China from primitive times to the present day. London, N.Y. [etc.] Cassell, 1915. 2 v. illus. 134 plates (part col.) 25 cm.

Edition of 1500 copies. The standard work on this subject despite its age. Contents: (1) Pottery and early wares; (2) Ming and Ch'ing porcelain. Bibliography v. 1, p. xxvii–xxx. Index v. 2, p. 309–26.

1775

Honey, William Bowyer. The ceramic art of China, and other countries of the Far East. London, Faber and Hyperion Press [1945]. 238 p. illus. (incl. map), 192 plates. 26 cm.

Covers China, Indo-China, Korea, and Japan. "Chinese dynasties and reigns" p. 226–27. Bibliography p. 218–26. Index p. 229–38.

1776

Lane, Arthur. Early Islamic pottery; Mesopotamia, Egypt and Persia. London, Faber, 1947. 52 p. [100] plates (part col.) 26 cm. (Faber monographs on pottery and porcelain)

One of the best introductory books on the subject. Number 1777 below is a companion volume on later Islamic pottery. Bibliography p. 49. Index p. 51–52.

1777

Lane, Arthur. Later Islamic pottery: Persia, Syria, Egypt, Turkey. London, Faber and Faber [1957]. 133 p. 103 plates (3 col.) on 53 l., map. 26 cm. (Faber monographs on pottery and porcelain)

Bibliography p. 124–27. Index p. 151–53.

Spain

1778

González Martí, Manuel. Cerámica del Levante español, siglos medievales. Barcelona [etc.] Editorial Labor, 1944–52. 3 v. illus. (part col.), plates (part col.), plans. 28 cm.

A very well-illustrated treatment of Spanish pottery. Contents: [t. 1] Loza; t. 2, Alicatados y azulejos; t. 3, Azulejos, "socarrats," y retablos. Includes bibliographies. Elaborate indexes.

United States

1779

Barber, Edwin Atlee. Marks of American potters . . . with facsimiles of 1000 marks, and illustrations of rare examples of American wares. Philadelphia, Patterson and White, 1904. 174 p. illus. 21 cm.

Contents: Pennsylvania potteries; New Jersey potteries; New York potteries; New England potteries; Ohio potteries; Potteries of the southern states; Potteries of the western states. Index p. 169–74.

1780

Barber, Edwin Atlee. The pottery and porcelain of the United States; an historical review of American ceramic art from the earliest times to the present day, to which is appended a chapter on The pottery of Mexico . . . 3d ed., rev. and enl., with 335 illustrations. N.Y., Putnam, 1909. 621 p. illus. 24 cm.

1st ed. 1893; 2d ed. 1901. "The main purpose of this work is to furnish an account of such of the earlier potteries as, for any reason, possesses some historical interest, and of those manufactories which, in later days, have produced works of originality or artistic merit . . . I have endeavored to present a condensed but practically complete record of the development of the fictile art in America during the three centuries since the first attempts."—*Pref.*

American marks and monograms p. 392–414. Index p. 601–17.

1781

Laidacker, Samuel H. The standard catalogue of Anglo-American china. 1938 ed. Scranton, Pa. [1938]–51. 2 v. illus. 24 cm.

Volume 2 published at Bristol, Pa., has title: *Anglo-American china*. A useful book for collectors giving current auction prices. Contents: [pt. 1] From 1810 to 1850: Printed and decorative ware made in England by the Staffordshire potters for the American trade; pt. 2, Other than American views appearing on transfer-decorated wares produced by Staffordshire and other English potters during the period from 1815 to 1860. "An index to views and patterns" at end of v. 2, p. 137–44.

Techniques

1782

Hetherington, Arthur Lonsdale. Chinese ceramic glazes. [2d rev. ed.] South Pasadena, P. D. and Ione Perkins [c1948]. 114 p. 14 plates (part col.) 22 cm.

An important discussion of the technical aspects. "Selected bibliography" p. [110]. Glossary p. 111–14. Index p. 115–16.

1783

Leach, Bernard Howell. A potter's book; with introductions by Soyetsu Yanagi and Michael Cardew. N.Y., Transatlantic Arts [1948]. 294 p. illus., diagrs., plates (part col.) 23 cm.

A fundamental book for the understanding of the technical aspects of pottery, both Eastern and Western. Well illustrated by diagrams and plates. Appendix: Potter's terms, tools and materials p. 261–83. Index p. 284–94.

1784

March, Benjamin. Standards of pottery description. . . . With an introductory essay by Carl E. Guthe. Ann Arbor, Mich., Univ. of Michigan Press, 1934. 55 p. illus., 2 plates. 23 cm. (Michigan. Univ. Museum of Anthropology. Occasional contributions, no. 3)

Contents: A method of ceramic description; (1) Introduction; (2) Body description; (3) Hardness; (4) Color; (5) Surface texture, glazed ware; (6) Surface texture, unglazed ware; (7) Crackle; (8) A ceramic pantograph; (9) Records.

1785

Rhodes, Daniel. Clay and glazes for the potter. N.Y., Greenberg [c1957]. 219 p. plates. 27 cm.

A technical book whose purpose is "to present in as clear and understandable form as possible the important facts about ceramic materials and their use in pottery."—*Pref.* Bibliography p. 213. Index p. 215–19.

1786

Searle, Alfred Broadhead. An encyclopedia of the ceramic industries, being a guide to the materials, methods of manufacture, means of recognition, and testing the various articles produced in the clayworking and allied industries . . . arranged in alphabetical order for rapid reference . . . London, Benn, 1929–30. 3 v. illus., tables, diagrs. 29 cm.

Gives many recipes and much technical detail, as well as historical information. "Works of reference, with symbols" v. 1, p. xi–xxvii.

Glass

Biography

1787

Drake, Wilfred James. A dictionary of glasspainters and "glasyers" of the tenth to the eighteenth centuries. N.Y., Metropolitan Museum of Art, 1955. 224 p. illus. 29 cm.

For each artist, wherever possible, it gives name, date, and place, what is known of his activities, and a diagram to scale of his signature. Although the dictionary is arranged alphabetically there is also a listing of artists arranged by country and then by century of activity.

Appendix I, Glassmakers (makers of white and colored glass) p. 207–10; II, Designers of stained glass (known to have designed stained glass but not, as far as is known, glasspainters) p. 211–15; III, Signatures of glasspainters not yet identified p. 217–20. Bibliography p. 221–24.

SEE ALSO: Gnoli. Pittori e miniatori nell'Umbria (1164).

Glassware

1788

Angus-Butterworth, Lionel Milner. British table and ornamental glass. London, Hill, 1956. 123 p. illus. 26 cm.

Traces the history and development of glass, describes how it is made and decorated, and discusses the principles of design involved. "Annals of glass in Britain" p. 105–09. "A glossary of terms used in the glass industry" p. 110–19. Index p. 121–23.

1789

Buckley, Wilfred. European glass, a brief outline of the history of glass making, with notes on various methods of glass decoration, illustrated by examples in the collection of the author . . . with a foreword by Bernard Rackham . . . and with an essay on Dutch glass engravers by Dr. Ferrand Hudig . . . Boston, Houghton Mifflin, 1926. 96 p. illus., 110 plates. 29 cm.

Excellent halftone plates. "Literature on diamond engraving" p. xxxiv. "Authoritative works" p. xxxvi.

1790

Dillon, Edward. Glass. London, Methuen; N.Y., Putnam [1907]. 373 p. 49 plates (part col.) 26 cm. (The connoisseur's library)

Covers glass from primitive times and the Egyptians to the beginning of the 20th century. "Selected bibliography" p. xxii–xxviii. Index p. 361–74.

1791

Eisen, Gustav. Glass, its origin, history, chronology, technic and classification to the sixteenth century . . . assisted by Fakim Kouchakji. N.Y., Rudge, 1927. 2 v. illus., plates (part col.) 26 cm.

Edition of 500 copies. Paged continuously. A well-illustrated basic book for old glass. Bibliography v. 2, p. 751–61. Index v. 2, p. 763–68.

1792

McKearin, George Skinner, and McKearin, Helen. American glass ... 2000 photographs, 1000 drawings by James L. McCreery. N.Y., Crown [c1941]. 622 p. illus., plates, facsims., tables. 28 cm.

"Chronological chart of American glass houses" p. 583–613. Glossary p. xv–xvi. Bibliography p. 615–17. Index p. 618–22.

1793

McKearin, Helen, and McKearin, George S. Two hundred years of American blown glass ... Garden City, Doubleday, 1950. 382 p. 115 plates (part col.) 29 cm.

Edition of 500 copies. A general history of the subject including "notes on the modern renaissance of the art of glass." Bibliography p. 361–66. Index p. 367–82.

1794

Moore, Hannah Hudson. Old glass, European and American ... with two hundred and sixty-five illustrations. N.Y., Tudor, 1935. 394 p. illus. 25 cm.

A reprint of the 1924 ed. Contents: pt. 1, European glass; pt. 2, American glass. "American glass factories" p. 369–82. Index p. 385–94.

1795

Pazaurek, Gustav Edmund. Kunstgläser der Gegenwart, mit 4 Kupferdrucktafeln, 4 Farbentafeln, einer Markentafel und 253 Textabbildungen. Leipzig, Klinkhardt & Biermann, 1925. 264 p. illus., 8 plates (part col.) 26 cm. (Monographien des Kunstgewerbes, Bd. XIX/XX)

An account of glass production in the 20th century, with a table of marks p. 251. Bibliography p. 22–25. Index p. 261–64.

1796

Pazaurek, Gustav Edmund. Moderne Gläser. Leipzig, Seemann [1910]. 133 p. 149 illus., 3 col. plates. 26 cm.

An account of glass at the end of the 19th century, covering art nouveau, etc. Index p. 134.

1797

Thorpe, William Arnold. English glass. 2d ed. London, Black, 1950. 304 p. illus. 22 cm. (The library of English art)

"Intended to be a survey of taste in domestic and fancy glass from the second century to the present."—*Pref.* "The principal British museums for glass" p. 273–79. "List of

works cited" p. 263–71. "Index of principal proper names and descriptive terms" p. 281–301.

1798

Thorpe, William Arnold. A history of English and Irish glass. London, Medici Society; Boston, Hale, Cushman & Flint, 1929. 2 v. illus., 168 plates. 27 cm.

Edition of 500 copies printed. "A history of fine glass in England and Ireland from the 13th century until the second quarter of the 19th century."—*Pref.* Contents: v. 1, Text; v. 2, Plates (halftones). "Terminology" v. 1, p. 335–40. "Select bibliography" v. 1, p. 341–49. Index to v. 1 and 2, v. 1, p. 351–72.

1799

Watkins, Lura (Woodside). American glass and glassmaking, with 55 reproductions in color and monochrome and 3 diagrams in line. N.Y., Chanticleer, 1950. 104 p. illus. (part col.) 23 cm. (American crafts series)

A short survey illustrated with good plates. "Important public collections" p. 104. Bibliography p. 103. No index.

SEE ALSO: Garnier. Histoire de la verrerie et de l'émaillerie (1812).

Stained Glass

1800

Arnold, Hugh, and Saint, Lawrence B. Stained glass of the Middle Ages in England and France ... London, Black, 1925. 269 p. col. plates. 24 cm.

A reprint of the 1st ed., 1913. Also reprinted 1955. A rather general survey leaning toward the popular. Index p. 267–69.

1801

Connick, Charles Jay. Adventures in light and color; an introduction to the stained glass craft ... foreword by Charles D. Maginnis. N.Y., Random House [c1937]. 428 p. illus., plates (part col.) 32 cm.

A rather chatty book by one of the recognized practitioners of the art today. Valuable for techniques. "How to share a glassman's holiday," p. 267–377, lists where important glass may be found in churches and museums in Europe and America. "Books from a glassman's library" p. 378–91. Index p. 415–28.

1801A

Corpus vitrearum Medii Aevi. Sponsored by UNESCO under the patronage of the Union

Académique Internationale. Publisher varies by country. 1956–(58). (2 v.) illus., plates (part col.) 33 cm.

Projected are 15 volumes for Germany, 25 for France, five for Italy, four for Austria, four for Switzerland, and one each for Sweden and the United States. Volumes for Belgium, Holland, and Spain also are in prospect. To date, one volume for Switzerland and one for Germany have appeared.

A systematic inventory of stained glass still extant, arranged by countries, with emphasis on history and iconography. Profusely illustrated and thoroughly indexed by place, persons, and subjects. Contains bibliographies.

1802

Day, Lewis Foreman. Windows; a book about stained & painted glass. 3d ed. rev. and enl. London, Batsford, 1909. 420 p. 300 illus. 23 cm.

1st ed. 1897; 2d ed. 1902. "In Book I [the work attempts] to trace the course of workmanship, in Book II to map out the course of design, in Book III to discuss questions which, even though they may have something to do with design or workmanship, would have hindered or confused the strict account of it."—*Pref.*

"List of places mentioned, arranged alphabetically under countries and periods" p. 405–08. Index p. 409–20.

1803

Drake, Maurice. A history of English glass-painting, with some remarks upon the Swiss glass miniatures of the sixteenth and seventeenth centuries, illustrated by 36 plates from drawings by Wilfred Drake. N.Y., McBride, 1913. 226 p. 33 plates (part col.) 35 cm.

Catalogs of Swiss stained glass collections p. 197. A list of Swiss artists in glass of the 15th, 16th, and 17th centuries p. 198–206. Unidentified Swiss signatures p. 207–08. List of places where windows or important fragments may be seen p. 211–22. Bibliography p. 187–91. Index p. 223–26.

1804

Fischer, Josef Ludwig. Handbuch der Glasmalerei für Forscher, Sammler und Kunstfreunde, wie für Künstler, Architekten und Glasmaler; mit 48 Textabbildungen und 151 Abbildungen auf 135 Tafeln. Leipzig, Hiersemann, 1914. 318 p. illus., 135 plates. 24 cm. (Hiersemann's Handbücher, Bd. VIII)

A standard German handbook on glass painting, which is well illustrated. "Die

wichtigste Literatur über die Glasmalerei" p. 301–11. Index p. 312–17.

1805

Read, Herbert Edward. English stained glass. London and N.Y., Putnam [1926]. 259 p. incl. illus., plates. 30 cm.

Contents: (1) Introductory; (2) The age of reason; (3) The age of sentiment; (4) The age of fancy; (5) William Morris and the modern movement. Appendix: A brief survey of the earlier stained glass remains in England together with a discussion of selected examples of later glass p. 231–49. Bibliography p. 250–53. Index p. 255–60.

1806

Westlake, Nat Hubert John. A history of design in painted glass. London, Parker, 1881–94. 4 v. illus. 35 cm.

Standard 19th century history of stained glass. Bibliographical footnotes. Index (principally of names and places) v. 4, p. 183–93.

1807

Whall, C. W. Stained glass work; a text-book for students and workers in glass. With diagrams by two of his apprentices and other illustrations. London, Pitman, 1931. 380 p. illus., plates p. 337–68. 19 cm.

A reprint of the 1905 ed. Illustrated by halftones. Glossary p. 369–72. Index p. 374–81.

Enamels

1808

Chamot, Mary. English medieval enamels . . . with fifty-three illustrations in collotype. London, Benn, 1930. 49 p. 20 plates. 25 cm. (University College [London] monographs on English medieval art, II)

A survey of the whole field of English enameling. Catalog, p. 21–48, gives size. "Bibliography of general works" p. 19–20. Index p. 49–50.

1809

Cunynghame, *Sir* Henry Hardinge. European enamels . . . London, Methuen; N.Y., Putnam [1906]. 187 p. illus., 48 plates (4 col.) 27 cm. (The connoisseur's library [ix])

Contents: (1) Introduction (meaning of the word and nature of the materials); (2) Enamelling in ancient times. (3) Early Gaulish enamelling in Europe after the Christian era; (4) Byzantine enamels (cloisonné); (5) Medieval enamels; (6) Enamelled bas-reliefs;

(7) Painted enamels; (8) The miniaturists; (9) Landscapes on snuff-boxes and fancy ware; (10) Enamelled jewellery; (11) Modern enamellers. Index p. 177–88.

1810

Dawson, Edith B. Enamels. Chicago, Mc-Clurg, 1908. 207 p. 33 plates. 16 cm. (Little books on art. General ed.: Cyril Davenport)

First published in 1906. "An appreciation rather than a technical book."—*Introd.* Contents: Cloisonné enamels; Champlevé enamels; Painted enamels; Oriental enamels; Irish enamels; Modern enamels. "A list of books and articles on enamels" p. 199–201. Index p. 203–07.

1811

Day, Lewis Foreman. . . . Enameling, a comparative account of the development and practice of the art. . . . With 115 illustrations. London, Batsford, 1907. 222 p. illus. 22 cm.

At head of title: The course of art and workmanship. Descriptive list of illustrations p. xi–xxv. Index p. 215–22.

1812

Garnier, Édouard. Histoire de la verrerie et de l'émaillerie, illustration d'après les dessins de l'auteur, gravure de Trichon. Tours, Mame, 1886. 573 p. illus., 8 plates (4 col.) 29 cm.

An old history of glass and enamels. Index p. 557–65.

1813

Hasenohr, Curt. Email; Goldschmiedeemail, Maleremail, kunsthandwerkliches Gebrauchsemail, neue Emailtechniken. Dresden, Verlag der Kunst, 1955. 71 p. 28 plates (6 col.) 25 cm.

An illustrated German work on the techniques of various types of enamel work. "Literatur" p. 66. Index p. 67–69.

1814

McClelland, Ellwood Hunter. Enamel bibliography and abstracts, 1928 to 1939, inclusive, with subject and coauthor indexes. Columbus, Ohio, The Am. Ceramic Soc., 1944. 352 p. 28 cm.

A bibliography arranged alphabetically by author, with abstracts of articles, dealing with all aspects of enamels.

Subject index, p. 312–335, lists numerous entries under art on p. 314.

Index to coauthors p. 351–52.

1815

Marquet de Vasselot, Jean Joseph. Les émaux limousins de la fin du XVe siècle et de la première partie du XVIe; étude sur Nardon Pénicaud et ses contemporains. Paris, Picard, 1921. 412 p. *and* atlas of 85 plates. 27 cm.

Contents: Introduction (discussion of various schools) p. 1–210; Liste des émaux (catalog) p. 211–364. Appendices: (1) Documents relatifs à Nardon et à Jean Ier Pénicaud; (2) Liste des émailleurs limousins; (3) Le groupe violet.

Bibliography p. [385]–96. Index p. [403]–09.

1816

Molinier, Émile. Dictionnaire des émailleurs depuis le moyen âge jusqu'à la fin du XVIIIe siècle; ouvrage accompagné de 67 marques et monogrammes. Paris, Rouam, 1885. 113 p. illus. 18 cm. (Guide du collectionneur)

Contents: Dictionnaire p. 7–93; Essai d'une bibliographie des livres relatifs à l'histoire des émaux p. 93–104; Liste des principales collections publiques ou privées renfermant des émaux p. 105–13.

SEE ALSO: Clouzot. Dictionnaire des miniaturistes sur émail (1146); Marquet de Vasselot. Bibliographie de l'orfèvrerie (1853); Maryon. Metalwork and enamelling (1826).

Mosaics

1817

Anthony, Edgar Waterman. A history of mosaics. Boston, Sargent [c1935]. 332 p. 80 plates. 27 cm.

A general history, with numerous plates, covering mosaics from their earliest appearance until the present day. Glossary p. 316. Bibliography p. 299–314. Index p. 317–33.

1818

Berchem, Marguerite van, and Clouzot, Étienne. Mosaïques chrétiennes du IVme au Xme siècle. . . . Dessins de Marcelle van Berchem. Genève, "Journal de Genève," 1924. lxii, 253 p. illus., plates (1 col.) 30 cm.

Well illustrated by halftones. Contents: Introduction; (1) L'art de la mosaïque chrétienne; (2) Le costume; (3) La technique p. ix–lix; Notices p. 1–253, arranged by century and then by the monument discussed. Bibliography p. 254.

1819

Demus, Otto. Byzantine mosaic decoration; aspects of monumental art in Byzantium. London, Kegan Paul [1948]. 97 p. 64 plates. 26 cm.

Contents: (1) The classical systems of middle Byzantine church decoration; (2) History of the middle Byzantine system; (3) The imprint of the system of later art. Bibliography included in notes p. 87–94. Index p. 95–97.

1820

Demus, Otto. The mosaics of Norman Sicily. London, Routledge and Paul, 1950. 478 p. 120 plates. 26 cm.

Contents: (1) Monuments; (2) Iconography; (3) The development of style. Includes bibliographical references. Index of names p. 458–65. Iconographical index p. 466–71. General index p. 472–78.

1821

Fischer, Josef Ludwig. Deutsches Mosaik und seine geschichtlichen Quellen. Mit 97 Tafeln, davon 13 farbig. Leipzig, Hiersemann, 1939. 119 p. plates (part col.) 30x24 cm.

A well-illustrated treatment of German mosaics. Index p. 116–[20].

1822

Galassi, Giuseppe. . . . Roma o Bizanzio . . . Roma, Libreria della Stato [1930]–1953. 2 v. 425 illus., 166 plates (19 col.) 30 cm.

Volume 1, edition of 750 copies; v. 2, edition of 1000. A well-illustrated work on Byzantine mosaics considered as the origin of Italian artistic culture.

Contents: v. 1, I musaici di Ravenna e le origini dell'arte italiana; v. 2, Congedo classico e l'arte nell'alto medio evo. Each volume has an index of places and works, and v. 2 an index of persons.

1823

Powers, Harry Huntington. The art of mosaic. Newton, Mass., The University prints, 1938. 215 p. incl. illus. 21 cm.

A general survey of mosaics from early times to the end of the 13th century. No index.

1824

Sherrill, Charles Hitchcock. Mosaics in Italy, Palestine, Syria, Turkey and Greece; with 17 illustrations in black and white. London, Lane [1933]. 304 p. plates. 23 cm.

Written as a guidebook and containing basic information. Index p. 293–304.

SEE ALSO: Wilpert. Die römischen Mosaiken und Malereien (1234).

Metalwork
General

1825

Clouzot, Henri. Les arts du métal; métaux précieux, le bronze et le cuivre, le fer, les armes, la parure . . . Paris, Laurens, 1934. 524 p. 270 illus. 26 cm. (Manuels d'histoire de l'art)

Standard French text on the subject of metalwork. "Bibliographie sommaire" p. [485]–94. "Index des noms cités" p. 495–511.

1826

Maryon, Herbert. Metalwork and enamelling; a practical treatise on gold and silversmiths' work and their allied crafts. 3d ed. rev. N.Y., Dover, 1955. 331 p. illus. 23 cm.

Useful for techniques. Index p. 323–31.

1827

Perry, John Tavenor. Dinanderie; a history and description of mediaeval art work in copper, brass and bronze . . . N.Y., Macmillan; London, Allen, 1910. 238 p. illus., 28 plates. 27 cm.

A general survey of this field. Bibliography p. 221–22. Index p. 225–38.

Gold and Silver

1828

Anderson, Lawrence Leslie. The art of the silversmith in Mexico, 1519–1936. N.Y., Oxford Univ. Press, 1941. 2 v. illus., plates. 31 cm.

1st ed. Also published in Spanish (N.Y., Oxford Univ. Press, 1941). A sound treatment of this subject. Chapter X discusses marks on Mexican silver. Dimensions are given under the illustrations.

Contents: v. 1, Text; v. 2, Plates. Appendix I, List of silversmiths in Mexico; Appendix II, Ordinances relative to the silversmith's art. Bibliography v. 1, p. [435]–51. Index v. 1, p. 452–60.

1829

Avery, Clara Louise. Early American silver. N.Y., London, Century [1930]. 378 p. illus., 63 plates (incl. facsims.) 22 cm. (Century library of American antiques)

A general treatise on the subject covering the chronological development of silver in various states and cities, and the evolution of the principal forms in early American silver. "Bibliographical note" p. 361–64. Index p. 365–78.

1830
Bigelow, Francis Hill. Historic silver of the colonies and its makers . . . N.Y., Macmillan, 1917. 476 p. illus. 21 cm.
Various chapters devoted to different forms. Bibliography p. xxiii–xxiv. Index to silversmiths p. 445–48. General index p. 449–76.

1831
Bradbury, Frederick. British and Irish silver assay office marks, 1544–1954, with notes on gold markings, and marks on foreign imported silver and gold plate. Old Sheffield plate makers' marks, 1743–1860. 9th ed. Sheffield, Eng., Northend, 1955. 90 p. illus. 15 cm.
2d ed. 1928; 3d ed. 1932; 4th ed. 1936; 6th ed. 1943. A useful pocket volume of hallmarks. Bibliographical references in the Preface.

1832
Braun, Joseph. Meisterwerke der deutschen Goldschmiedekunst der vorgotischen Zeit . . . München, Riehn und Reusch, 1922. 2 v. illus. 26 cm. (Sammelbände zur Geschichte der Kunst und des Kunstgewerbes, hrsg. von Adolf Feulner, Bd. VIII)
Each volume contains 12 or 13 pages of text and plates and a catalog which gives size and bibliographical description. Contents: v. 1, 9.–12. Jahrhundert; v. 2, 12. und 13. Jahrhundert. Bibliography v. 1, p. 11 and v. 2, p. 1.

1833
Carré, Louis. A guide to old French plate . . . with a foreword by E. Alfred Jones . . . London, Chapman & Hall, 1931. 270 p. illus., 2 plates. 19 cm.
This concise handbook "traces the history of marking gold and silver plate in France, not only in Paris, but also at the great number of provincial guilds . . . [It includes an] account of the regulations of these guilds which numbered at least 178 in 1785."—*Introd.*
The first part is devoted to marks before the Revolution and the second part to those in use from 1797 to the present. Plates show choice pieces of the art. Each part has a glossary of marks. Index of marks p. 221–70.

1834
Carré, Louis. Les poinçons de l'orfèvrerie française du quatorzième siècle jusqu'au début du dix-neuvième siècle. Paris, Carré, 1928. 355 p. illus., 14 plates (incl. map, tab.) 33 cm.
Published in a limited edition of 1020 copies.
A useful work on French goldsmiths' hallmarks from the 14th to the beginning of the 19th century. Appendix: Poinçons de garantie en usage du 19 juin 1798 au 9 mai 1838, p. 332–36. Index of hallmarks p. 336–55.

1835
Chaffers, William. Hall marks on gold & silver plate, illustrated with revised tables of annual date letters employed in the assay offices of England, Scotland and Ireland . . . 10th ed. Extended and enl., and with the addition of new date letters and marks, and a bibliography. Also incorporating makers' marks from "Gilda aurifabrorum," ed. by Major C. A. Markham . . . London, Reeves, 1922. 395 p. illus., plates. 26 cm.
3d ed. 1868; 4th ed. 1872. Contains material on English goldsmiths, table of statutes and ordinances, table of marks, chronological list of English plate, London gold and silversmiths, provincial assay offices, etc. Bibliography p. [373]–83. General index p. 385–95.

1836
Churchill, Sidney John Alexander. The goldsmiths of Italy; some account of their guilds, statutes, and work, compiled from the published papers, notes, and other material collected by the late Sydney J. A. Churchill . . . by Cyril G. E. Bunt. London, Hopkinson, 1926. 182 p. 21 plates. 32 cm.
Contains bibliographies p. 161–73. Index p. 175–82.

1837
Cripps, Wilfred Joseph. Old English plate; ecclesiastical, decorative and domestic: its makers and marks. 10th ed. London, Murray, 1914. 538 p. 122 illus., 9 plates. 24 cm.
1st ed. 1878; 2d 1881; 3d 1886; 4th 1891; 5th 1894; 6th 1899; 7th 1901; 8th 1903; 9th 1906. An old work which has been somewhat superseded.
Appendices: A, Chronological list of examples used as authority for London date-letters and makers' marks p. 417–92; B, Im-

proved tables of the date-letters used by all the English, Scotch and Irish assay-halls from the earliest times p. 493–519. Bibliography p. 33–34. Index p. 521–38.

1838

Cripps, Wilfred Joseph. Old French plate; its makers and marks . . . 3d ed. with illustrations. London, Murray, 1920. 115 p. illus. 23 cm.

1st ed. 1880; 2d ed. 1893. An old work which has been somewhat superseded.

Contents: (1) French weights and standards; (2) The goldsmiths of France, and the marks used in Paris till 1789; (3) Provincial marks till 1789; (4) The hall-marks used in Paris and the departments since 1797. Appendix: Examples of old French plate with makers' names and marks p. 102–10 (arranged chronologically). Index p. 111–15.

1839

Currier, Ernest M. Marks of early American silversmiths, with notes on silver spoon types & list of New York City silversmiths 1815–1841. Illustrated with many of [the author's] drawings. Edited with introductory note by Kathryn C. Buhler. Portland, Me., Southworth-Anthoensen Press; London, Quaritch, 1938. 179 p. illus., plates, facsims. 28 cm.

Edition of 750 copies. Marks are arranged alphabetically by name of artist. Silversmiths of New York City 1815–41 with their dates p. 173–76. Bibliography p. 177–79.

1840

Dawson, Nelson. Goldsmiths' and silversmiths' work. N.Y., Putnam, 1907. 266 p. illus., 50 plates. 26 cm. (The connoisseur's library)

The subject is approached "from the side of the artist and craftsman" (*Pref.*) and covers from Mycenean and Roman to modern times. Index p. 263–67.

1841

De Castro, John Paul. The law and practice of hall-marking gold and silver wares, with a chapter on the licenses to be taken out by auctioneers, pawnbrokers and dealers in gold and silver plate . . . London, Lockwood, 1926. 372 p. 34 plates. 24 cm.

A technical book on the subject of hall-marks. "This book prepared . . . for the convenience of manufacturers in close contact with the hall-marking authorities, and for the assistance of dealers in gold and silver plate, at home and abroad, whose activities call for a competent knowledge of hall-marks

and of the main requirements of the British hall-marking enactments."—*Pref.*

Contents: (1) Introduction, Marks, Exemptions from marking, The seven state-recognized assay offices, Methods of assay, Advantages of the hall-marking system, Miscellaneous, Frauds and offences, Licenses to deal in plate; (2) Reports of decided cases: civil and criminal; (3) Statutes, revised and annotated; statutory rules and orders; Appendices.

"Bibliography and abbreviations" p. xiii–xiv. Index p. 366–72.

1842

Ensko, Stephen G. C. American silversmiths and their marks III. N.Y., Ensko, 1948. 285 p. illus. 24 cm.

Series I, 1927; Series II, 1937. "Only silversmiths and allied craftsmen who can be identified with known examples of their craftsmanship have been included in this list. With names of silversmiths are earliest working dates; hyphenated double dates indicate birth and death; and locations of business mentioned are followed by records of marriage, freemanships, apprenticeships and other pertinent information."—*Pref.*

Contents: (1) Names of early American silversmiths 1650–1850, p. 11–146; (2) Marks of early American silversmiths 1650–1850, p. 149–252; (3) Location of silversmith shops p. 253–71. Bibliography p. 281–85.

1843

Ensko, Stephen G. C., and Wenham, Edward. English silver 1675–1825. N.Y., Ensko [c1937]. 109 p. illus. 24 cm.

In this "handbook, an effort has been made to describe, concisely, the changes in style and form that have taken place in English silver during the period 1675 to 1825, and the sources from which those changes sprang."—*Foreword*. Illustrated with line drawings. Assay marks p. 99–109. Bibliography p. 14–15.

1844

Frederiks, J. W. Dutch silver, embossed plaquettes, tazze and dishes from the Renaissance until the end of the eighteenth century. The Hague, Nijhoff, 1952. 540 p. with 476 illus. 32 cm.

A well-illustrated corpus of Dutch silver covering the period from the Renaissance through the 18th century. Arranged by artist giving biographical data whenever possible. Indexes: of masters p. 529–31; of sources of designs p. 532; of representations p. 533–38.

1845

Frederiks, J. W. Dutch silver, wrought plate of North and South-Holland from the Renaissance until the end of the eighteenth century. The Hague, Nijhoff, 1958. xxxvi, 211 p. 624 illus. on 313 plates. 33 cm.

A well-illustrated corpus which "covers plaques, medals, boxes, book covers, knives, spoons, tazze, beakers, tankards, flagons, cups, bowls, porringers, dishes, basins, salvers, table-ware, candlesticks, braziers, tea-pots, tea-kettles, coffee-pots, milk jugs and tea caddies."—*Pref.* Gives biographical material for each artist listed.

Contents: (1) Print engravers p. 3–36; (2) Silversmiths p. 37–201. List of abbreviations p. xxxiii–xxxv. Indexes: of masters p. 205–08; of sources of design p. 209; of objects p. 210–11.

1846

French, Hollis. . . . A list of early American silversmiths and their marks, with a silver collectors' glossary. N.Y., Walpole Society, 1917. 164 p. illus. 25 cm.

Only 200 copies printed. Glossary p. 133–64.

1847

Havard, Henry. Histoire de l'orfèvrerie française. Paris, May & Metteroz, 1896. 472 p. illus., 40 plates (part col.) 45 cm.

A standard French history of goldsmithing covering from the earliest times through the 19th century. No index.

1848

Heal, *Sir* Ambrose. The London goldsmiths, 1200–1800; a record of the names and addresses of the craftsmen, their shop-signs and trade cards, compiled . . . from the records of the Goldsmiths' company and other contemporary sources; published under the patronage of the Worshipful Company of Goldsmiths of London. Cambridge [Eng.] The University Press, 1935. 279 p. 80 facsims. 33 cm.

"List of London goldsmiths' shop-signs" p. 49–89, with dates. "A list of the London goldsmiths, jewellers, bankers and pawnbrokers up to the year 1800, setting out their names, addresses and dates" p. 93–275. Index p. 277–80.

1849

Jackson, *Sir* Charles James. English goldsmiths and their marks; a history of the goldsmiths and plate workers of England,

Scotland, and Ireland; with over thirteen thousand marks reproduced in facsimile from authentic examples of plate, and tables of date-letters and other hallmarks used in the assay offices of the United Kingdom. 2d ed. rev. and enl. London, Macmillan, 1921. 747 p. illus., plates, tables. 31 cm.

Index p. 719–47.

1850

Jackson, *Sir* Charles James. An illustrated history of English plate, ecclesiastical and secular, in which the development of form and decoration in the silver and gold work of the British isles, from the earliest known examples to the latest of the Georgian period, is delineated and described, with a coloured frontispiece, seventy-six photogravure plates and fifteen hundred other illustrations . . . London, Country Life, 1911. 2 v. illus., 76 plates. 34 cm.

Paged continuously. Very well illustrated, with a "Chronological list of illustrations" v. 1, p. [xxix]–xxxviii. Bibliography is in the Preface. Index v. 2, p. 1065–85.

1851

Johnson, Ada Marshall. Hispanic silverwork. . . . With 266 illustrations. N.Y., Hispanic Society, 1944. 308 p. illus. 23 cm. (Hispanic notes and monographs; essays, studies and brief biographies issued by the Hispanic Society of America. Catalogue series)

Covers the Gothic through the 19th century. "Catalogue of silverwork in the collection of the Hispanic Society of America" p. 147–283. Bibliographical references included in "Notes" p. 284–94. References p. 294–300. Index p. 301–08.

1852

Jones, Edward Alfred. Old silver of Europe & America from early times to the nineteenth century . . . Philadelphia, Lippincott, 1928. 376 p. illus., 96 plates. 26 cm.

"An attempt to compile . . . a brief historical account of the old domestic silver of Europe and America."—*Introd.* Index p. 343–76.

1853

Marquet de Vasselot, Jean Joseph. . . . Bibliographie de l'orfèvrerie et de l'émaillerie françaises . . . Paris, Picard, 1925. 293 p. 23 cm. (Soc. Française de Bibliographie. Publications [12])

More than 2700 references to books and articles which treat directly of the history of French goldsmithing and enamels.

Contents: (1) Généralités; (2) Technique; (3) Métier (Organization of work, teaching, and competitions); (4) Poinçons; (5) Modèles, sujets; (6) Époques (arranged chronologically by objects described); (7) Localités; (8) Musées; (9) Expositions; (10) Collections privées; (11) Trésors (of churches, abbeys, etc.); (12) Artistes; (13) Objets. Under these headings works are listed alphabetically by authors.

Index of names of authors, persons, and places p. 261–93.

1854

Nocq, Henry. . . . Le poinçon de Paris, répertoire des maîtres-orfèvres de la juridiction de Paris depuis le moyen-âge jusqu'à la fin du XVIIIe siècle. Paris, Floury, 1926–31. 5 v. illus. (incl. facsims.), plates. 29 cm.

Edition of 620 copies printed. A standard work on Parisian hallmarks from the Middle Ages to the end of the 18th century. Contents: v. 1, A–C; v. 2, D–K; v. 3, L–R; v. 4, S–Z; v. 5, Supplement.

Volume 3 also contains: Résumé chronologique p. 127–96; Brèves indications p. 197–200; Listes des gardes p. 201–19; Poinçons des fermiers p. 220–42; Itinéraire des gardes (notice topographique) p. 243–55; Notice sur les orfèvres de la généralité de Paris . . . p. 256–79.

Volume 5 also contains: Tables; Poinçons de maîtres rangés d'après les initiales dans l'ordre alphabétique p. 35–65; Poinçons dans lesquels la dernière lettre n'est pas l'initial du nom de famille, tel qu'il s'écrit habituellement p. 66–71; Table des différents p. 73–96. "Principales sources de l'histoire des orfèvres de Paris" v. 4, p. 283–90.

1855

Okie, Howard Pitcher. Old silver and old Sheffield plate, a history of the silversmith's art in Great Britain and Ireland, with reproductions in facsimile of about thirteen thousand marks. Tables of date letters and other marks. American silversmiths and their marks. Paris marks and Paris date letters with a description of the methods of marking employed by the Paris guild of silversmiths. Hallmarks, and date letters when used, of nearly all the countries of Continental Europe, reproduced in facsimile. A history of old Sheffield plate and a description of the method of its production, with the names and marks, in facsimile, of every known maker. With twelve full-page illustrations. N.Y., Doubleday, 1928. 420 p. illus., plates. 26 cm.

"First edition." "Purpose [of the book is] of enabling the reader to establish the origin and authenticity of antique silver and 'old Sheffield plate.' "—Foreword. General index p. 415–20.

1856

Pollen, John Hungerford. Gold and silver smiths' work. London, Chapman and Hall; N.Y., Scribner and Wilford [1879]. 160 p. illus. 20 cm. (South Kensington Museum art handbooks, ed. by W. Maskell)

A general survey from the ancients through the 18th century with a chapter explaining hallmarks. Illustrated by a few line engravings in the text. Index p. 158–60.

1857

Ris-Paquot, Oscar E. Dictionnaire des poinçons, symboles, signes figuratifs, marques et monogrammes des orfèvres français et étrangers, fermiers généraux, maitres des monnaies, contrôleurs, vérificateurs, etc. Paris, Laurens, 1890. 382 p. 20 cm.

Contains 1557 monograms, hallmarks; includes list of coats of arms of jewelers' guilds, list of jewelers from 1337–1710.

Contents: pt. 1, Statuts et privilèges du corps des marchands orfèvres et joyailleurs de la ville de Paris; pt. 2, Armorial de la corporation des orfèvres de France; pt. 3, Poinçons et marques figuratives ou symboliques; pt. 4, Dictionnaire des noms des gardes de l'orfèvrerie de Paris de 1337 à 1710; pt. 5, Dictionnaire des noms des fermiers généraux, contrôleurs, maitres des monnaies, orfèvres, villes dont les poinçons, symboles, signes figuratifs, marques et monogrammes sont contenus dans l'ouvrage.

1858

Rosenberg, Marc. Der Goldschmiede Merkzeichen. 3. erweiterte und illustrierte Aufl. Frankfurt am Main, Frankfurter Verlags-Anstalt, 1922–28. 4 v. illus., 117 plates. 25 cm. Reprinted 1955.

Arranged alphabetically by city and then by artist. For each artist gives dates and cites works, as well as giving marks. Includes size of works and bibliography. Good clear halftone plates showing examples of the art.

Contents: 1–3, Deutschland: v. 1, A–C; v. 2, D–M; v. 3, N–Z; v. 4, Ausland und Byzanz. At end of each volume an index of marks and one of names of goldsmiths.

1859

[Tardy] Les poinçons de garantie internationaux pour l'argent. 4e éd. réunie par

Tardy. Paris, Tardy, n.d. 353 p. facsims. 17 cm.

2d ed. [1944] (Paris, Tardy, 148 p.). Hallmarks arranged by country and then by city. "Table alphabétique des lieux cités" p. 267–80. "Index analytique des poinçons contenus dans le volume" p. 281–348.

1860

Taullard, Alfredo. Platería sudamericana ... Buenos Aires, Peuser, 1941. 285 p. incl. illus., plates. 33 cm.

Edition of 800 copies. Comprises 112 pages of text and 167 of plates. Bibliography p. 7–8. "Nómina de plateros; época colonial [y época independiente]" p. 279–83.

1861

Thorn, C. Jordan. Handbook of American silver and pewter marks; preface by John Meredith Graham II. N.Y., Tudor [1949]. 289 p. illus. 24 cm.

Popular rather than scholarly but a useful manual. Contains 3500 American silver and pewter marks, arranged alphabetically by name of maker.

1862

Upmark, Gustaf. Guld- och silversmeder i Sverige, 1520–1850. Stockholm, Fröleen [1943]. 951 p. illus., plates, facsims. 26 cm.

Swedish gold- and silversmiths, arranged geographically and then alphabetically. Index of marks p. 821–914. Index of artists p. 915–45.

1863

Voet, Elias, Jr. Nederlandse goud- en zilvermerken 1445–1951. Met afbeeldingen tussen de tekst en 3 platen. 2. verm. druk, bewerkt door P. W. Voet. 's Gravenhage, Nijhoff, 1951. 73 p. illus. 22 cm.

A useful small handbook of Dutch hallmarks by the foremost authority on the subject. The author has written a number of more detailed studies of hallmarks in various cities of the Netherlands, i.e.: Haarlem, 1928; Amsterdam, 1912; Friesland, 1932; and The Hague, 1941.

"Wetten, koninklijke besluiten enz." p. 48–67.

1864

Wenham, Edward. Domestic silver of Great Britain and Ireland. N.Y., Oxford Univ. Press, 1935. 186 p. 95 plates on 48 l. 26 cm.

1st ed. 1931. A cheaper ed. 1935. A standard work on the subject. "Recent auction prices" p. 148–75. "Works of reference" p. 176. Index p. 177–86.

1865

Wenham, Edward. The practical book of American silver, with line illustrations by Edgar Holloway and reproductions from photographs. Philadelphia, Lippincott [1949]. 275 p. illus., plates. 24 cm.

"Books of reference" p. 265–67. Index p. 269–75.

1866

Wyler, Seymour B. The book of old silver, English, American, foreign; with all available hallmarks including Sheffield plate marks. N.Y., Crown [c1937]. 447 p. incl. illus., plates. 26 cm.

Pages 1–162 are devoted to text covering various aspects of the subject in 19 chapters. Pages 165–443 are devoted to hallmarks, divided by country of origin and with three indexes, by country and geographical location, p. 291–443. Bibliography p. 444. General index p. 445–47.

Pewter

1867

Bell, Malcolm. Old pewter . . . London, Newnes; N.Y., Scribner [1905]. 186 p. 106 plates. 23 cm. (Half-title: Newnes library of the applied arts)

Reprinted in 1913 (London, Batsford; N.Y., Scribner). Contains a chapter on how pewter was made, a historical survey of pewter, and a chapter on the collecting and displaying of pewter. Index p. 165–86.

1868

Cotterell, Howard Herschel. Old pewter, its makers and marks in England, Scotland and Ireland; an account of the old pewterer & his craft, illustrating all known marks and secondary marks of the old pewterers, with a series of plates showing the chief types of their wares. London, Batsford [1929]. 432 p. incl. illus., plates, facsims. 6 fold. plates. 29 cm.

"Historical introduction" p. 1–19. "Alphabetical list of pewterers" p. 145–344, giving their marks. Alphabetical list of "Initialled marks" p. 345–83; of "Obscure marks" p. 384–89. Bibliography p. 423. General index p. 425–32. Index to devices p. 391–415; to hallmarks p. 416–21.

1869

Denman, Carolyn. A bibliography of pewter. Boston, Pewter Collectors' Club of America [c1945]. 21 p. 28 cm. (*Its* Bulletin, no. 15)

Covers books and periodical articles, divided into: General, American, English, Scotch, Continental, Asiatic, and Modern.

List of museums containing collections p. 20–21.

Supplements to be issued from time to time.

1870

Hintze, Erwin. Die deutschen Zinngiesser und ihre Marken . . . Leipzig, Hiersemann, 1921–31. 7 v. illus. 28 cm.

A monumental work on German pewter marks. Contents: v. 1, Sächsische Zinngiesser; v. 2, Nürnberger Zinngiesser; v. 3, Norddeutsche Zinngiesser; v. 4, Schlesische Zinngiesser; v. 5–7, Süddeutsche Zinngiesser: (1) Aalen-Kronach; (2) Kunzelsau-Sulzbach; (3) Tauberbischofsheim bis Zwiesel, mit Anhang: Elsass, Österreich, Schweiz, Ungarn.

Each volume is a complete unit, arranged by geographical district and then by city, under which is given in four parallel columns: (1) Lfde. Nr. (number assigned); (2) Stadtzeichen; (3) Meisterzeichen; (4) Meister-Gegenstand-Eigentümer.

Each volume has indexes: (1) Meisterverzeichnis; (2) Register der Marken: a, Vereinigte Stadt- und Meisterzeichen; b, Stadtzeichen; c, Meisterzeichen; d, Qualitätzeichen für Probezinn, Lauterzinn, Feinzinn, Englisch Zinn; (3) Verzeichnis der Eigentümer.

1871

Jacobs, Carl. Guide to American pewter. Illus. by Marion B. Wilson. N.Y., McBride, 1957. 216 p. illus., plates, facsims. 24 cm.

"This book, although primarily a price guide, also includes concise information that will be useful to collectors and dealers."— *Collecting pewter*, p. 20. Arranged alphabetically by name of pewterer. Appendix of "Characteristic pewter forms" p. 205–16.

1872

Kerfoot, John Barett. American pewter . . . with illustrations from photographs by the author of specimens in his own collection. Boston, N.Y., Houghton Mifflin, 1924. 239 p. plates. 29 cm.

A standard book on this subect. Well illustrated. Index p. 231–39.

1873

Laughlin, Ledlie Irwin. Pewter in America, its makers and their marks. Boston, Houghton Mifflin, 1940. 2 v. illus., 78 plates (incl. facsims.) on 39 1. 33 cm.

The definitive work on the subject. Ap-

pendices: (1) Check list of American makers of pewter, Britannia, or block tin; (2) Representative inventories of American pewter shops. Bibliography v. 2, p. 161–92. Index v. 2, p. 193–242.

1874

Tischer, Friedrich. Böhmisches Zinn und seine Marken, mit 1258 Abbildungen von Zinngiessermarken und 16 Tafeln. Leipzig, Hiersemann, 1928. 329 p. 1258 illus., 16 plates, facsims. 31 cm.

A scholarly work on Bohemian pewter and pewterers' marks, covering both German and Czech workers. "Literaturverzeichnis" p. xiv–xv. Indexes of places p. vii–x; of masters p. 295–304; of marks p. 309–26; of coats of arms of owners p. 327–29.

Iron

1875

Ayrton, Maxwell, and Silcock, Arnold. Wrought iron and its decorative use. London, Country Life [1929]. 196 p. illus. (incl. plans, facsims.) 32 cm.

A well-illustrated survey of this field. Bibliography p. 188. Index p. 189–96.

1876

Blanc, Louis. Le fer forgé en France. La régence; aurore, apogée, déclin. Oeuvres gravées des anciens maîtres serruriers, architectes, dessinateurs et graveurs . . . Paris et Bruxelles, van Oest, 1930. 24 p. 96 plates. 33 cm.

A survey of French wrought ironwork. "Notices biographiques" p. 9–19. "Table des noms d'auteur dans l'ordre chronologique" p. 21–22. "Table des sujets reproduits" p. 23–24.

1877

Blanc, Louis. Le fer forgé en France aux XVIe et XVIIe siècles; oeuvres gravées des anciens maîtres, serruriers, architectes, dessinateurs et graveurs. Paris, van Oest, 1928. 27 p. 96 plates. 28 cm.

A collection of reproductions of original engravings of metalwork done by the creators. In portfolio. "Notices biographiques" p. 9–23. Alphabetical list of artists p. 25. List of subjects reproduced p. 26–27.

1878

Byne, Arthur, and Byne, *Mrs.* Mildred (Stapley). Spanish ironwork . . . with one hundred and fifty eight illustrations. [N.Y.] Hispanic Society, 1915. 143 p. illus., plates. 23 cm. (Hispanic Society publications, no. 89)

"Catalogue of ironwork in the collection of the Hispanic Society of America" p. [137]–43. Index p. 131–36.

1879

Ferrari, Giulio. . . . Il ferro nell'arte italiana; centosettante tavole riproduzioni in parte inedite di 368 soggetti del medio evo, del rinascimento, del periodo barocco e neo-classico raccolte e ordinate con testo esplicativo . . . 3. ed. aumentata. Milano, Hoepli [1927]. 197 p. 160 plates. 32 cm. (Collezione artistica Hoepli)

Primarily a picture book but a good survey of Italian ironwork from medieval times through the neo-classic period. "Indice" is just a list of the illustrations.

1880

Ffoulkes, Constance Joselyn. Decorative ironwork from the eleventh to the eighteenth century. London, Methuen, 1913. 148 p. illus., plates. 32 cm.

"Names of smiths and ironworkers" p. 141–44.

1881

Frank, Edgar Black. Old French ironwork; the craftsman and his art. Cambridge, Mass., Harvard Univ. Press, 1950. 221 p. illus., 96 plates. 25 cm.

A translation of *Petite ferronnerie ancienne*. Devoted to small pieces, i.e., locks, keys, hinges, bolts, padlocks, caskets, tinder boxes, sewing accessories, knives, seals and candlesticks, etc. Bibliography p. 217–18. Index p. 219–21.

1882

Gardner, John Starkie. English ironwork of the XVIIth and XVIIIth centuries; an historical & analytical account of the development of exterior smithcraft . . . with 88 collotype plates from photographs chiefly by Horace Dan, architect, and upwards of 150 other illustrations. London, Batsford [1911]. 336 p. illus., 88 plates. 25 cm.

A standard work on this subject. Contents: Medieval ironwork; The evolution of gates; Railings, balustrades, balconies, stair-ramps and grilles; Lampholders, brackets, signs and vanes; Lists of smiths and designers (p. 321–23).

General index to the text p. 324–36. Brief subject list of examples illustrated p. xv–

xviii. Topographical list of examples illustrated p. xix–xxvi.

1883

Gloag, John, and Bridgwater, Derek. A history of cast iron in architecture. With a foreword by Sir Charles Reilly. London, Allen & Unwin [1948]. 395 p. illus. (part col.) 29 cm.

A well-illustrated treatment of the subject. Includes bibliographies. Index p. 379–95.

1884

Hoever, Otto. An encyclopedia of ironwork; examples of hand wrought ironwork from the Middle Ages to the end of the 18th century, with an historical introduction by Otto Hoever. N.Y., Weyhe, 1927. 29 p. illus., 320 plates on 160 l. 32 cm.

Good halftone plates representing ironwork from the Gothic through classicism. Contents: (1) Introduction: ornamental ironwork; (2) Gothic; (3) Late Gothic and Renaissance; (4) Baroque and classicism.

1885

Sonn, Albert H. Early American wrought iron, with 320 plates from drawings by the author. N.Y., Scribner, 1928. 3 v. illus. (incl. facsims.), 320 plates. 33 cm.

Bibliography v. 3, p. 243–44. General index v. 3, p. 247–63, covering all three volumes.

Medals

1886

Armand, Alfred. Les médailleurs italiens des quinzième et seizième siècles . . . 2d. éd. rev., corrigée et considérablement augmentée. Paris, Plon, 1883–87. 2 v. and suppl. 25 cm.

1st ed. 1879. An attempt to make a manual in which all the Italian medals of the 15th and 16th centuries will be found, which contains 2600 medals.

Part 1 comprises the work of medalists whose names, initials, or marks are known (about 178). Under each artist medals are arranged alphabetically with a description of each, as well as indication of where it has been reproduced. Locations of unpublished medals are given. Part 2 treats of anonymous medalists and for them gives: names and dates of persons represented, diameter and legends of both sides, references to reproductions, and location of unpublished ones.

A 3d v. contains supplement and indexes. Bibliography v. 1, Pref. p. 17–18, and v. 3, Pref. p. 8. Volumes 2 and 3 have indexes of personages represented and legends inscribed on the medals. Volume 2, p. 307–31, has an alphabetical list of medalists referring to v. 1 and 2.

1887

Fabriczy, Cornelius von. Italian medals. Trans. by Mrs. Gustavus W. Hamilton. N.Y., Dutton, 1904. 223 p. 40 plates. 28 cm.

Contents: (1) The medals of the Quattrocento; (2) The struck medals of the Cinquecento. Index p. 213–[24].

1888

Forrer, Leonard. Biographical dictionary of medallists; coin, gem, and seal-engravers, mint-masters, etc., ancient and modern, with references to their works B.C. 500–A.D. 1900 . . . London, Spink, 1902–30. 8 v. illus., 6 plates. 25 cm.

300 copies printed. Sources are given at the end of almost every entry. Contents: v. 1–6, A–Z; v. 7, A–L Supp.; v. 8, M–Z, 2d Supp. Bibliography: v. 1, p. xxxix–xlviii and v. 8, p. [368]. Index of illustrations v. 8, p. 369–461.

1889

Friedländer, Julius. Die italienischen Schaumünzen des fünfzehnten Jahrhunderts (1430–1530). Ein Beitrag zur Kunstgeschichte . . . Berlin, Weidmann, 1882. 223 p. illus., 42 plates. 35 cm.

An important early work on Italian Renaissance medals. Alphabetical index of artists p. 216–17; of medals represented p. 218–23.

1890

Habich, Georg, ed. Die deutschen Schaumünzen des XVI. Jahrhunderts, hrsg. mit Unterstützung der Bayerischen Akademie der Wissenschaften und der Notgemeinschaft der Deutschen Wissenschaft im Auftrag des Deutschen Vereins für Kunstwissenschaft. München, Bruckmann [1929–34]. v. 1¹⁻², 2¹⁻² and index in 5 v. illus., 334 plates. 40 cm.

No more published. A scholarly corpus with excellent illustrations and bibliographies. Covers German medals of the 16th century arranged by masters and schools.

1891

Habich, Georg. Die Medaillen der italienischen Renaissance . . . Stuttgart und Berlin, Deutsche Verlags-Anstalt [1923]. 168 p. illus., 100 plates. 36 cm.

The basic work on the subject. Excellent

plates. Bibliography (of six items) p. xii. Indexes: "Tafelrückweis" p. 151–59; "Verzeichnis der Medailleure" p. 160–61; "Verzeichnis der auf den Medaillen dargestellten Personen" p. 162–67.

1892

Hill, *Sir* George Francis. A corpus of Italian medals of the Renaissance before Cellini . . . London, British Museum, Printed by order of the Trustees, 1930. 2 v. illus., 201 plates. 41 cm.

"The object of this work is to classify and describe the known varieties of medals produced by Italian artists from 1390 to about 1530." Dimensions are given to half a millimeter.

Contents: v. 1, Text; v. 2, Plates. List of museums and collections v. 1, p. xv–xvi. List of the more important catalogs of auction-sales consulted v. 1, p. xvii. Bibliography v. 1, p. xii–xiv.

1893

Hill, *Sir* George Francis. Medals of the Renaissance. Oxford, Clarendon Press, 1920. 204 p. 30 plates. 30 cm.

"An attempt to give a general summary of the whole" (*Pref.*) which covers Italian, German, French, English, and Netherlandish medals. Key to the plates p. 183–93. Bibliography p. 174–82. Index p. 194–204.

1894

Lenormant, François. Monnaies et médailles. Nouv. éd. Paris, Quantin [1885?]. 328 p. illus. 21 cm. (Bibliothèque de l'enseignement des beaux-arts)

A reissue of the 1st ed., 1883. Appendixes: (1) Liste des médailleurs italiens des XVe et XVIe siècles dont on possède des oeuvres signées p. 319–22; (2) Médailleurs et graveurs monétaires français depuis la renaissance p. 323–24; (3) Les procédés actuels de la fabrication monétaire p. 325–26. "Table des matières" p. [327]–28.

Gems and Jewelry

1895

Davenport, Cyril James Humphries. Cameos. London, Seeley; N.Y., Macmillan, 1900. 66 p. illus., 28 plates (8 col.) 27 cm. (The Portfolio artistic monographs [no. 41])

Contents: (1) The materials used for cameos and the processes employed in cutting them; (2) Early cameos and glass pastes; (3)

Graeco-Roman and medieval cameos; (4) Renaissance and later cameos. Index p. 63–66.

1896
Evans, Joan. A history of jewellery, 1100–1870. London, Faber [1953]. 240 p. illus., plates (part col.) 27 cm.
Bibliography p. 204–14. Index p. 215–40.

1897
Hansford, S. Howard. Chinese jade carving. [London], Humphries, 1950. 145 p. illus., maps, 32 plates. 26 cm.
A useful book on the technique of Chinese jade carving which covers the material, sources of supply of the jade stone, methods of jade carving, and the progress of the craft in China. Bibliography p. 125–39. Index p. 140–45.

1898
Laufer, Berthold. Jade; a study in Chinese archaeology and religion. [2d ed., with a new foreword by the Chicago Natural History Museum], South Pasadena, Perkins; London, Routledge, 1946. 370 p. illus., col. plates. 24 cm.
1st ed. 1912 (Chicago, Field Museum of Natural History, Pub. 154, Anthropological series v. 10).
The standard work on jade. Bibliography p. 355–60. Index p. 361–70.

1899
Osborne, Duffield. Engraved gems, signets, talismans and ornamental intaglios, ancient and modern . . . with thirty-two full-page plates. N.Y., Holt, 1912. 424 p. illus., 32 plates. 26 cm.
Contents: pt. 1, History of gem engraving—characteristics and development of each period; pt. 2, The deities and other personages common or liable to be found on engraved gems, with their appearance, attributes etc.; pt. 3, Technique—materials—historical and mythological signets. "Alphabetical list of attributes, aspects and sacred or sacrificial animals, trees and flowers" p. 393–98. Index p. 399–424.

1900
Salmony, Alfred. Carved jade of ancient China. Berkeley, Gillick Press, 1938. 85, [85] p. 72 plates on 38 1. 33 cm.
Edition of 250 copies. The description of the plates includes the size of the objects. Chinese dynasties and periods p. 83. Collec-

tions represented p. 85. Bibliography p. 77–82.

1901
Smith, Harold Clifford. Jewellery. London, Methuen; N.Y., Putnam [1908]. 409 p. illus., 54 plates (3 col.) 27 cm. (The connoisseur's library, gen. ed.: C. Davenport)
A general history of jewelry from ancient times to the present day. Bibliography p. 371–79. Index p. 381–410.

1902
Steingräber, Erich. Antique jewelry. N.Y., Praeger; London, Thames [1957]. 191 p. illus., part col. 29 cm.
A German ed. titled *Alter Schmuck; die Kunst des europäischen Schmuckes* published in Munich, Rinn [1956]. An illustrated survey of European jewelry from 800–1900. "Select bibliography" p. 185–86. Index p. 187–91.

Rugs and Carpets

1903
Dilley, Arthur Urbane. Oriental rugs and carpets; a comprehensive study. N.Y., London, Scribner, 1931. 303 p. illus. (maps), 79 plates (part col.) on 47 1. 29 cm.
Index p. 297–303.

1904
Faraday, Cornelia Bateman. European and American carpets and rugs; a history of the hand-woven decorative floor coverings of Spain, France, Great Britain, Scandinavia, Belgium, Holland, Italy, the Balkans, Germany, Austria and early America; and of the machine-made carpets and rugs of modern Europe and of the United States. With more than 400 illustrations of antique and modern European and American carpets and rugs, with thirty-two plates in full color. Grand Rapids, Mich., The Dean-Hicks Co., 1929. 382 p. illus., plates (part col.) 29 cm.
The standard work on carpets, other than Oriental. Index p. 379–82.

1905
Hawley, Walter Augustus. Oriental rugs, antique and modern . . . with 11 full-page plates in colour, 80 halftone engravings and 4 maps. N.Y., Tudor, 1937. 320 p. illus., plates (part col.), maps, tables. 28 cm.
Copyright 1913. "New edition, May, 1937." Chapters on "How to distinguish rugs" and "Purchasing rugs" are aimed at collectors or

buyers. The book also contains a chapter on weaving. Index p. 309–20.

1906

Holt, Rosa Belle. Oriental & Occidental rugs, antique & modern; with 33 full-page illustrations, 12 full color, and other drawings in the text, and a map of the Orient. New and rev. ed. Garden City, Garden City Pub. Co. [c1937]. 208 p. illus., plates (part col.), map. 28 cm.

1st ed. 1901; 2d ed. 1908 (Chicago, McClurg), of which this is a reprint. Previously published under title: *Rugs, Oriental and Occidental,* half-title of the present edition.

Contents: (1) History and details of rug weaving; (2) Rug weaving in Egypt, Persia and Turkey; (3) Rug weaving in India, Afghanistan, Beluchistan, Central Asia and the Caucasus region; (4) Miscellaneous oriental rugs; (5) Rug weaving in Europe and the U.S.; (6) Miscellaneous information (symbols and inscriptions) and geographical influences. Supplement 1927 p. 181–88.

"List of authorities" p. 175–78. Index p. 189–208.

1907

Kendrick, Albert Frank, and Tattersall, Creassey Edward Cecil. Hand-woven carpets, Oriental and European . . . with 205 plates, of which 19 are in colour. N.Y., Scribner, 1922. 2 v. 205 plates (part col.), map. 29 cm.

Edition of 1000 sets. Contents: (1) Historical; (2) Technical: v. 1, Text; v. 2, Plates. Bibliography v. 1, p. 193–94.

1908

Lewis, George Griffin. The practical book of Oriental rugs . . . new rev. ed., with 32 color plates, 80 halftones and numerous line designs. Philadelphia, N.Y., Lippincott [1945]. 317 p. illus., 112 plates (part col.) 22 cm.

6th rev. ed. 1st ed. 1911. A useful one-volume handbook which covers material of rugs, dyes, weaving, designs and their symbolism, and the identification of rugs (their classification). Bibliography p. 307–09. Index p. 310–17.

1909

Martin, Frederik Robert. A history of Oriental carpets before 1800 . . . Vienna, Printed for the author in the I. and R. State and Court Printing Office, 1908. 159 p. illus. (part col.), 33 plates (part col.) 67 cm.

Edition of 300 copies printed. "The text has been made as concise as possible, and must be considered as the first attempt to write a History of Oriental carpets and as a supplement to the great work published in Vienna 15 years ago [1916]. These two books will together form a history, as far as our knowledge now permits, of the most charming products of the Eastern Art."—*Pref.* Profusely illustrated both in the text and by excellent collotype plates.

"Notes" (bibliography) p. 147–52. List of text illustrations p. 153–57. List of plates p. 157. Index of principal names p. 158–59.

1910

Mumford, John Kimberly. Oriental rugs . . . N.Y., Scribner, 1929. 278 p. 32 plates (part col.), 2 maps, 2 fold. tables. 26 cm.

First published 1900; 4th ed. 1915. Covers material and dyes, design, history and classification, and discussion of the output of various countries where they are produced. Index p. 269–78.

1911

Neugebauer, Rudolf, and Troll, Siegfried. Handbuch der orientalischen Teppichkunde, mit 128 einfarbigen und 16 mehrfarbigen Tafeln, 5 Textfiguren, 8 Motivblättern und 1 Karte. 14. gänzlich neubearb. Aufl. Leipzig, Hiersemann, 1930. 111 p. illus., plates (part col.), map. 24 cm. (Hiersemanns Handbücher, Bd. IV)

"Das Handbuch der orientalischen Teppichkunde von Rudolf Neugebauer und Julius Orendi [pub. 1909] ist in vorliegendem Buch erneuert worden."—*Vorwort.* A German handbook of Oriental rugs.

Contents: (1) Der orientalische Teppich vor 1800; (2) Der orientalische Teppich nach 1800; (3) Die Technik des orientalischen Teppichs; (4) Die orientalischen Teppiche als Kunstwerk; (5) Einkauf und Behandlung des Orientteppichs.

"Motivblätter" p. 110–11 and eight plates. Index p. 105–09.

1912

Ripley, Mary Churchill. The Chinese rug book, with seventeen half-tone illustrations. N.Y., Stokes, 1927. 66 p. illus., plates. 22 cm.

Contents: (1) Historic periods in Chinese art; (2) Materials used in Chinese rugs; (3) Methods of weaving Chinese rugs; (4) Colors employed by Chinese weavers; (5) Designs found in Chinese rugs; (6) The classification of rugs according to design; (7) Classification of rugs according to color.

1913

Tattersall, Creassey Edward Cecil. A history of British carpets, from the introduction of the craft until the present day . . . Benfleet, Essex, Eng., Lewis [1934]. 182 p. illus., 116 plates (part col.) on 58 l. 33 cm.

A well-illustrated treatment by a recognized authority. "List of British carpet manufacturers" p. 178–82.

1914

Vienna. Österreichisches Museum für Kunst und Industrie. Ancient Oriental carpets . . . being a supplement to the Oriental carpets, pub. 1892 to 1896 by the Imperial Royal Austrian Commercial Museum, Vienna. . . . With a preface by the editor A. von Scala, introduction by Wilhelm Bode, text by Friedrich Sarre. Leipzig, Hiersemann, 1908. 8 p. 25 col. plates. 67 cm.

Excellent color combination prints. Contents: Text p. 1–8; Description of the carpets p. [9–13].

1915

Vienna. Österreichisches Museum für Kunst und Industrie. Old Oriental carpets; with text by Friedrich Sarre and Hermann Trenkwald, translated by A. F. Kendrick . . . Vienna, Schroll, 1926–29. 2 v. illus., 120 plates (part col.), tables, diagrs. 60 cm.

This work is based on *Orientalische Teppiche*, published 1892 (1916), and *Altorientalische Teppiche*, published 1908 (1914). A scholarly publication with magnificent reproductions, many of which are in color.

Volume 1 consists of "Carpets of the Austrian Museum for Art and Industry," text by Hermann Trenkwald. Volume 2 contains "The most important carpets in the older work, with the exception of those now in the Austrian Museum, as well as additional examples hitherto unknown or inadequately published," text by Friedrich Sarre and others. Bibliography v. 2, p. 37–42, by Kurt Erdmann.

1916

Vienna. Österreichisches Museum für Kunst und Industrie. Oriental carpets. English ed. by C. P. Clarke. London, Cousins, 1892–96. 3 v. illus., 101 plates (74 col.) 66 cm.

Edition of 400 copies printed, the first 200 in German and the remainder in French and English. Interesting and good early photomechanical color plates. Issued in ten parts.

Text: (1) Modern Turkey carpets, a monograph by J. M. Stoeckel; (2) Decorative animal figures in old Oriental carpets by Wilhelm Bode; (3) Indian carpets by Vincent J. Robinson; (4) Notes on the history of Oriental carpet-weaving in France by M. Gerspach; (5) The present state of the carpet industry in Persia by Sidney T. A. Churchill; (6) . . . Oriental manufacture of sumptuary carpets by Sir George Birdwood; (7) Monograph on Oriental carpets by C. Rudaon Clarke. Text to the plates.

SEE ALSO: Marquet de Vasselot. Bibliographie de la tapisserie, des tapis et de la broderie en France (1927).

Tapestries

1917

Ackerman, Phyllis. Tapestry, the mirror of civilization . . . N.Y., Oxford Univ. Press, 1933. 451 p. 48 plates. 24 cm.

"This book is an attempt to make tapestries living objects of aesthetic perception by revealing them as part of life."—*Pref.* Though not strictly a reference book, it contains much factual information. "Guild regulations" p. 312–17. "Some collectors and collections" p. 318–42. Notes p. 343–429. Bibliography p. 431–33. Index p. 435–51.

1918

Demotte, G. J. La tapisserie gothique; préface de Salomon Reinach. Paris, N.Y., Demotte, 1924. 10 p. 100 mounted col. plates. 55 cm.

Issued in four parts 1922–24. A collection of 100 mounted color plates with short descriptive notes and bibliographical references, including many details. "Bibliographie" leaf preceding p. 1.

1919

Göbel, Heinrich. Tapestries of the Lowlands, trans. by Robert West [pseud.] N.Y., Brentano, 1924. 97, 24 p. illus., plates (part col.) 32 cm.

A translation of pt. 1 of the author's *Wandteppiche* (1920). A section of 24 plates of marks at end of volume.

1920

Göbel, Heinrich. Wandteppiche. Leipzig, Klinkhardt und Biermann, 1923–24. 3 v. in 6. illus., plates (part col.), facsims. 32 cm.

This work covers technique as well as the history of tapestry and is well illustrated. It also gives signatures or marks. Contents: Teil I, Die Niederlande; Teil II, Die romanischen Länder; Teil III, Die germanischen und slavischen Länder. In Teilen I and II the first volume is text and the second plates. Teil III is divided geographically and each volume contains both text and plates for its districts.

Elaborate bibliographies are arranged as footnotes. Indexed by: (1) Manufacturers; (2) "Wandteppichfolgen"; (3) "Wirker und Wirkereihändler"; (4) Painters; (5) Historical personages; (6) Author names.

1921
Guiffrey, Jules Marie Joseph, and others. Histoire générale de la tapisserie. Paris, Société Anonyme de Publications Périodiques, 1878–85. 25 pts. in 3 v. illus., 105 mounted plates (part col.) 56 cm.

A standard work. Contents: pt. 1, Tapisseries françaises par M. Jules Guiffrey; pt. 2, Tapisseries italiennes, allemandes, anglaises, danoises, espagnoles, russes etc. par M. Eugène Müntz; pt. 3, Tapisseries flamandes par M. Alexandre Pinchart.

1922
Guiffrey, Jules Marie Joseph. . . . La Tapisserie . . . Paris, Picard, 1904. 128 p. 25 cm. (Bibliothèque des bibliographies critiques, pub. par la Société des Études Historiques, 20.)

A classified bibliography of 1083 items including books, periodical articles, and sales catalogs, with some annotations.

"Table alphabétique," p. 109–28, includes proper names, geographical names, and subjects.

1923
Hunter, George Leland. The practical book of tapestries . . . with 8 illus. in colour and 220 in double-tone. Philadelphia and London, Lippincott, 1925. 302 p. plates (part col.) 23 cm.

A generally useful book on the subject, discussing design and techniques as well as historical development, which covers the periods from the Egyptian to the modern. "Public collections" p. 279–80. "Descriptive list of books" p. 281–92. Index p. 293–302.

1924
Hunter, George Leland. Tapestries, their origin, history and renaissance. N.Y., Lane, 1913. 438 p. illus., 4 col. plates. 29 cm.

Large paper ed. of 550 copies. Tapestries treated from various angles other than the historical, including repair and cleaning. Poor illustrations.

Bibliography found in Chapter XV, "Tap-

estry museums, collections, inventories, sales, books," p. 323–66. Index of bibliography p. 437–38. General index p. 417–36.

1925
Kurth, Betty. Die deutschen Bildteppiche des Mittelalters. Wien, Schroll, 1926. 3 v. illus., 344 plates (part col.) 38 cm.

A scholarly work with bibliographical footnotes. Contents: Die Technik; Vorgotische Bildwirkereien; Gotische Bildwirkereien; Katalog; Quellenanhang. Indexes: of location of the tapestries p. 303–08; by subjects represented p. 309–14; of places and names p. 315–20.

1926
Lejard, André, ed. French tapestry. London, Elek [1946]. 107 p. illus., col. plates. 32 cm.

A series of articles, written by various authors, on the history and various aspects of French tapestry. Well illustrated and contains a good article on technique, as well as one on the modern revival of tapestry in France. Bibliography p. 107.

1927
Marquet de Vasselot, Jean Joseph, and Weigert, Roger-Armand. . . . Bibliographie de la tapisserie, des tapis et de la broderie en France. Paris, Colin, 1935. 354 p. 23 cm. (Archives de l'art français, pub. par la Société de l'Histoire de l'Art Français. Nouv. pér., t. XVIII)

A classified bibliography of more than 2700 items, including both books and periodical articles up to 1932, and covering tapestry, rugs, and embroidery in France.

Contents: Tapisserie p. 3–240; Tapis p. 243–54; Broderie p. 257–313.

Table alphabétique p. 317–46; Table des sujets représentés p. 347–51.

1928
Müntz, Eugène. A short history of tapestry. From the earliest times to the end of the 18th century. . . . Tr. by Louisa J. Davis. London, N.Y., Cassell, 1885. 399 p. illus. 20 cm. (The fine-art library)

This translation was made from the 2d French ed. A standard French work, illustrated by line drawings. "A guide for the amateur of tapestries," listing marks and chief monograms, p. 367–85. "List of the chief centres of manufacture" p. 387–88. "List of painters who designed cartoons for tapestry, or whose pictures were reproduced in tapestry" p. 389–90. "List of tapestry workers mentioned" p. 391–92.

1929

Müntz, Eugène. La tapisserie. 6. éd. Paris, Picard [189?]. 390 p. 21 cm. (Bibliothèque de l'enseignement des beaux-arts)

A standard French general history of tapestries. Appendix gives the principal marks and monograms p. 360–80. List of the principal centers of manufacture p. 381–82. List of painters who have made cartoons p. 383–84. List of tapestries mentioned in the work p. 385–86. Analytical table of contents at end of volume.

1930

Schmitz, Hermann. Bildteppiche; Geschichte der Gobelinwirkerei. Berlin, Verlag für Kunstwissenschaft [1919]. 352 p. illus. 25 cm.

A general German history of tapestry covering the 15th through the 18th centuries in Germany, the Netherlands, and France; and to a lesser degree, Italy, England, Denmark, Sweden, Spain, and Russia.

Tapestry marks in facsimile p. 333–37. Bibliography p. 349–52. Index of names p. 345–49.

1931

Schuette, Marie. Gestickte Bildteppiche und Decken des Mittelalters. Leipzig, Hiersemann, 1927–30. 2 v. 114 double plates (part col.) 51 cm.

A scholarly work on German embroideries of the Middle Ages with excellent plates, many in color. Contents: Bd. 1, Die Klöster Wienhausen und Lüne; Das Lüneburgische Museum, 1927; Bd. 2, Braunschweig; Die Klöster Ebstorf und Isenhagen; Wernigerode; Kloster Drubeck; Helberstadt, 1930.

1932

Thomson, William George. A history of tapestry from the earliest times until the present day. Rev. ed. N.Y., Putnam, 1931. 550 p. illus., plates (part col.) 30 cm.

First published 1906; entirely revised and reissued 1930. The standard English language work covering from pre-Christian times to the present.

"Tapestry marks" p. 501–12, with facsimiles. Indexes: (1) List of chief centers of manufacture p. 513–15; (2) Subjects of tapestries p. 516–28; (3) List of *tapissiers* and painters, merchants, founders, and directors of manufactories p. 529–42; (4) List of owners, authorities, collections, and sales p. 543–50.

SEE ALSO: Christie. Embroidery and tapestry weaving (1963).

Textiles

1933

Algoud, Henri. La soie, art et histoire. Paris, Payot, 1928. 255 p. illus., 16 plates. 24 cm. (Collection d'art et le goût)

A history of silks. Contents: (1) L'âge antique et des hautes époques; (2) La floraison italienne du moyen-âge et de la renaissance; (3) Le métier de la soie en France du XVe au XVIIe siècle; (4) L'ère française de la soie au XVIIIe siècle; (5) Les temps modernes.

1934

Baker, George Percival. Calico painting and printing in the East Indies in the XVIIth and XVIIIth centuries. London, Arnold, 1921. 78 p. 9 plates (1 col.), map. 58 cm. *and* portfolio of 37 plates (36 col.) 77 cm.

A de luxe work with excellent illustrations. "Les toiles peintes de l'Inde" p. 60–72, signed Henri Clouzot. Appendix on cotton p. 73–75. Bibliographical footnotes. Index p. 76–78.

1935

Clouzot, Henri. Painted and printed fabrics; the history of the manufactory at Jouy and other ateliers in France 1760–1815. . . . Notes on the history of cotton printing, especially in England and America by Francis Morris. New Haven, Yale Univ. Press, 1927. 108 p. 92 plates (part col.) 28 cm.

At head of title: The Metropolitan Museum of Art. Edition of 2000 copies printed. Contents: History of the manufactory at Jouy p. 1–44; Other important centers of cotton printing in France 1760–1815; Notes on the history of cotton printing, especially in England and America p. 75–89. Appendix: List of centers of cotton printing in France 1760–1815, p. 91–96.

"A brief bibliography" p. [xv]–xvii. Index p. 97–108.

1936

Cole, Alan Summerly. Ornament in European silks. London, Debenham & Freebody, 1899. 220 p. illus., plates. 26 cm.

A well-illustrated treatment of European silks. Index p. 207–20.

1937

Copenhagen. Danske Kunstindustrimuseum. Bibliotek. . . . Tekstil . . . [København, Petersen] 1930. 158 p. illus. 22 cm. (*Its* Bogfortegnelser II)

A listing, by broad subjects, of the books on textiles in this library. Author index p. 145–55 and series index p. 157–58.

1938

Falke, Otto von. Decorative silks . . . New ed. N.Y., Helburn, 1922. 47 p. illus., 126 plates (10 col.) 35 cm.

First published in 1913, in German, as the text to J. Lessing's *Gewebesammlung des Königlichen Kunstgewerbe-Museums zu Berlin* in 2 v.

A collection of good collotype plates with 47 pages of introductory text tracing the historical development of silk weaving from the 4th century to 1800, with an introductory chapter on Oriental tapestries and early Greek woven patterns.

1939

Glazier, Richard. Historic textile fabrics, a short history of the tradition and development of pattern in woven & printed stuffs . . . illustrated by 83 photographs and over 120 drawings chiefly by the author, together with 4 plates in colour. London, Batsford; N.Y., Scribner [1923] 119 p. illus., plates (part col.) 26 cm.

"The purpose is to give a short, but nevertheless a comprehensive history of figured weaving; tracing its development through what is termed characteristics or styles of certain periods."—*Pref.* Well illustrated with line drawings and diagrams in the text and halftone plates.

"A short reference list of books on textile design" p. 115–16. Index to plates and text illustrations p. ix–xiv; to text p. 117–20.

1940

Gunsaulus, Helen Cowen. Japanese textiles. [N.Y.] Priv. printed for the Japan Society of N.Y., 1941. 94 p. 16 plates (part col.) 31 cm.

Edition of 1000 copies printed. Excellent illustrations. Selected bibliography p. 93–94.

1941

Harmuth, Louis. Dictionary of textiles. 2nd enl. ed. N.Y., Fairchild, 1920. 222 p. 26 cm.

First published 1913.

Contains more than 8500 terms and definitions.

1942

Heiden, Max. Handwörterbuch der Textilkunde aller Zeiten und Völker für Studierende, Fabrikanten, Kaufleute, Sammler und Zeichner der Gewerbe, Stickereien, Spitzen, Teppiche und dergl., sowie für Schule und Haus. . . . Mit 16 Tafeln und 356 in den Text gedruckten Abbildungen. Stuttgart, Enke, 1904. 664 p. illus., 16 plates. 26 cm.

A German dictionary of textiles and the textile industry, which also covers the history of textiles. Old but still useful.

1943

Hunter, George Leland. Decorative textiles; an illustrated book on coverings for furniture, walls and floors, including damasks, brocades and velvets, tapestries, laces, embroideries, chintzes, cretonnes, drapery and furniture trimmings, wall papers, carpets and rugs, tooled and illuminated leathers; with 580 illustrations, 27 plates in colour. Philadelphia and London, Lippincott; Grand Rapids, Mich., The Dean-Hicks Co., 1918. 457 p. illus. (part col.) 33 cm.

"This is the first comprehensive book on the subject to be published."—*Pref.* Profusely illustrated. Bibliography p. 438–[47]. Index and glossary p. 448–58.

1944

Hunton, W. Gordon. English decorative textiles; tapestry and chintz, their design and development from the earliest times to the nineteenth century. London, Tiranti [1930]. 9 p. illus., plates. 32 cm. (Decorative arts series)

A collection of plates with very brief introductory text. Bibliography of works consulted p. [10].

1945

Jaques, Renate. Deutsche Textilkunst; ihrer Entwicklung bis zur Gegenwart, mit einem Geleitwort von Hans Croon. Berlin, Rembrandt Verlag [1942]. 319 p. illus., 6 col. plates. 27 cm.

A well-illustrated treatment of German textiles from their beginnings to the present. Index of subjects and names p. 301–12. Index of places p. 313–18.

1946

Jaques, Renate, and Flemming, Ernst. Encyclopedia of textiles, decorative fabrics from antiquity to the beginning of the 19th century including the Far East and Peru. N.Y., Praeger; London, Zwemmer, 1958. 32 p. 500 illus., 16 col. plates. 29 cm.

A new and entirely rev. ed. of the Flemming *Encyclopedia,* first published 1927. A German ed. published in 1958 by Verlag Ernst Wasmuth, Tübingen.

Contains a collection of textile designs

from Europe, China, Japan, Persia, and Peru. List of sources p. xxvii–xxx.

1947

Kendrick, Albert Frank. English decorative fabrics of the sixteenth to eighteenth centuries . . . Benfleet, Eng., Lewis [1934]. 88 p. 52 plates. 29 cm.

Covers embroideries, carpets, and tapestries. The descriptive text to the plates includes size. An index of 6 p. at the back.

1948

Lawrie, Leslie Gordon. A bibliography of dyeing and textile printing, comprising a list of books from the sixteenth century to the present time (1946). London, Chapman & Hall, 1949. 143 p. 23 cm.

Although a rather specialized and technical bibliographical work, it can be useful to the art historian for the inclusion of early books on the subject of dyeing and for its relation to the subject of textiles.

Contents: pt. 1, List of books printed from the sixteenth century until the present time in alphabetical order according to authors p. 17–100; pt. 2, Short-title list of works in chronological order p. 101–37. "Sources of information" p. 10–12. Classified index p. 139–43.

1949

Linton, George Edward. The modern textile dictionary. [1st ed.] N.Y., Duell, Sloan and Pearce [1954]. 772 p. illus., 32 plates, diagr. 24 cm.

"Significant terms, old and new, domestic and foreign—commonplace, or peculiar to some particular area—have been included."—*Pref.*

Covers terms for apparel, asbestos, color, costume, dyeing, fabrics, fashion and style, fibers and yarns, finishes and finishing processes, knitting, labor, lace, leathers, manmade and synthetic fibers, manufacturing processes of many textiles, plastics, printing, sciences used in trade, spot and stain removal, and care of clothing.

Appendix: Selected list of the better semitechnical and technical books on textiles p. 771–72.

1950

Little, Frances. Early American textiles . . . N.Y., London, Century [c1931]. 267 p. plates, facsims. 22 cm. (Century library of American antiques)

"Important dates in the history of Amer-

ican textiles" p. 255–56. Bibliography p. 249–53. Index p. 257–67.

1951

Migeon, Gaston. Les arts du tissu . . . nouv. éd., revue et augmentée. Paris, Renouard, 1929. 468 p. illus. 26 cm. (Manuels d'histoire de l'art)

Originally published 1909. A general history of the subject with numerous illustrations in the text.

Contents: (1) Les tissus de soie decorée de laine et de coton; (2) La broderie; (3) La tapisserie; (4) La dentelle. Contains bibliographies.

1952

Percival, MacIver. The chintz book . . . London, Heinemann [1923]. 103 p. 1 illus., plates (4 col.) 26 cm.

"Contains not only an account of the fabrics which were made in England in bygone days, but also of their prototypes, the 'painted callicoes' imported from India in vast quantities in the 17th and 18th centuries, and of their rivals the French 'toiles de Jouy' . . . The illustrations are chosen from the cottons of many countries and periods and form a guide to the styles in use at different times."—*Pref.*

Glossary p. 96–103. "Some books of interest to lovers of old chintzes" p. 79–80.

1953

Podreider, Fanny. Storia dei tessuti d'arte in Italia, secolo XII–XVIII. Bergamo, Istituto Italiano d'Arti Grafiche, 1928. 312 p. illus., plates (part col.), facsim. 27 cm.

A well-illustrated history of textiles in Italy from the 12th to the 18th century.

"Guida descrittiva per la visita delle collezione di stoffe d'arte nei musei italiani" p. [303]–07. "Indice per materia in base alle illustrazioni" p. 308–12.

1954

Reath, Nancy Andrews, and Sachs, Eleanor B. Persian textiles and their technique from the sixth to the eighteenth centuries, including a system for general textile classification. New Haven, Pub. for Penn. Museum of Art by Yale Univ. Press; London, Milford, Oxford Univ. Press, 1937. 133 p. illus., plates. 29 cm.

Edition of 500 copies printed. A scholarly work well illustrated by collotype plates.

Contents: Table of textile classification; Introduction; pt. 1, (1) Distinctive Persian types; (2) Sasanian and early Islamic weaves;

(3) Seljug weaves; (4) 14th and 15th centuries; (5) Safavid weaves; (6) Post-Safavid weaves; (7) Conclusion; pt. 2, Definition of terms; pt. 3, Analyses of textiles; pt. 4, Diagrams and plates. Index of 5 p. following the plates.

1955

Schmidt, Heinrich J. Alte Seidenstoffe; ein Handbuch für Sammler und Liebhaber. Braunschweig, Klinkhardt & Biermann, 1958. 483 p. 399 illus., 16 col. plates, 2 maps. 24 cm. (Bibliothek für Kunst- und Antiquitäten Freunde, v. 10)

Covers silk weavings from the earliest preserved specimens to the period of 1800. Index of illustrations p. 465–78; subject index p. 479–81.

1956

Volbach, Wolfgang Friedrich, and Kühnel, Ernst. Late antique Coptic and Islamic textiles of Egypt. N.Y., Weyhe, 1926. 15 p. 100 plates (part col.) 34 cm.

Primarily a collection of excellent plates with a few pages of introductory text.

1957

Walton, Perry. The story of textiles; a bird's-eye view of the history of the beginning and the growth of the industry by which mankind is clothed. N.Y., Tudor [1937]. 274 p. illus., plates. 25 cm.

First published 1925. 2d ed. 1936, of which this is a reprint. Covers the textile development in both Europe and America, but with special emphasis on America. Index p. 235–74.

1958

Weibel, Adèle Coulin. Two thousand years of textiles; the figured textiles of Europe and the Near East. N.Y., Pantheon, 1952. 169 p. plates (part col.) 31 cm. (Pub. for the Detroit Institute of Arts)

A scholarly well-illustrated work. Contents: (1) Introduction: Material and technique; (2) History. Catalog p. 73–164, giving size. Bibliography p. 165–67.

Embroidery and Needlework

1959

Antrobus, Mrs. Mary (Symonds), and Preece, Louisa. Needle work through the ages; a short survey of its development in decorative art, with particular regard to its inspirational relationship with other methods of craftsmanship. London, Hodder and Stoughton, 1928. 413 p. 103 plates (part col.) 32 cm.

Plates are arranged chronologically so as to form a pictorial survey of the development. Bibliography p. 391–98. Index p. 399–413.

1960

Byne, Mrs. Mildred (Stapley). Popular weaving and embroidery in Spain . . . with one hundred and seventy-five illustrations made expressly for and by the author. N.Y., Helburn [c1924]. 60 p. illus., 124 plates (3 col.) 26 cm.

A collection of plates with short text.

1961

Caulfeild, Sophia Frances Anne, and Saward, Blanche C. The dictionary of needlework, an encyclopaedia of artistic, plain and fancy needlework. Dealing fully with the details of all the stitches employed, the method of working, the materials used, the meaning of technical terms, and, where necessary, tracing the origin and history of the various works described . . . 2d ed. London, Gill [1885]. 528 p. illus., col. plates. 28 cm.

Arranged in dictionary form, giving definitions and descriptions of various fabrics, stitches, etc. Old but extremely useful and well illustrated.

1962

Christie, A. G. I. English medieval embroidery, a brief survey of English embroidery dating from the beginning of the tenth century until the end of the fourteenth: together with a descriptive catalogue of the surviving examples: illustrated with one hundred and sixty plates and numerous drawings in the text . . . Oxford, Clarendon Press, 1938. 206 p. illus., 159 plates. 40 cm.

The work is "a corpus of the existing embroideries produced in England before the close of the 14th century" with "a general survey of what was achieved by English embroiderers during this period."—Pref.

Appendix I: Some embroidery workers and purchases of embroideries recorded in medieval documents p. 31–37. Appendix II: Contemporary records of medieval embroideries p. 38–41.

Descriptive catalog p. 45–198 gives bibliographical references. Index of persons p. 199–200; of museums, libraries, treasuries and collections p. 200. General index p. 201–03.

1963

Christie, Grace. Embroidery and tapestry weaving; a practical text-book of design and workmanship . . . with drawings by the author and other illustrations. London, Hogg, 1906. 414 p. incl. illus., plates. 19 cm. (The artistic crafts series of technical handbooks, ed. by W. R. Lethaby)

4th ed. 1933 (London, Putnam, 403 p. incl. illus., plates, 19 cm.). "An introduction and text-book not only on the side of workmanship, but also on . . . design."—*Introd.* Well illustrated with diagrams of stitches, etc. Contents: pt. 1, Embroidery; pt. 2, Tapestry weaving. Index.

1964

Christie, Grace (*Mrs.* A. H. Christie). Samplers and stitches; a handbook of the embroiderer's art, with many designs and other illustrations by the author. 2d ed. rev. and enl. London, Batsford; N.Y., Dutton [1929]. 144 p. illus., 34 (i.e., 38) plates. 26 cm.

1st ed. 1920. A very useful book in which various stitches and methods "have been classified and presented . . . by means of working diagrams."—*Pref.*

1965

Dillmont, Thérèse de. Encyclopedia of needlework. New ed. rev. and enl. Mulhouse (France), T. de Dillmont [19–]. 809 p. illus., 13 col. plates. 14 cm. (D. M. C. library)

1st ed. 1886. Covers machine work as well as handwork. Includes embroidery, plain sewing, knitting, tapestry, crochet work, tatting, macramé, netting, laces, and needlework trimmings.

1966

Farcy, Louis de. La broderie du XIe siècle jusqu'à nos jours d'après des spécimens authentiques et les anciens inventaires. Angers, Belhomme [etc.] 1890–1900. In 3 portfolios. 214 plates. 58 cm.

"Supplément à La broderie . . ." p. [139]–46 and 34 plates in 3d portfolio. An important history of embroidery, comparable to Guiffrey's *Histoire générale de la tapisserie* (1921). Bibliographical footnotes.

1967

Kendrick, Albert Frank. English embroidery. London, Newnes; N.Y., Scribner [1905]. 125 p. 60 plates (4 col.) 23 cm. (Newnes' library of the applied arts)

A general treatment covering from the Anglo-Saxon period through the 18th century. "Some useful books of reference" p. 107–08. Index p. 109–[26].

1968

Lotz, Arthur. Bibliographie der Modelbücher; beschreibendes Verzeichnis der Stick- und Spitzenmusterbücher des 16. und 17. Jahrhunderts. Mit 213 Abbildungen auf 108 Tafeln. Leipzig, Hiersemann, 1933. 274 p. 108 plates (incl. facsims.) on 54 l. 25 cm.

A scholarly bibliography of needlework pattern books, arranged according to the country of origin and then chronologically. Index of names and cities p. 261–71. Index of publishers, places of publication, and presses p. 272–74.

1969

Seligman, G. Saville, and Hughes, Talbot. Domestic needlework, its origins and customs throughout the centuries. London, Country Life [etc.] 1926. 95 p. illus., 131 plates (part col.) 37 cm.

English ed. limited to 500 copies. Arranged by objects, e.g., samplers, pockets, bookbindings, pictures, caskets, etc.

1970

Wheeler, *Mrs.* Candace (Thurber). The development of embroidery in America. N.Y. & London, Harper, 1921. 151 p. plates (part col.) 25 cm.

Contents: Introductory: The story of the needle; Beginnings in the New World; The crewelwork of our Puritan mothers; Samplers and a word about quilts; Moravian work, portraiture, French embroidery and lacework; Berlin woolwork; Revival of embroidery, and the founding of the Society of Decorative Art; American tapestry; The Bayeux tapestries.

SEE ALSO: Marquet de Vasselot. Bibliographie de la tapisserie, des tapis et de la broderie en France (1927); Schuette. Gestickte Bildteppiche und Decken des Mittelalters (1931).

Lace

1971

Brooke, Margaret L. Lace in the making with bobbins and needle . . . with line illustrations by Winifred M. A. Brooke and photographs of lace in the Victoria and Albert museum. London, Routledge, 1923. 164 p. illus., diagrs., plates. 22 cm. (Routledge's modern trade-book series)

"Laces and their centres" p. 143–47. Glossary p. 148–54. Bibliography p. [156–58]. Index p. 159–64.

1972

Clifford, Chandler Robbins. The lace dictionary. Pocket edition, including historic and commercial terms, native and foreign . . . N.Y., Clifford & Lawton [1913]. 156 p. illus. 18 cm.

Topical index p. 149–56.

1973

Moore, Hannah Hudson. The lace book . . . with seventy engravings showing specimens of lace, or its wear in famous portraits, and with border by Charles E. Cartwright and decorations after Bodoni. N.Y., Stokes [1904]. 206 p. 58 plates (incl. ports.) 28 cm.

Includes: The growth of lace, Italian lace, Flemish lace, French and Spanish laces, English and Irish laces. Index p. 201–06.

1974

Morris, Frances, and Hague, Marian. Antique laces of American collectors. N.Y., Pub. for the Needle and Bobbin Club by William Helburn, 1920–26. 5 v. 36 cm. and 51 cm.

"A comprehensive study of the art of lace making in Italy, France and the Netherlands from the 16th through the 18th centuries." "Books of reference" v. 5, p. 131–35. Index v. 5, p. 137–43.

1975

Palliser, Fanny M. History of lace, entirely revised, rewritten and enlarged under the editorship of M. Jourdain and Alice Dryden, with 266 illus. London, Sampson Low, Marston, 1910. 536 p. illus., plates. 25 cm.

3d ed. 1875; 4th ed. 1902, of which this is a reprint. A standard work on the history of lace. Glossary of terms p. 503–06. Index p. 507–36.

1976

Pethebridge, Jeanette E. A manual of lace. London, Cassell [1947]. 71 p. illus. 28 cm.

Gives stitches and method of making nine different types of lace, i.e., Carrickmacross, Point de Venise, Bruges, etc., as well as a few sentences on the history and origin, care and restoration of lace.

1977

Powys, Marian. Lace and lace-making. Drawings by the author. Boston, Branford, 1953. 219 p. illus. 26 cm.

A well-illustrated and useful general book on lace, which describes various types and how to distinguish them. Also gives directions for making, mending, and cleaning lace. "Pedigree of needlepoint laces" p. 7. Index p. 217–19.

1978

Ricci, Elisa. Old Italian lace. Philadelphia, Lippincott, 1913. 2 v. illus., plates. 37 cm.

Limited edition of 300 copies. Well illustrated with a list of plates at the end of each volume. Contents: v. 1, (1) Modano or lacis, drawn-thread work, Buratto; (2) Punto a reticello; (3) Punto in aria; v. 2, Bobbin laces: Venice, Genoa, Milan, Abruzzi.

1979

Vanderpoel, Emily Noyes. American lace and lace-makers . . . ed. by Elizabeth C. Barney Buel. New Haven, Yale Univ. Press, 1924. 14 p. 110 plates. 33 cm.

Mostly a picture book with 14 pages of introductory text. Description of each plate on verso of previous plate.

1980

Whiting, Gertrude. A lace guide for makers and collectors; with bibliography and five-language nomenclature, profusely illustrated with halftone plates and key designs . . . N.Y., Dutton [c1920]. 415 p. illus. 26 cm.

A technical book with extensive bibliography, clear illustrations of various types of lace, and instructions for making them. "Explanation and nomenclature" p. 36–68 lists in parallel columns terms in English, French, Italian, Spanish, and German. Bibliography p. 243–401.

CHAPTER 17

Documents and Sources

THIS SECTION CANNOT POSSIBLY CLAIM completeness, but it endeavors to identify the basic, frequently recurring sources to which the worker in the art field has to turn. The earlier sources run to 1800, the later to the present. Documents include published collections of archival material and letters. Indication has been given only of the most important or frequently used editions. For a further treatment of the various editions and a more exhaustive study of the subject the reader is referred to Schlosser's *La letteratura artistica* (44).

Original Sources and Early Works

1981

Alberti, Leone Battista. De pictura praestantissimae artis et nunquam satis laudatae, libri tres. Basel, 1540.

The 1st ed. of the influential Renaissance treatise on painting. The first English translation is included in Leoni's translation of *De re aedificatoria*, 1726. A modern translation by John R. Spencer published 1956 (New Haven, Yale Univ. Press; London, Routledge, Paul, 141 p.), which is not too free of misunderstandings.

1982

Alberti, Leone Battista. [De re aedificatoria libb. X] Florence, Laurentius, 1485. [204] 1. 27 cm.

The 1st ed. of the famous Renaissance treatise (the first printed book) on architecture. The first English ed. by James Leoni, in 1726, was reissued in 1955 (London, Tiranti).

SEE ALSO: Androuet du Cerceau. Les plus excellents bastiments de France (843).

1983

Armenini, Giovanni Battista. De veri precetti della pittura . . . Ravenna, Francesco Tebaldini, 1587. 232 p. (3 v. in 1). 21 cm.

A 2d ed., Venice, 1678; reprinted in Milan, 1820 and Pisa, 1823. A complete treatise on design, draftsmanship, and painting technique which is useful for understanding the Mannerist painters. Also contains anecdotes and other information on artists and works of art of this period.

A fairly detailed index of 15 p. precedes the text.

1984

Baglione, Giovanni. . . . Le vite de' pittori, scultori, architetti, dal pontificato di Gregorio XIII. del 1572, fino a' tempi di Papa Urbano VIII nel 1642. Roma, Fei, 1642. 304 p. 26 cm.

2d ed., Rome, Manelfi, 1649; 3d ed. (Naples, 1733) also contains a life of Salvator Rosa, written by Passeri, and one of Baglione. A facsimile ed. made from the 1642 copy in the library of the Accademia dei Lincei, Rome, containing marginal notes of G. P. Bellori, was issued by the R. Istituto d'Archeologia e Storia dell'Arte, Rome, in 1935, edited by Valerio Mariana, with an index.

Valuable for the lives of the artists of the period leading up to the Baroque with special emphasis on Roman artists, but including some foreign artists such as Rubens, Elsheimer, Bril, and Goltzius.

1985

Baldinucci, Filippo. Cominciamento e progresso dell'arte dell'intagliare in rame, colle vite di molti de' più eccellenti maestri della stessa professione. Firenze, P. Matini, 1686. 124 p. 27 cm.

With this work is bound the author's *Vocabolario toscano* . . . Firenze, 1681. A 2d ed., with notes of D. M. Manni, Florence, G. B. Stecchi, 1767.

Articles on about 20 important masters of engraving, such as Durer, Lucas van Leyden, Raimondi, etc. "Indice delle cose notabili" p. 113–22.

1986

Baldinucci, Filippo. Notizie de' professori del disegno da Cimabve in qva, per le qvali si dimostra come, e per chi le bell' arti di pittura, scultura, e architettura lasciata la rozzezza delle maniere greca, e gottica, si siano in questi secoli ridotte all' antica loro perfezione; Opera di Filippo Baldinucci Fiorentino distinta in secoli, e decannali . . . Firenze, Per Santi Franchi, 1681–1728. 6 v. in 3. geneal. tables, 26 cm.

Subtitle and imprint vary. 2d ed. with notes by D. M. Manni (Florence, 1767–74, 21 pts. in 10 v.); 3d ed. prepared by Giovanni Piacenza (Turin, 1768–1817, 5 v.). Also appeared in *Classici italiani* (ed. 1811–12, Milan). An ed. with notes by F. Ranalli (Florence, 1845–47, 5 v.); an ed. of Baroque artists only with title: *Dal baroccio a Salvator Rosa, vite di pittori italiani del seicento, scelte e annotate da Guido Battelli, con XV tavole,* Firenze, Sansoni, 1914, 20 cm. (Biblioteca scolastica di Classici italiani).

Treats artists from northern countries as well as Italy and devotes a separate article to each artist. Contents: v. [1] Dedication to Cosimo III de' Medici; preface; privilegia of Pope Innocent XI, Duke Cosimo III, and Carlos II, king of Spain: approbations; Decades 1260–1300; v. [2] Decades 1300–1340; v. [3] Decades 1400–1550 (on title page 1400–1540); v. [4] Decades 1550–1580; v. [5] Decades 1580–1610; v. [6] Decades 1610–1670.

A separate index of all artists included in the work p. i–xx and an index of "cose più notabili" v. 6, p. 636–62.

1987

Baldinucci, Filippo. Vocabolario toscano dell'arte del disegno nel qvale si esplicano i propri termini e voci, non solo della Pittvra, Scvltvra & Architettvra; ma ancora di altre arti a quelle subordinare, e che abbiano per fondamento il Disegno, con la notizia de' nomi e qualità della Gioie, Metalli, Pietre dure, Marmi, Pietre tenere, Sassi, Legnami, Colori, Strumenti, ed ogn'altra materia, che servir possa, tanto allo costruzione di edifici e loro ornato, quanto alla stessa Pittura e Scultura . . . Firenze, Per Santi Franchi al Segno della Passione, 1681. 188 p. 30 cm.

Other editions: Florence, 1806, and Milan, 1809, *Classici italiani.*

An early dictionary of art terms in painting, sculpture, architecture, and the minor arts, arranged alphabetically. "Aggivnte dello stesso avtore" p. 185–88.

1988

Baruffaldi, Girolamo. Vite de' pittori e scultori ferraresi . . . Ferrara, D. Taddei, 1844–46. 2 v. 57 plates. 24 cm.

Written between 1697 and 1722 but not published until 1844. At end of v. 2: "Pubblicato nel settembre 1848."

The earliest history of the Ferrarese school of painting. A chapter devoted to each artist and usually a line portrait, arranged chronologically. A list of artists treated at end of each volume.

"Vita dell'autore" v. 1, p. ix–xx. "Quadro cronologico degli artisti ferraresi non rammentati dal Baruffaldi, e poco cogniti per opere" v. 2, p. 584–96. General index v. 2, p. 597–604.

1989

Bellori, Giovanni Pietro. Le vite de' pittori scvltori, ed architetti moderni. Parte prima. Roma, Il success. al Mascardi, 1672. 462 p. engr. plates. 24 cm.

2d ed., Rome, 1728, contains a biography of Luca Giordano. The biography of Carlo Maratti by Bellori, which was published in Rome in 1732, is included in the 3d ed., issued in Pisa, 1821, 3 v. This 1821 ed. is the one most commonly used. A facsimile ed. was published in Rome by the R. Istituto d'Archeologia e Storia dell'Arte in 1931. An ed. edited by Michelangelo Piacentini entitled *Vite de Guido Reni, Andrea Sacchi e Carlo Maratti* was published in Rome, 1942.

Invaluable as a source of information on the Carracci, Caravaggio, Barocci, Domenichino, etc. Rubens' and Poussin's art included with the Italian masters.

1990

Bie, Cornelis de. Het gulden cabinet vande edel vry schilder-const ontsloten door den lanck ghewenschten vrede tusschen de twee machtighe croonen van Spaignien en Vranckryck. [2. ed. Antwerpen, 1662] 3 pts. in 1 v. 584 p. incl. 88 engr. plates. 24 cm.

An early and more limited ed. 1661.

Paged continuously. An early source of biography and portraiture of artists, a good part of which is in rhyme. Some of the portraits are engraved by Hollar.

Part 2 covers painters and pt. 3 architects, sculptors, and engravers. "Tafel oft register van dit gulden cabinet" p. 578–84.

1991
Blondel, Jacques François. Architecture francoise, ou, Recueil des plans, elevations, coupes et profils des eglises, maisons royales, palais, hôtels & edifices les plus considérables de Paris, ainsi que des châteaux & maisons de plaisance, situés aux environs de cette ville, ou en d'autres endroits de la France, bâtis par les plus célébres architectes, & mesurés exactement sur les lieux. Avec la description de ces edifices, & des dissertations utiles & intéressantes sur chaque espece de bâtiment. Paris, C. A. Jombert, 1752–56. 4 v. in 3. illus., 500 plates (part. fold., incl. plans). 44 cm.

A prime source for French 18th century architecture, both in the text and the elaborate engravings. Succeeds the earlier Mariette (2019).

1992
Boschini, Marco. Le minere della pittura. Compendiosa informazione di Marco Boschini, non solo delle pitture publiche di Venezia: ma dell'isole ancora circonuicine . . . Venezia, Nicolini, 1664. 572 [i.e., 570] p. incl. plates. 16 cm.

2d ed. greatly enl., titled *Le ricche minere della pittura Veneziana*, Venezia, 1672.

The first real artistic guide to Venice, arranged by quarter of the city and then by the building containing the works. "Tauola di tutti i luoghi doue sone descritte le pitture nella presenta opera," 15 p. at beginning of volume.

1993
Bosse, Abraham. Sentimens sur la distinction des diverses manières de peinture, dessein & gravueure, & des originaux d'avec leurs copies, ensemble du choix des sujets, & des chemins pour arriver facilement & promptement à bien pourtraire . . . Paris, Chez l'Autheur, 1649. 114 p. 2 plates. 15 cm.

The original ed. of a treatise on painting, drawing, and engraving written by a follower of Callot.

1994
Campbell, Colin. Vitruvius Britannicus; or, The British architect, containing the plans, elevations, and sections of the regular buildings, both publick and private in Great Britain, with variety of new designs . . . by Colen Campbell. . . . Vitruvius britannicus;

ou, L'architecte britannique, contenant les plans, elevations, & sections des batimens reguliers, tant particuliers que publics, de la Grande Bretagne. London, The author [etc.] 1715–71. 5 v. plates (part double, incl. plans). 51 cm.

A main source of the English country house and secular architecture of the late 17th and 18th centuries. Volume 1 published 1715; v. 2, 1717; v. 3, 1725. J. Woolfe and James Gandoni published two more volumes 1767 and 1771. A further addition of 2 v. by G. Richardson with title *The new Vitruvius Britannicus*, 1802–08.

1995
Carducci, Vincenzio. Dialogos de la pintura; su defensa, origen, essēcia, definicion, modos y differencias, al gran monarcha de las Españas y Nuevo Mundo, don Felipe III. . . . Siguēse a los dialogos, informaciones, y paraceres en sabor del arte, escritas por varones insignes en todas letras. Madrid, Francisco Martinez, 1633. 229 p. 9 plates. 21 cm.

A new ed. was published by Villaamil, Madrid, 1665 (229 numb. 1. [22] incl. 9 plates, 21 cm.).

An important early Spanish source which consists of eight dialogues between a master and his pupil. Index p. [231–41].

1996
Cellini, Benvenuto. Due trattati uno intorno alle otto principali arti dell'oreficeria. L'altro in materia dell'arte della scultura; dove si veggono infiniti segreti nel lavorar le figure di marmo, & nel gettarle di bronzo. Composta da m. Benvenuto Cellini scultore fiorentino. In Fiorenza, Per Valente Paniaaija & Marco Peri, 1568. [146] p. 21 cm.

2d ed., Florence, Tartini e Franchi, 1731, reworked by Crusca with an interesting preface; a reprint of this appeared in Turin, 1795.

Text consists of two treatises on the techniques of goldsmithing and sculpture. Initial letters are woodcuts with scenes of castles or towns in the background. Table of contents on six pages following the dedication and preceding the body of the work.

1997
Chambers, *Sir* William. A treatise on civil architecture, in which the principles of that art are laid down, and illustrated by a great number of plates, accurately designed and elegantly engraved by the best hands. London, Printed for the Author by J. Haberkorn, 1759. 85 p. 50 plates. 52 cm.

Later eds. 1768, 1791 (with variant title), 1825, 1826, and 1862. Probably the most influential architectural treatise of the second half of the 18th century, which was widely used for three generations.

1998

Cumberland, Richard. Anecdotes of eminent painters in Spain during the sixteenth and seventeenth centuries; with cursory remarks upon the present state of arts in that kingdom. 2d ed. London, C. Dilly, 1787. 2 v. 16 cm.

1st ed. 1782 (London, J. Walter). Based on Palomino (2028). Index at end of each volume to artists mentioned therein.

1999

Delorme, Philibert. Le premier tome de l'architectvre de Philibert de l'Orme conseillier et avmosnier ordinaire du roy, & abbé de S. Serge lez Angiers. A Paris, Chez Federic Morel, 1567. 283 p. incl. illus., plate, plans, diagrs. 4 plates. 36 cm.

One of the early French statements on Renaissance architecture by its leading exponent.

2000

Descamps, Jean Baptiste. La vie des peintres flamands, allemands et hollandois, avec des portraits gravés en taille-douce, une indication de leurs principaux ouvrages, & des réflexions sur leurs différentes manieres . . . Paris, Jombert, 1753–64. 4 v. illus. 21 cm.

A reissue of this work, with material on French and Italian painters by Dézallier d'Argenville, was published in Marseilles, 1842, 5 v., 23 cm.

Covers Flemish, German, and Dutch painters, from the Van Eycks, in 1366, to 1706. Preface discusses limitations of the author's predecessors and outlines his own purpose, sources, etc. Biographies of artists are arranged chronologically and list their principal works. Works known to the author are evaluated; for other works their location only is noted.

According to Schlosser (44) this work is not much better than Weyerman's (2048), which plagiarized Houbraken (2008). Index at end of each volume. In v. 4 the index gives phonetic spellings in an attempt to give pronunciation of names.

√2001

Dézallier d'Argenville, Antoine Joseph. Abrégé de la vie des plus fameux peintres, avec leurs portraits gravés en taille-douce

. . . Paris, De Bure l'Aîné, 1745–52. 3 v. engr. plates. 26 cm.

1st ed. New ed., rev., corr., and augm., 1762 (Paris, De Bure l'Aîné, 4 v.). German ed. translated by J. J. Volkmann (Leipzig, 1767–68, 4 v.).

Articles arranged by schools, with an engraved portrait at the beginning of each biography. Contents: v. 1, Italian; v. 2, French, Dutch, Flemish, German, and Swiss; v. 3, Supplement.

Each volume has a "Table des matières."

2002

Dézallier d'Argenville, Antoine Nicolas. Vies des fameux architectes depuis la renaissance des arts, avec la description de leurs ouvrages. Paris, Deburé l'Aîné, 1787. 2 v. 22 cm.

Volume 2 has title: *Vies des fameux sculpteurs depuis la renaissance des arts* . . .

An important early source. Each volume contains an essay on architecture or sculpture, followed by lives of the artists. Index of names of architects v. 1, p. 486–88, arranged by countries; same for sculptors, v. 2, p. 416–19.

√2003

Dominici, Bernardo de. Vite de' pittori, scultori, ed architetti napoletani, non mai date alla luce da autore alcuno . . . Napoli, Ricciardi, 1742–44. 3 v. 24 cm.

A new ed., Naples, 1840–46, in 4 v. In spite of many errors, the principal source on the Neapolitan school. The value of this work has been unjustly minimized by modern scholars. At end of each volume an alphabetical index of persons and subjects.

2004

Doppelmayer, Johann Gabriel. Historische Nachricht von den Nürnbergischen Mathematicis und Künstlern . . . Nürnberg, Monath, 1730. 2 v. plates. 38 cm.

Book 1 devoted to mathematics and bk. 2 (p. 177–314) to artists of Nuremberg. Engraved plates of various works of art at the end.

Bibliographical footnotes. Index in v. 2: latter half of pt. 1 covers artists treated in the volume (9 p.); pt. 3 covers notable material for both volumes.

2005

Du Fresnoy, Charles Alphonse. De arte graphica. The art of painting. With remarks. Translated into English, together with an original preface containing a parallel betwixt painting and poetry. By Mr. Dryden. As also

A short account of the most eminent painters, both ancient and modern, continu'd down to the present times. . . . By another hand . . . London, Printed by J. Heptinstall for W. Rogers, 1695. lxiv, 355 p. 24 cm.

Written 1641–65 and first published in Latin, Paris, 1668. 2d ed. in Latin and French with a dialogue on color and notes by Roger de Piles, Paris, 1673; numerous subsequent eds. First English ed. 1695; later English eds. 1716, 1750, and 1769; rendered into verse by William Mason and published with notes by Sir Joshua Reynolds, London, 1783.

A 17th century treatise on painting which has had a tremendous influence. Includes the original poem in Latin, with title "De arte graphica liber," translated into English from the French translation of Roger de Piles, p. 1–77. "A short account of the most eminent painters . . ." by R. Graham, p. 227–349. Index of masters treated p. 350–55.

√ 2006

Félibien, André, *Sieur des Avaux et de Javercy*. Entretiens sur les vies et les ouvrages des plus excellens peintres, anciens et modernes. Paris, Mabre-Cramoisy, etc. 1666–88. 5 v. 24 cm.

1st ed. published: v. 1, 1666; v. 2, 1672; v. 3, 1679; v. 4, 1685; v. 5, 1688. 2d ed. 1685–88; frequently reprinted up to 1725. Published in German in Hamburg, 1711; in Italian in Venice, 1755.

A major source for the lives of French artists. Index at end of each volume.

2007

Gool, Jan van. De nieuwe schouburg der Nederlantsche kunstschilders en schilderessen; waer in de levens—en kunstbedryven der tans levende en reets overledene schilders, die van Houbraken, noch eenig ander schryver, zyn aengeteekend, verhaelt worden. s'-Gravenhage, gedrukt voor den autheur, 1750–51. 2 v. plates. 22 cm.

Continues Houbraken (2008) and contains his life, as well as biographical accounts of Netherlandish painters. Numerous engraved portraits of artists, usually four to a page. At end of each volume is an alphabetical index of artists treated in that volume.

2008

Houbraken, Arnold. De groote schouburgh der Nederlantsche konstschilders en schilderessen, zynde een vervolg op het Schilder-boek van K. van Mander. Amsterdam, 1718–21. 3 v. engr. illus., 48 engr. plates. 20 cm.

1st ed. 2d ed. 1753 (s' Gravenhage, Swart

[etc.]); a new ed. by P. T. A. Swillens 1943–53 (Maastricht, Leiter-Nypels). A German translation abbreviated by Wurzbach in *Eitelberger's Quellenschriften* XIV (2053).

This work is as valuable for the 17th century in the Low Countries as Van Mander is for the 16th. Index at end of each volume.

2009

Hüsgen, Heinrich Sebastian. Nachrichten von Frankfurter Künstlern und Kunst-Sachen enthaltend das Leben und die Werke aller hiesigen Mahler, Bildhauer, Kupfer- und Pettschier-Stecher . . . nebst einem Anhang von allem was in "öffentlichen und Privat-Gebäuden merkwürdiges . . . ist" . . . Frankfurt am Main, 1780. 378 p. 17 cm.

Contains biographical information on Frankfurt artists. Contents: Vorrede p. v–xxxii; Nachrichten von Frankfurter Künstlern und Kunst-Sachen p. 3–216; Anhang von allem was in öffentlichen und Privat-Gebäuden der Stadt Frankfurt am Mayn merkwürdiges von Kunst-Sachen . . . ist p. 221–366; Register aller hiesigen Künstler p. 367–78.

2010

Junius, Franciscus. De pictura veterum libri tres. Amsterdam, Blaeu, 1637. 3 v. in 1. 20 cm.

This is the first Latin ed.; the most useful Latin ed. is 1694, Rotterdam, Regneri, 38 cm., with index.

An early work by a member of Rubens' circle, which is a mine of information regarding antiquity.

2011

Knorr, George Wolfgang. Allgemeine Künstler-Historie; oder Berühmter Künstlere Leben, Werke und Verrichtungen, mit vielen Nachrichten von raren alten und neuen Kupferstichen beschrieben . . . Nürnberg, Bieling, 1759. 282 p. plates. 21 cm.

Notes on 127 northern artists, followed by some Italian ones (p. 184–282). A section p. 21–33 on Durer; p. 33–94 on his etchings and woodcuts. Portraits of various artists on 11 engraved plates, usually three to a page.

2012

Lafreri, Antonio. Speculum Romanae magnificentiae, omnia fere quaecunque in urbe monumenta extant, partim juxta antiquam, partim juxta hodiernam formam accuratissime delineata repraesentans . . . Rome [c.1574]. size and no. of plates vary from copy to copy. (The copy in Avery Library, which is one of the most complete, has 607 plates in 6 v.)

The great collection of 16th century engravings pertaining to ancient and Renaissance Rome. Only a few complete copies are known to exist. A printed catalog in the Biblioteca Marucelliana, Florence, dated 1573, lists the nucleus of the collection. *Cf.* Christian Huelsen in *Collectanea variae doctrinae Leoni S. Olschki Bibliopolae Florentino sexagenario obtulerunt.* Monachii, Jacques Rosenthal, 1921, p. 121–70.

2013

Lairesse, Gerard de. Het groot schilderboek . . . Amsterdam, Erfgenaamen van W. de Coup, 1707. 2 v. in 1. plates. 21 cm.

Also published in Amsterdam 1712, 1714, 1716, 1836; Haarlem, 1740; in French, Paris, 1787; in German, with title *Grosses Malerbuch,* Nürnberg, 1728 and 1780; in English, translation by Fritsch, London, 1738, 1778, and 1817.

Basically a book of artistic theory in the Baroque period. Each volume has an elaborate table of contents at the end, engraved plates, and many diagrams.

√2014

Lanzi, Luigi. Storia pittorica dell'Italia dal risorgimento delle belle arti fin presso al fine del XVIII secolo . . . Bassano, Remondini, 1795–96. 3 v. 23 cm.

1st ed., Florence, A. G. Pagani, 1792; 2d ed. Bassano, Remondini, 1795–96. The classic ed., Bassano, 1809, is the last ed. revised by the author. English eds. translated by Thomas Roscoe: London, Simpkin and Marshall, 1828, in 6 v.; London, Bohn, 1847; and London, Bell, 1854–88.

An early work on Italian painting. The 1824–25 ed. (Milano, Società Tipografica de' Classici Italiani, 4 v.) is based on the 3d rev. ed. of Bassano, 1809, and is amended, expanded, and in better order than the 1796 ed. It also contains some extra notes, especially for the Lombard schools, and a eulogy of Lanzi written by Giambattista Zannoni.

Contents: (1) Ove se descrivono le scuole della Italia inferiore, la Fiorentina, la Senese, la Romana, la Napolitana; (2) Ove se descrivono alcune scuole della Italia superiore, la Veneziana; e le Lombarde di Mantova, Modena, Parma, Cremona e Milano; (3) Ove se descrivono altre scuole della Italia superiore, la Bolognese, la Ferrarese, e quelle di Genova e del Piemonte.

Indexes in v. 3: of artists p. 387; of historical and critical books listed in the work p. 522–43; of subjects p. 543–52.

2015

Lomazzo, Giovanni Paolo. Trattato dell'arte della pittvra, scoltvra et architettvra . . . Milano, Per P. G. Pontio, 1584. 7 v. in 1 (700 p.) 22 cm.

Reprinted in 1585 and issued in Rome by Saverio Del-Monte in 3 v. in 1844 (Biblioteca artistica 1–3). English translation by R. Haydocke, London, 1598, entitled *A tracte containing the artes of curious paintinge, caruing & buildinge.*

Gives a complete picture of the theories of art, iconography, and beauty of the Mannerist artists. Book 7 is a veritable dictionary of iconography of the period. Contents: v. 1, Theory of proportion; v. 2, Emotions; v. 3, Doctrine of color; v. 4, Light and shade; v. 5, Linear perspective; v. 6, Painting, of kinds and of places; v. 7, Materials.

√2016

Malvasia, Carlo Cesare, *Conte.* Felsina pittrice; vite de' pittori bolognesi alla maesta christianissima di Lvigi XIII . . . con indice in fine copiosissimi. Bologna, Barbieri, 1678. 2 v. illus. 23 cm.

A third volume was issued by Luigi Crespi with title: *Vite de' pittori bolognesi non descritte nella Felsina pittrice,* Roma, 1769. The ed. of 1841, Bologna, is augmented with the life of Malvasia and notes by P. G. Zanotti, and is important because of the good index.

An important source for the history of painting in North Italy. At beginning of v. 1 a list of painters treated in this volume, arranged alphabetically by first name. At end of v. 2 indexes of churches mentioned in the work, of names of owners and others mentioned, of artists (p. 511), and of important subjects. Corrections for both volumes on last page of v. 2.

√2017

Mancini, Giulio. Considerazioni sulla pitture; pubblicate per la prima volta da Adriana Marucchi, con il commento di Luigi Salerno. Roma, Accademia Nazionale dei Lincei, 1956–(57). v. 1–(2). illus., facsims. 25 cm. (Fonti e documenti inediti per la storia dell'arte, 1)

An important source, written between 1614 and 1621, for the aesthetic theories of Caravaggio, Annibale Carracci, and their circle.

Contents: v. 1, Considerazioni sulla pittura, Viaggio per Roma, Appendice, Edizione critica e introduzione di Adriana Marucchi, Presentazione di Lionello Venturi; v. 2, Commento alle opere del Mancini di Luigi Salerno.

Bibliography v. 2, p. 225–30. General index to both volumes v. 2, p. 233–98.

2018

Mander, Carel van. Het schilder-boeck waer in voor eerst de leerlustighe jueght den grondt der edel vry schilderconst in verscheyden deelen wort voorghedraghen, daernae in dry deelen t'leven der vermaerde doorluchtighe schilders des ouden, en nieuwen tyds, eyntlyck d'wtlegghinghe op den Metamorphosen pub. Ouidij Nasonis oock daerbeneffens wtbeeldinghe der figueren; alles dienstich en nut den schilders constbeminders en dichters, oock allen staten van menschen . . . Haerlem, Paschier van Wesbvsch, 1604. 2 pts. in 1 v. engr. plates. 21 cm.

2d ed. with a biography of Van Mander was published in Amsterdam, 1618. The original biographies of Flemish, Dutch, and German artists, which are the most important part, were published with text by Jongh in Amsterdam, 1764. A modern ed. in Dutch published in Amsterdam, 1934; 2d ed. 1943; 3d ed. 1946. A French translation with notes by Hymans published in Paris, 1884. An English ed. with translation and introduction by Constant Van de Wall published in N.Y., 1936.

The lives of the artists begin on fol. [58] and have a title page which bears an Alckmaer imprint and the date 1603. An index to the lives on fol. [302–04], followed by Errata.

2019

Mariette, Jean. L'architecture françoise, ou Recueil des plans, elevations, coupes et profile des eglises, palais, hôtels & maisons particulieres de Paris, & des chasteaux & maisons de campagne ou de plaisance des environs, & de plusieurs autres endroits de France, bâtis nouvellement par les plus habils architectes, et levés & mesurés exactement sur les lieux. A Paris, Chez Jean Mariette, M.DCCXXVII. 2 v. plates. 45 cm.

The number of plates varies in this 1st ed. A reprint was issued in 1927–29 in 3 v. with 562 plates, published in Paris by Van Oest, with an introduction and index by Louis Hautecoeur.

A prime source for French classic architecture, both in text and engraving. It precedes the corpus by Blondel (1991).

2020

Marot, Jean. L'architecture française. [Paris? c. 1670] [4] p. 195 plates. 45 cm.

Called "Le Grand Marot." A collection of engravings forming a main source for the study of 17th century French architecture, as is Androuet du Cerceau (843) for the 16th century, and Mariette (2019) for the 18th century.

2021

Marot, Jean. Recueil des plans, profils et eleuations des plusieurs palais, chasteaux, eglises, sepultures, grotes et hostels batis dans Paris . . . et aux enuirons, auec beaucoup de magnificence, par les meilleũ architectes du royaume, desseignez, mesurés et grauez par Jean Marot, architecte parisien. [Paris? c. 1660–70] 116 plates (incl. plans). 24 cm.

Called "Le Petit Marot." A series of beautiful engravings of façades and plans of important French buildings and monuments.

2022

Martínez, Jusepe. Discursos practicables del nobilísimo arte de la pintura, sus rudimentos, medios y fines que enseña la experiencia, con los ejemplares de obras insignes de artífices ilustres. . . . Publicada la Real Academia de San Fernando, con notas, la vida del autor y una reseña histórica de la pintura en la corona de Aragon, por su individuo de número, don Valentin Carderera y Solano. Madrid, Impr. de M. Tello, 1866. 220 p. 24 cm.

A 17th century manuscript (c. 1675) on artistic theory, which was first published in the 19th century (in 1852 and 1866). Chapters I–XIV are theoretical, while chapters XV–XXI contain rather informal accounts of the lives of important artists.

2023

Orlandi, Pellegrino Antonio. Abcedario pittorico nel quale compendiosamente sono descritte le patrie, i maestri, ed i tempi, ne' quali fiorirono circa quattro mila professori di pittura, di scultura, e d'architettura diviso in tre parti. . . . Il tutto disposto in alfabetto per maggior facilità de dilettanti . . . Bologna, Costantino Pisarri, 1704. 436 p. illus. 25 cm.

2d ed.; enl. 1719. Other eds.: Florence, 1731, 1776, 1788; Venice, 1753; Naples, 1733 and 1763 (with numerous additions on Neapolitan artists and the biography of Solimena).

An early biographical dictionary containing one of the earliest bibliographies of art literature p. 390–407. At end of volume a "Tavola" which lists last names and Christian names of the artists.

Later editions have noteworthy bibliography and indexes of monogrammists, engravers, etc.

2024

Pacheco, Francisco. Arte de la pintura, su antigüedad y grandezas. . . . Segunda edición . . . copiada de la primera . . . de 1649. Dirígela D. G. Cruzada Villaamil. Madrid, Galiano, 1866. 2 v. 22 cm. (Biblioteca de el arte en España, v. 2–3)

1st ed. Seville, 1649.

In three books and 12 chapters, plus "Adiciones a pinturas sagradas" v. 2, p. 243–377. Index of paintings v. 2, p. 379–80, and a table of contents at end of each volume.

2025

Palladio, Andrea. I quattro libri dell'architettvra di Andrea Palladio. Ne' quali, dopo un breue trattato de' conque ordini, & di quelli auertimenti, che sono piu necessarij nel fabricare; si tratta delle case private, delle vie, de i ponti, delle piazze, de i xisti, et de' tempij. Con privilegi. In Venetia, Appresso Dominico de' Franceschi, 1570. 4 v. in 1. illus. (incl. plans, diagrs.) 30 cm.

The 1st ed. of the much-used handbook by the great Renaissance architect (facsimile ed., Milano, Hoepli, 1945). The first complete translation into English is James Leoni's of 1715.

2026

Palomino de Castro y Velasco, Acisclo Antonio. An account of the lives and works of the most eminent Spanish painters, sculptors and architects; and where their several performances are to be seen. Translated from the Museum pictoricum of Palomino Velasco. London, Printed for S. Harding, 1739. 175 p. 16 cm.

Alphabetical list of painters' names p. v–viii.

2027

Palomino de Castro y Velasco, Acisclo Antonio. El museo pictórico y escala óptica. Madrid, por la viuda de Juan Garcia Infancon, 1715–24. 2 v. 31 cm.

A new ed. 1795–97 in 3 v. A reprint ed., with "Prólogo de Juan A. Ceán y Bermúdez," published in Madrid by M. Aguilar, 1947.

A great textbook of art theory and practice. Contents: t. 1, Theorica de la pintura, en que se describe su origen essencia, especies, y qualidades, con todos los demas accidentes, que la enriquezen, è ilustran y se preveban, con demonstraciones mathematicas, y filosoficas, sus mas radicales fundamentos . . . ; t. 2, Practica de la pintura en que se trata de el modo de pintar à el olio, temple, y fresco, con la resolucion de todas las dudas, que en su manipulacion pueden ocurrir. Y de la perspectiva comun, la de techos, angulos, teatros, y monumentos de perspectiva, y otras cosas muy especiales, con la direccion, y documentos para las ideas, o assumptos de las obras, de que se ponen algunos exemplares.

Volume 1 has index of "los terminos privativos del arte" (18 p.) and "Indice de las cosas mas notables contenidas en este tome" (23 p.). Volume 2, pt. 3, gives lives of eminent Spanish painters and contains indexes at end of volume.

2028

Palomino de Castro y Velasco, Acisclo Antonio. Las vidas de los pintores y estatuarios eminentes españoles. Que con sus heroycas obras, han ilustrado la nacion: y de aquellos estrangeros ilustres, que han concurrido en estas provincias, y las han enriquecido, con sus eminentes obras. Londres, H. Woodfall [etc.] 1742. 325 [i.e., 221] p. 21 cm.

Covers 227 artists (each entry numbered in margin). Index of artists p. 213–17. Place index of works of art p. 218–325 [i.e., 221].

2029

Pascoli, Lione. . . . Vite de' pittori, scultori, ed architetti moderni, scritte e dedicate alla Maesta Vittorio Amedeo Re di Sardegna. Roma, Rossi, 1730–36. 2 v. 25 cm.

A facsimile ed. issued by the R. Istituto di Archeologia e Storia dell'Arte (Rome, Calzone, 1933) with an introduction by Corrado Ricci.

Pascoli also wrote a *Vite de' pittori, scultori ed architetti Perugini,* published in Rome in 1732, which is sometimes considered as a third volume of this important work.

Each volume is divided into three sections: painting, sculpture, and architecture.

2030

Passeri, Giovanni Battista. Vite de' pittori, scultori ed architetti che hanno lavorato in Roma, morti dal 1641 fino al 1673 . . . Roma, Barbiellini, 1772. 492 p. 28 cm.

1st ed., published posthumously by Giovanni Lodovico Bianconi with notes by Bottari. Reissued in 1934 as Bd. XI of the *Römische Forschungen der Biblioteca Hertziana* with notes by Jacob Hess (Vienna, Schroll). Baglione's Neapolitan ed. of 1733 contains Passeri's biography of Salvator Rosa (1984).

Consists of long biographical articles on Roman artists, arranged chronologically by death date, 1641–73. Continues where Baglione (1984) ends.

2031

Piles, Roger de. Abrégé de la vie des peintres etc. . . . avec des réflexions sur leurs ouvrages, et un traité du peintre parfait, de la connoissance des desseins & de l'utilité des estampes. Paris, Langlois, 1699. 540 p. 17 cm.

Also published in Paris, 1715, and in Amsterdam, 1767. Published in German by Marperger, Hamburg, 1710; in English in London, 1706 and 1744.

Contains general articles on painting, drawing, use of prints, and short articles on about 300 painters, as well as an article on taste.

French ed. of 1699 has an alphabetical list of painters treated, at end of volume. English ed. of 1706 contains sections on composition, design, expression, perspective, coloring, prints, landscape, etc., and the biographies. It also includes an "Essay towards an English school." English ed. of 1744 has an alphabetical list of painters covered in De Piles, at beginning of volume.

2032

Piles, Roger de. Cours de peinture par principes. Paris, Estienne, 1708. 493 p. 2 plates. 17 cm.

Published in Paris, 1708, 1720, 1791; in English, London, 1743. The German ed. is entitled *Einleitung in die Malerei aus Grundsätzen*, Leipzig, 1760. Also published in Dutch with *L'Aretino* of L. Dolce in Amsterdam, 1756.

This work contains at the end De Piles's famous classification of painters according to composition, design, color, and expression, "Balance des peintres."

2033

Piranesi, Giovanni Battista. Le antichità romane, opera del cavaliere Giambatista Piranesi, architetto veneziano, divisa in quattro tomi . . . Roma, Nella Stamperia di Angelo Rotilj, 1756. 4 v. 218 plates. 54 cm.

An invaluable record of Roman antiquity and architecture, and also the most spectacular collection by the great engraver.

Volume 1 contains the remains of ancient buildings in Rome arranged in topographical plates according to their present day existence, with a critical index of their types; also the ancient aqueducts in the vicinity of Rome, the Roman Forum, and Capitoline

Hill. Volumes 2 and 3 contain the sepulchral monuments existing in Rome and the Agro Romano, with the plans, elevations, external and interior views, as well as sarcophagi, funerary urns, bas reliefs, inscriptions, etc. Volume 4, bridges of Rome which are still in existence, remains of theaters, porches, and other monuments extant, with explanations.

For a bibliographical account of the various editions of this and his other works, see: Hind, A. M. *Giovanni Piranesi, a critical study*, 1922; and Focillon, H. *Giovanni-Battista Piranesi; essai de catalogue raisonné de son oeuvre*, 1918.

2034

Ponz, Antonio. Viage de España, ó cartas, en que se da noticia de las cosas mas apreciables, y dignas de saberse que hay en ella . . . Madrid, Joachin Ibarra, 1772. 18 v. 19 cm.

"Su autor D. Pedro Antonio de la Puente." A 2d ed., 1774–83; 3d ed., 1787–94; Italian ed., Parma, 1793–97 in 4 v. A modern reprint, *Viaje de España ed los dos tomos del Viaje fuera de España* (Madrid, Aguilar, 1947, 2039 p.), contains indexes of names and places and of works and authors, as well as a very detailed table of contents.

An early source which is a description of monuments in various parts of Spain.

2035

Pozzo, Bartolomeo dal. Le vite de' pittori, degli scultori ed architetti veronesi raccolte da varj autori stampati, e manuscritti, e da altre particolari memorie. Con la narratiua delle pitture e sculture che s'attrouano nelle chiese, case ed altri luoghi publici e priuati di Verona, e suo territorio . . . Uerona, G. Berno, 1718. 313 p. 24 cm.

Gives the lives of Veronese artists and descriptions of the art treasures of Verona. The contents of private collections are listed and painted decorations of various buildings are described.

Index of artists (4 p.) at beginning of volume.

———. Aggiunta alle Vite de' pittori, degli scultori ed architetti veronesi del signor fr. Bartolomeo . . . Verona, Stampa di P. A. Berno, 1718. 42 p. 24 cm.

2036

Ridolfi, Carlo. Le maraviglie dell'arte, ouero Le vite de gl'illvstri pittori veneti, e dello stato. Oue sono raccolte le opere insigni, i costumi, & i ritratti loro. Con la narratione delle historie delle fauole, e delle moralità da quelli dipinte . . . Venetia, Sgaua, 1648. 2 v. in 1. plates. 23 cm.

2d ed., Padua, 1835–37 in 2 v.; a new ed., rev. by Detlev von Hadeln, Berlin, 1914–24 in 2 v.

Next to Boschini (1992), the most important source for Venice of the seicento, treating not only Venetian painters but also some from the mainland. Contains engraved portraits.

Each volume has an index of artists mentioned, and one of "cose notabili."

2037

Sandrart, Joachim von. L'Academia todesca della architectura, scultura & pittura: oder, Teutsche Academie der Edlen Bau- Bild- und Mahlerey-Künste . . . Nürnberg, Sandrart; Frankfurt, Merian, 1675–79. 2 v. in 3. illus., plates, diagrs., map. 39 cm.

Volume 2 has title: Der Teutschen Academie zweyter und letzter Haupt-Theil (1679).

Latin ed. 1683; a new ed. of J. J. Volkmann, Nürnberg, 1768, in 8 v.; also a modern ed. with commentary by A. Peltzer, Munich, 1925.

Part 1 contains a general introduction based on Vasari, Palladio, Serlio, Van Mander, etc.; pt. 2 contains lives of artists; pt. 3 is an attempt at a general museography. Illustrated with numerous plates and portraits.

Index of artists and important subjects v. 1, p. 377–87.

2038

Scamozzi, Vincenzo. Idea dell'architettura universale . . . diuisa in x libri . . . Venetiis, expensis avctoris, 1615. 2 v. in 1. illus., plans. 35 cm.

Books 4–5, 9–10 were never published. The most elaborate and learned treatise on architectural history and theory from the viewpoint of the late Italian Renaissance.

2039

Serlio, Sebastiano. Il primo [-quinto] libro d'architettura di M. Sebastiano Serlio, Bolognese. [Venetia] 1551. 5 pts. in 1 v. illus., plans, diagrs. 35 cm.

The first complete ed. of the first five books of this important and much perused high Renaissance treatise on architecture; augmented by a sixth "libro extraordinario" published in Lyon, 1551, and a seventh (posthumous) published in Frankfurt, 1575. The first five books were originally published separately in Venice and Paris between 1537

and 1547 (v. 4, 1537; v. 3, 1540; v. 1–2, 1545; v. 5, 1547). The English translation of books 1–5 appeared in London in 1611. Unpublished manuscripts of another sixth book are in the Staatsbibliothek in Munich and at the Avery Library. *Cf.* Dinsmoor, W. B. in *Art bulletin,* v. 24, 1942, p. 55–91, 115–54.

2040

Soprani, Raffaele. Le vite de' pittori, scoltori, et architetti genovesi. . . . E de' forastieri, che in Genoua operarono. Con alcuni ritratti de gli stessi. Opera postvma, dell'illustrissimo Signor Rafaele Soprani. . . . Aggiontaui la vita dell'autore per opera di Gio. Nicolo Cavana . . . Genova, Bottaro e Tiboldi, 1674. 340 p. plates. 24 cm.

An expanded ed. (Genoa, 1768), with notes by Giuseppe Ratti, brings the work up to the middle of the 18th century.

Contains biographies of artists working in Genoa, with many engraved portraits. Indexes of Genovese artists, of foreign artists who worked in Genoa, and of other foreign artists mentioned in the work.

2041

Vasari, Giorgio. Le vite de' piv eccellenti architetti, pittori et scvltori italiani, da Cimabve insino a' tempi nostri: descritte in lingua toscana da G.- V.-, pittore Aretino. Con vna sua vtile e necessaria introduzione a le arti loro. Firenze, Torrentino, 1550. 3 v. in 2. plates. 22 cm.

This original ed., issued in 3 pts. in two quarto volumes (992 p.), with indexes, and dedicated to Duke Cosimo Medici, is now a bibliographical rarity.

A reprint, edited by Corrado Ricci, was issued in Rome by Bestetti and Tumminelli in 1927, in 4 v.

The key source of Renaissance biography.

2042

Vasari, Giorgio. Le vite de' piv eccellenti pittori, scvltori e architettori, scritte (di nuovo ampliate), de M. Giorgio Vasari pittore et architetto Aretino. Co' ritratti loro et con le nuoue vite dal 1550 insino al 1567, con tauole copiosissime de' nomi, dell'opere, e de' luoghi ou' ell sono. Firenze, Givnti, 1568. 3 v. illus. 25 cm.

This 2d ed. is especially noted for the fine woodcut portraits which were executed in Venice. It also contains some confusing typographical errors.

The classic ed. is that of Gaetano Milanesi, published by Sansoni, Florence, 1787–1818, in 8 v. and an index volume dated 1885. The most used English translation is that of Gaston du C. De Vere, London, The Medici Society, 1912–15, in 10 v. For other eds. of Vasari see Schlosser (44), 1956 ed., p. 332–46.

2043

Verci, Giovanni Battista. Notizie intorno alla vita e alle opere de' pittori, scultori e intagliatori della citta di Bassano. Venezia, E. Gatti, 1775. 328 p. 18 cm.

Painting covers p. 1–277; sculpture and engraving p. 278–313. Contains indexes of painting and sculpture to be found in the churches in Bassano and surrounding towns.

2044

Vertue, George. . . . Vertue note books. Oxford, Printed for the Walpole Society by John Johnson, 1930–(55). (7) v. plates, plans, facsims. 32 cm.

Notes on art and artists made by George Vertue between 1718 and his death in 1757. They originally filled 40 notebooks, 33 of which are now in the British Museum and have been printed in *The Walpole Society annual* (2357), volumes: 18, 1929/30; 20, 1931/32; 22, 1933/34; 24, 1935/36; 26, 1937/38 and Index, v. 29, 1947; 30, 1955.

2045

Vignola, Giacomo Barozzio, *called*. Regola delli cinqve ordini d'architettvra di M. Iacomo Barozzio da Vignola. [1562 n.p.] 32 plates. 37 cm.

The 1st ed. of the famous handbook of the orders often reprinted and reissued. The most frequently used ed. is by Arthur L. Tuckerman, N.Y., 1891.

2046

Vitruvius, Pollio. [De architectura. Roma, Herolt, 1486] 98 l. diagrs. 28 cm.

The 1st ed. of the great Roman sourcebook on Greek and Roman architecture. Countless later eds. follow, the first translation from the Latin into Italian, 1521; the first English translation, 1669. Recent usable translations by Granger (Loeb ed., 1931–34) and by Morgan (1914). Bibliography by Bodo Ebhardt, Berlin, 1918.

2047

Walpole, Horace, *Earl of Orford*. Anecdotes of painting in England; with some account of the principal artists; and incidental notes on other arts; collected by the late Mr. George Vertue; and now digested and published from his original mss. by Mr. Horace Walpole . . . Strawberry Hill, Printed by Thomas Farmer, 1762–71. 5 v. plates. 23 cm.

1st ed. For a modern supplement see Walpole (2058).

Lives of the artists arranged chronologically by reigns, containing much original observation by an eye-witness. Volume 4 also contains an article on "The history of the modern taste in gardening." Volume 5, with title *A catalogue of engravers who have been born, or resided in England*, includes also a "Life of Mr. George Vertue" and a list of his works.

Index of artists at end of each volume.

2048

Weyerman, Jacob Campo. De levensbeschryvingen der Nederlandsche konstschilders en konst-schilderessen, met een uytbreyding over der schilder-konst der ouden . . . Verrykt met de konterfeytsels der voornaamste konst-schilders en konstschilderessen, cierlyk in koper gesneden door J. Houbraken . . . 's Gravenhage, Boucquet, 1729–69. 4 v. illus. 21 cm.

Schlosser (44) notes that Weyerman is a plagiarizer of Houbraken (2008) and considers the work of little value. At end of each volume an index of artists treated therein.

Later Collections of Source Material

2049

Goldwater, Robert John, and Treves, Marco, ed. and tr. Artists on art, from the XIV to the XX century. [2d rev. ed. N.Y.] Pantheon Books [1947, c1945]. 499 p. illus. 24 cm.

Includes writings of painters and sculptors from the end of the Middle Ages to the Second World War, arranged chronologically. For each artist gives a portrait and a few identifying sentences, followed by excerpts from his writings on art. Nearly half of the writings have been translated into English by the compilers, and other passages have been edited.

Bibliography of sources p. 480–88. Index p. 493–500.

2050

Holt, Elizabeth Basye (Gilmore), ed. Literary sources of art history; an anthology of texts from Theophilus to Goethe. Princeton, Princeton Univ. Press, 1947. 555 p. illus. 25 cm.

An expanded and revised paperback ed. was issued by Doubleday (Anchor Books) under the title *A documentary history of art,* in 2 v. Volume 1, *The Middle Ages and Renaissance,* appeared in 1957 and v. 2, *Michelangelo and the Mannerists, the Baroque and the eighteenth century,* in 1958.

Translations of excerpts from original documents on the arts, including treatises, letters, and journals, from the middle of the 10th to the end of the 18th century. Each selection is preceded by a paragraph about the author.

Bibliographical footnotes. Index p. 551–55.

2051

Jones, Henry Stuart, ed. Select passages from ancient writers illustrative of the history of Greek sculpture, ed. with a translation and notes by Stuart Jones . . . London and N.Y., Macmillan, 1895. 231 p. 21 cm.

Parallel columns give both the original text and the translation. There is no attempt to be comprehensive. "As a rule, the inscriptions of artists (which may be read in Loewy's *Inschriften* . . . [2095]) have not been included."—*Pref.*

2052

[Pini, Carlo] La scrittura di artisti italiani (sec. XIV–XVII) reprodotta con la fotografia da Carlo Pini e corridata di notizie da Gaetano Milanesi. Firenze, Presso l'Editore, 1869–76. mounted facsims. 33 cm.

Issued in 11 fascicles and one dated 1876 which contains an alphabetical index of artists' names, additions and corrections, and a chronological index of artists. Includes 300 photogravures of specimens of artists' handwriting.

2053

Quellenschriften für Kunstgeschichte und Kunsttechnik des Mittelalters und der Neuzeit, mit Unterstützung des Österreichischen K. K. Ministeriums für Kultus und Unterricht . . . hrsg . . . I–XVIII Bd.; neue Folge, I.–15. Bd. Wien, Braumüller [etc.], 1871–1908. [Bd. 1, 1888]. 33 v. in 19. illus., map. 23 cm.

Editors: v. 1–18, R. Eitelberger von Edelberg; n. F. v. 1–8, A. Ilg; v. 9–15, C. List. Volumes 1–18 have title: Quellenschriften . . . des Mittelalters und der Renaissance.

Contents: (1) Cennini, Cennino. Das Buch von der Kunst . . . Neue Ausgabe, 1888; (2) Dolce, Lodovico. Aretino, oder Dialog über Malerei . . . 1871; (3) Dürer, Albrecht. Dürers Briefe, Tagebücher und Reime . . . 1872; (4) Eraclius. Heraclius, von den Farben und Künsten der Römer . . . 1873; (5) Biondo, Michelangelo. Von der Hochedlen Malerei . . . 1873; (6) Condivi, Ascanio. Das Leben des Michelangelo Buonarroti . . . 1874; (7) Theophilus, called also Rugerus. Theophilus Presbyter Schedula diversarum Artium, 1 Bd. . . . 1874; (8) Stockbauer, Jacob. Die Kunststrebungen am Bayerischen Hofe unter Herzog Albert V. und seinem Nachfolger Wilhelm V . . . 1874; (9) Semper, Hans. Donatello . . . 1875; (10) Neudörfer, Johann. Des Johann Neudörfer Schreib und Rechenmeisters zu Nürnberg Nachrichten von Künstlern und Werkleuten daselbst aus dem Jahre 1547 . . . 1875; (11) Alberti, Leone Battista. Leone Battista Alberti's kleinere kunsttheoretische Schriften, 1877; (12) Unger, F. W. Quellen der byzantinischen Kunstgeschichte, 1. Bd., 1878; (13) Prague. Malerzeche. Das Buch der Malerzeche in Prag . . . 1878; (14) Houbraken, Arnold. Arnold Houbraken's Grosse Schouburgh der niederländischen Maler und Malerinnen . . . 1880; (15–18) Leonardo da Vinci. Das Buch von der Malerei, Deutsche Ausgabe . . . 1882. Neue Folge: (1) Michiel, Marcantonio. Der Anonimo Morelliano . . . [1. Abth.] . . . 1896; (2) Paccioli, Luca da Borgo. Divina proportione . . . 1896; (3) Filarete, Antonio Averlino. Antonio Averlino Filarete's Tractat über die Baukunst . . . 1896; (4) Schlosser, Julius, Ritter von. Schriftquellen zur Geschichte der karolingischen Kunst . . . 1896; (5) Ilg, Albert. Beiträge zur Geschichte der Kunst und der Kunsttechnik aus Mittelhochdeutschen Dictungen, 1892; (6) Hainhofer, Philipp. Des Augsburger Patriciers Philipp Hainhofer Beziehungen zum Herzog Philipp II. von Pommern-Stettin . . . 1896; (7) Schlosser, Julius, Ritter von. Quellenbuch zur Kunstgeschichte des abendländischen Mittelalters . . . 1896; (8) Richter, J. P. Quellen der byzantinischen Kunstgeschichte . . . 1897; (9) Hollanda, Francisco de. Vier Gespräche über die Malerei geführt zu Rom 1538 . . . 1899; (10) Hainhofer, Philipp. Des Augsburger Patriciers Philipp Hainhofer Reisen nach Innsbruck und Dresden, 1901; (11–13) Hampe, Theodor. Nürnberger Ratsverlässe über Kunst und Künstler im Zeitalter der Spätgotik und Renaissance (1449) 1474–1618 (1633), 1904; (14) Ertinger, F. F. Des Bilderhauergesellen Franz Ferdinand Ertinger Reisebeschreibung durch Österreich und Deutschland . . . 1907; (15) Kallab, Wolfgang. Vasaristudien . . . 1908.

2054

Quellenstudien zur holländischen Kunstgeschichte. Haag, Nijhoff, 1893–1928. 15 v. plates, facsim. 25 cm.

A series of reprints of important texts of sources for Dutch art history.

Contents: (1) Hofstede de Groot, Cornelis. Arnold Houbraken und seine "Groote Schouburgh," kritisch beleuchtet, 1893; (2) Greve, H. E. De bronnen van Carel van Mander voor "Het leven der doorluchtighe Nederlandtsche en Hoogduytsche schilders," 1903; (3) Hofstede de Groot, Cornelis. Die Urkunden über Rembrandt (1575–1721), 1906; (4) Lilienfeld, Karl. Arent de Gelder, sein Leben und seine Kunst, 1914; (5–7, 10–14) Bredius, Abraham. Künstler-Inventare . . . 1915–22, 8 v.; (8) Mander, Carel van. Das Lehrgedicht des Karel van Mander, 1916; (9) Hirschmann, O. Hendrick Goltzius als Maler, 1600–1617, 1916; (15) Buchell, Arend van. Arnoldus Buchelius, "Res pictoriae," 1928.

2055

Sánchez Cantón, Francisco Javier. Fuentes literarias para la historia del arte español . . . Madrid [Imprenta Clásica Española] 1923–41. 5 v. 25 cm.

At head of title: Junta para ampliación de estudios e investigaciones científicas. Centro de estudios históricos. Publisher varies: v. 2, Bermejo.

Reprints texts of important sources such as Francisco de Hollanda, Vasari, Pacheco, Del Valle, etc. Each volume has indexes by person and place, and at end of v. 5 is an author index to all five volumes.

2056

Sánchez Cantón, Francisco Javier. Opusculos Gallegos sobre bellas artes de los siglos XVII y XVIII . . . publicados en facsimile, o transcritos, con notas preliminares. Compostela, 1956. 348 p. 24 cm. (Colleción de los bibliofilos Gallegos, 3)

Edition of 500 copies printed. The work consists of reprints of seven old Spanish treatises on the history of art, three of which are published for the first time.

Contents: (1) Vega y Verdugo, José. Memorial sobre obras en la Catedral de Santiago (1657–66, from the illustrated ms.); (2) Andrade, Domingo de. Excelencias, antiguedades y nobleza de la arquitectura (1695); (3) Feijoo, Fr. Benito Jeronimo. Razon del gusto (1733); (4) Feijoo, Fr. B. J. El no sé qué (1733); (5) Sarmiento, Fray Martin. Sistema de adornos de escultura del nuevo Real Palacio de Madrid (1743–47, from the ms. with facsimile of the inscriptions); (6) Castor, Felipe de. Dedicatoria de la lección de Varchi (1753); (7) Prado Marino, Melchor. Disertación ante la Real Academia de Bellas Artes (1796, ms. in facsim.). List of artists on one page following text.

2057

Venturi, Lionello. Les archives de l'impressionisme. Lettres de Renoir, Monet, Pissarro, Sisley et autres. Mémoires de Paul Durand-Ruel. Documents. Paris, N.Y., Durand-Ruel, 1939. 2 v. plates, facsims. 26 cm.

Letters and documents dealing with the impressionist school. Bibliography. "La critique de l'impressionisme de 1863 à 1880," v. 2, p. 273–342. Index and table of contents at end of v. 2.

2058

Walpole, Horace, *Earl of Orford.* Anecdotes of painting in England; 1760–1795, with some account of the principal artists; and incidental notes on other arts; collected by Horace Walpole; and now digested and published from his original mss. by Frederick W. Hilles and Philip B. Daghlian. . . . Volume the fifth and last. New Haven, Yale Univ. Press, 1937. 262 p. facsim. 24 cm.

Forms a supplement to his *Anecdotes of painting in England* (2047).

The bulk of the material has been selected from Walpole's *Book of materials,* in the Folger Shakespeare Library. Other selections are from the author's set of annotated catalogs of exhibitions, now owned by Wilmarth Lewis.

Contents: (1) Introduction, Principal artists, societies, and academies of art, Miscellaneous notes; (2) Painters of portraits; (3) Painters of history, landscape; (4) Painters in enamel and miniature; (5) Statuaries; (6) Architecture and architects; (7) Engravers and medallists; (8) Ladies and gentlemen distinguished by their artistic talents. "Index of names" p. 241–62.

Archives, Documents, and Letters

2059

Antwerp. St. Lucas Gilde. De liggeren en andere historische archieven der Antwerpsche Sint Lucasgilde, onder zinspreuk: "Wt ionsten versaemt" . . . afgeschreven en bewerkt door Ph. Rombouts en Th. van Lerius. Anvers, Baggerman [1872–76]. 2 v. 29 cm.

Excerpts from the archives of the St. Lucas Guild of Antwerp. Contents: (1) Liggere van 1453–1615. Volledige rekeningen van 1585–1586 en 1588–1589. Rekeningen van ontvangsten van 1616–1629; (3) Liggere van 1629–1729. Inschryvings register van 1749–1794. Rekeningen van ontvangsten van 1629–1736.

Volume 1 has "Table des prénoms" p. 681–98; "Table des professions mentionées dans ce volume" p. 698–706; and "Table des noms propres" p. 707–92. Volume 2 has "Table des professions" p. 869–76 and "Table des noms propres" p. 877–1002.

2060

Archief voor Nederlandsche Kunstgeschiedenis. Verzameling van meerendeels onuitgegeven berichten en mededeelingen betreffende Nederlandsche schilders, plaatsnijders, beeldhouwers, bouwmeesters, juweliers, goud- en zilverdrijvers, smeden, stempelsnijders, tapijtwevers, borduurwerkers, plateelbakkers, glasschilders, ingenieurs, landmeters, kaartmakers, verlichters, schoonschrijvers, boekbinders, enz., bijeengebracht door Fr. D. O. Obreen. Rotterdam, Van Hengel & Eeltjes [etc.] 1877–90. 7 v. plates. 21 cm.

A collection of previously unpublished documents relating to the fine arts in the Netherlands. Index at end of each volume, covering material in that particular volume.

2061

Bacci, Pèleo, ed. Documenti toscani per la storia dell'arte . . . [Firenze, Gonnelli, 1910–12] 2 v. 27 plates. 19 cm.

These documents refer almost exclusively to the history of art in Pistoia. Bibliographic footnotes. At end of each volume is a table of contents which lists the documents included.

2062

Bacci, Pèleo. Fonti e commenti per la storia dell'arte senese; dipinti e sculture in Siena, nel suo contado ed altrove. Siena, Accademia degli Intronati, 1944. 259 p. plates. 24 cm. (Collezione di monografie d'arte senese, Ser. 1)

Sources and comments relating to painting and sculpture in Siena and its surrounding area. At end of volume is a table of contents, and an index of names of artists specially mentioned in the documents.

2063

Becker, Felix. Schriftquellen zur Geschichte der altniederländischen Malerei nach den Hauptmeistern chronologisch geordnet. 1. Kritik und Commentar der Quellen . . . Leipzig, Sellmann & Henne, 1897. 94 p. 21 cm.

Published as a dissertation, University of Leipzig. A discussion of the various sources and documents available concerning early Netherlandish painters.

2064

Bertolotti, Antonio. Alcuni artisti siciliani a Roma nei secoli XVI e XVII. Notizie e documenti, raccolti nell' archivio di stato romano. Palermo, Virzi, 1879. 38 p. 28 cm.

Documents regarding Sicilian artists working in Rome in the 16th and 17th centuries, arranged by century and then by medium in which they worked. Bibliographical footnotes. No index or table of contents.

2065

Bertolotti, Antonio. Le arti minori alla corte di Mantova nei secoli XV, XVI e XVII; ricerche storiche negli archivi Mantovani. Milano, Giuseppe Prato, 1889. 257 p. 25 cm.

On verso of title page: "Estratto dall'Archivio Storico Lombardo anno XV–1888."

Extracts from the Mantuan archives covering goldsmithing, engraving in metal, alloys, wood and ivory, crystal and glass, embroidery, silversmithing, jewelry, seal cutting, enameling, niello work, and clockmaking. Index of artisans and others p. 241–57.

2066

Bertolotti, Antonio. Artisti belgi ed olandesi a Roma nei secoli XVI e XVII; notizie e documenti raccolti negli archivi romani. Firenze, Tipografia Editrice della Gazzetta d'Italia, 1880. 429 p. 18 cm.

Documents concerning Belgian and Dutch artists in Rome in the 16th and 17th centuries culled from the Roman archives. "Indice della cose principali" p. 387–91. "Indice degli artisti ed altri accennati" p. 393–426. "Errata-corrige" p. 427–29.

2067

Bertolotti, Antonio. Artisti bolognesi, ferraresi ed alcuni altri del già Stato Pontificio in Roma nei secoli XV, XVI, XVII. Bologna, Regia Tipografia, 1885. 295 p. 25 cm.

Subtitle: "Studi e ricerche tratte dagli archivi romani."

Covers architects, engineers, painters, sculptors, goldsmiths, engravers, intarsia workers, potters, etc. from Bologna and Ferrara, working in the Pontifical State from 1400 to 1700. Arranged by centuries and then by medium. Index at the end.

2068

Bertolotti, Antonio. Artisti lombardi a Roma nei secoli XV, XVI e XVII; studi e ricerche negli archivi romani . . . Milano, Hoepli, 1881. 2 v. 19 cm.

Documents concerning Lombard artists working in Rome in the 15th, 16th, and 17th centuries. Covers architects, painters, sculptors, goldsmiths, cabinetmakers, makers of clocks and musical instruments. Arranged by centuries and then by medium.

"Indice delle cose più notevoli nei due volumi" v. 2, p. 327–35. "Indice degli artisti e di altri accennati nei due volumi" v. 2, p. 337–87.

2069

Bertolotti, Antonio. Artisti modenesi, parmensi e della Lunigiana in Roma nei secoli XV, XVI e XVII. (*In* Deputazioni di storia patria per le provincie modenesi e parmensi. Atti e memorie, 1883, ser. 3, v. 1, pt. 1, p. [7]–193) 25 cm.

Includes material regarding all types of artists from Modena, Parma, and the Lunigiana, working in Rome in the 15th, 16th, and 17th centuries, arranged by medium.

"Indice delle cose più notevole" p. 175–78. "Indice nominale" p. 179–93.

2070

Bertolotti, Antonio. Artisti subalpini in Roma nei secoli XV, XVI e XVII. Mantua, Tip. Lit. Mondovi, 1884. 284 p. 26 cm.

Contains text and documents on artists of the Alpine provinces of Italy and their work in Rome. "Libri ed opuscoli dell'autore," 4 p. at end.

2071

Bertolotti, Antonio. Artisti svizzeri in Roma nei secoli XV, XVI e XVII; ricerche e studi negli archivi romani. Bellinzona, Tip. e Litografia Colombi, 1886. 71 p. 25 cm.

Documents from the Roman archives concerning Swiss artists in Rome in the 15th, 16th, and 17th centuries.

2072

Bertolotti, Antonio. Artisti urbinati in Roma prima del secolo XVIII; notizie e documenti raccolti negli archivi romani . . . Urbino, Tip. della Cappella per E. Righi, 1881. 69 p. 26 cm.

"Estratto dal periodico 'Il Raffaello.'" Contains documents relating to artists from Urbino working in Rome before the 18th century.

2073

Bertolotti, Antonio. Artisti veneti in Roma nei secoli XV, XVI e XVII. Studi e ricerche negli archivi romani. Venezia, A Spese della Società, 1884. 99 p. 30 cm.

Published in Reale Deputazione Veneta di Storia Patria. Monumenti storici, Ser. 4, v. 3.

Documents concerning artists from the Veneta, transcribed from Roman archives. Arranged by centuries and then by medium. Covers architecture, painting, sculpture, engraving, goldsmithing, wood carving, typography, music, etc.

2074

Bertolotti, Antonio. Figuli, fonditori e scultori in relazione con la corte di Mantova nei secoli XV, XVI, XVII; notizie e documenti raccolti negli archivi mantovani. Milano, Tip. Bertolotti di Giuseppe Prato, 1890. 115 p. 25 cm.

A collection of documents regarding potters, founders, and sculptors in relation to the court at Mantua in the 15th, 16th, and 17th centuries, culled from the archives in Mantua. Divided into: Ceramica, Fonderie, Scultura in marmo.

"Indice delle sezioni" p. 110. "Indice degli artisti e altri nominati" p. 111–15.

2075

Borghesi, Sapione, and Banchi, L. Nuovi documenti per la storia dell'arte senese raccolti da S. Borghesi e L. Banchi; appendice alla raccolta dei documenti pubblicata dal Comm. Gaetano Milanesi. Siena, Torrini, 1898. 702 p. 23 cm.

Contains 350 documents relating to Sienese art. "Tavola dei documenti," p. 649–76, lists chronologically (May 1297 to 1679) the documents included, with page numbers. Index of artists p. 677–93. Index of places and subjects p. 695–702.

2076

Bottari, Giovanni. Raccolta di lettere sulla pittura, scultura ed architettura scritte da' più professori che in dette arti fiorirono dal secolo XV. al XVII. Roma, 1754–73. 7 v. 22 cm.

Volume 7 compiled by Luigi Crespi. Title pages vary slightly. The 2d ed. (Milan, 1822–25) was greatly enlarged by Stephano Ticozzi and published in 8 v. with an index. An abridged French ed. (Paris, 1817) was translated by L. J. Jay.

A collection of letters concerning painting, sculpture, and architecture written by artists of the 15th, 16th, and 17th centuries.

2077

Braghirolli, Willelmo. Lettere inedite di artisti del secolo XV cavate dall'archivio Gonzaga. [With Note biografiche] Mantua, 1878. 152 p. 23 cm.

Edition of 150 copies. A collection of artists' letters of the 16th century, from the Gonzaga archives. No index.

2078

Bredius, Abraham, ed. Künstler-Inventare; Urkunden zur Geschichte der holländischen Kunst des XVIten, XVIIten und XVIIIten Jahrhunderts . . . Haag, Nijhoff, 1915–22. 6 v. & Nachtrag & Register. plates, facsims. 25 cm.

Inventories of estates of Dutch and Flemish artists, mentioning art objects. The Register has indexes of persons, places, pictures, and an alphabetical index of the inventories.

2079

Datos documentales para la historia del arte español . . . Madrid, 1914–43. 3 v. 23 cm.

At head of title: v. 1–2, Junta para ampliación de estudios e investigaciones científicas. Centro de estudios históricos; v. 3, Consejo superior de investigaciones científicas. Instituto Diego Velázquez.

A collection of documents dealing with the history of Spanish art. Contents: (1) Pérez Sedano, Francisco. Notas del archivo de la catedral de Toledo, 1914; (2) Zarco del Valle, M. R. Documentos de la catedral de Toledo, 1916, 2 v.; (3) Ferrandis, José. Inventarios reales (Juan II a Juana la Loca), 1943.

General index at end of v. 3.

2080

Dehaisnes, Chrétien César Auguste. Documents et extraits divers concernant l'histoire de l'art dans le Flandre, l'Artois et le Hainaut avant le XVe siècle . . . Lille, Danel, 1886. 2 v. 33 cm.

Paged continuously. Documents culled from various archives of France and Belgium. Arranged chronologically: v. 1, 627–1373; v. 2, 1374–1401.

Glossary p. 921–28. "Table des matières" p. 929–1006. "Table des noms des artistes et des fournisseurs d'objets d'art" p. 1007–65.

2081

Duverger, Jozef. Bijdragen en documenten tot de kunstgeschiedenis. Ghent, Vyncke, 1942. 64, 66 p. 21 cm.

A discussion of available Renaissance documents in the Netherlands. Contents: (1) Bijdragen tot de studie der renaissance in de Nederlanden; (2) Vorstelijke grafmonumenten uit het begin van de XVIe eeuw. (Two sections separately paged.)

2082

Filangeri, Gaetano Angerio Guglielmo, ed. Documenti per la storia, le arti e le industrie delle provincie napoletane . . . Napoli, Accademia Reale delle Scienze, 1883–91. 6 v. plates, facsim. 31 cm.

Edition of 250 copies. A collection of documents dealing with the history, art, and industry of the Neapolitan provinces.

Contents: v. 1, Effemeridi delle cose fatte per il duca di Calabria (1484–1491) di Joampiero Leostello . . . da un codice della Biblioteca nazionale di Parigi; v. 2–4, Estratti di schede notarile; v. 5–6, Indice degli artefici dell'arti maggiori e minori.

2083

Fontaine, André. . . . Conférences inédites de l'Académie Royale de Peinture et de Sculpture d'après les manuscrits des archives de l'École des Beaux-Arts . . . Paris, Albert Fontemoing [1903]. 232 p. 20 cm. (Collection "Minerva")

A collection of important 17th and 18th century discussions taken from the archives of the École des Beaux-Arts.

Contents: (1) La querelle du dessin et de la couleur; (2) Conférences de Le Brun, de Philippe et de Jean-Baptiste de Champaigne; (3) L'année 1672; Appendices: (A) Retouches XVIIIe siècle sur un discours de Philippe de Champaigne; (B) Conférence de M. Nocret sur le portrait du Marquis del Vasto, du Titien (7 septembre 1668).

2084

Gaye, Johann Wilhelm. Carteggio inedito d'artisti dei secoli XIV, XV, XVI, pubblicato ed illustrato con documenti pure inediti dal dott. Giovanni Gaye, con facsimile . . . Firenze, G. Molini, 1839–40. 3 v. fold. facsims. 23 cm.

A collection of documents and letters culled from the archives of Florence and other cities. Arranged chronologically: v. 1, 1326–1500; v. 2, 1500–1557; v. 3, 1501–1672.

Preface to v. 3 gives biography of Gaye. Each volume contains facsimiles of documents at end, and an index of documents. Volume 3 has index of the letter writers in the 3 v., and index of the titles of documents which are not letters.

2085

Golzio, Vincenzo. . . . Documenti artistici sul seicento nell'archivio Chigi; con presentazione di Roberto Paribeni. Roma, Palombi, 1939. 435 p. plates, plans, facsim. 28 cm.

At head of title: R. Istituto d'archeologia e storia dell'arte. These documents from the Chigi Archives in Ariccia are divided into those concerning works of art done for Cardinal Flavio Chigi, and those executed for Alessandro VII.

"Elenco dei libri esaminati" p. xii. Index of artists p. 425–28; of places p. 429–30; of illustrations p. 431–32.

2086

Gonetta, Giuseppe. Bibliografia statuaria delle corporazioni d'arti e mestieri d'Italia, con saggio di bibliografia estera. Roma, Forzani, 1891. 99 p. 25 cm.

500 copies printed.

A bibliography of old statutes which lists both printed and unprinted sources, arranged alphabetically by city.

Contents: (1) Statuti editi ed inediti, p. 19–77; (2) Bibliografia italiana, p. 78–88. Saggio di bibliografia estera, p. 89–99.

2087

Gualandi, Michelangelo, ed. Nuova raccolta di lettere sulla pittura, scultura ed architettura scritte da' più celebri personaggi dei secoli XV a XIX con note ed illustrazione . . . Bologna, A Spese dell'Editore ed Annotatore, 1844–56. 3 v. 24 cm.

A collection of letters by Italian artists, forming a continuation of Bottari (2076), with numerous contributions from the Medici and other archives. At end of each volume a list of letters contained in it.

2088

Guhl, Ernst. Künstlerbriefe, übersetzt und erläutert von Dr. Ernst Guhl. 2. umgearbeitete und sehr vermehrte Aufl. von Dr. Adolf Rosenberg. Berlin, Guttentag, 1880. 2 v. in 1. 24 cm.

A valuable collection of 311 artists' letters of the 15th, 16th, and 17th centuries, translated and extensively annotated. Alphabetical list of artists whose letters are included, with their dates, p. 369–82.

2089

Guiffrey, Jules, ed. Comptes des bâtiments du roi sous le règne de Louis XIV. Paris, Imprimerie Nationale, 1881–1901. 5 v. 29 cm. (Collection de documents inédits sur l'histoire de France. Series III [i.e., VI] v. 18)

A year-by-year record of building expenses and related matters in connection with art enterprises of the French crown. Contents: v. 1, 1664–1680; v. 2, 1681–1687; v. 3, 1688–1697; v. 4, 1696–1705; v. 5, 1706–1715.

Each volume has its own list of artists included, and an alphabetical index.

2090

Historical sources for the study of Flemish art . . . [Antwerp, De Sikkel, 1931–49] v. 1–5. plates, facsims., geneal. tables. 26 cm.

First 4 v. issued in both Dutch and English editions; v. 5 in Dutch only.

Contents: (1) Denucé, Jean. Art-export in the 17th century in Antwerp, 1931; (2) Denucé, Jean. The Antwerp art-galleries: inventories of the art-collections in Antwerp in the 16th and 17th centuries, 1932; (3) Denucé, Jean. Letters and documents concerning Jan Bruegel I and II, 1934; (4) Denucé, Jean. Antwerp art-tapestry and trade, 1936; (5) Denucé, Jean. Documenten uit den kunsthandel te Antwerpen in de XVIIe eeuw van Mattijs Musson.

2091

Knögel, Elsmarie. Schriftquellen zur Kunstgeschichte der Merowingerzeit. Darmstadt, Wittich'sche Hofbuchdruckerei, 1936. 258 p. 28 cm.

Also appeared in Bonner Jahrbücher *Jahrbücher des Vereins von Altertumsfreunden im Rheinlande* (Darmstadt, 1936, Hft. 140/141, 1. T., p. 1–258).

A valuable collection of documents or texts relating to Merovingian art, covering the years 500–750. Includes 60 pages of introductory text.

"Abkürzungen" p. 229–30. "Alphabetisches Verzeichnis der ausgezogenen Quellen" p. 230–36. "Verzeichnis der wichtigeren allgemeinen Literatur" p. 237.

"Register zur Textsammlung" p. 238–58, divided into: "Personennamen" p. 238–44; "Ortsnamen" p. 245–52; "Sachregister und Glossar" p. 252–58.

2092

Leblond, Victor. L'art et les artistes en Ile-de-France au XVI siècle (Beauvais & Beauvaisis) d'après les minutes notariales; avec 7 phototypies et 80 marques, signatures et monogrammes. Paris, Champion, 1921. 352 p. plates, facsim. 26 cm.

Contains more than 400 documents relating to the art and artists of the region: art fairs, contracts of apprenticeship of master masons, painters, image carvers, glassworkers, bell casters, embroiderers, organ makers, and clockmakers.

Signatures, marks, and monograms are on seven plates at the end. Bibliographic footnotes. Iconographic index p. 312–14. "Table" p. 315–52.

2093

Lehmann-Brockhaus, Otto, ed. Lateinische Schriftquellen zur Kunst in England, Wales und Schottland vom Jahre 901 bis zum Jahre 1307. München, Prestelverlag, 1955–(58). v. 1–(4). 24 cm. (Veröffentlichungen des Zentralinstituts für Kunstgeschichte in München, 1)

To be complete in 5 v. A collection of Latin sources for art in England, Wales, and Scotland from 901 to 1307. Sources comprise passages from chronicles, registers, etc. Pipe rolls, plea rolls, wills, and sources written after 1500 have been excluded.

Contents: Bd. 1, Quellen in topographischer Ordnung, A–K (nr. 1–2248); Bd. 2, Quellen in topographischer Ordnung, L–Z (nr. 2249–5072); Bd. 3, Quellen, die sich topographisch nicht einordnen lassen (nr. 5073–6773); Bd. 4, Quellennachweis, geographisches Register, Personenregister. Includes bibliographical references.

2094

Lehmann-Brockhaus, Otto. . . . Schriftquellen zur Kunstgeschichte des 11. und 12. Jahrhunderts für Deutschland, Lothringen und Italien . . . Berlin, Deutscher Verein für Kunstwissenschaft, 1938. 2 v. 24 cm.

Contains 3062 documents arranged according to medium, covering Germany, Lothringen, and Italy for the years 1002–1190. Contents: [v. 1] Text; [v. 2] Register. "Quellen-nachweis," [v. 2, p. 1]–54. Volume 2 also contains indexes of places, persons, saints and heathen gods, and subjects.

2095

Loewy, Emanuel. Inschriften griechischer Bildhauer mit Facsimiles. Gedruckt mit Unterstützung der Kaiserlichen Akademie der Wissenschaften zu Wien. Leipzig, B. G. Teubner, 1885. 410 p. illus., facsims., fold. tab. 30 cm.

For many years the standard work on inscriptions on Greek sculpture. Arranged chronologically by centuries and then geographically.

"Bibliographisches Register" p. [xxvii]–xxxvii. Artist index in Greek letters at the end.

2096

Marcadé, Jean. Recueil des signatures des sculpteurs grecs. Paris, Boccard, 1953–(57). v. 1–(2). illus., plates. 29 cm.

At head of title: "École française d'Athènes." Issued in portfolio form.

A modern attempt to replace Loewy (2095). It intends to give for each artist the sum of epigraphical testimony and a résumé of literary sources. Arranged alphabetically by name of artist. Volume 1 contains artists whose work at Delphi is proven by epigraphy. Volume 2 covers Delos.

2097

Milanesi, Gaetano. Documenti per la storia dell'arte senese, raccolti ed illustrati dal dott. Gaetano Milanesi . . . Siena, Porri, 1854–56. 3 v. 23 cm.

Documents concerning Sienese art. Contents: (1) Secoli XIII e XIV; (2) Secoli XV e XVI; (3) Secolo XVI. At end of v. 3 an index of the artists mentioned in the documents and notes (p. 353–420).

2098

Milanesi, Gaetano. Nuovi documenti per la storia dell'arte toscana dal XII al XV secolo raccolti e annotati da G. Milanese. Firenze, Dotti, 1901. 176 p. 23 cm.

Printed in an edition of 100 copies. A group of documents covering Tuscan art of the 12th to the 15th century, gathered by Milanesi in doing research for his edition of Vasari, mostly from the Archivio de' Contratti, Florence.

No index or table of contents.

2099

Mortet, Victor. Recueil de textes relatifs à l'histoire de l'architecture et à la condition des architectes en France, au moyen âge, publié avec une Introduction, des Notes, un Glossaire et un Répertoire archéologique . . . Paris, Picard, 1911. 515 p. 23 cm. (Collection de textes pour servir à l'étude et à l'enseignement de l'histoire [44])

A collection of texts concerning the history of architecture and the condition of architects in France in the Middle Ages. Documents are arranged chronologically covering the 11th and 12th centuries.

Appendix contains alphabetical indexes of persons, places, and archaeological material, and a glossary.

2100

Mortet, Victor, and Deschamps, Paul. Recueil de textes relatifs à l'histoire de l'architecture et à la condition des architectes en France, au moyen âge, XIe–XIIIe siècles . . . Paris, Picard, 1929. 407 p. 22 cm. (Collection de textes pour servir à l'étude et à l'enseignement de l'histoire [51])

A companion volume to Mortet above (2099).

2101

Müntz, Eugène. . . . Les arts à la cour des papes: Innocent VIII, Alexandre VI, Pie III (1484–1502); recueil de documents inédits ou peu connus, publié sous les auspices de l'Académie des Inscriptions et Belles-Lettres . . . Ouvrage accompagné de 10 planches tirées à part et de 94 gravures dans le texte. Paris, Ernest Leroux, éditeur, 1898. 303 p. incl. 14 plates. illus., 9 plates. 29 cm.

At head of title: Fondation Eugène Piot.

Documents concerning the arts of the papal court, arranged by name of the reigning pope and then by the medium. Alphabetical index of artists and monuments p. 293–99. Table of contents p. 301–03.

2102

Müntz, Eugène. Les arts à la cour des papes; nouvelles recherches sur les pontificats de Martin V, d'Eugène IV, de Nicolas V, de Calixte III, de Pie II et de Paul II. Rome, Imprimerie de la Paix de Philippe Cuggiani, 1884. 88 p. 25 cm.

From *Mélanges d'archéologie et d'histoire*, 1881–82, 1884–85, published by L'École Française de Rome.

Arranged chronologically. No index.

2103

Müntz, Eugène. . . . Les arts à la cour des papes pendant le XVe et le XVIe siècles; recueil de documents inédits tirés des archives et des bibliothèques romains . . . Paris, E. Thorin, 1878–82. 3 v. plates. 25 cm.

A collection of documents from the archives and libraries of Rome concerning the arts of the papal court, arranged chronologically by name of pope and then by monument or medium.

Contents: pt. 1, Martin V–Pie II, 1417–1467 (1878); pt. 2, Paul II, 1464–1471 (1879); pt. 3, Sixte IV–Léon X, 1471–1521: sect. 1, Sixte IV (1882).

Table of contents at end of each volume.

2104

Orbaan, Johannes Albertus Franciscus. Documenti sul barocco in Roma. Roma, nella sede della Società, 1920. clxvi, 659 p. 7 plates. 24 cm. (R. Società Romana di Storia Patria. Miscellanea [v. 6])

A collection of documents concerning Baroque art in Rome. Contents: Introduzione p. v–clxvi; Il diario del cerimoniere (anni 1605–62) p. 1–38; La Roma di Paolo V negli Avvisi p. 39–272; Notizie sulla vita artistica e intellettuale p. 273–91; La depositoria generale p. 293–361; Viaggio de pontefici p. 365–486; Appendice. Collezioni romane d'arte p. 489–522.

Indexes: "Indice dei nomi delle persone" p. 525–68; "Indice delle materie" p. 569–606; "Indice topografico" p. 607–59.

2105

Overbeck, Johannes. Die antiken Schriftquellen zur Geschichte der bildenden Künste bei den Griechen. Leipzig, Engelmann, 1868. 488 p. 24 cm.

Reprinted Hildesheim, 1958.

A collection of original documents relating to the history of fine arts in Greek times, which aims at completeness. No translations or commentary. Index of artists p. 477–88.

2106

Paris. Châtelet. . . . Artistes parisiens du XVIe et du XVIIe siècles; donations, contracts de mariage, testaments, inventaires etc. tirés des insinuations du Châtelet de Paris, publiés et annotés par Jules Guiffrey. Paris, Imprimerie Nationale, 1915. 379 p. 35 cm. (Histoire générale de Paris; collection de documents publiée sous les auspices de l'Édilité parisienne)

Archival materials on Parisian artists of the 16th and 17th centuries. Contents: (1) Les maîtres jurés saisies, élections, pièces diverses (1454–1581); (2) Les peintres (1534–1650); (3) Les sculpteurs (1521–1650); (4) Les tailleurs d'antiques (1571–1622); (5) Les fondeurs en sable (1543–1604); (6) Les architectes (1454–1647); (7) Les tapissiers (1519–1620); (8) Les graveurs en taille-douce (1560–1646); (9) Les graveurs de sceaux, de monnaies et de pierres fines (1454–1620); (10) Les peintres verriers (1534–1648); (11) Artistes divers—brodeurs, doreurs sur fer et sur cuivre, menuisiers en ébane, pâtenotriers en émail, jardiniers. "Table alphabétique" p. 323–79.

2107

Pinchart, Alexandre. Archives des arts, sciences et lettres; documents inédits . . . Gand, Hebbelynck, 1860–81. 3 v. plates (part col.) 23 cm.

Volume 3 has imprint; Gand, Vanderhaeghen.

A collection of documents relating to artists, etc., listed according to some 100 categories. Index at end of each volume, referring only to material in that volume.

2108

Pollak, Oskar. Die Kunsttätigkeit unter Urban VIII. Aus dem Nachlass hrsg. von Dagobert Frey unter Mitwirkung von Franz Juraschek. Wien, B. Filser, 1928. v. 1. 25 cm. (Quellenschriften zur Geschichte der Barockkunst in Rom)

A collection of selections from documents regarding the churches, palaces, etc. built under the pontificate of Urban VIII, arranged by type of monument.

Contents: Bd. 1, Kirchliche Bauten (mit Ausnahme von St. Peter) und Paläste. Indexes in v. 1: "Personenverzeichnis" p. 451–59; "Verzeichnis der benützten Archive und Bände" p. 460–79.

2109

Raccolta di fonti per la storia dell'arte . . . Firenze, Sansoni [1936–(50)]. v. 1–(7) in (8). plates. 24 cm.

Directed by Mario Salmi. A series of volumes which contain documents and reprints of sources concerning Italian art.

Contents: (1) Gronau, Giorgio. Documenti artistici urbinati; (2) Giannotti, Donato. Dialogi; (3) Emert, Giulio Benedetto. Fonti manoscritte inedite per la storia dell'arte nel Trentino; (4) Baroni, Costantino. Documenti per la storia dell'architettura a Milano nel rinascimento e nel barocco; (5) Francheschi, Pietro di Benedetto dei. De prospectiva pingendi, edizione critica a cura di Nicco Fasola (with atlas of 49 plates); (6) Filippini, Francesco. Miniatori e pittori a Bologna; documenti dei secoli XIII e XIV; (7) Alberti, Leone Battista. Della pittura; edizione critica, a cura di Luigi Mallè.

2110

Rambaud, Mireille. Les sources de l'histoire de l'art aux Archives nationales . . . avec une étude sur les sources de l'histoire de l'art aux Archives de la Seine par Georges Bailhache et Michel Fleury; avant-propos de Charles Braiband. Paris, Imprimerie Nationale, 1955. 173 p. 25 cm.

At head of title: Ministère de l'éducation nationale. Direction des archives.

A guide which intends to aid the art historian's research, not a repertory of art archives. Covers architecture, urbanism, plastic and decorative arts, theater, music, and dance.

Contents: I, Documents écrits; II, Documents iconographiques; III, Les sources de l'histoire de l'art aux Archives de la Seine. Index p. 161–73.

2111

Rathgeber, Georg. Annalen der niederländischen Malerei, Formschneide- und Kupferstecherkunst . . . Gotha, Müller, 1844. 5 pts. in 1 v. 34 cm.

A collection of documentary and other information about artists and their work, arranged chronologically, with references to previous literary work.

Contents: (1) Von den Brüdern Van Eyck bis zu Albrecht Dürers Anwesenheit in den Niederlanden; (2) Von Albrecht Dürers Anwesenheit in den Niederlanden bis zu Frans Floris Tod; (3) Von Frans Floris Tod bis zu Peter Paul Rubens Abreise nach Italien; (4) Von Peter Paul Rubens Abreise nach Italien bis auf Rubens Tod; (5) Von Rubens Tod bis auf Rembrandts Tod.

Parts 1–3, 4–5 paged separately.

2112

Reinach, Adolph Joseph. Recueil Milliet; textes grecs et latins relatifs à l'histoire de la peinture ancienne, pub., tr. et commentés, sous le patronage de l'Association des études grecques. . . . Avant-propos par S. Reinach . . . Paris, C. Klincksieck, 1921. v. 1. 25 cm.

Rev. and prepared for publication by Salomon Reinach. A collection of Greek and Latin texts concerning ancient painting. Old but still used.

Alphabetical index of painters mentioned p. 423–25. "Table des matières" p. 427–29.

2113

Richter, Jean Paul. Quellen der byzantinischen Kunstgeschichte. Ausgewählte Texte über die Kirchen, Klöster, Paläste, Staatsgebäude und andere Bauten von Konstantinopel . . . Wien, C. Graeser, 1897. 432 p. 23 cm. (Quellenschriften [für Kunstgeschichte] . . . n[eue] F[olge] VIII. Bd.)

"Sonder-Ausgabe aus Eitelberger-Ilgs Quellenschriften."

A collection of excerpts from documents dealing with Byzantine monuments, arranged chronologically and subdivided by monuments.

"Inhaltsverzeichnis" p. ix–xxiv. "Verzeichnis der benützten Schriftsteller" p. xxv–xxxix. "Chronologie der byzantinischen Kaiser" p. li–liii. Index p. 421–32.

2114

Rott, Hans. Quellen und Forschungen zur südwestdeutschen und schweizerischen Kunstgeschichte im XV. und XVI. Jahrhundert . . . Stuttgart, Strecker und Schröder, 1933–38. 3 v. in 6. illus., plates. 29 cm.

Sources and commentary dealing with southwest German and Swiss art history in the 15th and 16th centuries. Contents: Bd. 1A (Quellen), B (Text): Bodenseegebiet; Bd. 2 (Quellen und Text): Altschwaben und die Reichsstädte; Bd. 3A & B (Quellen), C (Text): Baden, Pfalz, Elsass, Schweiz (called Oberrhein on title page).

Bibliographical footnotes. Volume 3C contains a general index of artists by Gustav Rommel, p. 275–368, subdivided according to medium in which the artist worked. Other volumes have person and place indexes.

✓ **2115**

Schlosser, Julius, *Ritter* von. Quellenbuch zur Kunstgeschichte des abendländischen Mittelalters. Ausgewählte Texte des vierten bis fünfzehnten Jahrhunderts, gesammelt von Julius von Schlosser. Mit vier Abbildungen im Text . . . Wien, C. Graeser, 1896. 406 p. diagrs. 23 cm. (Quellenschriften für Kunstgeschichte . . . neue Folge, VII. Bd.) "Sonder-Ausgabe aus Eitelberger-Ilgs Quellenschriften."

A collection of excerpts from documents covering Western art from the early Christian period to the 15th century. Contents: I, Christliches Altertum und frühes Mittelalter; II, Hohes Mittelalter; III, Vierzehntes und fünfzehntes Jahrhundert.

Indexes: (1) Verzeichnis der Autoren p. 388–89; (2) Ortsregister p. 389–92; (3) Sachregister p. 392–94; (4) Verzeichnis der Künstlernamen p. 395; (5) Verzeichnis der technischen Ausdrücke p. 396–406.

2116

Schlosser, Julius, *Ritter* von. Schriftquellen zur Geschichte der karolingischen Kunst. Gesammelt und erläutert von Julius Schlosser . . . Wien, C. Graeser, 1896. 482 p. 23 cm. (Quellenschriften für Kunstgeschichte . . . neue Folge, IV. Bd . . . 1892) "Sonder-Ausgabe aus Eitelberger-Ilgs Quellenschriften."

A collection of excerpts from documents dealing with Carolingian art. Contents: Quellenverzeichnis p. ix–xvi; I, Architektur und Kleinkunst; II, Malerei und Plastik; III, Anhang: (1) Notizen über einzelne Künstler etc.; (2) Die Antike in karolingischer Zeit.

Indexes: (1) Ortsregister p. 445–51; (2) Sach- und Personenregister p. 452–63; (3) Heiligenverzeichnis p. 463–68; (4) Künstlernamen p. 469; (5) Glossarium der technischen Ausdrücke p. 470–82.

2117

Seville. Universidad. Laboratorio de Arte. . . . Documentos para la historia del arte en Andalucía. Sevilla, Facultad de Filosofia y Letras, 1927–(46). 10 v. 25 cm.

A series of monographs dealing with art in Andalusia, each of which has indexes of persons, places, and subjects.

Contents: v. 1–2, Documentos varios, 1927–28, 2 v.; v. 3, Sancho Corbacho, Heliodoro. Arte sevillano de los siglos XVI y XVII . . . 1931; v. 4, Muro Orejon, Antonio. Artifices sevillanos de los siglos XVI y XVII, 1932; v. 5, Bago y Quintanilla, Miguel de. Arquitectos, escultores y pintores sevillanos del siglo XVII, 1936; v. 6, Hernández Díaz, José. Arte y artistas del renascimiento en Sevilla, 1933; v. 7, Sancho Corbacho, Heliodoro. Arquitectura sevillana del siglo XVIII . . . 1934; v. 8, Muro Orejon, Antonio. Pintores y doradores . . . 1935; v. 9, Hernández Díaz, José. Arte hispalense de los siglos XV y XVI, 1937; v. 10, Marin, Enrique Respeto. Artifices gaditanos del siglo XVII, 1946.

2118

Troescher, Georg. Kunst- und Künstlerwanderungen in Mitteleuropa 800–1800; Beiträge zur Kenntnis des deutsch-französisch-niederländischen Kunstaustausches. Baden-Baden, Verlag für Kunst und Wissenschaft, 1953–54. 2 v. 23 cm.

A collection of documentary references to the activities and influence of German art and artists in France and the Netherlands (v. 1), and of French and Netherlandish art and artists in the German-speaking countries, i.e., Germany, Switzerland, Austria (v. 2), arranged by the places in which these exchanges occurred, chronologically within the place. Thoroughly indexed. "Schrifttumsverzeichnis" v. 1, p. xiii–xviii.

2119

Wildenstein, Georges. Rapports d'experts, 1712–1791; procès-verbaux d'expertises d'oeuvres d'art extraits du fonds du Châtelet, aux Archives Nationales, publiés par Georges Wildenstein. Paris, Les Beaux-Arts, 1921. 11 p., 170 columns, p. 174–186. 33 cm. (Études et documents pour servir à l'histoire de l'art français du dix-huitième siècle [no.2])

Accounts of the appraisement of works of art, culled from the Châtelet and the National Archives.

Contents: Introduction; Texte des rapports p. 1–172; Table des parties cités dans les rapports d'experts non publiés p. 173–79;

Table des matières contenues dans les rapports d'experts publiés p. 180–86.

Bibliography, p. [xii], is in "Table des abbréviations contenues dans les notes."

2120

Zarco del Valle, Manuel Remón. Documentos inéditos para la historia de las bellas artes en España. Madrid, Impr. de la Viuda de Calero, 1870. 438 p. facsims. 23 cm. (Publicado en los Documentos inéditos para la historia de España, LV)

Edition of 58 copies. A collection of documents relating to the history of Spanish art.

"Colección de pintores, escultores y arquitectos desconocidos, sacada de instrumentos antiguos y auténticos, por el r.p.m. fray Agustin de Arques Jover" p. [5]–112. Index of artists p. 429–38.

SEE ALSO: Archives de l'art français (2146, 2147); Nouvelles archives de l'art français (2295); Société de l'Histoire de l'Art Français, Paris. *Bulletin* (2340).

CHAPTER 18 | # Periodicals

THE FOLLOWING ALPHABETICAL LIST of 250 periodicals (museum bulletins have been omitted) attempts to include the outstanding titles for art research. Contrary to the usual form followed in this book, illustrations and plates have not been indicated in the collation, as almost all art periodicals are illustrated. The few exceptions are noted in the commentaries. Instead of the usual open-entry form for current periodicals, the last completed volume prior to January, 1958, has been indicated in parentheses, to give a better indication of the number of volumes which have been issued. In the case of a periodical which has ceased publication, the entry is closed and the parentheses omitted. Because libraries vary in their methods of binding periodicals, no attempt has been made to list the total number of volumes of each title.

Periodicals frequently change publishers. In this list the publisher given is usually the current one, or, in the case of an out-of-print title, the publisher who covered the longest span. Changes are indicated in the notes, but in case of frequent changes not all are listed. All changes of title, however, are indicated in the notes and are listed in the Index.

An attempt has been made to indicate where the various periodicals have been indexed. Inclusive dates of indexing are indicated for the *Art Index,* but dates are not indicated for other indexes. For abbreviations of names of indexes see list below.

Ann. mag. subj. ind.: Annual magazine subject index

B. d. d. Z.: Bibliographie der deutschen Zeitschriftenliteratur

B. d. f. Z.: Bibliographie der fremdsprachigen Zeitschriftenliteratur

Bibl. de Belgique: Bibliographie de Belgique

Can. index: Canadian periodical index

Catholic index: Catholic periodical index

Dansk tids.-index: Dansk tidsskrift-index

Eng. index: Engineering index

Hague. K. Bibl.: Hague. Koninklijke Bibliotheek. *Repertorium op de Nederlandsche tijdschriften*

Ind. arts index: Industrial arts index

Int. index: International index to periodicals

Italy. Parl. Cam. dei Deputati. Bibl.: Italy. Parlamento. Camera dei Deputati. Biblioteca. *Catalogo metodico degli scritti contenuti nelle pubblicazioni periodiche italiane e straniere*

Italy. Prov. Gen. dello Stato: Italy. Provveditorato Generale dello Stato. *Pubblicazioni edite dallo stato o col suo concorso*

Nijhoff: Nijhoff's Index op de Nederlandsche periodieken van algemeenen inhoud

P. A. I. S.: Public affairs information service. Bulletin of the Public Affairs Information Service

Poole's: Poole's Index to periodical literature

Readers' guide: Readers' guide to periodical literature

Rep. bibl.: Répertoire bibliographique des principales revues françaises

Rev. of revs.: Review of reviews

Subj. ind. to pers.: Subject index to periodicals

2121

Académie des Inscriptions et Belles-Lettres (Institut de France), Paris. Comptes-rendus des séances, 1–8, 1857–64; n.s., v. 1–7, 1865–71; s. 3, v. 1, 1872; s. 4, v. 1–27, 1873–99; s. 5, v. 1– , 1900–(56). Paris, Durand, 1857–(1956). 23 cm.

Monthly, with some variation. Contains various papers on art subjects, i.e., objects in the Louvre, architectural monuments, etc. Indexed in *B. d. f. Z.* and *Rép. bibl.*

———. Table des années 1857–1900. Dressée par M. G. Ledos. Paris, Picard, 1906. 232 p.

———. Table des années 1901–1930. Dressée par M. Fr. Renie. Paris, Picard, 1934. 229 p.

2122

Académie des Inscriptions et Belles-Lettres, Paris. Commission de la Fondation Piot. Monuments et mémoires publiés par l'Académie des Inscriptions et Belles-Lettres, t. 1–(49). Paris, Presses Universitaires de France, 1894–(1957). 36 cm.

Yearly through v. 47. Volume 48 covers 1954–56. Prior to 1940 published by E. Leroux. Lengthy, scholarly articles on ancient, Byzantine, medieval, and Renaissance art, with particular emphasis on archaeology. An index covering 1894–1913 is included in t. 20, pt. 2. In *Art index,* v. 29, pt. 2–v. 36, v. 40– . Also indexed in *B. d. f. Z.; Int. index.*

2123

Accademia Romana di Archeologia, Rome. Atti della Pontificia Accademia Romana di Archeologia, ser. 1–2, 30 v., 1821–1921; ser. 3, Memorie, v. 1–8, no. 3, 1923–48; ser. 3, Rendiconti, v. 1–(28), 1921/23–(55/56). Roma, Tip. Poliglotta Vaticana, 1821–(1957). 29–31 cm.

Annual, with some variation. Publisher varies. Ser. 1, v. 1–4, known as *Atti della Pontificia Accademia. . .* ; v. 5–15 and ser. 2, v. 1–15 called *Dissertazione . . .* Ser. 3, called *Memorie della Pontificia Accademia . . .* (36 cm.), and *Rendiconti* (26 cm.), have at head of title: *Atti della Pontificia Accademia . . . ser. III.* Useful primarily for articles on early Christian art, especially reports on recent excavations. Indexes: Ser. 1–3, 1821–1923; *Indice generale dal 1821 al 1938* in v. 14 of *Rendiconti. Rendiconti* is indexed in *B. d. f. Z.*

2124

Africa italiana; rivista di storia e d'arte a cura del Ministero delle Colonie, v. 1–8, 1927–Sept. 1941. Bergamo, Istituto Italiano d'Arti Grafiche, 1927–41. 28 cm.

Quarterly. None published 1936–39. Scholarly, well-illustrated articles on art and archaeology of the region. Reviews are included in first four volumes. Indexed in *Italy. Prov. Gen. dello Stato; Italy. Parl. Cam. dei Deputati. Bibl.; B. d. f. Z.*

2125

American Academy in Rome. Memoirs, v. 1–(25). Rome, Am. Academy, 1917–(57). 37 cm. Annual.

Continues the *Supplementary papers* of the American School of Classical Studies in Rome. Scholarly articles on work in progress; some volumes are monographs. In *Art index,* v. 7, 1929– . Also indexed in *B. d. f. Z.*

2126

The American architect, v. 1–152, 1876–Feb. 1938. N.Y., Hearst Magazines, Inc. [1876–1938]. 32–35 cm.

Monthly; frequency varies. Title varies; merged with *Architectural record,* March 1938. Publisher varies; v. 1–84 published in Boston by Ticknor. Short articles on all aspects of American architecture. Short book reviews. In *Art index,* v. 136–152. Also indexed in *Ind. arts index; B. d. f. Z.; Subj. ind. to pers.; Poole's.*

Besides the regular edition the following were issued with additional plates: Gelatine ed., 1885–88; Imperial ed., March 1886–Dec. 1899; International ed., 1890–1908.

———. Decennial index of the photolithographic and other illustrations, v. 1, 1876–85. Boston, Ticknor, 1888. 22 cm.

2127

American Institute of Architects. Journal, v. 1–(28). Washington, D. C., The Octagon [1944–(57)]. 20–29 cm. Monthly.

Preceded by *The Octagon,* a journal of the American Institute of Architects. As the official organ of the Institute, it contains short articles on various pertinent subjects and news notes in the field. Very brief book reviews. Indexed in *Art index; B. d. f. Z.; Ind. arts index; Subj. ind. to pers.*

2128

American journal of archaeology, ser. 1, v. 1–11, 1885–96; ser. 2, v. 1–(61), 1897–(1957). Cambridge, Mass., Archaeol. Institute of America, 1885–(1957). 24–27 cm.

Quarterly; frequency varies. Publisher and place vary. The journal of the Archaeological Institute of America, and as such contains articles on the latest discoveries being made. Section of plates at end of each volume. Signed reviews; from 1899–1931 contained an annual bibliography of archaeological literature. Volumes 1–54 contain summaries of original articles in current periodicals, superseded in v. 55–56 by "Archaeological bibliography": brief descriptions of recent publications, grouped according to area treated. Some volumes have lists of abbreviations of periodicals and societies, as used in the *Journal.* Indexed in *Art index,* v. 33– ; *Rev. of revs.; Poole's; Int. index; Subj. ind. to pers.; B. d. f. Z.*

————. Index . . . volumes I–X; with an appendix for v. XI. [Princeton] Princeton Univ. Press, 1899. 166 p. 26 cm.

————. Index to vols. I–X [2d ser.], 1897–1906. N.Y., Macmillan; London, Macmillan [1908]. 285 p. 24 cm.

2129
L'Ami des monuments et des arts parisiens et français. . . , v. 1–24. Paris, Comité des Monuments Français, 1887–1910. 26 cm.

Bimonthly; frequency varies. Articles deal with the study and protection of "monuments historiques" in France and elsewhere. From 1900– , includes proceedings of the Société des Amis des Monuments Parisiens. Contains brief unsigned reviews. Indexed in *B. d. f. Z.; Rép. bibl.*

2130
L'Amour de l'art, v. 1–32, mai 1920–53. Paris, Cercle français d'art, 1920–53. 31–38 cm.

Monthly, with some irregularities. Publisher varies. In 1933 and 1934 issued in two parts. In 1933 pt. 1, *Histoire de l'art contemporain,* consists of detailed chapters, universal in scope, written by specialists. Good biographies and bibliographies at end of each chapter. Part 2, *Bulletin mensuel* (comprising *L'Amour de l'art*). In 1934 pt. 1 comprised *Formes* and *L'Amour de l'art;* pt. 2 called *Revue mensuelle.* Volume 20, nos. 1–6, fév.-juil. 1939 have title *Prométhée. L'Amour de l'art n.s.* Suspended 1940–avr. 1945 (and v. 21–24 omitted in numbering). Covers all aspects and eras of art, especially modern. Well illustrated. From 1947– each issue is devoted to a special subject, e.g., Leonardo, Egypt, the Cinema. Signed reviews and notes on exhibitions, sales, etc. Oct. 1927–jan. 1952, short English summaries of articles appeared as supplements. In *Art index,* v. 15–20, nos. 9–10.

√**2131**
Annales archéologiques, t. 1–27, mai 1844–72; t. 28, 1881. Paris, Librairie Archéologique de Didron, 1844–81. 27 cm. Annual.

Suspended 1873–80. Treats medieval (mainly French) and Byzantine art and archaeology, with much emphasis on iconography. Contains a few color plates. Bibliographical notes. Index, t. 1–27: "Table analytique et méthodique" in t. 28.

2132
Apollo; the magazine of the arts for connoisseurs and collectors, v. 1–(66). London [1925–(57)]. 31 cm. Monthly.

Publisher varies. Subtitle varies. Articles on shows, collections, and single works of art. Has brief notes of events in the art world and sales, and currently a section "Views and news of art in America." Good color plates. Signed short reviews. In *Art index,* v. 9- . Also indexed in *B. d. f. Z.; Subj. ind. to pers.*

2133
Archaeologia; or miscellaneous tracts relating to antiquity, v. 1–(96). Oxford, Society of Antiquaries of London, 1770–(1955). 28–31 cm.

Annual. Volumes 1–61 published in London. Volumes 51– also called 2d ser., v. 1– . Treats archaeology in general, but especially Greek, Roman, and British, with some consideration of medieval and later subjects. Archival material frequently printed. Indexed in *Poole's; B. d. f. Z.; Subj. ind. to pers.*

————. Index to the first fifteen volumes . . . London, 1809. 290 p. 28 cm.

————. An index to Archaeologia . . . Volume XVI. to Volume XXX. inclusive . . . London, 1844. 309 p. 28 cm.

————. Index: v. 1–50. London, 1889. 806 p. 31 cm.

√**2134**
The Archaeological journal, v. 1–(113), March 1844–(1956). London, Royal Archaeological Institute of Gt. Brit. and Ireland, 1845–(1957). 22–24 cm.

Annual; frequency varies. Volumes 51–86 also called 2d ser., v. 1–36. Articles on archaeology and medieval art of Britain. Contains reviews and proceedings of meetings of the Institute. Indexed in *B. d. f. Z.; Subj. ind. to pers.*

————. Index: v. 1–25. London, 1878. 303 p. 23 cm.

2135
Archaeologische Mitteilungen aus Iran, Bd. 1–9, 1929–Sept. 1938. Berlin, Reimer, 1929–38. 25 cm.

Irregular. All articles written by Ernst

Herzfeld. Scholarly treatment of ancient art and texts of the Near East. Clear illustrations, maps, and charts. Some French articles included. Indexed in *B. d. d. Z.*

―――. Erster Ergänzungsband. Altpersische Inschriften. Berlin, Reimer, 1938. 384 p. 27 cm.

Old Persian texts compiled by Ernst Herzfeld. Index (glossary) by language. Section of clear reproductions of inscriptions at end of volume.

2136

Archaeology: a magazine dealing with the antiquity of the world, v. 1–(10), March 1948–(57). Cincinnati, Ohio, Archaeological Institute of America, c1948–(57). 27 cm.

Quarterly. Volumes 1–7 published in Cambridge, Mass. Fairly short articles, with somewhat popular approach, and brief news notes of activities in the field. Signed reviews. Indexed in *Art index.*

2137

Archaiologike ephemeris . . . [per. I] okt. 1837–60; per. II, v. 1–17, 1862–74; per. III, 1883–1915; 1916–(53/54). Athens, 1837–(1954). 32 cm.

1837–60, 1883–1909 have title: *Ephemeris archaiologike.* Subtitle varies. Not numbered in series after 1916. Not published July 1843–Oct. 1852, 1863–68, 1871, 1873, 1875–82. Written entirely in Greek, on Greek art and archaeology. Announcements of new books in the field (in various languages), and signed reviews. Indexed in *B. d. f. Z.*

2138

Architectural forum . . . v. 1–(107). N.Y., Time, inc. [1892–(1957)]. 30–35 cm.

Monthly. Publisher and place of publication vary. Volumes 1–25 have title: *The Brickbuilder;* subtitle varies. Absorbed *The Architects' world* Oct. 1938. From Jan. 1952 published as one of two parts (called editions) of *The Magazine of building;* sister publication of *House & home.* Both parts issued in one cover as sections of *Architectural forum, the magazine of building,* Dec. 1951. Articles emphasize actual construction and engineering of all types of buildings except homes. Some short reviews in more recent issues. In *Art index,* v. 51, July 1929– . Also indexed in *Ind. arts index; Eng. index; P. A. I. S.; Subj. ind. to pers.; B. d. f. Z.; Ann. mag. subj. ind.*

2139

The Architectural record; an illustrated monthly magazine of architecture and the allied arts and crafts, v. 1–(122), July 1891–(1957). N.Y., The Record and Guide [etc.] [1892–(1957)]. 25–27 cm.

Quarterly, July 1891–Apr. 1902; monthly, May 1902– . Subtitle varies; dropped with v. 71. Incorporated *The American architect and architecture* March 1938. Articles emphasize actual construction. In more recent issues there is a running series "Building types study," each issue being devoted to a particular type. *Great American architects series,* no. 1–6, May 1895–July 1899, issued at irregular intervals as extra nos. of the periodical (N.Y., The Archit. Record Co., 1895–99. 6 v. in 1. 25 cm.). In *Art index,* v. 66, July 1929– . Also indexed in *Readers' guide; Ind. arts index; B. d. f. Z.; P. A. I. S.; Subj. ind. to pers.; Poole's; Rev. of revs.; Eng. index.*

―――. Index; 1891–1906. N.Y., 1907. 16 p. 26 cm.

2140

The Architectural review, v. 1–(122), Nov. 1896–(1957). London, 1897–(1957). 33–35 cm. Monthly.

Title, vol. 1–11: *The Architectural review for the artist & craftsman.* Subtitle varies.

Discussions of recent architecture, as well as of great monuments of the past and on architectural theory, are supplemented by shorter notes pertaining to contemporary architectural developments. World-wide in scope, but with definite emphasis on England.

There are signed book reviews, and notes on exhibitions.

Richly illustrated.

Indexed in *Art index,* v. 66– ; in *Brit. subj. index;* and *B. d. f. Z.*

2141

The Architectural review, v. 1–16; v. 17, no. 1–4, Nov. 2, 1891–Apr. 1910; v. 18–[28] (n.s., v. 1–13), Jan. 1912–July 1921. Boston [Bates, Kimball & Guild, etc.] 1891–1921. 35 cm.

Eight numbers a year, Nov. 1891–Dec. 1898; monthly, Jan. 1899– . Publication suspended May 1910–Dec. 1911 and Apr. 1914–Aug. 1915. Publisher and place vary. Combined with *American architect* Aug. 31, 1921 under title *The American architect and the architectural review.* Supersedes *Technology architectural review.* A well-illustrated general architectural periodical similar in format to *International studio.*

2142

Architecture, v. 1–73, Jan. 1900–May 1936. N.Y., Scribner [c1900–36] 33 cm.

Monthly. Published by Forbes & Co., Ltd., 1900–17. Volumes 1–10 also numbered as whole nos. 1–60. Combined with *American architect* June 1936. Emphasis is on architecture in America. Richly illustrated, especially with photographs of New York City buildings. Occasional short book reviews. Index issued for every two volumes. In *Art index*, v. 59–Jan. 1936. Also indexed in *Ind. arts index; Subj. ind. to pers.; Ann. mag. subj. ind.*

2143

L'Architecture d'aujourd'hui, année 1–(28). [Boulogne (Seine), 1930–(57)]. 32 cm.

Monthly. Articles on contemporary architecture throughout the world; sometimes an entire issue is devoted to a specific subject. Includes sections: "Bibliographie" and "Revue des revues." Extensively illustrated, and has some English summaries. In *Art index*, v. 19– . Also indexed in *B. d. f. Z.*

2144

L'Architecture française; l'architecture–urbanisme–décoration, no. 1–(183/84). Paris, 1940–(57). 31 cm.

Monthly. "Organe de la reconstruction française." Most numbers are devoted to a special aspect of architecture: shops, hospitals, homes, etc. Some few short book reviews. Indexed in *B. d. f. Z.*

2145

L'Architettura; cronache e storia, anno 1–(2), magg./giugno 1955–(aprile 1957). Roma, 1955–(57). 32 cm. Monthly.

Supersedes *Metron, architettura urbanista.*

One of the brilliant new Italian architectural publications; its articles are world-wide in scope, with emphasis on contemporary developments. Discussions of work of the past and of technology round out the contents.

Richly illustrated with color and black-and-white photographs, plans, and diagrams.

Contains brief book reviews, and news of architectural conventions.

It also includes indexes of articles contained in earlier Italian periodicals, e.g., *Metron* (in the July and Aug. 1956 issues) and *Palladio* (in the Sept. 1956 issue).

English, French, Spanish, and German summaries of articles.

Indexed in *B. d. f. Z.*

2146

Archives de l'art français; recueil de documents inédits pub. par la Société de l'His-toire de l'Art Français, nouv. période, t. 1–(20), 1907–(45). Paris, Schemit [etc.] 1907–(46). 22 cm.

Preceded by *Archives de l'art français*, 1851–62, and *Nouvelles archives de l'art français*, 1872–1906. Publisher varies. Each volume publishes documents, valuable as source material on French art, as follows: v. 1–2, Miscellaneous; v. 3, Tuetey, Alexandre, and Guiffrey, Jean. *La commission du museum et de la création du Musée du Louvre (1792–1793)*, [1909]; v. 4, Miscellaneous; v. 5, Poussin, Nicolas. *Correspondance de Nicolas Poussin*, 1911; v. 6, Locquin, Jean. *Catalogue raisonné de l'oeuvre de Jean-Baptiste Oudry* . . . 1912; v. 7, Lemonnier, Henry. *Mélanges offerts à M. Henry Lemonnier*, 1913; v. 8, Guiffrey, Jules. *Mélanges offerts à M. Jules Guiffrey*, 1916; v. 9, Guiffrey, Jules. *Histoire de l'Académie de Saint-Luc*, 1915; v. 10, Ballot, M.–J. *Charles Cressent, sculpteur, ébéniste, collectionneur*, 1919; v. 11, Paris. Bibliothèque nationale. Dept. des estampes. *Catalogue des ouvrages relatifs aux beaux-arts du Cabinet des estampes de la Bibliothèque nationale (série Y)*, t. 1, 1921; v. 12, Courteault, P. *Une oeuvre de Gabriel en province. La place royale de Bordeaux*, 1921–22; v. 13, Guiffrey, Jean. *L'oeuvre de Pierre-Paul Prud'hon*, 1924; v. 14, Furcy-Raynaud, Marc. *Les sculptures exécutées au XVIIIe siècle pour la Direction de bâtiments du roi*, 1927; v. 15–16, Maumené, C. G. V. *Iconographie des rois de France*, 2 v., 1929–32; v. 17, Réau, Louis. *L'art français dans les pays du Nord et de l'Est de l'Europe (XVIII–XIX siècles)*, 1932; v. 18, Marquet de Vasselot, J. J., and Weigert, Roger-Armand. *Bibliographie de la tapisserie, des tapis et de la broderie en France*, 1935; v. 19, Réau, Louis; Messelet, Jean; and Adhemar, Jean. *Carle Vanloo, Jean Restout; les lithographies de paysages en France à l'époque romantique*, 1938; v. 20, Marquet de Vasselot, J. J. *Répertoire des vues des salles du Musée du Louvre*, 1946. Indexed in *B. d. f. Z.*

2147

Archives de l'art français; recueil de documents inédits relatifs à l'histoire des arts en France, t. 1–12, 1851–60; 2 sér., t. 1–2, 1861–62. Paris, Dumoulin [etc.] 1851–62 [i.e., 1866]. 22 cm.

Annual. Continued by: *Nouvelles archives de l'art français*, 1872–1906; *Archives de l'art français*, nouv. période, 1907–(46). Sér. 2 published by Librairie Tross. Contains source material and documents relative to French art. Odd-numbered volumes contain "Docu-

ments," t. 1–5; t. 6 "suivi d'une table complète des noms de personnes et de lieux com-
pris dans les six volumes." Even-numbered
volumes contain "Abecedario de P. J. Mariette et autres notes inédites de cet amateur
sur les arts et les artistes." Index: 1851–96,
in sér. 3, t. 12 of *Nouvelles archives.* . . .

2148
Archivio storico dell'arte, anno 1–7, 1888–94;
ser. 2, anno 1–3, 1895–97. Roma, Danesi,
1888–97. 34 cm.
    Monthly 1889–90; bimonthly 1891–97. Pub-
lisher varies. Superseded by *L'Arte.* Emphasis
is on the Italian Renaissance, but contemporary Italian art and art of other countries
is also considered. Many contributions by
well-known authorities. Signed book reviews.
Indexed with *L'Arte,* by author and subject;
also in *Italy. Parl. Cam. dei Deputati. Bibl.*

2149
Archivo español de arte, t. 14, no. 40–(t. 30,
no. 120). Madrid, Consejo Superior de Investigaciones Científicas. Instituto Diego Velázquez, 1940–(57). 28 cm.
    Bimonthly, t. 14–18; quarterly, t. 19– .
Continues (in part) *Archivo español de arte
y arqueología.* Scholarly considerations of
Spanish art, with signed book reviews. Indexed in *Art index; B. d. f. Z.*

2150
Archivo español de arte y arqueología, t. [1]–
13, no. 1–39. Madrid, Centro de Estudios Históricos [1925–37]. 28 cm.
    Three times a year. This scholarly journal
devoted to Spanish art and archaeology was
continued in 1940 by two separate publications: *Archivo español de arte,* t. 14, no. 40
– , and *Archivo español de arqueología,* t.
14, no. 40– . Contains signed book reviews
and brief notices of pertinent periodical articles. In *Art index,* nos. 1–39; also in *B. d. f. Z.*

2151
Arkhitektura SSSR. Moskva, 1951–(57). 33 cm.
Monthly.
    Organ of the Akademiia Arkhitektury SSSR,
Soiuz Sovetskikh arkhitektorov & Upravlenie
po delam arkhitektury pri Sovete ministrov
RSFSR. The leading architectural periodical
of Russia. Well illustrated.

2152
Ars islamica, v. 1–16. Ann Arbor, Mich.,
Univ. of Michigan Press [1934–51]. 31 cm.
    Semiannual. Published by the Research
Seminary in Islamic Art, Division of Fine

Arts, Univ. of Michigan, and the Detroit
Institute of Arts. Continued by *Ars orientalis.* Articles in English, with some in French
and German, are contributed by specialists
on Islamic arts and crafts. Volume 5 has
supplement: "Preliminary materials for a
dictionary of Islamic artists." Volume 8 is devoted to reviews of Pope's *Survey of Persian
art.* "Literature on Islamic art, 1939–1945"
published in v. 13–14, 1948, p. [150]–179, and
in v. 15–16, 1951, p. [151]–211. Entries arranged by country of publication and compiled by scholars in each country. Volume
15–16 also contains "Indices to 'Material for a
history of Islamic textiles up to the Mongol
conquest,' by R. B. Serjeant," p. [273]–305.
Signed book reviews are included. Indexes:
"Contents arranged according to subject" v.
1–5 and v. 1–10; v. 1–16 (by author and subject) in v. 15-16, p. [307]–28. In *Art index.*

2153
Ars orientalis; the arts of Islam and the East,
v. 1–(2). [Washington] 1954–(57). 32 cm. Irregular.
    Issued by the Freer Gallery of Art, Smith-
sonian Institution, and Fine Arts Dept., University of Michigan.
    It succeeds *Ars islamica.*
    Scholarly articles, copiously illustrated
with plates, line drawings, and maps are supplemented with signed book reviews and
bibliographies in the field.
    Volume 2 is the "Charles Lang Freer Cen-
tennial Volume."
    Indexed in *Art index.*

2154
L'Art; revue bi-mensuelle illustrée, année
1–35, t. 1–59. Paris, Librairie de l'Art, 1875–
1907. 30–43 cm.
    Subtitle and frequency vary; t. 1–35 have
subtitle: *revue hebdomadaire illustrée.* Suspended 1894–1901. Année 20, t. 56, 1894–
also called sér. 2, t. 1– . Particular emphasis
is placed on French art, as well as music
and some literature, with long articles on the
Salons. The signed reviews are quite long,
some illustrated. Indexed in *Italy. Parl. Cam.
dei Deputati. Bibl.*

2155
Art and archaeology; the arts throughout
the ages . . . v. 1–35, no. 3, July 1914–May/
June 1934. Washington, D.C., Archaeological
Society of Washington, D.C., 1914–[34]. 26–
28 cm.
    Frequency varies: bimonthly, 1914–15,
1918–19, 1932–34; monthly, 1916–17, 1920–

31. Publisher and place vary; 1914–21 pub. by The Archaeological Institute of America. Absorbed *Art and life,* May 1920. Contains fairly popular treatments of the fine arts and archaeology, with shorter news notes and some signed book reviews. It took over the nontechnical material formerly included in the *Quarterly bulletin* of the Archaeological Institute of America. In *Art index,* v. 27–35, no. 3, 1929–34. Also indexed in *B. d. f. Z.; Subj. ind. to pers.; Readers' guide; Ann. mag. subj. ind.*

2156

Art and auctions; international art dealers and collectors guide, v. 1– . Rotterdam, Van Kouteren, Feb. 1957– .

Fortnightly. Contains notices of forthcoming art auctions as well as the results of recent auctions, arranged by place of auction. The most important items are illustrated and their provenance given with a description. Prices are given in the currency of the country in which the sale is held. Includes parity tables.

2157

The Art bulletin, v. [1]–(39). N.Y., College Art Association of America, 1913–(57). 26 cm.

Quarterly. Place of publication varies. As the official publication of the College Art Association, it contains long scholarly considerations of all periods and fields of art history, as well as shorter notes on various subjects. Contains lengthy, signed book reviews. Volume 3, no. 1, 1920 includes "Books for the college art library," comp. by E. Louise Lucas. This classified list was revised and republished in v. 11, no. 3, 1929. Indexes: (1) v. 1–20 [1938. 11] p. Arranged by subject; (2) *An index of volumes I–XXX, 1913–1948.* Comp. by Rosalie B. Green under the direction of the editors. (N.Y., Columbia Univ. Press, 1950. 426 p.). This is done in one alphabet, and also contains the contents of each volume, chronologically. In *Art index,* v. 11– . Also indexed in *Subj. ind. to pers.; B. d. f. Z.*

2158

L'Art d'aujourd'hui, v. 1–6. [Paris] Morancé, 1924–[29]. 28 cm.

Quarterly (2 fascs. a year), v. 1; annual, v. 2–6. Contains short articles on individual artists, with good plates which are valuable for contemporary French art. There are more illustrations than text. Volume 6 has an alphabetical list of artists treated in v. 1–6, with numbers of the illustrative plates.

2159

Art et décoration, t. 1–67, 1897–1938; n.s., no. 1–2, 1939; [3. sér.] no. 1–(16), 1946–(50). Paris, Librairie Centrale des Beaux-Arts [1897–(1950)]. 30–32 cm.

Monthly through June 1938; bimonthly July–Dec. 1938; n.s. is quarterly. Suspended July 1914–June 1919, Feb. 1939–1946. Absorbed *L'art décoratif* in June 1922, *L'architecture* July 1925, and *L'architecte* Jan. 1936. Title 1936–39: *Art et décoration et l'architecte.* Subtitle varies. Well-illustrated articles treat modern art in general, architecture, and the decorative arts, especially house furnishings. Contains announcements of exhibitions and some book reviews. Supplements: "Nouvelles-concours"; "Les échos d'art" (1932–37). In *Art index,* v. 55–68, no. 2; no. 7, 1948– . Also indexed in *B. d. f. Z.*

———. Table des matières contenus dans les 12 premières années. Tomes I–XXIV (janvier, 1897–décembre, 1908). Paris, Librairie Centrale des Beaux-Arts [1910?]. 64 p. 31 cm.

2160

L'Art et les artistes, t. 1–23, no. 5, avr. 1905–fév. 1919; n.s. t. 1–38, no. 1–199, avr. 1919–juil. 1939. Paris, 1905–39. 32 cm.

Monthly. During World War I (t. 20–23) only special numbers were published. N.s., t. 1–38 also called ann. 14–34. Subtitle varies. Fairly popular coverage of painting, sculpture, and engraving, as well as some architecture and applied arts. Well illustrated. Various numbers are devoted to particular artists or subjects. In *Art index,* n.s., v. 18, March 1929– . Also indexed in *B. d. f. Z.; Subj. ind. to pers.*

2161

L'Art flamand & hollandais; revue mensuelle illustrée, t. 1–22. Anvers, Van Oest, 1904–14. 30 cm.

Monthly. Suspended 1915–20 (for which years see *Onze kunst*). Volume 23, 1921, called *La revue d'art,* which continues to 1929. Articles are contributed by specialists on Dutch and Flemish art of all periods. Signed book reviews and a section of short reviews of exhibitions, news of the art world, and résumés of important articles in the field are included. Illustrated with black and white halftones; almost no color plates. Indexed in *Bibl. de Belgique.*

2162

Art in America, v. 1–(45). N.Y., 1913–(Jan. 1958). 28 cm.

Bimonthly through v. 20; quarterly, v. 21– . Place of publication varies. Articles are on art in general, often by well-known scholars; but with v. 37, 1949– emphasis is wholly on American art. Beginning with v. 38, no. 1, Feb. 1950 it is "devoted each year to four special publications in the field of American art research, some in conjunction with coordinated exhibitions." Signed book reviews and occasional annotated lists of new art books are included. In *Art index*, v. 17– . Also indexed in *Ann. mag. subj. ind.; Subj. ind. to pers.; B. d. f. Z.*

2163

Art international, v. 1–( ). Zürich, James Fitzsimmons, 1956–(57). 25 cm.

Volume 1 called *European art this month*. Ten issues a year. There is an airmail edition. Not primarily a journal of criticism or art history, it gives up-to-date information on all phases of art in all parts of Europe: calendars of exhibitions, information on salons, competitions and prizes, announcements of auctions and prices paid, art-world news, check lists of art books, brief descriptions of collections in lesser-known museums, occasional reviews of exhibitions, and synopses of reviews in other publications. It is compiled from "the announcements and catalogues of more than 1000 museums and galleries," as well as reports of correspondents and contents of other periodicals.

2164

The Art journal, v. 1–74, no. 1–884, Feb. 1839–Feb. 1912. London, Virtue, 1839–1912. 28–34 cm.

Monthly. Volumes 1–10 called *The Art union; a monthly journal of the fine arts.* 1851–54 called n.s., v. 3–6; 1855–61 called n.s., v. 1–7; 1862–80 called n.s., v. 1–19; 1881–1902 called n.s. (without volume numbers). An American ed. was also published, with largely American emphasis in its articles. A popular review containing many very short pieces on a great variety of subjects: museums, collections, exhibitions, types of art. Some book reviews.

2165

The Art news, v. 1–(56). N.Y., Art News Foundation Press [1902–(Feb. 1958)]. 41–46 cm.

Monthly from Sept. to May; semimonthly through Feb. 1946. Nov. 29, 1902–Apr. 30, 1904 called *Hyde's Weekly art news;* Nov. 5, 1904–Feb. 10, 1923 known as *American art news*. Subtitles vary. Contains articles of interest to the art collector, as well as to artists and students, on special collections, exhibitions, and works of individual artists, of all times. Currently it includes a series on the work and technique of contemporary artists. Also contains calendars of exhibitions, short reviews of shows, news of art in the United States and abroad, and brief book reviews. Well illustrated. An annual number is also published, with good color plates and lengthy articles, sometimes several devoted to the same theme (42 cm.). In *Art index*, v. 27– . Also indexed in *B. d. f. Z.*

2166

The Art quarterly, v. 1–(20). [Detroit, Mich.] Detroit Institute of Arts [1938–(57)]. 28 cm.

Quarterly. Contains scholarly, well-illustrated articles on art of all periods, with notable pieces on drawings appearing v. 16, Winter 1953– . French summaries, v. 15– . Edited by W. R. Valentiner and E. P. Richardson. Beginning with v. 9 includes "Recent publications in the field of art," a collection of short unsigned reviews of recent books and museum catalogs, in many languages. "Archives of American art" is an important section, v. 17, Winter 1954– . Includes notes on and illustrations of recent important acquisitions of American (and sometimes Canadian and European) museums, giving descriptions, pertinent extracts from museum catalogs and periodical articles, etc. Indexed in *Art index* and *B. d. f. Z.*

2167

L'Art sacré; revue mensuelle, juil. 1935–(août 1957). [Paris, Éditions du Cerf, 1935–(57)]. 29 cm.

Monthly. Suspended 1939–46 and replaced in 1945–46 by *Cahiers de l'art sacré*. The articles here cover religious art, contemporary church architecture and decoration, iconography, and occasionally liturgical music. Contributors are largely Roman Catholic priests Book reviews and some summaries of periodical articles are included. Indexed in *B. d. f. Z.*

2168

Art studies; medieval, Renaissance and modern. [v. 1–8] Cambridge, Mass., Harvard Univ. Press, 1923–[31]. 32 cm.

Annual. Volumes 1–2 published by Princeton University Press. "Edited by members of the departments of the fine arts at Harvard and Princeton universities." Volumes 1–5 are called "an extra number of the *American journal of archaeology*." Lengthy articles treat art in general, but no book reviews are included. In *Art index*, v. 7–8. Also indexed in *B. d. f. Z.* and *Subj. ind. to pers.*

2169
L'Art vivant, no. 1–234, 1925–juil. 1939. Paris, Librairie Larousse [etc., 1925–39]. 31 cm.
Semimonthly 1925–30; monthly, 1931–39. 1925–30 called t. 1–6; 1931–39 not numbered. A popular review of contemporary French plastic art and "industries de luxe": fashion, decorative arts, etc.; also gives news of exhibitions and sales, with some longer articles devoted to contemporary painting and art of the old masters. Articles are also devoted to countries of the world, with a tourism angle. Indexed in *B. d. f. Z.*

2170
L'Arte, anno 1–(56). Roma, Torino, Danesi, 1898–(57). 34 cm.
Bimonthly through 1935; 1936– frequency varies. Supersedes *Archivio storico dell'arte*. Director is Alfredo Venturi, anno 1–n.s., anno 12 (with Lionello Venturi, n.s., v. 1–6). Anno 33–55 also called n.s., v. 1–20. A valuable publication on Italian art in general; it also contains signed reviews, notes on exhibitions and of the art world. In anno 8, 1905– there are classified summaries of books and periodical articles on Italian art ("Bollettino bibliografico"). English and German summaries of articles in n.s., v. 10 and 11. In *Art index*, anno 32–n.s., v. 11. Also indexed in *B. d. f. Z.* and *Italy. Parl. Cam. dei Deputati. Bibl.*
———. Serra, Beatrice, ed. Archivio storico dell'arte (1888–1897) e L'Arte (1898–1929) indice generale dei quarantadue volumi. Roma, Casa Editrice de L'Arte, 1930. 511 p.
Index by author, subject, and places.
Indice dei fascicoli dal 1944 al 1957. 28 p.
Contains separate indexes of articles, illustrations, and entries in the "Bollettino bibliografico" section.

2171
Arte cristiana, anno 1–(44). Milano, Società Amici dell'Arte Cristiana, 1913–(57). 30 cm.
Monthly. Publisher and subtitle vary. Contains brief articles on church art of all periods. Some short book reviews and summaries of periodical articles are included.

√2172
Arte español; revista de la Sociedad de amigos del arte, t. 1–(21). Madrid, 1912–(57). 28–30 cm.
Three times yearly since 1947. Frequency

varies; sometimes four nos. a year. Each volume covers two years, with the exception of v. 13, which covers six years (1936–41). Director: Enrique Lafuente Ferrari. Called *Revista española de arte* in 1932–June 1936. Official Spanish periodical on Spanish art of the past and present with papers by Spanish experts. Well illustrated and includes some color plates. Contains book reviews, sometimes signed. Indexed in *B. d. f. Z.*

2173
Arte lombarda; rivista di storia dell'arte, annata prima-(seconda). [Venezia] Alfieri [1955–(56)]. 30 cm.
Annual. Director: Paolo d'Ancona. Similar in style and scholarly purpose to *Arte veneta*, and contains studies of ancient and contemporary Lombard art. Richly illustrated. Contains notes of new books, and in ann. 1 a classified bibliography: "Appunti per una bibliografia dell'arte lombarda 1945–1954," p. 165–87.

2174
Arte veneta; rivista trimestrale di storia dell'arte, anno 1–(10). Venezia [1947–(56)]. 33 cm.
Quarterly, v. 1–7; annual, v. 8– . Subtitle varies. Editor: Rodolfo Pallucchini. "The aim of this review is to promote the study of Venetian Art in all countries and particularly its relationship with the other Italian and foreign traditions." Articles are written by well-known scholars. Volume 1 has English summaries. Publishes some archival material. "Bibliografia dell'arte veneta dal 1940 al 1946" appears in each issue of v. 1. This is a classified list of books and periodical articles. Volumes 2– have current bibliographies on Venetian art. Similar in format and style to *Arte lombarda*.
———. Indici analitici dal 1947 al 1951 (annate I–V). Ed. by Maria Angela Novelli. Venezia. [103] p.

2175
Artes; monuments et mémoires, v. 1–8. Copenhague, Haase, 1932–[40]. 31 cm.
Annual. Published under subvention from Ny Carlsberg Foundation. A useful publication on Danish classic art and foreign art in Danish collections, in French, German, and Italian. Bibliography of chief Danish books on art from Romanesque period on, v. 1, p. 17–52. Indexed in *B. d. f. Z.*

2176
Artes de Mexico, no. 1–(16), 1953–(57). Mexico, D. F., 1953–(57). 30–32 cm.

Bimonthly (irregular). Subtitle: *Revista bimestral editada por el Frente nacional de artes plasticas*, nos. 1–6. With no. 13 title changed to *Artes de Mexico in English*. English summaries up to no. 13. Covers all periods and types of fine arts, dance in Mexico, and some articles on art in other countries. Stress on modern developments. The majority of issues are devoted to a single subject or theme. A series of articles on mural painting in Mexico from the earliest to modern, in nos. 3–6.

2177

Le Arti, rassegna bimestrale dell'arte antica e moderna a cura della direzione generale delle arti, anno 1–5, ott./nov. 1938–43. Firenze, LeMonnier, 1938–43. 30 cm.

Replaced *Bolletino d'arte* during the war years. Long scholarly articles by important scholars covering ancient art and Italian art of all periods, including modern. Contains a section with elaborate illustrations concerning restoration of works of art in various Italian museums, a series of documents on Italian art published by Pèleo Bacci, some articles on music, and a little material on the current theater. During the war years there is a section devoted to the war and the doings of prominent people. Signed book reviews. In *Art index*, v. 1–2. Also indexed in *Italy. Prov. Gen. dello Stato.*

2178

Artibus Asiae, [v. 1]–(19). Ascona, Switzerland, Artibus Asiae publishers, 1925/26–(56). 30 cm.

Quarterly. Suspended 1938–39. Published Hellerau-Dresden, Avalun-Verlag, v. 1–8, fasc. 1. Alfred Salmony, editor, v. 9– . *"Artibus Asiae* considers as its main purpose the presentation of hitherto unknown excavations and objects as well as new theories concerning known material." Contains articles by scholarly contributors in German, French, and English on Asiatic art and archaeology. Each number contains signed book reviews in a section entitled "Bibliographia." A series of 17 monographs have been issued as supplements from 1937 to date. In *Art index*, v. 11, 1948– . Also indexed in *B. d. f. Z.*

2179

Arts, v. 1–(31), Nov. 1, 1926–(Sept. 1957). [N.Y.] The Art Digest, Inc., 1926–(57). 32 cm.

Semimonthly (except monthly June to Sept.), Nov. 1926–Sept. 1955; monthly Oct. 1955– . Title varies: Nov. 1926–July 1954,

Art digest; Aug. 1954–Sept. 1955, *Arts digest.* Subtitle varies. Absorbed *Argus* (San Francisco, 1927–29?).

Short articles on events and people in U.S. art world; calendars of exhibitions throughout the United States; and short reviews ot showings in New York galleries. In more recent issues, longer articles on individual artists, collections, shows; and summaries of art news from abroad. Emphasis is on the contemporary. Frequent signed book reviews. Indexed in *Art index.*

2180

The Arts, v. 1–18, no. 1, Dec. 4, 1920–Oct. 1931. N.Y., The Arts Pub. Corp. [1920–31]. 29 cm.

Monthly, except two nos. during the summer. Hamilton Easter Field, editor and publisher v. 1–2; Forbes Watson, editor v. 3–18. Followed by *The Arts weekly*, March–May 1932. Absorbed *Touchstone*, June 1921. A popular type of publication which contains some sound material with particular stress on American art but also covers European exhibitions. Signed book reviews. Good illustrations. In *Art index*, v. 15–18. Also indexed in *Int. index* and *Ann. mag. subj. ind.*

2181

Les Arts; revue mensuelle des musées, collections, expositions, année 1–16. Paris, Goupil, 1902–20. 36 cm.

Suspended 1914–16. A popular "picture book" review of contemporary conservative art with a wealth of halftone illustrations. The majority of the articles are devoted to private collections, recent acquisitions of some museums, and sales notes. English summaries of articles through 1905. Each volume is well indexed but no general index. Indexed in *B. d. f. Z.*

2182

Arts; spectacles, no. 1–(650). Paris, 1945–(57). 59 cm.

Weekly. Continues *Beaux-arts.* Called *Arts: beaux-arts, littérature, spectacles*, nos. 1–352. Georges Wildenstein, director, nos. 1–356, 1945–52. A weekly newspaper of the art world which also covers books, movies, and the theater. Some book reviews. In *Art index*, nos. 53–177.

2183

Les Arts anciens de Flandre, t. 1–6. Bruges, Association pour la Publication des Monuments de l'Art Flamand [1905–14]. 43 cm.

Quarterly. Useful for Flemish medieval,

Renaissance, and later artists. Also some articles on private collections.

2184
Arts and architecture, v. 1–(74). [Los Angeles, J. D. Entenza] 1910–(57). 31–35 cm.

Frequency varies: monthly 1910–March 1933 and 1935– . Title varies. Originally called *The Pacific coast architect*. Volumes 35–61, 1929–44, called *California arts and architecture*. Publication suspended March 1920–Feb. 1921. Useful for American architecture, with emphasis on the West Coast. Contains some book reviews.

2185
Arts & decoration, v. 1–55, no. 2, Nov. 1910–March 1942. N.Y., Adam Budge, 1910–42. 30–37 cm.

Monthly. Publisher and subtitle vary. Absorbed *The Art world* in March 1918; from May 1918–Jan. 1919 called *The Art world and arts & decoration*. Combined with *The Spur* in Aug. 1940. A popular magazine of decorative arts, which covers all aspects of gracious living including decoration, gardens, the stage, etc. Occasional short reviews. In *Art index*, v. 31–55. Also indexed in *Readers' guide* and *Ann. mag. subj. ind.*

2186
Arts asiatiques, t. 1–(4). Paris, Presses Universitaires de France [1954–(57)]. 28 cm.

Quarterly. Published under the auspices of the Musée Guimet and of the Musée Cernuschi, and has taken the place of the *Revue des arts asiatiques*. Contains scholarly articles on Asiatic art written by specialists, and signed book reviews in "Comptes rendus."

2187
Arts et métiers graphiques, no. 1–68, sept. 1927–mai 1939. Paris [1927–39]. 32 cm.

Bimonthly; frequency varies. Contains technical and critical articles on painting, typography, photography, illustrations, posters, and the art of the book of the contemporary period. Some fine color plates. Picture captions are also in English. A separate index of 8 pages (not paged) covers the entire run from 1927–39, but is more of a table of contents which lists all articles under several broad headings. Indexed in *B. d. f. Z.* and *Subj. ind. to pers.*

2188
Les Arts plastiques, année 1–4; ser. 5–(6). Bruxelles, Éditions des Arts Plastiques [1947–(54)]. 22 x 15 cm.

Frequency varies: 1947–48, monthly; 1949– , bimonthly. Publisher varies: 1947–no. 2, 1950, Éditions de la Connaissance. Covers art of all periods and countries. Signed book reviews. "Bibliographie internationale des catalogues d'exposition" beginning with no. 8–9 of 1947, arranged by country. "Répertoire international des films sur l'art" beginning with no. 1–2, 1949, arranged by country and then alphabetically by title, with indications of the type and origin of the film. "Flemish painting at the Royal Academy; an essay by Denys Sutton" forms no. 6, 1953.

2189
Ausonia; rivista della Società Italiana di Archeologia e Storia dell'Arte, anno 1–10. Roma, Loescher, 1907–21. 29 cm.

Annual, sometimes in two fascicles. Suspended 1914–18, 1920. More emphasis on archaeology than on art. Book reviews in "Recensioni" and "Bolletino bibliografico" (v. 1–6) with classified review of periodicals. "Notiziario bibliografico (1915–21)" in v. 10 has subject arrangement. Indexed in *B. d. f. Z.; Italy. Parl. Cam. dei Deputati. Bibl.*

2190
Baumeister; Monatshefte für Architektur und Baupraxis . . . 1–(54) Jahrg., Okt. 1902–(57). München, Callwey, 1903–(57). 34–40 cm.

Monthly. Publisher and place vary. Subtitle varies slightly: it is currently *Zeitschrift für Baukultur und Bautechnik*. Covers architecture of various countries, including the United States, but the emphasis is on Germany. Some book reviews, mostly signed. Well illustrated with photographs and plans. Indexed in *B. d. f. Z.*

2191
Beaux-arts; revue d'information artistique, année 1–[17]. Paris, Gazette des Beaux-Arts, 1923–39. 28–59 cm.

Frequency varies. Semimonthly, 1923–28; monthly, 1929–Dec. 1932, then weekly. Subtitle 1929– reads: *Chronique des arts et de la curiosité*. Continues *Chronique des arts*. Ceased publication 1940. Continued by *Arts* (2182). A review of art news, museum news, necrology, sales, exhibitions, etc., primarily for France. Short book-review section and, beginning with v. 7, summaries of articles in periodicals (up to Feb. 2, 1934). Combined with *Le Journal des arts* Dec. 1932. In *Art index*, v. 7, 1929–June 1, 1940. Also indexed in *B. d. f. Z.*

2192

Le Beffroi; arts, héraldique, archéologie, t. 1–
4. Bruges, Gailliard, 1863–73. 31 cm.

Annual. W. H. J. Weale, editor. Contains
few illustrations but is useful for Flemish
art, archaeology, heraldry, and archival information, especially for early Renaissance
painting. Index v. 1–4.

2193

Belvedere, 1–13 Jahrg. Zürich [etc.] Amalthea-
Verlag [1922–43]. 31 cm.

Monthly. Publisher and place vary. Subtitle varies. Contains material of interest to
collectors and news of sales and the art world,
as well as scholarly articles mostly dealing
with medieval and Renaissance art, with
many illustrations. Volumes 5–10, 1924–26
issued in two parts. Second part called "Forum." In v. 9–10 the parts are combined.
Signed book reviews as well as listings of
new publications in the field. In *Art index*,
v. 8–13. Also indexed in *B. d. d. Z.*

2194

La Biennale di Venezia; rivista trimestrale
dell'ente della Biennale, no. 1–(28/29), luglio
1950–(56). Venezia, Sansoni, [1950–(56)]. 32
cm.

Quarterly with some variation. Subtitle
varies. Numbers 1–24 published by Alfieri.
Devoted primarily to contemporary art, but
some articles on earlier artists. English,
French, and German summaries of articles.
Contains a section called "Bollettino del-
l'archivio storico d'arte contemporanea della
Biennale" which lists exhibits in Italy and
exhibitions of Italian art in other countries,
by the month, and then alphabetically by
artist. Also lists the books acquired by its
library and catalogs of exhibitions throughout the world, and gives prices. Bibliography
of the Biennale: 25th in no. 4; 26th in no.
13/14; 27th in no. 24. Index to nos. 1–24
contained in no. 24.

2195

Bollettino d'arte; notizie dei musei, delle
gallerie e dei monumenti, anno 1–14, genn.
1907–dic. 1920; ser. 2, anno 1–10, luglio 1921–
giugno 1931; ser. 3, anno 25–32, no. 4, luglio
1931–ott. 1938; ser. 4, anno 33–(42), 1948–
(57). Roma, Calzone [etc.], 1907–(57). 32 cm.

Monthly, 1907–38; quarterly, 1948– . Subtitle varies. Superseded *Gallerie nazionale
italiane*, 1893/94–1897/1902. Suspended 1939–
47; replaced by *Le Arti* during these years.
At the head of title, 1931–38: Ministero della

educazione nazionale. Direzione generale
delle antichità e belle arti. Genn. 1948– ,
Ministero della pubblica istruzione. Direzione
generale delle antichità e belle arti. Anni 8–
14 have supplement: "Cronaca delle belle
arti." Useful for Italian art of all periods,
including the classic. Museum notes at end
of each number. Some short book reviews in
ser. 4. In *Art index*, v. 30–32, July 1936–Oct.
1938. Also indexed in *Italy. Prov. Gen. dello
Stato; B. d. f. Z.*

2196

The British Museum quarterly, v. 1–(20),
May 1926–(55/56). London, The Trustees,
1927–(56). 26 cm.

Quarterly. Subtitle v. 16– : *A journal
dealing with recent acquisitions and research
concerning the museum's collections.* Suspended between Dec. 1940 and Jan. 1951. Index to v. 1–5 published 1931 (22 p.). Index to
v. 6–10 published 1937 (30 p.). In *Art index*,
v. 4–14, June 1929–Dec. 1940. Also indexed
in *Subj. ind. to pers.; B. d. f. Z.*

2197

British School at Athens. The Annual . . .
no. 1–(51), session 1894/5–(1956). London,
Macmillan, [1895–(56)]. 26 cm.

Annual. Publisher varies. Contains scholarly articles and reports of excavations. "A
short history of the British School at Athens,
1886–1911" by G. A. Macmillan in no. 17, p.
[ix]–xxxviii. "Bibliography of the work of
students of the School, coming within the
scope of the School's work but not published
in the second Annual" by J. ff. Baker-
Penoyre in no. 17, p. [xxxix]–liv. Has supplementary papers. In *Art index*, v. 29, 1927– .
Also indexed in *B. d. f. Z.* and *Subj. ind. to
pers.*

———. Index to nos. 1–16. London [1912].
144 p.

———. Index to nos. 17–32. London [193?].
77 p.

2198

British School at Rome. Papers, v. 1–(25).
London, The School, 1902–(57). 26 cm.

Annual. Published by Macmillan & Co.,
Ltd., v. 1–n.s., v.11. Volumes 14– also called
New series, v. 1– . Size varies. Scholarly
papers dealing with architecture, archaeology, inscriptions, etc. Indexed in *Subj. ind.
to pers.* and *Int. index.*

2199

. . . Bulletin de correspondance hellénique,
année 1–(81). Paris, Fontemoing, 1877–(1957).
26 cm. Semiannual.

At head of title: École française d'Athènes. Publisher and place vary. Scholarly articles dealing with Greek art and archaeology. In more recent issues, signed book reviews and news of excavations. Articles in Greek also, in earlier issues. Two supplements published. In *Art index*, v. 54–   . Also indexed in *Rép. bibl.* and *B. d. f. Z.*

――――. Table générale des dix premières années (1877–1886). Paris, Thorin, 1889. 216 p.

――――. Table quinquennale (1887–1891). Paris, Thorin, 1894. 157 p.

2200

Bulletin de l'art ancien et moderne, no. 1–819. Paris [Petit, 1899–1935]. 26–31 cm.

Monthly (irregular), 1922–1935. Weekly, 1899–1914. Semimonthly, 1919–1921. Published as a supplement to *Revue de l'art ancien et moderne.* Suspended Aug. 1914–Nov. 1919. Covers art news, museum acquisitions, necrology, sales, exhibitions, etc., primarily for France. "Extrait des tables du 'Bulletin' " in index to v. 27–71 of *Revue* . . . p. [193]–201. In *Art index,* 1929–35. Also indexed in *B. d. f. Z.*

2201

Bulletin des musées de France, année 1–[15]. Paris, Direction des Musées Nationaux [1929–50]. 28 cm.

Monthly, 1929–31; monthly (except Aug., Sept.), 1932–   . Title varies: 1948–50, *Musées de France.* Suspended 1939–45. Volume numbering dropped with v. 12, 1947. Replaced by *La Revue des arts.* The official organ of the French museums, containing news of these institutions and articles about their collections. Also includes news of L'École du Louvre and theses accepted there. Some short reviews up to 1946. In *Art index,* Jan. 1948–1950. Also indexed in *B. d. f. Z.*

✓**2202**

Bulletin monumental, v. 1–(115). Paris [etc.] 1834–(1957). 23 cm.

Frequency varies; quarterly, v. 91–   .

Published under the auspices of the Société française d'archéologie pour la conservation des monuments historiques.

Subtitle varies. Volumes 11–64 also numbered separately by series.

An important publication on French medieval art and architecture. Contains lengthy, signed reviews in "Bibliographie" section.

Several indexes have been published: v. 1–10, 1846; 11–21, 1861; 21–31, 1868; 31–39, 1873; 1834–1925 in Société Française d'Arché-

ologie. *Table alphabétique des publications de la Société* . . . *1834–1925.* Paris, Picard, 1930. 497 p.; 1914–1934 in v. 94, 1935, p. [524]–545; 1926–1954 in suppl. to v. 112, 1956. Indexed in *Rép. bibl.; Int. index.*

2203

Bullettino di archeologia cristiana, anno 1–7, genn. 1863–dic. 1869; 2. ser., anno 1–6, 1870–75; 3. ser., anno 1–6, 1876–81; 4. ser., anno 1–6, 1882–89; [5. ser., anno 1–4, 1890–94] Roma, Salviucci [etc.], 1863–94. 28–31 cm.

Monthly, 1863–69; quarterly, 1870–94. Edited by G. B. de Rossi. Superseded by *Nuovo bullettino di archeologia cristiana,* 1895–1922. Good for early Christian art.

――――. Indici generali della prima serie . . . 1863–69. Roma, 1870. 70 p. 33 cm.

――――. Indici generali per gli anni 1870–89 . . . Roma, 1876–91. 3 v.

2204

The Burlington magazine, v. 1–(99). London, 1903–(57). 32–33 cm.

Monthly. Issued in two volumes a year until v. 88, 1946. Volumes 1–89 called *The Burlington magazine for connoisseurs.* An important periodical covering the art of all periods and countries. In addition to articles by specialists it covers news of sales and exhibitions and correspondence. Contains signed book reviews and listings of "Publications received" and sometimes includes summaries of articles in periodicals. In *Art index,* v. 54–   . Also indexed in *Subj. ind. to pers.; B. d. f. Z.; Int. index; Ann. mag. subj. ind.*

2205

Byzantinische Zeitschrift, Bd. 1–(50). München, Beck, 1892–(1957). 25 cm.

Quarterly. Publisher and place vary. None published 1920–22, 1944–49. Scholarly publication, with articles in French and Greek as well as German, having to do with the Byzantine field. Lengthy reviews and shorter bibliographical notices. Indexed in *B. d. d. Z.*

――――. General Register zu Band I–XII, 1892–1903. Leipzig, Teubner, 1909. 592 p.

2206

Cahiers archéologiques, fin de l'antiquité et moyen âge, t. 1–(9). Paris. Éditions d'Art et d'Histoire, 1945–(57). 26 cm.

Annual (irregular). Publisher varies. André Grabar, editor. Contains original research on the art and archaeology of the last centuries of antiquity and of the Middle Ages. Volume 7 contains articles in English, German, and Italian as well as French. Indexed in *B. d. f. Z.*

2207

Cahiers d'art, année 1–(31/32), 1926–(56/57). Paris, Éditions "Cahiers d'art," 1926–(57). 32 cm.

Annual; frequency varies. Publisher varies. Christian Zervos, editor 1930– . One volume issued for the war years, covering 1940–44. Primarily for contemporary art, but also contains articles on older art periods allied to contemporary movements, with profuse and fine illustrations, and some color plates. Some articles also on contemporary music, book design, and cinema. In *Art index*, v. 5–15, no. 4, and v. 23– . Also indexed in *B. d. f. Z.*

2208

Les Cahiers techniques de l'art, v. 1–(3). Strasbourg, Le Tilleul, 1947–(56). 29 cm.

Three issues per volume. Volumes 1–2 published by F.-X. LeRoux. Scholarly, original studies in all the arts, with analyses of construction and iconography. "Notices bibliographiques" lists publications by field and then by period. "Bibliographie commentée" contains signed book reviews.

2209

Canadian art, v. 1–(14), Oct./Nov. 1943–(57). Ottawa, Society for Art Publications, 1943–(57). 25 cm.

Quarterly; v. 1–2 bimonthly, Oct.–June. Continues *Maritime art.* Published under the direction of a board representing the National Gallery of Canada, the Art Association of Montreal, the Vancouver Art Gallery, the Maritime Art Association, and the Federation of Canadian Artists. Deals primarily with art in Canada, but occasionally has an account of art in other countries. Signed book reviews. In *Art index*, v. 5– . Also indexed in *B. d. f. Z.; Can. index.*

2210

Casabella continuità, anno 1–(16), nos. 1–(187), 1928–(giuglio 1943); (199)–(217), (dic. 1953)–(1957). [Milano, Editoriale Domus] 1928–(43); (1953)–(57). 31 x 29 cm.

Monthly (irregular). Title: *Casabella costruzioni,* Jan. 1938–Dec. 1939; *Costruzioni casabella,* Jan. 1940–Dec. 1941. *Casabella; rivista mensile di architettura e di tecnica* to 1943.

Interrupted during the war years.

A well-illustrated architectural magazine with many plans. Emphasis is on contemporary developments, world-wide, but with special attention to Italy.

2211

Chinese Art Society of America. Archives, v. 1–(11), 1945/46–(57). [N.Y., 1946–(Feb. 1958)]. 31 cm.

Irregular. Contains scholarly articles and papers on Chinese art, many of which were given as lectures before the society. Short descriptions of objects acquired by American museums in the field.

2212

Die Christliche Kunst; Monatsschrift für alle Gebiete der christlichen Kunst und der Kunstwissenschaft sowie für das gesamte Kunstleben . . . 1–33 Jahrg., Okt. 1904–Sept. 1937. München, Gesellschaft für Christliche Kunst, 1904–37. 29 cm.

Subtitle varies slightly. Superseded by *Neue Saat,* 1938– . Covers Christian art of all kinds and periods. It is similar to, but more useful than, *Arte cristiana.* Contains some signed book reviews and some color plates. Indexed in *B. d. d. Z.*

2213

Chronique d'Égypte, v. 1–(32), dec. 1925–(57). Bruxelles, Musées Royaux d'Art et d'Histoire. Fondation Égyptologique Reine Élisabeth, 1925–(57). 24 cm. Semiannual.

Contains scholarly articles on subjects pertaining to Egypt and excavations there. Bibliography in section called "Bibliothèque," and, later on, signed book reviews in "Livres." Index to v. 1–10, 1925–35 [1937]. In *Art index,* v. 4–22, Dec. 1928–1947. Also indexed in *B. d. f. Z.*

2214

Der Cicerone; Halbmonatsschrift für die Interessen des Kunstforschers und Sammlers, 1–22 Jahrg.; 1949, Heft 1–4/5. Leipzig, Klinkhardt & Biermann, 1909–30; Köln, Greven, 1949. 25–32 cm.

Semimonthly; bimonthly in 1949. Publication ceased Dec. 1930. Merged with *Pantheon* . . . to Dec. 1944. Resumed publication in 1949. Subtitle varies. Rather popular, but some brief notes by well-known scholars. Contains articles on private and museum collections, individual works and artists, and sales news.

English translations are in v. 30. In 1928 and 1929 a "Sonderheft"; "Kunstliteratur," a classified group of short signed reviews: 1928, 56 p.; 1929, 48 p. Some book reviews. In *Art index,* v. 21–22. Also indexed in *B. d. d. Z.*

2215

College art journal, v. 1–(16), Nov. 1941–(57). [N.Y., College Art Association of America, 1941–(57)]. 23 cm.

Quarterly. Supersedes *Parnassus* and continues certain of its features. Primarily the organ of the Association. Lists programs of the annual meetings and sometimes contains abstracts of papers presented there. Contains notes on teaching appointments, college acquisitions, and exhibitions. Short signed book reviews. Also articles on art education. In general not illustrated. Winter 1951 issue has classified listing of pending Ph.D. theses in art history. Supplement: "The teaching of art in the colleges of the United States" by Robert J. Goldwater, in v. 2, no. 4. Indexed in *Art index; B. d. f. Z.*

2216

Commentari; rivista di critica e storia dell'arte, anno 1–(8). Roma, De Luca [1950–(57)]. 30 cm.

Quarterly. Edited by Mario Salmi and Lionello Venturi. Anno 1–2 published in Florence by Felice Le Monnier. Contains scholarly articles on art of all periods. "Recensioni," 1950–sett. 1954, contains signed book reviews. "Bollettino bibliografico" contains shorter signed reviews and from v. 2– list of books and periodical articles, arranged loosely by subject. "Documenti," v. 1–2, prints material of archival nature.

√ **2217**

Congrès Archéologique de France. Session tenue à . . . par la Société française d'archéologie [1]–(113). Paris, Picard [1834]–(1957). 23 cm. Annual.

Publisher and place vary. Title for 1843–1903 is *Séances générales tenues à* . . . 1908–12 issued in two parts: (1) Guide du Congrès; (2) Procès-verbaux et mémoires. Volumes 1–11 and 15 are included in the Society's *Bulletin monumental,* v. 1–10. Each volume deals with monuments of a different French locality, giving scholarly and detailed descriptions of architecture, sculpture, inscriptions, etc.

Indexed in: Société Française d'Archéologie. *Table alphabétique des publications de la Société française d'archéologie pour la conservation des monuments historiques, 1834–1925.* Paris, Picard, 1930. 497 p. 23 cm. Société Française d'Archéologie. *Table alphabétique des publications de la Société française d'archéologie: Congrès archéologique—Bulletin monumental, 1926–54.* Or-

léans, Pillault, 1956. [193] p. (Bulletin monumental, v. 112, fasc. 5, 1954)

2218

The Connoisseur; an illustrated magazine for collectors, v. 1–(140). [London] 1901–(57). 28 cm.

Frequency varies. 1901–41, monthly; 1942–49, quarterly; 1950–53, bimonthly; 1953– , appears nine times a year. Absorbed *International studio* in 1931. Contains articles on silverware, china, furniture, tapestry, paintings, sculpture, etc., and news of sales. Well illustrated and has good color plates. Book reviews, some signed by initials. "The Connoisseur in America" begins in v. 93 and contains news of exhibitions and acquisitions of private collectors and museums. Indexed for v. 1–12, 1901–05; v. 13–14, 1906–09. In *Art index*, v. 83, 1929– . Also indexed in *Rev. of revs.; Subj. ind. to pers.; Ann. mag. subj. ind.; Int. index; B. d. f. Z.*

2219

Copenhagen. Statens Museum for Kunst. Kunstmuseets aarsskrift, 1–(42) [1914]–(55). København, Langkjaersbogtrykkeri, 1914–(56). 30 cm.

Annual. Sometimes two years combined. Publisher varies. Contains rather long articles dealing mostly with Danish art or art of other countries in Danish museums. Since 1948 contains short résumés in French and English at the end of some articles. Occasionally, articles in English, French, or German. Indexed in *Dansk tids.–index; B. d. f. Z.*

———. Registre til Kunstmuseets aarsskrift I–XXX [1914–43]. København, 1945. 144 p.

2220

Country life . . . v. 1–(122). London [1897–(1957)]. 37 cm.

Weekly. Subtitle, v. 16–98: *The journal for all interested in country life and country pursuits.* While not an art or architectural periodical, it is invaluable for photographs and detailed descriptions of English country houses, their furnishings and collections. Also covers fashions, i.e., costume. Excellent clear illustrations. Volume 81 contains a list of country homes illustrated in v. 1–81. Each volume is carefully indexed and in addition indexes were published in July–Dec. 1933 and 1953. Indexed in *Subj. ind. to pers.*

2221

Creative art; a magazine of fine and applied art, v. 1–12, Oct. 1927–May 1933. [N.Y., Boni, 1927–33]. 30 cm.

Monthly. Volumes 1–8, no. 3 incorporate *The Studio* of London (v. 94, no. 415–v. 101, no. 456). Merged into *American magazine of art,* Jan. 1934. More popular than scholarly, but some scholars wrote for it. Contains short signed book reviews. Deals mainly with contemporary art, but also includes some articles on the past and some emphasis on the American art world. Gallery notes. In *Art index,* v. 4–12. Also indexed in *Ann. mag. subj. ind.*

2222

La Critica d'arte, v. 1–8, ott. 1935–1950; no. 1, genn. 1954–(no. 24, novembre/dicembre 1957). Firenze, Sansoni [1935–50], Vallecchi [1954–(57)]. 28 cm.

Bimonthly. Subtitle: *Rivista bimestrale di arti figurative,* v. 1–8. Long scholarly articles devoted to Italian and ancient art with a few on contemporary French and Italian art. Well illustrated. A few articles in German with Italian summaries; some French articles also. 1939–40 divides into two sections, one on ancient art and the other on medieval, Renaissance, and modern art. 1941 begins a new series devoted exclusively to ancient art, with particular stress on Greek art on Italian soil. Suspended publication with v. 7, 1942, and was resumed in May 1949 with "Terza serie, anno 8, no. 1, fasc. 27." This number covers medieval, Renaissance, and modern art. Articles in Italian, French, and English. New series began in 1954, called *Critica d'arte nuova rivista,* diretta da Carlo L. Ragghianti. Art of all periods covered. Unsigned book reviews, ser. 3, anno 8– . Indexed in *B. d. f. Z.*

2223

Dedalo; rassegna d'arte, anno 1–13, giugno 1920–giugno 1933. Milano-Roma, Bestetti e Tumminelli, 1920–33. 30 cm.

Monthly. Of general European art interest, covering the art of all periods and the applied arts. Scholarly articles. "Commenti" contains notes on publications and exhibitions and brief obituaries. In *Art index,* v. 10–13. Also indexed in *B. d. f. Z.*

2224

Deutsche Kunst und Denkmalpflege, v. 1–35, 1899–1933; n.s., 1–15, no. 7/8, 1934–42/43. Berlin, Deutscher Kunstverlag [etc.], 1899–1943. 24–35 cm.

Frequency varies. Title varies: 1899–Dec. 1922, *Die Denkmalpflege;* 1923–Dec. 1929, *Denkmalpflege und Heimatschutz;* 1930–32, *Die Denkmalpflege.* Absorbed *Heimatschutz* 1923, and *Zeitschrift für Denkmalpflege* 1930.

Covers the monuments of Germany, Austria, and other German lands. Contains signed book reviews and bibliographies. Index: v. 1–15, 1899–1913. Indexed in *B. d. d. Z.*

2225

Deutsches Archäologisches Institut. Athenische Abteilung. Mitteilungen, Bd. 1–(71/72). Berlin, Mann [1876]–(1957). 25 cm.

Quarterly, 1876–1913, 1915. Annual, 1914, 1918– . Issued 1876–1913 by the Abteilung under the Institute's earlier names: (1) Kaiserlich deutsches archäologisches Institut; (2) Archäologisches Institut des deutschen Reiches; (3) Deutsches archäologisches Institut. Publisher and place vary. Not published 1943–52. Long scholarly articles by specialists, on subjects pertaining to Greek art and archaeology. Indexes covering: Bd. 1–5, 1876–80; Bd. 6–10, 1881–86; Bd. 11–15, 1887–91; Bd. 16–20, 1892–96, each in one volume. In *Art index,* v. 55–64, 1930–39. Also indexed in *B. d. d. Z.*

2226

Deutsches Archäologisches Institut. Jahrbuch, Bd. 1–(71²), 1886–(1956). Berlin, De Gruyter, 1887–(1956). 28 cm.

Quarterly (sometimes combined). Publisher varies. Title varies: 1886–1917, *Jahrbuch des Kaiserlich deutschen archäologischen Instituts; Jahrbuch* supersedes the *Annali dell'Istituto di corrispondenza archeologica* (1829–85) and the *Archäologische Zeitung* (1843–85). "Archäologischer Anzeiger, Beiblatt zum Jahrbuch des . . . Instituts," containing reports of the Institute, proceedings of the Archaologische Gesellschaft zu Berlin, archaeological notices, bibliographies, etc., is issued serially with the numbers of the *Jahrbuch* (beginning with v. 4, 1889). The assembled numbers for each year form an independently paged section, usually bound with each volume of the *Jahrbuch.* Contains scholarly articles by specialists on subjects of archaeological interest. Includes bibliographies. Index issued for v. 1–10, 1886–95; v. 11–20, 1896–1905; v. 21–30, 1906–15; v. 31–40, 1916–25; v. 41–50, 1926–35, each in a separate volume. In *Art index,* v. 44–55, 1929–40. Also indexed in *Int. index* and *B. d. d. Z.*

2227

Deutsches Archäologisches Institut. Jahrbuch. Ergänzungsheft, 1–(18). Berlin, De Gruyter, 1888–(1955). 28 x 29 cm.

Publisher varies. A series of monographs by various authors, covering various subjects. (1) Strzygowski, Josef. Die Calender-bilder des Chronographen vom Jahre 354. 1888; (2) Bohn, Richard. Altertümer von Aegae. 1889; (3) Winnefeld, Hermann. Die Villa des Hadrian bei Tivoli. 1895; (4) Humann, Karl. Altertümer von Hierapolis. 1898; (5) Körte, Gustav. Gordion. 1904; (6) Wunsch, Richard. Antikes Zaubergerät aus Pergamon. 1905; (7) Führer, Josef. Die altchristlichen Grabstätten Siziliens. 1907; (8) Pagenstecher, Rudolf. Die calenische Reliefkeramik. 1909; (9) Conze, Alexander. Mamurt-Kaleh; ein Tempel der Göttermutter unweit Pergamon. 1911; (10) Diest, Walther von. Nysa ad Maeandrum. 1913; (11) Blümel, Carl. Griechische Bildhauerarbeit. 1927; (12) Messerschmidt, Franz. Nekropolen von Vluci. 1930; (13) Jantzen, Ulf. Bronzewerkstätten in Grossgriechenland und Sizilien. 1937; (14) Züchner, Wolfgang. Griechische Klappspiegel. 1942; (15) Kleiner, G. Tanagrafiguren. 1942; (16) Literaturberichte für die Jahre 1939–1947. 1950 (a classed bibliography including both books and periodical articles); (17) Neutsch, Bernhard. Studien zur vortanagräischattischen Koroplastik. 1952; (18) Budde, Ludwig. Severisches Relief in Palazzo Sacchetti. 1955.

2228

Deutsches Archäologisches Institut. Mitteilungen, Bd. 1–6, 1948–53. München, Bruckmann [1950–53]. 27 cm.

Annual. Superseded as a merger Archäologisches Institut des deutschen Reichs. *Athenische Zweiganstalt, Mitteilungen,* and *Römische Zweiganstalt, Mitteilungen,* while they were suspended. Scholarly treatments of archaeology in general. Indexed in *B. d. d. Z.*

2229

Deutsches Archäologisches Institut. Römische Abteilung. Mitteilungen. Bullettino, Bd. 1–(64). Heidelberg, Kerle, 1886–(1957). 24–26 cm.

Frequency varies. Publisher and place vary. Slight variation in spelling of title. Supersedes *Bullettino,* issued 1829–85 by Deutsches archäologisches Institut under an earlier name. Issued 1886–1915 and first half of 1917 under the Institute's earlier name, K. Deutsches archäologisches Institut. Not published 1945–52, during which time it was continued in part by the *Mitteilungen* issued by the Institute. Scholarly articles by specialists dealing with subjects of Roman archaeology and art. Indexes published covering: v. 1–10, 1886–95; v. 1–30, 1886–1915 (as

v. 31); v. 32–55, 1917–40 (as v. 56). In *Art index,* v. 44–54, 1929–39. Also indexed in *B. d. d. Z.*

2230

La Diana; rassegna d'arte e vita senese, anno 1–9. Siena [etc., 1926–34]. 33 cm.

Quarterly. Deals exclusively with Sienese art with greatest emphasis on painting, but also includes music and literature. Each volume has indexes of subjects, persons and places, and illustrations. Long articles by well-known scholars. Volumes 2 and 3 have lists of Sienese painters of the 13th to 15th centuries.

2231

Domus; l'arte nella casa . . . anno 1–(no. 337). Milano, Domus, 1928–(57). 30 cm.

Monthly. Subtitle varies. Covers architecture and the decorative arts, and also theater, cinema, music, and literature both modern and traditional; with a few articles on the fine arts. Well and profusely illustrated. Contains book reviews, some of which are signed. Indexed in *B. d. f. Z.*

2232

Eastern art . . . v. 1–3, July 1928–31. Philadelphia, College Art Association, c1928–31. 31 cm.

Quarterly, v. 1; annual, v. 2–3. Contains articles by recognized authorities in the field and lists of museum accessions. Volume 1 includes sections "Book reviews" and "Oriental abstracts" which are brief reviews of the current literature arranged by country and then by subject. Indexed in *Art index; Ann. mag. subj. index.*

2233

Emporium, v. 1–(126). Bergamo, Istituto Italiano d'Arti Grafiche [1895–(1957)]. 26–28 cm.

Monthly. Subtitle varies. A well-illustrated popular review which deals primarily with modern Italian art and culture. Contains a section "Chronache" with notes on exhibitions throughout the world. Book reviews, signed after v. 60, 1924. In *Art index,* v. 69–107. Also indexed in *B. d. f. Z.* and *Italy. Parl. Cam. dei Deputati. Bibl.*

———. Indice venticinquennale della rivista Emporium (1895–1919). Comp. a cura dell dott. Nello Tarchiani. Bergamo [192?]. 111 p.

2234

Fasti archaeologici . . . [v.] 1–[(10)], 1946–(57). Firenze, Sansoni, 1948–(57). 28 cm. Annual.

Subtitle: *Annual bulletin of classical archaeology*. Published by the International Association for Classical Archaeology and sponsored by UNESCO and the Metropolitan Museum of Art. It is a classed bibliography of publications in the field of archaeology and bulletin of discoveries throughout the classical world, with an author index to each volume. English, French, German, and Italian items included. Contents: (1) Generalia (by countries); (2) Prehistoric and classical Greece; (3) Italy before the Roman empire; (4) The Hellenistic world, and Eastern provinces of the Roman empire; (5) The Roman West; (6) Christianity and late antiquity. Lists of abbreviations and of contributors and their affiliations. Indexed in *B. d. f. Z.*

2235

Felix Ravenna, fasc. 1–(75). Ravenna, Tipografia Arti Grafiche [1911–(57)]. 25–26 cm.

Quarterly, 1911–17; irregular, 1919–29; three nos. a year, 1930– . None published in 1918, 1920–24, 1928, 1933, 1935–37, 1940–49. Subtitle and publisher vary. No. 34– called "Nuova serie." "Terza serie" begun 1950. The articles deal with the art of Ravenna and the surrounding country, and include much archival material. Includes section "Rassegna bibliografia." Three monographic supplements issued in 1914, 1916, 1928. An occasional article written in English or German. "Indici generali della prima quattro annate [1911–14]" in fasc. 16, p. 723–34. "Indici delle annate V e VI (fasc. XVII–XXIV)," 7 p. at end of fasc. 24.

——. Indici della prima serie, 1911–1929 (fasc. I–XXXIII). Ravenna, Arti Grafiche, 1933. 95 p.

2236

Figura; studies edited by the Institute of Art History, Univ. of Uppsala, 1–(8). Stockholm, Almqvist & Wiksell [1951–(56)]. 27 cm. Annual.

"This publication presents the results of researches carried out at the Institute of Art History of Uppsala University." Scholarly articles on art history in general in various languages, with English predominating. Volumes 2– are monographic.

2237

Formes; revue internationale des arts plastiques, no. 1–33, 1930–mars 1933. Paris, Éditions des Quatres Chemins [1930–33]. 28 cm.

Appeared ten times a year in both a French and an American ed. Reappeared for 1934 in *L'Amour de l'art*, année 15, 1934, pt. 2. Covers contemporary art of international scope and also some art of other periods. Well illustrated. Some few book reviews, some of which are signed. Indexed in *Art index; B. d. f. Z.*

2238

Formes et couleurs, année 1–(12, no. 1). Lausanne, Held, 1939–(54). 32 cm.

Frequency varies; usually bimonthly. Covers art, literature, theater, etc. Popular rather than scholarly, but well illustrated with good color plates. Each number is devoted to a particular topic, i.e., Medicine, Children, War, etc. Contains book reviews. In *Art index* since 1948, année 10.

2239

France. Comité des Travaux Historiques et Scientifiques. Bulletin archéologique, année 1883–(1954). Paris, Imprimerie Nationale, 1883–(1956). 24 cm. Annual.

At head of title: Ministère de l'instruction publique et des beaux-arts. Supersedes *Revue des sociétés savantes*, 1856–81, and their *Bulletin historique et philologique*, 1882. Contains scholarly articles on archaeology in general, especially French and North African. An index for 1916–40, and indexes at the end of each recent volume. Indexed in: *Rép. bibl.; B. d. f. Z.*

——. Tables générales, 1883–1915. Paris, 1923. 1083 p. 25 cm.

2240

Gazette des beaux-arts, t. 1–25 (1.–10. année), 1859–68; 2. pér., t. 1–38 (11.–30. année), 1869–88; 3. pér., t. 1–40 (31.–50. année), 1889–1908; 4. pér., t. 1–15 (51.–61. année), 1909–19; 5. pér., t. 1–18 (62.–70. année), 1920–28; 6. pér., t. 1–(50) (71.–(99.) année), jan. 1929/déc. 1957. Paris, N.Y., 1859–(1957). 28–30 cm.

Monthly in general, except for some irregularities. Publication suspended Oct. 1870–Sept. 1871, Sept. 1914–May 1916, July 1939–Sept. 1942, July 1955–Oct. 1956. Publisher varies. Pér. 6, t. 22–33, Oct. 1942–1948 published in N.Y. in English; pér. 6, t. 34, 1948 – published in Paris and N.Y. in French and English. From 1929– English summaries for French, and French summaries for English, articles. An important French periodical containing scholarly articles on all phases and periods of art. *La Chronique des arts et de la curiosité* has been issued as a supplement since 1861; in recent years, incorporated in the magazine, covers sales, museum acquisitions, exhibitions, and notes on the art world. Includes considerable bibliographical information and signed book reviews. In *Art index*, pér. 6, t. 1– . Also indexed in *Rép. bibl.; B. d. f. Z.; Subj. ind. to pers.*

――――. Tables générales des cinquantes premières années . . . 1859–1908, par Charles du Bus . . . Paris, 1910–15. 2 v. 29 cm.

――――. Table alphabétique et raisonnée du t. 1–3. pér., t. 8, 1859–92. Paris, 1866–95. 4 v.

2241

Gentsche bijdragen tot de kunstgeschiedenis, deel 1–(16). Antwerpen, "De Sikkel" [1934–(56)]. 26 cm.

An annual published under the auspices of the Hooger Instituut voor Kunstgeschiedenis en Oudheidkunde of the University of Ghent. Long scholarly articles, mostly on Flemish art, but some few on Egyptian, Sumerian, etc. In Flemish, with French and some English résumés. Each volume lists contents of previous volumes.

2242

Goya; revista de arte, no. 1–(21), julio-agosto 1954–(57). Madrid, Fundación Lazaro Galdiano, 1954–(57). 31 cm. Bimonthly.

A well-illustrated Spanish journal of the arts, covering all periods of painting, sculpture, and architecture. Contributors are from various countries but all the material is in Spanish. Contains book reviews. Short notices of exhibitions throughout the world, and longer articles on art happenings in Europe and the United States.

2243

Graphis; international bimonthly for graphic and applied art, v. 1–(13), Sept./Oct. 1954–(57). Zürich, Amstutz & Herdeg-Graphis Press [1944–(57)]. 30 cm. Bimonthly.

A profusely illustrated periodical with emphasis on the graphic and applied arts, i.e., posters, calligraphy, cartoons, and packaging; but some few articles on painting and art in general. Articles in German, French, and English. Signed reviews of books (predominantly Swiss) in German and English. In *Art index*, v. 4, no. 21, Jan. 1949– . Also indexed in *B. d. d. Z.*

2244

Die graphischen Künste, v. 1–56, 1879–1933; n. F. 1–5, no. 2, 1936–40. Baden bei Wien, Rohren, 1879–1940. 40 cm.

Volumes 1–56 published in Wien, Gesellschaft für vervielfältigende Kunst.

Great emphasis on contemporary graphic arts, book illustration, etc. Many signed and profusely illustrated book reviews, with mention of the processes used and the illustrators. "Mitteilungen der Gesellschaft für vervielfältigende Kunst" is included.

Volumes 24–55 contain "Anzeigen neuer Erscheinungen" which lists: (1) illustrated books and the literature of the graphic arts; (2) periodical references to the graphic arts. In *Art index*, v. 52–56 and n. F. v. 1–5, no. 2. Also indexed in *B. d. d. Z.*

2245

Hesperia; journal of the American School of Classical Studies at Athens, v. 1–(26). Cambridge, Mass., Harvard Univ. Press, 1932–(57). 29 cm. Quarterly.

Publisher and place vary. Long scholarly articles reporting on the work of the School and of excavations of the Agora in Athens, and on other related subjects, Latin as well as Greek. Supplements (9) are monographic. In *Art index*, v. 17, 1948– . Also indexed in *B. d. f. Z.*

――――. Index, v. I–X, Supplements I–VI. [Cambridge, Mass.] Am. Sch. of Classical Studies at Athens, 1946. 266 p.

2246

House and home, v. 1–(12). N.Y., Time, Inc., 1952–(57). 31 cm. Monthly.

Issued 1952– as one of the two parts (called editions) of the *Magazine of building*. Both parts issued in one cover as sections of *Architectural forum; the magazine of building* in Dec. 1951.

Emphasis on practical architecture in America today, dealing with home construction. Sister publication of *Architectural forum*. Indexed in *Art index; Ind. arts index; P. A. I. S.*

2247

Indian Society of Oriental Art. Journal, v. 1–(19), June 1933–(52/53). [Calcutta, 1933–(53?)]. 28 cm.

Twice a year, v. 1–8; then annual. Supersedes *Rupam*.

Contains articles by recognized scholars dealing with Indian art, with good plates, some in color. Includes fairly long, signed book reviews in v. 1–4 and 12. A table of names and terms of Buddhist iconography in Sanskrit, Chinese, and Japanese in alphabetical order, according to the Sanskrit, in v. 6, p. 57–62.

2248

The International studio. v. 1–99, March 1897–Aug. 1931. N.Y., Lane, 1897–1931. 30–33 cm. Monthly.

From 1897 to 1921 it forms the American ed. of *The Studio*, v. 1 of *The International studio* corresponding to v. 10 of *The Studio*. Part of each number was printed in England and joined with an American section. From 1922, produced entirely in America. Combined with *The Connoisseur* Sept. 1931.

A well-illustrated, popular type of art journal covering all phases of art and including some book reviews. In *Art index*, v. 92–99. Also indexed in *Ann. mag. subj. ind.; B. d. f. Z.; Readers' guide; Poole's.*

2249

Iskusstvo; organ Ministerstva Kultury SSSR i Org' Komiteta Soiuza sovetskikh khudozhnikov SSSR, 1933–(57). Moskva, Leningrad, Ogiz Izogiz [1933–(57)]. 25 cm. Bimonthly.

Publisher and subtitle vary. Contains articles on Russian art, chiefly of the contemporary period. It is well and profusely illustrated and has bibliographical notes and a section of news of the Russian art world. Indexed in *B. d. f. Z.*

2250

Istituto Nazionale di Archeologia e Storia dell'Arte, Rome. Rivista, anno 1–9, 1929–42; n.s. 1–(5/6), 1952–(56/57). Roma, "L'Erma" di Bretschneider, 1929–(57). 30 cm.

Three fascicles a year, anno 1–9; n.s. is annual. Anno 1–9 have title: Istituto d'Archaeologia e Storia dell'Arte, Roma. *Rivista*. Publisher varies. Suspended 1942–51.

Long scholarly articles on art and archaeology in Italy. Valuable for material on Italian excavations, and Renaissance and Baroque art. Well illustrated. Indexed in *B. d. f. Z.*

2251

Italy. Istituto Centrale del Restauro. Bollettino, nos. 1–(30). [Rome] Istituto poligrafico dello stato; Libreria dello stato, 1950–(57). 25 cm. Quarterly.

At head of title: Ministero della pubblica istruzione. Cesare Brandi, editor, no. 1– .

Contains articles and shorter notices on preservation and restoration of architecture, sculpture, and painting; mostly Italian, but sometimes of other countries. Scholarly approach, with much illustration.

There are signed reviews of books and periodical articles, and English summaries, in the last number of each year. No. 14–15 is devoted to restoration of Sienese paintings.

2252

Jahrbuch der kunsthistorischen Sammlungen in Wien, Bd. 1–36, 1883–1925; n. F. 1–13, 1926–[44]; Bd. 50–(53), 1953–(57). Wien, Tempsky [etc.] 1883–(1957). 38 cm. Annual.

Called *Jahrbuch der kunsthistorischen Sammlungen des allerhöchsten Kaiserhauses*, v. 1–34.

Long scholarly articles by specialists covering all types of art and periods. The last number of v. 1–34 usually contains sources for the history of the Viennese collections. Well illustrated.

Supplements issued: Ehrenpforte des Kaisers Maximilian I, 1885–86; Triumph des Kaisers Maximilian I, 1883–84; Das Heroon von Gjölbaschi-Trysa, 1889; Die Wiener Genesis, edited by Hartel and Wickhoff, 1895: these are of varying sizes. Volume 8 is devoted solely to "Der Theuerdank."

Index: v. 1–36 in v. 36; 55 p. In *Art index*, n. F. 1–12. Also indexed in *Int. index* and *B. d. d. Z.*

2253

Jahrbuch der preussischen Kunstsammlungen, Bd. 1–64. Berlin, Grote, 1880–1943. 35 cm. Quarterly.

Publisher varies. Long, scholarly, well-illustrated articles covering the art of various periods and countries.

"Amtliche Berichte aus den königlichen Kunstsammlungen" appears at beginning of v. 1–28. Thereafter it appears as a separate publication and contains articles dealing with objects in the museum collections. From 1902–18 each volume has a supplement containing archival material.

Indexes published covering: v. 1–10, 1891; v. 11–20, 1900; v. 21–30, 1910; v. 31–50, 1934 (Berlin, Grote). In *Art index*, v. 50–61, no. 1. Also indexed in *B. d. d. Z.* and *Int. index.*

2254

Jahrbuch für Kunstwissenschaft. Leipzig, Klinkhardt & Biermann, 1923–30. 31–33 cm. Annual.

Supersedes *Monatshefte für Kunstwissenschaft*. Merged with *Repertorium für Kunstwissenschaft* and *Zeitschrift für bildende Kunst* to form *Zeitschrift für Kunstgeschichte*.

Scholarly articles dealing with all types of art and all periods. Long signed book reviews at end of each *Heft*, and a classified bibliography of current literature in the 1926 and 1928 volumes. In *Art index*, 1929–30. Also indexed in *B. d. d. Z.*

2255
Journal of Egyptian archaeology, v. 1–(43). London, The Egypt Exploration Fund, 1914–(57). 29 cm.

Annual, 1940– ; quarterly, 1914–34; two numbers a year, 1935–39. Supersedes the *Archaeological report* published by The Egypt Exploration Fund. Bibliographies included, which also cover bibliographies of Greek inscriptions. In *Art index*, v. 27, 1941– . Also indexed in *Subj. ind. to pers.; B. d. f. Z.*

——. Indexes to volumes I–XX [1914–1934]. London, Egypt Exploration Society [1934]. 17 p.

2256
The Journal of Hellenic studies, v. 1–(77). London, The Council of the Soc. for the Promotion of Hellenic Studies [1880]–(1957). 23–28 cm. *and* atlas of 39 cm.

Semiannual, 1880–1939; annual, 1940– .
A wide variety of articles covering literature, archaeology, art, etc. Also contains signed book reviews.

In v. 1–8, 1880–87, the plates were published separately and numbered I–LXXXIII; 39 cm. Index to v. 1–8 in v. 8, p. 541–75. In *Art index*, v. 50, 1930– . Also indexed in *Poole's; B. d. f. Z.; Subj. ind. to pers.*

——. Index to v. 9–16 and supplements I & II. London, 1898. 56 p.

——. Index to v. 17–42 and supp. papers III. London, 1923. 103 p.

——. Index to v. 43–60. London, 1941. 93 p.

2257
The Journal of Indian art, v. 1–17, 1884/6–1915/6. London, Griggs, 1886–1916. 39 cm. Quarterly.

A rather popular type of journal published under the patronage of the Government of India, which covers Indian art as well as Indian industry. Well illustrated with many full-page plates. Indexed in *Subj. ind. to pers.*

2258
The Journal of Roman studies, v. 1–(47). London, The Soc. for the Promotion of Roman Studies, 1911–(57). 28 cm. Semiannual.

Contains scholarly, well-illustrated articles dealing with Roman civilization, including much on Roman Britain. Proceedings of the Society, Reports of the council, etc., are also included. Signed book reviews of varying lengths are given.

Indexes published: v. I–XX, 1911–30 with v. 20, p. 129–[227]; v. XXI–XL, 1931–50, published separately. In *Art index*, v. 18,

1928– . Also indexed in *Subj. ind. to pers.* and *B. d. f. Z.*

2259
The Kokka, no. 1–(789), Oct. 1889–(1957). Tokyo, The Kokka Co. [1889–(1957)]. 39 cm. Monthly.

None published 1945. Subtitle: *an illustrated monthly journal of the fine and applied arts of Japan and other eastern countries.* Nos. 1–337 (Oct. 1889–June 1918) were published in both Japanese and English editions. From no. 338, July 1918, down to the present, a Japanese ed. only, with English summaries.

Contains beautiful full-page black and white plates and colored tip-ins, representing Japanese and other Eastern arts. Indexed in *B. d. f. Z.*

2260
Konsthistorisk tidskrift; revy för konst och konstforskning . . . årgång 1–(26). Stockholm [1932–(57)]. 28 cm. Quarterly.

"Utgiven av Konsthistoriska sällskapet."
Contains articles in German, French, and English as well as Swedish. Most articles in Swedish have English or German summaries. Primarily covers art of the past, but some few articles on contemporary work. Includes book reviews, some of which are signed, of books in all Western languages, but a predominance of German literature. Indexed in *B. d. f. Z.*

2261
Kritische Berichte zur kunstgeschichtlichen Literatur, v. 1–7. Leipzig, Poeschel & Trepte [1927–38]. 26 cm. Quarterly.

Publisher varies.
A periodical devoted to criticism of art-historical literature, with long scholarly reviews written by specialists, and almost no illustration. While the first five volumes cover books only, v. 6 contains some periodical literature. Includes a few articles which are not reviews. Indexed in *B. d. d. Z.*

2262
Kroniek van kunst en kultuur, jaarg. 1–10. Amsterdam, Uitgeverij Contact, 1936–49. 28 cm.

Monthly; sometimes combined. Suspended 1942–Oct. 1945.
A rather popular type of Dutch review covering literature, music, stage, and screen as well as the fine arts. Emphasis on modern art, but not restricted to this field. Signed book reviews and notes. Indexed in: *Nijhoff; B. d. f. Z.*

2263

Die Kunst und das schöne Heim, Jahrg. 1–(55), Okt. 1899–(Sept. 1957). München, Bruckmann, 1899–(1957). 30 cm.

Monthly; frequency varies. Subtitle varies. Published as *Die Kunst; Monatshefte für freie und angewandte Kunst* from 1899–1944, in two volumes a year. The odd-numbered volumes 1–59 comprise *Die Kunst für Alle,* which covers the fine arts; and the even-numbered volumes 2–60, *Dekorative Kunst.* Beginning with v. 61, 1930 the odd-numbered volumes are *Freie Kunst* and the even-numbered ones *Angewandte Kunst.* Publication suspended Oct. 1944–April 1949.

A well-illustrated journal which rather leans toward the popular. Its scope is international in the earlier years but recently tends to be primarily German. Contains articles on contemporary work, exhibitions, etc. Some short book reviews. In *Art index,* v. 59–84, 1929–June 1941. Also indexed in *B. d. d. Z.*

2264

Kunst und Künstler, Jahrg. 1–32, 1902–Juni 1933. Berlin, Cassirer, 1902–33. 30–33 cm. Monthly.

Subtitle varies. A rather popular journal, but containing some serious articles by well-known scholars and some signed book reviews. Covers largely 19th and 20th century European art. In *Art index,* v. 27–32. Also indexed in *B. d. d. Z.*

2265

Kunstchronik; Nachrichten aus Kunstwissenschaft, Museumswesen und Denkmalpflege, Jahrg. 1–(10), 1948–(57). Nürnberg, Carl [1948–(57)]. 21 cm.

Monthly; sometimes combined. "Herausgegeben vom Zentralinstitut für Kunstgeschichte in München."

Contains news of museums, exhibitions, institutes, congresses, obituaries, research, etc. in the field of art history. It is particularly valuable for tracing the fate of museum collections after the war.

"Bibliographie" lists German books currently appearing; and each volume also contains lists of publications of the year, both German and foreign. Signed book reviews, as well. A supplement, "Nachweis ausländischer Litteratur," published 1949–50, lists books in the fields of archaeology and Occidental art published outside Germany since 1939, and where they are located in German libraries. Entries are marked consecutively and are alphabetical in each issue. Each vol-

ume has a detailed index of authors, artists, and places. Indexed in *B. d. d. Z.*

2266

Kunsten idag, v. 1–([11]), Vinteren 1946/47–(57). Oslo, Per Rom [1947–(57)]. 31 cm. Quarterly.

A Norwegian periodical dealing with contemporary art of Norway and other countries and containing articles on artists and on types of art: e.g., tapestries, Negro sculpture, art of India, etc. English summaries at end of each issue. Well illustrated, with many color plates. Indexed in *Dansk tids.-index.*

2267

Kunstgeschichtliche Anzeigen. Neue Folge, Jahrg. 1–(2), 1955–(57). Graz-Köln, Hermann Böhlaus Nachf., 1955–(57). 23 cm.

Publisher and place vary.

Continues *Kunstgeschichtliche Anzeigen,* 1904–13 and *Kritische Berichte zur kunstgeschichtlichen Literatur,* 1927–38 (2261). It is a publication of the Kunsthistorisches Institut der Universität Wien, and of the Institut für Österreichische Geschichtsforschung (which published the original *Kunstgeschichtliche Anzeigen*).

Each issue is devoted to a review of current research on a particular subject.

Lists of recent books, arranged by period covered, and containing prices, are also included.

2268

Kunstgewerbeblatt; Monatsschrift für Geschichte und Litteratur der Kleinkunst, Jahrg. 1–5 [Okt. 1884–Sept.] 1889; n.F. 1–28 Jahrg. [Okt.] 1889–Sept. 1917. Leipzig, Seemann, 1884–1917. 29–34 cm. Monthly.

Subtitle varies. Issued as supplement to *Zeitschrift für bildende Kunst.* Contains short articles and news notes on industrial arts. Some book reviews. Indexed in *B. d. d. Z.*

2269

Kunsthistorisches Institut, Florenz. Mitteilungen, Bd. 1–(7). Berlin, Leipzig, Cassirer, 1908–(56). 27 cm. Irregular.

Publisher and place vary. None published 1914–15, 1918, 1942–52.

Scholarly articles dealing with Italian art and German artists working in Italy. Contains "Berichte über das Institut." In *Art index,* v. 3 (no. 3)–v. 6. Also indexed in *B. d. d. Z.*

2270

Das Kunstwerk; eine Zeitschrift über alle Gebiete der bildenden Kunst, Jahrg. 1–(10).

Krefeld und Baden-Baden, Agis-Verlag, 1947–(56). 27 cm.

Frequency varies. As of v. 11, no. 1, July 1957, monthly. Publisher and subtitle vary.

A well-illustrated periodical covering the art of all countries and periods, but particularly valuable for material on contemporary German artists. Contains reviews of exhibitions in various places, obituaries, and some signed book reviews. Some issues are devoted to a particular subject. Indexed in *B. d. d. Z.*

2271

Lalit Kalā; a journal of Oriental art, chiefly Indian, nos. 1/2–(3/4), April 1955/March 1956–(April 1956/March 1957). New Delhi, Lalit Kalā Akadami [1956?–(1957?)]. Semi-annual. 35 cm.

This publication is "devoted mainly to Indian art and archaeology but also [embraces] in its scope all aspects of Oriental art and archaeology which have any connection with the culture of this country."—*Editorial.*

Scholarly contributions, original research, discussions of recent museum acquisitions and of contemporary Indian art also.

"Each issue will contain several accurate colour plates of paintings, manuscript illustrations, etc. which hitherto have not been reproduced in colour . . ."—*Editorial.*

Signed reviews of books in the field.

2272

Liturgical arts; a quarterly devoted to the arts of the Catholic church, v. 1–(25), Fall 1931–(57). N.Y., The Liturgical Arts Society, 1932–(57). 31 cm. Quarterly.

Contains articles by well-known scholars dealing with the art of the Catholic church. Includes some book reviews, mostly signed. In *Art index,* v. 4, 1935– . Also indexed in *Catholic index.*

2273

Maandblad voor beeldende kunsten; tevens orgaan der "Vereeniging van Vrienden der Aziatische Kunst," jaarg. 1–26. Amsterdam, de Bussy, 1924–50. 29 cm.

Well-illustrated, fairly scholarly articles on all phases and periods of art. Much Oriental art is contained in the earlier volumes, and the "Bulletin" of the Vereeniging van Vrienden der Aziatische Kunst is included in jaarg. 6–21. Occasional signed book reviews. Indexed in *B. d. f. Z.* and *Nijhoff.*

2274

Magazine of art, v. 1–46, no. 5, 1909–May 1953. Washington, D.C., The American

Federation of Arts [1909–53]. 25–31 cm.

Monthly, Oct.–May. Called *Art and progress,* Nov. 1909–Dec. 1915; *American magazine of art,* Jan. 1916–Aug. 1936. Absorbed *Creative art,* Jan. 1934.

Particularly useful for American art although not confined to this subject. Articles by recognized writers. Contains book reviews, usually signed, and notes of exhibitions. In *Art index,* v. 20–46. Also indexed in *Ann. mag. subj. ind.; Readers' guide; B. d. f. Z.; Int. index.*

2275

The Magazine of art, v. 1–25, n.s., 1–2, 1878–July 1904. London, Paris, N.Y., Cassell [1878]–1904. Monthly.

Publisher varies. Issued in both an American and an English ed.

Contains material on some lesser English 19th century artists and some descriptions of English country homes and landscape. Emphasis is on contemporary art and artists. Short notes on the art world: sales, exhibitions, and book notices and reviews. Indexed in *Poole's; Readers' guide; Rev. of revs.*

2276

Marburger Jahrbuch für Kunstwissenschaft, Bd. 1–(16). Marburg/Lahn, Verlag des Kunstgeschichtlichen Seminars der Universität, 1924–(55). 29 cm. Annual.

Edited by Richard Hamann and others. Publisher and place vary. Suspended between 1949/50 and 1955.

Scholarly articles covering sculpture, painting, architecture, and the graphic arts of all periods, with emphasis on the Middle Ages. Occasional articles in English and French. In *Art index,* Bd. 1–13. Also indexed in *B. d. d. Z.*

2277

Marg, a magazine of architecture and art, v. 1–(10). Bombay [1947–(57)]. 32 cm. Quarterly.

Issued by the Modern Architectural Research Group. Covers various aspects of Indian art, including dance, photography, music, etc. It is well illustrated and contains good color illustrations. French résumés of articles. Some book reviews. Sometimes a whole number is devoted to a special area, e.g., Goa, Kashmir. Contains notes on exhibitions.

2278

Marsyas; a publication by the students of the Institute of Fine Arts, New York University, v. 1–(7). N.Y., N.Y. Univ. Press, 1941–(57). 28 cm. Irregular.

Subtitle varies. Scholarly articles written by students of the Institute. Gives list of subjects of dissertations and M. A. essays done at N.Y.U. In v. 5, a "Checklist of graduate theses in the fine arts presented in American universities, 1940–48." Indexed in *Art index*.

2279

Mélanges d'archéologie et d'histoire, année [1]–(69). Paris, DeBoccard; Roma, Spithöver [etc., 1881–(1957)]. 25–27 cm.

Annual; frequency varies. At head of title: École française de Rome.

Long scholarly articles which are valuable for Italian art and archaeology from prehistoric to the Renaissance periods. Bibliographies and signed reviews in the earlier volumes.

"Table des vingt premières années de *Mélanges,* 1881–1900," in année 20, p. [333]–74. Indexed in *Rép. bibl.; B. d. f. Z.*

————. Tables des tomes XXI–XXXVIII, 1910–20; tables des tomes I–XXXVIII, 1881–1920. Paris, 1920. 56 p.

————. Table des tomes XXXIX–LVII, 1921–40. Paris [1949]. 44 p.

2280

Minotaure, année 1–6, no. 1–12/13, 1933–mai 1939. [Paris, Skira, 1933–39] 32 cm.

Five times yearly, nos. 1–5; quarterly, no. 6–13. Année 4–6 also called troisième série. Number 2 has special title: "Mission Dakar-Dijibouti, 1931–33." A very well-illustrated periodical covering the literary and artistic tendencies of the present day. Much material on primitive art, and anthropological articles. An index to the 13 numbers has been compiled by Julia Sabine of the Newark (N.J.) Public Library and can be obtained from her.

2281

Mir iskusstva, t. 1–12. S.–Peterburg, 1899–1904. 31–34 cm.

Semimonthly, 1899–1900; monthly, 1901–04. Edited by Sergeĭ Diagilev and A. Benua.

Important as the organ of the Russian impressionists (who got their name, "miriskussniki," from the title of the periodical; they denied the importance of "realism" and subject in the creation of art, proclaimed by the old school of "peredvizhniki," and announced the new approach to art for art's sake).

2282

Moderne Bauformen; Monatshefte für Architektur und Raumkunst, Jahrg. 1–43, no. 9. Stuttgart, Hoffmann [1902]–44. 30–36 cm. Monthly.

Subtitle Jahrg. 1–5: *eine Sammlung von Details, Interieurs, und Facaden für Architekten und Bauhandwerker.*

More illustrations than text. Useful for pictures of contemporary architecture and decorative art, mostly German. Supplement: "Mitteilungen aus der Fachwelt." In *Art index*, v. 29–40, Jan. 1920–May 1941. Also indexed in *B. d. d. Z.*

2283

Monatshefte der kunstwissenschaftlichen Literatur, Jahrg. 1–3. Berlin, Meyer, 1905–07. 27 cm. Monthly.

A review of art literature with book reviews and bibliographies, which was superseded by *Monatshefte für Kunstwissenschaft.* Each number contains signed book reviews and a classed bibliography of recent books and periodical articles, dating from 1904. Indexed in *B. d. d. Z.*

2284

Monatshefte für Baukunst & Städtebau, Jahrg. 1–26. Berlin, Wasmuth [1914–42]. 32 cm. Monthly.

Title varies: *Wasmuths Monatshefte für Baukunst,* Jahrg. 1–14. Absorbed *Der Städtebau,* Jan. 1930. Publisher varies.

Articles by scholars on architecture of the past and present, but latterly more emphasis on present-day architecture. Contains reviews and summaries of periodical articles. In *Art index,* v. 15–24, Sept. 1931–May 1941. Also indexed in *B. d. d. Z.; Subj. ind. to pers.*

2285

Monatshefte für Kunstwissenschaft, Jahrg. 1–15, 1908–Sept. 1922. Leipzig, Klinkhardt & Biermann [1908–22]. 25–28 cm. Monthly.

Like *Monatshefte der kunstwissenschaftlichen Literatur,* with the addition of articles on European art history. Emphasis in the articles on German artists. Contains long signed book reviews and lists of periodical articles in the field, arranged by broad subjects. Superseded by *Jahrbuch für Kunstwissenschaft.* Indexed in *B. d. d. Z.*

2286

Mouseion, année 1–14, avr. 1927–45 [Paris, Institut International de Coopération Intellectuale] 1927–45. 24 cm.

Frequency varies. Main publication issued three times a year to v. 4, no. 12; thence quarterly. Published by Presses Universitaires de France, v. 1–2. Subtitle varies. Multigraphed until 1933.

The main part of the publication contains material on various museums throughout the world, on restorations, and on archaeological techniques. Volumes 1–3 contain English summaries of articles; v. 5 has supplements in English, German, Spanish, and Italian. Notes on museum personnel, annual reports, etc.

Two supplementary series exist: *Informations mensuelles,* mars 1932–sept. 1935; *Supplément mensuel,* oct. 1935–46. These are 23–27 cm. Both main publication and supplements have reviews and bibliographies. Indexed in *Art index,* v. 1–14, no. 2 (main pub.); *B. d. f. Z.*

———. Indexes: v. 1–50 [main pub.]; index to the supps. [Paris, Office International des Musées, 1946] 312 p.

2287
Münchner Jahrbuch der bildenden Kunst, Bd. 1–13, 1906–23; n.F., Bd. 1–12, 1924–39; 3. Folge, Bd. 1–(7), 1950–(56). München, Prestel, 1906–(56). 29 cm.

Annual; frequency varies. Suspended 1939–50. Publisher varies.

Covers ancient, medieval, Renaissance, and modern art through the 18th century. Contains a section which gives news of the state museums and their activities and acquisitions. In *Art index,* n.F. v. 6–13, 1929–39. Also indexed in *B. d. d. Z.*

2288
Museum; a quarterly review, v. 1–(10). [Paris, UNESCO, 1948–(57)] 30 cm. Quarterly.

Superseded *Mouseion.* Contains well-illustrated articles on museums in various countries, and problems of interest to museum workers. Notes on the contributors on inside of the back cover. Text in French and English. Indexed in *Subj. ind. to pers.; B. d. f. Z.*

2289
Museum; revista mensuel de arte español antiguo e moderno y de la vida artistica contemporanea, v. 1–7, no. 7. Barcelona, Thomas, 1920–28. 31 cm. Monthly.

A well-illustrated periodical covering modern Spanish art primarily. Contains book reviews and art notes.

2290
The Museum news, 1–(35). [Washington, D.C., American Assoc. of Museums, Smith-

sonian Institution, 1924–(57/58)] 28 cm. Semimonthly.

A newssheet publication containing short paragraphs of information regarding American museums. Contains reviews. Index to special articles v. 1–30, issued as a supplement to v. 30, Apr. 15, 1953. In *Art index,* v. 6, 1929– .

2291
Museums journal; the organ of the Museums Association, 1–(57), July 1901–(57/58). London, The Museums Assoc., 1902–(57/58). 22–27 cm. Monthly.

Publisher varies. Supersedes the Association's *Report of proceedings.*

Contains articles on museums in various parts of the world, but predominantly English. Some few book reviews and short news items. "Indexes to papers read before the Museums Association 1890–1909" in v. 9. In *Art index,* v. 29, July 1929– . Also indexed in *Subj. ind. to pers.*

2292
Museumskunde; Zeitschrift für Verwaltung und Technik offentlicher und privater Sammlungen, Bd. 1–17, 1905–Aug. 1924; n.F., Bd. 1–11, 1929–39. Berlin, Deutscher Museumsbund, 1905–39. 29 cm.

Quarterly after 1929. Subtitle varies. None published 1925–28.

Contains articles on museums throughout the world, but special emphasis on German ones, with a section covering literature in the museum field. Bibliographies included. Indexed in *B. d. d. Z.*

2293
Nederlands Historisch Instituut te Rome. Mededeelingen, deel 1–10, 1921–25; tweede reeks, deel 1–10, 1931–40; derde reeks, deel 1–(9), 1942–(57). 's Gravenhage, 1921–(57). 22–24 cm. Annual.

In Dutch but with French résumés. Scholarly articles on Italian art and archaeology, and the relationship between Dutch artists and Italy. "Résumés des études" in each volume. In *Art index,* v. 9–3d ser., v. 5, 1929–47.

2294
Nederlands kunsthistorisch jaarboek, v. [1]–(8). 's Gravenhage, Daamen, 1947–(57). 28 cm. Annual.

Volumes 5– published in Bussum, by Dishoeck, and bear title: *Nederlands kunsthistorisch jaarboek; Netherlands year-book for history of art.*

A scholarly, well-illustrated periodical

treating all phases of art history, with emphasis on Netherlandish art. Articles in English, French, German, and Italian, as well as Dutch, with English summaries of the latter.

2295

Nouvelles archives de l'art français . . . 1872–78; 2. sér., t. 1–6, 1879–85; 3. sér., t. 1–22, 1885–1906. Paris, Baur [etc.], 1872–1907. 22 cm.

Frequency varies; sér. 3 monthly. Preceded by *Archives de l'art français*, 1851–62 [*i.e.,* 66]. Continued as *Archives de l'art français . . . pub. par la Société de l'Histoire de l'Art Français*. Nouvelle période.

Subtitle varies; sér. 3 is called *Nouvelles archives de l'art français . . . revue de l'art français ancien et moderne,* and is in two sections, the second devoted to current sales, acquisitions, and books.

Séries 2, v. 4–6 are "Scellés et inventaires d'artistes," pub. par Jules Guiffrey, ptie. 1–3; sér. 3, v. 19–20, "Correspondance de M. de Marigny avec Coypel, Lépicié et Cochin," pub. par M. Marc Furcy-Raynaud, ptie. 1–2; sér. 3, v. 21–22, "Correspondance de M. d'Angiviller avec Pierre," pub. par M. Marc Furcy-Raynaud, ptie. 1–2; sér. 3, v. 17–18, "Procès-verbaux de la commission des monuments," t. 1–2.

"Table générale des documents contenus dans les *Archives de l'art français* et leurs annexes (1851–1896) [par Maurice Tourneux], sér. 3, v. 12, p. [253]–428.

2296

Nuovo bullettino di archeologia cristiana, anno 1–28. Roma, Libreria Spithover, 1895–1922. 28 cm.

Two double, or four, fascicles issued yearly. Publisher varies. Supersedes *Bulletino di archeologia cristiana* and was superseded by *Rivista di archeologia cristiana*.

From 1898–1922: Ufficiale per i resoconti della Commissione di archeologia sacra sugli scavi e su le scoperte nelle catacombe romane.

Useful for material on Early Christian art and archaeology. Contains reviews. Indexed in *B. d. f. Z.*

2297

L'Oeil; revue mensuelle d'art, no. 1–(36). Lausanne, Sedo [1955–(57)]. 31 cm. Monthly.

Edited by George and Rosamond Bernier. A well-illustrated periodical, with numerous color plates, covering art of all periods. Contains an interesting selection and range of articles and unusual side lights.

2298

Old master drawings, v. 1–14. London, Batsford, 1926–40. 28 cm. Quarterly.

Subtitle: *a quarterly magazine for students and collectors.* Editor: K. T. Parker.

Contains short articles by recognized scholars in the field and many excellent halftone reproductions of drawings. For each drawing gives size and provenance. Each volume has index of authors, subjects, artists, and collections. In *Art index,* v. 4–14.

2299

Onze kunst; geillustreerd maandschrift voor beeldende en decoratieve kunsten, deel [1]–46, jaarg. 1–25, 1902–juni 1929. Antwerpen, Burton; Amsterdam, Veen [1902–29]. 30 cm. Semiannual.

Supersedes *De Vlaamsche school.* Subtitle varies. None published 1921, 1923–24, 1927–June 1928. Publisher varies.

A semipopular journal of Flemish art which also contains information about exhibitions of other art in Flanders and the Netherlands. Contains book reviews and reviews of periodicals. Index: v. 1–20, 1902–11. Indexed in *B. d. f. Z.; Bibl. de Belgique; Hague. K. Bibl.*

2300

Oriens christianus; Hefte für die Kunde des christlichen Orients, Jahrg. 1–8; neue Serie, Bd. 1–14; dritte Serie, Bd. 1–14; vierte Serie, Bd. 1–(5). Wiesbaden, Harrassowitz, 1901–(57). 29 cm.

Semiannual; 4. ser., Bd. 1– annual. Publisher and place vary. Subtitle varies. Founded by the Priestercollegium des Deutschen Campo Santo in Rom im Auftrag der Görresgesellschaft. Not published 1942–52.

Scholarly articles on Christian culture in the East, and almost no illustrations. Contains long, signed book reviews. Indexed in *B. d. d. Z.*

2301

Oriental art, a quarterly journal devoted to the study of all forms of Oriental art, v. 1–3 [1948–51]; n.s., v. 1–(3), 1955–(57). [London] The Oriental Art Magazine Ltd. [1948–(57)]. 30 cm. Quarterly.

Contains scholarly articles by specialists on various aspects of Oriental art, news about museums and exhibitions of Oriental art throughout the world. Signed book reviews and a section called "Bibliography" which lists books and periodicals under general headings such as: Asia, Middle East, Greater India, and Far East. Indexed in *Subj. ind. to pers.*

2302

Ostasiatische Zeitschrift, Jahrg. 1–28, Apr. 1912–1942/43. Berlin und Leipzig, De Gruyter, 1912–43. 28 cm.

Quarterly, v. 1–14, then six times a year. Subtitle varies. Publisher varies. Volumes 11–28 also called n.F., v. 1–18.

Includes articles on Eastern art in German, French, and English, and is especially valuable for book reviews and bibliographies on Far Eastern art. Gives lists of periodical articles pertaining to Oriental studies in German and foreign periodicals, listed by place of publication. Lists new publications according to geographical area they cover. Includes sales notes and notes of the art world of this field, and lists catalogs dealing with Oriental art.

Volumes 15– include "Mitteilungen der Gesellschaft für Ostasiatische Kunst." In *Art index*, n.F., v. 15–16, 1929–40. Also indexed in *B. d. d. Z.*

2303

Österreichische byzantinische Gesellschaft. Jahrbuch, 1–(5). Wien, Verlag Herder, 1951–(56). 24 cm. Annual.

Publisher and place vary.

Contributions—in English, French, German, or Italian—by internationally known scholars on Byzantine history and art. It contains signed book reviews.

2304

Österreichisches archäologisches Institut in Wien. Jahreshefte, Bd. 1–(43 Beiblatt). Baden bei Wien, Rohrer, 1898–(1956). 29 cm. Annual.

Publisher varies.

Contains scholarly articles on archaeological subjects and epigraphy. Has a separately paged "Beiblatt" which contains news or notes on excavations, and shorter articles.

Index to Bd. 1–5 in Bd. 5, Beiblatt; Bd. 6–10 in Bd. 10, Beiblatt. Indexes to Bd. 19–20 and 21–22 issued as a combined volume. In *Art index*, v. 24–31, no. 2, 1929–39. Also indexed in *B. d. d. Z.*

2305

Oud-Holland, jaarg. 1–(72). Amsterdam, De-Bussy, 1883–(1957). 28 cm.

Annual to v. 41; now quarterly. Publisher varies. Subtitle varies.

A scholarly Dutch periodical dealing with Dutch art but also including articles on history and literature. Some material in German, French, and English. English summaries. Contains signed book reviews.

Beginning with v. 65 for 1950, also includes "Mededelingen van het Rijksbureau voor Kunsthistorische Documentatie." Volumes 42–54 contain "Overzicht der literatuur betreffende Nederlandsche kunst," by country of origin. Supplement to v. 3: "Dagboek van Constantyn Huygens . . . door J. H. W. Unger," 1885.

Indexes covering v. 1–40, 1883–1922, in v. 40; v. 41–50, 1923–33, in v. 50. In *Art index*, v. 46–57. Also indexed in *B. d. f. Z.; Nijhoff; Hague. K. Bibl.*

———. Oud-Hollands systematische inhoudsopgave van den 1sten–60sten jaargang, 1883–1943 door C. Bille. [1946?] 76 p.

Indexes years 1–60.

2306

Palladio; rivista di storia dell'architettura, anno 1–5, 1937–41; n.s. 1–(7), 1951–(57). Milano, Hoepli, 1937–(57). 32 cm. Bimonthly.

Suspended 1942–50. Covers architecture from the prehistoric to the 20th century in Italy and elsewhere. Includes brief signed book reviews. Beginning with n.s., no. 2, April 1951, sometimes includes summaries in English, French, and German of important articles.

2307

Pallas; international art and archaeology news bulletin, v. 1–15. Geneva, Switzerland, 1937–51. 22 cm.

Weekly, often combined. Reproduced from typewritten copy. Title varies: v. 1–2, 1937–38 in German and called *Neue Pallas*; v. 3–10, 1939–46 *The New Pallas*, in English.

Gives news of the art world including: museums and collections, acquisitions and loans, exhibitions, discoveries, excavations, losses and thefts, art dealers' news, and obituaries. Useful for news of the art world during the last war. Items arranged by place under the above headings. No illustrations and no indexes.

2308

Pantheon; Monatsschrift für Freunde und Sammler der Kunst, Bd. 1–32. München, Bruckmann [1928–44]. 32 cm. Monthly.

Cicerone merged with it in v. 7, Jan. 1931.

A well-illustrated periodical with short articles by recognized authorities covering European and some Oriental art, with English summaries. Some color plates. Includes museum and art world notes. Signed book reviews from v. 2 on. Occasional articles in English and French. In *Art index*, v. 1–27. Also indexed in *B. d. d. Z.*

2309

Paragone; mensile di arte figurative e letteratura, anno 1–(8). Firenze, Sansoni, 1950–(57). 22 cm. Monthly.

Issued in two sections: odd-numbered parts called *Arte;* even-numbered, *Letteratura.* Editor: Roberto Longhi.

Arte section is a general Italian art periodical including articles on art of various countries and periods, reviews of exhibitions, and signed book reviews. Sometimes includes a section "Antologia di critici" which reprints art criticism of various countries and periods; "Antologia di artisti" gives notes on works of art in various museums. Indexed in *B. d. f. Z.*

2310

Paris. Musée national du Louvre. Laboratoire de recherches scientifiques. Bulletin, année 1–(2), juin 1956–(oct. 1957). Paris, Conseil des musées nationaux [1956–(57)]. 28 cm.

Edited by Germain Bazin and Madeleine Hours. Supplement to *La Revue des arts.* First issue has a bibliography of works issued by the Laboratory, 1936–55.

2311

Parnassus, v. 1–13. [N.Y., College Art Association of America, 1929–41] 29 cm.

Monthly, Oct.–May. Replaced by the *College art journal.*

Less scholarly than the *Art bulletin* and contains short signed book reviews, lists of exhibitions in New York, recent museum acquisitions, and programs of the College Art Association meetings. Indexed in *Art index* and *B. d. f. Z.*

2312

Pictures on exhibit; world wide views of the art shows, v. 1–(20), Nov. 1937–(June 1957). N.Y., Pictures Pub. Co., 1937–(57). 20 cm.

Monthly, except July–Sept. Subtitle varies. Contains short articles on various exhibitions and lists the current exhibitions in the United States, gallery news, etc. In *Art index*, v. 6, Nov. 1944–Apr. 1945.

2313

Die Plastik; illustrierte Zeitschrift für die gesamte Bildhauerei und Bildnerei und ihre Beziehungen zu Architektur and Kunstgewerbe, Jahrg. 1–12. München, Callwey, 1911–22. 28 cm. Monthly.

A popular, well-illustrated journal of modern sculpture which covers pottery also. Emphasis is on German works. Some book reviews. Indexed in *B. d. d. Z.*

2314

The Portfolio; an artistic periodical, [v. 1–24]. London, Seeley and Co., Ltd., 1870–93. 36 cm. Monthly.

Publisher varies. Superseded by *The Portfolio; monographs on artistic subjects,* 1894–1907. 27 cm.

Contains some useful articles, particularly on contemporary English art, but on the whole not very scholarly. Also contains material on the English countryside and places. Some book notices are included, and news of the English art world. Indexed in *Poole's.*

2315

The Print-collector's quarterly, v. 1–30, Feb. 1911–Aug. 1951. N.Y. and London, Keppel [etc.] 1911–51. 18 cm. Quarterly.

Publisher and place vary. Combined with *Print, a quarterly journal of the graphic arts,* with v. 30, no. 3. Suspended 1918–20, Oct. 1936–Feb. 1937, Apr. 1942–Nov. 1948.

A profusely illustrated journal containing articles by recognized authorities on individual artists of all times. Contains book reviews in v. 11–23. In *Art index,* v. 16–30. Also indexed in *B. d. f. Z.; Int. index; Subj. ind. to pers.; Ann. mag. subj. ind.*

———. General index, v. I–XIII, 1911–1926. London, Dent, 1927. 78 p.

———. Complete index, v. I–XXIII, 1911–1936. London, Dent [1936]. [96] p.

2316

Progressive architecture; pencil points, v. 1–(38). [N.Y., Reinhold, etc.] 1920–(57). 30 cm. Monthly.

Title varies: 1920–Sept. 1945, *Pencil points;* June 1942–Dec. 1943, *New pencil points.* In 1932 absorbed the *Monograph* series, records of early American architecture, which was published six times a year. Through 1940 it was retained as a section with its own volume numbering.

A periodical covering artistic aspects of architecture, as well as technical matters of interest to draftsmen, designers, and specification writers, with emphasis on contemporary architecture. In *Art index,* v. 10, Jan. 1929– . Also indexed in *B. d. f. Z.; P. A. I. S.*

2317

Proporzioni; studi di storia dell'arte, 1–(3). Firenze, Sansoni [1943–(50)]. 26 cm.

Annual, but irregular. Edited by Roberto Longhi. Scholarly articles with emphasis on Italian art of all periods. Volume 3 is a festschrift honoring Pietro Toesca; contains a bibliography of his writings.

2318

Quadrum; revue internationale d'art moderne, no. 1–(4). Bruxelles, L'Association pour la Diffusion Artistique et Culturelle (A.D.-A.C.), 1956–(57). 27 cm.

Appears in May and Nov. In English, German, French, and Italian, with English and French summaries. Lavishly illustrated, often in color. Well-known contributors. Emphasis on contemporary art. Contains news of figures in the art world, museum acquisitions, and exhibitions; and some book reviews.

2319

Rassegna bibliografia dell'arte italiano . . . anno 1–19, 1898–1916. Ascoli Picino, Tassi, 1898–1917. 23 cm. Monthly.

Publisher and place vary. Gives abstracts of books and periodical articles. Index at end of each volume.

2320

Rassegna d'arte, anno 1–19. Milano, Martinelli [etc., 1901–19]. 35 cm. Monthly.

Merged with *Rassegna d'arte antica e moderna*, anno 1–6, 1914–19. Discontinued as a separate periodical with 1920.

Quite scholarly articles which are valuable for Italian art, chiefly painting. Contains some color plates of masterpieces. Signed book reviews. An index covering 1901–10. Indexed in *Italy. Parl. Cam. dei deputati. Bibl.*

2321

Rassegna d'arte antica e moderna, anno 1–9. Roma, Milano, Alfieri & Lacroix, 1914–22. 30 cm. Monthly.

Volume 1 of years 1–6, 1914–19, is *Rassegna d'arte*, v. 14–19. Volume 2 of years 1914–19 has subtitle: *Vita d'arte (moderna)*. Has a wider scope than *Rassegna d'arte*. Contains exhibition and art notes.

2322

La Renaissance de l'art français et des industries de luxe, année [1]–23, no. 1, mars 1918–mars 1940. Paris, Les Éditions Nationales [1918–40]. 32 cm. Monthly.

Publisher varies. A popular French journal, similar to *International studio*. Quite a bit of emphasis on decorative arts but also some information on lesser-known French painters. Many illustrations, some in color. Contains information on sales, acquisitions, exhibitions, and some book reviews. Frequently has English translations or summaries. In *Art index*, v. 12–22. Also indexed in *B. d. f. Z.*

2323

Repertorium für Kunstwissenschaft, Bd. 1–52. Berlin [etc.], De Gruyter, 1876–1931. 25–29 cm.

Irregular (4–6 nos. a year). Publisher varies. Volumes 36–45 also called n.F., Bd. 1–9. Merged with *Zeitschrift für bildende Kunst* and *Jahrbuch für Kunstwissenschaft* to form *Zeitschrift für Kunstgeschichte*.

An important scholarly periodical. A section of book reviews is arranged according to broad groups, i.e., architecture, painting, sculpture, and contents of periodicals. Lists recent publications (both books and periodical articles) and also necrologies from 1876–1903. In *Art index*, v. 50–52. Also indexed in *B. d. d. Z.*

———. Register zu Band I–XVI . . . Berlin und Stuttgart, Spemann, 1893. 164 p.

2324

Revue archéologique, année [1]–16, 15 avril 1844–mars 1860; n.s., année 1–23, t. 1–44, mai 1860–déc. 1882; sér. 3, t. 1–41, jan. 1883–déc. 1902; sér. 4, t. 1–23, jan. 1903–juin 1914; sér. 5, t. 1–36, jan. 1915–déc. 1932; sér. 6, t. 1–(50), jan. 1933–(57). Paris, Leroux, 1844–(1957). 25 cm.

Frequency varies; currently quarterly. Publisher varies.

A valuable publication on archaeology in general, but especially of Greece and Rome. Each number has news notes, necrologies, and bibliographies.

Indexes: v. 1–10 in v. 10, p. [771]–836; v. 11–16 in v. 16, p. [771]–84; n.s. 1860–69; 1870–90 as sér. 3, t. 23. In *Art index*, sér. 5, t. 30– . Also indexed in *Rép. bibl.; B. d. f. Z.; Subj. ind. to pers.*

———. Tables des années 1900–1945. Paris, Presses Universitaires de France, 1949. 692 p. 26 cm.

2325

Revue belge d'archéologie et d'histoire de l'art, t. 1–(25). Anvers, Burton [1931–(56)]. 25 cm. Quarterly.

Publisher and place vary. Published by L'Académie Royale d'Archéologie de Belgique as successor to its *Bulletin* and *Annales* which ran from 1842 to 1930.

Articles are predominantly on Flemish painting, sculpture, architecture, and tapestry, as well as archaeological findings. Scholarly treatment. Articles in French mainly, with some in Flemish. Signed reviews in "Bibliographie." In *Art index*, t. 1–17, no. 2, 1931–48. Also indexed in *Bibl. de Belgique; B. d. f. Z.; Int. index.*

2326

La Revue d'art, t. 23–30. Anvers, Burton, 1921–29. 30 cm. Monthly.

Publisher and place vary. Subtitle varies. Continues *L'Art flamand & hollandais* and has same format. For 1915–20 see *Onze kunst*. Suspended Apr. 1921–March 1922.

Covers Flemish and Dutch art from Middle Ages to modern times. Includes list of recently published books. Indexed in *B. d. f. Z.* and *Bibl. de Belgique*.

2327

Revue de l'art ancien et moderne, t. 1–71, avr. 1897–1937. Paris [1897–1938]. 31 cm.

Monthly, t. 1–35, 1897–juin 1914; t. 36 covers juil. 1914–déc. 1919; t. 37–71, ten numbers a year. Suspended 1914–19. Has supplement: *Bulletin de l'art*.

Covers architecture, painting, sculpture, as well as some music and dance—of all periods. Also contains short exhibition and art world notes, book reviews, and bibliographies. In *Art index*, v. 56–71. Also indexed in *Rép. bibl.; B. d. f. Z.*

————. Tables de 1897 à 1909. Paris, 1910. 150 p. 29 cm.

————. Tables, t. II (1910–1937). Paris, 1939. 201 p. 31 cm.

2328

Revue de l'art chrétien, t. 1–64, jan. 1857–juin 1914. Paris, Pringuet, 1857–1914. 25–29 cm.

Monthly, t. 1–20; quarterly, t. 21–39; bimonthly, t. 40–64. Subtitle varies. Volumes 18–32 also called 2. sér., t. 1–15; v. 33–39, 3. sér., t. 1–7; v. 40–54, 4. sér., t. 1–15; v. 55–64, 5. sér., t. 1–10.

Contains articles on early Christian architecture, artifacts, archaeology, and iconography, mainly with reference to France, but also Europe in general and the Holy Land. There are signed reviews and précis of periodical articles. Indexed in *B. d. f. Z.; Rép. bibl.*

————. Table méthodique des articles publiés dans la Revue . . . depuis l'origine (janvier 1857) jusqu'au 31 décembre 1881. 56 p.

————. Table analytique générale de la Revue . . . années 1883 à 1895. [Supplement to Nov. 1895 issue]

————. Table alphabétique 1883–1909. Paris, Champion [etc.], 1914. 112 p.

2329

La Revue des arts, 1951–(57). [Paris, Conseil des Musées Nationaux, 1951–(57)] 28 cm. Quarterly.

Edited by Jean Charbonneaux. Replaces *Musées de France*.

Quite scholarly articles and notes treating objects in French museums. Supplement: Paris. Musée National du Louvre. Laboratoire de Recherches Scientifiques. *Bulletin*. Indexed in *Art index*.

2330

Revue des arts asiatiques, année 1–13, mai 1924–1939/42. Paris, Les Éditions d'Art et d'Histoire [1924–42]. 27 cm.

Ten times a year to March 1925; thence quarterly. Subtitle varies; v. 5– , *Annales du Musée Guimet*. Publisher varies.

Scholarly articles, with some colored plates, on Oriental art. Signed book reviews are included. Issues from March 1925– contain the "Bulletin" of the Association Française des Amis de l'Orient. Indexed in *B. d. f. Z.*

2331

Rivista d'arte, anno 1–(31), 1903–(56). Firenze, Olschki [1903–(58)]. 25 cm.

Monthly, 1903–05; bimonthly (irregular), 1906–42; annual, 1950– . Publisher varies. Title in 1903 was *Miscellanea d'arte*. Suspended 1908–11; 1943–49. Anno 11–25 called ser. 2, anno 1–14; anno 26– is ser. 3, anno 1– .

Scholarly articles by specialists treat Italian art, especially Tuscan Renaissance painting. Lengthy signed reviews, v. 26– . Archival material is published, as well as shorter signed articles publishing single, little-known works of art. "Bibliografia" lists important books and articles in the field, classified by artists or subjects treated. Museum acquisitions and restorations are also noted. In *Art index*, anno 11 (ser. 2, v. 1)–21, ser. 2, v. 11. Also indexed in *B. d. f. Z.*

————. Indice generale dei XXIV volumi, 1903–42. Firenze, Olschki, 1950. 446 p. [Issued as v. 25]

2332

Rivista di archeologia cristiana, anno 1–(32). Roma, Pontifica Commissione de Archeologia Sacra, 1924–(56). 28 cm. Quarterly.

Publisher varies. Supersedes *Nuovo bullettino di archeologia cristiana*. Valuable for material on Early Christian archaeology, with news notes and reviews of books in the field. From 1929– includes a classified bibliography of books and periodical articles on the subject. Indexed in *B. d. f. Z.*

2333

Römische Quartalschrift für christliche Altertumskunde und für Kirchengeschichte,

Jahrg. 1–(52). Freiburg, Herder, 1887–19(57). 25 cm. Quarterly.

Publisher and place vary. Volumes 48– issued by Deutsches Priesterkolleg am Campo Santo, Römisches Institut der Görres-Gesellschaft.

Not primarily an art periodical, but treats Early Christian architecture, inscriptions, monuments, archaeological findings, and manuscripts throughout the Mediterranean area. Some signed reviews and a few illustrations and plates. Includes 28 monographic supplements. In v. 15–46, "Anzeiger für christliche archäologie" containing bibliographical notes. Indexed in *B. d. d. Z.*

2334
Römisches Jahrbuch für Kunstgeschichte, Bd. 1–(7). Wien, Schroll, 1937–(55). 31 cm. Annual.

Publisher and place vary. Published under the auspices of the Bibliotheca Hertziana in Rome, except for v. 3–6 which were "Veröffentlichung des Kaiser-Wilhelm-Instituts für Kunstwissenschaft im Palazzo Zuccari zu Rom." Volumes 1–2 have title: *Kunstgeschichtliches Jahrbuch der Bibliotheca Hertziana.* Suspended 1945–54.

Has long scholarly articles on Italian medieval and Renaissance art. Occasional articles are written in Italian. Indexed in *B. d. d. Z.*

2335
Roopa-lekhā; a bi-annual art journal, v. [1]– 4, no. 1–13, 1929–34; n.s., v. 1–3, no. 1, July 1939–46; v. 20, no. 1–2, 1948; v. 22–(27), 1948/ 49–(56). Delhi [All-India Fine Arts & Crafts Soc., 1929–(56)]. 36 and 34 cm.

Two numbers a year; formerly quarterly (irregular). Suspended 1935–June 1939; 1941– 42; July 1943–45.

Subtitle varies. Contains articles on Indian painting and arts in general, with much stress on contemporary developments. Includes many color plates, not always related to the text. "Art notes" give information on art education, societies, etc. Short signed book notices.

2336
Royal Institute of British Architects. Journal, 3d series, v. 1–(64), 1893/94–(1957). London, 1894–(1957). 28–29 cm.

Fortnightly during sessions of the Institute, monthly during recess, v. 1–46; monthly, v. 47– . Half-title: *The Architectural journal.* . . . Preceded by *Transactions* and *Journal of Proceedings* which combined in 1893 to form the *Journal,* 3d series.

Contains papers read at meetings of the Institute, news items, fairly long signed reviews, and articles by specialists on art and architectural history. In *Art index,* ser. 3, v. 38, Nov. 8, 1930– . Also indexed in *Subj. ind. to pers.; Eng. index; B. d. f. Z.*

2337
Rūpam; an ilustrated quarterly journal of Oriental art chiefly Indian, no. 1–44. Calcutta [O. C. Gangoly, 1920–30]. 33 cm.

Scholarly contributions treat Indian and other Asiatic art, with good color plates and long signed reviews. Number 10, April 1922, p. 57–8, contains "Bibliography of Indian painting (not including Moghul)" by A. K. Coomaraswamy. In *Art index,* no. 38–44. Also indexed in *B. d. f. Z.; Subj. ind. to pers.*

2338
Sele arte, anno 1–(5), luglio/agosto 1952–(57). [Firenze, Studio Italiano di Storia dell'Arte, 1952–(57)] 21 cm.

Bimonthly (six times a year). Editor is Carlo L. Ragghianti.

Rather popular in treatment, it contains listings and reviews of exhibitions, notes on the cinema, numerous unsigned book reviews, and in each issue two or three longer articles (usually unsigned) on artists or phases of art history. It covers architecture, sculpture, painting, graphic and decorative arts. International in scope. Illustrated with many very small halftones, and a few larger color plates. Numbers 12 and 24 are devoted to the Venice Biennale of 1954 and 1956 respectively.

2339
Sociedad Española de Excursiones. Boletin, año 1–(58), marzo 1893–(1954). Madrid, Hauser y Menet [1893–(1954)]. 29 cm.

Monthly, año 1–15, 1893–1907; quarterly, año 16, 1908– . Publisher varies. Individual issues are numbered by "año" instead of "tomo." Tomo 44 comprises año 44, 1–2 trimestre, marzo–junio 1936 and año 48, 3–4 trimestre, 1936–40; t. 45–50, therefore, comprise año 49–54. Tomos 51–(57), however, are numbered año 51–(57).

Covers Spanish art, archaeology, history, and literature, with brief notices of pertinent books and longer signed reviews año 13– . Indexes: 1893–1906, in año 14. In *Art index,* v. 37–44. Also indexed in *B. d. f. Z.*

2340
Société de l'Histoire de l'Art Français, Paris. Bulletin, année 1–4, 1875–78; 1907–(57).

Paris, Colin, 1878 [i.e., 1875]–(1958). 23 cm.

Quarterly, 1875–78, with a title page for each year and a general title page for the four years. 1875 is paged separately; 1876–78 paged continuously. Annual, 1907–11, 1915–19, 1926– ; quarterly, 1912–14; semiannual, 1920–25; 1938 in two fascicles. Suspended 1879–1906. Publisher varies.

Contains news of the Society, publishes archival material, and from 1907–35 lists works recently published by members. Index: "Table du Bulletin, de 1875 à 1878, par M. Anatole de Montaiglon" in année 4, 1878, p. [221]–56.

——. Répertoire des publications de la Société . . . (1857–1927). Paris, 1930. 219 p.

——. Répertoire des publications de la Société . . . (1928–56). Paris, 1958. 135 p.

Lists articles in its *Archives, Nouvelles archives, Bulletin,* and other publications, by subject with an author index.

2341

Society of Architectural Historians. Journal, v. 1–(16). Charlottesville, Va., Univ. of Virginia, Grad. School of Business Admin. [1941–(57)]. 28 cm. Quarterly.

Place of publication varies. Issued 1941–50 by the Society under an earlier name: American Society of Architectural Historians. None published in 1945. First eight volumes are mimeographed (with exception of v. 5); v. 9– printed, and well illustrated.

Articles by specialists on a wide variety of topics dealing with architectural history. Contains signed book reviews. Volumes 1–8 have current bibliographies on architectural history. In *Art index,* v. 5, 1945– .

2342

Speculum; a journal of mediaeval studies, v. 1–(32). Cambridge, Mass., Medieval Academy of America [1926–(57)]. 26 cm. Quarterly.

While not an art periodical, its scholarly treatments of all phases of medieval life and culture frequently contain material of interest to the art historian. Long signed reviews. Lists pertinent books, v. 1– ; and has bibliographies of periodical literature, v. 9– . In *Art index,* v. 4, 1929– ; selectively indexed, however, v. 25– . Complete indexing in *Int. index,* v. 4, no. 4, 1929– . Also indexed in *B. d. f. Z.; Subj. ind. to pers.*

2343

Sredi kollektsionerov, v. 1–4. Moskva [1921–24]. 22–27 cm. Weekly.

Forms a valuable history of art collections in Russia before and after the Revolution,

for book collectors, museums, and art specialists. Gives information about conferences, exhibitions, auctions, and where and to whom objects of art were sold. Monthly bibliographies and book reviews.

2344

Städel-Jahrbuch, Bd. 1–9. Frankfurt am Main, Prestel-Verlag, 1921–35/36. 29 cm. Annual.

Publisher varies. Editors: Georg Swarzenski and Alfred Wolters. Articles deal mostly with objects in the Städelsches Kunstinstitut, although there are treatments of other German art, or objects in other German collections. In *Art index,* v. 6–9. Also indexed in *B. d. d. Z.*

2345

Studies in conservation. Études de conservation, v. 1–(2), Oct. 1952–(56). [London, Nelson, 1952–(56)] 25 cm.

Appears twice a year; four numbers to each volume. Supersedes *Technical studies in the field of the fine arts;* its signed book reviews cover material published since the demise of *Technical studies.* Subtitle: *the Journal of the International Institute for the Conservation of Museum Objects.*

French summaries of articles; some articles are written in French with English summaries. Each number gives information on contributors.

2346

Studies in the history of mediaeval Italian painting, v. 1–(2), Spring 1953–(56). Florence, 1953–(56). 31 cm. Biennial.

At head of title: E. B. Garrison. Each issue contains about four long, detailed, and scholarly articles written and published by E. B. Garrison. Excellently illustrated.

2347

The Studio; an illustrated magazine of fine and applied art, v. 1–(154), April 1893–(1957). London, The Studio Ltd.; N.Y., The Studio Pubs., Inc., 1893–(1957). 30 cm. Monthly.

Publishers vary. Subtitle varies. Founded in London, and for certain years an American ed. appeared concurrently with the English ed., as follows: 1897–1921, *The International studio,* N.Y., was part of each issue; Oct. 1927–March 1931, *Creative art, incorporating The Studio of London,* N.Y.; April 1931–Feb. 1932, *Atelier,* N.Y.; March 1932–Jan. 1939, *The London studio,* N.Y.; Feb. 1939– , *The Studio,* published in London and N.Y. and continuing *The Studio* volume numbering (v. 117, no. 2–).

A popular, well-illustrated review, it surveys all phases of art, especially modern and British. Index: v. 1–42. In *Art index* as follows: *Atelier*, v. 1, 1931–*The Studio* (v. 152, 1956). Also indexed in *B. d. f. Z.; Poole's; Ann. mag. subj. index* (*Atelier* and *London studio* also); *Rev. of revs.; Subj. ind. to pers.*
————. General index to the first twenty-one volumes of "The Studio" 1893–1901. London, N.Y. [1902?]. 135 p.

2348
Syria; revue d'art oriental et d'archéologie, t. 1–(34). Paris, Geuthner, 1920–(57). 29 cm. Quarterly.
Published under the auspices of L'Institut Français d'Archéologie de Beyrouth, t. 24, fasc. 3– .
Treats Syrian art and archaeology from classic to Mohammedan and modern times. Signed reviews in "Bibliographie" section. Indexes: v. 1–10 [1920–29] in v. 10, p. [371]–84; v. 11–20 [1930–39] in v. 20, p. [389]–412. Indexed in *B. d. f. Z.*

2349
Technical studies in the field of the fine arts, v. 1–10, July 1932–April 1942. [Lancaster, Pa., 1932–42] 27 cm. Quarterly.
Continued by *Studies in conservation*, 1952– . Published for the William Hayes Fogg Art Museum, Harvard University. Deals with scientific analysis and problems of restoration of works of art. Includes book reviews and abstracts of periodical articles. Volume 10 has author index of v. 1–10. In *Art index*.

2350
Techniques et architecture, année [1]–(17), sept./oct. 1941–(janvier 1958). Paris [1941–(58)]. 32 cm. Bimonthly.
Emphasis is on contemporary architecture, from the construction aspect, each issue being devoted to a special subject, e.g., roads, bridges, pools, etc. Extensively illustrated with photographs and plans. Some short book reviews are included. Indexed in *B. d. f. Z.*

2351
Il Vasari; rivista d'arte e di studi vasariani e cinquecenteschi, anno 1–(14, no. 2). Arezzo, Casa Vasari [1927–(43)]. 27 cm. Irregular.
Confined solely to Italian art of the 16th century, with special reference to Vasari. Much archival material is published. Almost no illustration.

2352
Verve; an artistic and literary quarterly, v. 1–(7), no. 1–(34), Dec. 1937–(56). Paris [Éditions de la Revue *Verve*, 1937–(56)]. 36 cm. One double no. a year.
Publisher and subtitle vary. Numbers 1–8 published in English; no. 9– in French. Numbers 29/30– also have American editions published in N.Y. by Harcourt, Brace and Co.
A de luxe publication, devoted to art of all periods, Eastern as well as Western, with excellent color reproductions. From nos. 7 and 9– (except no. 27–28) it is monographic. In *Art index*, v. 5– .

2353
XXe [i.e., Vingtième] siècle, année 1–2, no. 1, mars 1938–39; no. 1–(9), 1951–(57). Paris, Éditions des Chroniques du Jour [1938–(57)]. 32 cm. Irregular.
G. di San Lazzaro is director. An Eng. edition was published for v. 1, nos. 4–5/6. Nouvelle série begun in 1951.
Devoted exclusively to contemporary art, and includes many contributions written by artists themselves. In n.s. each issue is devoted to a specific theme: art and poetry, space, etc. Splendid illustrations in black and white and color. There are signed book and exhibition reviews in "Chroniques du jour" section.

2354
Vizantiiskii vremennik [v. 1–25] 1894–1927; n.s., 1–(12), 1947–(57). Moscow, Acad. Nauk, 1894–(1957). 27 cm.
Quarterly, v. 1–25; n.s. is annual. Volumes 1–25 published in St. Petersburg (Petrograd) and Leipzig by C. Ricker. Suspended 1928–46. New series, v. 1–2 also called v. 26–27.
This Russian periodical is devoted to Byzantine studies, with illustration of articles beginning in n.s., v. 2– , and bibliographies of current works together with long signed reviews. Index: v. 1–15 in v. 16. Indexed in *B. d. f. Z.*

2355
De Vlaamsche school, jaarg. 1–[33] 1885–87; nieuwe reeks, jaarg. 1–14, 1888–1901. Antwerpen, Buschmann, 1885–1901. 30–34 cm. Annual.
Publisher and place vary. Subtitle varies. Title is *De Vlaamse school*, n.r., jaarg. 10– . Continued by *Onze kunst*. Somewhat popular treatment of art and letters of the Netherlands. Short book notices are included.

2356

Wallraf-Richartz-Jahrbuch, Bd. 1–(19). Köln, Seemann, 1924–(57). 27–33 cm. Annual.

Publisher and place vary. Issued under the auspices of the Wallraf-Richartz museum. No issues 1929, 1931–32, 1935, 1944–51. Volumes 6–8 also called n.F. 1–3; "n.F." dropped thereafter. Volumes 9–13 called *Westdeutsches Jahrbuch für Kunstgeschichte;* with v. 14– this becomes the subtitle.

Deals mainly with German art of the Rhineland and contain news of Rhenish museums. Signed reviews in v. 14– . In *Art index*, v. 6–11. Also indexed in *B. d. d. Z.*

2357

Walpole Society, London. The first–(35th) volume of the Walpole Society. Oxford, 1912–(59). 32 cm.

Annual (irregular). Volumes 31 and 32 published in London. Publication since World War II has been somewhat delayed, so that v. 29, for 1940–42, came out in 1947; v. 30, covering 1951–52, published 1955; v. 31, for 1942–43, published 1946; v. 32, for 1946–48, published 1951; v. 33, covering 1948–50, published in 1953; etc.

Treats British art, especially painting, from the Middle Ages on. Several volumes are monographic. Volumes 18, 20, 22, 24, 26, and 30 reprint the *Notebooks* of George Vertue; v. 29 is an index to the first five volumes of these *Notebooks*. Volume 15 has contents of v. 1–14; "Contents of vols. I to XXVIII" in v. 31, p. 113–17. Indexed in *Subj. ind. to pers.*

2358

Warburg Institute. Journal of the Warburg and Courtauld Institutes, v. 1–(20), July 1937–(57). London, 1937–(57). 28 cm.

Annual, 1945–49; quarterly (with some irregularity), 1937–44, 1950– . Title varies: July 1937–Apr. 1939 called the *Journal of the Warburg Institute.*

Long scholarly articles consider medieval, Renaissance, and 17th and 18th century art, as well as literature, with emphasis on iconography, especially the perpetuation of classical motifs. Editors: Rudolf Wittkower, Anthony Blunt, T. S. R. Boase, Frances A. Yates, E. H. Gombrich. Index: v. 1–12, 1937–49, 6 p. In *Art index*, v. 10– . Also indexed in *B. d. f. Z.* and *Subj. ind to pers.*

2359

Wendingen; maandblad voor bouwen en sieren van Architectura et Amicitia, ser. 1–12. Santpoort, Mees, 1918–31. 35 x 35 cm.

Published in Amsterdam, "De Hooge Brug," ser. 1–5. None published 1922 and 1926. "Orgaan van het genootschap Architectura et Amicitia te Amsterdam."

Articles treat modern architecture, sculpture, design, etc., and especially art nouveau. Interesting modern format: double column, loose-leaf pages. More illustrations than text; excellent reproductions. Some articles done in English.

2360

Das Werk; schweizer Monatsschrift für Architektur, freie Kunst, angewandte Kunst . . . Jahrg. 1–(44). [Winterthur, Buchdruckerei Winterthur, 1914–(57)] 30 cm. Monthly.

Subtitle varies. "Offizielles Organ des Bundes schweizer Architekten BSA und des schweizerischen Werkbundes SWB."

Covers architecture and the fine and applied arts. Contains book reviews, generally signed, and French summaries of articles (in the earlier issues). In *Art index*, v. 40, Sept. 1953– . Also indexed in *B. d. d. Z.*

2361

Wiener Beiträge zur Kunst- und Kulturgeschichte Asiens; Jahrbuch des Vereines der Freunde asiatischer Kunst und Kultur in Wien, Bd. 1–11. Wien, Krystall-Verlag, 1925/26–37. 30 cm. Annual.

Each volume contains three or four scholarly pieces on various aspects of Oriental art or culture. Signed brief book reviews, v. 4– . In 1936 a special publication was issued: *Sammlung Baron Eduard von der Heydt, Wien; Ordos-Bronzen, Bronzen aus Luristan und dem Kaukasus, Werke chinesischer Kleinkunst aus verschiedenen Perioden.* Bearbeitet von Viktor Griessmaier. 110 p.

2362

Wiener Jahrbuch für bildende Kunst; die bildenden Künste, Jahrg. 1–5, 1916/18–22. Wien, Schroll [1918–22]. 32 cm. Annual.

Volumes 1–4 issued as *Die bildenden Künste; Wiener Monatshefte.* Jahrgang 1 is combined with *Der Architekt*, which latter is paged separately. Hans Tietze, editor, v. 2– . Emphasis here is on contemporary German art, with some short signed reviews. Rather popular treatment. Indexed in *B. d. d. Z.*

2363

Wiener Jahrbuch für Kunstgeschichte, Bd. 1–(30). Wien, Zentralstelle für Denkmalschutz im Bundesministerium für Unterricht. Kunstgeschichtliches Institut, 1907–(54). 30–31 cm.

Preceded by: Austria. Zentral-Kommission zur Erforschung und Erhaltung der Kunst- und historischen Denkmale. *Jahrbuch.* Title reads variously: *Kunstgeschichtliches Jahrbuch; Jahrbuch des kunstgeschichtlichen Instituts; Jahrbuch für Kunstgeschichte.* Volumes 1–14 edited by Max Dvorak. Volumes 15– also called n.F., v. 1– .

Long scholarly articles, chiefly on Austrian art. "Beiblatt," Bd. 1–15, 1907–22, issued as appendix. In *Art index,* v. 8–11, 1932–37. Also indexed in *B. d. d. Z.*

————. Generalregister, 1903–1912. 1913. 112 p. Also covers the *Jahrbuch* of the Zentral-Kommission.

2364

Zeitschrift des deutschen Vereins für Kunstwissenschaft, Jahrg. 1–10. Berlin, 1934–43. 31 cm. Quarterly.

Comparable to and continued by *Zeitschrift für Kunstwissenschaft* (2368). Volumes 1–10 contain "Photoverzeichnis," no. 1–22, "Neuaufnahmen des kunstgeschichtlichen Seminars in Marburg." Indexed in *B. d. d. Z.*

2365

Zeitschrift für bildende Kunst, Jahrg. 1–24, 1866–Sept. 1889; n.F., Jahrg. 1–33, Okt. 1890–1922; Jahrg. 58–65, 1924/25–31/32. Leipzig, Seemann, 1866–1932. 29–34 cm. Monthly.

In 1932 merged with *Repertorium für Kunstgeschichte* and *Jahrbuch für Kunstwissenschaft* to form *Zeitschrift für Kunstgeschichte.*

Treats art in general and includes book reviews (sometimes signed) and classified bibliographies of current books and articles. Has numerous good illustrations, with notes as to who made the plates and (usually) an identification of the process employed. In late 1880's and 1890's contains heliogravures made by Albert and Hanfstaengl. Includes various supplements: Kunstchronik, Kunstgewerbeblatt, Kunstmarkt und Kunstchronik, Monatsrundschau, Kunstliteratur (from 1925– , and reviewing the literature of general art-historical and archaeological interest), Kunstchronik und Kunstliteratur. Registers published every four or six years. In *Art index,* v. 63–65. Also indexed in *B. d. d. Z.*

2366

Zeitschrift für Kunst; Vierteljahreshefte für künstlerische Gestaltung, Malerei, Plastik, Architektur, Kunsthandwerk, Jahrg. 1–(4). Leipzig, Seemann [1947–(50)]. 30 cm. Quarterly.

Suspended as of Jan. 1951. Covers art of all ages, and is quite valuable for articles on contemporary German artists. Also has a few articles on Russian art. Well illustrated, and contains signed reviews. Indexed in *B. d. d. Z.*

2367

Zeitschrift für Kunstgeschichte, Bd. 1–(20). München, Berlin, Deutscher Kunstverlag, 1932–[(57)]. 28 cm.

Bimonthly, 1932–42; annual, 1949–51; semiannual, 1952–55; three issues a year, 1956. Publisher and place vary. This is "neue Folge von *Repertorium für Kunstwissenschaft, Zeitschrift für bildende Kunst, Jahrbuch für Kunstwissenschaft.*" Suspended 1943–48.

Covers the whole field of art in scholarly fashion. Well illustrated. Long signed reviews and, in v. 12– , classified bibliographies of current art books and articles. In *Art index,* v. 1–8. Also indexed in *B. d. d. Z.* and *Subj. ind. to pers.*

2368

Zeitschrift für Kunstwissenschaft, Bd. 1–(11). Berlin, Deutscher Verein für Kunstwissenschaft, 1947–(57). 27 cm.

Quarterly (two fascs. a year). Continues *Zeitschrift des deutschen Vereins für Kunstwissenschaft.* Contains scholarly articles on German subjects predominantly, with some few on Italian or Netherlandish art. Well illustrated. Indexed in *B. d. d. Z.*

2369

Zeitschrift für schweizerische Archaeologie und Kunstgeschichte, Bd. 1–(17). Basel, Birkhäuser [1939–(57)]. 31 cm. Quarterly.

This publication is the official organ of the Verband der Schweizerischen Altertumssammlungen and the Gesellschaft für Schweizerische Kunstgeschichte, and is published under the direction of the Schweizerische Landesmuseum in Zürich. Supersedes *Anzeiger für schweizerische Altertumskunde.*

Exhaustive treatments of Swiss art history and archaeology. Most articles are in German. Signed book reviews. Each issue contains a section: "Nachrichten, herausgegeben von der Gesellschaft für schweizerische Kunstgeschichte," which gives news of restorations, etc., in the various cantons. Indexed in *B. d. d. Z.*

2370

Zodiac; revue internationale d'architecture contemporaine; international magazine of contemporary architecture, v. 1– . Milano.

Edizioni di Comunità [1957]– . 27cm. Semi-annual.

Published under the auspices of L'Association pour la Diffusion Artistique et Culturelle, Bruxelles, and Società Ing. C. Olivetti & C., Ivrea, Italy.

A new magazine reflecting contemporary architectural thinking, with articles written in English, French, Italian, or German. There are English and French translations at the end of each issue.

Contains book reviews.

CHAPTER 19

Series

THIS CHAPTER CONTAINS A SELECTIVE LIST-ing of some of the most important and most frequently used series of art books. It would have been desirable to give a complete listing of the works published in each series, but this proved impracticable. In choosing the various examples illustrating each series, an effort was made to select titles which would indicate the scope and range covered.

2371

[Albertina Facsimiles] Vienna, Schroll, 1922–ca. 1928. plates. 38–61 cm.

Size varies. A series of large collotype color reproductions of drawings in the Albertina in Vienna. Excellent collotype plates made by Jaffé and Lowy, with texts by specialists such as Joseph Meder and Alfred Stix. Examples: *Handzeichnungen französischer Meister des XVI.–XVIII. Jahrhunderts*, 1922; *Dürers grüne Passion* [1924].

2372

Les Albums d'art Druet. Paris, Librairie de France, 1928–31. illus. 32 cm.

Monographs on French painters and sculptors of the 19th and 20th centuries. Each volume contains a short text and 24 photogravures of the artist's work. 32 volumes issued.

Examples: (1) *Cézanne* [1928]; (9) *Despiau* [1927]; (32) *André Lhote* [1931].

2373

American Artists Group, New York. N.Y., American Artists Group Inc., 1939–46. illus., plates (part col.) 24 cm.

An unnumbered series which varies somewhat in format. The purpose of the series is "to present an authoritative parallel literature of contemporary American art, the authors of various books in the series to be, wherever possible, the artists themselves."—*Pref.* of Sloan's *Gist of art,* 1939.

Examples: DuBois, Guy Pène. *Artists say the silliest things,* 1940; McCausland, Elizabeth. *George Innes,* 1946; Müller, Hans Alexander. *How I make woodcuts and wood engravings,* 1945; Schmeckebier, Laurence Eli. *John Steuart Curry's Pageant of America,* 1943.

2374

American Artists Group, New York. Monographs. N.Y., American Artists Group Inc., 1945–46. illus., plates. 16 cm.

Small inexpensive monographs of about 64 pages, each covering the work of a prominent American artist. Each volume contains a short text written by the artist himself and is illustrated by rotogravures, with a portrait of the artist on the cover.

Among artists included are: John Sloan, Rockwell Kent, Thomas Hart Benton, Max Weber, Waldo Peirce, Stuart Davis, Eugene Speicher, Edward Hopper, Alexander Brook, Gladys Rockmore Davis, Yasuo Kuniyoshi, Bernard Karfiol, Charles Burchfield, John Steuart Curry, William Zorach, Doris Lee, Leon Kroll, Arnold Blanch, Raphael Soyer, and Frederic Taubes.

2375

American artists series. N.Y., Privately printed, 1911–26? plates. 26 cm.

Privately printed by Frederic Fairchild Sherman, in limited editions of about 250 copies. Not all volumes bear the series note, but they are identifiable by uniform format and a list of titles published in the front of the monograph on J. Francis Murphy, 1926. The format is predominantly text with several full-page plates, bibliographies, lists of awards, exhibitions, etc.

Included are: *George Innes* by Elliott

Daingerfield, 1911; *Fifty paintings by George Innes*, introd. by E. Daingerfield, 1913; *Homer Martin* by Frank Jewett Mather Jr., 1912; *Fifty-eight paintings by Homer Martin*, introd. by Dana Carroll, 1913; *Alexander Wyant* by Eliot Clark, 1916; *Sixty paintings by Alexander Wyant*, introd. by E. Clark, 1920; *Ralph Albert Blakelock* by Elliott Daingerfield, 1914; *Winslow Homer* by Kenyon Cox, 1914; *Albert Pinkham Ryder* by Frederic Fairchild Sherman, 1920; *John Twachtman* by Eliot Clark, 1924; *J. Francis Murphy* by Eliot Clark, 1926.

2376

American artists series. N.Y., Whitney Museum of American Art [c1931–32]. illus. 26 cm.

An unnumbered series of monographs on American painters of the 19th and 20th centuries, written by well-known critics. The material is primarily illustrative (halftones) with a short biography, an essay, and a bibliography. Each volume has a portrait of the artist as a frontispiece.

About 21 volumes issued. Examples: *Mary Cassatt* by Forbes Watson [c1932]; *John Sloan* by Guy Pene DuBois [1931]; *Arthur B. Davies* by Royal Cortissoz [c1931].

2377

American artists series. N.Y., Crown [1942]. illus. (part col.) 26 cm.

Publications bear note: "Published under the supervision of André Gloeckner in collaboration with Addison gallery of American art, Andover . . . and many other collections." Aimee Crane did photo research and bibliographies. Illustrated by halftones with a few in color.

Included are: *George Bellows* by Peyton Boswell Jr.; *Whistler* by James W. Lane; *Thomas Eakins* by Roland J. McKinney; *Winslow Homer* by Forbes Watson, all issued in 1942.

2378

Archäologische Studien zum christlichen Altertum und Mittelalter. Freiburg, Mohr, 1895–99. 5 v. plates. 24 cm.

Continued as *Studien über christliche Denkmäler. Neue Folge der archäologischen Studien zum christlichen Altertum und Mittelalter* (2476). A numbered series. Examples: (3) Stuhlfauth, Georg. *Die Engel in der altchristlichen Kunst*, 1897; (5) Vopel, Hermann. *Die altchristlichen Goldgläser*, 1889.

2379

Architetti del movimento moderne. Milano, Il Balcone, 1947–(56). v. 1–(16). illus. 17 cm.

A series of small biographies of modern architects, many treated thus for the first time. Includes bibliographies.

Contents: (1) Carlo, Giancarlo de. *William Morris*, 1947; (2) Labò, Mario. *Giuseppe Terragni*, 1947; (3) Zevi, Bruno. *Frank Lloyd Wright* [2. ed. ampliata] 1954; (4) Veronesi, Giulia. *Tony Garnier*, 1947; (5) Labò, Giorgio. *Alvar Aalto*, 1948; (6) Zevi, Bruno. *Erik Gunnar Asplund*, 1948; (7) Veronesi, Giulia. *Joseph Maria Olbrich*, 1948; (8) Pevsner, Nikolaus. *Charles R. Mackintosh*, 1950; (9) Veronesi, Giulia. *J. J. Pieter Oud*, 1953; (10) Zevi, Bruno. *Richard Neutra*, 1954; (11) Argan, Giulio Carlo. *Pier Luigi Nervi*, 1955; (12) Bill, Max. *Ludwig Mies van der Rohe*, 1955; (13) Rogers, Ernesto N. *Auguste Perret*, 1955; (14) Nicoletti, Manfredi. *Raimondo d'Aronco*, 1955; (15) Melograni, Carlo. *Giuseppe Pagano*, 1955; (16) Munz, Ludwig. *Adolf Loos*, 1956.

2380

Ars Asiatica: études et documents publiés sous la direction de Victor Goloubev. Brussels, Van Oest, 1914–35. illus. 35 cm.

A numbered series of volumes written by specialists on various subjects relating to Eastern art. Illustrated with good collotypes.

Contents: (1) Chavannes, Édouard. *La peinture chinoise au Musée Cernuschi avril–juin 1912*, 1914; (2) *Six monuments de la sculpture chinoise*, 1914; (3) *Sculptures civaites*, 1921; (4) Parmentier, Henri. *Les sculpteurs chames au Musée de Tourane*, 1922; (5) Coedès, Georges. *Bronzes khmèrs*, 1923; (6) Binyon, Laurence. *Asiatic art in the British Museum*, 1925; (7) Sirén, Osvald. *Documents d'art chinois de la collection Osvald Sirén*, 1925; (8) Krom, N. J. *L'art javanais dans les musées de Hollande et de Java*, 1926; (9) Binyon, Laurence. *Chinese paintings in English collections*, 1927; (10) Golubev, V. V. *Documents pour servir à l'étude d'Ajanta*, 1927; (11) Hall, H. R. *Babylonian and Assyrian sculpture in the British Museum*, 1928; (12) Coedès, Georges. *Les collections archéologiques du Musée national de Bangkok*, 1928; (13) Coomaraswamy, A. K. *Les miniatures orientales de la collection Goloubeu au Museum of Fine Arts de Boston*, 1929; (14) Odin, Ulrich. *Peintures chinoises et japonaises de la collection Ulrich Odin*, 1929; (15) Vogel, J. P. *La sculpture de Mathurâ*, 1930; (16) Groslier, George. *Les collections khmères du Musée Albert Sarraut à Phnom-penh,* 1931; (17) Godard, André. *Les bronzes du Luristān,* 1931; (18) Coomaraswamy, A. K. *La sculpture de Bodhgayā,* 1935.

2381

Ars una: species mille. London, Heinemann; N.Y., Scribner, 1909–28. illus. 19 cm.

Seven volumes were issued 1909–28, intended to form a general history of art. Small handbooks with texts written by specialists and profusely illustrated with tiny illustrations. Examples: Rooses, Max. *Art in Flanders,* 1914; Hourticq, Louis. *Art in France,* 1911; Dieulafoy, Marcel. *Art in Spain and Portugal,* 1913; Ricci, Corrado. *Art in northern Italy,* 1911; Maspero, Sir Gaston. *Art in Egypt,* 1913.

2382

L'Art français: Collection dirigée par Georges Wildenstein. Paris, Les Beaux-Arts, *ca.* 1927–34. plates. 33 cm.

14 volumes issued from 1927 to 1934. Monographs devoted to a single artist or a specific geographical region. Contain detailed bibliographies and good plates. Subjects included: Germain Pilon; L'Afrique méditerranéenne; La Tour; L'art en Provence; Louis Tocque; Girardon; Les châteaux de la renaissance; L'art en Normandie; Pater; Manet; Largillière; Les Lemoyne; Chardin; Lancret.

2383

El Arte en España. v. 1–36. Barcelona, Thomas, n.d. [1913?]. plates. 16 cm.

Small monographs on Spanish art and architectural monuments, each containing 25–30 pages of text in Spanish, French, and English with 48 plates.

Examples: (1) Lampérez y Romea, V. *Catedral de Burgos;* (3) Doménech Gallissá, R. *La Casa del Greco;* (6) Beruete y Moret, A. de. *Velázquez en el Museo del Prado;* (18) Gómez Moreno, M. *Valladolid;* (27) Quintero y de Atauri, P. *Museo de Bellas Artes de Cádiz.*

2384

Arts, styles et techniques; collection publiée sous la direction de Norbert Dufourcq. Paris, Larousse, 1942–(57). illus. 17 cm.

A series of small volumes written by specialists, unfortunately printed on poor paper. Good illustrations considering the low price. They cover art in various countries and various media of French art.

Examples: Dorival, Bernard. *La peinture française,* 2 v., 1942; Aubert, Marcel. *Le vitrail en France,* 1946; Devambez, Pierre. *Le*

style grec, 1944; Réau, Louis. *L'art russe,* 1945; Colomb, Simone. *L'art anglais,* 1947.

2385

Basler Studien zur Kunstgeschichte, ed. by J. Gantner. Basel, Birkhauser, 1943–(57). illus. 24 cm.

A numbered series with more emphasis on text than illustrations; 15 have appeared to date.

Examples: (1) Murbach, E. *Form und Material in der spätgotischen Plastik,* 1943; (2) Cahn, H. *Die Münzen der sizilischen Stadt Naxos,* 1944; (3) Fromer-Im Obersteg, L. *Die Entwicklung der schweizerischen Landschaftsmalerei* . . . 1945; (7) Maurer, Emil. *Jacob Burckhardt und Rubens,* 1951; (10) Kaufmann-Hagenbach, Annie. *Die Basler Plastik des fünfzehnten und frühen sechzehnten Jahrhunderts,* 1952.

2386

Bauhausbücher; Schriftleitung: Walter Gropius, L. Moholy-Nagy, eds. München, Langer, 1925–29. 14 v. illus. (incl. plans). 23 cm.

A useful series of monographs on modern architecture. Examples: (1) Gropius, Walter. *Internationale Architektur;* (2) Klee, Paul. *Pädagogisches Skizzenbuch;* (8) Moholy-Nagy, Ladislai. *Malerei, Photographie, Film;* (10) Oud, J. J. *Holländische Architektur;* (14) Moholy-Nagy, Ladislai. *Von Material zu Architektur.*

2387

Beiträge zur Kunstgeschichte, 1–8, n.F. 1–41. Leipzig, Seeman, 1878–1914. 49 v. in 13. illus., plates. 24 cm.

A numbered series of scholarly works on art history covering all countries and periods. Very few illustrations. Examples: (1) Schultz, Alwin. *Die Legende vom Leben der Jungfrau Maria und ihre Darstellung in der bildenden Kunst des Mittelalters,* 1878; (15) Wilisch, Erich. *Die altkorinthische Thonindustrie,* 1892; (38) Krommes, R. H. *Studien zu Federigo Barocci,* 1912.

2388

Beiträge zur vergleichenden Kunstforschung, hrsg. vom Kunsthistorischen Institut der Universität Wien (Lehrkanzel Strzygowski). Vienna, 1920–(28). 24–33 cm.

A numbered series in which seven volumes were issued 1920–28. Publisher varies.

Examples: (1) Glück, Heinrich. *Das Hebdomon,* 1920; (2) Strzygowski, Josef. *Kunde, Wesen, Entwicklung,* 1922; (7) Strzygowski, Josef. *Die Holzkirchen in der Umgebung von Bielitz-Biala,* 1927.

329

2389

Berner Schriften zur Kunst, hrsg. von Prof. Dr. Hans R. Hahnloser. Bern, Bentelli, 1944–(57). illus., plates (part col.) 29–43 cm.

A numbered series with scholarly texts, good halftones, and some color plates.

Examples: (1) Mollwo, Marie. *Das Wettinger Graduale*, 1944; (3) Roth, Alfred G. *Die Gestirne in der Landschaftsmalerei des Abendlandes*, 1945; (4) Scheidegger, Alfred. *Die Berner Glasmalerei von 1540 bis 1580*, 1947; (5) Hahnloser, Hans Robert. *Chorfenster und Altare des Berner Münsters*, 1950.

2390

Bibliothek der Kunstgeschichte. Leipzig, Seeman, *ca.* 1921–23. illus. 18 cm.

Edited by Hans Tietze. At least 55 volumes were issued. Small, thin picture books with short text by well-known authorities, covering Eastern as well as Western art. Example: Hartlaub, G. F. *Die Maler von Siena im XV. Jahrhundert* [1923].

2391

Bibliothek für Kunst- und Antiquitätensammler. Berlin, Schmidt, 1920–(30). illus., plates. 23–25 cm.

A numbered series of standard works covering various aspects and fields of collecting. Subjects included are: medals, bronzes, ivories, amber, paintings, drawings, and various minor Oriental arts. Examples: (1) Bernhart, Max. *Medaillen und Plaketten*, 1920; (9) Donath, Adolph. *Psychologie des Kunstsammelns*, 1920; (33) Burger, Willy. *Abendländische Schmelzarbeiten*, 1930.

2392

Bibliothèque d'histoire de l'art. Paris, Van Oest, 1926–(31). plates. 26 cm.

Edited by A. Marguiller. An unnumbered series which covers a variety of subjects, i.e., Chinese sculpture, Egyptian art, Dutch painting, early Christian and Byzantine art, etc. Texts are written by authorities in the field and the plates are clear and numerous.

Examples: Brière-Misme, Clotilde. *La peinture hollandaise*, 1927; Ardenne de Tizac, Henri d'. *La sculpture chinoise*, 1931 (which contains a list of the volumes issued to date).

2393

Die blauen Bücher. Königstein im Taunus und Leipzig, Langewiesche, 1909–(56). illus. 27 cm.

Slim paper-bound volumes of about 110 p.

dealing with architecture, painting, and sculpture. Primarily illustrative material but some text written by competent scholars.

Examples: Pinder, Wilhelm. *Deutsche Barockplastik*, 1932, 1940; Boeckler, Albert. *Deutsche Buchmalerei vorgotischer Zeit*, 1942; Hegemann, Hans Werner. *Deutsches Rokoko*, 1956.

2394

Buenos Aires. Universidad Nacional. Instituto de Investigaciones Historicas. Estudios y documentos para la historia del arte colonial . . . Buenos Aires, Peuser, 1934–(44). plates, plans. 33 cm.

Edition of 1000 copies printed. Contents: v. 1, *Arquitectura virreinal* por Martin S. Noel & *Adición documental* por José Torre Revello, y una advertencia por Emilio Ravignani, 1934; v. 2, *Los artistas pintores de la expedición Malaspina* por José Torre Revello, 1944.

2395

Chapters in art. London, Tiranti, 1944–(57). plates. 19 cm.

A publisher's series of thin, small, inexpensive volumes, written by competent authors. Mostly plates with a short text. Frequently include bibliographies. Some are numbered and others are not. Some do not bear the series note but are recognizable by their format and are listed in the series by the publisher in advertisements.

Examples: Jarnecki, Jerzy. *English Romanesque sculpture 1066–1140*, 1951; Natanson, Joseph. *Gothic ivories of the 13th & 14th centuries*, 1951; Broadbent, A. T. *Sculpture today in Great Britain 1940–43*, 1944; Newton, Eric. *British sculpture 1944–1946*, 1947; Jarnecki, Jerzy. *Later Romanesque sculpture 1140–1210*, 1953.

2396

Codices e Vaticanis selecti phototypice expressi, 1902–(42), 1–(27). 45–48 cm.

Publisher varies. A series of excellent facsimile editions of manuscripts in the Vatican library, some of which are important for art history.

Examples: (1) Vergilius Maro, Publius. Mss. (Cod. Vat. 3223) *Fragmenta et picturae Vergiliana* . . . 1930; (2) Vergilius Maro, Publius. Mss. (Cod. Vat. 3867) *Picturae ornamenta* . . . 1902; (3) Vatican. Biblioteca Vaticana. Mss. (Ottoboni 501) *Le miniature del ponteficale ottoboniano* . . . 1903; (5) Codex Vaticanus palatinus graecus 431. *Il rotulo di Giosuè*, 1905; (8) Greek church. Liturgy and ritual. Menologion. *Il Menologio di Basilio*

II, 2 v., 1907; (10) Cosmas Indicopleuste. *Le miniature della topografia cristiana (Cod. vat. greco 699*), 1908; (11) Sangallo, Giuliano de. *Il libro di Giuliano da Sangallo*, 2 v., 1910; (18) Terentius Afer, Publius. *Terentivs Cod. vat. lat. 3868*, 1928; (24) Villani, Giovanni. *La cronaca figurata*, 1936; (25) Jerphanion, Guillaume. *Les miniatures du manuscrit syriaque no. 559 de la Bibliothèque vaticane*, 1940.

2397
Colección Labor. Sección LV.—Artes plásticas. Barcelona, Edición Labor, 1929–36. 19 cm.
A series of monographs on various aspects of Spanish art, as well as about 20 others covering the art of other countries. Examples: Mayer, A. L. *La pintura española*, 2d ed., 1929; Sola, M. *Arte hispano americano*, 1935; Sola, M. *Arte precolombiano*, 1936.

2398
Colección Síntesis de arte. Madrid, Dossat [c1950–51]. plates. 25 cm.
Contains: Chueca Goitia, F. *Breve historia de la arquitectura española* [c1950]; Gómez-Moreno, Maria Elena. *Breve historia de la escultura española*, 1951; Lafuenta Ferrari, E. and Niño Mas, F. *Breve historia de las artes industriales españolas* [195?]; Lafuente Ferrari, E. *Breve historia de la pintura española* [c1951]. Together these volumes form a good history of Spanish art.

2399
Collection Ars et historia, publiée sous la direction de J. et R. Wittmann. Paris, Éditions d'Histoire et d'Art, Plon, 1931?–(55). 25 cm.
An unnumbered series containing books on a variety of subjects, including music, medicine, and the dance.
Examples: Faure, Élie. *Histoire de l'art*, 5 v., 1939–40; Deschamps, Paul. *La peinture murale en France*, 1951; Jamot, Paul. *La peinture en France*, 1934; Grousset, René. *La Chine et son art*, 1951; Pradel, Pierre. *Michel Colombe*, 1953; Verlet, Pierre. *Le mobilier royal français*, 1955.

2400
Collection Écrits de peintres, dirigée par Pierre Cailler. Genève, Cailler, 1944–(47). plates. 19 cm.
After the first few volumes it becomes a numbered series. Contains reprints or translations of important texts. Most of the volumes have a few plates, some reproducing the title page of the original ed. Examples:

Barraud, Maurice. *Reflexions à perte de vue*, 1944; Liotard, Jean E. *Traité des principes et des règles de la peinture*, 1945; Bellori, Giovanni Pietro. *Vie de Nicolas Poussin*, 1947; Félibien, André. *Entretiens sur la vie et les ouvrages de Nicolas Poussin*, 1947.

2401
Collection Les grands artistes vus par eux-mêmes et par leurs amis. Genève, Cailler, 1945–(51). 20 cm.
A numbered series of monographs on French painters. Made up chiefly from writings of the artist's friends and his own letters. Each volume contains a bibliography and bears after the series note: "Dirigée par Pierre Courthion avec la collaboration de Pierre Cailler."
Artists included: (1) *Manet*, 1945; (2) *Daumier*, 1945; (3) *Corot*, 2 v., 1946; (4) *Géricault*, 1947; (5) *Ingres*, 2 v., 1947; (6) *Courbet*, 2 v., 1948–50; (10) *Van Gogh*, 1947; (11) *Toulouse-Lautrec*, 1951.

2402
Collection Prométhée, pub. sous la direction de René Huyghe et Germain Bazin. [Paris] Tisné, 1944–(51). illus. (part col.) 26 cm.
A series of monographs on individual artists written by scholars. Many illustrations but some (especially those in color) of rather poor quality. Each volume contains bibliography, chronological index (according to works cited, museums and collections, and other names). Other features vary from volume to volume.
Examples: Drucker, Michel. *Renoir*, 1944; Combe, Jacques. *Jérôme Bosch*, 1946; Adhémar, Hélène. *Watteau*, 1950; Lemaire, Jean. *Van Gogh*, 1951; Bazin, Germain. *Corot*, 1951; Dorival, Bernard. *Cézanne*, 1949. Some are also issued in an English edition, e.g., *Cézanne* and *Bosch*.

2403
Collezione Silvana, monumenti della civiltà pittorica italiana. Milano, Pizzi or Hoepli, 1945–(54). plates (part col.) 38 cm.
A numbered series of picture books containing a few pages of text and about 30 plates, mostly in color. Color plates are offset and quite good in quality. A few contain some color halftones. Each volume includes a short bibliography.
Subjects include: Giotto, la Cappella degli Scrovegni; Masolino a Castiglione Olona; Mantegna, la Cappelle Ovetari nella Chiesa degli Eremitani; Tiepolo, la Villa Valmarana. I Vivarini.

2404

Collezione "Valori plastici." Milan, Hoepli, 1926–(50). plates. 21–28 cm.

Series edited by Mario Broglio. Originally the series bore the imprint "Roma, Casa Editrice d'Arte 'Valori plastici.'" These volumes were 28 cm. and were illustrated by collotypes. Examples: Venturi, Adolfo. *Michelangelo,* 1926; Colasanti, Arduino. *Donatello,* 1930; Cecchi, Emilio. *Trecentisti senese,* 1928. Hoepli bought out this house and the Cecchi item in the new series is called "nuova edizione, riveduta e accrescitua," 1948.

The new format is 21 cm. and the illustrations are halftones of good quality. About half of each volume is text. Examples: Ortolani, Sergio. *Cosmè Tura, Francesco del Cossa, Ercole de' Roberti,* 1941; Ortolani, Sergio. *Il Pollaiuolo,* 1948; Galassi, Giuseppe. *La scultura fiorentina del quattrocento,* 1949.

2405

Les Demi-dieux. Paris, Éditions du Dimanche. 1945–(55). illus. 32 cm.

Publisher varies: Au Divan, Éditions du Dimanche. An unnumbered series of monographs on important painters. Texts by good writers. Illustrations are rotogravures and include numerous details. Each volume has bibliography and biography of the artist, as well as a critical essay. Dimensions of the paintings discussed are given.

Examples: Gide, André. *Poussin,* 1945; Cassou, Jean. *Delacroix,* 1947; Maurois, André. *David,* 1948; Fargue, L. Paul. *Velazquez,* 1946; Alain [pseud.] *Ingres,* 1949; MacOrlon, Pierre. *Courbet,* 1951.

2406

Deutscher Verein für Kunstwissenschaft, Berlin. Denkmäler deutsche Kunst. Berlin, Deutscher Verein für Kunstwissenschaft, 1912–(55). 31–49 cm.

An unnumbered series of monographs on German art written by recognized specialists. Sektion II covers Plastik and Sektion III, Malerei. Size and format vary. Many volumes issued in the 1920's and 1930's and resumed again in the 1950's.

Examples: Goldschmidt, Adolf. *Die Elfenbeinskulpturen,* 4 v., 1914–26; Martin, Kurt. *Die Nürnberger Steinplastik im XIV. Jahrhunderts,* 1927; Wesenberg, Rudolf. *Bernwardinische Plastik,* 1955.

2407

Deutscher Verein für Kunstwissenschaft, Berlin. Forschungen zur deutschen Kunstgeschichte, 1935–(51). Berlin, Deutscher Verein für Kunstwissenschaft, 1935–(51). 31–36 cm.

A numbered series dealing with German art. Format varies. Many of the volumes also have the legend: "Jahresgabe des Deutschen Vereins für Kunstwissenschaft" (followed by year).

Examples: Winkler, Friedrich. *Dürer und die Illustrationen zum Narrenschiff,* 1951 (Bd. 36); Hessig, Edith. *Die Kunst des Meisters E. S. und die Plastik der Spätgotik,* 1935 (Bd. 1).

2408

... Documentos de arte argentino ... Buenos Aires [Talleres gráficos de la casa J. Peuser, ltda., 1939–47] 25 v. plates. 28 cm. (Publicaciones de la Academia Nacional de Bellas Artes)

A series of well-illustrated monographs dealing with various phases of Argentine art. Some have English and French summaries.

Examples: (1) [Noel, M. S.] *La iglesia de Yavi,* 1939; (3) [Noel, M. S.] *Por la ruta de los Inkas y en la Quebrada de Humahuaca,* 1940; (15) Noel, M. S. *En los senderos misionales de la arquitectura cordobesa,* 1942.

2409

Documents of modern art. N.Y., Wittenborn, 1944–(55). illus., plates (part col.) 26 cm.

Editor: Robert Motherwell. Contents: (1) Apollinaire, G. *The Cubist painters,* rev. ed. 1949; (2) Mondrian, P. *Plastic art and pure plastic art,* 1945; (3) Moholy-Nagy, L. *The new vision,* 4th ed. rev. 1949; (4) Sullivan, L. H. *Kindergarten chats,* 1947; (5) Kandinsky, W. *Concerning the spiritual in art,* 1947; (6) Arp, Jean. *On my way,* 1948; (7) Ernst, Max. *Beyond painting,* 1948; (8) Motherwell, R. *The Dada painters and poets: an anthology,* 1951; (9) Kahnweiler, D. H. *The rise of Cubism,* 1949; (10) Reymond, Marcel. *From Baudelaire to surrealism,* 1949; (11) Duthuit, G. *The Fauvist painters* 1950; (12) Giedion-Welcker, Carola. *Contemporary sculpture,* 1955.

2410

Drawings of the great masters. London, Benn, 1926–27. plates. 26 cm.

A series of volumes covering the drawings of various schools of art. Each consists of about 70 collotype plates and about 35 pages of text by a well-known author, with a catalog of the drawings represented, giving their size and a bibliography.

Examples: Edge, H. *Florentine drawings of the Quattrocento*, 1926; Mellaart, J. N. J. *Dutch drawings of the seventeenth century*, 1926; Muchall-Viebrook, T. W. *Flemish drawings of the seventeenth century*, 1926; Parker, K. T. *Drawings of the early German schools*, 1926; Parker, K. T. *North Italian drawings of the Quattrocento*, 1927; Popham, A. E. *Drawings of the early Flemish school*, 1926.

2411

Egypt Exploration Fund. Memoirs. London, Egypt Exploration Fund, 1885–1934. no. 1–41. illus., plates (part col.), plans, facsims. 32–46 cm.

Contains reports on the excavations carried out by the Fund. In general, each volume is devoted to a particular site or monument.

2412

Encyclopédie Alpina illustrée. Paris, Alpina, c1935–(39). plates. 35 cm.

A numbered series of good clear rotogravure plates issued in portfolios forming monographs, without text, on various subjects, e.g., Pompeian frescoes, Florentine sculpture, French drawings, Greek sculpture, and various cathedrals.

Examples: Maiuri, Amedeo. *Les fresques de Pompéi*, 1936; Verrier, Jean. *Notre-Dame de Paris* [c1939].

2413

Encyclopédie photographique de l'art. The photographic encyclopaedia of art . . . Paris, Éditions "Tel" [c1936–49]. 5 v. illus., plates, maps. 33 cm.

The first three volumes have a commentary by Amedée Ozenfant; v. 4 has text by Michèle Beaulieu; v. 4 published under the supervision of Marcel Aubert. Predominantly plates with short explanatory text in French and English. Excellent rotogravure plates.

Contents: v. 1, Le Musée du Louvre: Égypte, Mésopotamie; v. 2, Le Musée du Louvre: Mésopotamie (suite), Canaan, Chypre, Grèce; v. 3, Le Musée du Louvre: Grèce (suite), Rome; v. 4, Le Musée du Louvre: Sculptures du moyen âge; v. 5, Le Musée de Caire.

2414

English master painters, edited by Herbert Read. London, Kegan Paul (and others), [1940]–(55). plates. 26 cm.

An unnumbered publisher's series of monographs on individual English painters.

Examples: Shirley, Andrew. *Bonington*, 1940; Waterhouse, Ellis K. *Reynolds*, 1941; Beckett, R. B. *Lely*, 1951; Constable, W. G. *Richard Wilson*, 1953; Garlick, Kenneth John. *Sir Thomas Laurence*, 1955.

2415

Études d'art et d'ethnologie asiatiques (Collection publiée sous le patronage de L'École Française d'Extrême-Orient). Paris, Van Oest, Les Éditions d'Art et d'Histoire, 1944–(51?). 28 cm.

A numbered series which has supplanted *Ars Asiatica* (2380). Contents: (1) Coral Rémusat, G. *L'art khmer, les grandes étapes de son évolution*, 1951; (2) Marchal, Henri. *L'architecture comparée dans l'Inde et l'Extrême-Orient*, 1944; (3) Marchal, Henri. *Le décor et la sculpture khmers*, 1951.

2416

Études sur l'art de tous les pays et de toutes les époques. Strasbourg, Heitz, 1920–(29). plates. 29 cm.

Some are published in German, others in French; some have plates and others do not. A list of the first eight to appear is found in Gysin, Fritz. *Delacroix*, 1929. Example: Marle, Raimond van. *Simone Martini et les peintres de son école*, 1920.

2417

Florence. R. Galleria degli Uffizi. I disegni della R. Galleria degli Uffizi in Firenze . . . Firenze, Olschki, 1912–21. 5 ser. in 20 pts. 498 plates. 56 cm.

In portfolios. Cover title. A series of very good collotype reproductions of drawings in the Uffizi collections, with a sentence or two describing each.

Contents: Serie I. (fasc. 1), *Jacopo Carrucci, detto il Pontormo*; (2) *Tiziano Vecellio e Jacopo Robusti, detto il Tintoretto*; (3) *Paolo Uccello, Antonio Pollaiolo, Piero Pollaiolo, Andrea del Verrocchio, Sandro Botticelli*; (4) *Adamo Elsheimer, Matteo Brill, Paolo Brill, Cornelio Poelenburgh, Hermann van Swanevelt, Giovanni Both, Jacques Callot, Claude Lorrain, Giusto Sustermans, Gaspero Vanvitelli*. Serie II. (fasc. 1), *Lodovico Cardi, detto il Cigoli, Iacopo Chimenti, detto l'Empoli, Cristofano Allori, Francesco Furini*; (2) *Baccio della Porta, detto Fra Bartolommeo*; (3) *Scuole Emiliana e Cremonese, disegni di Ercole Roberti, Francesco Francia, Lorenzo Costa, Boccaccio Boccaccino, Amico Aspertini, Giovanni Luteri, detto Dosso Dossi, Antonio Allegri, detto il Correggio, Giulio Campi,*

Gervasio Gatto, detto il Sojaro, Francesco Primaticcio, Francesco Massola, detto il Parmigianino, Nicolò dell'Abate; (4) *Jacopo Callot e Stefano della Bella.* Serie III. (fasc. 1), *Scuola veneta;* (2) *Raffaello;* (3) *Scuola tedesca e fiamminga;* (4) *Disegni di pittori fiorentini del secolo XVII.* Serie IV. (fasc. 1), *Filippino Lippi e Piero di Cosimo;* (2) *Disegni di pittori bolognesi dei secolo XVI–XVIII;* (3) *Andrea d'Agnolo, detto Andrea del Sarto;* (4) *Scuola fiorentina (secoli XV e XVI).* Serie V. (fasc. 1), *Maestri tosco-romani del secolo XVI;* (2) *Maestri umbro-senesi;* (3) *Disegni di Leonardo da Vinci;* (4) *Disegni ornamentali.*

2418
The Gallery of masterpieces. N.Y., Scribner; London, Hamilton; Paris, Amiot-Dumont, 1954–(57). col. plates. 44 cm.

A series of monographs of color plates devoted to individual artists. Plates made by Annibale Belli in Italy. Each volume consists of about 20 pages of text, including bibliography and 20 color plates.

Artists included: Fra Angelico, Giotto, Rembrandt, Van Eyck, and Goya.

2419
I Grandi musei del mondo. Bergamo, Istituto Italiano d'Arti Grafiche, *ca.* 1909–n.d. col. plates. 36 cm.

A numbered series, each containing about 50 colored halftone plates of good quality, reproducing masterpieces from one of the important museums, with a short text for each picture. 13 volumes issued.

Contents: (1) Ricci, Corrado. *La Galleria degli Uffizi;* (2) Ricci, Corrado. *La Galleria Pitti e la Galleria dell'Accademia;* (3) Hermanin, Federico. *Le Gallerie Nazionali di Roma; La Galleria Borghese; La Galleria Nazionale d'Arte Antica nel Palazzo Corsini;* (4) Frizzoni, Gustavo e Ricci, Corrado. *Le Gallerie di Milano;* (5) Steenhoff, W. *Il Museo d'Amsterdam;* (6) Réau, Luigi. *I Musei di Pietroburgo;* (7) Ricci, Corrado. *Le Regie Gallerie di Venezia;* (8) Mourey, Gabriele. *I Musei di Londra;* (9) Pinetti, Angelo. *Il Museo di Berlino;* (10) Voss, Hermann. *Le Gallerie del Belgio;* (11) De Beruete, Don Aureliano. *Il Museo del Prado;* (12) Philippi, A. *Le Gallerie di Dresda;* (13) Reber, Francesco. *La Pinacoteca Antica di Monaco.*

2420
Les Grands sculpteurs français; collection dirigée par Francis Salet. Paris, Tisné, 1950–(51). illus., plates. 25 cm.

Scholarly type of monograph with good clear halftone illustrations and detailed bibliography. Contents: David, Henri. *Claus Sluter,* 1951; Réau, Louis. *J. B. Pigalle,* 1950.

2421
Graphische Gesellschaft. Berlin, Cassirer. Veröffentlichungen 1–25, 1906–22. Ausserordentliche Veröffentlichungen 1–5, 1908–14. illus. 36–39 cm.

Size varies slightly. The majority of the illustrations are photogravures, but some are collotypes. Each volume mentions process used and tells who made the plates.

Veröffentlichungen consists of reproductions of such works as the *Biblia Pauperum* (no. 2), 1906; *Dance of Death* (no. 12), 1910; and also works on various periods of engraving such as Kristeller, Paul. *Eine Folge Venezianischer Holzschnitte* (no. 9), and on collections such as *Berlin, K. Museen Kupferstichkabinett* (no. 21), 1915.

Ausserordentliche Veröffentlichungen contain Kristeller, Paul. *Die Tarocchi,* 1910, and a monograph on Schongauer, 1914.

2422
The Great centuries of painting. Geneva; N.Y., Skira, 1952–(57). col. plates. 29 cm.

Albert Skira, editor. Translated into English from the original French text. A series of volumes illustrated by good color plates, each covering a century or the scope of a particular civilization in ancient art. Texts by well-known authors. Each volume has a bibliography.

Contents: Jacques Dupont and François Mathey. *The 17th century* [1951]; Maurice Raynal. *The 19th century* [1951]; Georges Bataille. *Lascaux,* 1955; Jacques Dupont and Cesare Gnudi. *Gothic painting,* 1954; André Grabar. *Byzantine painting,* 1953; Giulio Carlo Argan and Jacques Lassaigne. *The 15th century,* 1955; Amedeo Maiuri. *Roman painting,* 1953; Arpag Mekhitarian. *Egyptian painting,* 1954; Massimo Pallottino. *Etruscan painting,* 1952; Georges de Traz. *The 18th century,* 1952; Lionello Venturi. *The 16th century* [1956]; Carl Nordenfalk and André Grabar. *Early medieval painting,* 1957.

2423
Great masters in painting and sculpture. London, Bell, 1900–1914. illus. 21 cm.

Series edited by G. C. Williamson. 31 volumes issued. Monographs consisting of about 40 halftone illustrations and a catalog of works of the artist, usually arranged geographically by place of exhibition. Examples: Brinton, Selwyn. *Correggio*, 1903; Stevenson, Robert A. M. *Velasquez*, 1914.

2424

Grosse Kulturen der Frühzeit. Ed. by H. Bossert. Stuttgart, Kilpper, 1954–(57). plates. 27 cm.

Each volume is written by a scholar in the field which he covers and contains about 150 pages of text, and 150 to 225 illustrations, a bibliography, and an index.

Contents: (1) Riemschneider, M. *Die Welt der Hethiter*, 1954; (2) Schmökel, H. *Ur, Assur und Babylon*, 1955; (3) Wolf, W. *Die Welt der Aegypter*, 1955; (4) Matz, F. *Kreta, Mykene, Troja*, 1956; (5) Osten, H. H. van der. *Die Welt der Perser*, 1956; (6) Jirku, A. *Die Welt der Bibel, 5000 Jahre in Palästina und Syrien*, 1957.

2425

Harvard-Radcliffe fine arts series. Cambridge, Mass., Harvard Univ. Press, 1936–(57). size varies.

Scholarly monographs devoted to various subjects of art history. Contents: Burroughs, Alan. *Limners and likenesses*, 1936; Wethey, H. E. *Gil de Siloe and his school*, 1936; Darby, D. F. *Francisco Ribalta and his school*, 1938; Neilson, K. B. *Filippino Lippi*, 1938; Warner, Langdon. *Buddhist wall-paintings*, 1938; Lucas, E. L. *Books on art*, 1938; *Medieval studies in memory of A. Kingsley Porter*, 2 v., 1939; Grace, F. R. *Archaic sculpture in Boetia*, 1939; Post, Chandler Rathfon. *A history of Spanish painting*, 1930–(57); Schroeder, Eric. *Persian miniatures in the Fogg museum of art*, 1942; Starr, R. F. S. *Nuzi*, 2 v., 1937–39; Hersey, C. K. *The Salmantine lanterns*, 1937; Mongan, Agnes and Sachs, Paul. *Drawings in the Fogg museum of art*, 3 v., 1940.

2426

Hiersemanns Handbücher. Leipzig, Hiersemann, *ca.* 1905–32. plates. 24 cm.

A numbered series of which at least 13 volumes were published between 1905 and 1932.

Examples: (3) Kisa, A. C. *Das Glas im Altertum*, 1908; (4) Neugebauer, Rudolf. *Handbuch der orientalischen Teppichkunde*, 1920; (7) Doering, Oscar. *Deutschlands mittelalterliche Kunstdenkmäler als Geschichtsquelle*, 1910; (8) Fischer, J. L. *Handbuch der Glasmalerei*, 1914 (2. Aufl. 1937); (10) Mols-

dorf, Wilhelm. *Christliche Symbolik der mittelalterlichen Kunst*, 2. Aufl., 1926; (13) Singer, H. W. *Die Fachausdrücke der Graphik*, 1932.

2427

[Hyperion books] Paris, London, N.Y., Hyperion Press, 1936–44. illus., col. plates. 32 cm.

Editor, André Gloeckner. Originally published in both English and French. During the war they were issued in New York by Harper's and Random House. Some also came out in Paris in the early 1940's.

Primarily picture books with short texts and bibliographies. Black and white illustrations are rotogravures. Halftone color plates are rather poor in quality. Some later American plates are printed by offset.

Contents: Bazin, Germain. *Italian painting in the XIV and XV centuries*, 1938; Borenius, Tancred. *La peinture anglaise au XVIIIe siècle*, 1938; Harris, E. *Spanish painting*, 1937; Michel, Édouard. *La peinture flamande au XVIIe siècle*, 1939; Réau, Louis. *French painting in XIV, XV, & XVI centuries*, 1939; Rocheblave, Samuel. *French painting of the 18th century*, 1937; Rocheblave, Samuel. *French painting of the 19th century*, 1936; Roger-Marx, Claude. *French original engravings from Manet to the present time*, 1939; Terrasse, Charles. *French painting in the 20th century*, 1939; *French impressionists and their contemporaries represented in American collections*, 1944.

2428

[Hyperion monographs] N.Y., Hyperion Press, 1937–45. illus. 33–35 cm.

A series of monographs devoted to individual artists of various periods and countries. Short text by recognized authors, but the approach is popular rather than scholarly. Illustrations are not particularly good.

Examples: Jacz, G. de. *Raphael's colours*, 1937; Glück, Gustav. *Pieter Brueghel*, 1937; Legendre, Maurice. *El Greco*, 1937; Lassaigne, Jacques. *Daumier*, 1938; Reinhardt, Hans. *Holbein*, 1938; Rewald, John. *Gauguin*, 1938; Rey, Robert. *Manet*, 1938; Mauclair, Camille. *Turner*, 1939; Rewald, John. *Maillol*, 1939; Cassou, Jean. *Picasso*, 1940; Boswell, Peyton. *Varnum Poore*, 1941; Perls, K. G. *Vlaminck*, 1941; Vargo, Margaret. *Waldo Peirce*, 1941; Vaughan, Malcolm. *Derain*, 1941; Breuning, Margaret. *Mary Cassatt*, 1944; Jewell, E. A. *Paul Cézanne*, 1944; Mauclair, Camille. *Edgar Degas*, 1945; Fierens, Paul. *James Ensor*, 1943.

2429

Italy. Direzione Generale delle Antichità e Belle Arti . . . Catalogo delle cose d'arte e di antichità d'Italia . . . 1–11. Roma, La Libreria dello Stato, 1911–39. 31 cm.

Contents: (1) Toesca, Pietro. *Aosta*, 1911; (2–3) Papini, Roberto. *Pisa*, 2 v., 1912–[32?]; (4) Cecchelli, Carlo. *Zara*, 1932; (5) Serra, Luigi. *Urbino*, 1932; (6) Gigliolo, Odoardo. *Fiesole*, 1933; (7) Coletti, Luigi. *Treviso*, 1935; (8) Brizio, Anna M. *Vercelli*, 1935; (9) Zocca, Emma. *Assisi*, 1936; (10) Santangelo, Antonino. *Cividale*, 1936; (11) Morassi, Antonio. *Brescia*, 1939.

2430

Italy. Direzione Generale delle Antichità e Belle Arti . . . Inventario degli oggetti d'arte d'Italia. v. 1–9. [Roma] La Libreria dello Stato, 1931–38. 27 cm.

Contents: (1) *Provincia di Bergamo*; (2) *Calabria*; (3) *Parma*; (4) *Aquila*; (5) *Pola*; (6) *Mantova*; (7) *Padova*; (8) *Ancona e Ascoli Piceno*; (9) *Sondrio*.

2431

Klassiker der Kunst in Gesamtausgabe. Stuttgart und Leipzig, Deutsche Verlags-Anstalt, 1904–37. illus. 26 cm.

38 volumes published. A numbered series of monographs on important painters and a few sculptors, which contain a wealth of halftone illustrations as well as text. Each volume has a section of works attributed to the artist or copies of lost works, as well as a chronological index of the works, a listing by place, and a subject index.

Many of the volumes were issued in French by Hachette, Paris, as the series, *Classiques de l'art.*

2432

Die Kunst des Ostens. Berlin, Cassirer, 1921–25. illus. 26 cm.

Edited by William Cohn. 11 volumes issued 1921–25. A numbered series dealing with the art of Egypt and the East. Profusely illustrated. A French ed. of this series was also issued.

Examples: (5) Sarre, Friedrich. *Die Kunst des alten Persien*, 1923; (9) Kühnel, Ernst. *Maurische Kunst*, 1924; (11) Glaser, Curt. *Ostasiatische Plastik*, 1925.

2433

Kunstgeschichtliche Monographien. Leipzig, Hiersemann, 1904–32. illus. 27 cm.

20 volumes were published 1904–32. Schol-

arly monographs on painters with numerous collotype illustrations. Examples: (no. 9) Sievers, Johannes. *Pieter Aertsen*, 1908; (no. 15) Weigelt, C. H. *Duccio di Buoninsegna*, 1911; (no. 20) Spahn, Annemarie. *Palma Vecchio*, 1932.

2434

Kunsthistorisches Institut, Florence. Italienische Forschungen. Berlin, Cassirer, 1906–12, 1925–26. Bd. 1–2, 4–5. N.F. Bd. 1–2. 27 cm.

Band 3 never published. Scholarly publications dealing with Italian Renaissance art.

Contents: Bd. 1, *Das Aktenbuch für Ghibertis Matthäus-Statue an Or San Michele zu Florence . . . I Solari, architetti e scultori lombardi del XV secolo . . . Venezianischer Hausrat zur Zeit der Renaissance . . . Restello, Spiegel und Toilettenutensilien in Venedig zur Zeit der Renaissance . . .*; Bd. 2, *Il duomo di Firenze: documenti sulla decorazione della chiesa e del campanile tratti dall'archivio dell'opera . . .*; Bd. 4, *Archivalische Beiträge zur Geschichte der venezianischen Kunst . . .*; Bd. 5, *Geschichte der Peruginer Malerei bis zu Perugino und Pinturicchio . . .*; Neue Folge, Bd. 1, Posse, Hans. *Der römische Maler Andrea Sacchi*, 1925; Bd. 2, Biehl, Walther. *Toskanische Plastik des frühen und hohen Mittelalters*, 1926.

2435

Künstler-Monographien. Bielefeld und Leipzig, Velhagen und Klasing, 1895–1940. illus. 26 cm.

Edited by Hermann Knackfuss. 121 volumes had appeared by 1940. A numbered series of monographs on famous painters and sculptors, each containing about 150 pages well-illustrated with numerous halftones. Text by recognized authorities. Some were also published in English as "Monographs on Artists."

Examples: (24) Steinman, Ernst. *Botticelli*, 1897; (74) Schubring, Paul. *Luca della Robbia*, 1921; (121) Schürer, Oskar. *Michael Pacher*, 1940.

2436

Library of great museums. N.Y., Abrams, 1952–[57]. illus., col. plates. 23–33 cm.

An unnumbered series of monographs devoted to important museums. The text describes the history of the museums, and the plates reproduce in color the important paintings.

Contents: Huyghe, René. *Art treasures of the Louvre*, 1951; N.Y. Metropolitan Museum of Art. *Art treasures of the Metropolitan*, 1952; Wehle, Harry. *Art treasures of the Prado Museum*, 1954; Bardi, P. M. *Art treasures of the Sao Paulo Museum* [1954]; Hendy, Philip. *Art treasures of the National Gallery, London*, 1955; Rossi, Filippo. *Art treasures of the Uffizi and Pitti* [1956]; Buchner, Ernst. *Art treasures of the Pinakothek*, 1957; Grigson, Geoffrey. *Art treasures of the British Museum* [1957].

2437
The Library of great painters. N.Y., Abrams, 1950–(57). col. plates. 34 cm.
An unnumbered series of monographs on individual painters, made up of text by recognized authorities and about 50 good color plates. Contents: Schapiro, Meyer. *Paul Cézanne*, 1952; Rich, Daniel Catton. *Edgar Hilaire Germain Degas*, 1951; Schapiro, Meyer. *Vincent van Gogh*, 1954; Pach, Walter. *Pierre Auguste Renoir*, 1950; Bronstein, Leo. *El Greco*, 1950; Münz, Ludwig. *Rembrandt* [1954]; Cooper, Douglas. *Toulouse-Lautrec* [1955]; Pittaluga, Mary. *Raphael* [1955, c1954].

2438
The Library of great painters. Portfolio edition. N.Y., Abrams, 1951–(57). col. plates. 33 cm.
An inexpensive series of monographs which consist of short text and nine color plates of the same caliber as in the main series. Many of the titles are the same as in the larger series and are a sort of abridgment of those works. However, some titles have appeared only in this series.
Examples: Thompson, James W. *Masterpieces of Italian painting*, 1951; Held, Julius Samuel. *Flemish painting*, 1953; Held, Julius Samuel. *Peter Paul Rubens*, 1953.

2439
Les Maîtres du moyen âge et de la renaissance. Paris, Michel, 1924–(49). illus. 28 cm.
Édouard Schneider is editor of the series, in which 11 volumes have been issued. Volumes are half text, half collotype reproductions, and contain bibliographies.
Examples: Schneider, Édouard. *Fra Angelico da Fiesole*, 1924; Du Colombier, Pierre. *Albert Dürer* [c1927]; Dimier, Louis. *Le Primatice* [c1928]; Mesnil, Jacques. *Botticelli* [1938]; Du Colombier, Pierre. *Jean Goujon*, 1949.

2440
Manuels d'histoire de l'art. Paris, Laurens, 1908–(35). illus. 25 cm.
An unnumbered series of which 15 volumes had appeared by 1935. "Object of the series is to trace the evolution of each art from the earliest efforts to the present state, covering the various places and periods in which it was developed." Illustrated by halftones in the text.
Examples: Picard, Charles. *La sculpture antique de Phidias à l'ère byzantine*, 1926; Gillet, Louis. *La peinture de Poussin à David*, 1935.

2441
Marées Gesellschaft. Drucke. München, Piper, 1911?–25? plates. 53–64 cm.
Publications of large, excellent collotype reproductions of drawings and water colors. Plates were made by various firms such as Frisch, Jaffé, etc.
Examples: *Cézanne und seine Ahnen* [1921]; *Antike Fresken*, by Theodor Wiegand [1922].

2442
Masterpieces of French painting; collection directed and published by Albert Skira. Paris, 1934–(48). col. plates. 39 cm.
Appeared in both French and English eds. before the war. Some few of the monographs bear the imprint London, Zwemmer for the English ed. During the war the series was issued in Geneva by Skira.
Each volume contains six to 16 loose color plates illustrating the history of French painting, and six to eight pages of text. The series is unnumbered but divided by centuries. Some volumes cover the whole century or school, others cover three or four artists, but the majority are individual monographs.

2443
Masters of etching. London, Studio, 1924–32. plates. 25 x 31 cm.
A numbered series of monographs on important etchers. Artists of various countries are included but the emphasis is on British. 32 volumes were issued 1924–32. Each consists mainly of plates with a short text. Some volumes called *Modern masters of etching*.
Examples: *Frank Brangwyn*, 2 v., 1924–32; *J. L. Forain*, 1925; *Arthur Briscoe*, 1930.

2444
Masters of modern art. N.Y., Dodd Mead, 1925–27. illus. 20 cm.

12 volumes were issued in this series covering French painters and sculptors. Each volume contains a text translated from the French, about 40 rotogravure illustrations, and a very short bibliography.

Artists included: Rodin, Manet, Renoir, Morisot, Millet, Fantin-Latour, Toulouse-Lautrec, Monet, Gauguin, Bayre, and Pissarro. Example: Mauclair, Camille. *Claude Monet*, 1925.

2445

Meister der Graphik. Leipzig, Klinkhardt & Biermann, 1919–32? illus., plates. 31 cm.

Editor, Hermann Voss. A numbered series of monographs on graphic artists, uniform in format. 15 were published 1919–32. Examples: (no. 2) Geisberg, Max. *Die Anfänge des Kupferstiches* [1923]; (no. 10) Geisberg, Max. *Der Meister E. S.* [1924].

2446

Meister der Zeichnung. Leipzig, Baumgartner, 1912– . plates. 30 cm.

Editor, H. W. Singer. At least seven volumes issued. Imprint varies sometimes. Good collotype reproductions with short text. Artists covered include: Max Klinger, Albert Besnard, Emil Orlik.

2447

Meisterwerke der bedeutendsten Galerien Europas. Munich, Hanfstaengl, 1903–23. plates. 24–25 cm.

11 volumes issued. Only European museums are included, with special emphasis on those in Germany. Illustrated with halftone plates.

Contents: (1) Hanfstaengl, Eberhard. *Die Ältere Pinakothek in München*, 1922; (2) Hanfstaengl, E. *Die Neue Pinakothek, Staatsgalerie und Schackgalerie in München*, 1922; (3) Voll, Karl. *Die Gemälde Galerie in Dresden*, 1922; (4) Voll, K. *Die National Gallery in London*, 1922; (5) Voll, K. *Das Rijks-Museum in Amsterdam*, 1903; (6) Voll, K. *Die K. Galerie im Haag und die Galerie der Stadt Haarlem*, 1903; (7) Voll, K. *Die Gemäldegalerie in Kassel*, 1904; (8) Weiner, P. P. *Die Eremitage in St. Petersburg*, 1923; (9) Fischel, Oskar. *Das Kaiser Friedrich Museum in Berlin*, 1922; (10) Ganz, Paul. *Die Öffentliche Kunstsammlung in Basel*, 1923; (11) Mayer, August. *Meisterwerke der Gemäldesammlung des Prado in Madrid*, 1922.

2448

Die Meisterzeichnung. Bd. 1–5. Freiburg im Breisgau, Urban-Verlag [1928–36]. plates. 31 cm.

A collection of good collotype plates with a short introductory text of about 25 pages and a "Verzeichnis" which describes the plates, gives size, and suggests bibliographical references.

Contents: (1) Hugelshofer, Walter. *Schweizer Handzeichnungen des XV. und XVI. Jahrhunderts*, 1928; (2) Parker, K. T. *Elsässische Handzeichnungen des XV. und XVI. Jahrhunderts*, 1928; (3) Schilling, Edmund. *Nürnberger Handzeichnungen des XV. und XVI. Jahrhunderts*, 1932; (4) Winkler, Friedrich. *Mittel- Niederrheinische und Westfälische Handzeichnungen des XV. und XVI. Jahrhunderts*, 1932; (5) Benesch, Otto. *Oesterreichische Handzeichnungen des XV. und XVI. Jahrhunderts*, 1936.

2449

Modern painters. N.Y., Abrams [1954]–(57). illus. (part mounted col.), plates, facsims. 30 cm.

A series of sound monographs on modern painters, written by recognized authorities and well illustrated. Each contains bibliography and sometimes documents. Contents: *Paul Klee* by Will Grohmann; *Piet Mondrian* by Michel Seuphor [pseud.]; *Pablo Picasso* by Wilhelm Boeck and Jaime Sabartés; *Kandinsky* by Will Grohmann.

2450

The Monograph series recording the architecture of the American colonies and the early republic. v. 1–(26). [July 1915–Oct. 1940] N.Y., Whitehead, 1916–(40). 24 v. in 10. illus., plates, plans. 28 cm.

Title varies: v. 1–18, The White pine series of architectural monographs. Volumes 18–26 published in the periodical *Pencil points*.

These monographs "present classified illustrations of wood construction, critically described by representative American architects, of the most beautiful and suggestive examples of architecture, old and new, which this country has produced."

Good illustrations and many measured drawings of architectural details.

2451

Monumenta Cataloniae; materiales para la historia del arte en Cataluña. Barcelona, Editorial "Alpha," 1932–(56). illus., plates. 33 cm.

Elaborate publications with excellent collotype plates, bibliography, and bibliographical footnotes.

Contents: (1–2) Durán y Sanpere, A. *Los*

retablos de piedra, 2 v. [1932–34]; (3) Gudiol y Ricart, J. *Els vidres catalans* [c1936]; (4) Pijoán y Soteras, J. *Les pintures murals romàniques de Catalunya* [1948]; (5–7) Puig y Cadafalch, J. *L'escultura romànica a Catalunya*, v. 1–3 [1949–54]; (8) Olivar, Marçal. *La ceràmica trecentista a Aragó, Catalunya i València* [1952]; (9) Folch i Torres, J. *La pintura romànica sobre fusta*, 1956.

2452
Monumenti della pittura antica scoperti in Italia . . . Roma, La Libreria dello Stato [1936]–(55). illus., plates (part col.), plans. 52 cm.

Each fascicle treats of the ancient paintings in a single tomb or house and consists of scholarly text, with bibliographical notes, and good plates, most of which are in color.

Contents: (Sezione prima), La pittura etrusca: Clusium, 1939; Tarquinii, v. 1–4, 1937–55; (Sezione terza), La pittura ellen-istico-romana: Centuripae, v. 1, 1940; Pompeii, v. 1–5, 1937–41; Roma, v. 1–3, 5, 1936–41.

2453
I Monumenti italiana. [ser. 1] fasc. 1–17/18, 1934–39; ser. 2, fasc. 1–(2), 1947–(53). Roma, La Libreria dello Stato, 1934–(53). illus., plates, plans. 50 cm.

Serie 1 has subtitle: *rilievi raccolti a cura della Reale accademia d'Italia*. Serie 2 has at head of title: Accademia nazionale dei Lincei.

Elaborate plans and renderings of individual monuments of ancient and later Italian architecture, issued by fascicles.

2454
Monumenti vaticani di archeologia e d'arte pubblicati . . . a cura della Pontificia Accademia Romana d'Archeologia, 1–(9), 1922–(51). Roma, Bardi, 1922–(51). 36 cm.

A numbered series covering material in the Vatican collections. Examples: (1) *Le stanze di Raffaello*, 1922; (2) *Vasi antichi dipinti del Vaticano* [1924]; (4) *Sculture magazzino del Museo vaticano*, 2 v., 1936–37.

2455
Nederlands Historisch Instituut te Rome. Studiën, 1931–(42). Haag, Nijhoff, 1931–(42). plates.

Contents: (1) Fokker, T. H. *Werke Niederländischer Meister in den Kirchen Italiens*, 1931; (2) Post, R. R. *Supplieken gericht aan de Pausen, Clemens VI, Innocentius VI en Urbanus V, 1342–1366*, 1937; (3) Hoogewerff, G. J. *Nederlandsche kunstenaars te Rome (1600–1725) uittreksels uit de parochiale archieven*, 1942.

2456
N.Y. Museum of Modern Art. [Publications] illus. 26 cm.

Since its founding in 1929 the museum has issued a catalog for each of its major exhibitions. These are written by specialists, are well illustrated, and usually contain valuable bibliographies. Some—such as *Cubism and abstract art*, 1936; *Fantastic art, Dada, surrealism*, 1936; *Ancient arts of the Andes*, 1954; *Indian art of the U.S.*, 1941; and *Arts of the south seas*, 1946—contain the best summaries and information available on the subject.

Other catalogs such as *Matisse*, 1951, *Picasso*, 1939, 1946, and 1957, etc. become valuable monographs on individual artists. From 1947 to 1958 Simon and Schuster distributed the museum's publications, which form an important record of modern art and are extremely useful for art reference work. Since May 1958 Doubleday has taken over the distribution.

2457
Nouvelle encyclopédie illustrée de l'art français. Paris, LePrat, 1943–[51]. illus. 29 cm.

An unnumbered series, cheaply bound, on not very good paper. Rotogravure illustrations (some bleeding the page), many by Jean Roubier, are quite good. Altogether the series forms a rather popular type of pictorial history of French art. Covers architecture, painting, and minor arts.

Contents: Lantier, Raymond Jubert J. *Les origines de l'art français* [1947]; Lefrançois, Louise (Pillon). *L'art roman* [1943]; Réau, Louis. *L'art gothique* [1945]; Du Colombier, Pierre. *L'art renaissance* [1945]; Mauricheau-Beaupré, Charles. *L'art au XVIIe siècle en France*, 2 v., 1946– ; Dacier, Émile. *L'art au XVIIIème siècle en France*, 1951.

2458
L'Opera del genio italiano all'estero. Roma, La Libreria dello Stato, 1934–(43). ser. 1. illus., plates. 30 cm.

Each volume of the series printed in 550 copies. Scholarly works dealing with Italian artists working in other countries. Each volume contains text, bibliographies, and lists of the artists, as well as indexes and plates.

Contents: Budinis, Cornelio. *Gli artisti italiani in Ungheria*, 1936; Morpurgo, Enrico. *Gli artisti italiani in Austria*, v. 1, 1937; Lavagnino, Emilio. *Gli artisti in Portogallo*,

1940; Hermanin, Federico. *Gli artisti in Germania,* 3 v., 1934–43; Lo Gatto, Ettore. *Gli artisti italiani in Russia,* 3 v., 1934–43; Maggiorotti, L. A. *Architetti e architetture militare . . . ,* 3 v., 1933–39.

2459

Orbis pictus: Weltkunst-Bücherei. Berlin, Wasmuth, 1920–24. plates. 26 cm.

P. Westheim, editor. 19 volumes issued. Small books of about 50 pages, one half of which is halftone plates. Covers Oriental as well as Western art. Example: Weber, Otto. *Assyrische Kunst,* 1924.

2460

Painting, colour, history. Geneva; N.Y., Skira, 1949–(57). col. illus. 35 cm.

Albert Skira, editor. An unnumbered series with colored illustrations and including bibliographies.

Contents: Venturi, Lionello. *Italian painting,* 3 v., 1950–52; Lassaigne, Jacques. *Spanish painting,* 2 v., 1952; Goya y Lucientes, Francisco José de. *The frescoes in San Antonio de Florida in Madrid, historical and critical study* by Enrique Lafuente Ferrari, 1955; Raynal, Maurice. *History of modern painting,* 3 v., [1949–50] (1 v. edition, 1953); Leymarie, Jean. *Dutch painting* [1956]; Lassaigne, Jacques. *Flemish painting: v. 1, The century of Van Eyck,* 1957.

2461

Pan American Institute of Geography and History. Commission on History. Publications. Mexico, 1950–(53). 23 cm.

The same volumes are also listed as Publications of the Pan American Institute of Geography and History, with varying numbers. A series devoted to monographs on historical and archaeological monuments in various countries in this area. Usually contain bibliographies.

Examples: (23) Rubio y Muñoz-Bocanegra, Angel. *Panama,* 1950; (30) Lee, Ronald F. *United States,* 1951; (35) Andrade, Rodrigo Melo Franco de. *Brasil,* 1952; (38) Montandón, Roberto. *Chile,* 1952; (41) Pressoir, Catts. *Haiti,* 1952; (42) Rubín de la Borbolla, Daniel Fernando. *Guatemala,* 1953; (43) Rubín de la Borbolla, Daniel Fernando. *México,* 1953; (44) Rubín de la Borbolla, Daniel Fernando. *Honduras,* 1953; (61) Vargas, José Maria. *Ecuador,* 1953.

2462

Pantheon series of the Pegasus Press. N.Y., Harcourt Brace; Florence, Pantheon [1927–31]. plates. 32 cm.

This useful series was published in French, German, English, Italian, and Spanish. The volumes are made up predominantly of very good collotype plates with text written by specialists, and include bibliographies and biographical material on artists.

Included are: Borenius, T., and Tristram, E. W. *English medieval painting;* Saunders, O. Elfrida. *English illumination,* 2 v.; Porter, A. K. *Spanish Romanesque sculpture,* 2 v.; Goldschmidt, A. *German illumination,* 2 v.; Ricci, Corrado. *North Italian painting of the Cinquecento;* Toesca, Pietro. *Florentine painting of the Trecento;* Fiocco, Giuseppe. *Venetian painting of the Seicento and Settecento;* Aubert, M., and Vitry, P. *French Gothic sculpture,* 2 v.; Rinaldis, Aldo de. *Neapolitan painting of the Seicento;* Domínguez Bordona, J. D. *Spanish illumination,* 2 v.; Weigelt, C. H. *Sienese painting of the Trecento;* Deschamps, P. *French sculpture of the Romanesque period, XI to XVI centuries;* Baker, C. H. Collins and Constable, W. G. *English painting of the 16th and 17th centuries;* Venturi, Adolfo. *North Italian painting of the Quattrocento;* Haseloff, A. *Pre-Romanesque sculpture in Italy;* Lemoisne, P. A. *Gothic painting in France: 14th and 15th centuries;* Gómez-Moreno, M. *Renaissance sculpture in Spain;* Hadeln, Detlev von. *Handzeichnungen von G. B. Tiepolo,* 2 v.

2463

Les Peintres français nouveaux. Paris, Éditions de la "Nouvelle Revue Française," 1925–30. 17 cm.

47 volumes issued 1925–30. Small monographs on individual contemporary French painters. Each volume of about 60 pages contains a very brief biography, a short critical essay, a few quotations from various critics, and numerous illustrations. Example: Carco, Francis. *Utrillo,* 1929.

2464

Petites monographies des grands édifices de la France, pub. sous la direction de Marcel Aubert. Paris, Laurens, 1909–(50). illus. 20 cm.

An unnumbered series of small illustrated monographs, each on an individual French monument, written by a recognized scholar and containing a bibliography. The series was founded by E. Lefevre-Pontalis and contains cathedrals, churches and chapels, abbeys, chateaux, and civil buildings. 89 volumes had appeared by 1950.

Examples: Lécureux, L. T. *Saint-Pol-de Léon*, 1909; Anglès, Auguste. *L'abbaye de Moissac*, 1911; Terrasse, Charles. *Le château d'Ecouen*, 1925; Gobellot, René. *La cathédrale de Sées*, 1937; Blanche-Le Bourhis, Magdeleine. *Le château de Cheverny*, 1950.

2465

Phaidon Press books. Vienna, Phaidon Press; London, Phaidon Press; N.Y., Oxford Univ. Press, 1936–(57). illus.

Originally published by the Phaidon Press, Vienna, but at the beginning of World War II transferred to England. Earlier volumes published in German. Some of the German editions were later issued by Oxford with a few slight changes.

Size and format vary, but the illustrations are of high quality and the texts written by reputable scholars. The majority of the books are monographs on individual artists, but some are surveys of the art of a particular country or period. In 1944 a "Pocket editions" series was begun with Burckhardt, Jacob. *Civilization of the Renaissance*, and numerous other titles have been brought out in this size.

Examples: Tietze, Hans. *Titian paintings and drawings*, 1937; Uhde, Wilhelm. *The impressionists*, 1937; Ironside, Robin. *Pre-Raphaelite painters*, 1948; Benesch, Otto. *The drawings of Rembrandt*, 6 v., 1954–57; Wittkower, Rudolf. *Gian Lorenzo Bernini*, 1955; Blunt, Anthony. *The drawings of G. P. Castiglione & Stefano della Bella in the collection of Her Majesty the Queen at Windsor Castle* [1954].

2466

Prestel-Bücher. Frankfurt am Main, Prestel-Verlag [1935–(50)]. illus., plates (part col.) 25 cm.

A series of moderately priced volumes covering mostly drawings, with good illustrations and short text (c. 50 p.) by recognized authorities.

Since the last war some of the titles are issued in French by Les Éditions Holbein in Bâle, and Harper in New York has brought out some in English as Harper's Art Library.

Examples: Regteren Altena, Johan Q. van. *Holländische Meisterzeichnungen des siebzehnten Jahrhundert* [1949]; Delen, Adrien J. J. *Flemish master drawings of the seventeenth century* [1950]; Gradmann, Erwin. *Dessins de maîtres espagnols* [194?]; Winzinger, Franz. *Deutsche Meisterzeichnungen der Gotik* [1949].

2467

Prestel Gesellschaft. Frankfurt am Main, Prestel Verlag. Veröffentlichung 1–16, 1912–37. illus. 21–54 cm.

A numbered series containing facsimiles of drawings in various collections reproduced in collotype of high quality, with short text. Some bear the imprint: Voightländer-Tetzner.

Some volumes reproduce drawings in a collection, such as: (no. 3–5), Bremen. Kunsthalle. *Zeichnungen alter Meister . . . 3 v.*, 1914–16.

Others reproduce the work of a single artist, such as: (nos. 10–11), *Daniel Chodowiecki*. Volume 16 covers the Brussels. *Musées royaux des beaux-arts de Belgique*, 1937.

2468

K. Preussisches Historisches Institut, Rome. Kunstgeschichtliche Forschungen. Leipzig, Hiersemann, 1910–12. 3 v. illus., plates. 32 cm.

Contents: (1) Erbach-Fürstenau, Adalbert, Graf zu. *Die Manfredbibel*, 1910; (2) Wackernagel, Martin. *Die Plastik des XI. und XII. Jahrhunderts in Apulien*, 1911; (3) Friedländer, Walter F. *Das Kasino Pius des Vierten*, 1912.

2469

Princeton monographs in art and archaeology. Princeton, Princeton Univ. Press, 1912–(57). 31 cm.

Size varies. A numbered series of scholarly monographs covering the art of all periods and fields. 36 volumes have appeared to date. Examples: (3) Marquand, Allan. *Luca della Robbia*, 1914; (18) Roosval, Johnny. *Swedish art*, 1932; (26) Weitzmann, Kurt. *The fresco cycle of S. Maria di Castelseprio*, 1951; (36) Krautheimer, Richard. *Lorenzo Ghiberti*, 1956.

2470

Problems of contemporary art. N.Y., Wittenborn, 1945–48. 26 cm.

Size varies. "A series, with no general editor, being a catch-all for texts relating to the immediate tensions in the arts." Contents: (1) Paalen, W. *Form and sense*, 1945; (2) Read, H. *The grass roots of art*, 1947; (3) Dorner, A. *The way beyond 'art,'* 1947; (4) *Possibilities; an occasional review*, v. 1, 1947/48; (5) Vantongerloo, G. *Paintings, sculptures, reflections*, 1948.

2471

Rome. Kaiser Wilhelm-Institut für Kunst- und Kulturwissenschaft. Römische Forschungen der Bibliotheca Hertziana. Leipzig, Keller, 1912–38(?). illus., plates, facsims. 29 cm.

Size varies.

14 volumes issued by 1938. Examples: (1) Steinmann, Ernst, and Wittkower, Rudolf. *Michelangelo Bibliographie, 1510–1926,* 1927; (7) Hager, Werner. *Die Ehrenstatuen der Päpste,* 1929.

2472

Les Sculpteurs français nouveaux. Paris, Gallimard, Nouvelle Revue Française, 1924–30. 17 cm.

No imprint on title page. Some published by Nouvelle Revue Française, others by Gallimard.

Small monographs of about 65 pages devoted to contemporary French sculptors. Made up mostly of reproductions with a very brief biography, a short critical article, and a few quotations from critics. Among the artists included: Bernard, Pompon, Maillol, Orloff, Lipchitz, Zadkine, Manolo, Gimond.

2473

Société Française de Reproductions de Manuscrits à Peintures, Paris. Bulletin . . . année 1–21 [1911–38]. Paris, 1911–38. 21 v. and portfolio of plates. 32 cm.

Année 4 covers 1914–20. A valuable series of annual publications devoted to reproducing and publishing important illuminated manuscripts in the libraries of various countries. Both Western and Eastern manuscripts are included. The text is by recognized scholars and the illustrations are very good. In general each annual volume is devoted to the manuscripts in a particular library.

"Liste des recueils de fac-similés et des reproductions de manuscrits conservés à la Bibliothèque Nationale," année 1, p. 55–83, 116–551, with an alphabetical index p. 152–57.

"Bibliographie des publications relatives aux manuscrits à peintures parues 1911–1932" by Ph. Lauer, année 3, p. 68–79; année 4, p. 150–75; année 6, p. 96–109; année 11, p. 25–44; and année 16, p. 63–78, was also published separately, and includes both books and periodical articles.

2474

I Sommi dell'arte italiana. Milano, Martello, 1952–(57). illus., plates. 31 cm.

A series of monographs on individual Italian painters; also issued with English text by the same publisher with title: *Great Italian artists.*

Contents: Moschini, Vittore. *Francesco Guardi,* 1952; Moschini, Vittore. *Canaletto,* 1954; Paccagnini, Giovanni. *Simone Martini,* 1954; Pergola, Paolo della. *Giorgione,* 1955; Pallucchini, Rodolfo. *Piazzetta,* 1956; Acqua, Gian Alberto dell'. *Tiziano* [1955]; Carli, Enzo. *Sassetta* [1957?].

2475

Studien der Bibliothek Warburg. Leipzig, Berlin, Teubner, 1922–32. nos. 1–24. illus. 27 cm.

A numbered series of scholarly works, many of which deal with art and mythological or iconographical problems. Continued by the same series published in London as *Studies of the Warburg Institute* (2481).

Examples: (5) Panofsky, Erwin. *"Idea" ein Beitrag zur Begriffsgeschichte der älteren Kunsttheorie,* 1924; (8) Saxl, Fritz. *Antike Götter in der Spätrenaissance . . .* 1927; (9) Schmidt-Degener, F. *Rembrandt und der holländische Barock,* 1928; (23) Stechow, Wolfgang. *Apollo und Daphne,* 1932.

2476

Studien über christliche Denkmäler. Neue Folge der archäologischen Studien zum christlichen Altertum und Mittelalter. Leipzig, Dieterich, 1902–37. Heft 1–24. illus., plates, plans. 24–25 cm.

Editor, J. Ficker. Examples: (no. 5/6) Rott, Hans. *Kleinasiatische Denkmäler aus Pisidien Pamphylien, Kappodokien und Lykien,* 1908; (23) Elliger, Walter. *Zur Entstehung und frühen Entwicklung der altchristlichen Bildkunst,* 1934; (24) Schlee, E. *Ikonographie der Paradiesesflüsse,* 1937.

2477

Studien zur deutschen Kunstgeschichte. Strassburg, Heitz, 1894–(1955). nos. 1–(311). illus. 23–27 cm.

Size varies. Over 300 volumes published. A numbered series dealing with German art. Some volumes are illustrated and others not. Illustrations in general are not remarkably clear.

List of nos. 1–152 in Secker, H. F. *Die Skulpturen des Strassburger Münsters . . . ,* 1912. List of nos. 242–64 in Heine, A. F. *Asmus Jakob Carstens,* 1928. Number 311 is Jedding, Herman. *Der Tiermaler Joh. Heinr. Roos (1631–1685),* 1955.

2478

Studien zur spätantiken Kunstgeschichte. Leipzig, De Gruyter, 1925–(41). 28 cm.

Edited by H. Lietzmann and G. Rodenwaldt. Volume 12 appeared in 1941. Example: Delbrueck, Richard. *Die Consulardiptychen und verwandte Denkmäler*, 1929.

A numbered series covering late antique and early Christian art.

2479

Studies in manuscript illumination. Princeton, Princeton Univ. Press, 1947–(54). 31 cm.

A numbered series. Contents: (1) Goldschmidt, Adolph. *An early manuscript of the Aesop fables of Avianus*, 1947; (2) Weitzmann, Kurt. *Illustrations in roll and codex*, 1947; (3) Weitzmann, Kurt. *The Joshua roll*, 1948; (4) Weitzmann, Kurt. *Greek mythology in Byzantine art*, 1951; (5) Martin, John R. *The illustration of The heavenly ladder of John Climacus*, 1954.

2480

Studies in the history and criticism of sculpture. Photographs by Clarence Kennedy. Northampton, Mass., Smith College, 1928–[32]. phot. 51 cm.

Seven volumes issued, 1–6 without text. Portfolios of unusually fine and carefully mounted photographs. Fields covered are Greek and Italian Renaissance. Size varies. Contents: (1) Kennedy, Clarence. pt. 1, *Three Greek bronzes*; pt. 2, *The Erechtheion*, 1928; (2) Desiderio da Settignano. *The tomb of Carlo Marsuppini*, 1928; (3) Kennedy, Clarence. *Certain portrait sculptures of the Quattrocento*, 1928; (4) *The treasury of the Siphnians at Delphi*, 1929; (5) Desiderio da Settignano. *The tabernacle of the sacrament*, 1929; (6) Desiderio da Settignano. *The Magdalen and sculptures in relief*, 1929; (7) [Wilder, Elizabeth] *The unfinished monument by Andrea del Verrocchio to the Cardinal Niccolo Forteguerri at Pistoia*, 1932.

2481

Studies of the Warburg Institute. London, Warburg Institute, University of London, 1936–(57). nos. 1–(21). illus. 25–27 cm.

A numbered series of scholarly works dealing mainly with iconographical problems, art theory, or the work of individual artists. Continues the series begun in Germany as *Studien der Bibliothek Warburg* (2475).

Examples: (2) Buchthal, Hugo. *The miniatures of the Paris Psalter*, 1938; (6) Hinks, Roger Packman. *Myth and allegory in ancient art*, 1939; (10) Katzenellenbogen, Adolf. *Allegories of the virtues and vices in medieval art from early Christian times to the thirteenth century*, 1939; (16) Mahon, Denis. *Studies in seicento art and theory*, 1947; (19) Wittkower, Rudolf. *Architectural principles in the age of humanism*, 1949.

2482

Taste of our time. [N.Y.] Skira, 1953–(57). col. illus. 18 x 17 cm.

A popular series which is divided into three sections. All volumes are available also with French and German text.

(1) *Monographs:* A series of monographs on individual painters, with 50 to 60 small color reproductions. The texts are written by well-known authors. Each volume contains a chronology of the artist, bibliography, and an index, as well as the biographical and critical study. Contents: *Botticelli* by Giulio Carlo Argan; *Cézanne* by Maurice Raynal; *Chagall* by Lionello Venturi; *Degas* by François Fosca [pseud.]; *Dufy* by Jacques Lassaigne; *Fra Angelico* by Giulio Carlo Argan; *Gauguin* by Charles Estienne; *Goya* by Pierre Gassier; *El Greco* by Paul Guinard; *Lautrec* by Jacques Lassaigne; *Manet* by Georges Bataille; *Picasso* by Maurice Raynal; *Piero della Francesca* by Lionello Venturi; *Renoir* by Denis Rouart; *Van Gogh* by Charles Estienne and C. H. Sibert.

(2) *Famous places as seen by great painters:* Reproductions of views of various cities as represented by various artists. Includes: *Paris in the past; Paris in our time; Venice; Montmartre.*

(3) *The Great art revolutions: Impressionism* by Jean Leymarie, 2 v.

2483

Les Trésors des bibliothèques de France: manuscrits, incunables, livres rares, dessins, estampes, objets d'art, curiosités bibliographiques . . . Paris, Van Oest, 1926–(46). 6 v. illus., plates, facsims., geneal. tab. 30 cm.

Issued in fascicles of which 26 have appeared so far. Edited by M. R. Cantinelli and Émile Dacier. The series attempts to publish the treasures of the various French libraries. Illustrations are accompanied by text. Each volume has an index to its contents, but so far there has been no general index.

2484

Tübinger Forschungen zur Archäologie und Kunstgeschichte. Reutlingen, 1924–[35]. illus. 27 cm.

15th volume issued in 1935. Well-illustrated volumes printed on coated paper.

Example: Weise, Georg. *Spanische Plastik,* 3 v. in 5, 1925–29.

2485

Tübinger Forschungen zur Kunstgeschichte. Tübingen, Kunsthistorisches Institut der Universität, 1952–(56). plates. 23 cm.

A numbered series of small volumes (varying from 20 to 72 pages each) with or without illustrations. Each volume contains a bibliography.

Examples: (1) Hell, Hellmut. *Melchior Binder,* 1952; (4) Weise, Georg. *Die spanischen Hallenkirchen der Spätgotik und der Renaissance,* 1953; (8) Fleck, Walther-Gerd. *Schloss Weikersheim und die Hohenlohischen Schlösser der Renaissance,* 1954.

2486

Utrechtse bijdragen tot de kunstgeschiedenis. 's Gravenhage, Nijhoff, 1952–(54). 24–27 cm.

Contents: v. 1, Hoogewerff, G. J. *De Bentvueghels,* 1952; v. 2, Slive, S. *Rembrandt and his critics,* 1953; v. 3, Noé, Helen. *Carel van Mander en Italië,* 1954.

2487

Vasari Society for the reproduction of drawings by old and modern masters. Oxford Univ. Press, 1905–35. plates. 42–48 cm.

Parts 1–10, 1905/06–1914/15. Series 2, pts. 1–16, 1920–35. Collotype reproductions of drawings in various collections with a short text describing each plate. Index for pts. 1–

10 in pt. 10, p. 7–15. A separate index to the first series was also published in 1920.

2488

Die Zeichnung. Munich, Delphin-Verlag [1923?–28?]. plates. 33 cm.

A collection of good collotype plates with an introductory text of about 40 pages with an index of artists, giving brief biographical details, and an index of plates, giving location and size of drawings. Reihe 1, Die Deutschen; Reihe 2, Die Italiener.

Examples: Reihe 1, Bd. 4, Muchall-Viebrook, Thomas W. *Deutsche Barockzeichnungen* [1925]; Reihe 2, Bd. 4, Voss, Hermann. *Zeichnungen der italienischen Spätrenaissance* [1928].

2489

Zur Kunstgeschichte des Auslandes. Strassburg, Heitz, 1900–35. illus. 29 cm.

More than 132 volumes issued. Monographs on special artists and books covering whole periods of Italian, French, Flemish, and other art. Emphasis on text rather than on illustrations, which are collotypes.

Examples: (59) Jacobsen, Emil. *Das Quattrocento in Siena,* 1908; (136) Fraenckel, Ingeborg. *Andrea del Sarto,* 1935.

SEE ALSO: Handbuch der Kunstwissenschaft (444); Historia del arte Labor (447); Die Kunstdenkmäler der Schweiz (751); Pelican history of art (452); Propyläen-Kunstgeschichte (454).

Special Collections and Resources

Art Research Libraries in the United States and Western Europe

THE FOLLOWING LIST OF LIBRARIES WITH short descriptions of their holdings points out the most important collections for the researcher. In the United States the emphasis has been on a few eminent collections, with information on the areas in which they are particularly strong. It should be borne in mind, however, that practically all of the large universities maintain art libraries or collections of art books. Likewise, all large public libraries have art divisions, many of which can be considered outstanding, such as the Enoch Pratt Free Public Library in Baltimore and the Cincinnati Public Library. Almost all museums have their own libraries, which usually are particularly strong in the fields represented in the museums but contain also the basic reference tools. For further information on art libraries the reader is referred to the chapter on "Directories" which lists directories of libraries and museums with their resources.

The material for the European libraries was gathered chiefly firsthand by the author (with a few exceptions) and represents the latest figures available as of June, 1957. Dr. Walter W. S. Cook has kindly supplied the information on Spanish libraries; that for the Belgian and Swedish libraries unfortunately had to be secured by correspondence. The information on American libraries has been compiled since July, 1957, with the generous assistance of the individual librarians.

The entries for libraries in the Appendix follow the form given by the individual librarians in charge or on their letterheads rather than that used by the Library of Congress in cataloging.

United States

Cambridge, Mass.

2490

Harvard University. Fogg Museum Library
Fogg Museum of Art
Cambridge 38, Mass.
E. Louise Lucas, Librarian
Founded 1927

The Harvard University resources in the field of fine arts consist of about 150,000 volumes, which are divided among the Fogg Museum Library. (c. 35,000 volumes), the Harvard College Library (founded 1638), the School of Design, the Houghton Library, and the Peabody Museum. The Fogg catalog contains entries for all art and archaeology books in the Harvard College Library as well as its own holdings. It serves the Harvard faculty, students, visiting scholars, and the students of Radcliffe College.

While the collection basically covers all aspects of art history, it is particularly strong in the fields of drawings, the graphic arts, the Italian Renaissance, and the field of conservation. Likewise the Fogg Museum Library has outstanding collections of museum publications, exhibition catalogs, and art auction catalogs. A noted collection of original drawings in the Fogg Museum is extremely important for research in this field.

An extensive collection of nearly a quarter of a million classified and cataloged photographs and 78,000 lantern slides, covering the entire range of art history, supplements the book holdings.

Chicago, Ill.

2491
Ryerson and Burnham Libraries
Art Institute of Chicago, Chicago 3, Ill.
Ruth E. Schoneman, Librarian
Founded: Ryerson 1901; Burnham 1912

A library of about 64,000 volumes which serves the museum staff, the faculty and students of the School of the Art Institute, the faculty and students of the Department of Architecture, Illinois Institute of Technology, visiting faculty and students, and the general public. The particular fields of interest are 19th and 20th century painting, decorative arts, prints and drawings, Oriental art, and the architecture of Chicago and vicinity. The library maintains indexes to periodicals and pamphlets and to art auction sales catalogs.

Supplementing the book collection is an architectural microfilm archive which contains microfilm of sketches, drawings, blueprints, specifications, and other documents related to the architecture of Chicago and vicinity, 1880–1915.

A collection of about 65,000 photographs, 18,400 color prints, 57,500 mounted reproductions, and c. 47,000 slides covers the fields of architecture, painting, sculpture, decorative and graphic arts.

Detroit, Mich.

2492
Archives of American Art
The Detroit Institute of Arts
Detroit 2, Mich.
E. P. Richardson, Director
Mrs. Miriam Lucker Lesley, Archivist
Founded 1954

An attempt to collect in one central place the original records of American painters, sculptors, and craftsmen. It is planned that the archives will contain both original and secondary sources (manuscripts, letters, notebooks, records, sketchbooks, clippings, an-

nouncements, exhibition catalogs, membership lists, cards, films, etc.) as well as printed material (directories, biographies, monographs, art auction sales catalogs, publications of societies and institutions, periodicals, and other printed items dealing with American art). In addition there is microfilm or other exact copy of the above types of material, and photographs of works of art. The collection covers material pertaining to artists, collectors, dealers, critics and historians, museums, societies, and institutions. The time scope is from the landing of the first European to the present, and the term "American artist" is defined as one who was born in America or who was born elsewhere but who worked in America.

Although it is a young and growing institution the Archives already possesses more than 17,000 photographs, nearly 3000 reproductions, 217 rolls of 35 mm. film with approximately 1200 frames per roll, nearly 1700 catalogs, more than 2000 letters, and more than 10,000 clippings. Its resources are open to accredited research scholars and writers in the American field. Reports on its growth are published regularly in the *Art Quarterly* (2166).

Los Angeles, Calif.

2493
The Elmer Belt Library of Vinciana
1893 Wilshire Boulevard
Los Angeles 37, Calif.
Mrs. Kate Trauman Steinitz, Librarian
Originated 40 years ago but extensive collecting since 1945

A private library of 10,000 volumes dealing with Leonardo da Vinci and the Renaissance, and 2000 volumes on the history of medicine, which is bequeathed to the University of California at Los Angeles. The collection is used by the faculty and students of U.C.L.A. and other schools, colleges and universities, and maintains a reference correspondence with the international world of Da Vinci scholars. The book collection is supplemented by unpublished contemporary manuscripts on Leonardo, slides, photographs, records, films, and a microfilm archive, thus forming an outstanding collection of documentary material on Leonardo. A multigraphed finding list (now out of print) was published in 1946, and a definitive catalog of the library is in preparation.

New Haven, Conn.

2494
Yale University Art Library
56 High Street, New Haven, Conn.
Phyllis A. Reinhardt, Librarian
Date of founding uncertain

A collection of about 15,000 volumes, covering the history of art, architecture, planning, design, and the graphic arts. This is a working library and is supplementary to some 40,000 volumes in the Yale University Library. The Yale Libraries serve primarily their own faculty and students but are also available to scholars. The book resources are augmented by pamphlet files of exhibition catalogs, architectural materials, etc., and collections of more than 91,000 mounted reproductions of works of art and 106,000 slides, both encompassing the history of art in general.

The Yale resources are particularly rich in the field of early American painting because of their collection of letters and manuscripts which includes extensive material on John Trumbull and Samuel Morse. In the field of modern art the Gertrude Stein Collection, the Katherine Dreier bequest, and the Steiglitz archives offer unique research material. In addition, the University possesses a collection of manuscript writings of John Ruskin.

New York, N.Y.

2495
Avery Architectural Library
Columbia University, New York 27, N.Y.
Prof. James Grote Van Derpool, Librarian
Founded 1890

One of the outstanding architectural research libraries of the world, comprising 58,000 volumes on architecture, archaeology, city planning, and the various decorative arts. Also it contains a collection of about 10,000 original architectural drawings, with emphasis on American work. The collection is particularly strong in early works on architecture, including rare incunabula and original manuscripts. An extensive index of periodical articles and restorations and an obituary file are maintained. The library is open to the architectural profession, to scholars, and to qualified readers in general.

These resources are augmented by Columbia's Fine Arts Library of 24,000 volumes covering the fields of painting, sculpture, drawings, and illuminated manuscripts, which is housed in Schermerhorn Hall.

2496
Frick Art Reference Library
10 East 71st Street, New York City
Mrs. Hannah Johnson Howell, Librarian
Founded 1920

A library of 122,000 volumes and 36,000 sales catalogs covering Western European painting of the Christian era to about 1860, American painting, sculpture, drawings, illuminated manuscripts, and other books related to these fields, which is open to all serious students of art history and accredited scholars.

The 36,000 catalogs of art auctions are thoroughly organized and cataloged. Each sale is indexed by the name of the collection, the place, and the date of sale.

The archive of about 334,000 photographs and reproductions is unique in that it is so thoroughly indexed. Each photograph is indexed by artist, subject, and collection with cross references from variant attributions. Portraits are indexed by name of sitter. The information on the verso of the reproduction contains the date, source of the reproduction, records of exhibition, a history of the collections through which it has passed, descriptive notes and opinions of various authorities as to attribution, and a bibliography of books and articles. 63,000 of these reproductions represent illuminated manuscripts. In addition the library possesses 143,000 photographs which are in process and 55,000 negatives.

2497
N.Y. Metropolitan Museum of Art Library
Fifth Avenue at 84th Street, New York City
James Humphry III, Librarian
Founded 1881

A reference collection of 136,000 volumes covering ancient and modern art, archaeology, and the industrial arts, which is open to the museum staff, graduate students, members of the museum, and qualified research workers upon application to the Librarian.

A large collection of European and American sales catalogs is partially indexed by names of collectors, and an index compiled by Florence N. Levy covers the artists represented in the American sales catalogs. The library also possesses a card catalog of early art imprints up to 1800 (excluding architecture) compiled by Dr. Hans Tietze, which indicates the location of copies in various New York City libraries. A photostatic copy of the Princeton Index of Christian Art cards (without the photographs) is housed in the library, but it is not complete.

The museum also has a reference collection of 223,000 photographs and a lending service of 6020 color prints, 52,000 photographs, 141,890 black and white slides, 4000 stereos, 9874 color slides, and 24,635 kodachromes, which cover ancient and modern civilization, architecture, sculpture, painting, and the minor arts.

2498

N.Y. Museum of Modern Art Library
11 West 53d Street, New York 19, N.Y.
Bernard Karpel, Librarian
Founded 1932

A library which serves primarily the museum staff but is also open to members and the general public. The field covered is modern art from about 1875 to date, comprising painting, sculpture, architecture, the graphic arts, film, photography, industrial and theatrical design. The collection consists of about 15,000 books, pamphlets, and bound periodicals, clipping files containing approximately 11,200 units, a reference photo archive of about 22,500 units, and a collection of nearly 20,000 lantern slides; thus forming what is probably the most extensive repository in the world dealing with modern art.

In addition the library maintains a photographic service which consists of about 50,000 photos representing the material in its collections, its exhibitions, installations, etc. Photostat and microfilm facilities are available. The card catalog includes selective entries to unindexed periodicals and in 1956 a photographic index to picture materials was begun.

The museum publishes extensively in the field of modern art (2456), and the library furnishes bibliographies for these volumes.

2499

The New York Public Library
Fifth Avenue and 42d Street, New York 18, N.Y.
Karl Kup, Chief of Art and Print Divisions
Founded 1895

The Art Division comprises an excellent reference collection of about 96,000 volumes covering painting, drawing, sculpture, architecture, and the applied arts, which serves scholars, authors, research workers, and the general public. In addition to the book collection the division maintains an Inside File of about 100,000 cards locating illustrations of works of art and architecture in printed sources. It also includes miscellaneous information gathered during many years of research. The file is divided into: (1) General subject file, including artists and craftsmen and their works, as well as subjects such as costume, interiors, saints; (2) Architectural Index, including architects, buildings arranged by type, and architectural elements such as columns and doorways. A Clipping File of some 350,000 items of illustration and text is arranged by artists, architects, craftsmen, and designers, in one alphabet. A Pamphlet File contains material published by art societies, institutions and galleries, and newspaper items relating to them. Also about 600 scrapbooks on artists and subjects supplement the book collection.

The Prints Division, which was established in 1899, contains 11,000 books and 110,000 prints covering the prints of six centuries in general and especially fine prints, Japanese prints, Americana, political caricature, ornament prints, and bookplates. In addition to the main catalog the Print Division maintains an Illustrators' Catalog of book illustration, a printmakers' catalog, and a bookplate catalog (of bookplates in books). It also has indexes of subjects in prints, of portraits, of views, and of political caricature. A collection of portraits is arranged alphabetically in 200 boxes, and various clippings on artists are kept in envelopes. The library also contains some unpublished, typescript catalogs of the work of printmakers.

2500

The Pierpont Morgan Library
29–33 East 36th Street, New York 16, N.Y.
Frederick B. Adams, Jr., Director
Founded 1906

Although it is not actually an art reference library, the Pierpont Morgan Library is recognized as the outstanding collection of illuminated manuscripts in the Western Hemisphere and is therefore very valuable for the advanced scholar in these fields. In addition, more than 55,000 reference volumes cover the fields represented in the collection. These resources are available to accredited scholars and research workers upon written application to the Director.

Fields of interest to art historians covered are: Assyrian and Babylonian seals, cylinders, and cuneiform tablets; Egyptian, Greek, and other papyri; medieval and Renaissance manuscripts from the 6th to the 16th centuries (comprising about 900 items), bookbindings, prints, and drawings. The collection of drawings, the core of which was the Fairfax Murray collection, comprises from 2500 to 4000 items and represents artists from the 14th to the 19th centuries. The print resources include examples of nearly all of Rembrandt's etchings in the first as well as later states, and there are also rich holdings of English and other mezzotints from their beginnings through the 19th century.

Princeton, N.J.

2501 609|452.3773

Index of Christian Art, Department of Art & Archaeology, Princeton University
231 McCormick Hall, Princeton University
Princeton, N.J. 452-3000
Rosalie B. Green, Director
Founded 1917 once code 609

An important iconographical tool which consists of 500,000 index cards plus 100,000 photographs covering Early Christian and medieval iconography. The card file is arranged by the subject matter of Christian art, under about 25,000 headings, and is supplemented by the photograph file, which is arranged by medium and location. For a more detailed description see Woodruff, Helen. *The Index of Christian Art at Princeton University; a Handbook.* Princeton, Princeton Univ. Press, 1942.

Two copies of this index are to be found in the Dumbarton Oaks Research Library of Harvard University in Washington, D.C. (2504) and in the Pontifical Institute for Christian Archaeology in Rome (known as the Vatican copy). The Metropolitan Museum Library (2497) owns a facsimile, without illustrations, which is not up to date.

This index is available to graduate students and independent scholars.

M - F

2502
Princeton University. Marquand Library
McCormick Hall, Princeton University
Princeton, N.J.
Frederica Oldach, Librarian
Founded 1908

The art library of Princeton University, comprising about 50,000 volumes, which serves the faculty and students of Princeton,

members of the Institute for Advanced Study, and visiting scholars and students. While the library covers art in general, special fields of interest are medieval and Christian art, particularly illuminated manuscripts, the history of architecture, and classical archaeology.

Supplementing the resources of the Marquand Library is a collection of 450,000 photographs, which belongs to the Department of Art and Archaeology and covers all fields of art. The Dan Fellows Platt Collection is included in this number.

San Marino, Calif.

2503
Henry E. Huntington Library and Art Gallery. Art Reference Library
San Marino 9, Calif.
Mrs. Margaret Truax Hunter, Librarian
Founded 1928

A collection of more than 10,000 volumes on art history serving the Curator of Art Collections and other members of the Huntington staff, research fellows, and scholars. The Art Reference Library specializes in the fields covered by the Huntington art collections, i.e., English 18th century paintings, French sculpture of the 18th century, English and French decorative arts of the 18th century, Italian small bronzes of the 16th century, and Italian and Flemish paintings of the Renaissance.

Likewise the Art Reference library maintains a collection of art auction catalogs which consists of a complete run of Christie's and Sotheby's since 1937, with a fairly complete run from 1900–36 and scattered 19th century numbers; American Art Galleries Association—Anderson Galleries 1907–35; and Parke Bernet since v. 1, which are indexed by names of the owners who are selling.

A growing photograph archive now includes 30,000 items covering mainly English 18th century painting and portraits of British men, women, and children of any period by any artist.

The Manuscript Department of the Huntington Library is particularly rich in medieval illuminated manuscripts, all of which are described in the Seymour De Ricci *Census of Medieval and Renaissance Manuscripts in the U.S. and Canada*, N.Y., Wilson, 1935–40, in 3 v. In addition this division possesses numerous letters of English artists, including Aubrey Beardsley, Thomas Bewick, William Blake, George Cruikshank, A. H. Forrester, Benjamin Haydon, and the Pre-Raphaelite Group. There are also a large collection (618 items) of John Ruskin, and a collection of both letters and drawings of William M. Thackeray, which add considerably to the resources for art research.

Washington, D.C.

2504
Dumbarton Oaks Research Library and Collection
1703 32d Street, N.W., Washington 7, D.C.
Margaret Rathbone, Administrative Librarian
Founded 1940

A division of Harvard University with a library of 50,000 volumes covering the medieval field, particularly Early Christian and Byzantine. All subjects within this field are covered, such as art, archaeology, history, religion, literature, music, law, science, palaeography, papyrology, and numismatics. Its facilities are available to scholars and any member of the public working in the medieval field. Among the resources are a copy of the Princeton Index of Christian Art (2501), The Dumbarton Oaks Census of Early Christian and Byzantine Art in American Collections, Monuments of Byzantine Art in Greece (a collection of Greek photographs), and a card catalog of all bibliographic references noted in the periodical *Byzantinische Zeitschrift* (2205). A collection of 16,000 photographs covers Byzantine art and archaeology, with many on mosaics.

2505
Freer Gallery of Art. Library
Smithsonian Institution
Washington 25, D.C.
Mrs. Bertha M. Usilton, Librarian
Founded 1906, opened 1923

A collection of 35,000 titles of which about 50 per cent are in Chinese and 10 per cent in Japanese. There are also books in Persian, Arabic, and Hindu, as well as all Western languages. The scope of the library is "to supplement the objects in the gallery" and therefore it covers the arts and culture of the Far East, Near East, and India; Biblical manuscripts; and works on James McNeill Whistler, Abbott Thayer, Thomas Dewing,

Winslow Homer, D. W. Tryon, and others of that period, including some of their letters to Mr. Freer. While the library is used principally by the research staff of the Freer, it is open to anyone who wishes to use it. An index of periodical articles of interest to the Gallery is maintained. Three jumbo files of photographs covering the subject field of the library, but not duplicating the objects owned by the Gallery, are arranged by subject.

2506
Library of Congress
First and East Capitol Sts., S.E.
Washington 25, D.C.
L. Quincy Mumford, Librarian of Congress
Edgar Breitenbach, Chief, Prints and Photographs Division
Founded 1880

The U.S. national library, with holdings of 35 million volumes and pieces, has 124,300 art books which are assigned to the classification of art, aside from art books which form part of a series. The Library attempts to acquire all current scholarly fine arts publications, whether domestic or foreign; gaps in its holdings of older publications, notably source material, are filled within the limits of available funds. All of this material is available in the Main Reading Room, with a reference collection in fine arts available on open shelves and current periodicals shelved in the Periodical Reading Room. The Library is open to all adults, and stack privileges may be granted to scholars upon application to the superintendent of the Reading Room.

The Prints and Photographs Division (founded 1897) contains 583,200 prints and 2,927,000 photographs. The strength of the collection lies in its vast numbers of prints and photographs documenting American history and civilization in its broadest aspects, and in its modern and contemporary fine prints purchased with the income from the J. and E. R. Pennell bequest. For a description of its holdings see the *Guide to the special collections of prints and photographs* (170). This collection maintains a self-indexing single picture file classified by subjects, including a portrait and a topographic file; a dictionary catalog describing groups of pictures (lots) by author and subjects; and an inventory of the fine and historical prints, arranged by author and subjects, is in preparation. This division provides both reference and reproduction services.

Special collections pertaining to fine arts and architecture in the Library of Congress Prints and Photographs Division include: 19th century American lithographs, including Currier and Ives; Civil War pen and ink and pencil drawings by Waud, Forbes, and others; Cabinet of American Illustration (original drawings and watercolors) of late 19th and early 20th century; political cartoons and caricatures of the 18th–20th centuries; early American architecture, including original drawings by Latrobe, Thornton, Bulfinch, and others, the Historic American Buildings Survey, and photographs of the Deep South by Frances Benjamin Johnston; Gardiner Greene Hubbard collection of engravings and etchings by old masters; J. and E. R. Pennell collection containing Joseph Pennell's own work, Whistleriana, and modern and contemporary prints, especially by American artists (about 250 prints are acquired annually); Archive of Hispanic Culture (photographs and color slides); Chadbourne collection of original 19th century Japanese woodcuts, representing Japanese artists' interpretation of Westerners; and "Victories of the Emperor Ch'ien Lung," engravings produced in China and France, late 18th century.

Belgium

Antwerp

2507
Museum Plantin-Moretus Library
Vrijdagmarkt 22, Antwerp
Dr. L. Voet, Librarian
Founded in 16th century

This library, which was founded by Christoph Plantin in the 16th century, has been open to the public since 1876 and serves scholars and students. Its collection consists of 40,000 old and modern books covering the art of printing and bibliography. Two catalogs have been published:

Denucé, J. *Inventaire des Archives Plantiniennes.* Anvers, 1926.

Denucé, J. *Catalogue des manuscrits* [conservés au] *Musée Plantin-Moretus.* Anvers, 1927.

In addition the library possesses 525 manuscrits dating from the 9th to the 18th century and a collection of 1600 photographs covering the collections of the Plantin-Moretus Museum and typography.

2508
Rubenshuis
Rubensstraat 9–11, Antwerp
F. Baudouin, Curator
Founded 1946

A library of 2500 volumes covering Rubens and 17th century Flemish painting, which is open to scholars working in this field. In addition the library possesses a small collection of manuscript material including five Rubens letters, the contract and receipt for the "Assumption of the Virgin" in the Antwerp Cathedral, and documents about Rubens and his relatives. An important collection of Rubens engravings and 5000 photographs covering Rubens and 17th century Flemish painting adds to the resources.

England

London

2509
British Museum Library
Great Russell St., London W.C.1
Sir Thomas Kendrick, Director
Founded 1753

As in the case of all the great national libraries, the chief value for art research lies in the fact that it is a depository library and thus possesses a copy of all books published in Great Britain among its 6,000,000 printed books.

The Department of Prints and Drawings, which contains a magnificent collection of prints, drawings, and reproductions, as well as books relating to these subjects, is particularly valuable for research in these fields and is open to the public.

Likewise, for anyone working in the field of illuminated manuscripts, the Department of Manuscripts is of major importance, with its collection of 60,000 manuscripts.

2510
Courtauld Institute of Art. Library
University of London
20 Portman Square, London
Rhoda Welsford, Librarian
Founded 1932

A collection of about 24,000 books and 24,000 pamphlets covering the general history of art in the Western world. It is particularly strong in the field of illuminated manuscripts and sales catalogs. The library serves the students, staff, and professors of the university, the staffs of art galleries, and accredited scholars.

Conway Library contains 365,740 photographs and 116,860 negatives covering the fields of illuminated manuscripts, medieval wall paintings, stained glass, architectural drawings, and metalwork.

Witt Library contains three-quarters of a million photographs and reproductions covering European and American painting, drawing, and the graphic arts from 1250 to the present.

2511
India Office Library
Commonwealth Relations Office
King Charles Street, London S.W.1
Mr. S. C. Sutton, Librarian
Founded 1801

A library of about 300,000 volumes dealing with Indic studies and related fields, i.e., Islam, Buddhism, and the surrounding countries and former dependent territories such as Burma and the Persian Gulf. The library is open to bona fide students upon presentation of proper credentials.

It includes books in both European and Oriental languages and is rich in manuscript material, much of which is illuminated. The library also contains a collection of drawings, both Oriental and European, as well as a collection of photographs and negatives. *A Guide to the India Office Library* by S. C. Sutton, [London] Her Majesty's Stationery Office, 1952, describes the holdings in detail. Microfilms and photographs of much of the material are available.

2512
Percival David Foundation of Chinese Art.
  Library
University of London
53 Gordon Square, London W.C.1
Miss B. W. D. Martin, Librarian
Founded 1951

A collection of 4122 volumes in Eastern and Oriental languages dealing with the art and culture of the Far East, with emphasis on art. The nucleus of the collection was the private library of Sir Percival David. At the present time books and periodicals dealing with ceramics and jade of China and Japan are being acquired.

The library is assembling a collection of photographs and lantern slides covering the objects in its museum.

2513
Royal Institute of British Architects Library
66 Portland Place, London W.1
James C. Palmes, Librarian
Founded 1834

A library of more than 60,000 volumes dealing with architecture, building, and town planning. It is generally used by architects, architectural students, and anyone seriously interested in architecture. A catalog in two volumes was published in 1937 (22).

The library contains a periodical subject index, in all languages, concerned with architecture and allied subjects, and a collection of 15,000 architectural drawings, to which a handlist is to be published shortly, probably in 1959.

2514
School of Oriental and African Studies. Art
  Library
School of Oriental Studies, University of
  London
Woburn Square, London W.C.1
Margaret Medley, Librarian
Founded 1912

A collection of about 3000 volumes which was originally the Eastern section of the Courtauld Institute, covering the art and archaeology of the East. The library is open to all students of the university and other interested persons, upon application to the Librarian. It also includes a photograph collection of about 15,000 items covering the same fields as the book holdings.

2515
Victoria and Albert Museum Library
South Kensington, London S.W.7
Mr. A. W. Wheen, Keeper
Founded 1837

A library of more than 300,000 volumes covering the entire field of the fine and applied arts of all countries and periods. It is open to the public, but rare material is limited to ticket holders.

In addition the library contains a miscellaneous collection of manuscripts on the visual arts, as well as several special collections not always related to art, i.e., the Dyce and Forster collections. The library is particularly strong in art periodicals and is currently receiving about 1000.

A photograph collection of more than 250,000 covers the same fields as the printed material.

2516

Warburg Institute. Library
University of London
Woburn Place, London W.C.1
Dr. Otto Kurz, Librarian
Founded in late 19th century as a private library

A collection of 100,000 volumes covering the whole field of civilization with emphasis on the survival of the classical tradition. Open to research workers and students of the university, and accredited scholars.

There is also a collection of more than 100,000 photographs covering painting, sculpture, architecture, and illuminated manuscripts which forms an important iconographical tool dealing with pagan as well as Christian subjects.

2517

Westminster Reference Library
St. Martin's Street, London
Lionel R. McColvin, C.B.E., F.L.A.
Founded 1857

An art library of 30,000 volumes which is a part of the Westminster Public Library (which has a collection of 257,165 volumes in the lending division and 100,913 for reference). The fields covered by the art division are: sculpture, painting, engraving, art history and aesthetics in general, theater, cinema, ballet, opera, and design. The library is used by art students and research workers, press illustrators, film, theater, and costume designers, as well as the general public.

The library also contains an extensive reference collection of reproductions of famous paintings which comprises most of those listed in the UNESCO catalogs.

France

Paris

2518

Bibliothèque d'Art et d'Archéologie de l'Université de Paris
3 Rue Michelet, Paris Ve
Suzanne Damiron, Librarian
Founded 1906, given to University 1918

A library of 250,000 volumes covering the art of all times and countries, both Eastern and Western. Open to professors and advanced students of the university, museum personnel, and other scholars with the permission of the Librarian.

In addition the library has a collection of 12,000 prints and engravings of the 18th and 19th centuries, and about 365 manuscripts including the Journal of Delacroix, his student sketchbook, and correspondence with various people. There are also 71 boxes of autographs, 75 boxes of documents relating to artists, and 91 volumes of copies of documents from archives. A photograph collection of 200,000 items covers the same fields as the books.

2519

Bibliothèque de la Conservation des Musées Nationaux
Palais du Louvre, Paris Ier
Mme. André Chamson, Librarian
Founded 1871

A collection of about 100,000 volumes covering the various fields represented in the various French museums. The library is open to the personnel of the national museums and to accredited scholars. The library also possesses the archives of the Musées Nationaux dating back to the founding of the Louvre. This collection comprises inventories, accessions lists, and files as well as autographs and notes.

2520

Bibliothèque de l'École Nationale Supérieure des Beaux-Arts
14 Rue Buonaparte, Paris VIe
Mme. Bouleau-Rabaud, Librarian
Founded 1864

A collection of about 100,000 volumes covering fine arts and archaeology with special emphasis on technical books. Oriental art is covered in general. Open to students of the school and to anyone interested in art. The library also possesses a collection of about 500,000 photographs and 10,000 drawings of various masters, as well as the archives of the Académie Royale de Peinture et Sculpture and a collection of illuminated manuscripts of the Middle Ages.

2521

Bibliothèque de l'Union Centrale des Arts Décoratifs
107 Rue de Rivoli, Pavillon de Marsan, Palais du Louvre, Paris Ier
Paul Ratouis de Limay, Conservateur
Founded 1864

A reference library devoted to art with emphasis on the decorative arts. The collection comprises about 75,000 volumes which include sales catalogs and exhibition catalogs, and a collection of 5000 albums of pictures covering painting, architecture, and sculpture as well as the decorative arts. In addition there is a collection of 700 albums of samples of textiles, laces, etc., and a collection of 60,000 drawings of architecture, furniture, and the decorative arts. The personal library of James Hazen-Hyde has been added to the holdings.

2522
Bibliothèque du Musée Guimet
6 Place d'Iéna, Paris XVIe
Antoinette Hauchecorne, Librarian
Founded 1879

A collection of 46,000 volumes dealing with art and archaeology of India and the Far East, as well as history, geography, religion, and iconography. The material is in both European languages and the vernacular. The library also possesses manuscripts of Pelliot, Hackin, etc., and a collection of prints brought back by Chavannes from his expedition.

In addition the museum has a photographic collection of 50,000 prints and 15,000 negatives.

2523
Bibliothèque Municipale d'Art et d'Industrie Forney
12 Rue Titon, Paris XIe
Mme. Jacqueline Viaux, Librarian
Founded 1886

A public library serving mostly students, residents of the district, furniture designers, etc. The collection of about 35,000 volumes covers art with emphasis on techniques, applied arts, and costume. In addition the library contains a collection of mounted pictures, samples of textiles, prints, and drawings.

2524
Bibliothèque Nationale
Rue de Richelieu 58, Paris IIe
Julien Cain, Librarian
Jean Vallery-Radot, Conservateur, Dept. de Estampes
Jean Porcher, Conservateur, Dept. des Manuscrits

Since 1537 the Bibliothèque Nationale has been a depository library, so that it includes all books on art published in France. In addition the Dept. des Manuscrits contains many valuable illuminated manuscripts and some archival material. The Dept. des Estampes contains original drawings, engravings, and books relating to drawings, engravings, and some painting, as well as a tremendous collection of photographs and reproductions.

Germany
Berlin

2525
Ehemals Staatliche Museen Berlin. Die Kunstbibliothek
Jebensstrasse 2, Berlin-Charlottenburg 2
Dr. Paul Ortwin Rave, Director
Founded 1867

A reference collection of about 81,000 volumes covering the arts of all periods, countries, and media, but with special emphasis on costume and the applied arts. It is open to the public.

The library contains the famous Lipperheide collection of books and prints on costume (1651), a special collection of prints, drawings, sketchbooks, and engravings of ornament which is contained in 1250 boxes, and a collection of book arts, posters, and East Asian woodcuts amounting to about 1500 items.

In addition the library has 4700 portfolios containing about 230,000 classified and indexed photographs and 21,000 lantern slides.

Bonn

2526
Kunsthistorisches Institut der Universität Bonn
Liebfrauenweg 1, Bonn
Dr. Georg Kauffmann, Librarian

One of the outstanding art libraries of Germany, consisting of a collection of about 80,000 volumes and 100,000 photographs covering the field of art history in general and serving students in this field.

Marburg

2527
Marburg (Philipps) Universität. Kunstgeschichtliches Seminar
Ernst von Huelsen-Haus, Wolfstrasse, Marburg
Gisela Coch, Librarian
Founded 1913

A collection of 22,000 books covering the general history of Western art from the Carolingian period to the present. The library serves primarily the students of the institute but it is open to town people as well. The collection is supplemented by libraries belonging to three other institutes housed in the same building and covering prehistoric, classical, and Christian archaeology.

Also in the same building is the Bildarchiv Foto-Marburg which is a collection of 300,-000 photographs covering the entire field of art, ancient and modern, Eastern and Western, with particular emphasis on German material. This archive was founded in 1923 and is under the supervision of Herbert G. Schmidt. Negatives are available for all of these photographs; and slides, photographs, and enlargements may be ordered.

Munich

2528

Zentralinstitut für Kunstgeschichte in München
Arcisstrasse 10, Munich 2
Prof. Dr. L. H. Heydenreich, Director
Dr. Otto Lehmann-Brockhaus, Librarian
Founded 1947

A reference library for students and art historians, of 55,000 volumes covering European art history and including architecture, sculpture, painting, engraving, and the applied arts. It also houses the library of the Pinakothek (20,000 volumes), which is shelved separately in one section.

In addition the institute contains an "Index of Baroque Iconography" with references to sources and works of art of the 17th and 18th centuries in Germany and Austria; an "Index of Pre-Romanesque Art" corresponding to the French Fichier Préroman of the Sorbonne in Paris; and an "Index to Medieval Treasure Inventories in Germany," which collects material up to the mid-16th century in Germany with special attention to the inventories up to the mid-13th century.

The institute also contains a collection of 75,000 photographs covering European art history.

Greece

Athens

2529

American School of Classical Studies. Library
54 Souidias Street, Athens
Mrs. John L. Caskey, Librarian
Founded 1881

The working library of the School, which contains 18,800 volumes and is intended for the use of the members of the School but also welcomes Greek archaeologists, members of other foreign schools in Athens, and visiting American scholars and students, with the permission of the Librarian. Special fields of interest are: excavation reports, sculpture, vase painting, numismatics, and all prehistoric archaeology (particularly as connected with Greece and the Near East). In addition to the book collection the library possesses a fairly good map collection, a good collection of prehistoric sherds from sites in Greece, and a modest group of vases from Corinthian down to Roman times. A topographical index of the archaeological sites in Greece is maintained, as well as a collection of about 9000 photographs of the School's excavations at Corinth and elsewhere, excepting those at the Agora in Athens.

2530

Gennadius Library
61 Souidias Street, Athens
Peter Topping, Librarian
Founded 1926

A library of about 50,000 volumes serving the students and professors of the University of Athens, and Greek and foreign scholars in medieval and modern Greek history, literature, art and archaeology, and the Greek Orthodox Church. Its special fields of interest include: Byzantium, medieval and modern Greece, Ottoman Empire and modern Turkey, Balkan history, Early Christian and Byzantine archaeology and art, and the continuation of the tradition of Byzantine architecture and painting in Greece after 1453. In addition the library possesses about 300 manuscript items relating mainly to medieval and modern Greek history and literature, and a collection of original works of art consisting mostly of water color sketches and drawings of Greek and Turkish subjects by Edward Lear, William Haygarth, and others, and Greek monastic bindings.

The American School publishes a series of monographs dealing with materials in the Gennadian.

Italy

Florence

2531

Biblioteca Berenson
I Tatti, Settignano, Florence
Baronese Alda Anrep, Librarian
Founded 1890

The private library of Bernhard Berenson, but it is open to all students who have been introduced. The collection of about 50,000 volumes, not counting sales catalogs, covers primarily Renaissance painting and drawing but also includes material on Oriental art, literature, history, philosophy, etc. The library also possesses a large collection (number not known) of photographs covering all fields of art history.

2532
Biblioteca della Galleria degli Uffizi
Via della Ninna 5, Florence
Prof. Cesare Fasola, Librarian
Founded 1770

A library of about 40,000 volumes covering the general history of art with special emphasis on Italian art, serving students of art history. In addition the library possesses about 365 manuscripts but has no organized photograph collection.

2533
Biblioteca Marucelliana
Via Cavour 43–45, Florence
Dr. Carlo Angeleri, Librarian
Founded 1752

A library of 400,000 volumes which was devoted in the 19th century to applied and fine arts but now covers general culture with emphasis on the applied arts. It is used primarily by professors and students of the university but is open to the public. In addition to the printed books the library has a manuscript collection of about 20,000 items dating from the 12th to the 19th century (but mostly from the 17th and 18th centuries), 40 of which are illuminated, a collection of 20,000 engravings dating from the 15th to the 19th century, and an important collection of opera librettos.

2534
Kunsthistorisches Institut in Florenz.
  Biblioteca.
Piazza S. Spirito 9, Florence
Prof. Dr. Ulrich Middeldorf, Librarian
Founded 1888

A collection of 40,000 volumes dealing with Italian art and general history relating to Italy, which is open to all students and accredited scholars. The library has an especially fine topographical section and contains papers of a number of famous scholars and the archive abstracts of Gustav Ludwig and others. A unique collection of about 180,000 photographs covers architecture, sculpture, painting, drawing, and the minor arts in Italy, and a few related fields.

Rome

2535
Biblioteca Apostolica Vaticana
Città del Vaticano, Rome
Abbot Anselmo M. Albareda, Librarian
Founded c. 1450

A research library for advanced students and scholars containing more than 500,000 volumes covering manuscripts and historical and humanistic fields. Although there is no separate art division the library is extremely important for this subject, as it contains about 6000 manuscripts, many of which are illuminated. The Cicognara library (1) forms a part of the collection and is shelved as a unit.

2536
Biblioteca dell'Istituto Nazionale di Archeologia e Storia dell'Arte
Piazza Venezia 3, Rome
Dr. Guido Stendardo, Director
Founded 1921

A library of 250,000 volumes covering archaeology, history of art, classical philology, epigraphy, and numismatics, which is open to members of the institute, professors, and accredited scholars. Some 19th century manuscripts, including the writings of Rudolfo Lanciani and an important collection of plans of Rome from the 16th to the 19th century, as well as a collection of 60,000 photographs, are contained in the holdings.

2537
Biblioteca Nazionale Centrale Vittorio Emanuele
Via Collegio Romano 27, Rome
Dr. Prof. Laura De Felice Olivieri, Librarian
Founded 1870

This national library, which has no separate art division, is useful for art research in that it has been a depository library since 1870 and thus includes all art books published in Italy since that date.

2538
Bibliotheca Hertziana
Via Gregoriana 28, Rome
Dr. L. Schudt, Librarian
Founded 1913

A library of 47,000 volumes serving international scholars and art historians. The collection specializes primarily in the history of Italian art with emphasis on Rome, but also covers the art of other European countries, and contains a remarkably complete file of fine arts periodicals both past and current. A collection of 50,000 photographs covers the same subjects as the book holdings, though not as widely.

2539
Bibliothek des Deutschen Archäologischen Institut, Rome
Via Sardegna 79, Rome
Dr. Hans Riemann, Librarian
Founded 1829

A reference library of 70,000 volumes covering archaeology, philology, ancient history, and allied fields, which is open to professors, students, and anyone interested in archaeology. In addition to the printed material the library has a collection of about 120,000 photographs and 42,000 negatives.

2540
Library of the American Academy
Via Angelo Masina 5, Rome 28
Col. Peter de Daehn, Librarian
Founded 1894

A collection of 62,000 volumes serving members of the Academy and accredited scholars of all nationalities. The subjects covered are classical archaeology and allied fields including philology and history, history of art with special emphasis on Italy and modern art, architecture and landscape architecture, guidebooks, and material pertaining to Rome. In addition the library has a photographical corpus of topographical and architectural monuments of Rome and vicinity, a file of photographs of works of former Fellows of the Academy, and a photographical aerial survey of Northern Italy.

2541
Library of the British School at Rome
Valla Giulia, Rome
Michael Ballance, Librarian
Founded 1902

A library of 45,000 volumes serving British holders of Rome fellowships and accredited scholars. The subjects covered include ancient and medieval history, archaeology, and the fine arts. The Ashby Library, which is an excellent collection of books on ancient topography, is kept as a unit. Among the photographs held by the library are a complete set of Parker photographs (c. 1880) covering Roman topography and a collection of aerial photographs of the whole of Italy with emphasis on the south (complementing

the holdings of the American Academy), which are indexed.

Venice

2542
Archivio Storica d'Arte Contemporanea della Biennale
Cà Giustinian, Venice
Umbro Apollonio, Librarian
Founded 1928

A collection of 12,000 books covering painting, drawing, and engraving of modern Italian and foreign artists of the 19th and 20th centuries, modern music, and modern theater and cinema. The collection is available to art students, critics, artists, and collectors. A valuable asset of this library is a collection of folders which contain forms filled in by the exhibiting artists, in which are listed: education, prizes received, exhibitions in which works have been shown, museums whch contain works of the artist, and a bibliography. In addition the library possesses a collection of letters of contemporary artists and a collection of 120,000 photographs and 20,000 negatives covering modern art of every country.

2543
Biblioteca d'Arte del Museo Correr
San Marco Square 52, Venice
Dr. Terisio Pignatti, Librarian
Founded 1834

A library of 78,000 volumes devoted primarily to Venetian art with a secondary interest in Italian art, and also covering Venetian history, economics, and politics (from 1000 A.D. to 1800). While it is a public library, it is used chiefly by students of art history and architecture. The collection also includes about 25,000 prints, 8000 drawings, and 11,000 manuscripts of which 700 are illuminated. A photographic archive of about 110,000 items is composed mostly of reproductions of the entire art collection of the Museo Correr and its library.

2544
Fondazione Giorgio Cini. Biblioteca
Isola di San Giorgio Maggiore, Venice
Dr. Alessandro Bettagno, Librarian
Founded 1954

A modern art research library, in the process of being assembled, covering Italian art but concentrating especially on Venice, which is housed in a library designed by

Michelozzo and adjoining rooms. The major part was the personal library of Professor Giuseppe Fiocco, which is particularly rich in offprints, and to this has been added the personal library of the late Raimond van Marle.

The book collection is supplemented by a photo-archive which already exceeds 130,-000 items, as well as a large collection of negatives. Among the special resources is an "Index of Byzantine and Post-Byzantine Art."

Netherlands

Amsterdam

2545
Kunsthistorische Bibliotheek Rijksmuseum
Amsterdam
Marjorie H. Bottenheim, Librarian
Founded ca. 1885

A library of about 40,000 volumes which is open to the public. The subjects covered are art history and aesthetics, painting, sculpture, decorative art, drawings, prints, and books from their beginnings until the middle of the 19th century. A collection of photographs covering painting, drawing, and prints belongs to the Printroom rather than to the library.

A printed catalog was issued in 1935 (6).

The Hague

2546
Rijksbureau voor Kunsthistorische Documentatie (Netherlands Institute for Art History)
Korte Vijverberg 7, The Hague
Miss W. M. C. Juynboll, Librarian
Founded 1932

A library of 15,000 books and periodicals and 77,000 catalogs covering Dutch and Flemish art of all periods, the history of collecting, and catalogs of museums, exhibitions, and sales. Open to students of art history. The library possesses the collection of sales catalogs assembled by Fritz Lugt and many others, all of which are indexed by artist. In addition the library contains notes by Hofstede de Groot, A. Bredius, and others taken from archives, as well as a collection of newspaper clippings with emphasis on modern Dutch and Flemish art.

The library publishes the Netherlands Institute for Art History Bibliography (68) and the "Iconographic Index of Dutch and Flemish Painting" to which many libraries subscribe. The Index reproduces on post-cards all the photographs and reproductions of the Institute, representing biblical, mythological, allegorical, and historical subjects, with references in English.

There is a photographic collection of 550,000 items covering paintings, drawings, and prints of all periods with emphasis on Dutch and Flemish, as well as some sculpture and applied art.

Utrecht

2547
Ikonologisch Instituut der Rijksuniversiteit te Utrecht
Drift 25, Utrecht
Helen Noë, Librarian
Founded 1923

A library of several thousand volumes devoted to the study of iconography with emphasis on emblematical conceits, and a collection of books on early Christian art.

2548
Kunsthistorisch Instituut der Rijksuniversiteit te Utrecht
Drift 25, Utrecht
Helen Noë, Librarian
Founded 1923

A library of about 13,000 volumes, open to students of the university, covering Western art in general. The Instituut also has a collection of about 100,000 photographs covering Western art in general, including architecture.

The archaeological Instituut of the university is housed in the same building and also has a library of about 5000 volumes.

Scandinavia

Copenhagen, Denmark

2549
Kunstakademiets Bibliotek
Charlottenborg, Copenhagen
Dr. A. Marcus, Director

The library of the Danish Academy of Fine Arts which contains about 40,000 volumes on art history, as well as collections of architectural drawings, photographs, etc.

Oslo, Norway

2550
Nasjonalgalleriet Bibliotek
Universitetsgaten 13, Oslo
Vivi Greftegreff, Librarian

The most important library in Norway for art research, covering art in general and consisting of about 11,000 volumes.

Stockholm, Sweden

2551
Kungl. Akademien för de fria Konsterna. Bibliotek
Fredsgaten 12, Stockholm

The library of the Swedish art academy, which is important for early literature and original drawings in the field of architecture.

2552
Kungl. Biblioteket
Stockholm 5
Dr. Uno Willers, State Librarian
Founded early 17th century

The Royal Library of Sweden, with a total holding of more than 1,000,000 volumes, contains about 25,000 volumes devoted to art. In addition to being the national library it serves as the University Library of Stockholm in the fields of the humanities, social sciences, and theology. The collection is particularly rich in early literature on emblems and architecture as well as books concerning medieval miniatures, fine printing, and bookbinding. There is also a large collection on royal entrances and similar festivities of the 16th to the 18th centuries. In addition the manuscript division contains various correspondences which are important for Swedish 19th century art history.

Printed catalogs have been issued for some sections.

2553
Kungl. Vitterhets Historie och Antikvitets Akademiens Bibliotek
Storgatan 41, Stockholm
Dr. Adolf Schück, Librarian
Founded 1786

A special library of about 100,000 volumes covering Scandinavian and classical archaeology and medieval art, which is open to the public.

2554
Nationalmusei Bibliotek
Stockholm 16
Mrs. Sia Påhlman, Librarian
Founded 1868

The library of the National Museum contains about 77,000 volumes covering the fine arts, classical art, Far Eastern art, and the decorative arts, but excluding architecture. In addition there is a collection of about 200,000 clippings.

Another division of the Museum maintains a photograph collection of about 200,000 items covering all of the fine arts.

Uppsala, Sweden

2555
Uppsala University Library
Uppsala
Dr. Tönnes Kleberg, Librarian
Founded 1621

A library of 1,200,000 books, 500,000 dissertations, 20,000 manuscripts, and an unknown number of pamphlets, covering all fields of interest except technology and agriculture, which serves university scholars.

For art research the library has a collection of reference books in art literature, collections of 15,000 engravings, 6000 drawings, 100 sketchbooks, and 75,000 topographical and historical plates. Card catalogs of the portraits, engravings, drawings, etc., belonging to the library are maintained. Some printed catalogs of the collection of drawings and manuscript maps of the library have been issued.

Spain

Barcelona

2556
Instituto Amatller de Arte Hispánico
Paseo de Gracia 41, Barcelona
Dr. José Gudiol Ricart, Director

A specialized art library which contains excellent holdings of international periodicals and a bibliographical artistic index.

A photographic collection of 400,000 prints and negatives covers Spanish art (including architecture, sculpture, painting, and the minor arts) in Spain as well as in England, Belgium, Holland, France, Italy, and the United States. It also includes the set of negatives formed by the Archivo Mas and that of the Archivo de Arqueológia Catalana, made under the direction of D. José Gudiol.

Madrid

2557
Fundación Lázaro Galdiano
Sarrano 122, Madrid
Antonio Rodriguez-Monino, Librarian

An excellent art library with a good collection of periodicals.

2558
Instituto Arqueológico Alemán
Serrano 159, Madrid
Dr. Helmut Schlunk, Director

A rich library for prehistoric, classical, and medieval Spanish art, with a fine collection of photographs and wonderful books.

2559
Instituto Diego Velázquez de Arte
Diego Angulo Iñiguez, Director

Instituto Arqueológico y Prehistórico "Rodrigo Caro"
Antonio Garcia y Bellido, Director

Dunque de Medinaceli 4, Madrid

Both institutes are housed in the same building and constitute the most important center for art research. They contain an excellent library of art books and periodicals and a considerable assemblage of auxiliary photographic material.

Pamplona (Navarre)

2560
Institución Principe de Viana
Diputación Foral de Navarra, Pamplona
José E. Uranga, Sec. of the Institute

A large collection of photographic material dealing with art in Navarre. Gradually as this takes form, it is being published in the periodical *Principe de Viana*.

Santiago de Compostela

2561
Seminario de Estudios Gallegos
Santiago de Compostela
Dr. Jesús Caro Garcia, Director

A collection of books and photographs dealing with the province of Galicia.

Seville

2562
Archivo General de Indias
Seville
José M. de la Peña y Cámara, Director

A collection which contains the great mass of documentary material dealing with Central and South America from which Dr. Diego Angulo Iñiguez' work was written.

2563
Laboratorio de Arte
Fábrica de Tabacos
Universidad de Seville, Seville
Dr. Enrique Marco Dorta, Director

A magnificent library and photographic collection, especially rich in the art of the province of Seville.

Valencia

2564
Universidad Biblioteca
Valencia

Contains a wonderful collection of Italian illuminated manuscripts.

Valladolid

2565
Seminario de Estudios de Arte
Universidad de Valladolid, Valladolid

An important art library and photographic collection.

Index

Index

Index

Index

Index

Index

A book of sporting painters. Sparrow, W. S., 1295

Books on Latin America and its art. N.Y. Metropolitan Museum of Art, 64

Borenius, T., and Tristram, E. W. English medieval painting, 2462

Borghesi, S., and Banchi, L. Nuovi documenti per la storia dell'arte senese, 2075

Born, W. American landscape painting, 1457; Still-life painting in America, 1458

Borovka, G. I. Scythian art, 663

Borroni, F. "Il Cicognara," 27

Borton, H. A selected list of books and articles on Japan, 70

Bosc, E. Dictionnaire de l'art, de la curiosité et du bibelot, 1613

Boschini, M. Le minere della pittura, 1992

Bošković, D. Medieval art in Serbia and Macedonia, 911

Bosse, A. Sentimens sur la distinction des diverses manières de peinture, dessein & gravueure, 1993

Bossert, H. T. The art of ancient Crete, 484; An encyclopedia of colour decoration, 1624; Geschichte des Kunstgewerbes, 1625; Grosse Kulturen der Frühzeit, 2424; Ornament in applied art, 1626; Peasant art in Europe, 1627

Boston. Museum of Fine Arts. Ancient Egypt, 479; Bibliographies of Indian art, 71

Bottari, G. Raccolta di lettere sulla pittura, scultura ed architettura, 2076

Bouchot, H., and Duplessis, G. Dictionnaire des marques et monogrammes de graveurs, 1519

Bourcard, G. Graveurs et gravures, 1510

Bovy, A. La peinture suisse, 1449

Bowes, J. L. Japanese marks and seals, 1770

Bowie, H. P. On the laws of Japanese painting, 1382

Bradbury, F. British and Irish silver assay office marks, 1831

Bradley, J. W. A dictionary of miniaturists, illuminators etc., 1143

Bradley, M. C. The treatment of pictures, 1471

Braghirolli, W. Lettere inedite di artisti, 2077

Branden, F. J. van den. Geschiedenis der Antwerpsche schilderschool, 1339

Braun, J. Meisterwerke der deutschen Goldschmiedekunst, 1832; Tracht und Attribute der Heiligen, 346

Breasted, J. H. Oriental forerunners of Byzantine painting, 1214

Bredius, A. Künstler-Inventare, 2078

Bréhier, L. L'art byzantin, 512; L'art chrétien, 513; L'art en France, 578; La sculpture et les arts mineurs byzantins, 982

The Brickbuilder, 2138

Bridgwater, D., and Gloag, J. A history of cast iron in architecture, 1883

Brieger, P. English art, 603

Briggs, M. S. Baroque architecture, 835; Muhammadan architecture, 901

Brinckmann, A. E. Barock-Bozzetti, 990; Barockskulptur, 444, 991; Die Baukunst des 17. und 18. Jahrhunderts, 444; Stadtbaukunst, 444

Briquet, C. M. Les filigranes, 1531

The British antique trades and collectors' directory, 108

The British architect see Campbell, C. Vitruvius Britannicus, 1994

British Museum. Dept. of Prints and Drawings. A handbook to the drawings and water-colours, 1090; Index of artists, 92; An index of Chinese artists, 93

British Museum Library, 2509

The British Museum quarterly, 2196

British School at Athens. The Annual, 2197

—— Library, 2541

British School at Rome. Library, 2541

—— Papers, 2198

Britten, F. J. Old clocks and watches, 1732

Britton, J. The architectural antiquities of Great Britain, 864; Cathedral antiquities, 865; A dictionary of the architecture and archaeology of the Middle Ages, 769

Brøndsted, J. Early English ornament, 1628

Bronzes: techniques, 957

    Chinese, 410

    German, 1013, 1024

    Greek, 972

    Italian, 1042, 1052

    Roman, 972

Brooke, M., and Dubester, H. J. Guide to color prints, 157

Brooke, M. L. Lace in the making, 1971

Brown, A. V. V., and Rankin, W. A short history of Italian painting, 1306

Brown, B. Lithography for artists, 1592

Brown, G. B. The art of the cave dweller, 557; The arts in early England, 596

Brown, M. W. American painting, 1459

Brown, P. Indian architecture (Buddhist and Hindu periods), 902; Indian architecture (the Islamic period), 903; Indian painting, 1383; Indian painting under the Mughals, 1384

Brown, W. T., and Gotch, J. A. Architecture of the Renaissance in England, 870

Bruckmanns Deutsche Kunstgeschichte, 590

Bruhn, W., and Tilke, M. A pictorial history of costume, 1660

Index

Index

Index

deutschen Bildhauerkunst, 1016

Dekorative Kunst, 2263

Delacre, M., and Lavallée, P. Dessins de maîtres anciens, 1092

Delen, A. J. J. Histoire de la gravure, 1578

Delogu, G. Essai d'une bibliographie internationale d'histoire de l'art, 28

Delorme, P. Le premier tome de l'architectvre, 1999

Delteil, L. Manuel de l'amateur d'estampes des XIXe et XXe siècles, 1534; Manuel de l'amateur d'estampes du XVIIIe siècle, 1535; Le peintre-graveur illustré, 1536

De Mazia, V., and Barnes, A. C. The French primitives and their forms, 1249

Les Demi-dieux, 2405

Demmin, A. F. Encyclopédie historique etc., 176

Demotte, G. J. La tapisserie gothique, 1918

Demus, O. Byzantine mosaic decoration, 1819; The mosaics of Norman Sicily, 1820

Denkmäler der Malerei des Altertums, 1203

Denkmäler deutsche Kunst, 2406

Denman, C. A bibliography of pewter, 1869

Deonna, W. La sculpture suisse, 1077

Deroko, A. Monumentalna i dekorativna arkitektura u srednjevekovnoj Srbiji, 913

Descamps, J. B. La vie des peintres, 2000

Deschamps, P. French sculpture of the Romanesque period, 2462

—— and Mortet, V. Recueil de textes relatifs à l'histoire de l'architecture . . . XIe–XIIIe siècles, 2100

Desgodets, A. B. Les édifices antiques de Rome, 812

Design see Decoration and ornament

De Tolnay, C. History and technique of old master drawings, 1093

Detroit. Public Library. Costume, a list of books, 1649; Furniture, a list of books, 1685

Deusch, W. R. Malerei der deutschen Romantiker, 1264; Deutsche Malerei des 13. und 14. Jahrhunderts, 1261; Deutsche Malerei des 15. Jahrhunderts, 1262; Deutsche Malerei des 16. Jahrhunderts, 1263

Deutsche Kunst und Denkmalpflege, 2224

Deutsche Kunstgeschichte, 590

Deutscher Verein für Kunstwissenschaft, Berlin. Denkmäler deutsche Kunst, 2406

—— Forschungen zur deutschen Kunstgeschichte, 2407

—— Zeitschrift, 2364

Deutsches Archäologisches Institut

Jahrbuch, 2226

—— Ergänzungsheft, 2227

Mitteilungen, 2228

Deutsches Archäologisches Institut. Athenische Abteilung

Mitteilungen, 2225

Deutsches Archäologisches Institut. Römische Abteilung

Bibliothek, 2539

—— Katalog, 14

Mitteilungen. Bullettino, 2229

Devigne, M. La sculpture mosane, 1007

Deville, E. Index du Mercure de France, 84

Dézallier d'Argenville, A. J. Abrégé de la vie des plus fameux peintres, 2001

Dézallier d'Argenville, A. N. Vies des fameux architectes, 2002

Dialogos de la pintura. Carducci, V., 1995

La Diana, 2230

Dickins, G. Hellenistic sculpture, 968

Dickinson, H. A. S. German masters of art, 1265

Dickson, H. E. A working bibliography of art in Pennsylvania, 81

Dictionaries see subdivision "dictionaries" under specific subjects, e.g., Art: dictionaries

The dictionary of English furniture. Macquoid, P., and Edwards, R., 1712

Dictionary of modern painting, 1140

The dictionary of needlework. Caulfeild, S. F. A., and Saward, B. C., 1961

Dictionnaire de la peinture moderne, 1140

Dictionnaire raisonné du mobilier français. Viollet-le-Duc, E. E., 1618

Didron, A. N. Christian iconography, 350

Diederichs, E. Deutsches Leben der Vergangenheit in Bildern, 1564

Diehl, C. L'art chrétien primitif et l'art byzantin, 516; Manuel d'art byzantin, 517; La peinture byzantine, 1215

Diepenbroick-Grüter, H. D. von, firm, Hamburg. Allgemeiner Porträt-katalog, 100

Diez, E. Die Kunst der islamischer Völker, 444; Die Kunst Indiens, 444

Dilley, A. U. Oriental rugs and carpets, 1903

Dillmont, T. de. Encyclopedia of needlework, 1965

Dillon, E. Glass, 1790; Porcelain, 1749

Dimier, L. Histoire de la peinture de portrait, 1251; Les peintres français du XVIIIe siècle, 1252

—— and Réau, L. Histoire de la peinture française, 1253

Dinanderie. Perry, J. T., 1827

Dinsmoor, W. B. The architecture of ancient Greece, 813

Directories see subdivision "directories" un-

Index

Index

Farbman, M. S. Masterpieces of Russian painting, 1408

Farcy, L. de. La broderie, 1966

Fashion dictionary. Picken, M. B., 1654

Fasti archaeologici, 2234

Faure, E. History of art, 439

Félibien, A. Entretiens sur les vies et les ouvrages des plus excellens peintres, 2006

Félice, R. de. French furniture of the Middle Ages and under Louis XIII, 1701; French furniture under Louis XIV, 1702; French furniture under Louis XV, 1703; French furniture under Louis XVI and the empire, 1704

Felix Ravenna, 2235

Felsina pittrice. Malvasia, C. C., 2016

Fenaroli, S. Dizionario degli artisti bresciani, 260

Fenollosa, E. F. Epochs of Chinese and Japanese art, 669

Ferguson, G. W. Signs and symbols in Christian art, 354

Ferguson, J. C. Chinese painting, 1386

Fergusson, J. A history of architecture, 791; History of Indian and Eastern architecture, 906; Tree and serpent worship, 402

Ferrari, G. Catalogo delle pubblicazioni periodiche, 91; Il ferro nell'arte italiana, 1879; Il legno nell'arte italiana, 1046

Fett, H. P. Billedhuggerkunsten i Norge under Sverreaetten, 1069

Feuchtwanger, F., and Groth-Kimball, I. The art of ancient Mexico, 631

Feulner, A. Die deutsche Plastik des sechzehnten Jahrhunderts, 1017; Die deutsche Plastik des siebzehnten Jahrhunderts, 1018; Kunstgeschichte des Möbels, 454, 1694; Skulptur und Malerei, 444

—— and Fischer, O. Geschichte der deutschen Malerei, 590

Ffoulkes, C. J. Decorative ironwork, 1880

Fielding, M. American engravers, 1520; Dictionary of American painters, sculptors and engravers, 301

Fierens, P. La peinture flamande de Bruegel au XVIIIe siècle, 1349; La peinture flamande des origines à Quentin Metsys, 1350

Fierens-Gevaert, H. Histoire de la peinture flamande, 1351; Les primitifs flamands, 1352

Figura, 2236

Filangeri, G. A. G. Documenti per la storia, le arti e le industrie delle provincie napoletane, 2082

Filov, B. D. Early Bulgarian art, 704; Geschichte der altbulgarischen Kunst, 705; Geschichte der bulgarischen Kunst, 706

Fine art reproductions. New York Graphic Society, inc., 163

Finlay, I. Art in Scotland, 597

Fiocco, G. Venetian painting of the Seicento and Settecento, 2462

First flowers of our wilderness. Flexner, J. T., 1462

First reader for antique collectors. Drepperd, C. W., 1632

Firth, R. W. Art and life in New Guinea, 561

Fischel, O. Die Zeichnungen der Umbrer, 1113

Fischer, J. L. Deutsches Mosaik, 1821; Handbuch der Glasmalerei, 1804

Fischer, O. Die Kunst Indiens, Chinas und Japans, 454; Geschichte der deutschen Zeichnung und Graphik, 590

—— and Feulner, A. Geschichte der deutschen Malerei, 590

Fitch, J. M. American building, 934

Flemming, E., and Jaques, R. Encyclopedia of textiles, 1946

Fletcher, Sir B. F. A history of architecture, 792

Fleury, Jules see Champfleury, J. F. H.

Flexner, J. T. American painting, 1462

Flipo, V. Mémento pratique d'archéologie française, 849

The floating world. Michener, J. A., 1584

Florén Lozano, L. Bibliografía de la bellas artes en Santo Domingo, 61

Florence. R. Galleria degli Uffizi. I disegni della R. Galleria degli Uffizi in Firenze, 2417

—— Kunsthistorisches Institut, 2534

Flower painting, 1189, 1372

Fogg Museum Library, 2490

Fokker, T. H. Roman baroque art, 618; Werke niederländischer Meister in den Kirchen Italiens, 1353

Folk art
American, 1079, 1461, 1465, 1629
European, 1627
Mexican, 649
Swedish, 725

Fondation Piot see Académie des Inscriptions et Belles-Lettres, Paris

Fondazione Giorgio Cini. Biblioteca, 2544

Fontainas, A.; Vauxcelles, L.; and Mourey, G. Histoire générale de l'art français, 582

Fontaine, A. Conférences inédites de l'Académie Royale, 2083

Fontenay, L. A. de B. see Bonafons, L. A. de

Forgeries of works of art, 1099; bibliography, 42

Index

Gardner, J. S. English ironwork, 1882

Garnier, É. Dictionnaire de la céramique, 1737; Histoire de la verrerie et de l'émaillerie, 1812

Garrison, E. B. Italian Romanesque panel painting, 1311; Studies in the history of mediaeval Italian painting, 2346

Garrison, J. J., and Robb, D. M. Art in the western world, 456

Garrucci, R. Storia della arte cristiana, 519

Garzarolli-Thurnlackh, K. Die barocke Handzeichnung, 1110

Gatti, F., and Pellati, F. Annuario bibliografico di archeologia e di storia dell'arte per l'Italia, 57

Gay, V., and Stein, H. Glossaire archéologique, 183

Gaya Nuño, J. A. Historia del arte español, 742; Historia y guía de los museos de España, 125

Gaye, J. W. Carteggio inedito d'artisti, 2084

Gayet, A. J. L'art copte, 520

Gayley, C. M. The classic myths, 314

—— and Scott, F. N. A guide to the literature of aesthetics, 29

Gaynor, F., and Pei, M. A. Liberal arts dictionary, 200

Gazette des beaux-arts, 2240

Geck, F. J. Bibliography of Italian art, 59

Gedanken zur Kunstgeschichte. Wölfflin, H., 434

Geiger, B. Handzeichnungen alter Meister, 1095

Geisberg, M. Bilder-Katalog, 1565; Der deutsche Einblatt-Holzschnitt, 1566

Gelder, H. E. van. Kunstgeschiedenis der Nederlanden, 655

—— and Duverger, J. Kunstgeschiedenis der Nederlanden, 656

Gelsted, O. Kunstner-lesikon, 280

Gems see Jewelry

Gennadius Library, 2530

Genootschap Architectura et Amicitia te Amsterdam see Wendingen, 2359

Gentsche bijdragen tot de kunstgeschiedenis, 2241

George, W. Le dessin français, 1103

The Georgian period, 935

Georgian Society, Dublin. Records of eighteenth-century domestic architecture and decoration in Dublin, 869

Gérard, C. Les artistes de l'Alsace, 237

Gerstinger, H. Die griechische Buchmalerei, 1217

Geschichte der deutschen Kunst, 591

Geschichte der russischen Kunst, 707

Gesellschaft für schweizerische Kunstgeschichte see Zeitschrift für schweizerische Archaeologie . . . , 2369

Gestoso y Pérez, J. Ensayo de un diccionario de los artífices que florecieron en Sevilla, 290

Gettens, R. J., and Stout, G. L. Painting materials, 1476

—— and Usilton, B. M. Abstracts of technical studies in art and archaeology, 30

Getty, A. The gods of northern Buddhism, 403

Geymueller, H. von, and Stegmann, C. M. The architecture of the Renaissance in Tuscany, 889

Giani, G., and Barbaroux, V. E. Arte italiana contemporanea, 612

Giedion, S. Space, time and architecture, 837

Giedion-Welcker, C. Contemporary sculpture, 992; Modern plastic art, 992

Giglioli, G. Q. L'arte etrusca, 490

Gilbert, D. B. American art directory, 106

Gilbey, Sir W. Animal painters of England, 1285

Giles, H. A. A Chinese biographical dictionary, 274

Giraldo Jaramillo, G. Bibliografía selecta del arte en Colombia, 62; La pintura en Colombia, 1329

Giraudet, E. Les artistes tourangeaux, 238

Girodie, A.; Vial, H.; and Marcel, A. Les artistes décorateurs du bois, 244

Glaser, C. Die altdeutsche Malerei, 1266; Gotische Holzschnitte, 1538; Les peintres primitifs allemands, 1267

Glass: histories, 1790, 1791, 1812
  American, 1792–1794, 1799
  British, 1788, 1797, 1798
  European, 1789, 1794
  Irish, 1798
  Modern: 20th century, 1795, 1796

Glassmakers, 1787

Glass painters, 1787

Glass painting and staining see Stained glass

Glazier, R. Historic textile fabrics, 1939; A manual of historic ornament, 1634

Gloag, J. Guide to western architecture, 793; A short dictionary of furniture, 1689

—— and Bridgwater, D. A history of cast iron in architecture, 1883

Glück, G. Die Kunst der Renaissance in Deutschland, 454

Glück, H. Die Kunst des Islams, 454

Gnoli, U. Pittori e miniatori nell'Umbria, 1164

Göbel, H. Tapestries of the Lowlands, 1919; Wandteppiche, 1920

Godefroy, J. Geschiedenis van de bouwkunst in Nederland, 897

The gods of northern Buddhism. Getty, A., 403

Index

Index

Index

Index

Index

Index

Index

Monumenta Cataloniae, 2451

Monumenti della pittura antica scoperti in Italia, 2452

I Monumenti italiani, 2453

Monumenti vaticani di archeologia e d'arte, 2454

Monumentos arquitectónicos de España, 927

Monuments de l'art byzantin, 535

Moon, B. E. Mycenaean civilization publications, 40

Moore, C. H. The medieval church architecture of England, 877

Moore, H. H. The lace book, 1973; Old glass, 1794

Moore, W. The story of Australian art, 574

Morey, C. R. Early Christian art, 536; Medieval art, 537

—— Mather, F. J., and Henderson, W. J. The American spirit in art, 759

Morley, S. G. The ancient Maya, 640

Morris, F., and Hague, M. Antique laces, 1974

Morrison, A. The painters of Japan, 1393

Morrison, H. S. Early American architecture, 940

Morse, J. D. Old masters in America, 1136

Mortet, V. Recueil de textes relatifs à l'histoire de l'architecture, 2099

—— and Deschamps, P. Recueil de textes relatifs à l'histoire de l'architecture . . . XIe–XIIIe siècles, 2100

Mosaics, 1234, 1822, 1824; histories, 1817, 1823

  Byzantine, 1819

  Christian, 1818

  German, 1821

  Sicilian, 1820

Moss, R. L. B., and Porter, B. Topographical bibliography of ancient Egyptian hieroglyphic texts, reliefs, and paintings, 41

Motherwell, R. Documents of modern art, 2409

Mothes, O., and Müller, H. A. Illustriertes archäologisches Wörterbuch der Kunst, 195

Mourey, G.; Fontainas, A.; and Vauxcelles, L. Histoire générale de l'art français, 582

Mouseion, 2286

Mühsam, K. Internationales Lexikon der Preise, 149

Mulk-Rāj, A. The Hindu view of art, 684; Persian painting, 1394

Muller, F. De Nederlandsche geschiedenis in platen, 1580

Müller, H. A., and Mothes, O. Illustriertes archäologisches Wörterbuch der Kunst, 195

—— and Singer, H. W. Allgemeines Künstler-Lexikon, 222

Müller, I. P. E. von. Handbuch der klassischen Altertums-Wissenschaft, 196

Müller, S. F. C. Alte Möbel, 1697

Müller, T. Geschichte der deutschen Plastik, 590

Mumford, J. K. Oriental rugs, 1910

Münchner Jahrbuch der bildenden Kunst, 2287

Munro, T., and Guillaume, P. Primitive Negro sculpture, 997

Munsell, A. H. A color notation, 1493

Müntz, E. Les arts à la cour des papes, 2101; Les arts à la cour des papes; nouvelles recherches, 2102; Les arts à la cour des papes pendant le XVe et le XVIe siècle, 2103; A short history of tapestry, 1928; La tapisserie, 1929

Mural painting see Painting: mural

Muratov, P. P. L'ancienne peinture russe, 1414; Les icones russes, 1415

Murr, C. G. von. Bibliothèque de peinture, de sculpture, et de gravure, 4

Murray, M. A. Egyptian sculpture, 976

Musées de France, 2201

El museo pictorico y escala óptica. Palomino de Castro y Velasco, A. A., 2027

Museum. The care of paintings, 1494

Museum; a quarterly review, 2288

Museum; revista mensual de arte español, 2289

The Museum news, 2290

Museum Plantin-Moretus Library, 2507

Museums, 2413, 2419, 2436; directories, 111, 114–117, 119–127; periodicals, 2196, 2265, 2286, 2288, 2291, 2292

  American, 121; periodicals, 2290

  British, 119, 124

  Dutch, 127

  European, 123, 2447

  French, 122; periodicals, 2200, 2201, 2329

  German, 193

  Spanish, 125

The Museums Association. Journal, 2291

Museums journal, 2291

Museumskunde, 2292

Mustoxidi, T. M. Histoire de l'esthétique française, 50

Muther, R. The history of modern painting, 1241

Mycenae. Wace, A. J. B., 505

Myers, B. S. Mexican painting in our time, 1330; Modern art in the making, 1242

Mythology, 308, 310, 313, 314, 318, 323, 335, 397

  Buddhist, 408

  Chinese, 411, 412

  Classical, 336A–339

Index

Index

Répertoire international des archives photographiques. United Nations Educational, Scientific and Cultural Organization, 168

Répertoire international des musées. International Museum Office, 126

Repertorium für Kunstwissenschaft, 2323

Reproductions, 155–171; catalogs, 155–158, 163, 169, 171

American, 169

British, 164

French, 159, 165

German, 160

See also Color prints

Restoration *see* Conservation and restoration

Restorers: British, 1610

Revett, N., and Stuart, J. The antiquities of Athens, 822

Revista española de arte, 2172

Revista svizzera d'arte e d'archeologia, 2369

Revolution and tradition in modern American art. Baur, J. I. H., 753

Revue archéologique, 2324

Revue belge d'archéologie et d'histoire de l'art, 2325

La Revue d'art, 2161, 2326

Revue de l'art ancien et moderne, 2327

Revue de l'art chrétien, 2328

La Revue des arts, 2329

Revue des arts asiatiques, 2330

Revue suisse d'art et d'archéologie, 2369

Rewald, J. The history of impressionism, 1244; Post-Impressionism, 1245

Reymond, M. La sculpture florentine, 1054

Reynolds, G. Nineteenth century drawings, 1100; Twentieth century drawings, 1101

Rhodes, D. Clay and glazes for the potter, 1785

Le ricche minere della pittura Veneziana *see* Boschini, M. Le minere della pittura, 1992

Ricci, C. Art in northern Italy, 622; Baroque architecture and sculpture in Italy, 887; North Italian painting of the Cinquecento, 2462

Ricci, E. Mille santi nell'arte, 382; Old Italian lace, 1978

Rice, D. S., and Pearson, J. D. Islamic art and archaeology, 75

Rice, D. T. Byzantine art, 539; English art, 603; Russian art, 716

Rice, T. A. T. Russian art, 717

Rich, J. C. The materials and methods of sculpture, 1086

Richardson, E. P. Painting in America, 1468

Richert, G. La pintura medieval en España, 1444

Richmond, L., and Littlejohns, L. The technique of water-colour painting, 1497

Richter, G. M. A. Ancient furniture, 1698; Archaic Greek art, 498; The sculpture and sculptors of the Greeks, 978

Richter, J. P. Quellen der byzantinischen Kunstgeschichte, 2113

Rickert, M. Painting in Britain, 452

Ridolfi, C. Le maraviglie dell'arte, 2036

Riis, P. J. An introduction to Etruscan art, 499

Rijksbureau voor Kunsthistorische Documentatie, 2546

Rinaldis, A. de. Neapolitan painting of the Seicento, 2462

Rindge, A. M. Sculpture, 956

Ripley, M. C. The Chinese rug book, 1912

Ris-Paquot, O. E. Dictionnaire des poinçons, symboles, signes etc., 1857; Dictionnaire encyclopédique des marques et monogrammes, 204

Ritchie, A. C. Sculpture of the twentieth century, 995

Rivista d'arte, 2331

Rivista di archeologia cristiana, 2332

Rivoira, G. T. Lombardic architecture, 888; Moslem architecture, 908; Roman architecture, 818

Rizzo, G. E. Storia dell'arte greca, 500

Robb, D. M. The Harper history of painting, 1193

—— and Garrison, J. J. Art in the western world, 456

Robert, C. Die antiken Sarkophagreliefs, 959

Robert-Dumesnil, A. P. F. Le peintre-graveur français, 1561

Robertson, D. S. A handbook of Greek & Roman architecture, 819

Rodenwaldt, G. Die antiken Sarkophagreliefs, 959; Die Kunst der Antike, 454

Roeder, H. Saints and their attributes, 383

Roger-Marx, C. French original engravings, 1562

Roh, F. Holländische Malerei, 1368; Die Kunst des 20. Jahrhunderts, 590

Rohault de Fleury, C. Archéologie chrétienne, 384; L'évangile, 385; La messe, 386; La Sainte Vierge, 387

Rombouts, P. De liggeren en andere historische archieven der Antwerpsche Sint Lucasgilde *see* Antwerp. St. Lucas Gilde. De liggeren en andere historische archieven, 2059

Romdahl, A. L., and Roosval, J. A. E. Svensk konsthistoria, 732

Rome. Istituto d'Archeologia e Storia dell'Arte *see* Istituto Nazionale di Archeologia e Storia dell'Arte, Rome

—— Kaiser Wilhelm-Institut für Kunst-

Index

Salmi, M. Romanesque sculpture in Tuscany, 1055; *see also* Raccolta di fonti per la storia dell'arte, 2109

Salmony, A. Carved jade of ancient China, 1900

Saltillo, M. L. Artistas y artífices sorianos, 297

Salverte, F. de. Les ébénistes du XVIIIe siècle, 1693

Samlerens kunstnerleksikon, 281

Samplers and stitches. Christie, G., 1964

Sánchez-Camargo, M. Pintura española contemporánea, 1445

Sánchez Cantón, F. J. Fuentes literarias para la historia del arte español, 2055; Opusculos Gallegos sobre bellas artes, 2056

Sandrart, J. von. L'Academia todesca della architectura, scultura & pittura, 2037

Sanford, T. E. The story of architecture in Mexico, 894

Sanpere y Miquel, S. Los cuatrocentistas catalanes, 1446

—— and Gudiol y Cunill, J. G. Els trescentistes, 1447

Santos, R. dos. L'art portugais, 749

Sarcophagi, 959, 988

Sauer, J., and Kraus, F. X. Geschichte der christlichen Kunst, 528

Sauerlandt, M. Die deutsche Plastik, 1028

Saunders, O. E. English illumination, 1294, 2462; History of English art, 604

Savage, G. Ceramics for the collector, 1757; Porcelain through the ages, 1758

Saward, B. C., and Caulfeild, S. F. A. The dictionary of needlework, 1961

Saylor, H. H. Dictionary of architecture, 777

Scamozzi, V. Idea dell'architettura universale, 2038

Scandinavian art, 734

The scepter of Egypt. Hayes, W. C., 477

Schäfer, H. Die Kunst des alten Orients, 454

Schapiro, M. Style, 429

Scheen, P. A. Honderd jaren Nederlandsche schilder-en teeken-kunst, 1169

Schiaffino, E. La pintura y la escultura en Argentina, 645

Schlesinger, M. Geschichte des Symbols, 331

Schlosser, J. von. Die Kunstliteratur, 44; La letteratura artistica, 44; Quellenbuch zur Kunstgeschichte, 2115; Schriftquellen zur Geschichte der karolingischen Kunst, 2116

Schmeckebier, L. E. A handbook of Italian renaissance painting, 1322; Modern Mexican art, 1334

Schmid, F. The practice of painting, 1499

Schmidt, G. Schweizer Malerei und Zeichnung, 1454

Schmidt, H. J. Alte Seidenstoffe, 1955

Schmidt, M. Kunst und Kultur von Peru, 454

Schmidt, P. F. Geschichte der modernen Malerei, 1246

Schmidt, R. Möbel, 1699; Porcelain as an art and mirror of fashion, 1759

Schmitt, O. Reallexikon zur deutschen Kunstgeschichte, 205

Schmitz, H. Bildteppiche, 1930; The encyclopedia of furniture, 1700

Schneider, R. L'art français, 585

Schnier, J. P. Sculpture in modern America, 1081

Die schöne alte Schweiz. Nicolas, R., 752

A school of ivory carvers in Provence. Smith, E. B., 388

Schottmüller, F. Bronze Statuetten und Geräte, 957; Furniture and interior decoration of the Italian Renaissance, 1717

Schramm, A. Pantheon, 118

Schramm, P. E. Herrschaftszeichen und Staatssymbolik, 332

Schraubstadter, C. W. Care and repair of Japanese prints, 1603

Schreiber, W. L. Manuel de l'amateur de la gravure, 1553

Schrifttum zur deutsch-baltischen Kunst, 52

Schrifttum zur deutschen Kunst, 51

Schubert, O. Geschichte des Barock in Spanien, 789

Schubring, P. Cassoni, 1323; Die italienische Plastik des Quattrocento, 444, 1056; Die Kunst der Hochrenaissance in Italien, 454

Schuette, M. Gestickte Bildteppiche und Decken, 1931

Schultz, A. Untersuchungen zur Geschichte der schlesischen Maler, 1157

Schwab, G. B. Gods & heroes, 337

Schwabe, R., and Kelly, F. M. Historic costume, 1670

Schweinfurth, P. Geschichte der russischen Malerei, 1417

Schweizerischer Werkbund *see* Das Werk, 2360

The scientific examination of pictures. Wild, A. M. de, 1509

Scott, F. N., and Gayley, C. M. A guide to the literature of aesthetics, 29

La scrittura di artisti italiani. Pini, C., 2052

Les sculpteurs célèbres nouveaux, 2472

Sculptors, 2002
  American, 304
  British, 251, 946, 947, 1032
  Dutch, 944, 1168
  Flemish, 267, 944
  Florentine, 1041
  French, 239, 244, 948, 1156, 2420, 2472
  German, 1158

Index

Tucci, G. Tibetan painted scrolls, 1402

Tuckerman, A. L. A selection of works of architecture and sculpture, 890

Tuckerman, H. T. Book of the artists, 304

Tudor artists. Auerbach, E., 1278

Twining, L. Symbols and emblems, 393

Two thousand years of textiles. Weibel, A. C., 1958

Tyler, R., and Peirce, H. L'art byzantin, 538

Ubbelohde-Doering, H. The art of ancient Peru, 653

—— and Lehmann, W. The art of old Peru, 639

Umanesimo e rinascimento. Ancona, P. d', 610

A union list of holdings of foreign art periodicals. American Library Association. Art Reference Round Table, 82

United Nations Educational, Scientific and Cultural Organization. Catalogue de reproductions en couleurs de peintures antérieures à 1860, 166; Catalogue de reproductions en couleurs de peintures—1860 à 1957, 167; Répertoire des bibliothèques de France, 133; Répertoire international des archives photographiques, 168

U.S. Copyright Office. Catalog of copyright entries, 169

—— Library of Congress. Reference Dept. Guide to the special collections of prints and photographs, 170

—— National Gallery of Art. Index of American design, 1629

Universal catalog of books on art see South Kensington Museum, London. National Art Library. First proofs of the Universal catalogue of books on art, 45

Universidad Biblioteca (Valencia), 2564

University of London. Percival David Foundation of Chinese Art. Library, 2512

—— School of Oriental and African Studies. Art Library, 2514

—— See also London. University.

University prints, Boston: fine art reproductions for students, 171

Upjohn, E. M.; Wingert, P. S.; and Mahler, J. G. History of world art, 460

Upmark, G. Guld- och silversmeder i Sverige, 1862

Uppsala University Library, 2555

Usilton, B. M., and Gettens, R. J. Abstracts of technical studies in art and archaeology, 30

Utrechtse bijdragen tot de kunstgeschiedenis, 2486

Vaillant, G. C. Aztecs of Mexico, 654; Indian arts in North America, 570

Valgimigli, G. M. Dei pittori e degli artisti Faentini, 263

Valladares, J. Arte brasileira, 66

Vanderbilt, P. Guide to the special collections of prints and photographs, 170

Vanderpoel, E. N. American lace, 1979

Vandier, J. Manuel d'archéologie égyptienne, 480

Varagine see Jacobus de Varagine

Vargas Ugarte, R. Ensayo de un diccionario de artífices coloniales, 266

Varille, M. Les peintres primitifs de Provence, 243

Vasari, G. Vasari on technique, 763; Le vite de' piv eccellenti architetti, pittori et scvltori italiani, 2041; Le vite de' piv eccellenti pittori, scvltori e architettori, 2042

Il Vasari, 2351

Vasari Society for the reproduction of drawings, 2487

Vase painting, 1138, 1195–1201

Vatican. Biblioteca Apostolica, 2535

—— Biblioteca Vaticana. Centro Bibliografica della Copia Vaticana del "Princeton art index." Catalogo delle pubblicazioni periodiche, 91

Vaticanische Miniaturen. Beissel, S., 1210

Vatter, E. Religiöse Plastik der Naturvölker, 1003

Vauxcelles, L.; Fontainas, A.; and Mourey, G. Histoire générale de l'art français, 582

Les ventes publiques en France, 153

Venturi, A. North Italian painting of the Quattrocento, 2462; A short history of Italian art, 625; Storia dell'arte italiana, 626

Venturi, L. Les archives de l'impressionisme, 2057; History of art criticism, 432

Verband der Schweizerischen Altertumssammlungen see Zeitschrift für schweizerische Archaeologie und Kunstgeschichte, 2369

Verci, G. B. Notizie intorno alla vita e alle opere de' pittori, scultori e intagliatori, 2043

Vereeniging van Vrienden der Aziatische Kunst. Bulletin, 2273

Verein der Freunde asiatischer Kunst und Kultur in Wien. Jahrbuch, 2361

Vermeulen, F. Handboek tot de geschiedenis der Nederlandsche bouwkunst, 898

Vertue, G. Vertue note books, 2044

Verve, 2352

Verwey, E. de la F. Aawinsten op het gebied van de beeldende kunsten, 15

Index

Index